MW01040827

CAREER DEVELOPMENT INTERVENTIONS

FIFTH EDITION

Spencer G. Niles
The College of William & Mary

JoAnn Harris-Bowlsbey
Kuder, Inc., Adel, Iowa

Boston Columbus Indianapolis New York San Francisco
Amsterdam Cape Town Dubai London Madrid Milan Munich Paris Montréal Toronto
Delhi Mexico City São Paulo Sydney Hong Kong Seoul Singapore Taipei Tokyo

Vice President and Editorial Director: Jeffery W. Johnston
Vice President and Publisher: Kevin M. Davis
Editorial Assistant: Marisia Styles
Executive Field Marketing Manager: Krista Clark
Senior Product Marketing Manager: Christopher Barry
Project Manager: Pamela Bennett
Program Manager: Janelle Criner
Operations Specialist: Deidra Skahill

Cover Design Director: Diane Ernsberger
Cover Photo: Shutterstock/©Markus Gann
Full-Service Project Management: Mohinder Singh,
  iEnergizer Aptara®, Ltd.
Composition: iEnergizer Aptara®, Ltd.
Printer/Binder: RR Donnelley/Crawfordville
Cover Printer: RR Donnelley/Crawfordville
Text Font: 10/12 ITC Berkeley Oldstyle Pro

Library of Congress Cataloging-in-Publication Data
Niles, Spencer G., author.
  [Career development interventions in the 21st century]
  Career development interventions / Spencer G. Niles, JoAnn Harris-Bowlsbey.—Fifth edition.
   pages cm
  Earlier editions published as: Career development interventions in the 21st century.
  ISBN 978-0-13-428630-3 – ISBN 0-13-428630-8
  1. Career development.   2. Career development–Case studies.   I. Harris-Bowlsbey, JoAnn, author.   II. Title.
  HF5381.N547 2017
  650.14–dc23
                                                                      2015031672

10 9 8 7 6 5 4 3 2

PEARSON

ISBN 10:   0-13-428630-8
ISBN 13: 978-0-13-428630-3

Preface

We have taught career courses to students in numerous universities in the United States as well as in Canada, Japan, Denmark, Portugal, England, Turkey, Australia, United Arab Emirates, Ireland, Qatar, and Spain, to mention just a few. Wherever students are interested in learning about career development theory and practice, we are eager to go! In each instance, however, not only are we teaching students about career development interventions, but students also teach us. The idea for this book began in response to student requests (pleas) for a career development textbook that was readable, useful, and interesting. These are high but reasonable expectations, which have served as our guiding principles as we composed the chapters of this book.

New to This Edition

In addition to consistently updating this textbook to reflect the most cutting-edge research, trends, and pedagogy, we have made the following changes to this edition:

- Greater use of case studies representing clients from diverse contexts in all chapters
- Extensive updates of current literature applying to each chapter
- Updated statistics related to demographic trends related to labor market participation and an expanded discussion of the implications of these trends for career development interventions
- Separate chapters addressing career development interventions in elementary school, middle school, and high school
- Expanded discussion of the changing landscape of career development interventions in higher education
- Expansion of the research and work of recent theorists, with an eye toward their applicability for diverse populations
- Incorporation of the 2016 CACREP Standards and the 2015 National Career Development Association Code of Ethics
- Extensive rewriting of the chapter on the use of technology in career guidance (Chapter 7) to discuss the use of social media in the job-seeking process

- New in-text student assignments and activities to encourage application and practice of the theoretical concepts presented in each chapter
- Continued use of student assignments based upon video content we created for this book

The video feature continues to be unique to this career development text. The videos provide outstanding examples of how leading career development experts conduct career counseling with diverse career counseling clients. The clients are real clients with genuine career concerns. The career counseling sessions were not scripted, rehearsed, or edited in any way. The career counselors had very little information, and in some cases none, about their clients prior to their career counseling sessions. Thus, the videos offer a realistic view of how nationally recognized career counseling experts conduct career counseling. We also provide video interviews with leading career development theorists and/or representatives of the leading theories who were close collaborators with the theorists they represent. These videos are designed to show how theory translates to practice and can be accessed through the Video and Resource Library on the MyCounselingLab® Web site. (See below for more information about MyCounselingLab.)

One important goal of this text is to convey to our readers the deep respect and long-term commitment we have for career development theory and practice. We emphasize this goal in Chapter 1. As we note in the book, few things are more personal than career choice, and we remained cognizant of this fact as we wrote each chapter. Making career decisions involves deciding how we will spend one of the most precious commodities we have—our time on Earth. We realize that these decisions are often difficult and overwhelming. Thus, we draw upon the work of our colleagues in the field to present readers with state-of-the-art career theory and practice. However, the current situation evolved from the past contributions of many leaders in the field. We acknowledge their important foundational contributions in Chapter 1.

Although we cover a wide variety of theoretical perspectives in the book (especially in Chapters 2 and 3), we emphasize that careers develop over time. A decision point in one's career development is just that: a point in time at which one makes decisions based on previous and current career development experiences. Although knowing how to help people at these important points in their career development is crucial, career practitioners can also intervene proactively in the lives of children, adolescents, and adults in ways that facilitate positive career development prior to the occurrence of career crises. Being able to provide assistance in both instances is critical.

We are especially concerned that career development theory and practice be inclusive. Constructing culturally inclusive career development interventions should be standard practice within the field. Unfortunately, this has not traditionally been the case. In part because of their historical context, career theories and practices have focused primarily on the career experiences of European American middle-class males. Although we devote a chapter to providing culturally competent career development interventions (Chapter 4), throughout the book we also address the need for inclusive career interventions. Our case studies highlight the career experiences of clients from diverse backgrounds. We think both approaches (having a single chapter devoted to the topic and infusing diversity throughout the book) are needed to begin to more adequately address the career development needs of all people. We are proud of the career counseling videos we produced for this book as they provide excellent examples of career counseling with diverse clients.

The need to provide clients with culturally sensitive career interventions provides an important foundation for discussing career counseling interventions in Chapter 8 and career assessment approaches in Chapter 5. The career counseling process and outcomes information provided here reflect the most recent work within the field. We also provide career information, resources, and Web site references (Chapters 6 and 7) that represent important aspects of the career development process. We highlight the essential considerations in designing and implementing career development programs in Chapter 9. We also emphasize in Chapter 9 the importance of engaging in the ongoing evaluation of career services. This is important for improving service delivery. However, when resources are limited, as they are in many situations, the need for both accountability and the ability to demonstrate effectiveness is great. Finally, we highlight developmental approaches to providing career assistance in the schools (elementary, middle, and high), higher education, and community settings in Chapters 10 through 14.

Of course, the desire to engage in ethical practice is also a standard in the field. However, there are many challenges confronting career practitioners. Web-based services such as career counseling and career assessment, the possibility of dual relationships, and theories with deeply rooted value sets present challenges to practitioners as they engage in ethical practice. Thus, we address many of these current ethical challenges in Chapter 15 using the 2015 National Career Development Association (NCDA) Code of Ethics. This is the first, and still one of the few, career development textbooks with a chapter devoted to ethical practice.

To make the book even more useful to readers, we use a framework developed by the NCDA. Specifically, we use the NCDA's career counseling competencies and the 2016 Council for Accreditation of Counseling and Related Educational Programs (CACREP) Standards to guide us in the identification of chapter topics. These competencies and standards appear in the appendices at the end of the book.

Please note that printed on the inside front cover is a grid identifying the chapters that are most relevant to each competency category and the 2016 CACREP standards. For those focused on career interventions in K–12 settings, we also incorporate the National Career Development Guidelines into Chapters 10 (elementary school), 11 (middle school), and 12 (high school).

We hope that we have accomplished the goals that motivated us to write this book. We also hope that we have fulfilled our students' expectations. In teaching our career courses, we consider it high praise when students tell us that they have a new respect and appreciation for career development interventions as a result of the class experience. This is what we hope occurs with this book. We invite readers to send us their feedback directly (sgniles@wm.edu; bowlsbeyj@kuder.com). We are committed to improving the book in any way that we can. Although collectively we have nearly a century devoted to the study and practice of career development, we have much yet to learn and we are eager to do so. Your comments will guide us in the revisions that we make. We are also happy to speak (either in person or virtually) to classes that are using our text. Simply contact us with such requests, and we will arrange for a time to make this happen. Finally, we wish you the very best as you embark on an exciting adventure with regard to your ongoing professional development.

Also Available with MyCounselingLab®

This title is also available with MyCounselingLab–an online homework, tutorial, and assessment program designed to work with the text to engage students and improve results. Within its structured environment, students see key concepts demonstrated through video clips, practice what they learn, test their understanding, and receive feedback to guide their learning and ensure they master key learning outcomes.

- **Learning Outcomes and Standards measure student results.** MyCounselingLab organizes all assignments around essential learning outcomes and national standards for counselors.
- **Video- and Case-Based Assignments develop decision-making skills.** Video- and Case-based Assignments introduce students to a broader range of clients, and therefore a broader range of presenting problems, than they will encounter in their own pre-professional clinical experiences. Students watch videos of actual client-therapist sessions or high-quality role-play scenarios featuring expert counselors. They are then guided in their analysis of the videos through a series of short-answer questions. These exercises help students develop the techniques and decision-making skills they need to be effective counselors before they are in a critical situation with a real client.
- **Licensure Quizzes help students prepare for certification.** Automatically graded, multiple-choice Licensure Quizzes help students prepare for their certification examinations, master foundational course content, and improve their performance in the course.
- **Video Library offers a wealth of observation opportunities.** The Video Library provides more than 400 video clips of actual client-therapist sessions and high-quality role plays in a database organized by topic and searchable by keyword. The Video Library includes every video clip from the MyCounselingLab courses plus additional videos from Pearson's extensive library of footage. Instructors can create additional assignments around the videos or use them for in-class activities. Students can expand their observation experiences to include other course areas and increase the amount of time they spend watching expert counselors in action.
- **Comprehensive online course content.** Filled with a wealth of content that is tightly integrated with your textbook, MyLab lets you easily add, remove, or modify existing instructional material. You can also add your own course materials to suit the needs of your students or department. In short, MyLab lets you teach exactly as you'd like.
- **Robust gradebook tracking.** The online gradebook automatically tracks your students' results on tests, homework, and practice exercises and gives you control over managing results and calculating grades. The gradebook provides a number of flexible grading options, including exporting grades to a spreadsheet program such as Microsoft Excel. And, it lets you measure and document your students' learning outcomes.

Access to MyCounselingLab can be packaged with this textbook or purchased standalone. To find out how to package student access to this website and gain access as an Instructor, go to www.MyCounselingLab.com, email us at counseling@pearson.com, or contact your Pearson sales representative.

Acknowledgments

I am grateful for and humbled by the support and love I have received from my family members and mentors. My mother, Pauline, taught me at an early age about the importance of Donald Super's life-space theory segment as she balanced work and family demands as a single parent. She was a pioneer who lived with grace and dignity, despite substantial challenges presented both to professional women and single parents.

My children, Jenny and Jonathan, teach me about love each day and help to make me a better person. I am fortunate to have the opportunity to watch as their careers unfold. I am particularly thrilled that they both work in the field of education, one as an elementary school counselor (Jenny) and one as a trainer in the area of career development (Jonathan). I am profoundly proud of the people they are and the important work that they do.

My professional mentors and cherished friends have guided me through multiple career development tasks. Edwin L. Herr was the first to provide support and guidance, and he has continued to do so for more than 25 years. He embodies the best of what a mentor should represent. I will forever be indebted to Ed for his personal and professional assistance. Mark L. Savickas and Donald E. Super have also provided guidance, and I am honored that, at various times in my career, they have cared. Finally, I have been honored to coauthor this book with JoAnn Harris-Bowlsbey. She is incredibly knowledgeable, wise, gracious, and kind. She too, is a valued mentor and dear friend. I look forward to future editions and opportunities to work together.

Spencer G. Niles

Like Spencer, my life was molded by a mother who was a single parent and who worked incredibly hard to ensure that I had a level of education and access that she never enjoyed. She taught me the principles of faith, responsibility, commitment, and service. I want to acknowledge her role in laying the foundation that made my present life and contributions possible.

My most valued professional mentor was Donald E. Super, who was kind enough to share his writings and thoughts with me for 30 years. I have personally enjoyed the fullness of his career rainbow in my life. Nancy Schlossberg and David Tiedeman also contributed mightily to my conception of the process of career development and have enriched the well from which the content of this book flows.

My professional contributions would not have been possible without the ongoing support of my late husband, Stan. For the 33 years of our marriage, he placed a very high priority on my career and helped all that he could—editing, proofreading, doing home chores—to nourish it, never pressuring for more of my time. Finally, my ongoing friendship with and respect for Spencer Niles deepens as we experience the authorship of this book and other professional pursuits together.

JoAnn Harris-Bowlsbey

We both appreciate the dedicated assistance and support provided by Kevin Davis and Lauren Carlson at Pearson.

We wish to thank those who reviewed the fourth edition and made suggestions for improvement that we have incorporated into this fifth edition of the book: Stephanie Tursic Burns, Western Michigan University; James M. O'Neil, University of Connecticut; Chester R. Robinson, Texas A&M University–Commerce; and Joan N. Strutton, The University of Texas at Tyler.

Brief Contents

Contents

INTRODUCTION TO CAREER DEVELOPMENT INTERVENTIONS

Like it or not, what we do for money is a big part of our lives. In many ways it defines who we are, and it's how most of us pay for the basic needs of day-to-day living, such as food, shelter, and transportation. In time, if you're lucky, your job can provide more quality leisure time, investments for the education of your children, and a home. Every day we get up and go to work—there's no getting out of it. So it's imperative to choose a field or endeavor that will enrich your life. And whether you're a contractor building a house, a doctor repairing a heart, or a teacher educating students, you need to focus on the finished product and take pride in the process that achieves that finished product. You should never settle for anything less than your best effort, because it matters. It matters to the homeowner, the patient, and the students, and it most certainly should matter to you.

David H., Contractor

Work is something I do because I have to. If I won the lottery, I wouldn't work. As a single parent of two young children, I have to be responsible. I do it for them. Can work be meaningful? I hope to experience that someday. Right now, it's how my family and I get by—that's the most important thing. And most days it's not fun.

Ann D., Food service worker

My work means everything to me—well, almost everything. As an oncologist, I am dedicated to my work and my patients. I feel a tremendous responsibility to be the best physician that I can be. I also feel a responsibility to be the best I can be as a representative of my family and the African American community. I have dedicated much of my life to this activity. It is what gives me meaning and purpose. I feel fortunate to do the work I do.

Camille S., Physician

MyCounselingLab®

Visit the MyCounselingLab® site for *Career Development Interventions*, Fifth Edition, to enhance your understanding of chapter concepts. You will have the opportunity to practice applying what you learned in the chapter by completing the video- and case-based exercises in the MyLab. Taking the Licensure Quizzes will help you prepare for your certification exam.

Chandra and her colleagues were discussing their career development course and wondering why, as graduate students in counselor education, they were required to take it. José declared that he had no interest in providing career counseling and was not likely to need to know much about it. Jonathan added that he found the prospect of administering tests just plain boring. Beth was set on establishing a private practice and said that she would probably refer clients with career concerns to practitioners specializing in the field.

Chandra had a different take. She had witnessed the powerful impact of work on her family when her father's employer moved overseas and laid him off from his engineering job. While Chandra's father sought new employment, her mother struggled to keep her full-time nursing job while caring for Chandra and her two younger brothers. When her father had to settle for a position that provided less pay, challenge, and satisfaction than had his old one, she watched as he became depressed and tension mounted between her parents. No one was spared: Her brothers were getting into trouble at school, and Chandra, beset by anxiety, developed insomnia. Chandra understood all too well the link between work and well-being and hoped that learning about career development might empower her to help other families avoid what had happened to hers.

D avid H., Ann D., and Camille S. communicate some of the diverse values, purposes, and goals that people attach to work. Some view work as a way to express themselves and confer meaning and purpose on life. Others work to provide for their families and, often due to circumstances beyond their control, approach work strictly as a way to bring in money. Some, like Camille S., the physician, see work as a way to fulfill their responsibility to an ethnic or cultural group. Still others struggle simply to find work. The unemployment rate in the United States in December 2014 was 5.6%; in April 2011 it was 9%; and in April 2001 it was 4.4% (Bureau of Labor Statistics, 2014). These numbers, however, can be misleading. For example, if you were unemployed and stopped looking for work for a month, you would not have been counted as unemployed—and there are significant numbers of people who have given up trying to find work. Moreover, in April 2013 an estimated 22 million Americans were unemployed or underemployed (underemployed workers include those who are highly skilled and working in low-paying jobs, highly skilled and working in jobs requiring less skill, and those working part-time who want to work full-time). This is a global issue. The International Labour Organization estimates the number of unemployed workers worldwide to be a record 202 million (Moore, 2013).

Chandra's experience is not unusual. We live in uncertain times: Seasoned adults struggle to cope with their careers while recent college graduates have trouble landing their first job. Adolescents feel pressured to succeed but can't see how high school life connects to their future lives as working adults. Children are constantly exposed to occupational stereotypes—police officer, firefighter, doctor—that influence their perceptions of what opportunities await them. So let us be clear: Counselors are expected to, and indeed *must*, provide career assistance in every professional setting. Counselors in grade school, higher education, and community settings will, to varying degrees and at various times, encounter clients confronting career development issues. It is for good reason that the American School Counselor Association (2003) identifies career development as one of three areas essential to the work of school counselors. Survey results examining the concerns of college students consistently identify career planning assistance as their dominant issue. It's no different for working adults who find themselves out of work as their employers downsize.

Despite this, many students in counseling and related programs react with as little enthusiasm as did José, Jonathan, and Beth when required to take a career information course

(Heppner, O'Brien, Hinkelman, & Flores, 1996). Perhaps some think they'll be required to memorize blocks of data or spend hours learning how to administer and interpret occupational questionnaires. Perhaps they view career development interventions as separate from general counseling interventions, with the former involving information dissemination, advising, and test administration, and the latter employing more "sophisticated" therapeutic techniques. Maybe they envision mechanical career development interventions in which the counselor dictates a course of action and takes complete responsibility for the outcome. Or maybe, like Beth, they view career development interventions as irrelevant to their counseling careers.

No matter what their objections are to studying career development, we challenge them.

We believe (and think Chandra would agree) that competent career practitioners must possess expertise in a broad array of counseling-related competencies. The knowledge and skills required for providing effective career assistance encompass and transcend those required for general counseling (Blustein & Spengler, 1995; Gysbers, Heppner, & Johnston, 2009; Herr, Cramer, & Niles, 2004). For example, the competencies identified by the National Career Development Association* (National Career Development Association, 2009) include knowledge and skills in career development theory; individual and group counseling; individual and group assessment; career information and resources; program promotion, management, and implementation; career coaching and consultation; multicultural counseling; supervision; ethical and legal issues; and using technology effectively in the career intervention process. These competencies extend far beyond those required for career advising and test administration.

Moreover, areas of inquiry related to career development interventions are fascinating, challenging, and connected to recent psychological emphases on optimal human functioning, maximizing happiness, and fulfilling human potential (Hartung, 2002; Niles, Amundson, & Neault, 2011; Savickas, 2009). Career counselors meet their clients at the intersection of what has been and what could be in their lives; interventions help these clients consider how to develop and deploy their talents as their lives progress. Career development practitioners in the 21st century also seek to empower people to derive meaning from their unique life experiences and translate that meaning into rewarding occupational and other choices. Translating life experiences into rewarding choices requires self-awareness. Accordingly, career practitioners provide interventions that help people clarify and articulate how they see themselves. These interventions may include formal, standardized assessments as well as informal, nonstandardized activities that creatively engage clients in the process (Amundson, 2009). Because planning a career and sorting through related concerns are complex processes, competent counselors must be skilled at developing effective working alliances with their clients (Anderson & Niles, 2000; Multon, Heppner, Gysbers, Zook, & Ellis-Kalton, 2001; Perrone, 2005). When career counselors work collaboratively and innovatively with their clients to identify a clear career direction, both client and counselor experience the process as invigorating and fulfilling (Anderson & Niles).

We also realize that practitioners face multiple challenges in the career intervention process. Making career decisions is rarely simple, and good career counseling is never mechanistic or routine. People make decisions about work within the contexts of their other roles and responsibilities, and the complex and stressful nature of such decisions becomes clear (Perrone, Webb, & Blalock, 2005). What might seem to be a straightforward work decision can become frustrating

---

*Until 1985, the National Career Development Association was known as the National Vocational Guidance Association, or NVGA.

and overwhelming to someone who feels buffeted by limited work opportunities, family expectations, financial constraints, and multiple life-role commitments. Given the complexity of making career decisions, it isn't surprising that many people who seek career counseling experience substantial levels of psychological distress (Multon et al., 2001). Obviously, counselors must address clients' distress as they help them identify their values, skills, life-role priorities, interests, and motivations. When clients also experience low self-esteem, weak self-efficacy, and little hope that the future can be more satisfying than the past, the counselor's task becomes even more challenging (Lent, Brown, & Hackett, 2002). Such clients require more help resolving their career dilemmas than a test battery can provide. Given this fact, many clients describe a supportive and effective alliance with their career practitioner as one of the most helpful aspects of the counseling experience (Anderson & Niles, 2000; Multon et al., 2001). Obviously, the abilities to establish rapport, listen closely, and express empathic understanding are essential career counseling skills.

Working collaboratively and effectively with clients also requires career practitioners to possess advanced multicultural competencies (Leong, 1995). Clients operating from a collectivistic orientation, for example, engage in the career planning process differently than those coming from an individualistic orientation (Hartung, Speight, & Lewis, 1996). Thus, working within a client's cultural context is essential to providing effective assistance. Kim, Li, and Liang (2002) found that career counselors focusing on the expression of emotion were perceived as having greater cross-cultural competence than counselors focusing on the expression of cognition when working with Asian American college students with high adherence to Asian values. Leong (2002) found acculturation to be positively related to job satisfaction and negatively related to occupational stress and strain. Gomez and colleagues (2001) found that the career decisions of Latina clients were strongly influenced by sociopolitical, cultural, contextual, and personal variables: Socioeconomic status, family obligations, cultural identity, and the existence of a support network were all concerns of the Latinas participating in the Gomez et al. study. Madonna, Miville, Warren, Gainor, and Lewis-Coles (2006) highlight the importance of understanding a client's religious beliefs to effective career counseling. Paul (2008) describes the use of a constructive-developmental approach that incorporates a client's sexual identity into the career counseling process; Pepper and Lorah (2008) discuss the unique concerns of transsexual clients. Powell and Greenhaus (2012) offer a counseling framework that factors family influences into the career decision-making process.

Clearly, a client's constellation of cultural and contextual variables affects the career intervention process. Therefore, as with general counseling interventions, the career development intervention process is a dynamic, complex, and challenging one that requires practitioners to use multicultural counseling skills to help their clients.

Tips from the Field

Because there are few decisions more personal than choosing a career, it is important to remember that good career counselors are, first, good counselors.

In addition, indications are that the career development process will soon become more complex. Change, transition, and instability dominate the career development landscape. The Bureau of Labor Statistics (2015) reports that one in four workers has been with his or her current employer for less than a year. Also, in 2014, the median number of years that workers had been with their current employers was 4.6: 4.7 for men and 4.5 for women. This level of transition involves costs to companies, as they must train new employees, and to society, as transitioning workers claim benefits from government programs such as Temporary Assistance for Needy Families (TANF) and unemployment insurance.

In addition to decreased longevity with an employer, today's workers operate in a globalized economy. Thomas Friedman (2005) described this in *The World Is Flat: A Brief History of the 21st Century*, noting that technological advances have created a more level economic playing field, with previously disadvantaged countries now rivaling the knowledge and wealth of the United States and other world powers. Computer and communication technologies, previously a stronghold of developed countries, have been accessed and mastered by China and India, making these nations more competitive economically. This "flattening" of access and opportunity has had a major impact on the nature of work around the world, accelerating the economic interdependence of national economies so that what happens in one country impacts the economies of others. Recent global unemployment rates support this assertion.

Another effect of economic globalization is the outsourcing of jobs from one country to another. On the plus side, this improves the receiving country's economy and standard of living: Its workers have greater employment opportunities, and the country gains access to the latest technology. The outsourcing country benefits from lower labor costs, and consumers benefit as well because globalization increases competition, and companies then lower their prices. Friedman's theory is that these developments will continue until world economies are lateral— that is, they show a flat line. A flat world means we are economically dependent on one another and communicating more with one another.

What are the practical implications of the trends Friedman identifies? To compete effectively in a flat world, Friedman believes that 21st-century workers must focus on and develop some new capacities. First, they must be constantly engaged in learning: Workers must learn new ways of doing old things as well as new ways of doing new things. Second, they must cultivate a passion for, and curiosity about, life. Passion and curiosity are potent forces that infuse the workplace with energy and innovation. Third, they must expand their capacity to work collaboratively. Employees with strong interpersonal skills are valued as team players who cope well with workplace challenges. Finally, they must be able to balance analytical thinking with creative energy, bringing a fuller perspective to solving complex problems. Friedman's list of self-management skills for the 21st century can be expanded to include (a) the capacity to cope with change and tolerate ambiguity, (b) the ability to acquire and use occupational information effectively, (c) the ability to adjust quickly to changing work demands, and (d) a working knowledge of technology. Developing these capacities along with specific job content skills will enable workers to stay current in the expanding global economy.

Before leaving our discussion of globalization, we should note that the phenomenon is not strictly positive. Workers in manufacturing and some white-collar jobs have fewer opportunities in nations where this work has been outsourced: Computer programmers, editors, engineers, and accountants are some examples of the latter. Globalization has also led to the increased exploitation of workers in developing countries. A United Nations (UN) report (2000) asserts that globalization has increased inequality and discrimination, widening the gap between the haves and have-nots. Safety standards are often ignored to produce goods less expensively. Also, many developing countries lack child labor laws, and young workers often toil in inhumane conditions. Companies build factories in countries without environmental regulations and discharge pollutants into soil and waterways. Also, globalization has sparked increased human trafficking. Finally, the UN report notes that multinational companies have become increasingly influential in local politics, influencing legislation and public policies that are friendly to business but not to the people they employ.

Adding to the new problems are some old ones: discrimination and disparities in opportunities and income between men and women; workers from dominant and minority ethnic groups; heterosexuals and members of sexual minorities; those who are able-bodied and those who are physically challenged; those who have access to quality education and the doors it opens, and those for whom those doors are closed; and so on. Such issues highlight the need for career practitioners to advocate for social justice. In fact, we believe that the ability to advocate effectively for social justice is utterly essential for career practitioners in the 21st century.

Among other things, advocating for social justice requires career development practitioners to learn about legislation and public policies that support workers and provide career development services (the Workforce Investment Act and Americans with Disabilities Act, to name two). Relating to this, Friedman (2005) identifies the need for legislation that makes it easier for people to switch jobs by connecting retirement benefits and health insurance less to their employers and providing insurance that would help cover a possible drop in income. Friedman also believes we should put more energy into inspiring young people to pursue careers in science, technology, engineering, and math (STEM), as fewer of them are entering these fields. This provides implicit support for inserting career development language into the next iteration of the Elementary and Secondary Education Act, familiarly known as No Child Left Behind.

It follows that knowing how to shape public policy and legislation is an important skill for career development practitioners: Acquainting legislators with the importance of career services to their constituents, and reminding them of the benefits that accrue to the community, are powerful actions that career practitioners can take. Being multiculturally sensitive and aware is also an essential component of providing effective career interventions. The bottom line is that all people at some point must cope with career development tasks to successfully manage their lives and careers. We believe that all counselors, regardless of their work setting, must understand the career development process and be skilled at providing career interventions.

THE MEANING OF WORK ACROSS TIME

Understanding the career development process and being able to provide holistic, comprehensive, and systematic career development interventions across a worker's life span require practitioners to appreciate the role that work plays in people's lives. Substantial evidence indicates that the meaning of work for people around the world is changing (e.g., Ardichvili & Kuchinke, 2009; Borchert & Landherr, 2009; Ferrar et al., 2009). Unfortunately, many shifts are not positive for workers. Most workers in industrialized nations now enjoy the benefits of paid vacation time (typically about three weeks per year) and paid parental leave. Currently, 134 countries have laws establishing a maximum length to the work week. The exception is the United States. According to the International Labour Organization, Americans work 137 more hours per year than Japanese workers, 260 more than British workers, and 499 more than French workers. Currently, 85.8% of men and 66.5% of all women in the United States work more than 40 hours per week. So it should come as no surprise that Americans report sharply higher levels of work–family conflict than do citizens of other industrialized nations. Fully

90% of American mothers and 95% of American fathers report work–family conflict (Williams & Boushey, 2010).

The centrality of work to American life may have lessened since the 19th century, when the average citizen worked 70 hours per week, but current data indicate that work continues to dominate the lives of many Americans. This makes sense because the work you choose determines the people with whom you will associate for a major portion of your daily life; it also affects how much time off you will get and when you will get it, the sorts of continuing education and training you will engage in, the type of supervision you will labor under, the degree of autonomy you will experience, and the lifestyle you will enjoy. Thus, one of the first questions we ask a new acquaintance is, "What do you do?" Although people might respond by describing a variety of activities, they seldom do: There is an implicit, if not explicit, understanding that the query relates to what you do for a living. Such interactions reinforce the contention that occupation is one of the principal determinants in industrial society of social status (Super, 1976). They also support Sigmund Freud's statement that "work is the individual's link to reality." For better or worse, our choice of work colors the perceptual lens through which others view us and through which we view ourselves; we make different assumptions about people who say they are neurosurgeons compared to those who say they work at fast-food restaurants. In many countries, an occupational title tends to be used, correctly or incorrectly, to identify a person more than does any other single characteristic. It is important to note, however, that in some contexts and at different periods of history, one's choice of work was not as closely connected to one's identity as it is today; then, your surname or residence provided a primary means for self-identification.

How is it that work has become a core component of our identity? In primitive societies, work was taken for granted. You worked to survive. In classical societies, work was viewed as a curse insofar as it involved manual rather than intellectual labor. (It is interesting to note that the Greek word for *work* has the same root as the word for *sorrow*.) The early Christians viewed work as providing an opportunity to help those less fortunate by sharing the fruits of their labors. The notion that "idleness is akin to sinfulness" also emerged from early Christianity and was maintained throughout the Middle Ages, with the growing idea that work was appropriate for all people as a means of spiritual purification.

The Reformation brought little change to this attitude except for the influence of Martin Luther and John Calvin. Luther viewed work as a way to serve God: All work had equal spiritual value as long as you did it to the best of your ability. The meaning of work shifted dramatically in the theological perspective espoused by John Calvin and his followers. Calvin built on earlier traditions that viewed work as the will of God by adding the idea that the results of work— profits, for example—should be used to finance more ventures for more profit and, in turn, for more investment. In addition, Calvin's doctrine of predestination—that your fate after life is predetermined by God, not determined by you during your time on Earth—led his followers to search for visible signs in this life that they were predestined for eternal bliss in the next one. Success in work came to be viewed as a manifestation that one was predestined for eternal life. This evolved into the notion that one was obligated to God to achieve the most exalted and rewarding occupation; hence, striving for upward mobility became morally justified. This coincided with the belief that God rewards those who devote time and effort to work; thus was born the attitude known as the Protestant work ethic. The value attached to hard work, the need for all persons to work, and the justification of profit emerging from Calvinism would eventually form the basis of modern capitalism and industrialism. The values associated with the Protestant work ethic also served as the foundation of the 19th-century view of work labeled by Savickas (1993) as the "vocational ethic." This ethic valued independent effort, self-sufficiency, frugality, self-discipline, and humility, and it was brought across the Atlantic by the Puritans.

The meaning of work continued to evolve as some countries industrialized and increased their reliance on mechanically generated energy to perform it. The determination of a person's status became a question not only of how hard he worked but also a question of the type of work he did. In essence, *occupation* replaced *work* as a means of determining a person's status. Savickas (1993) noted that this shift in the nature of work occurred on the brink of the 20th century, when people turned their efforts toward organizing craftspeople into companies and building large cities around industries. The rugged individualism reflected in self-employment on farms and in small, craft-oriented businesses was replaced for many people by the challenge of working for a company and moving up the corporate ladder. Because people working for companies found little reward for independence, self-sufficiency, and self-management, a new work ethic emerged in the 20th century, described by Maccoby and Terzi (1981) as the "career ethic." The career ethic can be described as exhorting workers to "find your fit and don't quit." It defined successful careers as work of extended tenure within the same company, and successful career paths as those that ascended through organizational ranks. Today, this largely male, Caucasian middle- and upper-socioeconomic class model provides, at best, a minimally useful description of the careers most people experience.

Recent developments in the nature of work bring into question the viability of the career ethic (McCortney & Engels, 2003). Organizations served by the career ethic are downsizing in unprecedented numbers, with many workers finding that computers are performing the work they once did. Many employers view workers as expendable commodities. Workers who have lost their jobs to downsizing often feel betrayed and anxious about their prospects. After working long hours, and in some cases relocating to new communities to maintain their employment, many workers are less willing to sacrifice everything for their employers when their employers are so willing to sacrifice them. Survivors of downsizing realize that their situations are anything but secure (McCortney & Engels).

In addition, companies are flattening their organizational structures, leaving fewer career ladders to climb. The elimination of vertical hierarchies challenges the definition of a "successful" career. Hall and associates (1996) argue that changes in the structure of employment opportunities portend a future in which "people's careers will increasingly become a succession of 'ministages' of exploration-trial-mastery-exit, as they move in and out of various product areas, technologies, functions, organizations and other work environments" (p. 33). These shifts have led some people to suggest that "work has ended" and the "career has died" (Bridges, 1994; Rifkin, 1995). The tragic echoes of September 11, 2001, and the recent global economic downturn with resultant high unemployment reverberate widely, influencing politics, economics, international relations, and by logical extension, work. We are still sorting through how these events will shape people's approach to work. McCortney and Engels (2003) note that "it is essential to consider whether the current concept of the work ethic can be accurately, uniformly applied to all individuals in the 'salad bowl' of the United States today" (p. 135). Thanks to globalization, the question applies to nations outside the United States as well.

These changes in the work ethic highlight the fact that career development occurs amid relentless economic, social, cultural, technological, political, global, and historical change. These changes also underscore the fact that career development, like human development, is an evolutionary process. However, unlike biological development—which is ontogenetic and fairly predictable—career development is dynamic, interactive, contextual, relational, and often unpredictable.

LINKING WORK WITH WORTH

Despite historical changes in the meaning people attach to work and whether it is viewed as a blessing or a curse, work continues to play a central role in our lives (Brief & Nord, 1990; Mannheim, 1993). More recently, Doherty (2009) found that work provided vital social interactions for study participants, fulfilling social and personal needs and providing a sense of personal identity and meaning. Results supporting the primacy of work in the Doherty study were uniform across workplaces and occupations.

This phenomenon is not limited to the United States; results of cross-national studies suggest that many people in other countries view work as being more important than leisure, community, and even religion (Ardichvili & Kuchinke, 2009; Borchert & Landherr, 2009). Harpaz (1999) found that in several multinational studies, work was second in importance only to family activities. Not only do we continue to place an extremely high value on work, but people in the United States also tend to use psychological definitions of work. For example, Super (1976) defined work as:

> The systematic pursuit of an objective valued by oneself (even if only for survival) and desired by others; directed and consecutive, it requires expenditure of effort. It may be compensated (paid work) or uncompensated (volunteer work or an avocation). The objective may be intrinsic enjoyment of work itself, the structure given to life by the work role, the economic support which work makes possible, or the type of leisure that it facilitates. (p. 12)

Psychologically oriented definitions of work place the perceptions and motivations relative to work within a person's actions and control. Such definitions reflect a largely American view of work, which emphasizes individual control in career development (motivation, discipline, perseverance, goal-directedness) and deemphasizes the role played by sociological contextual variables (opportunity structure, the economy, socioeconomic status) in shaping one's career. Thus, if a person has a "successful career," we tend to attribute positive qualities to the person, regardless of whether we know him or her. The corresponding assumption is that a person without a successful career is inferior. Our denial of both the sociological factors affecting the trajectory of a person's career and the centrality of work in our culture becomes problematic because we link work with self-worth (Shanahan & Porfeli, 2002; Subich, 2001). Obviously, if our sense of self-worth is dependent on how we feel about our work contributions, our self-esteem can unravel quickly when work situations go awry (Herr, Cramer, & Niles, 2004). If you have ever felt undecided about your career choice, or if you have ever been fired from a job, or worked in a dissatisfying job, or been unable to find a job, or lived with anyone experiencing any of these events, you probably have a good sense of the bad feelings that often surface in negative work-related situations.

Linking work with self-worth also becomes problematic when we develop unrealistic expectations of work. For example, O'Toole (1981) suggests that "when it is said that work should be meaningful, what is meant is that it should contribute to the self-esteem, to the sense of self-fulfillment, through the mastering of one's self and one's environment, and to the sense that one is valued by society" (p. 15). These themes still inform the expectations that many people have for their careers. Although these are clearly desirable experiences, issues such as dehumanizing work conditions, unemployment, prejudicial hiring practices, downsizing, and mismatches between people and their jobs lead to the conclusion that work is anything but meaningful for many people. Denying contextual factors can lead people to blame the victim when work experiences are negative for reasons beyond their control.

Not only do many workers experience negative work situations and job dissatisfaction; they also do not know how to improve things. A 2011 Harris interactive survey sponsored by the National Career Development Association (2011) revealed that 59% of adults in the American workforce would try to get more and/or different information about career options if they could start their work life over. In the same poll, 45% of adult workers thought they needed more training or education to at least maintain their current earning power. An earlier National Career Development Association (NCDA) poll (NCDA, 1999) revealed that 39% of Americans did not have a career plan and 69% did not know how to make informed career choices. Obviously, many adults have information and skill deficits related to career planning and self-management. Many people also have limited opportunities to engage in systematic self-exploration for career development and are unclear about their training and educational needs. The same poll indicated that almost half of all U.S. workers experience job-related stress and think that their skills are being underutilized. Given the prevalence of these issues and our tendency to link work with self-worth, we may deduce that the need for competent career practitioners is substantial and urgent.

Difficulties in managing career tasks can be tracked developmentally. Mortimer, Zimmer-Gembeck, Holmes, and Shanahan (2002) offer evidence that many adolescents do not receive assistance in acquiring career development skills. Drawing on 69 interviews (43 females, 26 males) with participants in the Youth Development Project ($n = 1,000$), a longitudinal study of work through adolescence and early adulthood, researchers reported that the young participants had little formal instruction in how to find suitable work as they moved into postsecondary school. The lack of institutional support for young people making the school-to-work transition is perplexing given the centrality of work in people's lives. Mortimer and her colleagues contend that "more systematic efforts are needed to provide vocational information to youth in high schools" (p. 463) and that effort should be made to connect students with the schools and occupations in which they express an interest. Having actual experiences with potential occupations is important in differentiating between satisfied and dissatisfied entrants to the labor force, as well as those whose interests and jobs are congruent. "For youth who lack vocational direction, shifting schools and jobs can entail substantial economic, personal, and social costs" (Mortimer et al., p. 463).

High levels of career uncertainty and occupational dissatisfaction correlate with high levels of psychological and physical distress (Herr, 1989). High levels of unemployment are associated with increased rates of chemical dependency, interpersonal violence, suicide, criminal activity, and admission to psychiatric facilities (Herr et al., 2004; Kalton, 2001; Liem & Rayman, 1982). Difficult career situations often translate to difficult life situations. Fritzche and Parrish (2005) cite research supporting the "spillover hypothesis," which suggests that feelings in one area of life affect feelings in other areas. The ripple effect occurring when career situations go awry can be dramatic and tragic. Moreover, all counselors, regardless of work setting, will encounter these ripple effects either directly (by working with a client experiencing career difficulties) or indirectly (by working with a family member of a person experiencing career difficulties).

PROVIDING SYSTEMATIC CAREER DEVELOPMENT INTERVENTIONS

The need to provide systematic assistance to people trying to manage the influence of work on their lives is tremendous (National Career Development Association, 2011). The young, the elderly, the unemployed, the underemployed, the displaced worker, and members of diverse racial, ethnic, and socioeconomic groups all confront work-related issues that affect their lives. How well they can cope with these issues may be the difference between living a life that is meaningful and productive and one that is largely devoid of meaning and satisfaction.

Career counselors assist their clients in diverse ways. Counselors in high school, postsecondary, and community settings teach clients skills (self-assessment, job search, and career information acquisition) necessary for effective career planning and decision making. Counselors in all settings also help their students or clients realize that decisions about work influence one's life outside of work. Correspondingly, counselors can help clients develop realistic expectations of what work can provide in terms of personal satisfaction, and they can explain that activities and relationships outside of work can provide satisfaction when it isn't forthcoming on the job. Given our emphasis on intra-individual variables in career development, a major task confronting counselors is helping people see that their job doesn't have to define their self-worth, and that self-worth derives more from how they live than where they work.

More specifically, effective career counselors help their clients or students learn how to do the following:

1. Use both rational and intuitive approaches when making career decisions.
2. Achieve clarity about the importance they attach to their various life roles and the values they want to embody by inhabiting these roles.
3. Cope effectively with ambiguity, change, and transition.
4. Develop and maintain self-awareness, especially as it pertains to their interests, values, motivation, and aptitudes.
5. Develop and maintain occupational and career awareness.
6. Develop occupationally relevant skills and knowledge, and keep them up to date.
7. Access and participate in lifelong learning opportunities.
8. Search for jobs effectively.
9. Provide and receive career mentoring.
10. Develop and maintain skills in multicultural awareness and communication.

Skills related to these areas must be placed in a developmental context so that counselors working with children, adolescents, and adults can provide appropriate career interventions and respond to former labor secretary Elaine L. Chao's point that "To succeed in the 21st century, our nation must be prepared to adapt to changes in our economy—in how we work, where we work, and how we balance our professional and family lives. We cannot simply react to changes. We must anticipate them, thus helping all workers to have as fulfilling and financially rewarding careers as they aspire to have."

DEFINITION OF TERMS

A major issue in the career development field is the misuse of terminology by practitioners as well as clients. For example, it is common for counselors to use the terms *career* and *work* interchangeably; it is also common for counselors to talk about "doing career development" as if it were an intervention rather than the object of an intervention. Similarly, counselors often conflate *career guidance* with *career counseling*. This lack of precision confuses practitioners, students, and clients and compromises the efficacy of career development interventions. When people use language imprecisely, they imply that terminology does not matter. However, practitioners are "engaged in a verbal profession in which words and symbols frequently become the content of the interactions they have with clients" (Herr, 1997, p. 241). Their words have power, and they need to communicate with clarity and precision. This enhances the credibility of our profession and provides common ground for devising, implementing, and evaluating career development interventions. We define key terms in the following paragraphs.

Career

Rather than limiting the definition of career to work, we advocate viewing *career* as a lifestyle concept. Accordingly, we concur with Super's (1976) view of career as the course of events constituting a life, and Herr et al.'s (2004) notion of career as the total constellation of roles played over the course of a lifetime. These definitions are broader than the one offered by Sears (1982), which defines career as the totality of work one does in a lifetime. Broader definitions acknowledge both the multiple life roles people play and differences in the importance they assign to these roles, especially with regard to work (Richardson, 1993). Broad definitions of career include the life role of homemaker, for example, as well as community volunteer.

Career Development

Career development refers to the lifelong psychological and behavioral processes as well as contextual influences shaping a person's career over the life span. As such, it involves the person's creation of a career pattern, decision-making style, integration of life roles, values expression, and life-role self-concepts (Herr et al., 2004).

Career Development Interventions

Career development interventions, defined broadly, comprise activities that empower people to cope effectively with career development tasks (Spokane, 1991). Every activity that helps people develop self-awareness and occupational awareness, learn decision-making skills, acquire job-search skills, adjust to occupational choices after they have been implemented, and cope with job stress can be labeled career development interventions. These activities include individual and group career counseling, career development programs, career education, computer-assisted career development programs, and computer information delivery systems as well as other forms of delivering career information to clients.

Career Counseling

Career counseling is a formal relationship in which a professional counselor assists a client or group of clients to cope more effectively with career concerns (choosing a career, managing career transitions, coping with job-related stress, looking for a job). Career counselors typically establish rapport with their clients, assess clients' career concerns, establish goals for the counseling relationship, intervene in ways that help clients cope more effectively with career concerns, evaluate clients' progress, and, depending on clients' progress, either offer additional interventions or terminate counseling.

Career Education

Career education is a systematic attempt to influence the career development of students and adults through various kinds of educational strategies, including providing occupational information, worksite-based experiences, career planning courses, and infusing career-related concepts into the academic curriculum (Hoyt, Evans, Mackin, & Magnum, 1972).

Career Development Programs

Career development programs are defined as "a systematic program of counselor-coordinated information and experiences designed to facilitate individual career development" (Herr & Cramer, 1996, p. 33). These programs typically contain goals, objectives, activities, and methods for evaluating the effectiveness of the activities in achieving the goals.

Career Development Practitioners

A variety of practitioners provide career assistance in various settings. Doctoral-level psychologists specializing in career development interventions work in private practice, university counseling centers, corporate settings, and community-based agencies. They typically hold a doctorate in counseling psychology from a program accredited by the American Psychological Association and use the term *vocational* or *career psychologist* to describe themselves. Licensed professional counselors also provide career interventions in settings similar to those in which vocational psychologists work. In addition, they often work in school settings, introducing career information and providing assistance to students in elementary, middle, and high schools. Most practitioners have a master's and/or doctoral degree in counseling, often from a program accredited by the Council for Accreditation of Counseling and Related Educational Programs (CACREP). Career development facilitators (CDFs) may or may not have a postsecondary degree but have completed 120 hours of training with an approved provider that equips them to offer more entry-level career assistance, often focusing on job search skills (résumé writing, interview skills, networking) and using basic self-assessment activities. They work primarily in employment centers, schools, and postsecondary settings.

IMPORTANT EVENTS IN THE HISTORY OF CAREER DEVELOPMENT INTERVENTIONS

The rise of career development interventions accelerated in the late 1800s as the United States shifted from an agriculture-based national economy to one grounded in industry and manufacturing. This shift brought new industrial and manufacturing work opportunities, which in turn created new dilemmas for American workers. Workers were confronted with identifying and accessing these new jobs, which were often located in urban areas and required them to move away from their rural homes. In addition, large numbers of immigrants arrived in the United States seeking new lives and opportunities (Herr, 2001).

In the early part of the 20th century, emphasis was placed on helping people identify and choose appropriate occupations and vocations. The time frame was limited as guidance for vocational decision making emphasized the act of making a choice and viewed the process as a single point-in-time event. In his brief history of career counseling in the United States, Pope (2000) notes that this early phase continued until 1920 and emphasized job-placement services.

The early focus on job placement reflected the prevailing white, middle-class, male model of career development that dominated the field until recent times. This view involved choosing an occupation early in one's life (usually upon leaving secondary or postsecondary school) and staying in the chosen occupation until retirement. To help people cope with vocational decision making, practitioners used objectivistic methodologies, usually in the form of aptitude tests and interest surveys.

Important advances regarding the development and use of aptitude tests and interest surveys were identified and articulated in books such as *Aptitude Testing* by Clark Hull (1928); *Aptitudes and Aptitude Testing* by Walter Bingham (1937); and *Vocational Interests of Men and Women* by E. K. Strong (1943). For most of the 20th century, the process of matching a person to a job based on his or her traits and the job's demands dominated the ways practitioners helped people find suitable work.

FRANK PARSONS

The early approach to career development—with its emphasis on testing clients, providing them with information, and advising them on which choices seemed to offer a good chance of occupational success—evolved from the work of Frank Parsons. An engineer and social reformer in the early 1900s, Parsons merged his training and commitment to outline a systematic process of occupational decision making, which he referred to as "true reasoning." Zytowski (2001) noted that in 1906 Parsons delivered a lecture entitled "The Ideal City" to the Economic Club of Boston, in which he cited young people's need of assistance in choosing a vocation. The lecture generated requests by recent high school graduates for personal meetings with Parsons, from which he generated his systematic approach to vocational guidance. In his book *Choosing a Vocation* (1909), published a year after his death, Parsons enumerated principles and techniques he found useful in helping adolescents, first at Breadwinner's College at the Civic Service House, a settlement house in Boston, and later at the Boston Vocation Bureau. Here are Parsons's principles:

1. It is better to choose a vocation than merely to hunt for a job.
2. No one should choose a vocation without careful self-analysis, thorough, honest, and under guidance.
3. The youth should have a large survey of the field of vocations and not simply drop into the convenient or accidental position.
4. Expert advice, or the advice of men who have made a careful study of men and vocations and of the conditions of success, must be better and safer for a young man than the absence of it.
5. Putting it down on paper seems a simple matter, but it is one of supreme importance in study. (Parsons, 1909, p. viii)

These principles formed the basis for the techniques Parsons used to help young people choose a vocation. These techniques, including observing workers in their settings and reading biographies and existing occupational descriptions, were incorporated into the "Parsonian approach," which consisted of three steps or requirements that would help someone make an occupational choice:

1. Develop a clear understanding of yourself and your aptitudes, abilities, interests, resources, limitations, and other qualities.
2. Develop knowledge of the requirements and conditions of success, advantages and disadvantages, compensation, opportunities, and prospects in different lines of work.
3. Use "true reasoning" on the relations of these two groups of facts. (Parsons, 1909, p. 5)

Step one requires self-investigation and self-revelation, assisted by a career counselor when possible. The second step relies on accurate and comprehensive occupational information. Because the available occupational information rarely met these requirements during Parsons's time, he developed materials that described occupations in great detail (compensation, task requirements, work settings). The third step, true reasoning, relied on the person's capacity (with the help of a counselor) to integrate information acquired from steps one and two into a career decision—a task that appears straightforward but in practice proves challenging.

Parsons developed his model against a background of social upheaval (rapid urbanization, proliferation of child labor, immigration), economic change (the rise of industrialism and growing division of labor), and scientific advances (the emergence of human and behavioral sciences) occurring in the United States. These shifts required workers trained to perform jobs demanding specific skills and aptitudes, help for young people to develop career plans, and protection from abuse for young people in the labor force. Parsons's approach was also congruent with the dominant scientific thinking of the 20th century, which emphasized positivism and objective methodology—that is, the Parsonian model encouraged practitioners to use standardized assessment to identify clients' interests, values, and abilities, thereby helping discover where they fit into the occupational structure.

Parsons's three requirements formed the basis of what evolved into the *matching model* and *trait-and-factor* approaches to career development interventions, which is located within the *person-environment* tradition of psychology. These elements are essentially self-knowledge, occupational knowledge, and decision-making skills.

The basic assumptions of the person-environment tradition are:

1. As a result of one's characteristics, each worker is best suited to a specific type of work.
2. Groups of workers in different occupations have different characteristics.
3. Occupational choice is a single point-in-time event.
4. Career development is mostly a cognitive process relying on rational decision making.
5. Occupational adjustment depends on the degree of agreement between worker characteristics and work demands.

The matching model sought to address the challenges inherent in step three of Parsons's model. An initial solution to the challenge of matching persons to environments was the practice of clinical matching, in which expert clinical judgments were made to ascertain a person's chances of success within an occupational field based on the use of a psychograph. The psychograph, developed by Morris Viteles in 1932, was a graphic representation of a person's relevant characteristics (abilities, trainings, specific vocational skills) and strengths in each area, rated from 1 to 10. Job psychographs were also developed with a similar system to rate characteristics relevant to successful performance in a particular occupation. The two psychographs were then compared, and a person's "goodness of match" for the occupation was determined.

Next emerged the trait-and-factor approach, with its emphasis on a person's relevant traits and characteristics, usually identified through the use of standardized tests or inventories. The same approach is used to describe occupational factors or requirements (occupations are profiled according to the degree to which they require certain traits and aptitudes). Then the person's profile of traits is matched to requirements of specific occupations. The goal of this type of matching is to identify the degree of fit between a person and an occupation.

When conducting trait-and-factor career counseling, Williamson (1939) advocated a six-step process:

1. Analysis
2. Synthesis
3. Diagnosis
4. Prognosis
5. Counseling
6. Follow-up.

In this model, the counselor collects clinical data (using interview techniques) and statistical data (often using standardized assessment), synthesizes the information, and draws inferences about the client's strengths and weaknesses. These help clarify the client's presenting problem and identify its probable causes. For Williamson (1939), the client's presenting problems can be diagnosed as (a) no choice, (b) uncertain choice, (c) unwise choice, or (d) a discrepancy between interests and aptitudes. Once the client's problem is diagnosed, the counselor offers a prognosis that includes alternative courses of action or adjustments, and the degree of success the client is likely to encounter with each. Counseling in Williamson's model involves "helping the client marshal and organize personal and other resources to achieve optimal adjustment either now or in the future" (Isaacson, 1985, p. 82). Finally, the counselor follows up by asking the client to evaluate the effectiveness of the counseling and whether she or he requires further assistance.

In classic trait-and-factor approaches, the counselor is active and directive while the client is relatively passive. It is the counselor's responsibility to take the lead in the collection, integration, and organization of client data. Moreover, the counselor uses these data in conjunction with occupational information to help the client identify a plan of action.

The Theory of Work Adjustment (TWA), developed by René Dawis and Lloyd Lofquist at the University of Minnesota in the 1960s, is an excellent illustration of the person-environment tradition (Dawis, 1996). TWA addresses the "correspondence between the individual (abilities and needs) and the environment (ability requirements and reinforcer system)" (Dawis, England, & Lofquist, 1964, p. 11). TWA focuses on interactions between people and their environments, and posits "the person and environment attempt to maintain correspondence with each other" (Dawis, 1996, p. 81). Both the worker and the work environment have needs and requirements that must be satisfied. A person adjusts well to work when the person and the environment are corresponsive to each other's requirements. Such correspondence is not always achieved, however. The degree to which a worker is willing to tolerate discorrespondence defines the worker's flexibility. Work environments also possess varying degrees of flexibility. The worker's tenure in a job is influenced by the worker's satisfactoriness (the work environment's degree of satisfaction with the worker), the worker's satisfaction (the degree to which the work environment provides the worker with sufficient and appropriate reinforcers, or rewards), and the work environment's perseverance (Dawis et al., 1964). Thus, there are four scenarios that describe a worker's experience: The worker is satisfied and the worker's performance is satisfactory; the worker is satisfied but the worker's performance is unsatisfactory; the worker is dissatisfied but the worker's performance is satisfactory; or the worker is dissatisfied and the worker's performance is unsatisfactory (Dawis, 2005). The first condition (satisfied and satisfactory) theoretically leads to continued employment, whereas the latter three theoretically lead to actions to change the situation, also known as adjustment behavior (Dawis, 2005). Although research pertaining to TWA has generally supported the theory, TWA has failed to generate robust research, and few empirical tests of TWA have been published in the past 15 years (Swanson & Gore, 2000).

Dawis (2002) also describes a more generalized TWA in his Person-Environment Correspondence (PEC) theory. A basic assumption of PEC theory is that persons (P) interact with environments (E). Both P and E are active and reactive. Moreover, both P and E have requirements and expectations that they expect their interactions to fulfill. For example, a counselor (P) working within a counseling environment (E) expects to have the opportunity to help others by using her counseling skills. Likewise, the counseling environment (E) expects the counselor (P) to perform competently and successfully. To the degree that such expectations are met, both P and E are satisfied, and corresponding behaviors are maintained. When expectations are not met, however, dissatisfaction occurs and P and/or E must adjust. Adjustments are made until satisfaction is achieved or until P and/or E gives up. A good fit, or correspondence, occurs when the person's capabilities fulfill the environment's requirements. A bad fit, or discorrespondence, occurs when the person's capabilities do not fulfill the environment's requirements.

Recent studies on TWA are few, but there are some, and they tend to focus on the work experiences of adults. For example, Lyons, Velez, Mehta, and Neill (2014) used TWA in their study of work adjustment among economically distressed African American workers. Their participants reported that perceptions of person-organization (P-O) fit were positively related to job satisfaction and negatively related to turnover intentions, and that job satisfaction was negatively related to turnover intentions (the greater the satisfaction, the less likely it is that the worker would want to leave his or her job). They also found that perceptions of racial climate were positively related to perceptions of P-O fit and negatively related to turnover intentions (the more positive the racial climate, the greater the perceived fit and the less likely that one would want to leave the job). Not surprisingly, racial climate is an important factor in job satisfaction and turnover intentions. The implication for TWA is that context matters and often overrides more familiar indicators of job satisfaction.

Although current techniques used in person-environment approaches such as TWA and PEC are more advanced than those advocated by Parsons, his contributions remain significant. In *History of Vocational Guidance,* John Brewer (1942) offered this list of Parsons's innovations:

1. He paved the way for vocational guidance in the schools and colleges by advocating their role in it and offering methods they could use.
2. He began the training of counselors.
3. He used all of the scientific tools available to him at the time.
4. He developed "steps" to be followed in the vocational progress of the individual.
5. He organized the work of the Vocation Bureau in a way that laid the groundwork for groups to model in schools, colleges, and other agencies.
6. He recognized the importance of his work and secured for it the appropriate publicity, financial support, and endorsements from influential educators, employers, and other public figures.
7. He laid the groundwork leading to the continuance and expansion of the vocational guidance movement by involving friends and associates in it and preparing the manuscript for *Choosing a Vocation.* (p. 27)

But there were other contributors to the new field of vocational counseling. The testing movement born of the work of James Cattell, Alfred Binet, and Walter Bingham was a force in the growth of career development interventions and helped codify Parsons's emphasis on self-understanding.

Influential publications, organizations, and legislation also emerged in the early part of the 20th century. *The Vocational Guidance Newsletter* was first published by Boston's Vocation Bureau in 1911 (it opened in 1908 with Parsons as its first director and vocational counselor); the National Vocational Guidance Association (NVGA) was founded in Grand Rapids, Michigan, in 1913; the U.S. Department of Labor was organized in 1913; the *Vocational Guidance Bulletin* was first published in 1915 by NVGA; the Vocational Rehabilitation Act became law in 1918; and Harry D. Kitson of Teachers College authored *The Psychology of Vocational Adjustment,* published in 1925.

The Minnesota Employment Stabilization Research Institute was established in 1931. Among the institute's findings was that improved guidance services were needed to create a more stable labor force and foster recovery from the Great Depression. The U.S. Employment Service was created in 1933 by the Wagner-Peyser Act, and 1939 saw publication of the first edition of the *Dictionary of Occupational Titles,* in which 18,000 occupations were titled, coded, and defined.

In the early 1940s, personnel testing and placement activities were greatly expanded as a result of World War II (the G.I. Bill was enacted in 1944). An excellent example of the era's advances in testing appears in 1943 in E. K. Strong, Jr.'s *Vocational Interests of Men and Women,* in which he documents nearly 20 years of interest measurement research. Also, during World War II women entered the workforce in unprecedented numbers, with many finding successful employment in manual and technical jobs that had been previously held exclusively by men.

As testing and placement activities were expanding, Carl Rogers's *Counseling and Psychotherapy* (1942) appeared in print. In the book, Rogers highlighted the importance of attending to clients' verbalized feelings: "Among the significant developments which resulted were a revamping of the older cognitive concept of the client in vocational guidance to include the dynamics of affective and motivational behavior, the increased emphasis on self-acceptance, and self-understanding as goals of vocational counseling" (Borow, 1964, p. 57).

Another significant event occurred in 1951 when Donald E. Super launched the Career Pattern Study, one of the first longitudinal studies of career development. In his excellent historical review, Borow (1964) noted that Super more than anyone else had helped shift the focus of career development interventions from a "static, single-choice-at-a-point-in-time concept" (p. 60) focused on vocational choice toward a model that conceptualized career development as an ongoing process involving the congruent implementation of the person's self-concept in a compatible occupational role. Super was primarily responsible for changing the definition of vocational guidance from "the process of assisting an individual to choose an occupation, prepare for it, enter upon it, and progress in it" to

> [t]he process of helping a person to develop and accept an integrated and adequate picture of himself [sic] and of his role in the world of work, to test this concept against reality, and to convert it into reality, with satisfaction to himself and to society. (Super, 1951, p. 89)

Super's multidisciplinary approach to studying career development incorporated contributions from economics and sociology while placing career behavior in the context of human development.

The 1940s and 1950s also saw the emergence of professional organizations related to career development. In 1947, the American Psychological Association (APA) created organizational divisions resulting in the establishment of Division 17, which from 1947 to 1952 was known as the Division of Counseling and Guidance and later renamed Counseling Psychology. Since its creation, this division has served as the primary APA division for psychologists interested in career development interventions. More recently, a special interest group within Division 17 formed to focus more tightly on the topic of career development theory and practice.

The merging of the NVGA, the American College Personnel Association, the National Association of Guidance Supervisors and Counselor Trainers, and the Student Personnel Association for Teacher Education resulted in the formation of the American Personnel and Guidance Association in 1951. The American School Counselor Association was formed in 1953, and its primary focus was the provision of career services to young people. Finally, in 1957, the American Personnel and Guidance Association created the American Board on Professional Standards in Vocational Counseling, the functions of which "were to evaluate and certify qualified vocational counseling agencies and to foster the maintenance of high professional standards, including standards of ethical practice" (Borow, 1964, p. 62).

Still, the primary organization for professional career counselors has been the NCDA. Since its inception as the NVGA, the NCDA has dedicated itself to improving the quality of services provided by career development practitioners. As early as 1920, it established a code of principles to guide practitioners in the delivery of career-related services. In 1981 its board of directors approved the first policy statement for the roles and competencies of career counselors; it has been updated several times since, most recently in 2003. The most recent competencies are listed in Figure 1.1. This statement reflects a broad range of general counseling skills and specific career-related competencies. The competencies reflect the belief of the NCDA that professional career counselors are trained practitioners with specialized education in career development. The competencies also reflect the importance of providing a wide range of career development interventions to meet the needs of diverse client populations. An excellent history of the NCDA appears in *The Career Development Quarterly, 36,* 1988.

In the 1960s, the field expanded as new behavioral, developmental, and psychoanalytical theories of career development appeared; the number of career assessment instruments grew dramatically (see Kapes & Whitfield, 2002); and computer-assisted career guidance and information-delivery systems in secondary schools and higher education settings emerged (Bowlsbey, Dikel, & Sampson, 2002).

During the 1970s, career education became a federal priority, highlighting the importance of providing career development interventions to both young people and adults. "The term 'career education' also symbolized the need to address systematically a range of conditions that were changing the relationship between education and work, particularly with regard to preparing students to understand the linkages between educational opportunities and the subsequent implications of these in work choice and work adjustment" (Herr & Cramer, 1996, p. 34). Recent efforts in the 1990s by school-to-work transition proponents focused on imparting knowledge, skills, and attitudes essential to effective workforce participation that closely resembled the ideas of career education efforts initiated in the 1970s (Lent & Worthington, 1999).

Another recent critical development has been increased attention to the career development needs of diverse client populations. Research related to career development theory and practice has transcended addressing the needs of white, middle-class men. Issues of gender, class, ability status, sexual orientation, and cultural bias in career development theories, and practices have been exposed, resulting in greater attention to how such variables affect the

These competency statements are for those professionals interested and trained in the field of career counseling. For the purpose of these statements, career counseling is defined as the process of assisting individuals in the development of a life career with focus on the definition of the worker role and how that role interacts with other life roles.

Professional competency statements provide guidance for the minimum competencies necessary to perform effectively a particular occupation or job within a particular field. Professional career counselors (master's degree or higher) or persons in career development positions must demonstrate the knowledge and skills for a specialty in career counseling that the generalist counselor might not possess. Skills and knowledge are represented by designated competency areas, which have been developed by professional career counselors and counselor educators. The Career Counseling Competency Statements can serve as a guide for career counseling training programs or as a checklist for persons wanting to acquire or enhance their skills in career counseling.

Minimum Competencies

In order to work as a professional engaged in career counseling, the individual must demonstrate minimum competencies in 11 designated areas. These 11 areas are: Career Development Theory, Individual and Group Counseling Skills, Individual/Group Assessment, Information/Resources, Program Promotion, Management, and Implementation, Coaching, Consultation, and Performance Improvement, Diverse Populations, Supervision, Ethical/Legal Issues, Research/Evaluation, and Technology. These areas and their respective performance indicators are defined as follows:

Career Counseling Competencies and Performance Indicators

Career Development Theory

Theory base and knowledge considered essential for professionals engaging in career counseling and development. Demonstration of knowledge of:

1. Counseling theories and associated techniques
2. Theories and models of career development
3. Individual differences related to gender, sexual orientation, race, ethnicity, and physical and mental capacities
4. Theoretical models for career development and associated counseling and information-delivery techniques and resources
5. Human growth and development throughout the life span
6. Role relationships which facilitate life-work planning
7. Information, techniques, and models related to career planning and placement

Individual and Group Counseling Skills

Individual and group counseling competencies considered essential to effective career counseling. Demonstration of ability to:

1. Establish and maintain productive personal relationships with individuals
2. Establish and maintain a productive group climate
3. Collaborate with clients in identifying personal goals
4. Identify and select techniques appropriate to client or group goals and client needs, psychological states, and developmental tasks
5. Identify and understand clients' personal characteristics related to career
6. Identify and understand social contextual conditions affecting clients' careers
7. Identify and understand familial, subcultural, and cultural structures and functions as they are related to clients' careers
8. Identify and understand clients' career decision-making processes
9. Identify and understand clients' attitudes toward work and workers
10. Identify and understand clients' biases toward work and workers based on gender, race, and cultural stereotypes

Figure 1.1
Introduction to career counseling competency statements.

Source: Revised by the NCDA Board of Directors, 2009. © 2009 National Career Development Association. Retrieved March 8, 2015, from ncda.org.

11. Challenge and encourage clients to take action to prepare for and initiate role transitions by:

- locating sources of relevant information and experience
- obtaining and interpreting information and experiences
- acquiring skills needed to make role transitions

12. Assist the client to acquire a set of employability and job-search skills
13. Support and challenge clients to examine life-work roles, including the balance of work, leisure, family, and community in their careers

Individual/Group Assessment

Individual/group assessment skills considered essential for professionals engaging in career counseling. Demonstration of ability to:

1. Assess personal characteristics such as aptitude, achievement, interests, values, and personality traits.
2. Assess leisure interests, learning style, life roles, self-concept, career maturity, vocational identity, career indecision, work environment preference (e.g., work satisfaction), and other related lifestyle/development issues
3. Assess conditions of the work environment (such as tasks, expectations, norms, and qualities of the physical and social settings)
4. Evaluate and select valid and reliable instruments appropriate to the client's gender, sexual orientation, race, ethnicity, and physical and mental capacities.
5. Use computer-delivered assessment measures effectively and appropriately
6. Select assessment techniques appropriate for group administration and those appropriate for individual administration
7. Administer, score, and report findings from career assessment instruments appropriately
8. Interpret data from assessment instruments and present the results to clients and to others
9. Assist the client and others designated by the client to interpret data from assessment instruments
10. Write an accurate report of assessment results

Information/Resources

Information/resource base and knowledge essential for professionals engaging in career counseling. Demonstration of knowledge of:

1. Education, training, and employment trends; labor market information and resources that provide information about job tasks, functions, salaries, requirements and future outlooks related to broad occupational fields and individual occupations
2. Resources and skills that clients utilize in life-work planning and management
3. Community/professional resources available to assist clients in career planning, including job search
4. Changing roles of women and men and the implications that this has for education, family, and leisure
5. Methods of good use of computer-based career information delivery systems (CIDS) and computer-assisted career guidance systems (CACGS) to assist with career planning

Program Promotion, Management, and Implementation

Knowledge and skills necessary to develop, plan, implement, and manage comprehensive career development programs in a variety of settings. Demonstration of knowledge of:

1. Designs that can be used in the organization of career development programs
2. Needs assessment and evaluation techniques and practices
3. Organizational theories, including diagnosis, behavior, planning, organizational communication, and management useful in implementing and administering career development programs

Figure 1.1
(*Continued*)

4. Methods of forecasting, budgeting, planning, costing, policy analysis, resource allocation, and quality control
5. Leadership theories and approaches for evaluation and feedback, organizational change, decision making, and conflict resolution
6. Professional standards and criteria for career development programs
7. Societal trends and state and federal legislation that influence the development and implementation of career development programs

Demonstration of ability to:

8. Implement individual and group programs in career development for specified populations
9. Train others about the appropriate use of computer-based systems for career information and planning
10. Plan, organize, and manage a comprehensive career resource center
11. Implement career development programs in collaboration with others
12. Identify and evaluate staff competencies
13. Mount a marketing and public relations campaign on behalf of career development activities and services

Coaching, Consultation, and Performance Improvement

Knowledge and skills considered essential in relating to individuals and organizations that impact the career counseling and development process. Demonstration of ability to:

1. Use consultation theories, strategies, and models
2. Establish and maintain a productive consultative relationship with people who can influence a client's career
3. Help the general public and legislators to understand the importance of career counseling, career development, and life-work planning
4. Impact public policy as it relates to career development and workforce planning
5. Analyze future organizational needs and current level of employee skills and develop performance improvement training
6. Mentor and coach employees

Diverse Populations

Knowledge and skills considered essential in relating to diverse populations that impact career counseling and development processes. Demonstration of ability to:

1. Identify development models and multicultural counseling competencies
2. Identify development needs unique to various diverse populations, including those of different gender, sexual orientation, ethnic group, race, and physical or mental capacity
3. Define career development programs to accommodate needs unique to various diverse populations
4. Find appropriate methods or resources to communicate with limited-English-proficient individuals
5. Identify alternative approaches to meet career planning needs for individuals of various diverse populations
6. Identify community resources and establish linkages to assist clients with specific needs
7. Assist other staff members, professionals, and community members in understanding the unique needs/characteristics of diverse populations with regard to career exploration, employment expectations, and economic/social issues
8. Advocate for the career development and employment of diverse populations
9. Design and deliver career development programs and materials to hard-to-reach populations

Supervision

Knowledge and skills considered essential in critically evaluating counselor or career development facilitator performance, maintaining and improving professional skills. Demonstration of:

1. Ability to recognize own limitations as a career counselor and to seek supervision or refer clients when appropriate
2. Ability to utilize supervision on a regular basis to maintain and improve counselor skills
3. Ability to consult with supervisors and colleagues regarding client and counseling issues and issues related to one's own professional development as a career counselor

Figure 1.1
(Continued)

4. Knowledge of supervision models and theories
5. Ability to provide effective supervision to career counselors and career development facilitators at different levels of experience
6. Ability to provide effective supervision to career development facilitators at different levels of experience by:

- knowledge of their roles, competencies, and ethical standards
- determining their competence in each of the areas included in their certification
- further training them in competencies, including interpretation of assessment instruments
- monitoring and mentoring their activities in support of the professional career counselor and scheduling regular consultations for the purpose of reviewing their activities

Ethical/Legal Issues

Information base and knowledge essential for the ethical and legal practice of career counseling. Demonstration of knowledge of:

1. Adherence to ethical codes and standards relevant to the profession of career counseling (e.g., National Board for Certified Counselors [NBCC], NCDA, and American Counseling Association [ACA])
2. Current ethical and legal issues which affect the practice of career counseling with all populations
3. Current ethical/legal issues with regard to the use of computer-assisted career guidance systems
4. Ethical standards relating to consultation issues
5. State and federal statutes relating to client confidentiality

Research/Evaluation

Knowledge and skills considered essential to understanding and conducting research and evaluation in career counseling and development. Demonstration of ability to:

1. Write a research proposal
2. Use types of research and research designs appropriate to career counseling and development research
3. Convey research findings related to the effectiveness of career counseling programs
4. Design, conduct, and use the results of evaluation programs
5. Design evaluation programs which take into account the need of various diverse populations, including persons of both genders, differing sexual orientations, different ethnic and racial backgrounds, and differing physical and mental capacities
6. Apply appropriate statistical procedures to career development research

Technology

Knowledge and skills considered essential in using technology to assist individuals with career planning. Demonstration of knowledge of:

1. Various computer-based guidance and information systems as well as services available on the Internet
2. Standards by which such systems and services are evaluated
3. Ways in which to use computer-based systems and Internet services to assist individuals with career planning that are consistent with ethical standards
4. Characteristics of clients which make them profit more or less from use of technology-driven systems
5. Methods to evaluate and select a system to meet local needs

Figure 1.1
(*Continued*)

process and emphasizing the importance of including cultural context (Chung, 2001; Lee, 2012; Pope, 2012). Models of identity development as they relate to gender, race, sexual orientation, and disability status are increasingly being integrated into career development theory and practice (Pope, 2000). Career treatment outcome studies are also moving beyond traditional college student samples to examine intervention effects with more diverse populations (Luzzo, 2000).

Exposing the myriad ways that societal context artificially limits career development for many people has awakened career theorists and practitioners to the importance of addressing social justice in career development interventions (Blustein, 2013; Chope, 2006; O'Brien, 2001). Lee (1989) agrees, stating that career counselors must act as "career development advocates for disenfranchised clients by actively challenging long-standing traditions that stand in the way of equity in the workplace" (p. 219). Indeed, striving for social justice through career interventions commenced with the work of Frank Parsons and, therefore, is an important theme throughout the history of the field. In this regard, Herr and Niles (1998) note:

> for most of the last 100 years, whether or not it has been explicit, counseling and, in particular, career counseling and career guidance have become sociopolitical instruments, identified by legislation at the federal level, to deal with emerging social concerns such as equity and excellence in educational and occupational opportunities, unemployment, human capital development, persons with disabilities, child abuse, AIDS, teenage pregnancy, substance abuse, career decision making relative to the preparation for entrance into emerging skilled occupations, and the identification and encouragement of students with high academic potential to enter higher education in science and mathematics. (p. 121)

Revitalizing the spirit of social justice by maximizing opportunities for all members of society is becoming an essential aspect of career interventions for many practitioners (see Blustein, 2006).

Conducting career interventions for social change requires counselors to provide multifaceted approaches and expand their roles beyond traditional practice. Career counseling for social change begins with practitioners possessing the multicultural knowledge, skills, and attitudes necessary to understand how a client's environment influences the interpretations and meanings he or she attaches to work and employment opportunities. Multicultural competencies are the foundation for identifying social action strategies to facilitate career development.

Career practitioners engaged in social action also use community resources to give clients access to information and opportunities (employment offices, "one-stop career shops," support groups). These counselors serve as facilitators of social change by providing information, referrals, and encouragement to clients (Enright, Conyers, & Szymanski, 1996). To play this role effectively, career counselors are required to maintain files of useful resources, including names of potential mentors representing a diversity of backgrounds (African American; Asian American; persons with disabilities; members of the gay, lesbian, bisexual, and transgender community), information on accommodations for disabled persons with different functional limitations, names of employers willing to provide opportunities for job shadowing and internships, and names of persons willing to participate in informational interviewing experiences (p. 111).

Having a thorough knowledge of community career resources also empowers counselors to identify areas where services are lacking. When they do, counselors take on a strong advocacy role and seek to rectify service deficiencies in their communities (Lee, 1989).

Advocacy is also important when clients' career concerns are the result of external factors such as large-scale downsizing, wage stagnation, and salary inequities experienced by women, persons of color, and persons with disabilities. Women working full-time earn 77% of what their male counterparts earn (Pew Research Center, 2014). The inequities experienced by persons with disabilities are even greater. In February 2015, 8.7 million people were unemployed in the United States, 2.7 million of whom had been unemployed longer than 27 weeks (Bureau of Labor Statistics, 2015). Those who have not experienced job loss, either directly or indirectly through a family member or close friend, are acutely aware of the tenuous nature of job security and experience high levels of guilt, fear, and anxiety.

Career counselors concerned with social justice address community concerns as well as those of individual clients (Cahill & Martland, 1996), and they do it by integrating individual career counseling skills and community counseling skills. Integrating strategies is critical in rural communities where economic restructuring can threaten their very existence. Cahill and Martland argue that community career counseling builds on the strength of individual career counseling and offers assistance to people struggling to maintain their communities. Thus, in addition to individual career counseling skills, career practitioners need skills in facilitating group problem solving and consensus building, and an understanding of social and economic factors that affect careers in contemporary society. Finally, Ludwikowski, Vogel, and Armstrong (2009) point out the importance of career interventions that engage potential clients via their social networks, electronic and otherwise. The use of social media to communicate the importance of career counseling and normalize use of pertinent resources may help reduce the stigma of seeking counseling in the first place.

Career counselors who instill hope in their clients and empower them to manage their careers are multiculturally competent. They convey information and referrals; advocate for their clients when employment practices and community traditions impede equity in the workplace; and integrate individual career counseling skills with community counseling skills to help people maintain their communities and create opportunities for career development (Blustein, 2006; Chope, 2006).

FUTURE TRENDS IN CAREER DEVELOPMENT INTERVENTIONS

Bingham and Ward (1994) note that "if vocational counseling was born from the changing demographics and economic needs of this century, then clearly career counseling will need to change in response to the changing needs of the coming century" (p. 168). Indeed, technological advancement, the emergence of an interdependent global economy, and an increasingly diverse workforce demand that career development theory and practice be revised to meet the challenges confronting 21st-century workers.

Change is happening everywhere, all the time. News reports cite statistics about high levels of global unemployment, corporate downsizing, and a jobless economic recovery, suggesting that the social contract between employer and employee is gone. More companies are now offering day care and parental leave, more families require dual earners, and more and more people are working from home. This reflects the strong intertwining of work and family roles. Thus, career theories, career interventions, and career development professionals must respond to evolutionary shifts in the nature of work.

Moreover, career development interventions must reflect the shifts we are experiencing in work—that adults will change jobs and even careers numerous times during their lives, that lifelong learning is essential to maintaining marketability, that life roles interact with both work roles and one another, that rapid changes in the world of work are a given, and that everyone must become skilled at interacting with a diverse array of coworkers. In 2003, Herr contended that the demand for career assistance would expand due to rising unemployment rates and an increase in part-time work. His prediction is now a reality.

How we intervene in the lives of the clients we serve is guided by our understanding of how these contextual shifts influence what people must do to further their careers. Savickas (1993) offers an interpretation of what is required to move the profession forward—namely, that in the 21st century career development professionals will shift from supporting the 20th-century notion of careerism to fostering self-affirmation in their clients. People will need to be encouraged to make a commitment to their culture and community and learn how to develop and express their values in the real world. Rather than providing clients with predefined services in a one-size-fits-all approach, counselors will collaborate with them to help interpret their life experiences within the context of their evolving careers. Rather than emphasizing a singular truth or objective, counselors will move toward appreciating multiple realities, perspectives, and relationships (Savickas). A primary task of career practitioners involves clarifying rather than assuming how they can be *useful* to their clients. Achieving this basic and essential understanding requires them to be skilled at providing culturally appropriate career interventions.

In addition to the Savickas (1993) article, a special issue of *The Career Development Quarterly* (September 2003) is one of the few examples in the literature in which future directions for career counseling are identified. Building on these contributions, we identify several ways in which career development professionals can construct interventions that respond to clients' concerns.

MOVE TO VIEWING CAREER DECISIONS AS VALUES-BASED DECISIONS

Career decisions are values-based decisions. Some values will figure prominently, and others will be abandoned, subordinated, or distorted in a career transition. Indeed, career decisions entail determining what is to prevail and what is to be sacrificed (Cochran, 1997). Without the promise of gain and the threat of loss, there is no decision to make. One might seize what appears to be a perfect opportunity. Yet people must evaluate to decide, and their values influence who they will become and the lives they will live. Career practitioners can empower clients to make choices that implement their values by serving as counselor, coach, and advocate for their clients.

MOVE BEYOND OBJECTIVE ASSESSMENT

The increased emphasis on values clarification means that providing clients with information about themselves and the world of work through objective assessment is not enough. Whereas information about how one's interests compare with those of others and where one stands on the normal curve is helpful, most people don't think of themselves as locations on a curve. Rather, they focus on trying to extract meaning from their life experiences. Some experiences command more attention than others—usually the painful ones. A painful or negative experience creates a yearning for its opposite, which becomes an ideal toward which to strive (Watkins & Savickas,

1990). In this sense, our early preoccupations point us toward what may later become our occupation. Our experiences are the backdrop against which we identify our values, interests, and skills, which we then try to connect to career options. Contemporary career development interventions must help people clarify and articulate these experiences and their meaning.

MOVE TO COUNSELING-BASED CAREER ASSISTANCE

We have established that personal and career concerns are inextricably intertwined. Many adults who seek career counseling are struggling with uncertainty, ambiguity, low self-efficacy, and personal as well as occupational information deficits (Niles & Anderson, 1995). Clients also report valuing the relationship they have with their counselor, and often discuss general as well as career concerns (Anderson & Niles, 2000). Many conclude that few things are more personal than career choice, and that the overlap between career and general concerns is substantial (Anderson & Niles, 1995; Krumboltz, 1993; Savickas, 2010; Subich, 1993). Career development practitioners respond by offering counseling-based career assistance.

Practitioners offering counseling-based career assistance do not view their clients as the problem and the counselor as the solution (Savickas, 1993). Rather, they seek to empower clients to articulate their experiences and direct their own lives. Savickas noted that such practitioners function as collaborators in the process and pay special attention to the counseling relationship (Anderson & Niles, 2000). Moreover, Savickas (2010) contends that all career counseling involves helping clients make decisions by increasing their "(1) concern about work, (2) sense of control over their career, (3) curiosity about opportunities, and (4) confidence in their ability to make a choice" (p. 1843). We agree with Savickas but extend his recommendations to increasing the client's confidence beyond making a choice to implementing and adjusting to that choice. We also believe it is necessary for clients to become curious about themselves as well as their opportunities. Career counselors may express curiosity about a client's situation to foster and model curiosity within the client.

MOVE TO A STRONGER EMPHASIS ON MULTICULTURAL CAREER DEVELOPMENT THEORIES AND INTERVENTIONS

Meeting the career development needs of a diverse population has been a significant issue in the literature since the early 1980s (Sue et al., 1982). It becomes even more significant given the increasing diversity within society and the workforce (Parmer & Rush, 2003). Career development interventions must address the "effects of social and economic barriers such as economic hardship, immigration disruption, and racial discrimination on the career behavior of ethnic minority individuals" (Leong, 1995, p. 550). We can expand Leong's list to include persons with disabilities and persons who are gay, lesbian, bisexual, transgendered, or questioning (Hershenson, 2005). Moreover, career practitioners must be aware of the world views embedded in their interventions and offer assistance congruent with the client's worldview (Fouad & Byars-Winston, 2005). Byars-Winston and Fouad (2006) recommend that career counselors engage in self-reflection throughout the counseling process so they may examine how their personal cultural contexts influence it. Thus, providing multicultural career development interventions requires counselors to be culturally sensitive and aware of both their own values and how their cultural assumptions affect their clients. Pope-Davis and Dings (1995) noted that multiculturally competent counselors must also:

> consider factors such as the impact of the sociopolitical system on people of color in the United States, have knowledge and information about particular cultural groups, and be able to generate a wide range of appropriate verbal/nonverbal responses to client needs. (p. 288)

This contrasts with many career theories and practices with limited relevance for clients outside Eurocentric worldviews emphasizing individualism and self-actualization in career behavior (Byars-Winston & Fouad, 2006; Hershenson, 2005; Leong, 1995). It also reinforces the importance of context in career development. Blustein (1994) defined context as "that group of settings that influence developmental progress, encompassing contemporary and distal familial, social, and economic circumstances" (p. 143). Diversity among clients and their concerns requires that context be considered when constructing and implementing career development interventions. To do otherwise is to risk providing "culturally encapsulated" (Wrenn, 1962) career assistance.

MOVE TO FOCUSING ON MULTIPLE LIFE ROLES

Incorporating context into career development interventions also requires practitioners to acknowledge that the "boxes of life" metaphor does not reflect life as many people know it. We don't live in compartmentalized life-role "silos." For some people, work provides a structure for personality organization; for others, work is more peripheral. To understand a person's career, you must understand the person's web of life roles. How a person structures the basic roles of living organizes and shapes his or her engagement with society (Super, Savickas, & Super, 1996). Theories and interventions that don't acknowledge this are addressing life situations that don't exist. Life roles interact and influence each other so that the same job may hold different meanings for two workers who live in different contexts. People seek to express specific values in each of their life roles, so practitioners must encourage clients to clarify and articulate the values they seek to express. Once they clarify and articulate these values, clients can be encouraged to identify outlets for expressing them in their salient life roles (Super, 1980). The increase in work-family conflict reported by both men and women (Williams & Boushey, 2010) reinforces the need for career interventions to address a person's life structure. Career development interventions in the 21st century must address the totality of a client's career concerns so she or he can be empowered to not only make a good living but also make a good life.

MOVE TO ADVOCATING FOR SOCIAL JUSTICE

The NCDA Career Counseling Competencies (2009) identify the need for career counselors to engage in advocacy for social justice and note the following competencies:

- Identify community resources and establish linkages to assist clients with specific needs.
- Assist other staff members, professionals, and community members in understanding the unique needs/characteristics of diverse populations with regard to career exploration, employment expectations, and economic/social issues.
- Advocate for the career development and employment of diverse populations.
- Design and deliver career development programs and materials to hard-to-reach populations.

Such competencies require counselors to move beyond individual and group counseling interventions. Toporek (2006) also emphasizes the role of career counselors as social change agents and advocates. Toporek and Liu (2001) define advocacy as "action taken by counseling professionals to facilitate the removal of external and institutional barriers to clients' well-being" (p. 387). Toporek and Liu also note that advocacy involves counselor actions ranging from empowerment to social action. Empowerment tends to involve individual and group-level interventions; social action involves engaging in the political process via actions such as writing a letter to the editor, meeting with congressional representatives, conferring with lobbyists, collaborating with special interest groups to influence the legislative process, and organizing labor demonstrations or strikes. As we write this, Indiana and Arkansas are passing new legislation permitting businesses to discriminate against same-sex couples on religious grounds, sparking protests and boycotts by entities as diverse as Walmart, Apple, the NCAA, and entertainers canceling tour dates (Tabuchi & Barbaro, 2015). The broad-based reaction against this legislation has caused states to back away from religious freedom discrimination acts written in such a way as to allow discrimination against sexual minorities. When a popular restaurant chain engaged in discriminatory practices toward sexual minorities a few years ago, human rights groups organized protests at several of its locations. The negative publicity persuaded the chain to change its practices. Similar actions and congressional testimony have led to more stringent workplace safety standards, legislation protecting persons with disabilities, nondiscriminatory practices in hiring racial and ethnic minorities, and so on.

MyCounselingLab®

Start with Topic 1—Work and Topic 2—American Occupational Structure.

SUMMARY

Careers are person specific and created by choices we make throughout our lives. Careers emerge from constant interplay between people and their environments, and they include a person's activities both prior to entering the workforce and after. Careers are personal and encompass the constellation of life roles that we play. Thus, managing a career effectively involves integrating life roles effectively. Careers are manifestations of our attempts to derive meaning from our experiences. The career development process is a spiritual journey reflecting interactions between how we choose to spend our time on Earth and the opportunities we experience while we're here. Professional counselors must be mindful of this as they begin to intervene in the lives of their clients. If Chandra and her classmates were to read this, we hope they'd agree that helping others build a career is exciting and fulfilling work.

CASE STUDY

Carlos came to an urban career center for counseling. At his first appointment, he said he had heard that career counselors survey people's interests, and he wanted to take such a survey to find out what he should do with the rest of his life. He said that he decided to pursue career counseling because his wife had been urging him to get help.

Carlos said that he had been in the navy for the last 21 years and joined up after graduating from high school because there were no jobs in rural

Arizona, where he grew up. Carlos's expertise was in radar and sonar maintenance, and he spent most of his naval career on ships and submarines, managing crews of 15 to 50 people. He enjoyed the work but said that being a supervisor was very frustrating at times, and he often decided it was easier to do a job himself than to rely on others. When he was not promoted to a higher rank, he retired.

Carlos began looking for work as a manager, but after eight months of searching had received no offers. Although his retirement income and his wife's part-time job had been sufficient to meet the mortgage and basic utility bills, Carlos had borrowed heavily to meet other expenses. He and his wife were rapidly depleting the savings intended for the educa-tion of their children—two sons ages 16 and 18, and a daughter, 12.

Carlos reported that lately he had been feeling tired most of the time. Even horticulture, his hobby and passion since boyhood, was not satisfying now. He confessed that he had been drinking heavily for the past month and that some days he just stays in his bathrobe and watches television. He said he hopes that finding out about his interests will help him get back on track.

How would you work with Carlos if you were his career counselor? Would you give him the interest assessment he seeks? Would you refer him for personal counseling? What additional information would you elicit from Carlos were you to work with him?

STUDENT ACTIVITIES

1. What are your assumptions about career devel-opment interventions? Rate them on a scale of 1 (boring) to 10 (exciting). Discuss your reasons for your rating.

2. Have you ever received career counseling? What happened? What was helpful? What was not helpful?

3. Consider your own motivation for working. Do you think you work to live, or do you live to work? What are the pros and cons of these approaches?

4. Review the history of career development inter-ventions. Identify two ways in which cultural and historical events have influenced career de-velopment interventions.

5. Identify which of your life roles are most impor-tant to you. How do your life roles interact with one another? What is your most important life role now? What values do you try to express in your most important life role?

CHAPTER 2

UNDERSTANDING AND APPLYING THEORIES OF CAREER DEVELOPMENT

Don't Let Theories Boggle Your Mind!

It's easy to be intimated by the word theory. *A theory is just an explanation—an oversimplified explanation of what is going on.*

The real world is an extremely complicated place. Human beings and their behavior are so complex that no one understands completely why people think, feel, and act as they do. A theory is like a road map. Suppose you have a map of California and you want to drive from San Francisco to Los Angeles. You see a red line marked "101" stretching between the two cities. Aha, you think, I'll drive down that red highway 101. But when you get to the highway, you see it is black asphalt. Why does the map show it to be red? The map lies! Why does the map lie? Because the mapmaker wants to make it easier for you to see the path. You drive down the highway and see office buildings, gardens, and swimming pools, but none of them are indicated on the map. The map not only distorts reality—it also omits zillions of details. Why? Because all those details would make it too complicated to find the best route between two cities.

In the same way, a theory attempts to explain a complex situation by overemphasizing and distorting the importance of certain variables while ignoring completely other variables that the theory-maker considers irrelevant. Theories are oversimplifications, just as road maps are oversimplifications. Yet road maps are very useful for certain purposes—even with all their faults. Similarly, theories can be useful—even with their faults.

A theory is just a way of oversimplifying a complex situation so that it is easier for you to see the big picture. That picture is not reality itself—just one theory maker's version of it.

John Krumboltz
Professor, Graduate School of Education
Stanford University

MyCounselingLab®

Visit the MyCounselingLab® site for *Career Development Interventions*, Fifth Edition, to enhance your understanding of chapter concepts. You will have the opportunity to practice applying what you learned in the chapter by completing the video- and case-based exercises in the MyLab. Taking the Licensure Quizzes will help you prepare for your certification exam.

Juana is a 17-year-old Latina in 12th grade in a predominantly white, middle-class public school. She is highly intelligent but dislikes school. She associates with a group of girls who are often in trouble with the police; recently, some of them were arrested for possession of marijuana. It is your impression, however, that these friendships are superficial. Juana is not hostile or disrespectful. However, she routinely hands in school-work late, if at all. Her parents have asked you to help her make a good career choice.

Juana is apathetic in most of her classes, but she enjoys art (especially painting) and playing flute in the school band. She dislikes math but has fairly strong interests in politics and has strong language skills. Juana has two younger sisters, ages 12 and 14. Her mother works as a teacher's aide in a local elementary school, and her father works as a salesman in a local car dealership. Juana's current plans are to finish high school; she has no plans beyond that, although she has said she "might like to be in a rock band." She agrees to meet with you to discuss her future.

CAREER DEVELOPMENT THEORIES

As you read about career development theories in the pages ahead, we encourage you to keep John Krumboltz's comments in mind and reflect on how effectively each theory addresses Juana's potential career path. You will notice that the theories differ in their coverage of career development compared to career decision making. Savickas (2002) notes that theories emphasize either individual differences related to occupations (describing how people can find their fit within the occupational structure) or individual development related to careers (how people manifest career behaviors across time). For example, developmental theories (Super, Gottfredson) highlight the manifestation of career behaviors over time. Person-environment theories (Work Adjustment Theory, Holland) address the essential ingredients (occupational and self-information) for choosing an occupation. One reason for studying various approaches to career theory is that no one theory adequately explains the totality of individual or group career behavior. As Super (1992) observed, the question of which theory is better is specious because the theories complement one another in addressing various facets of career behavior. As John Krumboltz (1996) notes, theories are useful despite their faults. We encourage you to become familiar with research into career theories, integrating the literature and your own experience to determine how career development theories help you work effectively with students and clients.

Regarding career development theories, Richardson (1993) states that "the theoretical and research literature in vocational psychology career development is notably oriented toward the White middle class. Moreover, there is almost no acknowledgement that poor and lower class populations, regardless of race or ethnicity, are almost totally absent from the literature" (p. 426). Tinsley (1994) counters that a substantial body of research over the years has not provided support for sex or economic-level differences, and expresses concern that "there is a tendency to dismiss general models that have applicability to both sexes and all economic class levels as limited in applicability only to White, middle-class men" (p. 109). These varying views from leading scholars in the field merit serious consideration. Still, it is clear to us that understanding the career development experiences of women, persons of color, sexual minorities, persons with disabilities, and less affluent members of society is a priority for the field. Thus, we encourage you to consider the following questions as you read the theories presented in this chapter and the next one:

1. How well do the theories describe the career development processes of members of diverse groups?
2. How well do the theories describe the career development process in general?
3. How well do the theories describe the factors involved in making a career choice?
4. How well do the theories inform the practice of career counseling?

5. To what degree is there empirical support for the theories?
6. What gaps can you identify within the theories?

Because no single theory is likely to do it all, it is important to identify the strengths and limitations of each one. This will enable you to draw on the best ideas the field has to offer. If you are interested in career development research, identifying the gaps will steer you toward fertile new areas to explore.

There are many ways to present career theories. Chronological order is frequently used, beginning with the work of Frank Parsons and proceeding to the most recent theories. Theories are sometimes grouped by category (psychological, developmental, trait-factor, objective vs. subjective). In deciding how to present the theories, we chose to do it in a fashion that made sense to us as practitioners.

Tips from the Field

Theories seldom explain the whole story, but good theories guide you as you gather information and fill in the gaps to paint a more complete picture of a student's or client's career development experience.

We discussed the work of Parsons and subsequent trait-factor theorists in Chapter 1 because these models are intertwined with the historical roots of career development interventions. The work of contributors such as Parsons, Williamson, and Dawis and Lofquist highlights the importance of interactions between a worker's traits and the work environment in career decision making. Building on our discussion of Parsons's model and trait-factor approaches (TWA, for example) in Chapter 1, we begin Chapter 2 with Donald Super's theory for several reasons. First, Super's theory provides a useful framework for conceptualizing career development over the life span. Super also acknowledges the various personal (needs, values, abilities) and situational (peer groups, family, labor market) elements that influence career development. Super's theory places work in the context of multiple roles each of us plays in life. Finally, his theory addresses helping people clarify, articulate, and implement their life-role self-concepts.

To expand on the influence of personal and situational influences on career development, we briefly discuss Anne Roe's career theory and then describe Linda Gottfredson's theory. Roe's theory points to the importance of early life experiences in career development. Gottfredson's theory addresses how sex-role stereotyping influences the career aspirations of both men and women (Gottfredson, 1996, 2002). Her theory offers a developmental and sociological perspective focused primarily on the career development process as it relates to the types of compromises people make in formulating their occupational aspirations.

We then discuss John Holland's theory, which has generated the most research of all. Holland's typology arguably provides the most useful framework for understanding and predicting individual behavior (job satisfaction, job performance, and occupational stability) within work environments. Through the use of assessment instruments, Holland applies his typology to help people clarify and implement their vocational identities (Spokane, Luchetta, & Richwine, 2002).

There are times when faulty or irrational thinking impedes a person's career development. The cumulative effect of a person's learning experiences can result in varying degrees of functionality in his or her ability to make effective career decisions. When people receive adequate support and are exposed to positive role models, they often develop interests and skills leading to satisfying career options. Conversely, when people lack support or are misinformed, they often disregard good options because they lack confidence or adhere to beliefs—"I must decide now what I will do for the rest of my life"—that keep them stuck. In these cases, people need help developing more useful beliefs. John Krumboltz's work provides a framework for helping practitioners foster career development in their clients (we discuss Krumboltz's theory in the final section of this chapter). In Chapter 3, we will focus on emerging theories that promise to provide effective descriptions of career development processes and practices. Table 2.1 summarizes the theories discussed in Chapters 2 and 3.

SUPER'S LIFE-SPAN, LIFE-SPACE THEORY

The leading developmental approach is Donald Super's life-span, life-space theory (Super, 1990; Super, Savickas, & Super, 1996), which evolved over 40 years as he and his colleagues refined and elaborated on its various aspects (Super et al., 1996). Although it is primarily developmental, Super labeled it as a "differential-developmental-social-phenomenological career theory" (Super, 1969). This communicates Super's efforts to synthesize and extend extant developmental and career theories. He understood that describing a process as complex as career development requires synthesizing interdisciplinary research (psychology and sociology). Super synthesized work by Buehler (1933), Havighurst (1951), Kelly (1955), Miller and Form (1951), and Rogers (1951) in conceptualizing aspects of his theory.

Super extended career theories by addressing shortcomings he perceived in those propounded by both his predecessors and contemporaries. For example, Super's contemporaries Ginzberg, Ginsburg, Axelrad, and Herma (1951) proposed a theory asserting that career choice is a developmental process rather than a single decision in which compromises are made to accommodate a person's wishes and occupational possibilities. They viewed the developmental process as spanning three stages: (a) fantasy (birth to age 11), (b) tentative (ages 11 to 17), and (c) realistic (ages 17 to early 20s). They theorized that four factors (individual values, emotional factors, amount and kind of education, and effect of reality through environmental pressures) converged to shape a person's career decisions.

Super argued that the theory proposed by Ginzberg et al. (1951) was deficient in that it (a) did not take into account research related to the role of interests in career decision making, (b) failed to operationally describe choice, (c) made a sharp distinction between choice and adjustment, and (d) lacked a clear articulation of the process of compromise as it relates to career choice. Responding to conditions such as these, Super developed his differential-developmental-social-phenomenological career theory.

Rather than developing a unified theory, however, Super (1990) developed a segmental one. He noted that "there is no 'Super's theory'; there is just the assemblage of theories that I have sought to synthesize. In another sense, the synthesis is a theory" (p. 199). The result is really a segmental theory describing three key aspects of career development: (a) life span, (b) life space, and (c) self-concept. The theory culminates in an intervention called the Career Development Assessment and Counseling (C-DAC) model (Super, Osborne, Walsh, Brown, & Niles, 1992). We provide an updated version of the C-DAC model in this chapter. The C-DAC model translates the three theory segments into career practice to help people articulate their career concerns, examine their life-role salience, and clarify their self-concepts.

Table 2.1
Brief Overview of Career Theories

Theory	Theorists	Orientation	Key Constructs	Research Support	Multicultural Emphasis
Work Adjustment	René Dawis Lloyd Lofquist	Trait-factor Career choice/adjustment	Satisfaction Satisfactoriness Person-in-an-environment Correspondence	Moderate	Low
Life-Span, Life-Space	Donald Super	Developmental	Life span Career stages Career development tasks Life space Self-concept Career maturity Career adaptability	High	Moderate
Personality Theory of Career Choice	Anne Roe	Personality Theory/Psychodynamic	Early childhood experiences Needs hierarchies Field/Level	Low	Low
Circumscription, Compromise, and Self-Creation	Linda Gottfredson	Developmental/sociological Career choice/development	Circumscription Compromise	Low	High
Vocational Personalities and Work Environments	John Holland	Person-Environment Career choice	Congruence Consistency Differentiation Vocational identity	High	Low
Learning Theory of Career Counseling	John Krumboltz	Social learning Career choice development	Learning experience Self-observation generalizations World view generalizations Task-approach skills, actions Planned happenstance	Moderate	Moderate

(Continued)

Table 2.1
(Continued)

Theory	Theorists	Orientation	Key Constructs	Research Support	Multicultural Emphasis
Social Cognitive Career Theory	Robert Lent, Steven Brown, Gail Hackett	Social cognitive career choice development	Self-efficacy Outcome expectations Personal goals Triadic reciprocal model	Moderate	High
Cognitive Information Processing Approach	Gary Peterson, James Sampson Jr., Robert Reardon, Janet Lentz	Cognitive career choice	Pyramid of information processing CASVE cycle Executive processing domain Career thoughts inventory	Moderate	Moderate
Career Construction Theory	Mark Savickas	Differential, developmental, and dynamic perspective of careers	Vocational personality Life themes Career Adaptability Career Style Interview	Moderate	High
Integrative Life Planning	L. Sunny Hansen	Contextual career choice/adjustment	Social justice Social change Connectedness Diversity Spirituality Integrative life planning inventory	Low	High
Postmodern	Vance Peavey	Constructivist	Meaning-making	Low	High
	Larry Cochran	Narrative	Career problem Life history Future narrative	Low	High
Chaos Theory of Careers	Robert Pryor and Jim Bright	Self-organization and change; phenomenalist	Attractors Patterns Patterns and Fractals	Moderate	Low

Life-span, life-space theory builds on key assumptions proposed by Super (1953, 1990; Super & Bachrach, 1957). These assumptions contend that people differ in their important self-characteristics and self-concepts; that their respective self-characteristics make them suitable to a number of occupations; that each occupation requires specific worker traits and that these requirements are flexible enough to allow for a variety of persons within specific occupations; and that self-concepts evolve over time, making choice and adjustment continuous processes for everyone. Further assumptions are that the change process for each person may be categorized according to life stages (growth, exploration, establishment, maintenance, and decline or disengagement); that a person's occupational level and career pattern are influenced by contextual (family, socioeconomic status, educational opportunities, community) and personal (skills, personality, needs, values, interests) factors; and that people's readiness to cope with career development tasks (career maturity) is influenced by how well they coped with previous ones.

The life-span, life-space theory also builds on other factors, including the proposition that a person's career development can be facilitated by providing developmentally appropriate interventions across the life span; that choosing a career requires people to develop and implement their self-concept and involves a synthesizing and compromising process as they develop, interact with, and learn from their surroundings; that a person's life satisfaction depends on finding life-role opportunities that are congruent with his or her self-characteristics; and that it is important for each person to structure life-role involvements that reflect his or her preferences, values, and self-concept.

These propositions incorporate diverse theoretical perspectives (trait-and-factor, developmental, social learning, and psychodynamic), supporting Super's contention that his theory is not merely developmental. Super's propositions also introduce some novel concepts to career development literature, namely by proposing the notion that there is intraoccupational variability among workers; that multiple life-role development is an important consideration in career development, and that self-concepts evolve over time, making choice and adjustment a continuous process. Thus, when Super's propositions are placed in historical context, they provide the impetus for shifting the paradigm from one that focuses on vocation to one that focuses on career, and from one that emphasizes the content of a career choice to one that emphasizes the process of career development over the life span.

Life Span

Career development, like physical development, is a lifelong process; yet it differs in that it is not ontogenetic. Rather, careers develop within the context of psychosocial development and societal expectations and against the backdrop of the occupational opportunity structure. Early in life, career development is relatively homogeneous and age related. Most young people are enrolled in schools that require them to make decisions at each grade level: eighth-graders must select a high school curriculum, students leaving high school must decide what they will do after graduation. Thus, we use the term *career maturity* to refer to the career decision-making readiness of children and adolescents. Career development in adulthood, however, is heterogeneous and not as directly connected to age. Adult careers develop in response to changes in occupational opportunities and life-role participation. Accordingly, we use the term *career adaptability* rather than career maturity when referring to an adult's decision-making readiness. Career adaptability reflects the idea that "as adults cope with their changing work and working conditions, adults make an impact on their environments and their environments make an impact on them" (Niles, Anderson, & Goodnough, 1998, p. 273). Just as a person's self-concept evolves over time, making choosing and adjusting continuous processes, so do educational and work environments change over time, making choosing and adjusting continuous requirements. Complacency is the enemy of effective career self-management. In this sense, career adaptability parallels Piaget's model of adaptation based on assimilation and accommodation. Career adaptability also supports the view that adults are "responsible agents acting within dynamic environmental settings" to find ways to effectively manage their career development (Super & Knasel, 1981, p. 199). Others (Savickas, 2005) have elaborated on Super's use of the career adaptability construct. As Hartung (2013) notes, "recent research has advanced and supported career adaptability along the dimensions of planning, exploring, and deciding" (p. 97).

Although Super originally applied adaptability to adult career development, we believe career adaptability can also be applied to children and adolescents. Despite their relative homogeneity in career development when compared with adults, young people experience differences in their readiness to cope with career development tasks. Some young people encounter environmental obstacles (poverty, racism, sexism) that sabotage career development, whereas others receive environmental opportunities (enrollment in good schools, engaging in recreational and co-curricular activities) that enhance it. Differences in contextual "affordances" (Vondracek, Lerner, & Schulenberg, 1986) have implications for career development. Thus, career adaptability seems a more fitting term for young people than does career maturity. Savickas (1997) agrees and states that "career adaptability should replace career maturity as the critical construct in the developmental perspective" (p. 247). We concur. The development of an adaptability scale within the Career Maturity Inventory is an example of an effective measure of this construct for school populations up to grade 12 (Savickas & Porfeli, 2011).

Describing the process of career development over the life span, Super drew on the research of Buehler (1933), Havighurst (1953), and Miller and Form (1951). Super conceptualized career as "the life course of a person encountering a series of developmental tasks and attempting to handle them in such a way as to become the kind of person he or she wants to become" (Super, 1990, pp. 225–226). Super identified a sequence of developmental tasks that people typically encounter and related them to stages and substages of career development, as follows: growth (childhood), exploration (adolescence), establishment (early adulthood), maintenance (middle adulthood), and disengagement (late adulthood).

Growth (Childhood)

Children ages 4 to 13 are confronted with the tasks of developing a sense of self and basic understanding of the world of work. In so doing, they progress through the substages of fantasy, interest, and capacity by using their innate sense of curiosity, first to engage in occupational fantasies, and then through exploring their environment (home, school, parental and peer relationships). Their curiosity leads them to acquire information about work and their interests and capacities. When things go well, children develop a sense of mastery and control over their environment and their ability to make decisions. Moving through the growth stage, they grasp that their behavior now affects their future lives. Moreover, they are increasingly able to use what they have learned about themselves and work to measure the viability of various educational and occupational opportunities.

Exploration (Adolescence)

Combining what they have learned about the work world and themselves with growing awareness that the present influences what happens next, 14- to 24-year-olds start planning for the future.

Within the career development domain, this involves crystallizing and specifying occupational preferences. When a young person specifies a preference, she or he implements the choice. These tasks occur within the substages of tentative, transition, and trial (with little commitment), respectively.

In the crystallization stage, young people use occupational and self-information acquired in the growth stage to learn more about the world of work and determine what kinds of work they might enjoy. Thus, accurate self-understanding is essential for identifying appropriate occupational preferences.

Specifying preferences requires an ability to choose among different occupations. The process of implementing a choice varies, depending on what choice has been made. Some choices require further training and education. Others provide opportunities for direct entry into a field. Regardless of what people choose, implementing the choice requires that they get started, one way or another.

Establishment (Early Adulthood)

Getting established in a career generally occurs from ages 25 to 45. The career development tasks associated with this stage are stabilizing, consolidating, and advancing. Stabilizing begins immediately after entering an occupation as a person evaluates whether the occupational preference she or he has implemented provides adequate opportunity for self-concept expression. Specifically, one must assess the organizational culture and determine whether she or he possesses the skills and interests to succeed there.

As one stabilizes in an occupation, he or she turns away from wondering whether the choice was a good one and turns toward becoming a dependable producer and creating a solid reputation in the occupation (consolidating). Focusing on becoming a dependable producer often leads to a chance to move up and gain more responsibility, more money, or both (advancing).

At any time in this process, however, a person may decide that the job or field he or she chose is no longer the right one. If this occurs, he or she will revisit the exploration stage and eventually crystallize, specify, and implement a different choice.

Maintenance (Middle Adulthood)

During maintenance (ages 45 to 65), workers encounter the tasks of holding, updating, and innovating. Many must choose either to improve their performance by keeping up with advancements in their field or to change fields altogether. In the latter instance, workers must recycle through exploration- and establishment-stage tasks to find new occupations. In the former, workers must update their skills and apply them innovatively in their current occupations. Those who decide to stay without updating their skills often stagnate and become poor performers (they are "stuck" in the holding task). In these instances, interventions addressing career renewal are required. Those who update and innovate often become excellent mentors to less experienced workers.

Disengagement (Late Adulthood)

Toward the end of the maintenance stage, when physical capacities begin to decline (which, interestingly, was the original name Super assigned to this stage), interest in work activities begins to wane. Most workers become concerned with planning for retirement. Thus, as the disengagement stage begins (currently around age 65), people turn to tasks of deceleration, retirement planning, and retirement living, with emphasis on physical, spiritual, and financial well-being. A current trend for many people at this stage involves pursuing what some refer to as "encore careers." Encore careers are second-half-of-life career choices in which people emphasize using their passions, abilities, interests, and previous experiences to pursue work that provides a strong sense of life purpose (see encore.org).

Although career development stage theory originally represented a more linear vision of a person's work life, Super (1990) acknowledged that people recycle through career stages and tasks throughout their lives. We propose further refinement and make two recommendations for using Super's stage theory in career counseling. First, we suggest that career practitioners acknowledge that people may be confronted with multiple career development task and stage issues simultaneously. It is not hard to imagine, for instance, that a recently laid-off 55-year-old newspaper reporter may be uncertain about deciding what she might do next in her career (i.e., exploration) while also fretting about whether she will have enough money to retire in ten years (i.e., disengagement). Such a person is likely to explore more narrowly than another person who may only be concerned with exploration-stage tasks. Second, we recommend that career practitioners conceptualize stages in a fashion that is similar to the notion of "status." Status in this instance refers to the need to understand the total constellation of career concerns the person is experiencing at any point in time. Similar to a physician assessing your health status during an annual exam, career practitioners need to understand the career status of each of their clients in order to help them most effectively. We think that understanding the constellation of career concerns a client or student experiences at any point in time provides important information regarding the sort of support and resources the client will find useful. Viewing the client's career concerns from the perspective of status moves away from linear notions of career stage theory and helps reinforce the point that career tasks present themselves to persons in ways that are not always restricted by chronological age. Thus, Super's stages and tasks provide important information regarding the potential array of career concerns, or societal expectations, that a person may be attempting to cope with at any point in his or her life. Understanding the life-span segment of Super's theory in this way will foster a greater understanding of a person's career development experience.

Life Space

While people are busy earning a living, they are also busy living a life (Super et al., 1996). The "simultaneous combination of life roles we play constitutes the lifestyle; their sequential combination structures the life space and constitutes the life cycle. The total structure is the career pattern" (Super, 1980, p. 288). Life roles interact so that the same job holds different meanings for people living in different situations. The meaning and purpose your psychology professor derives from his or her job is influenced by previous life roles he or she has played (child, high school athlete, college student, part-time restaurant server, graduate assistant) as well as roles he or she is currently playing (adult child, parent, soccer coach, department chair, friend). Your psych professor's life roles—his or her dedication to family, career, and community—are different from those of your other professors, as is the meaning he or she derives from work.

The salience people attach to their constellation of life roles defines what Super referred to as the life structure. The life-space segment of Super's theory acknowledges that people differ in the degree of importance they attach to work. As we mentioned in Chapter 1, many people link work with self-worth in a way that devalues other life roles that might be a boon to their sense of self-esteem and self-efficacy (not to mention to society). Many models of career counseling have disregarded the effects of life-role interactions and the fact that engaging in multiple life roles maximizes a person's opportunities to express his or her values.

Super noted that people tend to play nine major roles during their lives: (1) son or daughter, (2) student, (3) leisurite (a term coined by Super), (4) citizen, (5) worker, (6) spouse or partner, (7) homemaker, (8) parent, and (9) pensioner. A person's career comprises a constellation of life roles played over his or her lifetime (Super, 1980). Life roles are generally played out in specific theaters. These theaters are (1) home, (2) school, (3) workplace, and (4) community.

Effective life-role participation is difficult to achieve because conflicting demands make it hard to fulfill several at once. We must prioritize our life roles. Sometimes it's easy (putting work first when your children are old enough to look after themselves), sometimes not (when your six-year-old wakes up with a fever the morning of your big presentation). Sometimes roles usually played in one theater spill over into another and create conflict (Eagle, Miles, & Icenogle, 1997; Loscocco, 1997; Perrone, 2005). When work spills over into home life, the roles of worker, partner, and parent become enmeshed and none receives enough attention. Thus, life roles interact in ways that can be extensive or minimal: supportive, supplementary, compensatory, or neutral. Life flows well when the roles we play nurture one another and offer opportunities to express our values. Life is stressful when the roles we play are in conflict and we cannot express our values.

Many career counseling clients appear seeking assistance in coping more effectively with changing life-role demands. Interventions that address only the role of work are inadequate for them. Super's theory embraces this by focusing on how clients structure the roles of work, play, friendship, and family into a satisfying life (Super et al., 1996).

Self-Concepts

Super (1963) defined self-concept as a "picture of the self in some role, situation, or position, performing some set of functions, or in some web of relationships" (p. 18). Super (1980) uses the Archway model and the Life-Career Rainbow to depict various personal (aptitudes, values, needs) and situational (the family, the community, the economy, society) determinants that shape the constellation of life roles that individuals play and that interact to influence the person's self-concepts. In these models, Super delineates both the longitudinal processes of career development and the more situation-specific content of career decision making. Career decisions reflect our attempts to translate our self-understanding—self-concepts—into career terms (Super, 1984).

Self-concepts contain both objective and subjective elements. Objectively, we develop self-understanding by comparing ourselves to others: "I am like an accountant because I'm good with numbers" or "I am in the ninety-fifth percentile in mechanical ability." Subjectively, we develop understanding from the life stories we construct to confer meaning on our life experiences. There is relative homogeneity in our objective career experience (almost everyone reading this book is focused on acquiring the occupational title of counselor or counseling psychologist). There is tremendous heterogeneity in our subjective career experience (everyone reading this book has a unique history that has led him or her to wanting to work in a helping profession). We use our objective and subjective understanding to identify appropriate career goals. Such understanding guides us as we make choices about the extent and nature of our life-role participation. Because self-concepts develop over time, the need to make choices and the process of adjusting to these choices are lifelong tasks.

Applying Super's Theory

Toward the end of his career, Super increasingly focused on translating his theory into practice (Super et al., 1992) and labeled his approach the Career Development Assessment and Counseling (C-DAC) model. Like other theorists (Holland, Krumboltz), Super translated his theory into practice partly through systematic application of career assessment instruments emanating from his theory segments. Although these assessment instruments are key elements in the C-DAC model, they are not required for addressing Super's theory segments in career counseling (many C-DAC assessment instruments are available at no cost at vocopher.com).

The primary emphasis of the C-DAC model (and the traditional focus of career counseling) is on helping clients cope with concerns in the exploration stage of the life-span theory segment (Super, 1957; Super et al., 1996). Many people associate exploration exclusively with adolescents at the preimplementation stage of career development; however, exploration continues throughout life: "Exploration has come to be expected not only in adults who are changing career direction, but also in adults who are responding to the demands of progressing in the career they have chosen and in which they wish to remain" (Phillips, 1982, p. 130).

Persons entering the exploration stage for the first time focus on clarifying their values, skills, and interests and on connecting these attributes to initial occupational options. Formal standardized assessments can be useful in providing initial career explorers with foundational self-information required for coping effectively with exploration stage tasks. However, persons recycling through the exploration stage use exploratory behavior to resolve a wide variety of career issues (Niles et al., 1998). For example, some people use exploratory behavior to maintain their current positions while they focus on retirement living. Others use exploration to start over in new occupations, whereas still others use exploratory behavior to become more innovative in their current positions. It is not uncommon for people to experience career concerns across multiple career stages concurrently. Therefore, understanding the full range of a client's career concerns provides important information regarding the career tasks with which the client is attempting to cope. Although exploration always involves learning more about our situation or ourselves, what needs to be learned depends on our developmental status and salient life roles (Super, 1983). Career development rarely occurs in a linear fashion. Thus, identifying each client's constellation of developmental task concerns is the crucial first step in constructing appropriate career interventions.

Juana, the high school student you met earlier, is an initial career explorer, confronting the tasks of crystallizing and specifying occupational preferences for the first time. To cope effectively, Juana will need to acquire more information about herself—her values, interests, and abilities—and about the world of work. She will also need to learn about the career decision-making process and get help translating the information into a career plan. Ideally, Juana will also be able to see the connection between her school activities and her future and will become more motivated at school. As Juana crystallizes her occupational self-concept, she will need to reality-test her choices. Role playing, joining school clubs, job shadowing, volunteering, and part-time employment will augment her knowledge of both the work world and herself.

To calibrate career development issues facing mature clients, Super and his colleagues developed the Adult Career Concerns Inventory (ACCI) (Super, Thompson, & Lindeman, 1988). The ACCI measures adult clients' concerns at each stage of life-span, life-space theory: exploration, establishment, maintenance, and disengagement (Super et al., 1988). Each stage comprises three tasks, which respondents rate using a 5-point Likert-type scale ranging from 1 (no concern) to 5 (great concern). For example, the exploration stage comprises the tasks of crystallization, specification, and implementation. Each stage's tasks are divided into five substages, yielding 60 items. Summing each set of three-task substage scores yields a total for the corresponding career stage.

The ACCI is useful at the onset of counseling to identify clients' developmental task concerns as well as resources to help them cope. Clients concerned with the maintenance substage task of updating can be encouraged to attend seminars on new methods in their fields, visit places where they can see these methods in action, conduct information interviews with knowledgeable people, and take refresher training (items 36 to 40, respectively, on the Updating Scale of the ACCI). Counselors can use ACCI scores to identify a client's status in his or her constellation of career concerns.

Some clients, however, may be unable to make career choices because they lack the resources necessary for choosing (adolescents may lack career maturity, whereas adults may lack adaptability). Individuals who are not ready to make good choices need to (a) develop positive attitudes toward career exploration and planning, (b) learn how to gather information about themselves and occupational options, and (c) learn how to make career decisions.

The Career Development Inventory (CDI) (Thompson, Lindeman, Super, Jordaan, & Myers, 1984) assesses whether high school and college students are ready to make career decisions. Specifically, the CDI assesses career planning, career exploration, world-of-work information, and knowledge of career decision-making principles. CDI scores can be used to answer questions such as these: Does the respondent know how to make career decisions? Is the respondent aware of the need to make career plans? Does the respondent possess both general information about the world of work and specific information about the preferred occupation? Does the respondent know how to make use of exploratory resources relevant to the career decision-making process?

High scores on the CDI indicate affirmative answers to these questions. In such instances, clients are often able to proceed with career decision making. Low scores on the CDI indicate deficiencies that must be remediated. For example, a low CDI score suggests that the client is not aware of the need to make a career choice and is not involved in planning for the future. Using the CDI with Juana will help identify areas in which she needs assistance—in developing career maturity, for instance.

The next step in applying the C-DAC model involves determining the priority clients attach to their life roles. This step distinguishes Super's approach from other models because it helps clients understand how they "structure the basic roles of work, play, friendship, and family into a life" (Super et al., 1996, p. 128).

Achieving this involves exploring the importance, or salience, clients attach to their life roles. It also means realizing that the problems clients present in career counseling cannot be neatly categorized as reflecting either personal or career concerns. Because few issues are more personal than those related to career choice and adjustment, career and noncareer concerns overlap substantially (Betz & Corning, 1993; Krumboltz, 1993; Subich, 1993; Super, 1993). Research indicates that clients experience high levels of psychological stress and discuss concerns related to nonwork roles throughout the career counseling process (Anderson & Niles, 1995; Lucas, 1993; Niles & Anderson, 1993). Such findings point to the importance of attending to the emotional issues clients encounter as they cope with problems in their unique life structures.

Counselors can encourage clients to examine the meaning they attach to their life roles by asking them these questions: How do you spend your time during a typical week? How important are your different life roles to you? What do you like about each life role you play? What life roles do you think will be important to you in the future, and what do you hope to accomplish in each of them? What do your family members expect you to accomplish in each of your life roles? What life roles do they play? What helpful (and not so helpful) lessons have you learned about playing each role? It would be important to ask Juana questions like these to help her consider what life roles will be important to her in the future and what she can do now to prepare for them. Asking clients to describe how they spend time during the week and to consider the values reflected therein is also a useful strategy for inviting them to examine life structure issues. Counselors can also encourage clients to describe how they would prefer to spend their time, say, five years in the future. The counselor can then help them develop strategies for increasing the odds that it will happen.

Counselors can also use the Salience Inventory (Super & Nevill, 1986) as a starting point for discussing life-role salience. The Salience Inventory measures the relative importance of five life roles (student, worker, citizen, homemaker, and leisurite) in three dimensions, one behavioral and two affective. The behavioral component—participation—assesses what the respondent does or has done recently in each life role. The first affective component—commitment—requires the respondent to indicate how he or she feels about each life role. The second affective component—values expectations—requires the respondent to indicate the degree to which there will be opportunities now or in the future to express values in each life role.

Finally, life-role activities can be examined using the Pie of Life exercise, in which clients divide a circle into slices symbolizing the amount of time they spend doing different things during a typical week. They then identify the values they think are reflected in their life pie and discuss them with their counselor. The counselor focuses on reinforcing the time spent on activities that clients feel good about and reducing time spent on activities that they don't feel good about. The counselor can also discuss with clients what they would like to accomplish in each important life role and can focus on how they might do this.

To further guide the self-concept crystallization process, career counselors can use the Values Scale (VS) (Nevill & Super, 1986). The VS measures 21 intrinsic (creativity, altruism) and extrinsic (economic rewards) values that people hope to express in their life roles. The VS is a useful supplement to measures of interests and abilities, and counselors can use VS results to help clients focus their exploration of life roles and occupational options.

With information provided by the Salience Inventory and the Values Scale, counselors help clients identify the life roles that take most of their time, those to which they are emotionally committed, the values they hope to express in these roles, and the roles they expect to be important to them in the future.

With regard to the latter, counselors can help clients construct strategies to prepare for their salient life roles. For example, if Juana expects the life role of worker to be salient in her future, she can discuss ways to plan and prepare for it by, for instance, identifying activities to help her develop her readiness to hold down a job. Special attention can be given to helping Juana make connections between her current life role of student and her future role of worker. Information from the Salience Inventory can also be used to encourage Juana to think about areas of potential role conflict and to discuss strategies for coping with excessive demands from multiple life roles.

Contextual Factors Influencing Life-Role Salience

Super's Archway model suggests that life-role self-concepts are shaped by our contexts (personal and situational determinants). However, many people lack awareness of how contextual factors (dominant culture, culture of origin) interact with identity development to shape life-role salience (Blustein, 1994).

Dominant Culture

People often inherit patterns of life-role salience from the dominant or popular culture. Such inheritances can be problematic when they are embedded in beliefs based on gender, racial, and other stereotypes. Researchers have consistently found gender bias in life-role salience and occupational sex-role stereotyping in portrayals of workers in popular culture. With regard to the former, Niles and Goodnough (1996) reported in a literature review that researchers have consistently found gender differences in role salience that coincide with traditional sex-role expectations (women involved more in home and family than men and expecting more from the home life role than men). Women with high worker-role salience put themselves at a disadvantage in the workforce by such expectations. Also, men limit their involvement in home and family when they adhere to traditional expectations for life-role salience. Coltrane and Adams (1997) found that women are typically portrayed in popular culture as unemployed or employed in service or clerical occupations, perpetuating sex-role stereotyping and workplace gender inequality. Raising clients' awareness of how the dominant culture influences life-role salience helps them dismantle their own racist and sexist attitudes as they make career decisions.

Culture of Origin

Discussing the influence of the dominant culture on life-role salience can lead to discussions of how clients' cultural backgrounds influence their career development. Counselors and clients can explore how cultures of origin influence the values expressed in life roles (seeking self-actualization through work for a person of Eurocentric cultural background, or seeking to express cultural identity through work for a person of Asian heritage). When these discussions occur in small groups, they stimulate increased awareness of, and sensitivity to, cultural diversity in life-role salience.

This can also lead to exploring various cultural prescriptions (Eurocentric men are good providers and upwardly mobile in their occupations) that are assigned to certain life roles. In these discussions, counselors can encourage clients to identify how they perceive and interpret role expectations emanating from their cultures of origin and how these expectations affect the importance they attach to different life roles. Counselors may pay special attention to exploring how these expectations influence the client's understanding of the behaviors required for effective role performance (men who define their parenting role primarily as being a good provider may consider whether this alone constitutes good parenting).

Borodovsky and Ponterotto (1994) suggest the family genogram as useful for exploring interactions between family background, cultural prescriptions, and career planning. The genogram provides a tool for tracking career decisions across generations and identifying sources of a person's career beliefs and life themes.

This technique can be expanded to address the same topics for other life roles. By using the genogram, counselors can help clients identify beliefs and life themes pertaining to specific life roles that they have acquired from their families. Counselors can also contrast the influences on clients' life-role salience emanating from group-oriented cultures with influences emanating from individualistic cultures. The counselor may introduce terms such as *cultural assimilation* and *cultural accommodation* in these discussions, and examine the effects of sex-role stereotyping on life-role salience. The goal of these interventions is to increase clients' awareness of the influences shaping their beliefs about their primary life roles so they can make informed decisions about their future life-role participation.

Although examining life-role participation holistically is important, the central concern in career development interventions is helping clients clarify their occupational self-concepts. In the C-DAC model, clients use their understanding of life-role salience as the foundation on which they base the clarification and articulation of their vocational identities.

Vocational identities are clarified using two methods: the actuarial method (Super, 1954, 1957) and the developmental method (Super, 1954, 1961). The actuarial method relates to the trait-and-factor approach of using test scores to predict future occupational performance and satisfaction. For instance, Juana might complete the Strong Interest Inventory (SII) (Harmon, Hansen, Borgen, & Hammer, 1994) to compare her interests with those of people employed in various occupations. Using the actuarial method, the counselor "acts like an actuary, consults tables, graphs, and formulas seeking the optimal prediction, in probability terms, based on the observed correlations with similar performances of other people" (Jepsen, 1994, p. 45). Juana's pattern of interests would be related to the patterns of workers within a variety of occupations. The counselor would focus on similar patterns (as starting points for further exploration) and dissimilar patterns (to identify types of occupations Juana is not likely to find satisfying). Ability tests could be used in the same way: to compare Juana's abilities to those required for successful performance in specific occupations. Occupations for which her interests and abilities merge to predict satisfying and successful performance could then be identified for further consideration.

Values inventory results or values card sorts can then be used to guide further exploration. Some occupations might be appropriate for a client's interests and abilities but may not provide sufficient opportunities for values expression. For clients like Juana who are attempting to crystallize occupational preferences, values inventories or values card sorts may be helpful supplements to measures of interests and abilities (Super et al., 1996).

Using the developmental method (which Super also described as the Thematic-Extrapolation Method), counselors act more like historians than actuaries by inviting clients to construct autobiographical chronologies of what they did in the past. These chronologies are then examined for recurrent themes or threads of continuity that are used to "make sense of the past, explain the present, and draw a blueprint for the future" (Super et al., 1996, p. 157). Whereas the actuarial method is based on traits (How do my traits compare with the traits of others? In what occupations do my traits predict success?), the developmental method is based on life patterns (What patterns are revealed in my life history? Which of these patterns and themes are important to incorporate in my future planning?). Jepsen (1994) has noted that the developmental or thematic-extrapolation method contains three steps:

1. Analyze past behavior and development for recurring themes and underlying trends;
2. Summarize each theme and trend, taking into account the other themes and trends;
3. Project the modified themes and trends into the future by extrapolation. (p. 45)

Inviting a client to envisage his or her life as a book and then asking the client to identify the chapters of his or her life is a strategy for identifying recurring themes and underlying trends. The future can then be envisioned as chapters that must be lived for the client to feel as if his or her life is complete, and the focus can shift toward identifying future goals and aspirations.

The actuarial and developmental methods may be incorporated into career counseling by using Super's (1957) cyclical model of nondirective and directive methods. Super noted that "Since vocational development consists of implementing a self-concept, and since self-concepts often need modification before they can be implemented, it is important that the student, client, or patient put his self-concept into words early in the counseling process. The client needs to do this for himself, to clarify his actual role and his role aspirations; he needs to do it for the counselor, so that the counselor may understand the nature of the vocational problem confronting him" (p. 308). Specifically, Super (1957) described the cycles of career counseling as follows:

1. Nondirective problem exploration and self-concept portrayal (the client tells his or her story);
2. Directive topic setting, for further exploring (the counselor and client clarify career concerns and identify which ones they will focus on first);
3. Nondirective reflection and clarification of feeling for self-acceptance and insight (the counselor uses empathic responding and basic counseling skills to help the client clarify his or her situation, feelings, and thoughts);
4. Directive exploration for factual data from tests, occupational pamphlets, extracurricular experiences, grades, and so forth, for reality testing (the counselor and client collect relevant information regarding the client's characteristics and potential occupational options; they also identify options for reality testing or trying out potential options via job shadowing, occupational information interviewing, volunteering, and externships);
5. Nondirective exploration and working through of attitudes and feelings aroused by reality testing (the client tries out potential options and reflects on the experiences with the counselor, focusing on thoughts and feelings and how the experiences may inform the client's next step); and
6. Nondirective consideration of possible actions, for help in decision making (the client identifies what she or he will do next to move forward in her or his career development). (p. 308)

Essentially, the career counseling model articulated by Super emphasizes helping clients to clarify and articulate their self-concepts and implement them in life-role activity. Specific career counseling interventions, such as the C-DAC model and the thematic extrapolation method, may be incorporated into Super's cyclical model (most likely at steps 3 through 6).

Evaluating Super's Theory

Super's theory has been key to the evolution of career development theory and practice. Numerous researchers have relied on Super's work for their own investigations of career development processes. Lewis, Savickas, and Jones (1996) used the Career Development Inventory (Super, Thompson, Lindeman, Jordaan, & Myers, 1981) to predict success in medical school. Their results supported Super's (1981) contention that thinking about the future and planning for it are necessary for achieving career maturity and adaptability.

Reviewing literature pertaining to Super's Work Importance Study led Niles and Goodnough (1996) to three conclusions. First, life-role salience and values must be viewed within specific developmental and cultural contexts. Second, in diverse settings and with different groups, women and men ranked the importance of various life roles and values differently. Third, in order to facilitate their clients' career development, practitioners must attend to life-role salience and values issues in career counseling (see also Parasuraman, Purhoit, Godshalk, & Beutell, 1996).

Salomone (1996) provided a historical perspective by tracing the evolution of three key segments of Super's theory over a 40-year period: (a) theoretical propositions, (b) conceptualization of the career stages, and (c) definition of career. Salomone's review led him to three conclusions. First, Super's theoretical propositions have not changed substantially in 40 years. Second, there is the need for more research related to Super's propositions and career stage model. Third, Super's contributions represent an unparalleled legacy in developmental career theory. Super's theory segments provide a framework for helping clients clarify their life-role identities and the values they seek to express therein as well as for researchers investigating life-role identity development.

Journal articles provide examples of the systematic application of the C-DAC assessment instrument. For example, articles by Nevill and Kruse (1996) (Values Scale), Nevill and Calvert (1996) (Salience Inventory), Savickas and Hartung (1996) (Career Development Inventory), and Cairo, Kritis, and Myers (1996) (Adult Career Concerns Inventory) provide literature reviews, test descriptions, and information concerning the practical application of each assessment. Hartung et al. (1998) describe strategies for appraising a client's cultural identity in the initial stages of the C-DAC model and offer techniques for considering cultural factors throughout the C-DAC process, thereby making the model more applicable to clients representing diverse contexts.

The large number of research studies using Super's theory has declined since his death in 1994. Osipow and Fitzgerald (1996) noted that it "has the virtue of building upon aspects of the mainstream of developmental psychology and personality theory and has considerable utility for practice and research" (p. 143). They also noted that "most of the research reported on Super's theory generally supports his model" (p. 143). Borgen (1991) noted that it "has splendidly stood the test of time" (p. 278); Brown (1996) wrote that it "will forever be the segmental legacy of a brilliant thinker" (p. 522).

ANNE ROE'S PERSONALITY THEORY OF CAREER CHOICE

Anne Roe (1904–1991), a clinical psychologist, initially became interested in career behavior by investigating personality factors related to artists' creative expression. Later, she expanded her research to include eminent scientists. Roe (1956, 1957) suggested that early childhood experiences influence career behavior. As Brown, Lum, and Voyle (1997) emphasize, however, from Roe's perspective the relationship between early childhood experiences and subsequent career behavior is mediated by the "structure of psychological needs that develop due to the pattern of frustrations and satisfactions experienced in childhood" (p. 284). Specifically, the resultant need structure orients a person either toward people or away from people. Drawing on Maslow's (1954) needs theory, Roe contended that unsatisfied needs are strong motivators for people making career choices.

The environment in which a child is reared shapes his or her early experiences. Roe (1956) identified three main kinds of child-rearing environments: emotional concentration, avoidance, and acceptance. Emotional concentration on the child ranges from overprotection to overly demanding behaviors. Whereas physical needs are met, psychological needs may be withheld as parents place conditions on their love and approval. Children reared in overly protective environments learn that conforming elicits rewards, and they subsequently develop a dependence on others for approval and self-esteem. Children reared in overly demanding environments develop perfectionist tendencies and embrace their caretakers' all-or-nothing standards. Avoidance of the child ranges from neglecting the child's physical needs to rejecting the child's emotional needs. Acceptance of the child involves environments in which the child's physical and psychological needs are met. Independence and self-reliance are encouraged in either an unconcerned, noninvolved way or an active, supportive one.

Each of these environments affects how well the child's needs are met, which in turn influences the adult child's choice of occupational field. Adults working in service occupations are oriented toward people and thus were likely reared in loving, overprotective early childhood environments. Adults in more scientific occupational fields are typically not oriented toward people and therefore were most likely exposed to rejecting and avoidant early childhood environments.

Roe (1956) developed an occupational classification system comprising eight fields based on arts and entertainment and general culture. Service fields include people-oriented occupations such as teaching, counseling, and social work. Business contact occupations involve interpersonal interactions of a persuasive nature such as sales. Organizational occupations emphasize systems and management. Technology involves occupations such as engineering. Outdoor occupations focus on the application of scientific principles to, for example, forest management. Science includes occupations such as chemist and physicist. Arts and entertainment include occupations in performing and visual arts. General culture includes occupations such as government and civil service employee. People choose occupational fields based on their need structures, which were influenced by their childhood environments. A person's genetic structure and socioeconomic background affects the level of his or her occupation.

Evaluating Roe's Theory

Researchers have struggled to validate assumptions of Roe's theory because of its retrospective nature. Differences in parenting style, early life environments experienced by members of the same occupation, and the challenge of trying to predict how causal factors influence future outcomes have produced meager empirical support. Because Roe's theory focuses on factors underlying career choice and offers little about interventions, it has largely faded from the current literature. Roe's theory does, however, highlight the influence that a person's parents and needs structure have on his or her career development process.

LINDA GOTTFREDSON'S THEORY OF CIRCUMSCRIPTION, COMPROMISE, AND SELF-CREATION

Linda Gottfredson's (b. 1947) theory of circumscription, compromise, and self-creation (Gottfredson, 2002, 2005) describes the process of formulating occupational aspirations in childhood and adolescence. Gottfredson developed her theory, in part, to address the question "Why do children seem to re-create the social inequalities of their elders long before they themselves experience any barriers to pursuing their dreams?" (2002, p. 85). She examines the compromises people make in their career aspirations, particularly as they relate to sex-typed learning and experiences. Compromise involves the process of limiting career choices due to prestige, sex type, and field of interest (Gottfredson, 1981). Gottfredson's theory emphasizes the view that "career choice is an attempt to place oneself in the broader social order" (Gottfredson, 1996, p. 181). Thus, she offers a developmental and sociological perspective of career development.

Gottfredson (2002) notes that people distinguish occupations according to the dimensions of "masculinity-femininity, occupational prestige, and field of work" (p. 88). Gottfredson (2005) further asserts that occupational prestige is positively correlated with the degree of intellectual capacity required for job performance. A person's self-concept interacts with his or her occupational stereotypes. When people make career decisions, they determine the suitability of an occupation by considering perceived gender appropriateness (most important), prestige (second in importance), and the degree to which the occupation will fulfill their preferences and personality needs (least important). The "zone of acceptable occupational alternatives" or "social space" (2002, p. 91) represents a person's perception of his or her fit in society. Gottfredson contends that people compromise because they typically search for a good enough occupation, rather than for a great one. This is because a great choice requires more intensive values clarification and determination of alternatives than a good enough one. People become indecisive when they perceive the options within their social space as undesirable. Occupational satisfaction hinges on the degree to which "the compromise allows one to implement a desired social self, either through the work itself or the lifestyle it allows self and family" (2002, p. 107).

Circumscription involves the process of eliminating unacceptable occupational alternatives based primarily on gender and prestige, and highlights the fact that young people begin eliminating occupational options "as soon as they are able to perceive essential distinctions among people and lives" (Gottfredson, 2002, p. 131). The circumscription process is guided by five principles (2002, pp. 94–95). The first notes that circumscription is guided by the growing capacity of children to understand and organize complex information about themselves and the world as they progress from magical to abstract thinking. The second principle reflects the belief that because occupational aspirations are inextricably linked with one's self-concept, occupational preferences reflect attempts to both implement and enhance it. The third principle is that children begin to grapple with more complex distinctions among people (for instance, perceptions related to prestige) while they are still in the process of integrating more concrete phenomena, such as sex roles, into their self-conceptions. The fourth principle emphasizes the belief that children progressively eliminate occupational options as their self-concepts become clearer and more complex. At the same time, Gottfredson notes that "people reconsider options they have ruled out as unacceptable in sextype [sic] and prestige only when they are prompted to do so by some formative new experience or some notable change in their social environment" (2002, p. 95). Finally, the circumscription process is gradual and not immediately obvious despite its strong effect on the person undergoing it.

These principles operate throughout the stages of cognitive development that Gottfredson (1996) delineated to describe the circumscription process.

Stage One: Orientation to Size and Power

The first stage occurs between ages 3 and 5 and reflects the onset of object constancy in cognitive development. At this stage, children classify people in simple terms such as *big* and *little*, orienting themselves to the size difference between themselves and adults.

Stage Two: Orientation to Sex Roles

This stage occurs between ages 6 and 8. Here, children become aware of the different sex roles of men and women. They think dichotomously—good–bad, rich–poor—and interpret sex-role stereotypes as behavioral imperatives. Their occupational aspirations reflect a desire to behave in ways that are appropriate to their sex, manifesting in their belief that certain jobs are for boys and certain jobs are for girls. It is during this stage that children develop their "tolerable-sextype [sic] boundary" (Gottfredson, 2005).

Stage Three: Orientation to Social Valuation

During this stage, which occurs between ages 9 and 13, children think more abstractly and become aware of social class and prestige. They reject occupations not in line with their perceived ability levels nor approved of by their social reference group. Social class and ability determine the tolerable-level boundary, which represents the lower limit of occupations they are willing to consider (which occupations are beneath them and, therefore, not worthy of their consideration). Children also establish a tolerable-effort level based on the upper limit of effort they are willing to exert and the risks they are willing to take (occupational goals that are not beyond their ability to achieve). Together, these levels determine the zone of occupations children consider acceptable (Gottfredson, 1996).

Stage Four: Orientation to the Internal, Unique Self

During this stage, which starts at age 14, adolescents become more introspective and self-aware. Engaging in more abstract thinking than before, adolescents begin identifying internally generated goals and self-concepts and explore occupational options congruent with these. As Gottfredson notes, "vocational development erupts into conscious awareness during Stage 4" (2005, p. 81). This stage features a shift as emphasis turns from eliminating unacceptable options to identifying those that are preferred and acceptable. It is now that the process of compromise appears. Compromise involves eliminating options because of factors such as their perceived inaccessibility ("I don't want to be a doctor because I'll never get into medical school"). Compromise may be anticipatory (prior to actual encounters with external barriers) or experiential (after actual encounters with external barriers).

Applying Gottfredson's Theory to Practice

Gottfredson (1996) noted that, traditionally, career development interventions occur during stage four, when people are attempting to crystallize and clarify their self-concepts. However, Gottfredson's theory highlights the importance of interventions to young people in earlier stages of development, often in the form of career education programs. Such programs should focus on helping young people explore a full range of occupational options to promote systematic exploration in career choice (Gottfredson). Interventions that address sex-role stereotypes and expose children to options across occupational levels should be cornerstones of such programs. Gottfredson posited that career education programs must be sensitive to students' levels of cognitive development, expose students to a wide range of career options, and foster awareness of the circumscription and compromise processes.

For Gottfredson, a major issue in individual career counseling is the degree to which clients have unnecessarily restricted their occupational options. "The problem in compromise is the failure to come to grips with reality, either by ignoring it or failing to deal with it effectively" (Gottfredson, 1996, p. 217). Gottfredson identified criteria to guide counselors attempting to measure how much their clients may have unnecessarily restricted their options. For example, she noted that clients should be able to identify occupational options and relevant self-characteristics required to perform those occupations; clients should not unnecessarily restrict their occupational options; and they should be aware of obstacles they may encounter in implementing occupational choices.

In examining these criteria with clients, career counselors can explore clients' tolerable level and effort boundaries, perceptions of barriers, and the contextual factors influencing clients' perceptions of acceptable career options. Gottfredson advocates incorporating discussions of ability more explicitly into the career counseling process. Despite the fact that ability is a strong predictor of career success, it is often not highlighted in career counseling. Gottfredson (2003) contends that avoiding a discussion of ability restricts the usefulness of career counseling. When counselors discuss ability with adolescent clients, it helps them to see the connection between doing well in school and career success, thereby increasing their academic motivation and engagement.

Applying Gottfredson's criteria to Juana's case, the counselor could explore with her the occupational options she had already considered and build on Juana's strengths and interests. Acknowledging Juana's artistic bent—she enjoyed painting and playing flute in the school band—would be a good starting point. In discussing these interests, the counselor could assess whether Juana had unnecessarily restricted her options and consider questions such as *Is Juana's ability sufficient for a career in the arts? Is Juana aware of the obstacles she is likely to encounter pursuing such a career? Has she considered other ways to express her values, interests, and abilities? What caused her to eliminate other options?* The counselor could support and challenge Juana as she becomes more aware of her emerging self-concept and attempts to identify congruent options.

Evaluating Gottfredson's Theory

Research on Gottfredson's theory is not extensive: Existing research has been equivocal, and new research is declining. Much of it has focused on circumscription related to social class, gender, and intelligence. Using a sample of Canadian twelfth-graders, Hannah and Kahn (1989) found that those from higher social classes had higher aspirations than those from lower classes. Helwig (2001) conducted two longitudinal studies testing the applicability of Gottfredson's theory to children's career development. The research followed students from 2nd to 12th grades. In the first study, Helwig examined children's occupational aspirations and found support for the theory of circumscription and compromise. Helwig found support in the second study as well, reporting that students abandoned unrealistic occupational ideals in favor of realistic ones toward the end of high school. Other researchers applaud Gottfredson's theoretical emphasis on career development in childhood and gender differences, noting that the theory fills an important gap in the literature (McLennan & Arthur, 1999).

Empirical results from a study conducted by Henderson, Hesketh, and Tuffin (1988) focusing on New Zealand students ages 5 to 14 did not support the importance of gender in Gottfredson's stage two (Orientation to Sex Roles) but did support the importance of social class in stage three (Orientation to Social Valuation). A study conducted by Hesketh, Elmslie, and Kaldor (1990) suggested an alternative model of compromise in which interests were more important in career choices than sex type or prestige because interests incorporated sex type and prestige. Leong and Plake (1990) found that women often opted for work across gender lines if it offered more prestige, whereas men seldom did. Blanchard and Lichtenberg (2003) studied Gottfredson's compromise process and found that participants engaged in a moderate or high degree of compromise placed equal importance on prestige and sex type, in contrast to what the theory propounds. The same study participants did, however, place more emphasis on prestige and sex type than they did on interests as they considered factors influencing the compromise process.

More recently, Cochran, Wang, Stevenson, Johnson, and Crews (2011) used data from a longitudinal sample to investigate the relationship between adolescent occupational aspirations and midlife career success using Gottfredson's theory. The results of this study lend support to the influence of socioeconomic status (SES) and ability in the formation of occupational aspirations. Occupational aspirations, ability, and gender were significantly related to career achievement later in life. They also found that adolescent girls achieved less career success when they reached midlife than adolescent boys did.

In evaluating Gottfredson's theory, Brown (1996) noted "the propositions relating to the factors that lead to circumscription and compromise are too general. The result is that we are left with questions about what actually occurs in the career choice and selection process" (p. 523). Nonetheless, Gottfredson's theory provides interesting concepts describing boundaries and motivational dimensions related to the formation of occupational aspirations (Herr, Cramer, & Niles, 2004). It also addresses significant gaps in career-related literature (career development in childhood and gender differences). Moreover, Gottfredson's (2005) more recent explication of her theory begins to address Brown's criticism. Research testing the theory using a longitudinal and cross-sectional design would be particularly useful.

JOHN HOLLAND'S THEORY OF TYPES AND PERSON-ENVIRONMENT INTERACTIONS

The theory espoused by John Holland (1919–2008) belongs to a long tradition of theoretical perspectives describing individual differences in personality types (Murray, 1938; Spranger, 1928). Holland's theory (1959, 1966, 1973, 1985a, 1997) has been described as structural-interactive "because it provides an explicit link between various personality characteristics and corresponding job titles and because it organizes the massive data about people and jobs" (Weinrach, 1984, p. 63). The theory is based on four basic assumptions:

1. In our culture, most persons can be categorized as one of six types: realistic, investigative, artistic, social, enterprising, or conventional.
2. There are six kinds of environments: realistic, investigative, artistic, social, enterprising, and conventional.
3. People search for environments that will let them exercise their skills and abilities, express their attitudes and values, and take on agreeable problems and roles.
4. A person's behavior is determined by an interaction between personality and the characteristics of the environment. (Holland, 1973, pp. 2–4)

A key to using Holland's theory is understanding his typology. A good start is to consider how personality types develop. To a large degree, "types produce types" (Holland, 1973, p. 11)— that is, personality types are both genetically and environmentally based:

A child's special heredity and experience first lead to preferences for some kinds of activities and aversions to others. Later, these preferences become well-defined interests from which the person gains self-satisfaction as well as reward from others. Still later, the pursuit of these interests leads to the development of more specialized competencies as well as to the neglect of other potential competencies. At the same time, a person's differentiation of interests with age is accompanied by a crystallization of correlated values. These events—an increasing differentiation of preferred activities, interests, competencies, and values—create a characteristic disposition or personality type that is predisposed to exhibit characteristic behavior and to develop characteristic personality traits. (Holland, 1973, p. 12)

Holland contends that, to a large degree, career interests are an expression of an individual's personality (Holland, 1959, 1966, 1973, 1985a, 1992). As Spokane (1996) elaborated, "Interests, however, are complex measures that reflect personality as well as preferences, values, self-efficacy and so on. Types, then, are complex theoretical groupings based upon personality and interests" (p. 40). Personality traits are identified by a person's choice of leisure activities, school subjects, avocational interests, and work. To varying degrees, everyone conforms to one (or more) of six basic personality types. The more you conform to a type, the more likely it is that you will manifest the behaviors and traits associated with that type (Weinrach, 1984). Biases exist within the descriptions, and it is not the case that every "deficit" is apparent in every person who reflects a particular type. Following is a discussion of each of the six personality types as Holland defined them (1973, pp. 14–18; 1994, pp. 2–3).

The Realistic Type

The realistic type of person prefers activities that entail explicit, ordered, or systematic manipulation of objects, tools, machines, and animals and has an aversion to educational or therapeutic activities. The realistic person has mechanical abilities but may lack social skills. Realistic types prefer jobs such as automobile mechanic, surveyor, farmer, and electrician. Realistic types are often described as:

> conforming, humble, normal, frank, materialistic;
>
> persistent, genuine, modest, practical, hardheaded, natural;
>
> shy, honest, and thrifty.

The Investigative Type

The investigative type of person prefers activities that entail observational, symbolic, systematic, and creative investigation of physical, biological, and cultural phenomena to understand and control such phenomena. Investigative types have an aversion to persuasive, social, and repetitive activities. These tendencies lead to acquisition of scientific and mathematical competencies and to a deficit in leadership ability. Investigative types prefer jobs such as biologist, chemist, physicist, anthropologist, geologist, and medical technologist. Investigative persons are often described as:

> analytical, independent, modest, cautious, intellectual;
>
> pessimistic, complex, introverted, precise, critical;
>
> methodical, rational, curious, and reserved.

The Artistic Type

The artistic type of person prefers ambiguous, free, unsystematized activities that entail manipulation of physical, verbal, and human materials to create art forms and products. Artistic people have an aversion to explicit systematic and ordered activities. These tendencies lead to acquisition of competencies in language, art, music, drama, dance, and writing and to a deficit in clerical or business-system competencies. Artistic types like jobs such as composer, musician, stage director, singer, dancer, writer, interior designer, and actor/actress. Artistic persons are often described as:

> complicated, imaginative, introspective, disorderly;
>
> impractical, intuitive, emotional, impulsive, nonconforming;
>
> expressive, independent, open, idealistic, and original.

The Social Type

People with a social personality prefer activities that entail manipulation of others to inform, train, develop, cure, or enlighten. They have an aversion to explicit, ordered, and systematic activities involving materials, tools, or machines. These tendencies lead to acquisition of human relations competencies such as interpersonal and educational skills and to a deficit in mechanical and scientific ability. Social types like jobs such as teacher, religious worker, counselor, clinical psychologist, psychiatric caseworker, and speech therapist. Social persons are often described as:

> convincing, idealistic, social, cooperative, kind;
>
> sympathetic, friendly, patient, tactful, generous;
>
> responsible, understanding, helpful, and warm.

The Enterprising Type

People with enterprising personalities prefer activities that entail manipulation of others to attain organizational or economic gain. They have an aversion to observational, symbolic, and systematic activities. These tendencies lead to acquisition of leadership, interpersonal, and persuasive competencies and to a deficit in scientific ability. Enterprising types like jobs such as entrepreneur, salesperson, manager, business executive, television producer, sports promoter, and buyer. Enterprising persons are often described as:

> acquisitive, domineering, optimistic, adventurous;
>
> energetic, pleasure-seeking, agreeable, extroverted;
>
> attention-getting, ambitious, impulsive, self-confident,
>
> sociable, and popular.

The Conventional Type

People with the conventional personality type prefer activities that entail explicit, ordered, and systematic manipulation of data, such as keeping records, filing and reproducing materials, organizing written and numerical data according to a prescribed plan, and operating computers to attain organizational or economic goals. Conventional types have an aversion to ambiguous, free, exploratory, or unsystematized activities. These tendencies lead to acquisition of clerical, computational, and business-system competencies and to a deficit in artistic competencies.

Conventional types like jobs such as bookkeeper, stenographer, financial analyst, banker, cost estimator, and insurance claims adjuster. Conventional persons are often described as:

conforming, inhibited, persistent, conscientious, obedient;

practical, careful, orderly, thrifty, efficient;

and unimaginative.

Holland (1973) used the same six types to describe occupational environments (pp. 29–33). For example, the realistic environment requires the explicit, ordered, or systematic manipulation of objects, tools, machines, and animals and encourages people to view themselves as having mechanical ability. It rewards people for displaying conventional values and encourages them to see the world in simple, tangible, and traditional terms.

The investigative environment requires the symbolic, systematic, and creative investigation of physical, biological, and cultural phenomena. It encourages scientific competencies and achievements and the perception of the world in complex and unconventional ways. It rewards people for displaying scientific values.

The artistic environment requires participation in ambiguous, free, and unsystematized activities to create art forms and products. It encourages people to view themselves as having creative abilities and to see themselves as expressive, nonconforming, independent, and intuitive. It rewards people for the display of artistic values.

The social environment requires participation in activities that inform, train, develop, cure, or enlighten others. It requires people to see themselves as liking to help others, being understanding of others, and seeing the world in flexible ways. It rewards people for the display of social values.

The enterprising environment requires participation in activities that involve the manipulation of others to attain organizational and self-interest goals. It requires people to view themselves as aggressive, popular, self-confident, sociable, and possessing leadership and speaking ability. It encourages people to view the world in terms of power and status and in stereotyped and simple terms. It rewards people for displaying enterprising goals and values.

The conventional environment requires participation in activities that involve the explicit, ordered, or systematic manipulation of data, such as record keeping, filing materials, and organizing written and numerical data according to a prescribed plan. It requires people to view themselves as conforming, orderly, nonartistic, and having clerical competencies. It rewards people for perceiving the world in stereotyped and conventional ways.

Congruence

The key construct in Holland's theory is that of congruence. Congruence describes the degree of fit between an individual's personality type and current or prospective work environment. A person is in a congruent work environment when his or her personality type matches the occupational environment (a social type working as a counselor). Conversely, incongruence occurs when people are in environments that do not match their personality types (a social type working as a computer programmer). Individuals tend to be more satisfied and perform better in environments that are congruent with their personality types. Thus, congruence reflects the adage that birds of a feather flock together as well as that "different types require different environments" (Holland, 1973, p. 4) and "environments are characterized by the people who occupy them" (Weinrach, 1984, pp. 63–64). To distinguish congruence from Holland's other constructs, students often find it helpful to view the *u* and *e* in congruence as indicative of the relationship between you and the environment.

Holland uses a hexagonal model to represent the relationships within and between types (Figure 2.1). The highest level of congruence occurs when there is direct correspondence between workers' personality types and their work environments (investigative personality types in investigative work environments). The next highest level of congruence exists when workers are in environments adjacent to their type on the hexagon (a realistic personality type in an investigative work environment). The lowest level of congruence exists when workers are in environments opposite their personality types on the hexagon (a social type in a realistic work environment). The primary goal of career counseling is to help clients identify and connect with congruent work environments.

Differentiation

To describe workers and their environments, Holland (1973) focuses on the three types the worker or environment most closely resembles. However, some people and environments are

Figure 2.1

The relationships among Holland types.

Source: Information from *Holland's Hexagon, ACT Research Report No. 29,* by J. L. Holland, D. R. Whitney, N. S. Cole, and J. M. Richards, Jr., 1969, Iowa City: The American College Testing Program. Copyright © 1969 The American College Testing Program. Reprinted by permission.

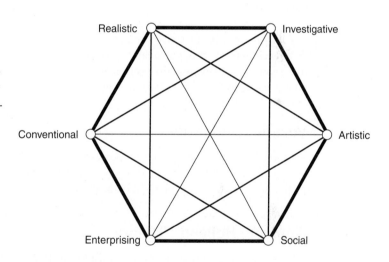

Degree of Consistency	Personality Patterns
▬▬▬▬ High	RI, RC, IR, IA, AI, AS, SA, SE, ES, EC, CE
———— Medium	RA, RE, IS, IC, AR, AE, SI, SC, EA, ER, CS, CI
———— Low	RS, IE, AC, SR, EI, CA

more clearly defined, or differentiated, than others. For example, a person may greatly resemble one Holland type and have little resemblance to others (a high level of differentiation), or a single type may dominate an environment. Other persons or environments may resemble multiple types equally and therefore be relatively undifferentiated or poorly defined. Holland (1973) referred to the degree of distinctness among types in someone's personality profile as "differentiation." Because people who are undifferentiated may have difficulty making career decisions, counselors often direct interventions toward helping them achieve greater differentiation among Holland types.

Consistency

The degree of relatedness within types is referred to as *consistency.* The hexagonal model shown in Figure 2.1 is useful in illustrating the similarities across types. For example, types located next to each other on the hexagon have more in common than types opposite each other. Higher degrees of consistency within personality types suggest more integration and harmony among traits, interests, values, and perceptions than do lower degrees of consistency. Holland assumes that consistent persons are more predictable in their behaviors and more likely to be higher career achievers than persons who are not consistent. However, it is not a goal of career counseling to make clients more consistent. Rather, the primary function of consistency in counseling is to foster awareness: clients with low consistency (a realistic-social personality type) must be aware that it may be difficult to find an occupational environment that allows them to express the diverse aspects of their personalities. In such cases, clients must identify avocational activities that allow them to express themselves outside of work. For example, a realistic-social personality type working as a social worker may choose to spend her leisure time in woodworking activities.

Vocational Identity

Vocational identity is defined as the "possession of a clear and stable picture of one's goals, interests, and talent" (Holland, 1985a, p. 5). Vocational identity is an important goal of many career development interventions and dependent on acquiring sufficient occupational and self-information.

Applying Holland's Theory

Congruence, differentiation, consistency, and vocational identity are the key theoretical constructs used to link Holland's theory to practice. "All things being equal, an individual with high identity who is congruent, consistent, and differentiated should be more predictable and better adjusted than one who is incongruent, inconsistent, and undifferentiated" (Spokane et al., 2002, p. 385). Assessment instruments developed by Holland and his associates are typically used to measure these constructs, and the results of these measures provide stimuli for career counseling content.

For example, the Self-Directed Search (SDS) (Holland, 1994) and the Vocational Preference Inventory (VPI) (Holland, 1985b) are used to translate clients' self-estimates of interests and competencies into Holland types. The SDS consists of an assessment booklet (used to identify a person's Holland type), an Occupations Finder (two versions are available, each listing 1,334 occupations classified according to either three-letter Holland codes or alphabetical order), and an interpretive guide titled *You and Your Career.* The latter provides people with information, activities, and readings for using Holland's theory in career decision making. The SDS, which is the most widely used interest inventory, is available in different versions based on reading level (SDS Form E), setting (SDS CP, Corporate Version), and language spoken by the respondent.

The SDS would provide a starting point for focusing Juana's career exploration and information gathering. First, Juana could use the assessment booklet to identify her three-letter summary code. (Because researchers have found a high error rate in summary code calculations [Miller, 1997], counselors must take precautions to prevent this.) Then Juana and her counselor could compare her summary code (ASI—artistic-social-investigative with low differentiation) to her abilities and interests.

It is especially important to discuss with the client his or her summary code when the code lacks consistency. A client with a code of RSA (realistic-social-artistic) may have trouble finding occupations that fit that combination (few jobs require workers to have equally strong mechanical, social, and artistic skills). Clients who do not understand this may experience pendulum shifting in their career choices. A man may opt for a realistic—R—occupation and be satisfied because it offers opportunities for engaging in R tasks and rewards R competencies. Over time, however, he may notice the absence of social—S—opportunities and become convinced that the R occupation should be replaced with one in the S environment. If he changes jobs, he may be satisfied with the new one—for a while—but over time he may feel that the new job is too S and not enough R, and the pendulum may shift back toward an R occupation.

Making low-consistency clients aware of the possibility of pendulum shifting is important because, if a congruent occupational environment is not available, avocational activities may compensate for the lack. In these instances, counselors may use the Leisure Activities Finder (Holmberg, Rosen, & Holland, 1990) to help clients identify opportunities to express dimensions of their personalities they may not be able to express through work. For example, a person with an RSA code may choose to work with things (R) at work, perhaps as a cook, but devote leisure time to the social (S) sphere, perhaps as youth group leader for a church. As we said before, it is important for practitioners to understand that consistency is not a goal of career counseling. Rather, consistency is a construct that helps clients understand who they are so they can make effective career decisions.

Clients with codes that lack differentiation (determined by subtracting the lowest score from the highest score among the six types, or by examining the numerical difference among the letters in the client's three-part code) often experience a lack of focus in their career direction. Lack of differentiation may occur because (a) clients lack exposure to activities across Holland environments, (b) they have trouble making decisions, (c) they have multipotentiality, or (d) they are depressed.

Clients lacking in exposure to Holland environments (e.g., young people with little or no work experience, homemakers returning to work after an extended absence) may need help increasing self-understanding as it relates to their interests, abilities, and values. With such clients, counselors may use values inventories, values card sorts, and skills checklists to foster understanding of these career decision-making variables. Persons returning to the labor market after a lengthy hiatus may find it useful to engage in an accomplishments exercise in which they list activities—accomplishments—about which they feel especially proud. As the client describes each activity, the counselor encourages him or her to list the skills embedded in the successful performance of the activity. After doing this for several activities, counselor and client will have generated a list of skills that they can categorize according to Holland type and can use to identify the type that embodies the client's dominant characteristics. Clients with limited work experience may also need to take steps to increase their self-understanding and differentiation, such as information interviewing, volunteering, and job shadowing.

Indecisive clients can be taught decision-making skills and encouraged to retake the SDS and/or to discuss which Holland types they think they most closely resemble. Instead of retaking the SDS, such clients may engage in a Holland card sort procedure during which they rank activities in order of preference (and the counselor observes how easy or difficult it is for them). The rankings are then reviewed to determine which Holland types they suggest. After learning decision-making skills, engaging in self-assessment activities, and reviewing occupational information, some clients may remain undecided. Clients may be fearful of choosing for many reasons, including failing, disappointing significant others, or even succeeding. In these instances, counselor and client need to engage in a counseling or therapy-like process to help the client understand his or her fears.

Elevated and undifferentiated SDS scores may indicate that a client has multiple interests and competencies, not decision-making problems. This was true of Holland himself, who had elevated and undifferentiated scores across almost all his types (Weinrach, 1996). Counselors may find it useful to focus on values instead of interests and abilities when working with such clients. Finally, counselors also must determine whether clients with low scores for all Holland types are having difficulty with depression or low self-esteem. Given Juana's youth and difficulties in school, her counselor would do well to explore all possible explanations of the low differentiation in her summary code.

With a general understanding of the Holland typology and a specific understanding of their own Holland summary codes, clients can peruse the Occupations Finder to find options that resemble their summary codes. Each client focuses on occupations resembling all combinations of his or her summary code, then identifies occupations within these categories that interest them (Juana would focus on occupations in the ASI, SIA, AIS, SAI, IAS, and ISA categories).

Next, counselors encourage clients to take action (information interviewing, researching occupational requirements, job shadowing) to learn about occupations that interest them. Clients then discuss what they've learned with their counselors and narrow their list of options. Counselors encourage clients to take additional steps (volunteering, taking courses related to a particular occupation, job searching) toward implementing tentative choices. Counselor and client also review how each option provides opportunities for expressing the types comprising the client's summary code. The goals of this process are to clarify the client's vocational identity and help the client make a congruent career decision.

In addition to the SDS, counselors can use the VPI to help clients identify their Holland type and connect their summary codes to congruent occupational environments. The VPI (Holland, 1985b) contains 160 occupational titles, the six Holland type scales, and five supplemental scales (self-control, masculinity/femininity, status, infrequency, and acquiescence). To assess vocational identity, counselors can use *My Vocational Situation* (MVS) (Holland, Gottfredson, & Power, 1980), a manual that measures vocational identity and perceived career development barriers. The MVS's Vocational Identity (VI) scale measures the respondent's awareness of and ability to specify his or her interests, personality characteristics, strengths, and goals with reference to career choices. The MVS's Occupational Information (OI) scale measures the respondent's need for occupational information.

Gottfredson and Holland (1996) also created the Position Classification Inventory (PCI) for classifying work environments according to Holland typology. Prior to the PCI, which uses individual worker judgments to classify his or her work environment, researchers and counselors used an actual census of workers to classify work environments according to the Holland types. Because variability exists across same-type occupations in different work environments, the PCI may be useful in helping clients understand their degree of congruence in a specific job. Miller and Bass (2003) found the PCI useful in classifying work environments in a paper manufacturing plant. Other inventories also use the Holland typology in reporting assessment results, among them the Strong Interest Inventory (SII) (Harmon et al., 1994), the Career Assessment Inventory (CAI) (Johannson, 1986), and the Armed Services Vocational Aptitude Battery (ASVAB) (U.S. Department of Defense, 1993).

Evaluating Holland's Theory

Holland's theory has inspired extensive research, and has arguably been subjected to more empirical tests than any other career theory (Spokane & Cruza-Guet, 2005). Gottfredson and Richards (1999) note that a major advantage of Holland's theory is that it provides a parallel way to describe people and environments. In 1996, Holland summarized research findings supporting the use of his typology to explain career certainty, change, and satisfaction. These findings focus on (a) relations between congruence and career outcomes, (b) methods for calculating constructs such as congruence, and (c) the application of Holland's theory to diverse populations.

Spokane et al. (2002) summarized the congruence-related research, noting that although results are somewhat mixed, there is a "modest relationship between person-environment fit and job satisfaction" (p. 400). Spokane, Fouad, and Swanson (2001) argued that most of the congruence-related research, especially in the early years, was correlational and therefore does not reflect the complexity inherent in person-environment interactions. Longitudinal, cross-sectional, and experimental studies are needed to more accurately represent person-environment interactions and measure the validity of the congruence construct.

Although there are data to support the importance of congruence to vocational satisfaction, research supporting the relationship between consistency and differentiation in vocational satisfaction has been weak. Research methodologies have not been sufficiently sophisticated to examine the complex processes related to consistency, differentiation, and relevant occupational outcomes (satisfaction, stability). To address this issue, Tracey, Wille, Durr, and Fruyt (2014) examined Holland's consistency and differentiation constructs by including the entire Holland profile (typically only the top two are used to determine consistency) and information on relative differences in all six scale scores, thus providing a more thorough definition of consistency and differentiation. They examined the relationship between these constructs and career certainty, career satisfaction, and occupational stability. Tracey et al. found support for the viability of consistency and differentiation as they relate to the outcomes used in the study (certainty, satisfaction, and stability). The methods used in this study suggest a potentially fruitful avenue for pursuing subsequent research related to consistency and differentiation.

Other studies provide intriguing data on the validity of Holland's theory. Miller (2002) investigated the degree of change in a male client's three-letter Holland code over 10 years (the client initially took the SDS at age 16). The man's code remained stable across a decade, supporting Holland's contention that SDS personality types remain stable over time. Lent, Brown, Nota, and Soresi (2003) examined the relationship of interest congruence to the occupational choices of 796 Italian high school students and found that interests were significant predictors of occupational choices for all Holland types.

Oleski and Subich (1996) studied 42 nontraditional students (mean age 34.4) in the process of changing careers. They found support for Holland's (1985a) assumption that people change careers to achieve greater congruence.

Lent and Lopez (1996) investigated the relationship between congruence indices and job satisfaction among adult workers. Although they found partial overlap among methods for calculating congruence, they noted the need for more research to understand the relations among indices of congruence, methods for coding work environments, and antecedents to congruence.

Tracey (2008) found that for college students enrolled in a career development class, the RIASEC model was linked to better career decision-making outcomes (students considering congruent career options have more career certainty and decision-making self-efficacy than those who do not adhere to the congruence principle). In a study comparing people who remain in the same career to those who change, Donahue (2006) found person-environment congruence to be related to career stability. Perdue, Reardon, and Peterson (2007) also found person-environment congruence to be associated with job satisfaction in a sample of 198 employees working for a multinational communications corporation.

Behrens and Nauta (2014) examined the effects of using Holland's Self-Directed Search as a stand-alone intervention with college students. One group (n = 39) received the SDS as a stand-alone treatment, and another (n = 41) received no treatment. Four weeks after taking the SDS, students were considering more career alternatives but experienced no significant change in career exploration, career decision-making self-efficacy, career indecision, or seeking of career counseling services. Behrens and Nauta concluded that using the SDS as a stand-alone treatment is not effective for increasing career exploration in college students.

Achieving congruence is partially dependent on the availability of occupations that enable a worker to express his or her personality. Downes and Kroeck (1996) hypothesized that there is a discrepancy between normative occupational interests and the number of existing positions in the United States. Using normative interest data from the SDS and data extracted from the *Monthly Labor Review*, Downes and Kroeck found a lack of interest in conventional- and enterprising-type jobs compared to the number of available positions. They found the opposite with regard to the remaining Holland categories. For instance, there was excess interest among high school students for social-, artistic-, and investigative-type jobs compared to the number of available positions. Investigative- and realistic-type jobs represented high-interest areas for the adults in the study. Based on their findings, Downes and Kroeck called for a concerted effort to reshape the interests and skills of U.S. workers to meet the labor needs of corporations and educational institutions.

Ryan, Tracey, and Rounds (1996) and Rounds and Tracey (1996) studied the generalizability of Holland's (1985a) model of vocational interests across ethnicity, gender, and SES. Ryan et al. found similar interest structures in the White and African-American high school students in their study. Ryan and her colleagues also found no differences in the structure of interests between low- and high-SES groups. A similar result was obtained when comparing low- and high-SES White groups. However, the low-SES African-American group was better fit by Holland's model than was the high-SES African-American group. Both male and female students fit Holland's model. Ryan and her colleagues concluded that Holland's model is generalizable across ethnicity, gender, and socioeconomic status as defined in their study. Oliver and Waehler (2005) found support for Holland's typology and its arrangement in circular RIASEC order in a sample of Native Hawaiians.

Mihalik (1996) examined whether clients' types predicted reactions to counselor intentions. Using a sample of undergraduate college students, Mihalik found that clients' vocational interests as measured by the SDS (Holland, 1987) were predictive of client reactions to counselor interventions. For example, participants with high enterprising-type scores responded positively to feeling challenged by their counselor, whereas participants with high social-type scores responded positively to feeling supported by their counselor.

Sverko, Babarovic, and Medugorac (2014) conducted a validation study of the Pictorial and Descriptive Interest Inventory (PDII). The PDII is a new measure of RIASEC interest types with photographs of people involved in typical job tasks, job titles, and short job descriptions. They found that the PDII, available online at careerassessment.eu, is a reliable measure of RIASEC types across the samples of middle school, high school, and university students they studied.

This brief compilation proves that Holland's theory has generated more research than any other career choice model, with much of the research supporting the theory (Holland, 1996; Spokane, 1985; Spokane et al., 2002). Holland's theory provides a clear link to practice: "The combination of empirical support and practical application accounts for the theory's popularity among the public as well as among professionals" (Spokane, 1996, p. 62). This being said, we believe that more research into the validity of Holland's method across cultural contexts is needed.

JOHN KRUMBOLTZ'S LEARNING THEORY OF CAREER COUNSELING

John Krumboltz (b. 1928) and his colleagues (especially Lynda Mitchell and G. Brian Jones) developed a learning theory of career counseling comprising two distinct parts. The first focuses on explaining the origins of career choice and is labeled the *social learning theory of career decision making* (SLTCDM) (Mitchell & Krumboltz, 1996). The second focuses on career counseling and is labeled the *learning theory of career counseling* (LTCC) (Krumboltz & Henderson, 2002; Mitchell & Krumboltz, 1996). Because the SLTCDM identifies factors influencing the career decisions people make (and is, therefore, subsumed under the LTCC part of the theory), and because the LTCC explains what career counselors can do to help clients make effective career decisions, Mitchell and Krumboltz labeled the entire theory the LTCC.

LTCC is based on the application of Bandura's (1977, 1986) social learning theory to career decision making. Bandura's theory emphasizes the influence of reinforcement theory, cognitive information processing, and classical behaviorism on human behavior. Social learning theory "assumes that people's personalities and behavioral repertoires can be explained most usefully on the basis of their unique learning experiences while still acknowledging the role played by innate and developmental processes" (Mitchell & Krumboltz, 1996, p. 234). Social learning theory also assumes that "humans are intelligent, problem-solving individuals who strive at all times to understand the reinforcement that surrounds them and who in turn control their environments to suit their own purposes and needs" (Mitchell & Krumboltz, 1984, p. 236). Bandura (1986) described the interaction of environment, self-referent thought, and behavior as the "triadic reciprocal interaction system" (p. 6).

Krumboltz and colleagues drew on these theoretical assumptions in developing LTCC. As noted, SLTCDM describes the factors influencing people's career decisions and LTCC describes what counselors can do to help them make effective career choices.

Social Learning Theory of Career Decision Making

The SLTCDM identifies four factors that influence how people make career decisions:

1. *Genetic endowment and special abilities.* Genetic endowments are inherited qualities such as sex, race, and physical appearance. Special abilities such as intelligence, athletic ability,

and musical and artistic talents result from the interaction of genetic factors and exposure to selected environmental events.

2. *Environmental conditions and events.* Factors in this category are generally outside our control and include a variety of cultural, social, political, and economic forces. For example, government-sponsored job-training programs such as the Comprehensive Employment Training Act and the Job Training Partnership Act provide opportunities for learning new skills and increasing employability. Technological developments (computer technologies) create new jobs and make others obsolete. Legislation affecting welfare policy, labor laws, and union policies influences job availability and facilitates or restricts job entry. Natural disasters can dramatically influence career opportunities and career paths. Family and cultural traditions, as well as neighborhood and community resources, can also affect individuals' career decisions. Job entry requirements may persuade or deter us from considering specific occupational opportunities. Where we live also influences the availability of job opportunities and how we choose among them (climatic differences between Maine and Florida result in differences in job opportunities; the availability of counseling jobs is greater in the United States than in countries where counseling is handled by spiritual leaders).

3. *Instrumental and associative learning experiences.* Instrumental learning experiences involve antecedents, behaviors, and consequences. According to Mitchell and Krumboltz (1996):

> Antecedents include the genetic endowments, special abilities, and environmental conditions and events previously discussed as well as the characteristics of a particular task or problem. Behavioral responses include cognitive and emotional responses as well as overt behavior. Consequences include immediate and delayed effects produced by the behavior as well as "self-talk" about those consequences. (p. 238)

Consider Jennifer, a master's-degree student in counselor education. She is highly competent socially (genetic endowment, special abilities, and skills) but feels anxious about taking a course in planned environmental conditions because statistics and research design intimidate her. The course is required; she must take it. The professor teaching the course, however, is well acquainted with counselor education students and knows that many of them are as anxious as Jennifer. Hence, the professor praises students when they master the material, and supports them when they're struggling. Jennifer decides to apply herself to master the course content (covert and overt action). She gets a B on her first exam—better than she imagined (consequences). She begins to think that research might be more fun than frightening and that she might become a competent researcher (covert reactions to consequences). As the semester progresses, Jennifer begins to tutor peers who are struggling in the course. In her second year, she serves as a graduate assistant in the course and enjoys helping students who feel anxious about being able to succeed (impact on significant others).

Associative learning experiences occur when a neutral stimulus is paired with a positive and/or negative stimulus or consequence. For example, Juana's school counselor encouraged her to attend a job fair at her high school because Juana was undecided about her options. Juana agreed to attend the fair. She had nothing solid in mind but decided she would browse to see what options seemed interesting. At the fair, Juana met a news anchor for a local TV station who happened to be Latina. Juana had never thought of TV journalism as a career (neutral stimulus) but enjoyed meeting the newswoman (positive stimulus), who invited her to tour the studio and sit in on a live broadcast. After taking the tour and observing the broadcast, Juana decided to enroll in the externship program her high school had established with the TV station (positive consequences).

4. *Task-approach skills.* Juana will need to use many skills to determine whether journalism is a good career for her. She must clarify her interests, values, and skills; gather occupational information; and know how to integrate this information into her decision making. In this process, Juana will consider her genetic characteristics, special abilities, and environmental influences (family support, training opportunities, financial resources, and occupational opportunities)—task-approach skills she must use to choose a career. Task-approach skills also include a person's work habits, mental set, emotional responses, cognitive processes, and problem solving. Of course, if Juana decides to pursue the career of TV newswoman, she also will need to develop journalism skills to achieve her goal. Thus, task-approach skills influence outcomes and are themselves outcomes.

Following are four factors that influence our beliefs about ourselves (e.g., what we are good at, what our interests are, what we value) and our beliefs about the world (e.g., hard work always pays off, accountants are nerdy, counselors value altruism over economic reward):

1. *Self-observation generalizations.* Overt or covert statements evaluating our actual or vicarious performance, or self-assessments of our interests and values, are defined as self-observation generalizations (Mitchell & Krumboltz, 1996). Learning experiences lead us to draw conclusions about ourselves. We compare our performance both to that of others and to what we expect of ourselves, and we use these comparisons to draw conclusions about our performance capabilities. We also draw conclusions about our interests and values from learning experiences. In SLTCDM, interests link learning experiences with specific actions (as when doing well in a research course leads to the decision to participate in research projects and tutor others). Self-observations about values are, in essence, statements about the desirability of specific outcomes, behaviors, and events (Mitchell & Krumboltz, 1996). The statement "It is important that my job provide me ample time off to be with my family" is a values-related self-observation generalization about desirable outcomes resulting from previous learning experiences.

2. *World view generalizations.* Likewise, generalizations about the nature and functioning of the world (it's not what you know, it's who you know; it's better to try and fail than to not try at all) are formed from learning experiences. The accuracy of worldview generalizations is dependent on the learning experiences shaping them.

3. *Task-approach skills.* Mitchell and Krumboltz (1996) define these outcomes as "cognitive and performance abilities and emotional predispositions for coping with the environment, interpreting it in relation to self-observation generalizations, and making covert and overt predictions about future events" (p. 246). As noted, task-approach skills influence career decision making and are outcomes of learning experiences that shape a person's career development. Task-approach skills critical to career development are those involved in decision making, problem solving, goal setting, information gathering, and values clarifying.

4. *Actions.* Learning experiences eventually lead people to take actions related to entering a career. These actions include applying for a job, entering a training program, applying to college and graduate school, changing jobs, and taking other steps to progress in one's career.

The SLTCDM suggests that career decision making is "influenced by complex environmental factors, many of which are beyond the control of any single individual" (Krumboltz, Mitchell, & Gelatt, 1976, p. 75). The theory also underscores "the interaction between innate predispositions and learning experiences within the intra-individual, family, social, educational and cultural context" (Krumboltz & Henderson, 2002, p. 43). Also, based on SLTCDM, Krumboltz (1994) noted that people will prefer an occupation if:

1. They have succeeded at tasks they believe are similar to tasks performed by practitioners of that occupation.
2. They have observed someone they admire being rewarded for performing activities similar to those performed by practitioners of that occupation.
3. A valued friend or relative praised its advantages, and/or they have observed positive words and images being associated with it. (p. 19)

Conversely, Krumboltz (1994) noted that people will avoid an occupation if:

1. They have failed at tasks they believe are similar to tasks performed by practitioners of that occupation.
2. They have observed someone they admire suffering negative consequences for performing activities similar to those performed by practitioners of that occupation.
3. A valued friend or relative stressed its disadvantages and/or they have observed negative words and images being associated with it. (p. 19)

Learning Theory of Career Counseling

The strength of SLTCDM is that it provides a description of factors influencing career decision making and identifies their outcomes. It is useful for understanding career paths retrospectively, which is helpful in making current decisions and in formulating future goals.

When career concerns arise, they typically involve one or more of the following: (a) the absence of a goal, or career indecision (Juana's presenting concern); (b) an expressed concern about high aspirations, or unrealism; and (c) a conflict between equally appropriate alternatives, or multipotentiality (Krumboltz & Thoresen, 1969). Krumboltz developed the learning theory of career counseling (LTCC) to guide counselors designing interventions addressing these three concerns. Counselors use LTCC to help clients (a) acquire more accurate self-observation generalizations, (b) acquire more accurate worldview generalizations, (c) learn new task-approach skills, and (d) take appropriate career-related actions. LTCC presumes counselor readiness to help clients cope with four career-related trends (Mitchell & Krumboltz, 1996, pp. 250–252):

1. People need to expand their capabilities and interests and not base decisions solely on existing characteristics. Interest inventories assess what we know and what we have experienced. To maximize a client's career choice options, counselors must encourage him or her to explore new activities, develop new interests, and consider new options based on newly formed interests and capabilities.
2. People need to prepare for changing work tasks and understand that occupations will not remain stable. Because change is constant, career counselors must help clients identify new skills and develop strategies for coping with the inherent stress.
3. People must be empowered to take action, not merely receive a diagnosis. For some clients, implementing a career choice is more challenging than making the choice. Many clients need ongoing assistance from their counselors as they attempt to adjust to the choice they have made.
4. Career counselors need to play a major role in dealing with all career challenges, not just selection. Many clients struggle with burnout, underemployment, low self-efficacy, conflicts with coworkers, and family members' reactions to their career choices.

These trends pinpoint the importance of providing clients with learning experiences to (a) correct faulty assumptions, (b) develop new skills and interests, (c) identify strategies for addressing problems emanating from work and other life-role conflicts, and (d) learn skills for coping with changing work tasks. Career counselors may use assessments to help clients identify both the characteristics (beliefs, skills, values, interests, personality) they have learned and opportunities for learning new ones. Thus, the career counselor's mission is to promote clients' learning and their ability to create satisfying lives for themselves (Krumboltz, 1996).

Applying LTCC

Krumboltz (1996) divides career development interventions into two categories: (a) developmental/preventive and (b) targeted/remedial. Developmental and preventive interventions include career education programs, school-to-work initiatives, job club programs, study materials, and simulations. They facilitate the acquisition of accurate occupational self-information and its deployment in the career decision-making process, and emphasize learning through active on-the-job participation (job shadowing, internships, and work-site observation).

Although many clients, including Juana, could benefit from these activities, clients must first receive targeted and remedial interventions, which include goal clarification, cognitive restructuring, cognitive rehearsal, narrative analysis, role playing, desensitization, paradoxical intention, and humor (Krumboltz, 1996). LTCC also emphasizes the importance of teaching decision-making skills to clients. Learning how to make career decisions helps clients resolve current career concerns and equips them with a powerful task-approach skill for coping with future changes in work and personal conditions (Krumboltz, 1976).

To help counselors identify problematic client beliefs associated with career problem categories (indecision, unrealism, and multipotentiality), Krumboltz (1988) developed the Career Beliefs Inventory (CBI). The CBI is based on the rationale that people make career decisions according to what they believe about themselves and the world of work. As Krumboltz (1994) wrote, "If their beliefs are accurate and constructive, they will act in ways that are likely to help them achieve their goals. If their beliefs are inaccurate and self-defeating, they will act in a way that makes sense to them but may not help them achieve their goals" (p. 424). The CBI helps counselors understand their clients' career beliefs and assumptions, and it is most useful when administered at the start of counseling. The CBI comprises 25 scales divided into five categories: My Current Career Situation, What Seems Necessary for My Happiness, Factors That Influence My Decisions, Changes I Am Willing to Make, and Efforts I Am Willing to Initiate. These categories, labeled in positive terms, are cognates of negative mental states that block people from taking action. As Krumboltz and Henderson (2002) remind us, meaningful journeys, including career journeys, pose obstacles that we must confront and surmount. Some clients allow discouragement and other problematic conditions to thwart their efforts to act. The CBI measures self-defeating beliefs that clients must address if they are to move forward. Cognitive restructuring and reframing are useful strategies for helping clients address these issues.

In career counseling, clients often refer to significant events in ways that suggest they had little or nothing to do with them. A client may say, "Oh, I just got lucky" or "I just happened to be in the right place at the right time." Krumboltz and his associates (Mitchell et al., 1999) assert that career counseling involves helping such clients acknowledge and exploit chance encounters, noting that "unplanned events are not only inevitable, they are desirable" (p. 118) and labeling this phenomenon "planned happenstance" (p. 115). Career counselors can foment planned happenstance by teaching clients "to generate, recognize, and incorporate chance events into the process of their career development" (Krumboltz & Henderson, 2002, p. 49). They may ask clients questions such as "How have unplanned events influenced your career in the past? How did you enable each event to influence your career development? How do you feel about encountering unplanned events in the future?" (2002, p. 50). Counseling interactions that intentionally address the role of chance in career development help normalize such occurrences, help clients see how serendipitous encounters can influence their careers, and help clients grow increasingly open to noticing and acting on unplanned events in the future. In essence, an internal locus of control and increased sense of personal self-efficacy are fostered.

Mitchell et al. (1999) focus on the skills that clients must develop to exploit unplanned events as they build their careers. Among them are developing and maintaining curiosity, persistence, flexibility, optimism, and a willingness to take risks.

Evaluating Career Development Interventions

Counselors usually evaluate the success of career development interventions by determining whether clients experience a reduction in career indecision. Krumboltz (1994) recommends that counselors consider revising these criteria. For example, counselors using LTCC view indecision as desirable for motivating clients to engage in new learning activities. Hence, Krumboltz recommends reframing indecision as open-mindedness.

Krumboltz (1994) also suggests that people striving for congruence between their work and work environments may be restricting themselves unnecessarily because proverbial birds of a feather do not always flock together; there is, after all, intra-occupational variability among people: an extroverted woman and a shy man can both be successful attorneys—especially if she's a personal injury litigator and he specializes in tax law. Krumboltz (1996) also argues that the congruence criterion is less useful today because it is based on stagnant definitions of occupational environments: "Heterogeneity, not homogeneity, within occupations is now more highly valued" (p. 242).

Krumboltz recommends measuring changes in client characteristics such as skills, values, beliefs, interests, and work habits. Counselors may ask themselves whether their interventions have stimulated their clients to engage in new learning activities. Process measures can focus on assessing the degree to which clients have made efforts to create more satisfying lives (have they explored options or sought information?).

Evaluating LTCC

There hasn't been much research into the efficacy of LTCC. There is, however, extensive research supporting the general social learning theory (Hackett, Lent, & Greenhaus, 1991). In addition, Krumboltz (1996) cites several studies supporting SLTCDM hypotheses related to development of educational and occupational preferences, task-approach skills, and action. Kim et al. (2014) conducted a validation study of the Planned Happenstance Career Inventory (PHCI) and were able to reduce the PHCI from 130 to 25 items across five factors (optimism, flexibility, persistence, curiosity, and risk taking). They also found a significant negative correlation between career stress and planned happenstance. People with higher levels of planned happenstance skills feel less stress and anxiety about their professional future. Career decision-making self-efficacy had significantly positive correlations with optimism, persistence, curiosity, and risk taking. The construct validity demonstrated in this study supports using the PHCI in career development interventions.

A strength of LTCC is that it addresses both environmental and intra-individual variables in career development. It is compatible with Super's (1990) Archway model of career development and offers a bit more in terms of specific ways that environmental and personal variables influence decision making. LTCC also can be used as a framework for understanding the development of interests leading to one's personal modal orientation as described by Holland's theory (1996). Finally, the development of the CBI and subsequent application of strategies such as cognitive restructuring and reframing provide useful applications of the theory to career development interventions.

MyCounselingLab®

Start with Topic 3—Career Development of Career Behavior and Choice.

Watch the video *21st Century Application of Holland's Theory.*

SUMMARY

The theories discussed in this chapter form the foundation for how leading theorists and practitioners have conceptualized the career development process for more than 50 years. The theories converge in some ways and diverge in others. They offer perspectives for conceptualizing how careers develop and how career choices are made. There is no one theory that adequately addresses all factors potentially influencing career development and all client career concerns, but they do provide a foundation upon which to expand our thinking about the career development process and interventions. An area ripe for expansion is how careers develop for a wider range of people, as most early theories of career development were based on the experiences of White men and often lack applicability to women and members of diverse racial, ethnic, socioeconomic, and religious groups. Another area for expansion is the content and process of career counseling. Most early theories of career development emphasize process rather than interventions. More treatment-outcome research into which interventions work for which clients is needed.

These theories provide an important stimulus in the evolution of theory development. As they continue to evolve and new theories emerge, we hope that theorists will continue to provide fuller, more detailed, and more comprehensive descriptions of the career development process so counselors can provide effective interventions to a wide range of people.

In the next chapter, we will discuss emerging theories providing evidence of such progress.

STUDENT ACTIVITIES

1. Review the Holland types. Which types do you most resemble? How do your activities reflect these types?

2. Review Super's career development tasks. Which tasks are you most concerned with now? What resources and support would help you cope effectively with them?

3. Review Gottfredson's theory. In what ways has sex-role stereotyping affected your career?

4. Consider the life role of worker. What have you learned about this role from your parents or guardians? What have you learned about this role from your relatives? In what ways have cultural influences shaped your understanding of the life role of worker?

5. Review John Krumboltz's theory. Identify two of your own worldview generalizations. Identify three self-observations (you might begin by stating "I'm the kind of person who …"; "One thing I value is … "; and "I'm really good at … ").

6. Reflect on your early life experiences and consider how well Anne Roe's theory describes your career choices thus far.

CHAPTER 3

UNDERSTANDING AND APPLYING RECENT THEORIES OF CAREER DEVELOPMENT

Career theory provides a framework through which to view the career situations of individuals. Theories help us understand individuals' career journeys, what factors along the way may have shaped their career development, what barriers and obstacles they may face now and in the future, and how to plot a course for the future. Like a prism, career theory enables us to view careers from many different angles. The constructs and concepts that comprise various theoretical approaches can serve as guides in helping us learn more about the unique characteristics of individuals. Theories can sensitize us to factors that may have negatively impacted a person's career development and strategies for moving forward in a positive direction. Some career theories help us learn about and see the connection between persons and their options, which include work, education, and leisure. Career theories also help us understand how work interacts with the other life roles an individual may pursue. Finally, career theories provide models to further our insight into the career decision-making and problem-solving processes. Theories come alive when they move beyond the written page and further inform our work with individuals who are making career choices and exploring career transitions.

Janet G. Lenz, Ph.D., MCC, NCC
President, National Career Development Association (2004–2005)
Associate Professor, Coordinator of Career Counseling
Florida State University

MyCounselingLab®

Visit the MyCounselingLab® site for *Career Development Interventions*, Fifth Edition, to enhance your understanding of chapter concepts. You will have the opportunity to practice applying what you learned in the chapter by completing the video- and case-based exercises in the MyLab. Taking the Licensure Quizzes will help you prepare for your certification exam.

Ronald, a 20-year-old African American male, presents for career counseling during the second semester of his sophomore year in college. In his initial appointment he states that he has not given much serious consideration to "life after college" and that he feels "confused" about his career goals. As the starting quarterback for the university's football team, Ronald had always thought he would play professional football. However, an injury and lackluster performance in the past season have left him feeling less confident about his ability to achieve this goal. He reports feeling "overwhelmed" and "doubtful" that he will be able to identify a suitable occupational alternative to professional football.

Ronald has a high grade-point average (3.6 out of 4.0) and has taken a wide variety of courses without declaring a college major. He is very personable and reports interests in math, literature, and music (he has played the piano since elementary school). He is also very involved in community service and is a mentor for two middle school students. From his comments, it is clear that Ronald has high expectations for himself. He now feels very anxious because he is not sure what he wants to do. Both of Ronald's parents are educators. His mother is employed as a high school math teacher, and his father is employed as a high school principal.

RECENT THEORIES

Theories are developed to address important questions that people ask about their career situations. The theories discussed in Chapter 2 rose to prominence because they provided effective responses to questions regarding how an individual's traits can be matched to work requirements (e.g., person-environment theories) and how people can develop their careers effectively across the life span (e.g., developmental theories). A number of career theories have emerged since the theories discussed in Chapter 2 were initially developed. In part, these recent theories tend to be more explicitly attuned to diverse populations and to the complexity involved in career decision making, especially as the latter relates to cognitive processes concerning career choice. As such, the theories we discuss in this chapter may be very relevant for a client such as Ronald.

Specifically, social cognitive career theory developed by Lent, Brown, and Hackett (Lent, 2013; Lent, Brown, & Hackett, 1996, 2002); the cognitive information processing theory developed by Peterson, Sampson, Reardon, and Lenz (1996), Peterson, Sampson, Lenz, and Reardon (2002), and Sampson, Reardon, Peterson, and Lenz (2004); the career construction model developed by Savickas (2005, 2009); the chaos theory of careers developed by Pryor and Bright (2011); and the integrative life-planning model developed by Hansen (1997) are each excellent examples of theories that have evolved to address cognitive and meaning-making processes that people use to manage their careers effectively within a global and mobile society. Theories seeking to help workers manage multiple job changes across their work lives without losing their sense of self and social identity are theories described as postmodern. Postmodern approaches to career development interventions address the client's "subjective" experiences of career development (Cochran, 1997). Approaches emphasizing the subjective career highlight the ways in which meaning is made out of life experiences and then translated into a career choice (Carlsen, 1988; Cochran, 1990, 1997; Savickas, 1995).

For the most part, most of these emerging theories draw upon a solid foundation of research support. Emerging career theories reflect two major trends within career theory and practice. One trend is the rising prominence of cognitive theories within the career domain. The second trend is the growing realization that career interventions must fit the client (rather than the other way around) and that clients are active agents in the career construction process. Finally, the theories discussed in this chapter are, for the most part, particularly useful in advancing career development practice.

Tips from the Field

Almost by definition, theories lag behind career experiences in the current context. Try to blend current experience with theories to bridge the gaps between what the theories describe and what the current career experiences of your student or client are. Keep striving to make your career theory and practice relevant for the current context.

LENT, BROWN, AND HACKETT'S SOCIAL COGNITIVE CAREER THEORY

The social cognitive career theory (SCCT) (Brown & Lent, 1996; Lent, 2005, 2013; Lent & Brown, 2002, 2006; Lent et al., 1996; Lent, Brown, & Hackett, 2002) provides a conceptual framework for understanding how people develop career-related interests, make (and remake) occupational choices, and achieve career success and stability. SCCT builds upon the assumption that cognitive factors play an important role in career development and career decision making. SCCT is closely linked to Krumboltz's learning theory of career counseling, or LTCC (Mitchell & Krumboltz, 1996). Lent et al. (1996) noted, however, that SCCT differs from Krumboltz's theory in several ways. For example, in comparison to LTCC, SCCT "is more concerned with the specific cognitive mediators through which learning experiences guide career behavior; with the manner in which variables such as interests, abilities, and values interrelate; and with the specific paths by which person and contextual factors influence career outcomes. It also emphasizes the means by which individuals emphasize personal agency" (p. 377). Lent (2013) views SCCT as a model that is complementary to trait-factor and developmental models of career behavior.

SCCT also draws heavily from Albert Bandura's (1986) social cognitive theory. Specifically, SCCT incorporates Bandura's triadic reciprocal model of causality, which assumes that personal attributes, the environment, and overt behaviors "operate as interlocking mechanisms that affect one another bidirectionally" (Lent et al., 1996, p. 379). Within this triadic reciprocal model, SCCT highlights self-efficacy beliefs, outcome expectations, and personal goals. Thus, SCCT also incorporates research, applying self-efficacy theory to the career domain (Hackett & Betz, 1981; Lent & Brown, 2002; Lent & Hackett, 1987).

Bandura (1986) defines self-efficacy beliefs as "people's judgments of their capabilities to organize and execute courses of action required to attain designated types of performances" (p. 391). Self-efficacy beliefs are dynamic self-beliefs and are domain specific. Self-efficacy beliefs provide answers to questions pertaining to whether we can perform specific tasks (e.g., Can I make this presentation? Can I pass the statistics exam? Can I learn person-centered counseling skills?). Our beliefs about our abilities play a central role in the career decision-making process. We move toward those occupations requiring capabilities we think we either have or can develop. We move away from those occupations requiring capabilities we think we do not possess or that we cannot develop.

Four sources shape self-efficacy beliefs: (a) personal performance accomplishments, (b) vicarious learning, (c) social persuasion, and (d) physiological states and reactions (Bandura, 1986). The most influential of these sources is the first (personal performance accomplishments). Successful accomplishments result in more positive or stronger domain-specific, self-efficacy beliefs, and failures lead to more negative or weaker domain-specific beliefs.

Outcome expectations are beliefs about the outcomes of performing specific behaviors (e.g., What is likely to happen if I apply for an internship at the university counseling center? What job opportunities am I likely to have if I earn a doctoral degree in counseling?). Outcome expectations include our beliefs about "extrinsic reinforcement (receiving tangible rewards for successful performance), self-directed consequences (such as pride in oneself for mastering a challenging task), and outcomes derived from the process of performing a given activity (for instance, absorption in the task itself)" (Lent et al., 1996, p. 381). Outcome expectations influence behavior to a lesser degree than self-efficacy beliefs (e.g., Even though I might like to have more job options, I am not likely to enroll in a doctoral program in counseling if I think there is a low probability that I will be successful in this program of study). Thus, outcome expectations are what we imagine will happen if we perform specific behaviors.

Personal goals also influence career behaviors in important ways. Personal goals relate to our determination to engage in certain activities to produce a particular outcome (Bandura, 1986). Goals help to organize and guide our behavior over long periods of time (e.g., I will persist in my research course because it is an important step along the way toward earning my master's degree in counseling and obtaining a job as a counselor).

The relationship among goals, self-efficacy, and outcome expectations is complex and occurs within the framework of Bandura's (1986) triadic reciprocal model of causality (i.e., personal attributes, external environmental factors, and overt behavior). In essence, this model describes how *person inputs* (e.g., predisposition, gender, and race) interact with contextual factors (e.g., culture, geography, family, gender-role socialization) and learning experiences to influence our self-efficacy beliefs and outcome expectations. Self-efficacy beliefs and outcome expectations in turn shape our interests, goals, actions, and, eventually, our attainments (Lent, 2013). However, these are also influenced by contextual factors (e.g., job opportunities, access to training opportunities, financial resources).

For example, our client Ronald stated that as a young child he was athletically gifted and large for his age (person inputs). Because he lived in the United States and because his father had been an outstanding football player (contextual factors), Ronald was encouraged to play football at an early age (persuasion). His physical size and talents led to success as a football player (positive reinforcement). He came to believe he was good at this sport (self-efficacy beliefs) and that if he continued playing it, he would continue to do well (outcome expectations). His interest in this activity led him to develop the goal of playing football in college at a major university (personal goal). To achieve this goal, Ronald continued to practice hard and develop his skills as a football player (actions). His family could financially afford to send him to the best football camps, where Ronald was able to further develop his skills and to be exposed to football coaches from the best university football programs (proximal contextual factors). Eventually, Ronald was awarded a football scholarship to a major university (performance attainment).

Obviously, Ronald's path may have been very different if he had possessed different person inputs (e.g., lacked athletic ability, been born a girl), had different contextual influences (e.g., been born in Europe), and experienced different learning experiences (e.g., received no support for participating in athletics, performed poorly as a football player). No doubt these differences would have resulted in different efficacy beliefs, outcome expectations, interests, goals, actions, and performance attainments.

Applying SCCT

SCCT is particularly useful in addressing two areas of career concern: performance attainment and persistence at overcoming obstacles. Performance is influenced by ability, self-efficacy, outcome expectations, and goals. Ability affects performance both directly and indirectly through influencing self-efficacy beliefs and outcome expectations. According to Lent and Brown (1996), "Higher self-efficacy and anticipated positive outcomes promote higher goals, which help to mobilize and sustain performance behavior" (p. 318). Problems in career development emerge when individuals prematurely foreclose on occupational options due to inaccurate self-efficacy beliefs, outcome expectations, or both, and when individuals forego further consideration of occupational options due to barriers they perceive as insurmountable (Lent, 2013).

For example, given Ronald's early and intense commitment to becoming a professional football player, it is possible that he did not fully explore a wide range of occupational possibilities prior to selecting professional football. His recent difficulties as a football player have caused him to realize that he has not explored other career options. In fact, Ronald reports feeling overwhelmed by the prospect of engaging in career exploration. He even questions whether there are occupations that will allow him to experience success and satisfaction. Thus, career development interventions in SCCT are often directed toward self-efficacy beliefs and outcome expectations.

To examine premature foreclosure on occupational options, Brown and Lent (1996) recommend that counselors encourage their clients to discuss those options that they have eliminated from further consideration. Specifically, in discussing occupations of low interest, counselors should analyze the experiences and beliefs upon which their clients' lack of interest is based. Here counselors focus on identifying any inaccuracies in their clients' self-efficacy beliefs and occupational information. Brown and Lent also state, "The basic processes for facilitating interest exploration are, therefore, fairly straightforward and include assessing discrepancies between self-efficacy and demonstrated skill and between outcome expectations and occupational information" (p. 357).

One approach used by Brown and Lent (1996) for facilitating interest exploration involves the use of a card sort exercise. In this exercise, clients sort occupations according to (a) those they would choose, (b) those they would not choose, and (c) those they question. Clients are then instructed to focus on the latter two categories by identifying occupations in these categories that they might choose if they thought they had the skills (self-efficacy beliefs), those they might choose if they thought the occupation offered them things they value (outcome expectations), and those they definitely would not choose under any circumstances. Occupations placed in the first two categories (relating to self-efficacy beliefs and outcome expectations) are then examined for accuracy in skill and outcome perceptions.

To analyze obstacles or barriers to their clients' career development, Lent (2005) recommends adapting Janis and Mann's (1977) decisional balance sheet procedure. Their adaptation of this procedure involves asking clients to first list their preferred career option(s) and then to identify the negative consequences they imagine will occur in pursuing any specific option. Negative consequences are explored as possible career-choice-implementation barriers by asking clients (a) to consider the probability of encountering each barrier and (b) to develop strategies for preventing or managing the barriers that clients are most likely to encounter.

For example, in career counseling, Ronald noted that he would be interested in becoming a math teacher but was reluctant to do so because teachers have to deal with a lot of "grief from students and parents." He also stated that teachers do not make a salary that is sufficient for raising a family. The counselor suggested to Ronald that much of the "grief" encountered from students represented opportunities to help them deal with difficulties in their lives (Ronald placed a high value on helping others). It was also suggested that teachers can receive skills training to learn how to respond effectively to many student and parent concerns. To explore the issue of salary, the counselor encouraged Ronald to conduct information interviews with teachers in several local school districts (his parents were employed in a district that was known for having below-average teaching salaries). When he learned that there can be significant salary differences between school districts, Ronald began to think that it might be possible to earn a decent wage as a teacher. Ronald also began to identify ways he could eventually increase his salary (e.g., coaching, moving into administration) if he were to become a teacher.

Clients can be helped to modify their self-efficacy beliefs in several ways. When ability is sufficient but self-efficacy beliefs are low due to factors such as racism and sex-role stereotyping, clients can be exposed to personally relevant, vicarious learning opportunities. For example, a woman who is African American and who possesses ability sufficient for a career in engineering, but has low self-efficacy beliefs, can be exposed to engineers who are also African American and female (Hackett & Byars, 1996). Clients with sufficient ability but low self-efficacy beliefs can also be encouraged to gather ability-related data from friends, teachers, and others to counteract faulty self-efficacy beliefs. Counselors can also work collaboratively with these clients to construct success experiences (e.g., taking specific academic courses, participating in volunteer experiences) to strengthen weak self-efficacy beliefs. In processing these success experiences, counselors can challenge clients when they identify external attributions for their successes and disregard internal, stable causes (e.g., ability) for their successes. Thus, the four sources of self-efficacy can be used as organizing structures for career interventions (Lent, 2005).

> **Tips from the Field**
>
> Career development occurs in a social learning context and is facilitated by the presence of supportive environmental conditions and the relative absence of barriers.
>
> **Lent, 2013, p. 143**

Evaluating SCCT

Most research related to SCCT focuses on self-efficacy. In summarizing this literature, Lent et al. (1996) noted support for the following theory-related conclusions: "(1) domain-specific measures of self-efficacy are predictive of career-related interests, choice, achievement, persistence, indecision, and career exploratory behavior; (2) intervention, experimental, and path-analytic studies have supported certain hypothesized causal relations between measures of self-efficacy, performance, and interests; and (3) gender differences in academic and career self-efficacy frequently help explain male-female differences in occupational consideration" (p. 397).

In addition, research findings indicate some support for SCCT's theorized relationships among self-efficacy beliefs, outcome expectations, goals, and interests (Lent, Brown, & Hackett, 1994). For example, Choi, Park, Yang, Lee, Lee, and Lee (2012) found that career decision-making self-efficacy correlated significantly with self-esteem, vocational identity, and outcome expectations among their study participants. Tang, Pan, and Newmeyer (2008) found career self-efficacy had a mediating effect on the career decision-making process for the 141 high school students participating in their research. Rogers, Creed, and Glendon (2008) surveyed 414 Australian high school students and found that career exploration was related to goals and social support (levels of exploration were highest when goals were clear and social support was strong), highlighting the fact that social cognitive variables are influenced by personal and contextual variables. Gibbons and Borders (2010) used SCCT to study college-related expectations in 272 seventh-grade students. Differences were found between prospective first-generation college students and nonprospective first-generation college students, "with the former group demonstrating lower self-efficacy, higher negative outcome expectations, and more perceived barriers" (p. 194). Self-efficacy directly affected outcome expectations, and both variables directly affected the students' strength of educational intentions. Gibbons and Borders suggest, however, that for their population of interest, the SCCT model may need to be revised as the effects of barriers and supports may directly influence outcome expectations rather than being mediated through self-efficacy.

Ali and Menke (2014) used social cognitive career theory to investigate the career development of 9th-grade students living in two rural communities with large numbers of Latino immigrants (55% of study participants). Study participants completed measures of vocational skills self-efficacy, career decision outcome expectations, career aspirations, and barriers to postsecondary education. Interestingly, Latino students in this study reported higher self-efficacy beliefs than did White students. Latino students also reported higher perceived barriers, but this did not seem to relate to their career aspirations. Ali and Menke suggest that results from their study indicate that school and career counselors should attend to Latino students' self-efficacy and outcome expectations as well as efficacy for overcoming barriers.

Raque-Bogdan, Klingaman, Martin, and Lucas (2013) also used social cognitive career theory as the basis for examining the person and contextual variables of gender, ethnicity, educational and career barriers, and career-related parent support for incoming first-year African American, Asian, Latino, and White college students. Their results indicate that women, as compared to men, perceived significantly higher levels of career barriers but similar levels of coping efficacy in dealing with these barriers. Women also reported receiving more career-related emotional support from parents than did men. For all participants, career-related parental support accounted for a significant portion of the variance for perceptions of educational and career barriers and coping efficacy with educational and career barriers. Among other things, this study reinforces the importance of career-related parental support relative to selecting academic majors and coping with perceived career barriers.

Shen, Liao, Abraham, and Weng (2014) examined the associations between culturally specific factors (i.e., parental pressure and support, living up to parental expectations, internalized stereotyping) and Asian American college students' occupational outcomes. Results of this study indicate that when Asian American students perceive their parents to be supportive, they are prone to follow parental expectations to choose certain occupations, which in turn is linked to their self-efficacy, outcome expectations, and interests in stereotypical occupations.

Based on these results, Shen et al. (2014) recommend that career counselors explore Asian parents' involvement in Asian American students' self-efficacy, outcome expectations, and interests in stereotypical and nonstereotypical occupations. For example, career counselors could assess parental involvement in terms of parental pressure versus support and discuss their differential role in occupational outcomes with Asian American students. Career counselors also could assist students in negotiating among parental expectations, occupational stereotypes and barriers, and their individual occupational interests in their career decision-making process. In addition, counselors should examine what academic and occupational stereotypes Asian American students have internalized and then investigate whether these serve as external and internal barriers in exploring nonstereotypical occupations.

Lent et al. (2001) investigated the applicability of SCCT to educational choices made by college students. They found that contextual barriers and supports indirectly affect educational choices through their influence on self-efficacy and the individual's willingness to convert interests into educational choices. Lindley (2005) found that her study participants had high rates of correspondence between the Holland codes for their career choices and their highest self-efficacy scores for their respective Holland types. Ochs and Roessler (2004) examined the relationship among career self-efficacy, career outcome expectations, and career exploration intentions of 77 special education students and 99 general education students.

They found career decision-making self-efficacy and outcome expectations to be significant predictors of career exploratory intentions in both student groups. Nauta, Kahn, Angell, and Cantarelli (2002) investigated the SCCT assumption that changes in self-efficacy precede changes in interests. Using a cross-lagged panel research design and structural equation modeling, they found a reciprocal relationship between self-efficacy and interests but no clear pattern of temporal precedence. Flores and O'Brien (2002) conducted path analyses on data acquired from a sample of 364 Mexican American adolescent women to assess SCCT's propositions related to the influence of contextual and social cognitive variables on career aspiration, career choice prestige, and traditionality of career choice. These researchers found partial support for SCCT as nontraditional career self-efficacy, parental support, barriers, acculturation, and feminist attitudes predicted career choice prestige. In addition, acculturation, feminist attitudes, and nontraditional career self-efficacy predicted career choice traditionality. Finally, feminist attitudes and parental support predicted career aspiration. Gainor and Lent (1998) examined the relations among SCCT, racial identity, math-related interests, and choice of major within a sample of 164 African American first-year university students. They found that self-efficacy and outcome expectations predicted interests, and interests predicted choice intentions across racial identity attitude levels. Diegelman and Subich (2001) found that raising outcome expectations among college students considering pursuing a degree in psychology resulted in an increased interest in pursuing this degree option for their study participants.

Hsieh and Huang (2014) investigated the relationship of family socioeconomic status and proactive personality to career decision self-efficacy in a sample of 336 Taiwanese college students. Their findings indicate support for the person input variables (i.e., socioeconomic status and proactive personality) as being predictive of career decision self-efficacy. Hsieh and Huang recommend that career counselors teach proactive thinking training programs for clients. Helping clients build skills that equip them to recognize and seize new opportunities, defend themselves against threats, and translate core competencies into competitive advantages are specific competencies recommended to build self-efficacy.

A number of studies have demonstrated positive outcomes for SCCT-based interventions used with diverse client groups. This provides strong support for the robustness of this theory as it is applied across diverse populations. An additional, and related, strength of SCCT is that it addresses both intra-individual and contextual variables in career development. Clearly, incorporating these two dimensions increases the applicability of the theory for diverse career development issues and populations. A recent literature review conducted by Patton and McIlveen (2009) indicates that SCCT is generating substantial research, especially in comparison to other career theories.

THE COGNITIVE INFORMATION PROCESSING APPROACH

The cognitive information processing (CIP) approach (Peterson et al., 1996; Peterson et al., 2002; Sampson et al., 2004) is rooted in the three-factor Parsonian model for making career choices (i.e., self-understanding, occupational knowledge, and bringing self-understanding and occupational knowledge together to make a choice). The CIP approach extends the Parsonian model, however, by incorporating more recent developments related to how people engage in cognitive information processing. Peterson and his associates apply what is known about cognitive information processing to career counseling.

There are four assumptions underlying the theory. The first assumption is that career-decision making involves the interaction between cognitive and affective process. Second, the capacity for career problem solving depends on the availability of cognitive operations and knowledge. Third, career development is ongoing and knowledge structures continually evolve. And fourth, enhancing information-processing skills is the goal of career counseling (Peterson et al., 2002).

The CIP approach to career intervention includes several dimensions: (a) the pyramid of information processing, (b) CASVE cycle of decision-making skills, and (c) the executive processing domain. First, the approach uses an information-processing pyramid to describe the important domains of cognition involved in a career choice. The first three levels of the pyramid reflect domains that are traditionally included in career theories: self-knowledge (values, interests, skills), occupational knowledge (understanding specific occupations and educational/training opportunities), and decision-making skills (understanding how one typically makes decisions). The fourth domain and top of the pyramid is metacognitions and includes self-talk, self-awareness, and the monitoring and control of cognitions (Sampson, Peterson, Lenz, & Reardon, 1992). Knowledge of self and occupations forms the foundation of the pyramid, and then decision-making skills and metacognitions build upon this foundation.

The second dimension of the CIP approach is labeled the CASVE cycle of career decision-making skills. The CASVE cycle represents a generic model of information-processing skills related to solving career problems and making career decisions. These skills are (a) communication, (b) analysis, (c) synthesis, (d) valuing, and (e) execution (CASVE).

The use of these skills is cyclical beginning with the realization that a gap exists between a real state and an ideal state (e.g., an existing state of career indecision and a more desired state of career decidedness). Becoming aware of such gaps can occur internally through the existence of ego-dystonic emotional states (e.g., depression, anxiety); the occurrence of behaviors such as excessive tardiness, absenteeism, or drug use; or the existence of somatic symptoms (e.g., headaches, loss of appetite). Or, we can become aware of such gaps through external demands (e.g., the need to select a curriculum of study in high school or college, the need to make a decision to accept or reject a job offer). Career problems, therefore, involve cognitive, affective, behavioral, and physiological components. Interpreting these internal and external cues involves *communication*. Specifically, clients must ask themselves two questions: (a) "What am I thinking and feeling about my career choice at this moment?" and (b) "What do I hope to attain as a result of career counseling?" (Peterson et al., 1996, p. 436).

Once we recognize that a gap or career problem exists, we must *analyze* what is required for problem resolution. For example, do we need more information about ourselves (e.g., values, interests) and/or the situation (e.g., my supervisor's expectations, job requirements)? What must we do to acquire the information or resources necessary to cope more effectively with the career problem (e.g., take an interest inventory, conduct an occupational information interview, seek counseling to understand our feelings related to our job situation)?

Synthesis involves two phases: (1) elaboration and (2) crystallization. During elaboration, clients seek to identify as many potential solutions to their career problems as possible (as in brainstorming, the focus is on quantity rather than quality solutions). During crystallization, clients identify those solutions that are consistent with their abilities, interests, or values. The outcome of these two phases that synthesis comprises is a manageable list of alternatives that are acceptable to the client.

Valuing involves examining and prioritizing each of the alternatives generated in light of one's value system, the benefits to be gained and the costs incurred with each alternative, each alternative's impact on significant others and society, and the probability that the alternative will result in a successful outcome (i.e., removing the gap). Once the alternatives have been prioritized, the optimal alternative is identified. The primary question for clients engaged in the process of valuing is "Which alternative is the best course of action for me, my significant others, and society?" (Peterson et al., 1996, p. 437).

The *execution* phase involves converting the optimal alternative into action. A plan of action is developed to implement the alternative and achieve its goal (e.g., I will enroll in psychology courses, study three hours per day, and take a course to improve my Graduate Record Examination scores in order to achieve my goal of gaining entry into a highly selective counselor education program). Thus, the execution phase requires clients to identify the specific steps necessary to operationalize the solution chosen in the valuing phase. The primary question in execution is "How can I transform my choice into an action plan?" (Peterson et al., 1996, p. 437).

Once the plan has been enacted, clients return to the communication phase to determine whether the alternative was successful in resolving the career problem. Once again, cognitive, affective, behavioral, and physiological states are assessed in evaluating the success of the alternative (e.g., Do I feel less anxious? Am I more content with my career situation? Has my class attendance improved?). If the evaluation is positive, then clients move on, but if the evaluation is negative, then clients recycle through the CASVE phases with the new information acquired from enacting the first alternative.

A third dimension of the CIP approach is the *executive processing domain*. The function of the executive processing domain is to initiate, coordinate, and monitor the storage of and retrieval of information (Peterson, Sampson, & Reardon, 1991). This domain involves metacognitive skills (Meichenbaum, 1977), such as self-talk, self-awareness, and control. Positive self-talk (e.g., "I am capable of making a good career choice") is required for effective career problem solving. Negative self-talk ("I can't make a good decision") leads to career indecisiveness. Self-awareness is necessary in monitoring and controlling internal and external influences on career decisions. Effective problem solvers and decision makers are aware of their values, beliefs, biases, and feelings. They use this awareness in generating and selecting problem solutions. Control and monitoring are essential for deciphering the information needed to resolve a career problem and for knowing when one is ready to move to the next phase in the CASVE cycle. The "control and monitoring of lower-order functions ensures that an optimal balance is met between impulsivity and compulsivity" (Peterson et al., 1991, p. 39), thereby providing a "quality control mechanism to ensure a complete, orderly, and timely progression through the CASVE cycle" (Peterson et al., 1996, p. 439).

Applying the CIP Approach

The pyramid model can be used as a framework for providing career development interventions. For example, the self-knowledge domain can be addressed through standardized and nonstandardized assessments. The occupational knowledge domain can be addressed by engaging in job-shadowing exercises and by reading occupational biographies (as when Ronald was encouraged to conduct occupational information interviews). The five steps of the CASVE cycle can be used to teach decision-making skills, and the executing processing domain provides a framework for exploring and challenging clients' dysfunctional metacognitions.

Peterson et al. (1991) have outlined a seven-step sequence for delivering individual, group, and classroom career development interventions. Step one involves conducting an initial interview with the client. During this step, the counselor attempts to understand the context and nature of the client's career problem. The counselor develops an effective working relationship with the client by responding empathically to client statements and by using basic counseling skills (e.g., clarification, summarization, reflection of affect, immediacy, and self-disclosure).

Counselors introduce clients to the pyramid model and the CASVE cycle to clarify client concerns and to provide clients with a model for understanding the career decision-making and problem-solving processes (Sampson et al., 1992). During this step, counselors focus on questions such as "What are the client's perceptions of the extent of development in each of the domains? How does the client typically make career decisions? Which metacognitions, if any, are dysfunctional and need changing? At which phase is the client currently focused?" (p. 73).

In Ronald's case, he was feeling stuck because he was not clear about the process typically used in making career decisions. He was also stuck because he believed that there were no occupational options that would be suitable for him (although he had not really engaged in any systematic exploration of occupational options). Moreover, he doubted his ability to make an effective occupational choice. Using the pyramid model to explain the decision process could provide Ronald with a sense of control and structure, thereby lessening his feeling of being "overwhelmed." Establishing an effective working relationship with Ronald and offering him a sense of hope that he could learn the skills necessary for managing his career could also help him to feel more confident and reassured that he could cope effectively with these career development tasks.

Step two involves conducting a preliminary assessment to determine the client's readiness for career decision making. The CIP approach uses the Career Thoughts Inventory (CTI) (Sampson, Peterson, Lenz, Reardon, & Saunders, 1996) to identify clients with dysfunctional career thoughts and, thereby, provide an indication of career development interventions that may be required to address the client's executive processing domain. For example, Ronald may be adhering to beliefs such as "I must absolutely certain an occupation will be satisfying to me before I can take action," "All teachers are paid poor salaries," or "I must decide now what I want to do for the rest of my life." Adherence to such beliefs will be problematic for Ronald as he engages in career planning. Thus, these beliefs need to be challenged and restructured for him to move forward (Lewis & Gilhousen, 1981).

In step three, counselors and clients work collaboratively to define the career problem(s) and to analyze potential causes of the problem. Here, counselors communicate nonjudgmentally their perceptions of clients' gaps between a real state of career indecision and the desired or ideal state of career decidedness (Cochran, 1997). Clients respond by agreeing with counselors' perceptions or by clarifying and restating the gap they are experiencing.

In step four, counselors and clients continue to collaborate by formulating achievable career problem-solving and decision-making goals. The formulation of goals leads to the development of an individual learning plan in step five. Individual learning plans provide clients with a guide concerning what activities they need to engage in and what resources they need to use to achieve their goals. Although individual learning plans provide a mechanism for monitoring and evaluating client progress, they may also be revised as clients acquire more information about themselves and their career concerns.

Step six in the CIP approach requires clients to execute their individual learning plans. Counselors can provide support, feedback, and assistance to clients as they complete their individual learning plans. Counselors can challenge clients with dysfunctional career thoughts to revise their thinking and then take action to complete their individual learning plans. Finally, during step seven, counselors and clients conduct a summative review of client progress and then generalize new learning to other current and future career problems.

Increasingly, CIP is being used with diverse client populations. For example, Watson, Lenz, and Melvin (2013) provide an excellent case example in which they apply CIP to an adult client experiencing career transition. Stein-McCormick, Osborn, Hayden, and Van Hoose (2013) and Strauser (2013) also provide excellent descriptions of how CIP can be used in career counseling with veteran and rehabilitation populations, respectively. Ledwith (2014) describes how CIP can be collaboratively integrated into academic advising and career counseling.

Evaluating CIP

Although research investigating CIP theory is not extensive, the number of studies based on CIP theory is growing. The development of the CTI should serve as a catalyst for CIP researchers investigating theoretical propositions related to the executive processing domain. The workbook accompanying the CTI, titled *Improving Your Career Thoughts: A Workbook for the Career Thoughts Inventory* (Sampson et al., 1996), is an excellent example of the translation of theory into practice. This more recent extension of the CIP approach builds on what one reviewer noted as the major contribution of the theory—the executive processing domain (Helwig, 1992). Brown and Lent (1996) noted that the description of the decision-making process outlined in Peterson et al. (1996) "is perhaps the clearest description of the variables involved in this process yet to emerge" (p. 521). Clemens and Milsom (2008) recommend using CIP with military families coping with transitions to new jobs in the civilian world. Hirshi and Lage (2008) used CIP as the theoretical framework for a career workshop delivered to 334 Swiss seventh-grade students. An evaluation of this workshop revealed that the students significantly increased their career decidedness, career planning, career exploration, and vocational identity. Osborn, Howard, and Leierer (2007) examined the effect of a CIP-based career development course on the dysfunctional thoughts of racially and ethnically diverse college freshmen. Using CTI scores as a springboard to discussing dysfunctional career thinking, Osborn and her associates found that students decreased their dysfunctional career thoughts as they related to career decision-making confusion, commitment anxiety, and external conflict. They also found that neither gender nor race/ethnicity was related to dysfunctional career thoughts. In a sample of adult Dutch and Belgian immigrants living in California, Ecke (2007) did find a significant relationship between a more secure attachment style and avoidance of career decision-making, as evidenced by less anxiety and less avoidance in response to attachment issues and lower career-thought dysfunction.

Strauser, Lustig, Cogdal, and Uruk (2006) investigated whether trauma symptoms in college students relate to dysfunctional career thoughts, vocational identity, and developmental work personality. Using a sample of 131 students, they found significant relationships between higher levels of trauma (e.g., parental divorce, death of a loved one) and higher levels of dysfunctional career thoughts and lower levels of developmental work personality (i.e., the degree to which an individual has successfully completed the tasks necessary for developing a healthy work personality, such as completing one's work on time in school). Among other things, this study highlights the personal-career connection and indicates that career counselors should be aware of post-traumatic stress disorder symptoms.

Strauser, Lustig, and Uruk (2004) examined career thoughts as measured by the CTI by comparing scores between college students with disabilities and students without disabilities.

Strauser and his associates found significant differences between individuals with disabilities and college students without disabilities on the CTI total and subscale scores. Specifically, individuals with disabilities had more negative thoughts than their nondisabled counterparts, pointing to the possible usefulness of the CIP model when providing career interventions to university students with disabilities.

Another study conducted by Yanckak, Lease, and Strauser (2005) explored the relationship between career thoughts and vocational identity using study participants diagnosed with cognitive and physical disabilities. Yanckak et al. found significant differences between individuals with cognitive impairments as compared to those with physical disabilities in their Decision-Making Confusion and External Conflict scores on the CTI. Individuals with cognitive impairments had more dysfunctional career thoughts than individuals with physical disabilities. A study conducted by Reed, Reardon, Lenz, and Leierer (2001) examined the effectiveness of a career-planning course based on the CIP approach. Using the CTI, results of this study indicated a significant decrease in negative career thoughts from pretest to posttest. Saunders, Peterson, Sampson, and Reardon (2000) used the CTI to investigate depression and dysfunctional career thinking as components of the state of career indecision among a sample of 215 undergraduate university students. They found a significant positive correlation between dysfunctional career thoughts as measured by the CTI and career indecision and, thus, recommend using the CTI in career counseling to help identify appropriate treatment strategies for clients experiencing career indecision.

Osborn, Peterson, Sampson, and Reardon (2003) used CIP as the theoretical framework for investigating client anticipations prior to using a computer-assisted career guidance system. Clients' most frequent anticipations for computer use included increased career options, enhanced self-knowledge, and strengthened occupational knowledge. Reardon and Wright (1999) describe how the CIP approach can be used in conjunction with Holland's theory to help a 19-year-old college student become aware of negative thought patterns serving as obstacles to choosing a college major. Similarly, McLennan and Arthur (1999) describe how CIP is useful for helping women to cope effectively with structural and individual barriers in their career development. In this study, a path model was used to explore how client thoughts influenced career exploratory behavior. A verified path model shows CIP's negative career thoughts inversely predict SCCT's career problem-solving self-efficacy, which in turn predicts career exploratory behavior. The model suggests that attending to client thoughts about career decision making is an important antecedent to engaging in career exploration. The model's suggested intervention sequence of steps appears to include addressing negative career thinking followed by adequately enhancing career problem-solving self-efficacy in order to successfully foster career exploration. This model demonstrates that both CIP and SCCT function in complementary ways. A hypothetical case of Sue, a client seeking assistance with her job search, is used throughout the McLennan and Arthur article to highlight the relevant theories and the practical implications of the research findings.

As predicted in a previous edition of this book, the fact that the CIP research team (i.e., Peterson, Reardon, Lenz, and Sampson) built their theory upon a solid foundation of research in cognitive psychology, have developed clear definitions of the different dimensions of the theory, and are committed to translating theory into practice suggests a bright future for the CIP approach to career development interventions. It can be argued that prediction has proven to be accurate. Plus, the CIP approach demonstrates robustness in addressing a wide array of client concerns and client populations (e.g., college students with disabilities).

SAVICKAS'S CAREER CONSTRUCTION THEORY

Career construction theory incorporates three perspectives—differential, developmental, and dynamic—into one approach. It incorporates a differential perspective by addressing what different people prefer to do in their work (Savickas, 2005, 2009, 2013). The developmental perspective in career construction theory emphasizes the various ways in which people cope with career development tasks and transitions. The dynamic perspective attends to the ways in which people use life themes to develop meaning in their career behavior as they fit work into their lives. As Savickas noted, "career construction theory asserts that individuals construct their careers by imposing meaning on their vocational behavior and occupational experiences. . . . Career construction theory posits that individuals construct representations of reality but do not construct reality itself. The concept of *career* imposes personal meaning on past memories, present experiences, and future aspirations by weaving them into a life theme that patterns the individual's work life" (Savickas, 2005, p. 43). Thus, career counselors using career construction theory replace an individual's assessment scores with an individual's personal stories. Assessment scores focus on the "psychology of possession" whereas personal stories emphasize a "psychology of use" (Savickas, 1998, p. 332). The assumption here is that it is *how* you use what you possess relative to abilities, interests, values, personality, and so on that matters relative to career behavior. A person's subjective career emerges from this active meaning-making process in which experiences are woven into a pattern that portrays a life theme. In career counseling, clients are helped to increase their awareness and understanding of the life projects embedded within their life themes and their life stories. Career construction counseling also helps clients understand the ways in which their life projects revealed in their life themes are important to them and to others.

Thus, career construction theory views the self from three perspectives: self as actor, self as agent, and self as author in the career development process (Savickas, 2013). We begin the self-construction process as children (actors), then in adolescence we become agents in which we direct actions, and finally we become authors who explain the actions we direct.

Within career construction, career-related "traits" such as interests, abilities, values, and so on are viewed as strategies for adapting to and connecting with the environment. Put another way, they are verbs rather than nouns (Savickas, 2013). Long-practiced traits (like playing football for Ronald) coalesce into tested styles. We use language to reflect upon our life experiences to inform what we want to become and what work we want to do (Savickas, 1998). In this sense, career is a relational construct that emerges from interpersonal processes and draws upon social constructionism.

Career adaptability is the third component of career construction theory. Life themes guide personality expression in work, but their expression is managed by the career adaptation process (Savickas, 2005, 2013). Transitions (e.g., from school to work, from job to job, from job to school) require adaptation, which is characterized by the following behaviors: orientation, exploration, establishment, management, and disengagement (Savickas, 2013). These behaviors form the cycle of adaptation. For example, Ronald is considering disengaging from football (his previous career goal) due to his poor performance. He is hoping to find new options to consider as he becomes reoriented to a new direction, which will subsequently involve exploring the nature of potential options, and then, if he chooses a new direction, will require him to manage the new role. Maintaining an adaptive approach to career construction involves: (a) being concerned about the future, (b) increasing personal control over the future, (c) displaying curiosity about exploring future scenarios and considering possible selves, and (d) developing the confidence to pursue identified aspirations (Savickas, 2013).

Applying Career Construction Theory

The general pattern of practice in career construction theory is to first construct or deconstruct a career story, then reconstruct an occupational plot or theme, and then co-construct the next career chapter (Savickas, 2013). The career counseling process commences with counselor-client exploration of the specific incident that spawned the need for career counseling (i.e., what dislocated the client from the current episode in his or her career story. This discussion also includes reference to the client's adaptive resources and readiness and, then, is followed by a discussion of the client's goals for career counseling. Career construction counseling also involves engaging the client in the Career Construction Interview (CCI; Savickas, 2005). The CCI helps clients clarify and articulate the private meanings they attach to their career behavior. Through the use of questions eliciting client preferences for self-expression within life contexts, career construction counselors help clients remember their pasts in ways that foster the construction of possible futures (Savickas). In addition to asking clients to share three specific early life recollections (ER), career construction counselors using the CCI ask the following questions to stimulate client consideration of their subjective career experience (i.e., meaning-making process):

1. Whom do you admire? Whom would you like to pattern your life after?

   Whom did you admire when you were growing up? Why?

   How are you like _____?

   How are you different from _____?

2. Do you read any magazines regularly? Which ones?

   What do you like about these magazines?

   Do you have any favorite television shows?

3. What do you like to do in your free time?

   What are your hobbies?

   What do you enjoy about these hobbies?

4. Do you have a favorite saying or motto?

   Tell me a saying that you remember hearing.

5. What are/were your favorite subjects in school?

   Why?

   What subjects do/did you hate?

   Why?

Responses to these questions are connected to the life themes revealed in the early life recollections to help clients clarify the life projects that guide their career behavior. Rehfuss, Cosio, and Del Corso (2011) investigated counselors' perspectives on using the CCI with clients who had career concerns. Specifically, they asked 34 counselors to describe their experiences with the CCI and to identify the benefits and challenges of the CCI. Results from this study indicated that counselors found the CCI to be a helpful resource in helping clients resolve their career concerns.

Specifically, counselors thought that the CCI was useful in helping clients identify their life themes, which they then could use to make meaningful career decisions. Moreover, counselors viewed the CCI as being helpful to clients in increasing self-understanding and developing a sense as to how work could provide opportunities for meaning making. Taber, Hartung, Briddick, Briddick, and Rehfuss (2011) provide a detailed description of how the CCI can be integrated into career counseling to help clients clarify their self-concepts and make their work lives more meaningful. Di Fabio and Maree (2012) used an Italian version of the CCI in a treatment outcome study with 72 participants and found that those exposed to the CCI reported a decrease in career decision-making difficulties and an increase in career decision-making self-efficacy. Cardoso, Silva, Gonçalves, and Duarte (2014) conducted an exploratory study of the change process in career construction theory and successfully tracked change processes across different phases of the career construction process in accordance with what the theory would predict. Finally, Savickas (2013) provides an excellent case example demonstrating the application of career construction theory with a 20-year-old client, named Elaine, across multiple sessions.

Evaluating Career Construction Theory

Career construction theory has largely been the result of the work of Mark Savickas and his international research team. Savickas and his colleagues have authored a number of articles in which the theoretical assumptions underlying career construction theory have been described and the usefulness of the Career Construction Interview has been analyzed (Di Fabio & Maree, 2012; Rehfuss, Cosio, & Del Corso, 2011; Savickas, 1997, 2005, 2009; Taber et al., 2011). The number of treatment outcome data and research studies directed toward theory validation is increasing, and more are welcomed—especially with regard to diverse client populations.

Hansen's Integrative Life Planning

Of all the theories discussed in Chapters 1 and 2, Hansen's integrative life planning model (ILP) (Hansen, 1997) is unique in that, rather than offering a theory that can be translated into individual counseling, Hansen contends that ILP is a new worldview for addressing career development. As such, ILP centrally addresses diversity issues related to ethnicity, race, gender, socioeconomic status, and spirituality. The "integrative" aspect of ILP relates to the emphasis on integrating the mind, body, and spirit. The "life planning" concept acknowledges, in a fashion similar to Super's (1980) life-space theory, that multiple aspects of life are interrelated. "Planning" is included in the title because, despite recent discussions about the value of planning in a time of uncertainty, it connotes a sense of personal agency in the career development process (Hansen, 2002). The ILP framework also draws upon psychology, sociology, economics, multiculturalism, and constructivism and takes a holistic approach by encouraging people to connect various aspects of life. Rather than a life-span model, ILP focuses on adult career development and is based on the following assumptions (Hansen, 2002):

1. Career professionals should help their clients think holistically about their lives.
2. Comprehensive life planning in the 21st century should blend self-knowledge and knowledge about society (e.g. the need for social justice).
3. Career professionals are agents for positive change.

Hansen (2002) also identifies six career development tasks confronting adults today. The six tasks reflect Hansen's emphasis on social justice, social change, connectedness, diversity, and spirituality. For example, the first task is labeled as "finding work that needs doing in changing global contexts" (p. 61). Here Hansen suggests that adults consider focusing on work that will result in a more socially just world (e.g., preserving the environment, understanding and celebrating diversity, advocating for human rights, and exploring spirituality). Similar to early notions of "bad" work and "good" work, Hansen encourages people to identify what they can do to contribute to positive change for social and environmental justice.

The second task Hansen (2002) identifies is "weaving our lives into a meaningful whole" (p. 61). This task emphasizes the point that few things are more personal than a career choice (Niles & Pate, 1989). Occupational choices are intertwined with other life-role choices and must be considered both holistically and within the greater context of one's life. This task also suggests that persons must draw upon their subjective experiences in clarifying and articulating their career choices.

Hansen's (2002) third task is an extension of the second. Labeled as "connecting family and work" (p. 61), it emphasizes life-role integration and the importance of negotiating roles and relationships (Hansen, 2002). This task also highlights the need to examine gender-role expectations and stereotypes. ILP envisions men and women as partners in the home and in the workplace. Hansen also advocates for valuing self-sufficiency and connectedness within men and women. Although not stated in ILP, one would expect that the same notions of equity in work and in home activities would also be applied to same-sex couples.

"Valuing pluralism and inclusivity" (Hansen, 2002, p. 61) represents the fourth task confronting adults. Hansen notes the importance of celebrating diversity and developing multicultural competencies as critical for work and nonwork activities. Valuing pluralism recognizes the importance of difference and establishes a foundation for celebrating diversity.

The fifth task (Hansen, 2002, p. 61) relates to "managing personal transitions and organizational change." Given the constancy of change in everyday experience and developing skills, the ability to cope effectively with transition is an essential task of adult development. In fact, Hansen (2002) suggests that transition counseling may be one of the most needed skills in career counseling. Tolerating ambiguity, developing personal flexibility, and being able to draw upon a reservoir of self-awareness and social support all help to negotiate life changes successfully. Finally, incorporating both rational and logical decision-making skills with intuitive orientations that value positive uncertainty (Gelatt, 1989) and planned happenstance (Mitchell, Levin, & Krumboltz, 1999) is also important for coping effectively with transitions in a time of change, instability, and ambiguity in career development.

The sixth task in ILP (Hansen, 2002) is that of "exploring spirituality and life purpose" (p. 61). Spirituality may or may not be defined as religion. Spirituality embraces purpose, meaning, connectedness, and a sense of community. Career choices are, at their best, spiritual in that they are expressions of one's gifts and talents. Career practitioners help their clients consider spiritual issues in career decision making when they explore questions such as "What does work mean in and for my life?" and "What do I want to mean to others through my work?" People engage in spiritually based career decision making when they examine the degree to which career options foster positive treatment of others, the environment, and themselves. The ILP approach joins Miller-Tiedeman's (1997) Lifecareer Theory and the work of Bloch and Richmond (1998) as a small but growing body of career development literature addressing the important topic of spirituality in career development.

Collectively, spiritual approaches to career development emphasize common themes that can be summarized as follows:

1. Career development intertwines with human development. Life cannot be compartmentalized into "silos" of activity; thus, careers should be viewed holistically.
2. Clients should be encouraged to embrace and celebrate their life journeys, rather than judging past experiences negatively. All life experiences provide opportunities for learning and growth.
3. Maintaining an attitude of flexibility and openness fosters development as well as the opportunity to identify new opportunities for growth and learning.
4. Change should be celebrated and embraced rather than feared and avoided.
5. Career development interventions that actively and collaboratively engage the client in career counseling; incorporate intuition as well as reason in decision making; and draw upon subjective assessment activities, imagery, meditation, and positive self-affirmations also engage the spirit in the career development process.

Applying ILP

ILP suggests that career counselors help their clients to understand these six tasks, see the interrelatedness of the various tasks, and prioritize the tasks according to their needs. The specifics of how ILP is applied in career counseling are still being developed. Hansen, Hage, and Kachgal (1999) developed the Integrative Life Planning Inventory to help clients identify where they are in relation to integrative thinking and planning. The assumptions and tasks of ILP also form the basis for career development programs aimed at teaching participants holistic career planning. Currently, ILP seems most useful as a framework for teaching an approach to life planning that emphasizes connectedness, wholeness, and community.

Evaluating ILP

ILP offers a creative approach to life planning. It appears to be a useful framework from which counselors can encourage clients to consider important life issues in their career decisions. It is one of the few models to include spirituality as an important aspect of the career development process. Similar to many recent models, ILP acknowledges the importance of context in career development. Moreover, it embraces social action by encouraging clients to consider the impact of their career choices on others and on the environment. More research on ILP is needed in terms of the model's concepts as well as the ways in which the model can be applied effectively in career development interventions. It is a concern that the research studies using ILP have dwindled in recent years. It is interesting to note, however, that ILP has much in common with the emerging postmodern approaches to career development interventions and, in many ways, could be placed in this category.

POSTMODERN APPROACHES

The label of *postmodern* can be used to refer to those approaches (e.g., narrative, contextual, constructivist) that emphasize the importance of understanding our careers as they are lived or, to put it another way, our subjective experience of career development. Postmodernism embraces multicultural perspectives and emphasizes the belief that there is no one fixed truth but, rather, that we each construct our own realities and truths. In this way, postmodern views include constructivist assumptions. Postmodern approaches also emphasize personal agency in the career construction process. For example, Cochran's (1994) narrative approach contends that career development theories should "provide systematic accounts of how persons become active agents rather than patients or victims of circumstances regarding career. The aim of career counseling is to enhance agency regarding career" (p. 209).

Creating Narratives

The narrative approach represents an example of a postmodern approach that highlights personal agency in career development. Specifically, career counseling from the narrative approach emphasizes understanding and articulating the main character to be lived out in a specific career plot (Cochran, 1997). This type of articulation uses the process of composing a narrative as the primary vehicle for defining the character and plot. Howard (1989) noted that "people tell themselves stories that infuse certain parts of their lives and actions with great meaning and de-emphasize other aspects. But had any of them chosen to tell himself or herself a somewhat different story, the resulting pattern of more-meaningful and less-meaningful aspects of his or her life would have been quite different" (p. 168). By constructing personal career narratives, we can come to see our movement through life more clearly and can understand our specific decisions within a greater life context that has meaning and coherence. Thrift and Amundson (2005) contend that "as career counselors come to grips with social justice and the growing inequities with society" (p. 18) they will increasingly move to narrative approaches in career counseling.

Cochran (1997) identified several ways in which narratives help people make meaning out of their life experiences. For example, he notes that narratives help to provide a sense of personal continuity across time (i.e., a beginning, middle, and end). As one becomes aware of how the past has influenced the present, one also can make decisions about the future. As Polkinghorne (1988) noted, a narrative is a "meaning structure that organizes events and human actions into a whole, thereby attributing significance to individual actions and events according to their effect on the whole" (p. 36). Cochran also highlighted the fact that a narrative helps give meaning to the plot of a person's story. Each story contains examples of behaviors and decisions that help to paint a portrait of who the person is relative to engaging in the world. Moreover, the plot contains story lines relative to problems encountered and how those problems either have or have not been resolved. Within each story line, there is a moral to the story (e.g., if I work hard and succeed, I learn that hard work pays off and am likely to continue working hard to succeed).

Career counseling from a narrative approach begins with the identification of a career problem. Career problems are defined as gaps between one's current career situation and a desired career future (Cochran, 1985). In the narrative sense, the career problem represents the beginning, and the middle relates to the way one is to move from the beginning to an end (Cochran, 1997). The career counseling process involves a number of episodes that are incorporated into counseling depending on each client's career concerns. For example, first a problem must be elaborated by the client and clarified through interactions between the client and the career counselor. Second, the counselor helps the client compose a life history to elucidate the client's career narrative. Techniques such as constructing a lifeline (Goldman, 1992), the life chapters exercise (Carlsen, 1988), the accomplishments interview (Bolles, 1998), and identifying early life-role models and early life recollections (Watkins & Savickas, 1990) facilitate the narrative construction process. The next episode builds upon and extends the narrative by creating a future narrative. Techniques include constructing a lifeline using the life chapters exercise, using guidance material such as the Self-Directed Search (Holland, 1985), using the accomplishments interview, and using guided fantasy. Testing the future narrative against reality becomes the next episode. Through job shadowing, volunteering, gaining internships and externships, conducting occupational information interviews, and working part-time, the person is able to acquire data that either support the constructed future narrative or lead to the revision of it based upon the new information the person has acquired. At this point, the person engages in making a choice that translates potentialities into actualities. To facilitate this process, clients can examine their values in light of specific career options via a career grid activity (Neimeyer, 1989), guided fantasy exercises, and life-themes identification (Watkins & Savickas, 1990). As clients crystallize a decision, they may encounter internal and external barriers or obstructions (e.g., Will I succeed? Will the option be satisfying? What will my family think?). They may also need assistance in identifying activities that provide opportunities to connect with their "new stories" constructed earlier in the career counseling process. Opportunities for making connections with new stories are labeled as *actualizations* by Cochran (1997).

Narrative approaches to describing career development and for providing career development interventions highlight the notion that we are the stories that we live. Career counseling from this perspective provides clients with opportunities to reconstruct a coherent life story. As Peavy (1992) writes, "Stories of self and career can be used by counselor and client to consolidate present self-knowledge and to help guide forward movement into anticipated futures" (p. 219).

The life chapters exercise mentioned earlier is very useful in helping clients construct narratives and in sensitizing them to the subjective experience of career (Cochran, 1997). In this exercise, clients are encouraged to consider their lives as if they were books by dividing their life events into chapters. Clients are asked to give titles to the chapters of their past. They are also invited to identify three important lessons they have learned by living each chapter of their lives. Clients are then asked to look ahead at the rest of their lives and create chapter titles that move from the present on through to death. They are asked to identify the chapters they expect to happen and the chapters they want to make sure happen if their lives are to be complete. In processing this activity, positive chapters are restored and negative chapters are reversed in the future.

Constructivist Career Counseling

People construct meaning through the decisions they make and the actions they take. This theme forms the basic assumption upon which Kelly (1955) developed his theory of personal constructs. Constructs represent personal theories that we develop regarding people and events; they are our perceptions of events, and they include the judgments and evaluations we make about others, the world, and ourselves. We use our theories, or personal constructs, to predict future events (e.g., "Because I value helping others and counseling provides the opportunity to help others, if I become a counselor, then I am likely to experience occupational satisfaction"). Constructs with greater predictive validity tend to be more stable than those that are not as useful in predicting events. Our constructs become refined over time, and we revise our perceptions based on life experience.

Peavy (1992) draws upon Kelly's theory in identifying four questions that are important for career counselors to consider in what he labels "constructivist career counseling":

1. How can I form a cooperative alliance with this client? (Relationship factor)
2. How can I encourage the self-helpfulness of this client? (Agency factor)
3. How can I help this client to elaborate and evaluate his or her constructions and meanings germane to this decision? (Meaning-making factor)
4. How can I help this client to reconstruct and negotiate personally meaningful and socially supportable realities? (Negotiation factor) (p. 221)

Herr and Cramer (1996) note that the questions posed by Peavy connect with Cochran's view that "agency in career, the willingness to act, to bring something about, to achieve life goals, should be the prime topic in career theory" (p. 191). This view, in turn, is consistent with Kelly's (1955) personal construct theory. Particularly useful here is Kelly's (1955) notion that personal constructs cohere to form a matrix of meaning or a system of hierarchically organized dimensions that can be adjusted to a range of events (Neimeyer, 1992). Personal constructs evolve across time. Life transitions (e.g., marriage, divorce, having children, children leaving home) often stimulate changes in our personal constructs. These assumptions led to the development of several career counseling interventions aimed at exploring and reconstructing the client's unique matrix of meaning.

One such technique is the laddering technique (Hinkle, 1965; Neimeyer, 1992). Neimeyer described the laddering technique as a strategy for helping clients identify their more important (superordinate) and less important (subordinate) constructs. The laddering technique can be initiated in a more open fashion, or it can be based on a specific dilemma confronting the client. For example, we could begin the laddering technique by asking our client, Ronald, to identify three occupations he is currently considering. Let's imagine that Ronald identified the occupations of engineer, social worker, and school administrator. We could then ask Ronald to identify any way in which two of the occupations he selected are alike, but different from, the third. Ronald might note that social workers and school administrators help people and that engineers might be helpful but only indirectly. We could then ask Ronald which he would prefer, helping people directly or indirectly. If Ronald noted that his preference was for working directly with people in a helping way, we would then ask Ronald why he preferred helping directly as opposed to indirectly. Ronald might state that it is important to him to see whether he is actually making a difference in people's lives as opposed to not knowing whether he has made a positive impact. The laddering technique would be continued with our asking Ronald why he would prefer each contrast. Laddering is completed when the elicited construct is so obvious that justification is evident and unnecessary.

A more elaborate technique for identifying personal constructs is called the *vocational reptest*. Based on Kelly's (1955) Role Construct Repertory Test, the reptest requires clients to systematically compare and contrast a set of career-related elements (e.g., occupations). This technique can be initiated in a fashion similar to the laddering technique. By considering several occupations at a time, clients identify ways in which two are similar to, but different from, the third. For example, construction worker and landscape architect are similar in that they involve working outdoors, and this makes them different from the work of an accountant, which involves working indoors. Another group of three occupations is then presented to the client and the client identifies how two of the occupations are similar to each other and different from the third. The ways in which the client identifies occupations as being similar and different represent the client's personal constructs. The client's personal constructs are used to help the client evaluate occupational options. Once seven to ten personal constructs (e.g., working indoors versus working outdoors) are identified, the client provides ratings for each of the occupations along each of the constructs he or she identified (e.g., using a scale of 1, *strongly dislike*, to 10, *strongly prefer*). Neimeyer (1992) noted that "when completed, the vocational reptest provides a useful window into the unique considerations that each person brings to bear in career decision making, as well as the interrelationship among those considerations" (p. 166).

Vocational card sorts can also be used within constructivist career counseling. For example, the career counselor can provide the client with a stack of cards, each containing an occupational title. The client can be instructed to sort the cards according to occupations she would consider, those that she would not consider, and those that she is uncertain about. Each occupation in the "would consider" and "would not consider" stacks can then be discussed with regard to reasons why the client would or would not consider the occupation. As each reason is discussed, the counselor listens for, and helps the client identify, important constructs the client uses in making decisions about occupational options (e.g., being able to engage in creative self-expression, having autonomy in work, having an occupation that provides job security). The constructs can then be reviewed and summarized.

From the constructivist perspective, career counseling outcomes are considered in terms of their fruitfulness. Fruitfulness refers to the assumption that counseling should result in a changed outlook or new perspective on some aspect of life (Peavy, 1992). Career development interventions are framed as "experiments," conducted both in session and out of session, that are directed toward helping clients think, feel, and act more productively in relation to their career concerns. Peavy noted that experiments can be conducted in the imagination of the client (e.g., guided fantasy), by engaging the client in critical self-reflection (e.g., laddering technique), by engaging the client in simulation or vicarious experiences (e.g., role playing or skill learning), and by engaging the client in real-world experiences (e.g., job shadowing, job interviewing).

Chaos Theory of Careers

Acknowledging the uncertainty and unpredictability of career development in the 21st century, Pryor and Bright (2011) offer a theory that responds to new realities, such as the speed of communication, the reshaping of organizations, the speed and extent of change, the need for lifelong learning, globalization, the emergence of contingent and contractually based work, and the rapidity of technological innovation. These new realities result in career challenges that are influenced by greater complexity, more chance events, and greater change than people experienced in the 20th century.

According to Pryor and Bright (2011), the complexity of the factors influencing career development highlights the need to avoid traditional approaches that attempt to explain career behavior in terms of one factor influencing another factor. To illustrate this point, Pryor and Bright note research conducted by Morrison (1994), who found that study participants with similar Holland codes diverged in their career paths over time in ways that were not predictable from descriptions of their Holland types. Pryor and Bright also point to their own research regarding complexity in career development. Specifically, Bright, Pryor, Wilkenfield, and Earl (2005) found that 70% of their research participants reported that their career development was influenced by unplanned events ranging from unplanned meetings, to illness, to messages from God. Given such complexity, it is more reasonable to focus on patterns in career development rather than attempting to use stable and isolated variables to predict career outcomes. Thus, Pryor and Bright (2011) view approaches such as Savickas's (2005) Career Construction Interview to be useful in career counseling. Although Pryor and Bright acknowledge that it is not possible to know fully what influences people or how they will respond in the future to the myriad influences they encounter in life, they suggest that by examining patterns across time, career counselors can help clients identify their emergent patterns of behavior.

The chaos theory of careers also highlights nonlinearity in career development. In nonlinear systems such as career behavior, small or seemingly trivial and unplanned events can have significant career implications. For example, on the day that Ron experienced his injury playing football, it had rained early in the morning. Although the sun was shining at the start of the game, the early morning rain resulted in the field being slightly slick during the game. The lack of sure footing caused Ron to slip during a rather routine run downfield. When he slipped, he also tore ligaments in his knee. Ron never returned to his pre-injury performance level, and it was that lackluster performance that led him to question (and consider) his future goals. Had the game started later in the day or, better yet, had it not rained at all, Ron's future might have been very different. In this way, the chaos theory of career development resonates with Krumboltz's planned happenstance concept. In fact, the same recommendations made by Krumboltz for addressing planned happenstance in career counseling (Mitchell et al., 1999) can be applied to helping clients cope successfully with nonlinearity as described in chaos theory and discussed by Pryor and Bright (2011).

Evaluating the Chaos Theory of Careers

The chaos theory of career development is an emerging theory that has excellent potential for addressing the career context of the 21st century. It is a theory that readily acknowledges the impact of change, uncertainty, and complexity in the career development process. It also is a theory that, like career construction theory, connects with spiritual dimensions of career development. That is, it is a theory that is directed toward meaning making, connectedness, purpose, and transcendence in career development (Pryor & Bright, 2011). For the potential of this theory to be realized, however, more theory validation research is needed. In addition, making the theory more accessible to career practitioners and more practical for career counseling will be required for greater adoption of this theory in the future.

MyCounselingLab®

Watch the videos *21st Century Application of Career Construction Theory with Student 1* and *21st Century Application of Career Construction Theory with Student 2* and complete Student Activity #2 at the end of this chapter.

Watch the video *21st Century Application of Holland's Theory with a College Student: Dr. Janet Lenz* and complete Student Activity #6 at the end of this chapter.

Watch the video *21st Century Career Construction Theory: A Dialogue.*

SUMMARY

Strengths in Recent Career Theories

The emerging career development theories discussed in this chapter reflect the vitality that exists within the field. Emergent theories maintain vitality within the career field by advancing new notions for career development theory and practice. Moreover, the theories discussed in this chapter fill numerous gaps in the literature. Strengths inherent in the emerging theories include (a) the theoretical propositions espoused are often applicable to diverse client populations, (b) most emerging theories have clear links with practice, and (c) many of the emerging theories incorporate and extend the theory and research base of preexisting theories (e.g., Bandura, 1986; Kelly, 1955; Rokeach, 1973).

Need for More Attention to the Career Experiences of Diverse Populations

Despite increased attention on constructing career theories that are applicable to diverse populations, there is much more work to be done in this regard. Not surprisingly, there is the need for more extensive research in testing the theoretical propositions and the practical applications of emerging career theories. Although the emerging theories generally incorporate a stronger emphasis on culture and context in career development, the need for more research investigating the applicability of the emerging models for diverse populations remains. A series of articles published in *The Career Development Quarterly* (September 2001) emphasized the need for career theorists and practitioners to pay greater attention to ways in which contextual factors (culture, gender, sexual orientation, sociopolitical events, etc.) shape career development. More than 15 years later, this need still exists.

Historically, career theories and practices in North America have deemphasized the person's context. This is a serious limitation as it restricts our ability to understand a person's career development. Context provides essential data to help us understand the dynamic interactions between the person and the environment that shape a person's career. Without context all we can hope for is to describe a career (e.g., she worked as a physician specializing in oncology; he pursued a major in electrical engineering and secured a position with Florida Power and Light Company upon graduation from college; he moved from job to job with no apparent direction or focus).

Although some career theorists (most often, those in the trait-factor category) seem to ignore the influence of discrimination in career development, other theories (many in the developmental and emerging theories categories) acknowledge the fact that there is not equal access to a full range of occupational opportunities. Understanding the dynamic interaction between the individual and various levels of environments (e.g., family, school, community) in which individual development and career behavior are embedded will deepen our capacity to understand career decisions and pathways.

Clearly, placing a greater emphasis on culture and context in career theory, research, and practice will increase our sensitivity to how factors such as racism, sexism, ageism, classism, and discriminatory behavior toward persons who are gay, lesbian, transgendered, or disabled influence career development by artificially constraining the opportunity structure for millions of people. Increased understanding of these processes should lead to increased effectiveness at counteracting negative effects of environmental influences in career development. This is a goal toward which all within the profession should strive.

Tips from the Field

In theory, there is no difference between theory and practice. In practice, there is.

Yogi Berra

Theory Summary and Integration

Although some (e.g., Patton & McMahon, 1999) contend that we are moving toward career theory convergence, others view it differently. It is clear that we have experienced the emergence of a paradigm shift from theories based in logical positivism (e.g., trait-factor) to postmodern perspectives emphasizing subjectivity, perspectivity, and counselor-client collaboration in career development interventions. It also is clear that although no one theory is superior, the field is stronger because of the multiple perspectives currently espoused. For example, Super's theory provides an overarching framework for understanding career development processes; Holland's theory offers a useful vocabulary to help the counselor and client engage in the complex activity of career decision making; Roe and Gottfredson remind us that careers develop from an early age and societal influences shape our thinking about future possibilities (often in negative ways); Krumboltz, Lent, Brown, and Hackett highlight how interactions between the person and the environment create self-beliefs that affect our career decisions; Peterson, Sampson, Lenz, and Reardon offer important descriptions as to how we make career decisions; Savickas highlights how careers are constructed by integrating the subjective dimension of career development in career counseling; Hansen urges us to consider a greater context that includes spirituality and cultural influences; Pryor and Bright encourage us to embrace the "chaos" that permeates 21st-century career development;

and the postmodern theorists remind us to never lose sight of the ways in which a person's unique life experiences provide meaning and purpose in career behavior. Each of the theories we have discussed in Chapter 2 and 3 are part of the rich tapestry that career practitioners can draw on systematically to guide their conceptualizations of their clients' career concerns and to inform their decisions regarding appropriate career interventions. Finally, we hope that future research results in even more clearly defined theoretical statements that are applicable to diverse populations and have strong connections with career development interventions.

Thus, the stage has been set for a bright future. Although learning about multiple theoretical perspectives can seem overwhelming at times, it is important to remember that these multiple perspectives also indicate the vitality that exists within the career development field. We encourage you to become more familiar with the theories that we have discussed and also to engage in the task of constructing your own career development theory. Draw on extant theory and reflect on how you think careers develop. Incorporate career development research results into your reflection process. Such personal reflections will be useful to you as a counselor and may even be useful to you in your own career development!

CASE STUDY

Denise is a 39-year-old, slender Caucasian female who presents herself professionally and is very well groomed. She is the oldest of three children in her family. She attended a suburban community college for two years; however, she did not earn a degree. Denise is currently working as an administrative assistant, which is her first full-time job in 15 years. Denise recently left her husband of 14 years as he would not allow her to work outside of the home or to pursue further education; he felt that he should be her job. She decided to seek career counseling because she thinks she "can be more than a secretary," but she is not sure of the possibilities. She is concerned that any change she makes will stretch her financially.

Denise is currently seeking a divorce from her husband. She stated he does not want a divorce and is encouraging her to enter counseling with him. She indicated she is "tired of being controlled" even though staying married would resolve her financial issues. She is struggling with the decision surrounding the divorce. Her family is supportive of her but does not have the resources to help her financially.

Denise is confident that her abilities surpass simply keeping house and taking care of her husband. She would like to grow as a person and feels this would be best accomplished by obtaining higher education. She is obviously struggling with her possible divorce and adjusting to the change in lifestyle.

As she has not been in the workforce for a number of years, she is not very knowledgeable about the world of work.

She has expressed an interest in the creative fields and stated she has often edited videotapes for herself and her family. She would like to explore educational programs related to this field.

She is battling the negative messages she has been receiving from her husband about the mean-inglessness of the position she holds. In her hobbies, she tends to take part in creative activities as well as in physically active activities.

Using one or more of the theories discussed in this chapter, describe Denise's career development. Which theory (or theories) discussed in this chapter would you use to provide Denise with career counseling? What are the limitations of these theories for Denise's situation?

STUDENT ACTIVITIES

1. Choose one theory from this chapter and write a one-page summary of how you would use this theory to describe the career development of Ronald (described in this chapter).

2. Refer to the Video and Resource Library and select the video entitled *21st Century Application of Career Construction Theory with a College Student: Dr. Mark Savickas*. What are the strengths of this approach? What do you view as the limitations of this model? Consider for yourself the questions Dr. Savickas posed to his client. How would you answer them? What do your answers suggest to you about your career goals? How would you describe your life project?

3. Think about one activity in your life right now for which you have very positive outcome expectations (i.e., you expect to be successful). Then, think about one activity in your life for which you have negative outcome expectations. Consider the contrast in your feelings about these two activities. What is your interest level for participating in each of these activities?

4. Complete the values sorting exercise provided in this chapter. Identify your top five values and define them for yourself. Consider the ways in which you express your top values on a daily basis. Ask yourself whether there are ways that you can increase the degree to which you express these values. If there are, then construct strategies for making this possibility reality.

5. After you have completed question 4, give the values exercise to a friend. Tell your friend to first identify his or her top 10 values, then his/her top 5, writing each one of his/her top 5 values on a separate slip of paper. Next, begin taking away a value one at a time. Each time you take away a value, be sure that your friend defines that value for her- or himself. Writing down the definition is important. Then, discuss the ways in which each of these values is manifested in the person's life. Discuss whether there are possibilities for increasing the degree to which the values can be manifested in the person's life. If there are, brainstorm strategies for making this occur.

6. Refer to the Video and Resource Library and select the video entitled *21st Century Application of Holland's Theory with a College Student: Dr. Janet Lenz*. In what ways does Dr. Lenz incorporate CIP theory in her work with her client? What are the advantages of integrating this theory with Holland's theory?

CHAPTER 4

PROVIDING CULTURALLY COMPETENT CAREER DEVELOPMENT INTERVENTIONS

The U.S. population and workforce have become increasingly diverse, and it is essential for career counselors and career development professionals to be multiculturally sensitive and competent. The multicultural counseling movement has matured from an exclusive focus on race/ethnicity to the inclusion of all cultural dimensions such as gender, gender identity, sexual orientation, disability, spirituality, religion, age, and social class. We all have multiple identities, and our personalities are built on many cultural identities. To become a multiculturally competent counselor requires a lifelong commitment to self-reflection and growth. It is also important to help all people and workers become multiculturally sensitive. Such sensitivity benefits not only oppressed group members but all people—only when everybody feels respected as a human and cultural being are we able to be free.

Y. Barry Chung, Ph.D.
Professor and Program Director of Counseling Psychology, Indiana University
President, National Career Development Association (2006–2007)

MyCounselingLab®

Visit the MyCounselingLab® site for *Career Development Interventions*, Fifth Edition, to enhance your understanding of chapter concepts. You will have the opportunity to practice applying what you learned in the chapter by completing the video- and case-based exercises in the MyLab. Taking the Licensure Quizzes will help you prepare for your certification exam.

Ju-Shin, a 28-year-old, first-generation Asian American (her parents were from Taiwan) presented for career counseling expressing concern about her current career choice. She was nearing completion of her doctoral degree in counseling. Initially, she planned on becoming a counselor educator. Recently, she was having second thoughts. Ju-Shin reported that, lately, her interest in counseling was fading. She also confided that she had enjoyed her research and statistics courses very much. One of her friends was enrolled in a doctoral program in educational research, and Ju-Shin was now wondering if this might be a better choice for her. As she spoke, the career counselor noticed that she was very anxious. As the session continued, Ju-Shin expressed a substantial amount of concern over how her parents would react if she were to switch degree programs. In fact, she seemed convinced that her parents would not approve of such a change. The more Ju-Shin discussed her concern, the more reluctant she seemed to consider changing her program of study. Yet, she also continued to note how much she seemed to enjoy her research-oriented courses.

A career counselor operating from a traditional trait-factor approach and an individual-istic orientation to career decision making might be inclined to provide Ju-Shin with a test battery that would offer her more self-information concerning her degree of fit for research-oriented programs of study and related occupations versus becoming a coun-selor educator. Once Ju-Shin had relevant information about traits such as interests, skills, and so on, the career counselor would encourage her to consider how well her traits fit with the factors required for success in the occupations Ju-Shin was considering.

Although the acquisition of such information would undoubtedly be useful to Ju-Shin, there are other issues surrounding her career dilemma. Ju-Shin's cultural back-ground is based in a collectivistic orientation to career decision making, in which she is not alone in her decisions. Her career decisions play out within the context of her family. It would be critical for Ju-Shin's career counselor to explore this contextual factor in career counseling. Ju-Shin's career counselor will need to understand how familial expectations interact with other factors (e.g., her interest in research) influencing Ju-Shin's career exploration. It would also be important for the career counselor to under-stand the degree to which cultural stereotypes and discriminatory behavior influence Ju-Shin's views as to what might be possible for her to achieve in her career. Individual and cultural interactions exist for all clients, and career counselors must develop the requisite multicultural knowledge, skills, and awareness for conducting culturally appro-priate career counseling.

Ju-Shin demonstrates the fact that cultural variables rest at the core of the career intervention process. To construct culturally appropriate career interventions, career professionals need to embrace this fact. Career counselors also need to be sensitive to the tremendous cultural and demographic shifts occurring in society. During the past four decades, the United States has been awash in cultural pluralism. According to Lee and Richardson (1991), the concept of cul-tural pluralism was spawned, in part, from societal, political, and economic events occurring in the 1960s. It is also the case that the world is becoming more demographically diverse. For example, throughout the 21st century, people of color will experience significant growth in num-bers while the White population will decline significantly. In fact, the White population was the only major racial group to decrease in population from 2000 to 2013, decreasing from 75% to 62.6% of the population in the United States across that time period (Colby & Ortman, 2015). On the other hand, the U.S. Census Bureau (2015) notes that the Hispanic population grew by 43% between 2000 and 2010, totaling 50.5 million people. The Asian population also increased by 43% between 2000 and 2010, growing from 10.2 million in 2000 to 14.7 million in 2010. The Black or African American population comprised 13.6% of the total population in the United States in 2010. In 2013, the population of African Americans including those of more than one race was estimated at 45 million or 15.2% of the total U.S. population (Colby & Ortman). The U.S. Census Bureau projects that in 2060 there will be 74.5 million African Americans including those of more than one race, comprising 17.9% of the population. By the year 2060 it is pre-dicted that people of color will represent the numerical majority in the United States (Byars-Winston, Fouad, & Wen, 2015; Colby & Ortman; Worthington, Flores, & Navarro, 2005).

The influx of new immigrants into the United States will also continue in large numbers (U.S. Census Bureau, 2015). Estimates are that between 820,000 and 1.2 million immigrants entered the United States annually between 1996 and 2006. In 2012, 40.7 million people living in the United States were foreign-born. Among this group, 11.6 million came to the United States from Mexico, 2.3 million from China, 2 million from India, 1.9 million from the Philippines, 1.3 million from Vietnam and El Salvador, and 1.1 million from Cuba and Korea (Center for American Progress, 2014). The percentage of homes in the United States in which a language other than English is spoken at home was 20.7% in 2013 (U.S. Census Bureau).

Obviously, the demographic changes experienced in the United States from 2000 to 2015 will continue to shape the composition of the labor force, which increasingly reflects the cultural pluralism existing within society. The U.S. Department of Labor's 2010–2011 edition of the *Occupational Outlook Handbook* (U.S. Department of Labor, 2010) offers projected changes in the labor force, which is comprised of those looking for work and those who are working, for the time period of 2008–2018. These projected changes indicate that among racial groups, Whites are expected to make up a decreasing share of the labor force, while Blacks, Asians, and all other groups will increase. Among ethnic groups, persons of Hispanic origin are projected to increase their share of the labor force from 14.3% to 17.6%, reflecting 33.1% growth. The male labor force is projected to grow by 7.5% from 2008 to 2018, compared with 9.0% for the female labor force. Today, women comprise 52% of the population in the United States and 47% of the total U.S. labor force, with the latter projected to increase to 51% by 2018 (Byars-Winston et al., 2015). The share of workers ages 16 to 24 is expected to decrease from 14.3% in 2008 to 12.7% by 2018. The primary working-age group, those between 25 and 54 years old, is projected to decline from 67.7% of the labor force in 2008 to 63.5% by 2018. Workers age 55 years and older, by contrast, are anticipated to increase from 18.1% to 23.9% of the labor force during the same period (Bureau of Labor Statistics, 2010).

Although future projected population shifts focus on more distant dates, the projected population shifts among school-age children are much more immediate. According to the Pew Research Center (2014), the number of U.S.-born Hispanic children ages 5 to 17 in the United States nearly doubled between 1997 and 2013. Public schools in the United States are now majority-minority. And White children today comprise nearly 75% of all private school enrollments (Hussar & Bailey, 2014), thereby giving rise to legitimate claims regarding the existence of racial/economic segregation in U.S. education.

In an extensive study of occupational population trends within the U.S. labor force, Byars-Winston et al. (2015) found that despite growing demographic diversity in the overall U.S. population, the labor force continues to reveal racialized and gendered disparities. More specifically, Byars-Winston and her colleagues identified three particularly disturbing trends in the U.S. labor force. First, American Indians continue to experience substantial employment, economic, and educational disadvantages when compared to Whites. Moreover, when controlling for factors such as age, sex, education, marital status, and state of residence, they are still 31% less likely to be employed than Whites. A second disturbing trend is that the proportional labor force participation of Black males was greater in 1970 than 2010. Black men are also nine times more likely than White men to be incarcerated. Finally, despite federal funding efforts to increase diversity within STEM occupations, racial/ethnic minority men and women have made little ground in gaining access to these occupations.

Changing demographics, multiple worldviews, and cultural plurality influence the career development intervention process. Despite these developments, there continues to be ample evidence to suggest that women, people of color, persons with disabilities, gay men, lesbian women, and transgender persons continue to encounter tremendous obstacles in their career development. For example, the wage gap between sexes still plagues the American workforce. Women earn 78 cents on a dollar for every dollar a man earns in a year (Arons, 2008). The gender wage gap has extreme costs for women over the course of their careers. The average female worker loses approximately $434,000 in wages over a 40-year period as a direct result of pay inequities. Out of 23 Organization for Economic Co-operation and Development (OECD) countries, the United States has the seventh-largest gender earnings gap. The gender wage gap in the United States is 21.6%, well above the OECD average of 18.5% (OECD, 2015). Despite the fact that women will soon comprise the majority of the labor force in the United States, the preponderance of evidence indicates that there are still substantial challenges to address if we are to achieve gender equity in career development (e.g., Bimrose, Watson, McMahon, Haasler, Tomassini, & Suzanne, 2014; Gati & Perez, 2014; Powell & Butterfield, 2015; Scheuermann, Tokar, & Hall, 2014).

The same exists for other demographic groups (e.g., Eggerth, DeLaney, Flynn, & Jacobson, 2012; Eggerth & Flynn, 2012; Lee & Ahn, 2012; Nassar-McMillan & Zagzebski-Tovar, 2012; Piña-Watson, Jimenez, & Ojeda, 2014). According to the Bureau of Labor Statistics (2015), 16.1% of African Americans and 11.8% of Latinos were unemployed in April 2011. This contrasts with 8% of Whites being unemployed. Nearly 25% of all teenagers were also unemployed in April 2011. With regard to postsecondary education, only 30% of African Americans ages 25 to 34, and less than 20% of Latinos in that age group, have an associate's degree or higher while students from the highest income families are almost eight times as likely as those from the lowest income families to earn a bachelor's degree by age 24 (Lewin, 2010).

Given these statistics, it is not surprising that Daire, LaMothe, and Fuller (2007) found that African American college students tend to place greater importance on future income, future status, and making a difference in society as influences in their career decision making than do White college students. Whites tend to be employed in managerial and professional specialty occupations (occupations that tend to have job security, decent salaries, due processes in hiring and firing, etc.). Only 23% of African Americans and 15% of Hispanics are employed in such occupations as compared to 32% of all Whites (Bureau of Labor Statistics, 2010). According to Herr, Cramer, and Niles (2004) "more than half of employed Latinas are either clerical workers or nontransport operatives (dressmakers, assemblers, machine operators, and so on)" (p. 277). The poverty rate of American Indian families is twice the rate (24.2%) of the general population in the United States (U.S. Bureau of Census, 2010). The unemployment rate for American Indians reached 13.6% in 2009. Moreover, occupational desegregation rates tend to be highest in occupations in which men are paid less and in which the number of workers is declining. African American as well as Hispanic families earn approximately 60% of the income of White, non-Hispanic families (U.S. Census Bureau, 2010).

Despite legislation aimed at protecting their rights (e.g., Public Law 93-112, Rehabilitation Act of 1973; Public Law 94-142, Education for All Handicapped Children Act of 1975; Public Law 95-602, Rehabilitation, Comprehensive Services, and Developmental Disabilities Amendment of 1978; Public Law 101-476, Education of the Handicapped Amendments of 1990; Public Law 101-336, Americans with Disabilities Act of 1990), Americans with disabilities have fared no better (e.g., Dipeolu, Sniatecki, Storlie, & Hargrave, 2013; Lindstrom, Doren, Post, & Lombardi, 2013; Siperstein, Parker, & Drascher, 2013). Persons with disabilities experienced an unemployment rate of 14.5% in 2011 (Bureau of Labor Statistics, 2010). About 56.7 million people in the United States in 2010 had a disability. According to the National Council on Disability (2000), 350,000 people between the ages of 18 and 25 receive Social Security income support (and, therefore, are not employed). Widen the age range to include all adult persons with disabilities, and the data are no more positive. In 2013, 17.6% of people with a disability were employed. This contrasts with 64% employment for those without a disability (Bureau of Labor Statistics, 2014).

Gay, lesbian, and bisexual individuals also experience discriminatory treatment in the labor force. Goleman (1990) suggested that the negative bias toward this group is often more intense than that directed toward any other group. Herr et al. (2004) noted that gay, lesbian, and bisexual persons are essentially barred from certain occupations and find vertical mobility blocked simply because of their sexual orientation. Career development theorists and practitioners are slowly beginning to construct theories and interventions that address these issues (e.g., Chung, 2003; Dispenza, Watson, Chung, & Brack, 2012; Heintz, 2012; Prati & Pietrantoni, 2014; Pope & Barret, 2002; Sangganjanavanich & Headley, 2013; Velez & Moradi, 2012).

It should be obvious from the above that increasing diversity does not equate to increasing equity. These statistics suggest that many women, racial/ethnic minorities, persons with disabilities, and gay/lesbian/bisexual/transgender individuals regularly experience discriminatory practices in hiring and promoting, insufficient financial resources, and a lack of role models and mentors. Thus, traditional approaches are often inadequate and/or inappropriate for assisting members of diverse groups in their career development (Pope, 2012). If so, then career development interventions in the 21st century must be reconceptualized to more adequately meet the career development needs of the members of an increasingly diverse society (Lee, 2012).

Clearly, career practitioners must possess strong multicultural competencies that include not only understanding the impact that discriminatory processes have on career development but also knowing how to intervene effectively when working with clients experiencing such processes. Thus, these competencies include and extend those typically included in multicultural counseling. Axelson (1985) defined *multicultural counseling* as a helping process that places the emphasis for counseling theory and practice equally on the cultural impression of both the counselor and client. Ivey, D'Andrea, Ivey, and Simek-Morgan (2009) emphasize the important role that cultural background plays in shaping a person's view of reality. These perspectives provide excellent starting points for career practitioners relative to cultural competencies. Important factors to address in designing and delivering culturally competent career development interventions include the degree to which interventions address universal and/or culturally specific variables, the degree of ethnocentrism embedded in career interventions, the client's level of acculturation, and the client's identity development. Of course, the career development practitioner must be aware of how these same factors influence his or her conceptualization of the clients and the identification of appropriate career interventions.

Tips from the Field

We are all alike, and we are all different from each other. Work to understand both and to incorporate that understanding in your career interventions.

TRADITIONAL ASSUMPTIONS OF CAREER THEORIES IN THE UNITED STATES

Historically, career development theories and interventions, especially in North America, have emphasized a psychological perspective highlighting the role that intra-individual variables (e.g., motivation, internal locus of control, perseverance, ability) play in shaping one's career.

Gysbers, Heppner, and Johnston (2014) point out that career development interventions in the United States, having arisen out of a specific context, tend to favor five tenets reflecting a European American perspective: (a) individualism and autonomy, (b) affluence, (c) structure of opportunity open to all, (d) the centrality of work in people's lives, and (e) the linearity, progressiveness, and rationality of the career development process. These tenets reflect specific assumptions that do not represent the contextual experiences many people encounter. Stead (2004) notes deficiencies in most extant career theories for their ethnocentrism and challenges the appropriateness of attempts at simply adapting existing theories to other cultures. He contends that from their beginnings culturally sensitive theories need to be grounded in specific cultural contexts to be relevant for those respective contexts. Young, Marshall, and Valach (2007) reinforce Stead's viewpoint by noting the variance in meaning attached to the word *career*, even in English-speaking, Western industrialized countries.

Although many early theories of career development acknowledged the influence of such person-environment interactions in shaping careers, descriptions of these interactions were not developed fully. Midway through the second decade of the 21st century, it is clear that a more diversified career counseling clientele and a heightened awareness of the important role that culture plays in career choice and career counseling highlight the need for theorists and practitioners to integrate multicultural perspectives into their theory descriptions and career interventions.

UNIVERSAL VERSUS CULTURE-SPECIFIC MODELS

Many statements pertaining to multicultural career development interventions reflect the tension between etic (i.e., universal) and emic (i.e., culturally specific) approaches to counseling. Etic perspectives maintain that career development interventions for members of minority groups should be the same as the career development interventions used for those representing the majority. As such, proponents of etic perspectives contend that current career theories and techniques are robust enough to have universal applicability.

Emic perspectives, on the other hand, highlight the importance of designing career development interventions that are specific to the client's culture. Wohl (1995) suggests that "culturally specific approaches are psychotherapeutic methods designed to be congruent with the cultural characteristics of a particular ethnic clientele, or for problems believed to be especially prominent in a particular ethnic group" (p. 76). By extension, then, culture-specific career development theories are required to provide more comprehensive and accurate descriptions of the career development process for diverse groups.

Several authors resolve the tension between etic versus emic approaches by incorporating useful elements of both perspectives into multicultural career development theory and practice (Arthur & Collins, 2011; Lee, 2012; Leong, 2014). For example, Leong and Pearce (2014) focus on similarities and differences in the career counseling process for majority and minority clients by adapting Kluckhohn and Murray's (1950) tripartite personality theory to the career counseling process. Kluckhohn and Murray contended that personality consists of universal (individuals are like all others in certain ways), group (individuals are like some others in certain ways), and individual (individuals are unique in certain ways) dimensions. Career counselors act in culturally encapsulated ways (Wrenn, 1962) when they attend to only the universal levels of their clients and ignore clients' important group, cultural, and individual dimensions. Leong and Brown (1995) emphasize that "effective cross-cultural counseling would consist of the appropriate shifting between dimensions as the counseling relationship develops" (p. 195).

Fischer, Jome, and Atkinson (1998) contend that researchers have focused a significant amount of attention on culturally specific (emic) counseling interventions, perhaps "at the expense of attention to common factors in multicultural counseling and research" (p. 528). Proposing a common factors perspective in multicultural counseling, Fischer and her associates suggest that "the curative properties of a given psychotherapy lie not in its theoretically unique components (e.g., insight for psychoanalytic approaches, modification of cognitions for cognitive approaches) but in components common to all psychotherapies" (pp. 529–530). Thus, Fischer and her associates identify four factors that appear to be "the universal elements of healing in all cultures" (p. 532). These factors are (a) the therapeutic relationship, (b) shared worldview, (c) client expectations, and (d) ritual or intervention. A cornerstone of the therapeutic relationship is the establishment of trust and rapport between the counselor and client. Fischer et al. cite the strong research support indicating that the establishment of an effective therapeutic relationship is a significant predictor of therapeutic outcome.

A key aspect in establishing the therapeutic relationship is a shared worldview between the counselor and client. This common factor reflects Rogers's (1957) notion of empathic understanding, which he defined as "trying to experience the client's world as if it were your own without losing the 'as if' quality" (p. 97). Fischer et al. (1998) suggest that understanding each other's worlds enables the client and counselor to establish the therapeutic relationship and sets the stage for positive expectations regarding counseling outcomes. Empathic understanding also minimizes the probability that counselors will operate on the myth of cultural uniformity, "which assumes that all individuals regardless of race, ethnicity, sex, age, and social class" have values and goals that are similar to the counselors' values and goals (Leong, 1993, p. 32). Thus, achieving this type of understanding is critical for providing effective multicultural career development interventions and requires the counselor to have adequate knowledge, skills, and awareness of the client's culture. Obviously, counselors must also be aware of their own cultural biases and assumptions within this process.

The third common factor identified by Fischer et al. (1998) is client expectations. "Counselors and healers raise client expectations and gain credibility through the setting in which they conduct therapy, the training and degrees they possess, working within a shared worldview with the client, and developing a therapeutic relationship with the client" (p. 538). When clients have positive expectations for their counseling experience, there is a greater likelihood that positive outcomes will occur (Torrey, 1986).

The first three common factors set the stage and are preconditions for the fourth common factor, which is ritual or intervention. Fischer et al. (1998) point out that "an intervention that is relevant and effective for one client may not be as relevant for another client, depending on the degree of relationship, shared worldview, and positive expectation" (p. 540). All of these factors are relevant to the career development intervention process, regardless of the career practitioner's theoretical orientation. Providing appropriate interventions requires career counselors to be aware of several important additional issues: ethnocentrism, acculturation, and identity development.

ETHNOCENTRISM

When career counselors assume that one value system (their own) is superior and preferable to another, they engage in ethnocentric behavior that is insensitive to their clients' worldviews. Ethnocentrism can easily occur in career development interventions when counselors assume that individualistic and self-sufficient actions are preferable to collectivistic actions reflecting interdependence and group loyalty. Individualists use individual attitudes, private interests, and personal goals to guide their behavior, whereas collectivists rely on shared interests, group norms, and common goals to inform their decision making (Hartung, Speight, & Lewis, 1996). For many people the emphasis on individualism found within numerous theories of career development generated in the United States does not mesh with worldviews in which the family or group is the principal arbiter of appropriate occupational choices.

Clearly, Ju-Shin, the client presented at the beginning of this chapter, is in the process of making a career decision from a collectivistic perspective. Another illustration of this point is provided by the career counseling case of Munier. Having recently relocated to the United States from Iraq, Munier came to the career services office during his first year in college concerned about whether poor performance in his physics and math courses would prevent him from being able to major in chemical engineering. In the course of meeting with Munier it became obvious that, although his concerns were projected toward a college major in engineering, his interests and abilities pointed toward a program of study in a nonscience area. In fact, he had failed physics in high school and just barely passed a math course in his first semester of college. He thoroughly enjoyed literature and had performed well in classes related to this area in both high school and college. When asked to discuss his tentative decision to pursue a major in engineering, it quickly became apparent that this decision was based in a collectivistic worldview. His father had made his career plans for him.

When asked about the appropriateness of this goal, given his prior academic performance and his interests, it was clear that Munier was not going to enlarge the range of options under consideration. In this case, a counselor blindly adhering to the need for students to develop traditional, Western career development values of individual action and an internal locus of control may decide to use a counseling strategy that would challenge Munier's tendency to adhere to the wishes of others (his father in this case) rather than to make decisions based on his own sense of what was right for him. The projected treatment plan may even include assertiveness training with the goal of having Munier confront his father about his career development goals. Unfortunately, this type of counseling strategy is not sensitive to Munier's culture of origin, in which it is not uncommon for fathers to dominate the career decision making of their sons. In fact, it is a responsibility that the father takes seriously and a duty about which the child feels strongly. Any attempts at influencing the career direction of Munier would need to be sensitive to this very important cultural dynamic. Culturally diverse students such as Munier must be provided with opportunities to sort through the implications of these cultural differences for their own career development and to learn coping strategies for dealing with differences in cultural expectations. Often, as in the case of Munier, this sorting process must occur within the context of the family.

Such value conflicts illustrate the point that decision making, the development of self-identity, and life choices do not occur in a vacuum. They occur within political, economic, and social conditions that influence the achievement images and belief systems on which individuals base their actions. There are numerous instruments available that can be used to assess the worldview construct. For example, the Career-in-Culture Interview (Ponterotto, Rivera, & Sueyoshi, 2000) and the Person-in-Culture Interview (Berg-Cross & Zoppetti, 1991) are examples of useful assessments for exploring worldview constructs.

ACCULTURATION

Although knowing that specific cultures are oriented toward individualism (e.g., European Americans) or collectivism (e.g., Asian Americans) is useful, it is also inappropriate to apply this knowledge to clients in a stereotypical fashion (e.g., "All European Americans are individualistic,"

"All Asian Americans are collectivistic"). Thus, another important variable to assess in understanding the client's worldview is that of acculturation. Acculturation can be defined as "the process of adopting the cultural traits or social patterns of another group" (Stein, 1975, p. 10). Results of acculturation research conducted in the United States have indicated that English-language proficiency is one of the best measures of acculturation (Fouad, 1993). However, acculturation is a complex and multifaceted process.

Early models of acculturation (e.g., Park & Burgess, 1921) were based on assumptions that reflected an either/or perspective toward acculturation (e.g., one either accepted the "new" culture and rejected the "old," or one rejected the "new" and maintained acceptance of the "old" culture). Inherent in such models is the notion of the *marginal person* (Park, 1928). The marginal person is someone who is psychologically caught between two cultures. Marginal persons hold negative views toward both their own culture and the host culture, such as when a Chinese American woman is unwilling to give unquestioned obedience to the traditional values of her Chinese parents but also finds it difficult to accept many of the values inherent in a European American culture associated with racist attitudes and behaviors (Leong & Brown, 1995). Such instances often result in the experience of an identity crisis characterized by chronic restlessness, self-consciousness, and feelings of inferiority (Atkinson, Morten, & Sue, 1993).

More recent models of acculturation, however, reflect a bicultural perspective toward acculturation. Such models embrace the notion that individuals can be highly acculturated to multiple cultures—a sort of both/and approach versus the earlier either/or models. Nguyen and Benet-Martinez (2013) conducted a meta-analysis examining the relationship between biculturalism and adjustment. Their analysis included 83 studies with a combined total of 23,197 participants. Results indicate a strong, significant, and positive relationship between biculturalism and adjustment (both psychological and sociocultural). Moreover, the link between biculturalism and adjustment is stronger than the association between a singular orientation with one culture and adjustment. These results invalidate those who viewed the bicultural person as a marginal person "caught between the conflicting values of two cultures and consequently feels little commitment to either" (Atkinson et al.). In contrast, the bicultural person "feels committed to both cultures and selectively embraces the positive aspects of each culture" (p. 23). Thus, the client's level of acculturation is an important within-group variable that must be addressed to provide appropriate career interventions.

It is important that counselors do not assume that the client's level of acculturation is at the same level as the client's family. Differences in this regard are important to address in the career development intervention process—especially for young people attempting to crystallize initial occupational preferences. Grieger and Ponterotto (1995) noted that it is not uncommon for first-generation, U.S. college students to experience cultural or bicultural strain and, consequently, conflict when their families' level of acculturation is at variance with their own. This could have been the case with Munier had he been oriented to more Western notions concerning the career decision-making process rather than the values inherent in his culture of origin.

IDENTITY DEVELOPMENT MODELS

Identity development models provide useful frameworks for understanding the process of identity development as it relates to key cultural variables, the individual, the environment in which the individual lives, and the ongoing interaction effects between the person and the environment.

Racial Identity Models

Models of racial identity help us understand that the status of racial identity (for both counselors and clients) can influence the career development intervention process at several levels. For example, Atkinson, Morten, and Sue (1989, 1993, 1998) describe five stages of racial identity development, each with corresponding counseling implications: (a) conformity, (b) dissonance, (c) resistance and immersion, (d) introspection, and (e) synergistic articulation and awareness.

Individuals in the *conformity* stage adhere to the dominant culture's value system, including its perception of racial/ethnic minorities. Their self-perceptions, as well as their perceptions of others, are viewed through the lens of the dominant culture. They tend to deny the existence of racism and discriminatory treatment on the part of the dominant culture and have a strong desire to "assimilate and acculturate" (Atkinson et al., 1993, p. 29). Moreover, their attitudes toward members of their own group may be very negative. In other words, individuals in the conformity stage may experience feelings of racial self-hatred as a result of cultural racism. Because of their strong identification with the dominant culture, individuals in the conformity stage may express a preference for a career counselor from the dominant culture. In the career development intervention process, they may display a high level of compliance and a need to please the counselor. Atkinson et al. (1993) suggest that these clients are likely to present career concerns that are most amenable to career development interventions focused on problem-solving approaches.

Individuals often move gradually into the *dissonance* stage, but the occurrence of significant events can serve as a catalyst for propelling a person into the dissonance stage. In either scenario, the process of movement into the dissonance stage typically occurs when the individual in the conformist stage encounters a person or situation that runs counter to conformist-stage beliefs (e.g., when an Asian American in the conformist stage, and thus adhering to negative stereotypes regarding the Asian culture, encounters a person who expresses pride in her Asian heritage, or when an African American in the conformist stage experiences racism on a personal level). In such instances, information is acquired that suggests alternative views toward the culture of origin (e.g., that there are positive aspects in cultural traditions, values, and customs) and the dominant culture (e.g., certain behaviors and practices in the dominant culture are discriminatory). Such information causes denial to break down and opens a window to further identity development. Specifically, individuals moving from conformity to dissonance may increasingly engage in self-exploration regarding self-concepts, identity, self-esteem, and group affiliation (Atkinson et al., 1989). Career development practitioners working with individuals in the dissonance stage need to have a thorough understanding of the individual's culture of origin.

Individuals adhering to beliefs and attitudes reflecting Atkinson et al.'s (1989) third stage of racial identity development, *resistance and immersion*, tend to reject the views and values of the dominant culture. They express a complete endorsement of the views and values of their culture of origin. In addition, their resolution of the confusion experienced in the dissonance stage often leads to intense anger as they become more aware of racism and how it has impacted their lives. Sue and Sue (1990) note that as individuals begin to question their feelings of cultural shame, they often experience guilt and anger for having "sold out in the past and contributed to his/her own group's oppression, and anger at having been oppressed and 'brainwashed' by the forces in the dominant society" (cited in Atkinson et al., 1993, p. 31). Individuals in this stage often view oppression as the primary source of their career development concerns. Atkinson et al. suggest that individuals in this stage tend not to seek counseling, but if they do it is likely to be with an ethnically similar counselor and for more crisis-like concerns. Individuals in the resistance and immersion stage may also prefer group career counseling that is action oriented and directed toward challenging racism. Sue and Sue point out that counselors, regardless of their degree of similarity to their clients, will be challenged concerning their own racism and role in society by clients in the resistance and immersion stage.

As individuals begin to experience discomfort with the rigidly held beliefs characterizing the resistance and immersion stage (e.g., "All Whites are bad"), they begin to focus on greater individual autonomy. That is, as they move into the *introspection* stage they begin to entertain the notion that perhaps not everything in the dominant culture is negative. Instead of holding on to blind adherence to positive or negative views toward cultural systems, there is a greater need to examine the merits of any particular cultural system on a more personal level. This notion emerges as a greater sense of security is experienced with one's own racial identity. As the individual becomes more autonomous, a more personal value system is developed. Atkinson et al. (1993) suggest that the emerging need for personal freedom in the face of a preponderant identification with their culture of origin often leads individuals to seek counseling to sort through the growing tension created by these conflicting dynamics. In such instances, career counselors who are similar to clients in race and ethnicity are often preferred; however, counselors from other cultures may be accepted if they share an appreciation for the client's cultural dilemma. Atkinson et al. suggest an approach that emphasizes self-exploration and decision making when working with clients in the introspection stage.

The final stage of the Atkinson et al. (1989) model is *synergistic articulation and awareness*. Individuals in this stage objectively examine the cultural values of their own group as well as those espoused by the dominant group. They accept or reject cultural values based on their experiences in earlier stages of identity development. They experience a genuine desire to eliminate all forms of oppression in society. Consequently, individuals in the synergistic stage tend to experience a sense of self-fulfillment regarding their cultural identity. Atkinson et al. suggest that because clients in this stage have developed "the internal skills and knowledge necessary to exercise a desired level of personal freedom ... attitudinal similarity between the client and counselor becomes a more important determinant of counseling success than membership-group similarity" (p. 36).

The model developed by Atkinson and his colleagues has similarities with Nigrescence theory of Black identity development first articulated by Cross (1971) in the early 1970s and then revised in 1995. Cross notes that Nigrescence theory essentially describes a resocializing experience that Cross (1995) describes as "the transformation of a preexisting identity (a non-Afrocentric identity) into one that is Afrocentric" (p. 97). The first stage in the Cross model is labeled as the *pre-encounter* stage. In this stage, persons often place values in things other than in their Blackness (e.g., religious beliefs, occupation). Some individuals, however, adhere to anti-Black attitudes reflected in hatred for other Blacks. Persons in the pre-encounter stage often favor Eurocentric cultural perspectives.

The *encounter* stage is the second stage in the Cross model. Cross (1995) notes that the encounter stage in the Nigrescence process "pinpoints circumstance and events that are likely to induce identity metamorphosis" (p. 104). Rather than a single event, the encounter stage more often involves a series of episodes that moves the person toward Nigrescence over time. These episodes create dissonance as the person discovers that there is another level of "Blackness" to which he or she should aspire. This realization tends to be accompanied by powerful emotional experiences (e.g., guilt, intense anger toward Whites). These experiences often create the opportunity for a more Afrocentric person to emerge.

The third stage in the Cross model is a transition stage labeled as *immersion-emersion*. Immersion reflects the process of immersing oneself in the "world of Blackness" (Cross, 1995, p. 107). The strong emotions emerging during the encounter stage provide the driving force for this intense *immersion* experience. Eventually, the person *emerges* from the emotionality of the immersion period and experiences a leveling off and greater control of his or her emotions. The new identity begins to be internalized.

The fourth stage in the Cross model is *internalization*. In this stage, the person ascribes high salience to his or her Blackness. Cross (1995) suggests:

> The internalized identity seems to perform three dynamic functions in the everyday life of a person: (a) to defend and protect a person from psychological insults that stem from having to live in a racist society, (b) to provide a sense of belonging and social anchorage, and (c) to provide a foundation or point of departure for carrying out transactions with people, cultures, and human situations beyond the world of Blackness. (p. 113)

The final stage is labeled as *internalization-commitment*. The main difference between blacks in the internalization or internalization-commitment stages is that in the latter there is a commitment to Black affairs that is expressed over an extended period of time. Future research in the Cross model will focus on fostering a more differentiated understanding of the internalization-commitment stage.

Cross and Strauss (1998) identified three functions of Black identity that describe how cultural identity statuses can help African Americans adapt to their environment: bonding, buffering, and bridging. Career counselors and their African American clients can clarify how clients' identity statuses function to support their affiliation with Black people (bonding) and non-Black people (bridging), and protect them from discriminatory encounters (buffering).

Gender Identity Models

Gender relates to differences in masculinity and femininity. Individual and societal expectations for men and women may differ across cultures, but we are all influenced by gender and gender expectations. Having a clear understanding of the influence of gender in career development is critical to providing appropriate career development interventions. Sex-role socialization exerts a powerful influence on girls and boys early in life (Gottfredson, 1981, 2002; Hageman & Gladding, 1983).

Stereotypically, this influence reinforces competition and skill mastery in boys and relationships and connectedness in girls (Gilligan, 1982). As men and women enter the workforce, sex-role socialization continues as women are often confronted with discrimination in selection and promotion practices. Such practices not only limit the opportunity for women to advance in the workplace, but they also limit opportunities to receive mentoring because women are excluded from the informal social networks often used by men to advance in their occupations. Greater than 90% of workers employed as secretaries, dental hygienists, preschool and elementary school teachers, and speech therapists are women (Bureau of Labor Statistics, 2010). Nearly the opposite is true with regard to women working in engineering and other science-related occupations.

The influence of socialization is not felt only by women, however. Men are expected to achieve and to be ambitious in their occupational pursuits. Many consider those men who are striving to achieve a balance in their life roles as lacking in ambition and the desire to work hard to achieve success. Moreover, men employed in occupations typically populated by women (e.g., men working as day care providers, nurses, or clerical workers) are often viewed as overly feminine. Many men who place a high value on family involvement and career achievement experience increased rates of depression as they struggle to fulfill roles in both of these life domains (Lease, 2003).

Differential socialization of the sexes has led to their unequal representation within occupations. As Herr et al. (2004) have written, "The fact that many occupations are sex-traditional simply perpetuates sex-role stereotypes, sustaining the division of labor as a self-fulfilling prophecy" (p. 260). Such sex-role stereotyping occurs beyond the life role of the worker. In a review of recent research related to life-role salience, Niles and Goodnough (1996) noted the significant influence of societal expectations on life-role participation. For example, it is a consistent finding that women place greater importance on the home and family than do men. It is also evident that those women who place importance both on work and on home and family are at risk for experiencing role conflict. For male-female couples, this conflict is exacerbated by the fact that men consistently report lower participation in the home and family role when compared with women. In this regard, it is important that men identify ways in which they can participate in activities within the home and family role that will allow them to express important values in this life role. Given the centrality of work in male identity, the exploration of fears and resistance to committing more time to home and family must often be addressed within the career development intervention process. Cook (1994) noted that in terms of life-role participation, "behaving differently may seem to be a practical option but it may feel like a gender role violation, or alternatively, a personal affirmation that had not been considered because of its novelty" (p. 90). To be clear, we are not suggesting that increased participation in home and family on the part of men will eliminate work-home role conflict; rather, a more likely outcome may be that this burden will be more equally shared.

To help achieve the goal of integrating gender in the career development intervention process, Gysbers et al. (2009) recommend using gender-related identity development models. For example, they cite a feminist identity development model proposed by Downing and Roush (1985). This model consists of five stages: (a) Stage 1: passive acceptance, (b) Stage 2: revelation, (c) Stage 3: embeddedness-emancipation, (d) Stage 4: synthesis, and (e) Stage 5: active commitment.

Stage 1 involves the passive acceptance of sexism and discrimination. There is an implicit, if not explicit, acceptance of sex-traditional gender roles. Stage 2 occurs when a life event exposes oppression of women in a way that cannot be denied (e.g., a woman may directly experience discrimination in job hiring or promotion). Stage 3 is characterized by the perception that men possess only negative traits (e.g., "Men are not trustworthy," "All men treat women unfairly") and women possess only positive traits. There is a strong desire to separate from men and bond only with other women. All men are viewed as oppressors, and all women are viewed as victims. In Stage 4, women view men as individuals rather than automatically considering all men to be members of an oppressive group. Women are also evaluated on an individual basis. The influence of internal and external factors is recognized in the behavior of both sexes. Finally, individuals in Stage 5 become actively involved in managing their career development and in changing oppressive environmental influences.

Oppressive environmental influences restricting the career development of women occur in the home, school, community, and workplace. Stereotypes are perpetuated pervasively in books, movies, television shows, and magazines. These stereotypes often result in women encountering issues such as the "glass ceiling" (i.e., the barring of women from upper levels of administration and leadership), a lack of available mentors, discrimination in hiring, sexual harassment, inadequate and unaffordable child-care options, and a general lack of support for women aspiring to nontraditional occupations. Gysbers, Heppner, and Johnston (2003) contend that "understanding feminist identity development may help us learn a great deal more about our clients' reactions to the gendered environment. For example, a woman whose attitudes and beliefs are at Stage 1 may either be unaware of, or actually accepting of, sex bias, whereas a client in the middle stages may prefer a female counselor and may benefit from processing the anger she feels about sexism" (p. 95).

To address inadequacies in career theories as they relate to the career development of women, Cook, Heppner, and O'Brien (2002) propose using an ecological perspective to help illuminate the dynamic interaction between the person and the environment. Cook and her associates suggest that an ecological perspective is particularly useful in addressing the White, male, and Western experiences and worldviews implicit in career counseling models. They note that an ecological perspective encourages greater sensitivity to ways in which environmental factors do not support the career development of women. Specifically, Cook et al. note the need for career counselors to address the following assumptions that are implicit in career development models: (a) the separation of work and family roles in people's lives, (b) the emphasis on individualism and autonomy, (c) the view that work is the central activity in people's lives, (d) the notion that career development is a linear and rational process, and (e) the White, male bias existing in the occupational opportunity structure. In addition, Cook and her colleagues emphasize the need for career counselors to address ways in which female clients experience the macrosystem imperatives concerning caring for others (i.e., how the client assigns importance to the needs of significant others and family members in her career development); how women might be able to influence their microsystems (e.g., the workplace) through learning or refining negotiation skills to enable them to ask for what they need (e.g., more flexible work hours, salary increases); how to identify and access quality child care; empowering women to handle sexual harassment in the workplace, and, therefore, lessen the likelihood of victimization; and helping women to access mentors. Of course, each of these issues provides opportunities for macrosystem (e.g., advocating for equitable workplace policies and treatment) and microsystem (e.g., within the career counseling relationship) interventions. Focusing on the career development experience of young women, Frome, Alfeld, Eccles, and Barber (2006) investigated why some young women who espouse occupational aspirations within male-dominated fields during adolescence relinquish these aspirations by the time they attain young adulthood. Their findings from a longitudinal data set indicate that the desire for a flexible job, the high time demands of an occupation, and the low intrinsic valuing of physical science predicted shifting occupational aspirations out of male-dominated fields. Concern for balancing family and career combined with a lower value for science-related domains (and perhaps a lack of societal and/or familial support) continue to influence women away from occupations in traditionally male-dominated fields, where, in fact, their abilities and goals may reside. Relatedly, Louis (2006) shared her personal experience as a scientist and mother. She contends that the confidence mothers have in their careers is correlated with the quality of their children's care and challenges employers to provide the necessary infrastructure that scientist-mothers need to succeed.

Integrating gender into the career development intervention process is important in working with men as well. Men are socialized to value power, competition, action, strength, logic, and achievement (O'Neil, 1982). They are taught to avoid emotional intimacy and to fear femininity (Skovholt, 1990). O'Neil contended that this type of socialization process results in men being restricted in self-disclosure and in experiencing various physical and emotional problems. The push toward achievement and success leads many men to overemphasize work activity and to minimize their activity in the home and family (Niles & Goodnough, 1996). Many men realize too late in life that they have frequently missed opportunities to connect more meaningfully with their partners and/or children. Providing men with opportunities (via individual and/or group career counseling) to explore how the socialization process influences their career behavior, to learn how to express their feelings, to learn how to manage and reduce stress, and to identify strategies for participating more fully in life roles beyond work are important components of career development interventions for this population.

Understanding the identity development status of men can help career development practitioners provide appropriate career development interventions. In this respect, it can be argued that a model of identity development similar to the one offered by Downing and Roush (1985) could also be applied to men. For example, a man whose attitudes and beliefs are at Stage 1 (i.e., passive acceptance) may be unaware of his acceptance of sex bias in his career behavior, whereas a client in the middle stages may prefer a male counselor and may benefit from processing the anger he feels about pressure to compete, achieve, and succeed at work. Men at Stage 5 (active commitment) may find male support groups helpful in maintaining behaviors that do not coincide with sex-role stereotyping (e.g., spending more time in nurturing activities related to the home and family role). Helping men to understand the importance of actively engaging in life roles beyond work and supporting them in these involvements (e.g., by offering support groups) may empower men to move toward a less constricted range of life-role involvements. This outcome benefits men, women, and children.

Lesbian/Gay/Bisexual/Transgender/Questioning Identity Models

There has been little research in the career development of lesbian, gay, bisexual, transgender, and questioning people (LGBTQ). Because each of these groups experiences oppression, Morgan and Brown (1991) suggested using minority career development theories to describe the career development experiences of persons who are LGBTQ. Although there is undoubtedly significant overlap due to oppressive environmental conditions, this suggestion offers, at best, a temporary solution to the lack of theory and research pertaining to these populations. However, as with racial and gender identity, the assessment of identity development levels of LGBTQ clients represents a crucial element in the career counseling process (Chung, 2003; Datti, 2009; Morgan & Brown, 1991; Paul, 2008; Pepper & Lorah, 2008; Pope, 1995). When working with LGBTQ clients, Orzek (1992) noted that counselors must understand the meaning that their clients attach to their sexual identity to construct career development interventions that mesh with their clients' stages of identity development.

According to Cass (1979), LGBTQ persons encounter six stages of identity development: (a) confusion, (b) comparison, (c) tolerance, (d) acceptance, (e) pride, and (f) synthesis. The stages in the Cass model parallel those in racial identity models. The Cass model proposes that, as progression is made through the six stages, LGBTQ persons experience an enhanced sense of self-acceptance and self-esteem; they become increasingly empowered to form a stronger community with other gay, lesbian, and bisexual individuals; they feel more comfortable in disclosing their sexual orientation; and they experience more congruence between their feelings and behaviors. Sophie (1986) proposed the following four-stage model of lesbian identity development:

1. Self-awareness of LGBTQ feelings without disclosing those feelings to others
2. Testing and exploration of emerging LGBTQ identity with limited disclosure to straight persons

3. Identity acceptance and preference for gay social interactions
4. Identity integration with movement from a dichotomous worldview to a more integrated worldview

Chapman and Brannock (1987) developed a five-stage model of lesbian identity development. Fassinger (1995) described this model as follows:

1. Being aware of a same-sex orientation but lacking a name for those feelings
2. Dissonance and confusion about dating men
3. Self-questioning and exploration of attraction to other women
4. Identification as a lesbian
5. Engaging in a long-term lesbian relationship (p. 151)

Chung (2003) conducted a strengths, weaknesses, opportunities, and threats (SWOT) analysis of the literature related to career counseling with LGBTQ persons. He identified several strengths within the existing literature. For example, Chung noted that recently numerous researchers have engaged in studying the career behavior of LGBTQ persons through the application of existing career theories (e.g., Holland, Super, and social cognitive career theory [SCCT]). Chung also noted the important contributions of researchers, such as Fassinger (1995) and Prince (1995), who have applied lesbian identity development and gay male identity development models, respectively, to career behavior. A third recent and important development within the literature noted by Chung has been the more focused attention given to career issues experienced by LGBTQ persons (e.g., sexual identity disclosure and management, work discrimination, and discrimination coping strategies). Future research is needed that integrates the latter body of research into theoretical models. In addition to the need for more theory-based research in this area, Chung calls for researchers to engage in more programmatic research efforts to advance understanding of the career development of LGBTQ persons. Finally, Chung highlights the fact that research related to the career development of lesbian and bisexual persons lags behind research efforts focused on gay men; thus, there is the important need for additional research in these areas in particular.

More recently, Chung, Williams, and Dispenza (2009) investigated the validity of Chung's (2001) work discrimination and coping strategy models for sexual minorities. Chung's Work Discrimination model describes work discrimination using three dimensions: (a) formal versus informal, (b) perceived versus real, and (c) potential versus encountered. Formal discrimination refers to official policies that affect an employee's employment status (e.g., being fired, promoted). Informal discrimination refers to the existence of a hostile workplace. Perceived discrimination refers to one's perceptions that behaviors are discriminatory. Real discrimination is based on actual experiences. Potential discrimination refers to possible discrimination that would occur should a person's sexual identity become known. "Encountered discrimination involves discriminatory acts that the person experiences. Collectively, these three dimensions (2 × 2 × 2) describe eight types of work discrimination (e.g., perceived-potential-formal discrimination, real-encountered-informal discrimination)" (Chung et al., p. 163).

The second dimension of Chung's model is the coping strategy framework. The first part of this framework involves the Vocational Choice model. Three vocational choice strategies are identified in this model. The first, self-employment, involves being one's own boss in order to avoid a discriminatory workplace. The second, job tracking, involves assessing whether an occupation and/or particular position is welcoming to sexual minorities. The third, risk taking, involves choosing a vocational option knowing that there is the risk for encountering discrimination. The second dimension of the coping strategy framework is the Identity Management model. This refers to "how a person decides to manage disclosure of information about his or her sexual identity for the purpose of dealing with potential discrimination" (Chung et al., 2009, p. 163). Strategies for identity management range from acting (pretending to be straight) to being explicitly out as a sexual minority.

Chung's third coping strategy model is Discrimination Management, which involves how a person responds to discrimination when it is encountered. Strategies here include quitting, remaining silent, drawing on social support, and confronting the discrimination directly. The Vocational Choice and Identity Management models deal with formal and informal potential discrimination. Discrimination Management focuses on responding to formal and informal discrimination. Coping strategies are selected based on the discrimination encountered. Chung et al. (2009) offer three important recommendations for career counselors working with clients who are sexual minorities. Specifically, they note that it is important to help clients understand that discrimination can be formal and informal regardless of nondiscrimination policies. Chung and his associates also suggest that it is important to help clients achieve realistic and accurate perceptions regarding discrimination and that they develop the capacity to accurately assess potential and encountered discrimination. Career counselors can help clients explore various options for coping with workplace discrimination using the strategies that Chung (2001) identifies. While engaging in such exploration with a client, it is very important that career counselors remain sensitive to the client's pace of identity development and cultural context. That is, career counselors should not push clients toward more self-affirming and assertive coping strategies if they are not ready for such strategies (Chung et al.).

Datti (2009) provides an example of how social learning theory can be used in career counseling with lesbian, gay, bisexual, transgender, and questioning young adults. Datti stresses the importance of including in initial assessments topics that adequately address issues that are significant to the career development of LGBTQ clients. For example, career counselors can help LGBTQ clients consider topics such as their perceived importance of separating personal and professional roles, their comfort in working with a variety of individuals, their interest in working for organizations that have tolerance and discrimination policies, their comfort level with disclosure of their sexual orientation, and whether they have developed a social support network. Assessing these factors can provide information about client attitudes as well as whether clients have developed career-related task-approach skills that are important for LGBTQ clients in managing their careers effectively.

Pope and Barret (2002) also note the need for more research related to the career development experiences of persons who are gay, lesbian, bisexual, or transgender. Using the extant literature, Pope and Barret identify several intervention strategies for career counselors working with gay and lesbian clients. For example, as a first step for career counselors, Pope and Barret stress the importance of counselors taking a personal inventory of ways in which subtle or unconscious biases may influence career counseling (e.g., when a heterosexually oriented career counselor attempts to move a young man toward becoming more masculine in his behaviors). Pope and Barret also stress the importance of becoming more familiar with gay and lesbian culture (e.g., by attending workshops, reading relevant literature, participating in lesbian/gay culture). They note the ethical necessity for career counselors who cannot be gay/lesbian affirmative to refer clients to a career counselor who has experience with sexual minorities and can work with clients in a more affirming manner. With regard to "client-focused" career interventions, Pope and Barret highlight helping clients to cope effectively with issues such as "coming out," dealing with workplace discrimination, negotiating dual-career couples' concerns (e.g., benefits issues, relocation issues), and the selection/use of assessment instruments. In addition to client-focused interventions, Pope and Barret discuss program-focused interventions. Recommended interventions in this category include sharing information on existing gay/lesbian community resources, offering special programming such as talks by gay/lesbian professionals, arranging career shadowing opportunities with gay/lesbian workers, maintaining a list of "out" gay/lesbian individuals who are available for information interviews, facilitating experiential opportunities (e.g., internships, externships) with gay/lesbian-owned or -operated businesses, and establishing mentoring programs with gay/lesbian mentors. Finally, Pope and Barret stress the importance of career counselors engaging in advocacy or social action interventions. For example, positive advocacy for gay and lesbian clients could include lobbying for the inclusion of sexual orientation in nondiscrimination policies of local employers.

Persons with Disabilities

Persons with disabilities represent another group that commonly experiences discrimination in career development. "Individuals with disabilities lag behind those without disabilities in virtually every indicator of economic activity" (Ettinger, 1996, p. 239). For example, only 31% of persons with disabilities who were also college graduates were employed in 2009 (compared with 81% of those who were not disabled and possessed only high school degrees) (Innovative Placements, 2010). The average annual income for a person with disabilities is about $33,000 compared to $44,269 for persons without disabilities. Despite these facts, career development researchers pay little attention to the career experiences of persons with disabilities. For example, an examination of the last ten reviews of the literature contained in the December 2014 issue of *The Career Development Quarterly*, considered by many career experts to be the most thorough annual review of the career development literature, revealed that more often than not, little attention is paid to the career literature pertaining to persons with disabilities. Even scholars who call on the profession to engage in more advocacy often fail to identify the near silence that exists on behalf of persons with disabilities. This is perplexing given that one in five Americans (54.4 million) has a disability (U.S. Census Bureau, 2015). Clearly, this is an embarrassing, and inexcusable, gap in the career development literature.

Herr et al. (2004) define a person with disabilities as "one who is usually considered to be different from a normal person—physically, physiologically, neurologically, or psychologically—because of accident, disease, birth, or developmental problems" (p. 280). The Americans with Disabilities Act of 1990 (ADA) identifies a person with disabilities as:

> A person who has physical or mental impairment that substantially limits one or more "major life activities," or has a record of such an impairment, or is regarded as having such an impairment. Examples of physical or mental impairments are contagious and noncontagious diseases and conditions such as orthopedic, visual, speech, and hearing impairments, cerebral palsy, epilepsy, muscular dystrophy, multiple sclerosis, cancer, heart disease, diabetes, mental retardation, emotional illness, specific learning disabilities, HIV disease, tuberculosis, drug addiction, and alcoholism. "Major life activities" include functions such as caring for oneself, performing manual tasks, walking, seeing, hearing, speaking, breathing, learning, and working. (U.S. Department of Justice, 1991, pp. 3–4)

The ADA stipulates that employers can consider only essential job functions when hiring or promoting employees. Employers may require prospective employees to demonstrate how they will perform specific job-related functions. Although employers can make employment decisions based on job-related qualifications, they cannot make employment decisions based on reasons that are related to the person's disability.

In addition, employers must provide reasonable accommodations to qualified individuals with disabilities to enable them to do the essential functions of a job, unless the change imposes undue hardship on the employers. Those desiring more information about the ADA can write to the Office of the Americans with Disabilities Act, Civil Rights Division, U.S. Department of Justice, Box 66118, Washington, DC 20035–6118. (See Figure 4.1.)

Zunker (2006) identifies several career development issues that typically confront persons with disabilities. Specifically, he notes that issues related to adjusting to disabilities (as when people experience physical trauma and then have difficulty adjusting to and accepting their disability) include confronting attitudinal barriers based on misinformation and discriminatory beliefs; overcoming generalizations formed as a result of being labeled disabled or handicapped; having a lack of role models and norm groups; coping with issues associated with the age of onset of disability; developing social/interpersonal skills; developing a positive self-concept; and developing skills for independent living. These issues each require specific career development interventions to facilitate the career development of persons with disabilities.

For those lacking role models, exposure to employed individuals with similar disabilities can serve as an important source of self-efficacy enhancement (Bandura, 1986). Cook (1981) noted that those having difficulty adjusting to their disability due to physical trauma might need assistance in coping with grief associated with losing their prior level of functioning. Zunker (2006) notes that those experiencing a disability at an early age may require assistance in developing assertiveness and independence, and those experiencing the onset of a disability in adulthood may need to be reintroduced to the overall career development process. Supported employment (e.g., sheltered workshops) opportunities may help persons with disabilities gain exposure to role models, experience enhanced self-esteem through work-related accomplishments, and develop important interpersonal skills.

Zunker (2006) and Levinson (1994) provide thorough descriptions of the assessment process for people with disabilities. For example, Levinson describes a comprehensive vocational assessment for persons with disabilities as including psychological, social, educational-academic, physical-medical, and vocational functioning assessments. Zunker suggests that vocational evaluations for persons with disabilities could include (in ascending order): gathering biographical data; conducting an evaluation interview; conducting psychological testing; providing opportunities to acquire occupational information and to engage in career exploration; completing work samples; completing situational or workshop tasks; conducting informal conferences with other staff members; offering job tryouts; holding formal staff conferences; and providing vocational counseling for career decision making, implementation, and adjustment to the career choice implemented.

Cummings, Maddux, and Casey (2000) note that much of the career literature related to persons with disabilities focuses on persons with physical disabilities and that little attention is directed toward those with learning disabilities. Persons with learning disabilities often experience challenges that negatively influence their career development. Some common challenges include a failure to understand how personal characteristics relate to career choice, low self-esteem, an inability to engage in self-advocacy, difficulties in establishing routines, difficulties in

General

- Public accommodations such as restaurants, hotels, theaters, doctors' offices, pharmacies, retail stores, museums, libraries, parks, private schools, and day-care centers may not discriminate on the basis of disability. Private clubs and religious organizations are exempt.
- Reasonable changes in policies, practices, and procedures must be made to avoid discrimination.

Auxiliary aids

- Auxiliary aids and services must be provided to individuals with vision or hearing impairments or other individuals with disabilities, unless an undue burden would result.

Physical barriers

- Physical barriers in existing facilities must be removed, if removal is readily achievable. If not, alternative methods of providing the services must be offered, if they are readily achievable.
- All new construction in public accommodations, as well as in "commercial facilities" such as office buildings, must be accessible. Elevators are generally not required in buildings under three stories or with fewer than 3,000 square feet per floor, unless the building is a shopping center, mall, or a professional office of a health care provider.
- Alterations must be accessible. When alterations to primary function areas are made, an accessible path of travel to the altered area (and the bathrooms, telephones, and drinking fountains serving that area) must be provided to the extent that the added accessibility costs are not disproportionate to the overall cost of the alterations. Elevators are required as previously described.

Employment

- Employers may not discriminate against an individual with a disability in hiring or promotion if the person is otherwise qualified for the job.
- Employers can ask about one's ability to perform a job, but cannot inquire if someone has a disability or subject a person to tests that tend to screen out people with disabilities.
- Employers will need to provide "reasonable accommodation" to individuals with disabilities. This includes steps such as job restructuring and modification of equipment.
- Employers do not need to provide accommodations that impose an "undue hardship" on business operations.

Who needs to comply

- All employers with 25 or more employees must comply, effective July 26, 1992.
- All employers with 15–24 employees must comply, effective July 26, 1994.

Transportation

- New public transit buses ordered after August 26, 1990, must be accessible to individuals with disabilities.
- Transit authorities must provide comparable paratransit or other special transportation services to individuals with disabilities who cannot use fixed route bus services, unless an undue burden would result.
- Existing rail systems must have one accessible car per train by July 26, 1995.
- New rail cars ordered after August 26, 1990, must be accessible.
- New bus and train stations must be accessible.
- Key stations in rapid, light, and commuter rail systems must be made accessible by July 26, 1993, with extensions up to 20 years for commuter rail (30 years for rapid and light rail).
- All existing Amtrak stations must be accessible by July 26, 2010.

Figure 4.1

Americans with Disabilities Act requirements specified in the Public Accommodations Fact Sheet.

Source: From *Americans with Disabilities Act Handbook* (Coordination and Review Section), U.S. Department of Justice, Civil Rights Division, 1991, Washington, DC: U.S. Department of Justice.

accurately observing and effectively imitating the work habits of role models, challenges related to information processing, and a tendency toward passive learning styles. Cummings and her associates identify several strategies that career practitioners can use to more effectively address the concerns of persons with learning disabilities. First, and foremost, they note the need for career practitioners to help secondary school students with learning disabilities engage in more systematic transition planning as they move from high school to postsecondary experiences. To achieve this goal, counselors must work to improve the coordination between high schools and postsecondary education and community agencies. Although the Individuals with Disabilities Education Act (IDEA) requires that each student's transition plan include information regarding postsecondary services (e.g., vocational rehabilitation, independent living options), linkages to these services are often not identified for students with learning disabilities. Because college students with learning disabilities often experience lower career decision-making self-efficacy and a more pessimistic attributional style for career decision making than their peers without disabilities (Luzzo, Hitchings, Retish, & Shoemaker, 1999), the need also exists to provide more systematic and adequate transition planning to students with learning disabilities who are moving from high school to postsecondary education. Finally, Cummings and her colleagues advocate for taking a K–12 approach to transition planning. In this regard, Levinson (1998) argues for a three-level transition assessment program for students with learning disabilities. Specifically, Levinson suggests a Level 1 assessment during the elementary school years that focuses on identifying the student's needs, values, abilities, interests, interpersonal skills, and decision-making skills. Assessment outcomes at this level should be connected to transition goals/objectives that focus on career exploration and self-awareness. Level 2 assessments should occur during the middle school years and should involve formal and informal measures related to interests, aptitudes, work habits, and career maturity. Assessment outcomes should be linked to additional career exploration moving toward a narrowing of tentative career options and goals. Level 3 assessment should include work samples and situational assessments and additional emphasis on identifying the student's skills, interests, and career goals. Empowering persons with learning disabilities to engage in effective self-advocacy is also essential.

The challenges experienced by persons with disabilities require career practitioners to work on multiple fronts to provide effective career assistance (Levinson, 1998). For example, because empirically supported career theories for persons with disabilities are lacking, career practitioners must consider how extant theories can be applied to foster understanding of the intra-individual and contextual factors that influence the career development of persons with disabilities. Hypotheses generated in this regard should be subjected to empirical validation to advance general understanding of career development processes for persons with disabilities. To generate sound hypotheses, career practitioners will need to possess specific knowledge that extends beyond a general familiarity with career theories. Specifically, career practitioners will need to have knowledge pertaining to the following:

1. Federal and state legislation, guidelines, and policies applicable to persons with disabilities
2. Types of disability classifications, diagnostic tools or processes, and their limitations
3. Informal assessment procedures for assessing interests, values, goals
4. Characteristics of different types of disabilities, their causes, and their likely effects on work behavior

5. Opportunities available in the local labor market for persons with different types of skills and different types of challenges
6. The meaning of functional limitation and its use in counseling
7. The effects of social stigma, labeling, and stereotyping on the self-concept of persons with disabilities
8. Essential employability skills, the availability of training programs, and occupational and educational opportunities
9. Ways to work effectively with other specialists to facilitate a comprehensive approach to career exploration, career preparation, and career placement of persons with disabilities
10. Examples of job redesign that employers use to accommodate the capabilities and/or functional limitations for persons with various types of disability
11. Methods of developing individual employment plans and individualized educational plans
12. Fears, concerns, and needs of parents or partners of persons with disabilities, and ways to work systemically to foster the career development of persons with disabilities
13. Models of developing daily living, mobility, job search, and work skills
14. Strategies for teaching self-advocacy skills related to accessing disability-related services

Persons with disabilities encounter specific obstacles in their career development that are often due to a lack of awareness and sensitivity on the part of employers, educational institutions, and the general public. Many employers adhere to the false (and stereotypical) beliefs that persons with disabilities will be absent more often, less productive, and less invested in their career development than their nondisabled peers. Evidence exists to suggest hiring discrimination is most often directed toward persons with physical or sensory impairments (McMahon et al., 2008). The provision of effective career development interventions requires practitioners to possess the requisite knowledge, skills, and awareness for adequately addressing the career concerns of persons with disabilities. Many times, this requires career development professionals to play an advocacy role with prospective employers and coworkers to dispel discriminatory myths.

ASSESSMENT

Our discussion of career development interventions for persons with disabilities leads into some important points to consider in conducting career assessments with diverse client populations. Walsh and Betz (1990) defined assessment as "a process of understanding and helping people cope with problems" (p. 12). Often, assessment involves using a test as a "method of acquiring a sample of behavior under controlled conditions" (p. 21). However, as we discussed previously, assessment can also involve activities such as observing client behaviors as they engage in specific work-related tasks, participating in job simulation activities, and engaging the client in a counseling interview to gather both important current information pertaining to the client's career concerns and relevant client biographical data.

Fouad (1993) notes that career counselors must be mindful of the fact that the client's culture plays a significant role throughout all phases of the assessment process. For example, analyzing the client's needs requires counselors to understand a client's worldview. Empathizing with the client from the client's perspective requires counselors to be aware of their own cultural backgrounds and how the client's culture may influence the assessment process. When encouraging clients to discuss their understanding of the assessment results, career counselors must be sure that the client's cultural context is factored into the review process. For example, because the history of Native American identity is typically maintained through oral tradition, a Native American client is likely to define words as powerful and value laden. Thus, the tendency to use words casually may be avoided at all costs (Sage, 1991) and silence may predominate in sessions. Such silences should be allowed to occur naturally and should not necessarily be determined as client resistance. In this regard, many of the points raised by Fischer et al. (1998) concerning multicultural counseling also pertain to conducting culturally appropriate career assessments.

When selecting a test, career counselors must ensure that the instrument is valid, reliable, and appropriate for the client's cultural and linguistic context. Fouad (1993) identified several important issues that must be considered in conducting career assessments across cultures. Specifically, Fouad noted that career counselors must determine whether a test is functionally and conceptually equivalent for the client's culture. Functional equivalence relates to "the role or function that behavior plays in different cultures" (p. 8). Conceptual equivalence "refers to the similarity in meaning attached to behavior or concepts" (p. 8). Fouad also identified metric equivalence (i.e., whether the scales of a test measure the same constructs across cultures) and linguistic equivalence (i.e., whether the translation of items results in equivalent language across cultures) as important areas to address in test selection.

Fouad (1993) also urges career counselors to consider whether systematic bias exists in any test being considered for use in career counseling. For example, content bias exists when test items are more familiar to members of one group than they are to another group. Lack of familiarity with item content obviously places a test taker at a significant disadvantage and leads to spurious test results. Internal structure bias exists when the relationships among items are not consistent across cultural contexts. Finally, selection bias occurs when a test has differential predictive validity across groups.

As with any career development intervention, selecting tests properly requires career counselors to be aware of their own worldviews, a client's worldview, and the psychometric concerns identified by Fouad (1993). Too many times, counselors have disregarded these factors when using tests in career counseling. In such instances, they do a disservice to the client and the profession. When used properly, assessments can provide clients with vital information for resolving their career concerns.

To conduct culturally competent career assessment, career counselors need to possess general counseling skills, multicultural counseling competencies, and career counseling competencies. Flores, Spanierman, and Obasi (2003) note important professional and ethical considerations for conducting career assessments with diverse client populations. Specifically, they remind career counselors that it is important to engage in information gathering, both formally and informally, that is culturally encompassing. Data that career counselors gather through assessment should help not only to identify the client's presenting career concerns but also to help the career counselor understand the client as a cultural being. Gathering data regarding culturally specific variables—such as racial/ethnic identity, acculturation, worldview, socioeconomic status, gender-role expectations, primary language, family expectations, and so on—will help set the cultural context for understanding the client's situation and concerns.

Ponterotto, Rivera, and Sueyoshi (2000) use a culturally sensitive semistructured protocol during career counseling intake sessions. Their "career-in-culture" (CiCl) interview incorporates recent theoretical advancements in multicultural counseling and social cognitive career theory (Lent, Brown, & Hackett, 2002). The CiCl interview focuses on understanding the client from five spheres of career development influence: culture, family, religion, community, and larger society self-view and self-efficacy; barriers and oppression; and narrative and relationship. Questions from each sphere foster a collaborative career counseling relationship and move from a focus on individual-based questions to those more broadly focused on family, religion, culture, and community. For example, the career counselor encourages the client to consider the following:

1. Is there anything you would like to know about me and my role as a career counselor?
2. Tell me about yourself.
3. Tell me about your career concerns and career goals.
4. What are some things that are important to you (and unimportant to you) in a career?
5. What types of occupations were you aware of growing up?
6. Name three things you are good at, and why.
7. Name three things you are not good at, and why you think you are not good at them.
8. Do you believe you can accomplish whatever goals you set for yourself? What might stop you from achieving your goals?
9. Tell me about your cultural background.
10. Tell me about your religious background.
11. How has your family influenced your career goals?
12. How do your career goals match with your family's expectations?
13. Draw a family genogram and tell me about the lives and work experiences of the family members identified.
14. What are some organizations in your community that have influenced you?
15. Who are some of the people in your community who have influenced you?
16. As a _____ (race/ethnicity, female/male, older/younger, gay/lesbian/bisexual/transgender/straight, abled/disabled) person, what do you see as your greatest challenges to pursuing your career goals?

The CiCl draws on social cognitive career theory (SCCT) and multicultural counseling to directly address essential spheres of influence in living and makes clear from the start that these topics are important in considering career concerns.

Scholl (1999) devised the Career Path Tournament as group intervention for middle school through university levels to help students consider the effects of sociological influences on career development. The tournament uses a round-by-round elimination format to achieve the following goals: (a) to stimulate awareness of sociological barriers to career advancement; (b) to increase participants' awareness of feelings (e.g., anger, anxiety, confusion); (c) to gain a better understanding of the career development process as it is reflected in education practices, professional training, and employment practices; and (d) to increase awareness of the need to intentionally cope with discriminatory practices. Herring (2002) provides excellent suggestions for additional group and classroom activities that engage students in the consideration of cultural and sociological influences in career development.

Leong, Hardin, and Gupta (2007) proposed a Cultural Formulation Approach to Career Assessment and Career Counseling (CF). Specifically, the CF encourages career practitioners to attend to the following five dimensions in the career counseling and assessment process: (a) cultural identity, (b) cultural conception of career problems, (c) cultural context and psychosocial environment, (d) cultural dynamics in therapeutic relationship, and (e) an overall cultural assessment. A special issue of the *Journal of Career Development* (Leong, 2010) illustrates the application of the Cultural Formulation Approach using five career counseling case studies involving

African American, Latina/Latino American, American Indian, Asian American, and international student clients.

Degges-White and Shoffner (2002) describe how the Theory of Work Adjustment can be used effectively to provide career counseling with lesbian clients. Casella (2002) describes how Super's theory can also be used to help lesbian clients advance in their career development. Additional interventions—such as those from postmodern theoretical perspectives (e.g., career laddering, "my life as a book," life-role salience questions that incorporate family and societal expectations)—can also be used to acknowledge the central role of culture in shaping identity and career development. Among the many different identities, values, and perspectives that career clients comprise, spiritual and religious dimensions should not be overlooked. First, it may be helpful to distinguish the differences as well as the areas of overlap between spirituality and religion. *Spirituality* can be viewed as a more encompassing term than *religion* in that it includes many different beliefs and practices that can be quite personal and individual. According to Cashwell and Young (2005), it includes "one's beliefs, awareness, values, subjective experience, sense of purpose and mission, and an attempt to reach toward something greater than oneself" (p. 13). Due to the highly individualized nature of the construct, spirituality and spiritual experiences can be difficult to define using strict categories and delineations.

Religion, conversely, is more concrete and comprehensible. It refers to a set of beliefs and practices that are part of a religious institution. It tends to be expressed in ways that are "denominational, external, cognitive, behavioral, ritualistic, and public" (Richards & Bergin, 1997, p. 13). It is a form of spirituality in that religious individuals may feel that they express their spirituality through practices and beliefs that are part of a religious institution (Cashwell & Young, 2005). Persons who identify themselves as spiritual and not religious tend to feel restricted by religious institutions and their dogmas, rituals, and practices, whereas religious persons may feel they identify closely with both terms.

In line with developments in career theory and practice, such as constructionist perspectives and an emphasis on meaning making for clients, religious and spiritual issues are important client components for career counselors to consider. A client's spiritual and/or religious beliefs may impact the way in which the client approaches choosing a major, a career, and switching careers and how he/she perceives career counseling. As with all cultural variables, counselor self-awareness is essential when working with clients from different spiritual and religious backgrounds. Career counselors will be most effective with a client if they deepen their own awareness of their beliefs regarding religion and spirituality as well as the prejudices that accompany those beliefs and how they may impact clients (Hayes, 2002).

RECOMMENDATIONS FOR CULTURALLY EFFECTIVE CAREER COUNSELING

Drawing upon what we have discussed in this chapter thus far, we offer the following recommendations for culturally effective career counseling:

1. Career counselors should, above all, possess essential counseling knowledge, skills, and understanding that reflect multicultural competencies. The possession of these attributes however, does not represent an end state. Rather, it represents a lifelong commitment to self-awareness, learning from others, and professional development.

2. Career counselors should be aware of their own attitudes and values generally, but they should also understand how their own attitudes and values may interact with their client's attitudes and values specifically. A helpful tool to deepen understanding of one's own identities, clients' identities, and the ways in which the two may interact is by using the ADDRESSING framework (Hayes, 2002). Briefly, the ADDRESSING framework stands for **A**ge and generational influences, **D**evelopmental or acquired **D**isabilities, **R**eligion and spiritual orientation, **E**thnicity, **S**ocioeconomic status, **S**exual orientation, **I**ndigenous heritage, **N**ational origin, and **G**ender. Hayes highlights the importance of paying close attention to our own dominant group identities and the ways in which power imbalances based on these dominant group memberships may negatively impact a client. For instance, if a career counselor is a White, Christian male and his client is a Middle Eastern, Muslim female, there might be ways in which the power differential negatively impacts the client and the career counseling relationship. The client may be more submissive and compliant to her career counselor than if her counselor had identities similar to hers. Because race- and culture-related conflicts can have pernicious effects on counseling outcomes (Constantine, 1997), career counselor preparedness for cross-cultural interactions is of utmost importance. Pope-Davis et al. (2002) note the importance of directly addressing counselor-client cultural differences. They found that clients are more satisfied with counseling and perceive their counselors as more multiculturally competent when this occurs.

3. Career counselors should be aware of their client's cultural context, but they should also understand that we are each first and foremost individuals and only secondarily representatives of our specific immediate and distal cultural contexts. Chan (1992) found that the salience of clients' identities fluctuate with the environment. This means that a career counselor working with a client who has multiple identities has to be tentative and refrain from prematurely drawing conclusions about the client's most salient identities. For instance, if a White, straight, male career counselor is working with an Asian American, gay, male, Buddhist college student who is majoring in math, the counselor may arbitrarily view the client's most salient identities as being Asian American and gay, when in reality the client's most salient identities within the career counseling relationship could be his being Buddhist and a math major. Sun (1995) found that when individuals can categorize others into multiple group memberships, they experience less prejudice toward the other. For instance, if a career counselor knows her client as "Lori, the young Native American woman," she may neglect to acknowledge other important aspects of Lori's identity. Lori may be a mother, a food-service worker, and a woman with a learning disability. With this more holistic view of Lori, the career counselor will have less tendency to generalize Lori's experience into a "Native American woman" experience and will in turn experience less prejudiced attitudes toward her and develop a more complete (and accurate) understanding of Lori.

4. Career counselors should empower clients who experience discrimination to "reject the rejection" within discriminatory attitudes and behavior. Discriminatory behavior always reveals much more about the perpetrator than it does about the person being discriminated against. The deficiencies do not reside in a person's skin color, sex, sexual orientation, or ethnicity but in the thinking and behavior of the person committing the discrimination.

5. Career counselors must be sure that they understand how experiences with racist, sexist, homophobic, classist, ageist, and discriminatory practices toward persons who are disabled influence their clients' career development. Certainly, reading can facilitate such understanding. Most times, however, career counselors will need to move to more active attempts at developing their

understanding of discrimination. Regardless of one's demographic characteristics, most of us have areas in which we need to learn more regarding discriminatory experiences. The young, middle-class, gay male with a learning disability most likely has experienced various forms of discrimination; however, he may not have developed an awareness of the ways in which a 45-year-old, Native American, single mother working in a factory experiences barriers in her career development. Participating in social action activities (e.g., volunteering at a homeless shelter if one has never been homeless) helps advance understanding in important ways. Expanding one's social network to include people who look, act, and believe differently can also advance understanding of differences.

6. Career counselors should engage in proactive programming to provide experiential opportunities, information resources, mentoring opportunities, and psychoeducational activities that are relevant to persons from diverse groups. They should provide services in nontraditional locations, enlist the support of leaders representing diverse groups, and implement strategies that make career services more accessible to more people.

7. Career counselors must engage in social action and advocacy to address systemic discrimination. Career counselors cannot simply talk about the importance of society becoming less discriminatory; they must also find ways to become actively engaged in addressing practices that result in artificial limitations being placed on the career development of a person and/or group.

8. Career counselors should engage in programmatic research efforts to develop and advance theories of career development that apply to diverse groups. Often researchers rely on samples of convenience, which, most often, are comprised of traditional college students. Moving beyond samples of convenience requires networking, using the Internet, contacting groups comprised of diverse persons to invite study participation, and using other more aggressive strategies for reaching out to potential study participants.

MyCounselingLab®

Start with Topic 4—Career Development and Counseling Special Populations.

SUMMARY

In the past decade many existing career development theories have been expanded to be more inclusive. New theories with a greater sensitivity toward describing the career development process for diverse populations are emerging (Leong, 2010). Career development practitioners are becoming increasingly sensitive to the fact that treating all clients in the same way is, in fact, discriminatory treatment because such an approach ignores the contextual factors shaping the client's career behavior.

Despite these advances, much more needs to be done. One area of concern in this regard, which has not received adequate attention, relates to the career development experiences of persons who are economically disadvantaged. Blustein (2013) is a leading researcher in this area and has proposed a useful framework that should stimulate more research addressing the career development of those who are economically disadvantaged. Career development interventions still need to be expanded to address both intra-individual and extra-individual variables influencing career behavior. Greater understanding is needed regarding how differences between the career counselor and the client regarding language, social class, ability, status, and, most important, culture, influence the career counseling process.

In short, our pluralistic society has provided an excellent catalyst to making career development theories and interventions more inclusive. It has also provided opportunities for the profession to grow while more effectively serving the needs of greater numbers of people. That said, there is much work yet to be done to increase the degree to which we provide culturally competent career development interventions to all clients and students.

CASE STUDY

Pat is a 17-year-old high school senior who attends a career-technical school in a large city and has taken courses in culinary arts. Pat notes that this decision was based on parental advice: "Dad says I needed to learn something practical." Pat also notes that there is parental pressure for Pat to be self-supporting after high school graduation. Pat's father (Frank) works as a truck driver and is away more than half of every month. Pat's mother (Marie) works as a cashier at a local grocery store. Pat is an only child and feels responsible for providing health care assistance to Marie who is not in good health.

Pat has worked bagging groceries at the same grocery store as Marie ever since age 16. Pat has always felt like a loner and spends much time alone at school. During free time he can often be found at Miller's Pond where he daydreams about writing poetry and acting. However, Pat has low self-efficacy related to both activities and states that "people usually make fun of my poetry and laugh at my dreams related to acting." He does not want to be a chef; he would like to do something that is meaningful but does not know what that would be. Pat states, "I probably am not smart enough to ever amount to much of anything." Frank (Pat's dad) has stated that he expects Pat to be independent when he turns 18 in six months. Pat has come to see you to get some help figuring out "what would be a good job" after high school.

How do you conceptualize Pat's situation? Would it make a difference if he were female or male? Would it make a difference if he were Caucasian or a member of a racial minority? What if Pat had a disability? What if he were gay? Do any of these possible demographic variables influence how you conceptualize Pat's career needs? Do any of them influence how you might work with him? If not, then what is your responsibility in helping Pat prepare for any discrimination he is likely to experience? Is it possible for these factors not to make a difference in a discriminatory world? If they could make a difference in how you conceptualize Pat's situation and how you might work with him, then identify some of the demographic categories and discuss how they would influence your work.

STUDENT ACTIVITIES

1. Identify ways in which you think culture and related factors have influenced your career development. Consider the ways in which your career development has been influenced by your family, your gender, your race, your socioeconomic status, your sexual orientation, your religion, the community in which you were raised, any disabilities you may experience, the area of the country in which you were raised, the country in which you lived, the time in history in which you grew up, and so on. Try to identify an influence from each of these factors. In what ways have these factors supported your career development? In what ways have they presented obstacles to you?

2. As you think about the factors you identified in question 1, imagine what your career

development experience might have been like had these factors been different (e.g., instead of being female you were male; instead of being raised in the United States you were raised in China; instead of being straight, you were gay). What obstacles might you have encountered? In what ways might your support systems have been different?

3. Engage in a discussion with a person who is different from you in terms of race, sex, sexual orientation, disability status, and/or national origin. Ask this person to describe her/his career development experiences. In what ways are your career development experiences similar to this person's? In what ways are they different?

4. Now that you have read about career development theories, consider how these theories may need to be expanded or revised to provide more inclusive descriptions of the career development experiences of more people.

CHAPTER 5

ASSESSMENT AND CAREER PLANNING

Assessment is a process by which you learn about your abilities, likes or interests, personality, and values or those qualities that give you personal satisfaction. I prefer using self-assessment procedures because they directly involve the person in a self-discovery process. I have found that most individuals like knowing more about themselves, creating self-motivation for the process. Another assessment process is the use of tests that some professionals believe are more scientific procedures than self-assessments. In this process, professionals learn information about the person and then filter the data back to that person. Tests rely on creating knowledge about a person in comparison with others. Depending on the situation, the comparability of the validity of either approach is equivalent.

I have been professionally associated with using ability, interest, personality, and value information to identify career goals. I like to remind people that this same information, however, is equally important for several other purposes. Abilities and personalities are involved in the development of self-concepts—critical dimensions of a person and his or her functioning. Also, consider the value self-knowledge plays in relationships. Awareness of similarities and differences, identifying commonalities of interests and values, and being sensitive to personal preference styles all contribute to the dynamics of developing relationships.

In sum, self-knowledge is a critical human development requirement. Assessment is a valuable skill that facilitates this goal.

Thomas Harrington, Ph.D. Professor Emeritus
Northeastern University

MyCounselingLab®

Visit the MyCounselingLab® site for *Career Development Interventions*, Fifth Edition, to enhance your understanding of chapter concepts. You will have the opportunity to practice applying what you learned in the chapter by completing the video- and case-based exercises in the MyLab. Taking the Licensure Quizzes will help you prepare for your certification exam.

The context for making career choices in the 21st century is decidedly different from that of the 20th century. The tasks of occupations are constantly changing. Some occupations are rapidly becoming obsolete while others are emerging. Some experts and agencies even predict that the concept of *occupation* will disappear altogether and that we will think of ourselves as possessing a set of skills that can be applied to work tasks in many different settings, which will produce a variety of products and services. Work is done in a different way in this century; we are now using a constantly expanding array of electronic equipment that has led to a variety of new settings, including working from home, working with team members electronically, and sending work to distant countries because it can be done less expensively there and can easily be sent electronically to a central source. The impact of global recessions and economic crises is that a larger percentage of people will be without a job for significant periods of time and that a larger percentage of people will have to work in jobs that do not coincide with their interests and values.

Not only are jobs different in the 21st century, but so are the people who perform the jobs. The United States is progressively moving from its tradition as a White, Christian nation to one of incredible diversity of all kinds, including age and racial-ethnic background. According to predictions released by the U.S. Census Bureau (2014) for 2012 to 2060, the number of U.S. residents 65 years of age and older will double between 2012 and 2060, changing from 43.1 million to 92.0 million.

Related to racial-ethnic diversity, the non-Hispanic white population is projected to peak in 2024, at 199.6 million, up from 197.8 million in 2012. The Hispanic population will more than double, from 53.3 million in 2012 to 128.8 million in 2060. Consequently, by the end of the period, nearly one in three U.S. residents will be Hispanic, up from about one in six in 2012. The Black population is expected to increase from 41.2 million to 61.8 million over the same period. Its share of the total population is expected to rise slightly, from 13.1% in 2012 to 14.7% in 2060. The Asian population is projected to more than double, from 15.9 million in 2012 to 34.4 million in 2060, with its share of the nation's total population climbing from 5.1% to 8.2% in the same period.

Among the remaining race groups, American Indians and Alaska Natives are predicted to increase by more than half from now to 2060, from 3.9 million to 6.3 million, with their share of the total population edging up from 1.2% to 1.5%. The Native Hawaiian and Other Pacific Islander population is expected to nearly double, from 706,000 to 1.4 million. The number of people who identify themselves as being of two or more races is projected to more than triple, from 7.5 million to 26.7 million over the same period.

The United States is projected to become a majority-minority nation for the first time in 2043. While the non-Hispanic White population will remain the largest single group, no group will make up a majority. Minorities, now 37% of the U.S. population, are projected to comprise 57% of the population in 2060, and the total minority population is expected to more than double, moving from 116.2 million to 241.3 million over the period.

Further, people of the 21st century face many more transitions in their work than their 20th-century counterparts. They need a broader base of general skills, a higher level of knowledge of technology, and a commitment to lifelong learning to upgrade and update their skills. They need to have a better knowledge of the career choice and planning process because they need to use it more often. They have to assume personal responsibility for their careers and financial security because the 20th-century model of the paternalistic corporation has disappeared. They increasingly view career development as an ongoing, lifelong process, one that needs to integrate the various life roles related to work, family, leisure, and community.

These changes in the context and core of career choice and development require a change in the purpose and use of assessment. The first model of career guidance is attributed to Frank Parsons (Miller, 1961), who founded the Boston Vocation Bureau. Parsons (1909) advocated a three-step process that became the basis for what is called the *trait-and-factor* approach of the 20th century. The steps include gaining knowledge of self, gaining knowledge of the world-of-work, and applying decision-making skill to making an occupational choice.

The development of many different kinds of tests in the 20th century, partly encouraged by two world wars during which it was important to identify specific levels of intelligence and ability, provided an array of instruments that people could use to gain knowledge of self. Similarly, it was easy in the 20th century to gain knowledge about the world-of-work. The tasks involved in occupations changed more slowly, and many individuals could assume that they would remain in the same occupation, even with the same organization, for a lifetime, while moving through the stages described by Super (1957) in his early theory. Typically, at least until the 1980s, education for life was attained between the traditional ages of 14 and 22 because the tools and tasks of work remained stable. For these reasons, accomplishing the second step of Parsons's formula for career guidance—gaining knowledge of the world-of-work—was feasible.

So it was that the trait-and-factor approach dominated the 20th century in helping individuals with career choice. The movement was led by giants in the field such as Thorndike, Hagen, Binet, Terman, Kitson, Strong, Kuder, Paterson, Super, and Williamson. Test development was promoted through funding from government agencies, such as the U.S. Employment Service, and by a myriad of for-profit and not-for-profit organizations.

Assessment—defined here as the use of any formal or informal technique or instrument to collect data about a client—should still be valued in the 21st century as a tool used by counselors or by clients themselves to gather data useful in the career planning process. Its most important use is to assist individuals at a given point in time to identify their current interests and skills in order to identify the next educational or vocational choice in the sequence that makes up career development. In the use of assessment there is a danger of leading the client to believe that the process of career planning and choice is simplistic.

Given the changes noted both in the context in which career planning occurs and in the experience of individuals, it is clear that the characteristics of the use of assessment should be markedly different in the 21st century in the following ways:

- The results of assessment tools (such as tests and inventories) should be viewed as *one* piece of data that the client and the counselor use as the client considers career options. Many other sources of data should also be used, including the client's self-knowledge and intentionality, past educational and vocational experience, and the best predictions possible about work demands of the future.
- Assessment should be used less for prediction of valid options, as the future will be different from the present, and more for identifying new concepts of self, needed areas for growth, and new possibilities for exploration.
- The client should be more involved in making a decision about whether to engage in assessment, and for what purposes, and should be viewed as an equal participant in the assessment process, rather than as the receiver of knowledge to which a counselor has some special access and ability to decode.

THE RELATIONSHIP OF ASSESSMENT TO THE CAREER PLANNING PROCESS

The process of career development is complex and continuous, comprising multiple cycles of decision making. Each time a person faces a new career choice in the process, that choice, if informed, is likely to include the steps illustrated in Figure 5.1.

Step 1: Become Aware of the Need to Make Career Decisions

At first glance, this step may appear unnecessary. Psychologists tell us that we are not motivated to take new actions until and unless we are aware that we need to do so. Depending on the work setting, clients may always come to counselors voluntarily. In that case, they do have some awareness of a need to make decisions, or they would not have initiated the contact. In other settings, such as in middle schools or high schools, students may be required to attend a career class or go to a counselor for help with career planning but may, in fact, have no awareness that they need such help or how it may affect their futures. There are some assessment instruments, described later in this chapter, that counselors may administer at this step of the individual's career planning process to provide some information about the degree of awareness that clients have and also about their specific needs as they enter the process.

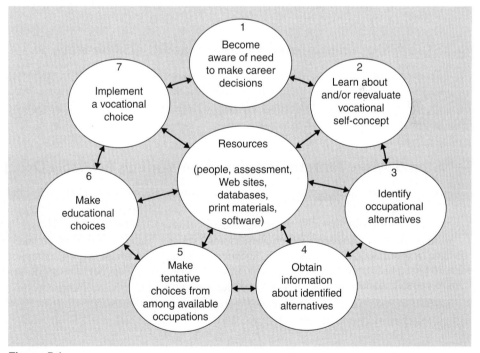

Figure 5.1
The career planning process.

Source: From *The Internet: A Tool for Career Planning,* 2nd edition, by JoAnn Harris-Bowlsbey, Margaret Riley Dikel, and James Sampson, p. 2, published by the National Career Development Association (2002). Used by permission.

Step 2: Learn About or Reevaluate Vocational Self-Concept

We know from the theories of Parsons, Holland, and Super that work is satisfying when people are doing what they like to do (using their interests), when they have the needed skills to do their work (using their abilities), and when they believe their work is important to do (attaining their values). Thus, it is essential to focus on the client, who must focus on self during this step of the process.

In addition to what the counselor learns or helps the client to learn through interviewing, it may also be beneficial to use formal or informal assessment to expand this knowledge or confirm it. Either purpose is very valuable. With informal assessment, the client might be asked to use a checklist, a card sort, or a fantasy. These may be especially effective with clients who have difficulty talking freely in an interview. If formal assessment is used, the counselor might choose inventories or tests of interests, skills, abilities, values, and/or personality characteristics.

Step 3: Identify Occupational Alternatives

At this stage, counselor and client are identifying occupations or jobs in which the client can implement his or her vocational self-concept (Super, Starishevsky, Matlin, & Jordaan, 1963). When assessment is administered in print form, typically there are accompanying manuals that link the client's results to titles of occupations. When assessment is administered by a computer, a customized list of related occupations can be provided as part of the score report.

Step 4: Obtain Information About Identified Alternatives

At this step of the career planning process, clients are encouraged to gather extensive information about possible occupations through reading print materials, using computer databases and Web sites, job shadowing, and information interviewing. Assessment is not typically used at this step of the process.

Step 5: Make Tentative Choices from Among Available Occupations

At this step the client, with the counselor's assistance, is comparing alternatives and attempting to discard some while placing others in priority order. One type of assessment that may be helpful at this stage is formal or informal assessment related to work values. Though occupational alternatives may be identified on the basis of interests, abilities, and/or personality type, values serve as a filter to determine which of many options have highest priority. At this stage a counselor might use a values card sort, checklist, or inventory such as *Super's Work Values Inventory—Revised* (Super & Zytowski, 2006). Follow-through would include the client's investigation to determine the potential of each occupation under consideration to satisfy the work values selected as most important.

Step 6: Make Educational Choices

Educational choices—high school courses, college major, and type and place of postsecondary education—should flow from selection of high-priority occupations. At this stage in the process,

Web sites such as ACT's Map of College Majors (act.org) or the College Board's site (bigfuture. collegeboard.org) might be used to assist the client in identifying possible majors or training specialties. Further, instruments such as the ACT college entrance test (ACT, 2015) or the Scholastic Aptitude Test (SAT) for college entrance (College Entrance Examination Board, 2015) are used for placement (in the case of the ACT) and/or for determining eligibility for entrance to specific schools. The *Armed Services Vocational Aptitude Battery* (see military.com; U.S. Department of Defense, 2005) is an instrument to provide guidance in selecting training programs in the branches of the military, using both interests and abilities as guidelines.

Step 7: Implement a Vocational Choice

At this step, clients enter the job market. Many organizations have their own instruments for screening applicants for jobs. Others use an instrument such as the *Position Classification Inventory* (Holland & Gottfredson, 1991), which determines a Holland code for a specific position, or *WorkKeys* (ACT, 2015b), which profiles a person's skills in 11 areas, comparing them to the level of skills needed in those same areas for specific jobs within an organization.

As indicated by the arrows between the steps of the model in Figure 5.1, the career planning process is cyclical and iterative. Note, for example, that a person may hold a job (Step 7) for a period of time and then move on to Step 1 again because of dissatisfaction with the job or a decision by the employer to reduce the number of employees. Also, note that career deciders may deal with the tasks of one step—such as identifying occupational alternatives (Step 3)—and then return to do more in-depth introspection (Step 2).

Let's use the case of Melissa to illustrate how assessment can be related to the steps of the career planning process described in Figure 5.1. Melissa is a college sophomore whose parents are insisting that she needs to declare a major that will help her get a good job when she graduates. Melissa finally makes an appointment to see a counselor at the university career center. Based on the confusion that she seems to have in the intake interview, the counselor decides to give Melissa a short assessment called the *Career Factors Inventory* (Chartrand, Robbins, & Morrill, 1997) which identifies which of four reasons—Need for Information, Need for Self-Knowledge, Career Choice Anxiety, and Generalized Indecisiveness—are making it difficult for an individual to make career choices. Melissa had very high scores on Need for Information and Need for Self-Knowledge, and these needs were obstructing her awareness (Step 1 of the Career Planning Process) that she needed to move ahead with making career choices.

Because of the high score on the Need for Self-Knowledge scale, the counselor asked Melissa to take the assessments of interests, values, and abilities that comprise the *Career Decision-Making System* (O'Shea & Feller, 2000), an assessment that can be taken in print form or online. Melissa's report from taking it online was sent to her counselor, and then the counselor spent time with Melissa interpreting the score report. The report identified her highest areas of interests and abilities and suggested occupations for her exploration (Steps 2 and 3 of the Career Planning Process).

Both from discussion and from Melissa's high score on Need for Information, the counselor knew that she needed to help Melissa gain information about how occupations are organized in the world of work and especially to learn in depth about the occupations suggested on her score report. So, she gave Melissa the assignment of reading about all of the occupations on her list by using the Web site CareerInfoNet, which not only gives information about job duties and education and training but also about annual salary and job demand in all geographic locations nationwide (Step 4 of the Career Planning Process). Using the results of the values assessment (part of the *Career Decision-Making System*) and a card sort, the counselor helped Melissa establish some criteria for rejecting some occupations and prioritizing the remainder. She also explained information interviewing to Melissa and helped her find at least one person who was working in each of her top three occupations. Through this process, Melissa accomplished Step 5, choosing top-priority occupations, of the Career Planning Process.

Now that Melissa was feeling much more confident about her self-knowledge and occupational knowledge, she was able to choose a major by using the *Educational Opportunities Finder* (Psychological Assessment Resources, 2015), which organizes majors by Holland codes, because she learned her Holland code and its meaning when she took the interest assessment as a part of the *Career Decision-Making System*. She was then able to declare her major, thus completing Step 6 of the Career Planning Process. In a couple of years she will be ready to search for a job (Step 7) that should be satisfying.

Purposes of Assessment

Assessment should not be used unless there is a specific reason for doing so, a reason that both the client and counselor understand. Often, the findings identified through formal or informal assessment could be learned through an interview, a type of informal assessment. Choosing to substitute interviewing for more formal assessment depends on whether the counselor possesses knowledge comprehensive enough to sample the domains (such as areas of career maturity, interests, skills, and values) typically covered by assessment and has sufficient time to devote to comprehensive interviewing. Given the demands of time and knowledge in multiple domains, counselors typically rely on assessment for data gathering, both to alleviate these time and knowledge demands and to take advantage of the considerable benefits that scientific rigor adds to assessment.

What are the reasons that counselors ask their clients to spend time and perhaps money to engage in assessment? They can be summarized in three main categories: (a) learning more about the needs of an individual or group, (b) learning more about the characteristics of individuals and helping them learn more about themselves, and (c) determining the change or progress of an individual or group.

Learning More About the Needs of an Individual or Group

School counselors are charged with helping all students with the career planning process through stages of career awareness (elementary school), exploration (middle school), and career preparation and decision making (high school and postsecondary). They typically accomplish this work through a systematic set of services offered to or required for all, though there is great variability in the needs of subgroups of the population.

In other settings in which more attention is given on a one-to-one basis, it is typical for counselors to ask clients to state the reasons for entering a counseling relationship. Many clients have sufficient awareness to be able to state their needs with considerable accuracy. Others are able to state the conditions they are experiencing without understanding the underlying reasons for these conditions (e.g., "I can't seem to make up my mind about a major" or "My boss and I are very different, and I can't seem to learn how to get along with him"). Still others are completely unable to state the specific problems they need to deal with.

A counselor may administer certain assessments, to be described fully later in this chapter, in order to define the needs of the student or client more precisely. Melissa appears to be a case in which using assessment for further exploration of her needs was warranted. Here are two additional examples:

A high school counselor who was responsible for 500 students in all areas of school guidance wanted to devise a program of career planning services that would optimally meet the varying needs of all sophomores. He administered the Career Decision Scale (Osipow, Carney, Winer, Yanico, & Koschier, 1997). This 19-item inventory measures the degree of an individual's certainty or indecision related to career choice. In this case, the counselor was less interested in students' individual scores (and indeed did not reveal them to students) than in forming groups of students with similar needs so that these needs could be addressed in the most cost-effective ways. Using the results of the Career Decision Scale, he formed three groups of students according to their level of career decidedness and designed programs of services with different components for each of the three groups.

Iantha came to a career counselor stating that she needed help to identify some possible occupations so that she could declare a college major. Using a common interest inventory, the counselor helped her to identify some possible occupations. After spending considerable time researching most of these, Iantha was still as undecided as she had been when she came in several sessions earlier. The counselor began to suspect that there were reasons for this continued indecisiveness and administered the Career Thoughts Inventory (Sampson, Peterson, Lenz, Reardon, & Saunders, 1996). This 48-item inventory is designed to measure a person's dysfunctional thinking that may affect the career decision-making process. These items provide scores related to three scales: Decision-Making Confusion, Commitment Anxiety, and External Conflict. By looking at the scores on these scales and at the client's response to specific items, the counselor was able to identify and deal with some specific barriers in the client's thought processes before attempting to provide further assistance with selection of a college major.

Learning More About the Characteristics of Individuals and Helping Them Learn More About Themselves

Since the initial theory of Frank Parsons, supported by preeminent theorists in the field such as Donald Super (Super et al., 1963) and John Holland (1997), self-knowledge has been hailed as an absolute requirement for exploration and choice of occupations, majors, and jobs. The self-attributes most often proposed by theorists are interests, abilities, skills, values, and personality characteristics. An abundance of instruments measure these characteristics. Sample instruments are described later in this chapter.

Knowledge of all of these characteristics can be helpful to both the client and the counselor in synthesizing a self-image that can be matched to an environment (using Holland's terminology) or implemented in an occupation (using Super's terminology). Counselors may ask clients to take only one instrument, take an instrument that measures two or three of these characteristics, or take several instruments whose combined results provide a more comprehensive picture. Here are two examples:

Roberto, a high school junior, came to his counselor for assistance in identifying some possible occupations. He stated that he wanted to go to work immediately after high school. The counselor decided to ask him to take the Campbell Interest and Skill Survey (Campbell, 2000), which measures both interests and skills related to the six Holland-like clusters. The results showed high skill in the Technical cluster and high interest in both the Technical (called Producing) and Science (called Analyzing) clusters. From these results the counselor was able to help Roberto find occupations he could enter immediately after high school with some changes in his planned courses for the next three semesters. He was also able to help Roberto learn about many additional occupations that he could consider if he were to attend a two- or four-year college.

Mary Sue, a 35-year-old woman reentering the workforce after 10 years of child rearing, sought the assistance of a career counselor in determining possible jobs she could pursue. She stated that she did not have time to engage in further training or education but needed to find a job that could use her present skills. The counselor decided to administer WorkKeys (ACT, 2015b), which measures an individual's current skills in 11 areas, including Reading for Information, Applied Mathematics, Listening, Business Writing, Locating Information, Applied Technology, Teamwork, Fit (interests and values inventories), Performance, Talent, and Workplace Observation. The counselor recommended that Mary Sue apply for jobs at three specific local companies that use the same instrument to profile the requirements of their positions. By talking with the human resource development personnel at these three companies, Mary Sue can identify jobs requiring her current level of skills and others that could be attainable in the future if she is willing to pursue additional training.

In both of these cases a counselor used the results of formal assessment to assist individuals to gain self-information that they had not been fully able to state or organize, as well as to gain information to guide their exploration.

Determining the Change or Progress of an Individual or Group

Some assessment instruments are designed to measure academic achievement, interests, or specific conditions, such as career maturity or career decidedness, over time, allowing the setting of benchmarks at specific points in a person's development. By comparing progress, change, or stability over time, it is possible to get a picture of a person's development. Following are two examples:

A middle school used the National Career Development Guidelines (ncda.org, described in Chapter 10), as a framework for integrating career development concepts and activities into its curriculum. The superintendent required that the program include an evaluation component that would measure the degree to which the competencies stated in the guidelines had been reached. A customized version of the Iowa Career Learning Assessment (Kuder, Inc., 1998) instrument was administered before delivery of the services and repeated afterward. There was a significant increase in scores in specific content areas after delivery of the program, providing objective data that the program was effective in building the desired competencies.

All of the students in a large, suburban school district took a series of tests called EXPLORE (8th or 9th grade), PLAN (10th grade), and the ACT (11th or 12th grade), all developed and published by ACT, Inc. (ACT, 2007, 2011, 2015). Each of these three batteries of tests measures academic achievement in English, Mathematics, Reading, and Science as well as current interests by means of a 90-item interest inventory called UNIACT. By looking at the results of this group of tests at three different grade levels, a counselor in a university counseling center was able to show a student that each of the three times he took the interest inventory he had made steady and good growth in the four academic areas, and that his most predominant area of interest was in the Social Service cluster. Based on these longitudinal results, the counselor felt secure in acquainting the student with the entire list of available university majors that relate to the Social Service cluster.

RESPONSIBILITIES AND COMPETENCIES OF THE COUNSELOR _____

Assessment and its interpretation can be harmful to clients if counselors are not adequately trained to deal with them. Counselors have responsibilities that are detailed specifically in the ethical guidelines that exist in the profession. Ethical guidelines, called the Code of Fair Testing Practices (Joint Committee on Testing Practices, 2004), have been developed by the American Education Research Association, the American Psychological Association, and the National Council on Measurement in Education. These are posted on the Web at apa.org and may be summarized into four areas: (a) developing and selecting tests, (b) administering and scoring tests, (c) reporting and interpreting test results, and (d) informing test takers. The Code of Professional Responsibilities in Educational Measurement (National Council on Measurement in Education, 1995), a document that covers the responsibilities of a wider audience—those who develop, market, select, administer, score, and interpret tests—is posted at ncme.org.

Possess General Knowledge About Assessment

Agencies that govern the accreditation of counselor education programs and the licensing of individuals require counselors to take a course in tests and measurements. According to the standards included in *A Counselor's Guide to Career Assessment Instruments* (Kapes & Whitfield, 2002), published by the National Career Development Association (NCDA), counselors should possess the knowledge and competencies related to assessment shown in Figure 5.2. Students who have already taken the required course on assessment may want to use this form as a checklist for their own competencies.

Have Detailed Knowledge About the Instruments Used

Besides the general knowledge of testing just summarized, counselors need to have very detailed knowledge about the assessments they select for use. This knowledge can be gained in a variety of ways. It is likely that counselors will initially consider an instrument because they have identified it through a search on a Web site, from reading about it on the Web site of its publisher, from publications such as *A Counselor's Guide to Career Assessment Instruments* (Wood & Hays, 2013), or because it was displayed at a conference. The first task, then, is to determine whether it has the characteristics—such as purpose, reading level, reliability, validity, and gender fairness—that it needs in order to qualify. These characteristics should be described in the technical manual that accompanies the instrument. The manual should report such important facts as the kind of research the instrument has undergone, what it is designed to measure, the norm groups that

Basic Concepts

Concepts important to the informal *use* of tests are listed below. Persons with final responsibility for *evaluating* and *selecting* assessment instruments will require knowledge beyond these basic concepts.

Use the following key in responding to the statements:

3 = I am able to apply the concept and explain it to others.

2 = I have some knowledge but little experience in applying the concept.

1 = I have little or no knowledge of this concept.

Enter the appropriate number in the blank at the left of each statement.

1. **Statistics used in testing and test manuals**

   _____ a. Measures of central tendency (mean, median, mode)

   _____ b. Measures of variability (range, variance, standard deviation)

   _____ c. Distributions (frequency, normal)

   _____ d. Scales of measurement (nominal, ordinal, interval, ratio)

   _____ e. Correlation coefficients (Pearson product-moment, point biserial)

2. **Types of instruments**

   _____ a. Measures of maximum performance

   _____ b. Measures of typical performance

   _____ c. Similarities and differences among measures of intelligence, aptitude, ability, achievement

   _____ d. Similarities and differences among self-reports, self-ratings, inventories, and tests

3. **Score reporting procedures**

   _____ a. Percentile ranks

   _____ b. Standard scores (including stanines)

   _____ c. Grade placement (equivalent) scores

   _____ d. Score profiles and profile analysis

   _____ e. Group similarity indices

   _____ f. Expectancy (experience) tables

   _____ g. Estimates of probability of success and/or level of success; standard error of estimate

4. **Standardization and norms**

   _____ a. Standardized administration and scoring

   _____ b. Limitations of raw scores

   _____ c. Types of norms (e.g., local, national, gender, grade); their applications and limitations

   _____ d. Norm-based versus criterion-referenced interpretation

Figure 5.2

Assessment knowledge and competencies.

Source: From *A Counselor's Guide to Career Assessment Instruments* (pp. 42–43), by J.T. Kapes and E.A. Whitfield. Published by the National Career Development Association (2002). Used by permission.

5. Reliability
    _____ a. Meaning of test reliability
    _____ b. Sources of measurement error
    _____ c. Types of test reliability (test-retest, parallel forms, internal consistency, including split-half, inter-rater)
    _____ d. Standard error of measurement and error bands

6. Validity
    _____ a. Meaning of test validity
    _____ b. Implications of test use for validation procedures
    _____ c. Types of test validity (content, criterion-related, construct)
    _____ d. Factors affecting test validity
    _____ e. Differential validity of test batteries for diverse criteria
    _____ f. Potential sources of bias affecting validity

Figure 5.2
(*Continued*)

have been used in testing its properties, and its reading level. If there is no technical manual, the counselor must be wary about the amount of research that has been applied to the instrument.

It is also useful to read the critiques that others have written about the instrument. Such critiques are found in *A Counselor's Guide to Career Assessment Instruments* (Wood & Hays, 2013), *The Nineteenth Mental Measurement Yearbook* (Carlson, Geisinger, & Jonson, 2014), and on the Web site of the Buros Center for Testing (buros.org). Also, discussions with other counselors who have used the instrument can provide their views of its strengths and weaknesses.

Evaluate the Instrument for Usefulness with Diverse Populations

This particular step of the process is designed to ensure that the instrument—in addition to having the purpose, reliability, and validity referred to in the previous section—is suitable for use with the diverse populations that you may want to assess. There are many kinds of diversity. Those relating to age, reading and comprehension level, race, ethnicity, gender, and disability must be considered when assessment instruments are selected. Related to age, instruments are developed and normed for persons of a specific age range and, thus, should be used to assess persons of that age range. Similarly, assessment instruments are written at a reading and comprehension level that can be determined. For example, there is a version of Holland's *Self-Directed Search, Form E* (1996) that is written at the fourth-grade reading level. This version of the instrument would, therefore, be the preferred version to administer to populations such as offenders or high school students with a reading deficit.

Further, race and ethnicity are important considerations when selecting instruments because cultural differences do affect the understanding and interpretation of inventory or test items. In a study with a sample of Mexican students, for example, Flores, Spanierman, Armstrong, and Velez (2006) found that the Holland typology did not fit Mexican American students well, especially males. Some instruments are accused of gender bias in the sense that their results encourage women toward certain occupational fields and men toward others. Learning style can also be a significant factor. Items on tests and inventories are typically presented as multiple-choice options working well for those who read well and think in a linear fashion. However, for persons of different learning styles, other methods of presentation might be far superior—such as analysis of vignettes provided as video clips, hands-on tasks or assignments, free-form essays, or oral presentations. Clearly, persons with specific kinds of disabilities need to be assessed in ways that accommodate their disabilities. When selecting instruments to respond appropriately to diversity, consider at least the nature of the items, the nature of the norm group, and the mode of administration and interpretation.

Items included on inventories measuring interests, skills, and values may be culture bound. It is important to review the test or inventory items to determine if they represent activities or concepts that are compatible with the context of your students or clients. Providing norm-referenced results—that is, comparing the scores of one person against those of a representative sample—is a useful thing to do. In order to make this activity meaningful, however, that sample group must contain a representative sample of those like your population. When considering an instrument, read its technical manual and/or call its publisher to determine what percentage of the norm group has characteristics like the people to whom you plan to administer the instrument.

Finally, consider the method of administration of the instrument as it relates to your population. Some people love to use a computer, and some don't. Some instruments are only available on the Web or delivered from a local computer, not in print form. Thus, a person who is uncomfortable with technology would be more comfortable and perhaps obtain more realistic results if administered an instrument that can be taken in print form. The Code of Fair Testing Practices (Joint Committee on Testing Practices, 2004) states the following two principles related to selection of instruments for persons of diversity:

- Make appropriately modified forms of tests or administration procedures available for test takers with disabilities who need special accommodations.
- Obtain and provide evidence on the performance of test takers of diverse subgroups, making significant efforts to obtain sample sizes that are adequate for subgroup analyses. Evaluate the evidence to ensure that differences in performance are related to the skills being assessed.

If the instrument passes this quality-control review, counselors may continue their exploration by taking the instrument themselves and getting a score report. This action will yield a firsthand knowledge of the kinds of items it has, the kind of score report it provides, and a sense of the accuracy of the instrument in measuring some characteristics about themselves. Next, the counselor may want to administer the instrument to a friend or to one or two individuals in order to become more familiar with it.

Prepare Students or Clients Adequately

Assuming that instruments have been selected, the counselor's next responsibility is to prepare those who will take the instrument for that experience. Such preparation consists of (a) explaining why they should take an assessment instrument, in other words, what they should expect to get from it; (b) getting agreement that they believe that its results will be helpful; (c) explaining what the items of the instrument are like and how long it will take to complete it; (d) telling them when the results will be available; (e) explaining what the score report will be like, perhaps by showing a mock score report; and (f) indicating what will happen to the results of the assessment—who will see them and where they will be stored.

Administer Instruments Properly

The manual provided with each formal assessment gives detailed instructions about the administration of the instrument. Some instruments, such as self-help interest inventories, can be given to an individual to take home. They are not timed, no supervision is needed, and there are no "right" or "wrong" answers. Other tests, such as college entrance examinations, are very high-stake tests and must be administered under the strictest conditions. These conditions include security of the test items prior to the testing session, identification of the examinee, room setup, lighting, silence, and exact timing. There are many other instruments that specify the conditions of administration somewhere between these two extremes. The point is to know, by reading the instructions provided with the instrument, what the appropriate conditions for administration are and then to meet those conditions.

Interpret Instruments Properly

Correct interpretation of any instrument relates to three different considerations: (a) an overall understanding of the relevance of assessment to the process of career planning and choice, (b) the reason the individual has taken the instrument, and (c) the guidelines provided by the publisher for use of the instrument and/or the instrument's technical manual.

This chapter began with discussion of how the context of career planning and choice has changed in the 21st century. The discussion indicated that, concomitant with that changed context, the old model of the trait-and-factor approach (often called the "test-'em and tell-'em" approach) should be replaced with a view of assessment that has the following characteristics:

- Assessment is *one* of several tools that are used to assist the client with career choices; others may include interviewing, use of Web-based career planning systems and sites, group work, and completion of specific assignments (such as informational interviewing, job shadowing, internships, and coursework). Any plans that may emerge from use of these approaches should take into account the learning that occurs from all of these approaches.
- Assessment should be administered with the person's full understanding of its purpose and with agreement that the activity may provide some helpful information that can be used to guide exploration.
- The counselor has the responsibility to prepare the client well, administer the instrument correctly, treat the results in a confidential manner, and interpret the results in a knowledgeable way. The counselor also has the responsibility to interpret the instrument flexibly; in other words, its results are not used as if they offer superior knowledge but, rather, as data that may be used to stimulate further exploration of alternatives, growth or change, or confirmation of information already possessed. Clients have the responsibility to evaluate the results of the assessment and determine whether they are appropriate representations of the self-attributes the instrument is designed to measure, and how, if at all, to use the results as a part of the data that guide personal decision making.

The reason why the counselor has asked the client to take the assessment also guides the appropriate interpretation of the instrument. For example, a counselor may suggest that a client take the *Strong Interest Inventory* (Strong, 2004) in order to confirm a tentative occupational choice he or she has made, in accordance with a scale on the *Strong Interest Inventory*. The counselor will have also suggested that the client engage in other activities—such as taking related coursework, having informational interviews with people in the occupation, and participating in job shadowing or an internship—that will or will not contribute to this confirmation. In this case, however, the counselor would provide a general interpretation of the inventory, but would also focus on the client's scores as they relate to the profile of the norm group for the specific occupation of the client's choice.

A second example: If the purpose for suggesting that a client take the *Myers-Briggs Type Indicator* (Myers & Briggs, 2012) was to help the client understand why she is having difficulty in relating to a supervisor, the counselor not only would interpret the instrument in general but also would ask the client how she would assess the supervisor on each of the four pairs of personality dimensions covered by the instrument. Where there were contrasts, the counselor would interpret the client's results in a way that would help the client to get a clearer picture of why the supervisor's style and expectations are different from her own.

Finally, it is imperative that counselors interpret instruments within the confines of the research and the intentions of the authors and publishers of the instrument. Some publishers offer—even require—thorough training on their instruments by means of a nationwide series of workshops. These publishers are demonstrably concerned about having their instruments interpreted correctly. Other publishers require that those who want to purchase their instruments have training related to the instrument before allowing them to make purchases.

If, however, counselors are using assessments without these requirements, they have the ethical responsibility to train themselves to have competence: reading the manuals that the publisher provides with the instrument, attending workshops or sessions offered at professional conferences, and/or acquiring training through a graduate course that focuses on career planning instruments.

Follow Through with Clients

Assessment is a waste of time and money if its results are not used to inform decision making. Counselors have an ethical responsibility to move beyond interpretation in order to assist the client or student to use the results in the clarification of self-concept and/or the making of informed career choices. This is the most difficult step in the process because it involves making a leap from presentation of objective data to making inferences about the meaning of those data. Such inferences must be made within the context of all that a counselor knows about a student or client, not from test data alone. Thus, there are no prescriptive answers, but here are some suggestions:

- Think about the characteristics (such as liking to work with people face-to-face and using verbal skills) that are measured by the instrument and then assist the individual to think broadly about how that combination of characteristics may relate to a wide array of occupations, not only to the specific titles provided in the publisher's materials.
- Assist the individual to think about the implications for education, training, and/or certification of the occupational options provided by the assessment, and discuss these.

- Assist the individual to think about the lifestyle implications of the occupational options identified by an instrument, including work hours, time to be with family, requirement for travel, income, and capability to merge dual careers.
- Prescribe near-to-reality ways for individuals to explore occupational options once they are identified. Such ways include related coursework, videos, job shadowing, internships, part-time jobs, informational interviewing, and mentoring.
- After individuals pursue one or more of these ways to do reality testing, follow through with interviews to help them evaluate what they have learned and to make choices about keeping specific occupations on a short list of options or discarding them.

Tips from the Field

Before you administer any assessment, either informal or formal, give careful thought to the purpose of the assessment and how you will help your counselee or client use its results.

INFORMAL ASSESSMENTS

Assessment instruments and techniques are commonly divided into two broad categories: *informal* and *formal*. Checklists, games, fantasies, forced-choice activities, card sorts, and structured interviews are examples of informal assessments. Some studies (Miller, 2007) indicate that very comparable results can be gained from informal assessment and formal assessment related to specific tasks, such as determining one's Holland code.

A *checklist* is a series of items that may relate to an individual's preferred work setting, job characteristics, work tasks, work values, or skills. Such a checklist may be developed by the counselor, or the counselor can borrow—with permission—one that someone else has developed or can purchase one. As an illustration, assume that you are working with a group of women who are planning to return to the workforce after some years of child rearing. Such women often have the perception that they have few or no work skills that employers would value. As a means of helping them change this perception, the counselor may give them a checklist containing the following items and ask them to check those that they believe they possess to a moderate or high degree:

_____ Manage multiple tasks at the same time

_____ Decide which among competing tasks has priority

_____ Manage time

_____ Budget and manage money

_____ Teach or train others

_____ Resolve conflicts between and among individuals

_____ Create and maintain an attractive environment

_____ Manage people

A *game* may be used with small or large groups to make individuals aware of realities related to career choice and planning. As a part of such a game, an individual may be asked to play a specific role in a simulated environment or become subject to a variety of opportunities and set-backs represented on the game board. One good example of this kind of informal assessment is the *Real Game Series* (Real Game, 2015), available in four versions for different age populations, ranging from grade 3 through adult. Information about these print and digital games is available at realgame.org. Though some versions of the game are classroom and print based, a Web-based version is available for secondary school students.

A *career fantasy is* an activity in which a counselor asks one or more individuals to relax, close their eyes, and imagine an ideal day that includes time at a worksite. Individuals' fantasies can be stimulated by using instructions, such as the following:

> I'd like you to relax, close your eyes if you wish, and put out of your mind any concerns that you may be dealing with. I want you to imagine that this is an ideal day of work. During this activity, you can have any job you want, and you have the skills and education to perform it.
>
> Imagine that you have completed breakfast and that you are now leaving your home to go to work. What kind of clothes are you wearing—informal clothes, some kind of uniform, a business suit? How are you getting to work—in your car, on a train, on an airplane, or are you working from home? How long does it take to get to work? What does your place of work look like? How many other people work directly with you? What is your relationship to these people?
>
> What are your work tasks today? Do you have any flexibility in how you perform them, or does someone supervise you closely? What kinds of tools or equipment do you work with? How much responsibility do you have for what you do? Is your pace frenetic, leisurely, or something in between?

This is a brief illustration. This fantasy can be embellished and expanded not only to include work activities but also to relate work to lifestyle, such as the kind of home, neighborhood, car, and leisure activities the person fantasizes. Discussion of this activity with individuals or small groups can help identify many characteristics that they desire in a job or lifestyle that the income from a job may impact. A *forced-choice activity is* one in which an individual is asked to make a choice between two options that are quite different from each other or to rank-order three or more activities. This kind of assessment may be applied to work values, job characteristics, and work settings, for example. Following are three illustrations of the kind of items that may be used for these three purposes:

Work values: Through your life's work, would you rather
_____ make a lot of money or _____ make a contribution to society?

Job characteristics: In your ideal job, would you rather
_____ tell someone else what to do or _____ have someone tell you what to do?

Work setting: In your ideal job, would you rather
_____ work outside or _____ work inside?

This technique might be used with any client whose interest assessment results are not definitive. Since it forces some choice, and therefore does not allow a series of responses such as "indifferent," it will reveal some interests.

A *card sort is* an activity in which an individual or a group is given a deck of cards. Each card represents something related to career choice, such as a work value, a skill, a work task, or a characteristic of a work setting. Typically, the card would contain the name of the characteristic (such as Variety, Managing People, or Making or Repairing Things) and a definition of it.

If the number of cards in the deck is relatively few (up to 15), clients may be asked to rank-order the cards, placing the one that is most important in first position, followed by all of the others in priority order. If the number of cards in the deck is large, clients are typically asked to sort them into three different stacks: those that are very important or essential, those that are somewhat important, and those that are not important. Such a card sort may be made by the counselor or may be purchased from those who have specialized in the development of such instruments. If it's self-made, it is important to cover the full range of possible values, skills, work tasks, or characteristics that clients might choose—a process that will require review of the literature.

Finally, in a *structured interview* a counselor asks questions that are related to some theoretical base. For example, during an intake interview, a counselor might ask a student to provide information about coursework, past jobs, or extracurricular or volunteer activities and prompt or organize the responses around the six clusters of occupations identified by John Holland or ACT. With sufficient knowledge about the characteristics of these six work environments, the counselor can formulate questions and analyze responses in skillful ways that yield an accurate assessment of a person's Holland code (see Chapter 2 for information about Holland's theory and codes) as well as acquire a great deal of information about the client. This approach would be very helpful with students or clients who have undifferentiated profiles of interest. Similarly, with sufficient knowledge of Jungian types (Jung, 1959), a skillful counselor might estimate a person's Jungian type without administering one of the instruments that measures personality type in these terms.

Informal assessment instruments have characteristics that are quite different from those of formal assessments, which we will examine next. Some of the characteristics of informal assessments are as follows:

- They have not been subjected to scientific rigor, nor do they have known *properties*, such as reliability and validity.
- They are not supported by any data that allow a person to compare his or her results with those of other people.
- Though inferences can be made by the client and the counselor, there are no documents that facilitate a connection between the choices made by the client and specific occupations.
- There is no standard way to interpret the results of these activities, which leaves such interpretation totally to the competence of the counselor.

The advantages of informal assessments include the following: (a) they are low cost or free of charge, (b) they may not require the ordering of materials in advance, (c) they may not require as much time to administer as formal assessments, and (d) they may be less anxiety producing for the client.

FORMAL ASSESSMENTS

Assessments labeled *formal* may be timed standardized tests or untimed standardized inventories. It is common to call an instrument an *inventory* if it is assessing content areas in which there are no right or wrong answers and to call it a *test* if the items do have right or wrong answers. Thus, an instrument measuring a person's interests is an inventory, whereas an instrument measuring a person's achievement in mathematics is a test.

The hallmark of formal assessments is that they have been subjected to scientific rigor—that is, authors and publishers have invested professional expertise, time, and money in order to develop a quality product. They have performed research on the instrument in an effort to ensure quality and to be able to know the *properties* that the instrument possesses. Some of the most important properties that counselors need to know when selecting instruments include the following:

- *Validity.* There are several types of validity, and it is beyond the scope of this book to define them. An instrument is said to have *validity* if it measures what it is supposed to measure. For example, if the instrument purports to measure interests, does it do so (as opposed to measuring skills or work values)? An ethical counselor will need to read the technical manual provided by the publisher in order to learn what procedures have been taken to ensure that it measures what its marketing literature says it does.

- *Reliability, often called test-retest reliability.* The construct of reliability deals with whether an instrument will measure what it is purported to measure reliably over time. In other words, if a client takes an interest inventory today and then takes it again three weeks from now, will the results be the same or approximately the same? Intervals of time used for testing reliability typically range from two weeks to several months. Obviously, some factors related to career choice, such as interests, skills, and work values, can and do change over time. Thus, the challenge with measuring reliability is to have a sufficient period of time between the first administration and a subsequent one so that the client is unlikely to remember the items or previous responses to them. On the other hand, if the period of time is too long, change in the way the client responds may be at least partially the result of normal development.

- Test-retest reliability is measured as a *correlation coefficient*, defined as the correlation between two measurements obtained in the same manner. A test-retest correlation coefficient of .8 is considered good and acceptable for selection of an instrument. Data about reliability should be provided in the technical manual as well as a description of how it was established, including the size and characteristics of the group used for this purpose.

- *Fairness related to diversity.* Increasingly in the 21st century counselors will deal with clients who represent a wide range of diversity—in gender, sexual orientation, ethnic background, race, age, and types of disability. It is important to know about the populations that are used to test and norm the instrument. The groups used for such testing need to be large enough to include a wide range of diversity, or the author and publisher need to state that the instrument has been tested only with selected populations. The former approach allows us to assume that the characteristics of clients are similar to those in the populations used for testing. This statement has profound implications for the use of instruments with members of diverse populations.

- *Comparison.* This property refers to whether or not the results that clients receive compare them to other people or rank-order characteristics related only to themselves. For example, some interest inventories are *norm-referenced*; an individual's scores are compared with those of one or more "norm" groups. For some inventories the score report will indicate that the examinee's responses place him or her, for example, at the 85th *percentile* compared with a norm group of persons of a similar age. This group of persons, or *norm group*, may be small or large, may be representative in various demographic ways of the population in general or only of a subset, may be national in scope or relatively local, or be comprised of both genders or one gender. In contrast, a different inventory may provide *raw scores*—that is, the total number of responses related to some category (right or wrong or assigned to some scale) is reported. Such data do not provide a picture of how examinees compare with others but do allow them to rank-order their own interests, values, abilities, or whatever is being measured. Further, if norms are being used, the individual's standing related to them may be expressed in a variety of ways, including percentiles, stanines, and standard scores, explained later in this chapter.

Types of Formal Assessments

Earlier in this chapter three different purposes for assessment were described: to identify clients' needs, to help clients and the counselor know more about the self, and to measure progress or change. This section of the chapter describes more specifically the types of instruments, and provides a sample list of the most common ones that can be organized into each of these three categories.

Identifying The Needs of Clients

Instruments that fall into this category may be administered to a single client or may be administered to a target group of clients. In the first case, the counselor is attempting to identify the needs of a specific client and may, therefore, interpret the results to that client as a part of the career counseling process. For example, if a counselor finds that the usual technique of assessing interests, identifying some occupations, and learning about those occupations does not seem to be helping a client to deal with career concerns, he or she may want to determine if this client has barriers, such as irrational beliefs, that prevent moving forward. Under these circumstances the counselor might choose *The Career Beliefs Inventory* (Krumboltz, 1991) and suggest that the client take it. If that inventory reveals that the client is invested in a belief that he or she cannot enter a specific occupational field because the opportunities are too limited, the counselor may suggest that the basis for this belief be investigated through some occupational research before further work is done to consider other possible career choices.

On the other hand, a counselor may be seeking to identify different levels of need for career services in the target population. He or she might administer *My Vocational Situation* (Holland, Daiger, & Power, 1980) to the entire group and then make some informed assumptions about the needs of those whose scores placed them in the top 25%, the middle 50%, and the lower 25% of the distribution. In this case, it is unlikely that the counselor would interpret individual scores for members of the group because that was not the designated purpose for the assessment.

Some examples of this type of instrument, with a brief description and information about the publisher, are listed next. However, new instruments emerge with frequency, and some cease to be published. When selecting an instrument, counselors should consult the latest versions of reference books that summarize what is currently available and the Web sites of major publishers.

Career Attitudes and Strategies Inventory (CASI), Holland and Gottfredson, 1994. A self-scored instrument designed to identify the attitudes, feelings, and obstacles that affect the careers of adults. The scales are Job Stability, Family Commitment, Risk-Taking Style, Geographical Barriers, Job Satisfaction, Work Involvement, Skill Development, Dominant Style Career Worries, and Interpersonal Abuse.

The Career Beliefs Inventory (CBI), Krumboltz, 1991. For persons over 13 years of age, designed to identify career beliefs that may be preventing them from reaching career goals. There are 25 scales organized under five categories: My Current Career Situation, What Seems

Necessary for My Happiness, Factors That Influence My Decisions, Changes I Am Willing to Make, and Effort I Am Willing to Initiate. Published by Mind Garden, Inc., Menlo Park, CA.

Career Factors Inventory (CFI), Chartrand et al., 1997. For persons over age 13, designed to identify persons' difficulties in the career planning and decision-making process. The scales are Need for Information, Need for Self-Knowledge, Career Choice Anxiety, and Generalized Indecisiveness. Published by Consulting Psychologists Press, Mountain View, CA.

Career Maturity Inventory (CMI), Crites and Savickas, 1995. Designed to measure how ready a student is to make a career decision. For students in grades 6–12. See vocopher.com.

Career Thoughts Inventory (CTI), Sampson et al., 1996. Designed to identify irrational thoughts that the client may have that could affect the career decision-making process. For use with students and clients from the high school level through adulthood. Available in print or digital form. Published by Psychological Assessment Resources, Odessa, FL.

Career Development Inventory (CDI), Super, Thompson, Lindeman, Jordaan, and Myers, 1984. Designed to measure career development and career maturity. For use with high school and college students. See vocopher.com.

Career Decision Scale (CDS), Osipow et al., 1997. Designed to measure the reasons for career indecision and inability to make a vocational choice. For use with high school and college students. Published by Psychological Assessment Resources, Odessa, FL.

Career Decision Profile (CDP), Jones, 1986. Designed to measure level of decidedness about career choice, self-knowledge, and knowledge about occupations and training. Published by Career Key, Inc. (careerkey.org).

My Vocational Situation (MVS), Holland et al., 1980. Designed to measure the degree to which lack of vocational identity, lack of information or training, and barriers may affect a person's ability to make a career choice. For use with students in grade 9 through adult years. Available free of charge for noncommercial use at the English version of http://saens.hi.is.

Most of the instruments just listed are designed for use with high school students and adults. This is the case because they measure constructs (such as career maturity, career beliefs, and decision-making skill) that are developmental in nature and should not be measured prior to the life stage in which their development is expected.

Learning More About Clients

In this category there is a rich array of inventories of interests, skills, abilities, work values, personality types, and combinations of these. In each case, the purpose is to allow the client and the counselor to explore characteristics that may help identify occupations or jobs for consideration. Following the theoretical work of Holland and Super, and of trait-and-factor theory in general, the purpose of these instruments is to identify personal characteristics that can be related to those of occupations or jobs in order to focus on exploration of options. The lists and short summaries provided next divide the most common instruments into those measuring interests, abilities, skills, work values, personality types, and combinations of any of these.

Interest inventories.   *Career Assessment Inventory (CAI)*, Johannson, 1986. Designed to measure interest in Holland's six personality types, 23 basic interest scales, and 111 occupations. Can be used with high school students, college students, and adults. Published by Pearson Assessments, Bloomington, MN.

Career Occupational Preference Survey (COPS), Knapp and Knapp, 1995. The COPS Interest Inventory consists of 168 items, providing job activity interest scores related to 14 different career clusters. Can be used with students in grades 7–12, college students, and adults. Published by EdITs, San Diego, CA.

Career Decision Making System – Revised (CDM-R), O'Shea and Feller, 2000. Designed to measure interest in Holland's six personality types, though names of scales have been changed. Different versions allow use from grade 7 to adulthood. Both print and online versions available. Published by Pearson Assessments, Bloomington, MN.

Interest Determination, Exploration, and Assessment System (IDEAS), Johansson, 1993. Two self-scored inventories—one for middle and high school students and one for adults—that measure interest in 16 areas. Published by Pearson Assessments, Bloomington, MN.

Interest Explorer, Riverside Publishing, 1998. For use with middle school students, high school students, and adults, the inventory measures interest in 14 career areas that are linked to the *Guide for Occupational Exploration, Occupational Outlook Handbook*, and *O*Net*. Published by Riverside Publishing, Rolling Meadows, IL.

Jackson Vocational Interest Survey (JVIS), Jackson, 1999. Designed to measure interests on 34 basic interest scales. For use with high school students, college students, and adults. Print and online versions available. Published by Sigma Assessment Systems, Port Huron, MI.

Kuder Career Interests Assessment (KCIA), Kuder, Inc., 2013a. Designed to measure interest in the six Holland occupational clusters or the 16 National career clusters and pathways; also compares the profile of the inventory taker with those of more than 2,000 real people and identifies and describes the specific jobs of the top matches. For use with high school students, college students, and adults. Available only on the Internet as a part of Kuder's career planning systems. Published by Kuder, Inc., Adel, IA.

O*Net Interest Profiler, U.S. Department of Labor, Employment and Training Administration, 2001a. Self-scored or Web-based instrument designed to measure interests by Holland's six personality types for persons in middle school through adult. May be printed out, copied, and distributed along with the score report and an interpretive booklet from onetcenter.org. Executable code may also be downloaded from this site. An online version is also available at MyNextMove.org.

Self-Directed Search (SDS), Holland and Messer, 2015. Designed to measure personality type and interest in six Holland occupational groups. There are multiple forms for different age ranges, languages, and reading levels. Can be used with high school students, college students, and adults. The assessment is also available on the Web at self-directed-search.com. Published by Psychological Assessment Resources, Odessa, FL.

The Strong Interest Inventory, Strong, 2004. Measures interests in eight different areas—occupations, school subjects, activities, leisure activities, types of people preferred as coworkers, preference between two activities, personal characteristics, and preference in the world-of-work. Provides a Holland code, scores on 30 basic interest scales, 5 personal style themes, and similarity of examinee's profile to the profile of workers in 244 occupations. Available in English, French, and Italian. Appropriate for use with high school juniors and seniors, college students, and adults. The assessment offers many different score reports, including those for high school students, those for college students, and reports combined with the results of the *Myers-Briggs Type Indicator* and the *Skills Confidence Inventory*. Published by Consulting Psychologists Press, Mountain View, CA.

Unisex Edition of the ACT Interest Inventory (UNIACT), Swaney, 1995. Measures interest in the six Holland types and uses the Holland code to suggest career areas on the World-of-Work Map for exploration. Due to different sets of items and norms, it is appropriate for use with high school students, college students, and adults. Included in ACT Profile (a Web-based system), and as a part of ACT's tests called *EXPLORE*, *PLAN*, *WorkKeys*, and the *ACT Assessment*. Published by ACT, Inc., Iowa City, IA.

Skills inventories.   SkillScan Professional Pack (1987), *Career Driver Online* (2009), and *SkillScan Express* (2014). The *SkillScan Professional Pack* provides the opportunity for users to sort manually a large number of skills by areas of competence, preference, and need for development and to identify skills with a combination of high competence and preference. Web-based versions, *Career Driver Online* and *SkillScan Express*, are available at skillscan.com. Appropriate for use with high school students, college students, and adults. Published by SkillScan, Martinez, CA.

WorkKeys, ACT, 2015b. Measures skills in 11 areas: Reading for Information, Applied Mathematics, Listening, Writing, Locating Information, Applied Technology, Teamwork, Motivation, Learning, Observing, and Speaking. Specific jobs can be profiled on the same skills, allowing the relationship of an individual's skills with the level required by specific occupations and jobs. Can be used with high school students and adults. Published by ACT, Inc., Iowa City, IA.

Kuder Skills Confidence Assessment (KSCA), Kuder, 2013b. Measures self-assessed skills that may be related either to the six Holland occupational groups or the 16 National career clusters. Reports strength of skills on a seven-point continuum and suggests occupations and programs of study related to the user's score report. Available only as a part of Kuder's Web-based Career Planning System. Published by Kuder, Inc., Adel, IA.

Combination of interests, aptitudes, and skills.   *Campbell Interest and Skill Survey (CISS)*, Campbell, 2000. Measures interests and self-reported skills in seven areas that are roughly parallel to the Holland six types and contains 25 basic scales and 60 occupational scales. The basic scales are subscales of the Holland types, expressed as Influencing, Organizing, Helping, Creating, Analyzing, Producing, and Adventuring. There are parallel skills scales for each of the interest scales. Available in print and on the Internet. Can be used with high school students, college students, and adults. Published by Pearson Assessments, Bloomington, MN.

The Armed Services Vocational Aptitude Battery (ASVAB), U.S. Department of Defense, 2005. Measures abilities in 10 content areas and includes measurement of interests by Holland typology and personal preferences (values). Designed for high school seniors, postsecondary students, and adults. Used for admission to various specialties in the armed forces but is also provided free of charge to high school seniors in general. The interest assessment is available as a part of the online Career Exploration Program at asvabprogram.com. Published by the U.S. Department of Defense.

The *COPSystem 3C*, Knapp and Knapp, 1995. An online career guidance assessment program for adults in career transition. It consists of three assessments: the COPS Interest Inventory, the CAPS ability battery, and the COPES work values survey. Print version also available for students in grades 6 to 12, college students, and adults. Published by EdITS, Inc., San Diego, CA.

Abilities.   *O*Net Ability Profiler*, U.S. Department of Labor Employment and Training Administration, 2001b. The O*Net Ability Profiler uses a paper-and-pencil format with optional apparatus parts and computerized scoring. Individuals can use O*Net Ability Profiler results to identify their strengths and areas for which they might want to receive more training and education, or to identify occupations that fit their strengths.

The O*Net Ability Profiler measures nine job-relevant abilities: Verbal Ability, Arithmetic Reasoning, Computation, Spatial Ability, Form Perception, Clerical Perception, Motor Coordination, Finger Dexterity, and Manual Dexterity. This instrument can be downloaded without charge from the O*Net Web site at onetcenter.org.

Inventories of personality type.   *The Personality Type Profiler*, Golden, 2004. The *Golden Personality Type Profiler* identifies both a Jungian four-letter type and a fifth element for stress, in addition to providing scores for 18 traits (facets) that help describe the unique personality of each person. Score reports can be provided either for individuals or for teams. The assessment is administered online at us.talentlens.com. Published by Pearson Publishing, San Antonio, TX.

The Myers-Briggs Type Indicator (MBTI) Step I and Step II (MBTI), Myers and Briggs, 2012. Measures the psychological types described by Jung, yielding a four-letter code that can be related to typical profiles of groups of people who work in specific occupations or that can be used to develop teams or understand the interactions among members of a team. The results of the assessment are expressed as an individual's preference along a continuum on scales titled Extraversion-Introversion, Sensing-Intuition, Thinking-Feeling, and Judging-Perceiving. Combined score reports for the MBTI and the Strong Interest Inventory are available. MBTI is available in Spanish, German, French, Dutch, Canadian French, Italian, Korean, Portuguese, Danish, Norwegian, Chinese, Swedish, and Russian. Can be used with high school students, college students, and adults. Can be taken in print form or on the Web at mbticomplete.com. Published by Consulting Psychologists Press, Mountain View, CA.

Note that as with the previous group of assessment instruments, these are targeted primarily to individuals in the high school, college, and adult years. This is the case because interests are not crystallized until the adolescent years, and the development of abilities and skills to support them typically occurs in the high school and college years.

Inventories measuring work values.   *O*Net Work Importance Profiler*, U.S. Department of Labor, Employment and Training Administration, 2001c. The *Work Importance Profiler* measures the importance of six work values—achievement, independence, recognition, relationships, support, and working conditions. Individuals who take the instrument begin by rank-ordering 21 work need statements by comparing them with one another. The results are linked to occupational titles. The instrument can be downloaded without charge either as a print document or as executable code from www.onetcenter.org.

Super's Work Values Inventory—revised, Super and Zytowski, 2006. Measures importance of 12 of Super's work values and provides percentile scores of level of importance. For use by high school students and adults. Available only in Web-based form as a part of the Kuder Career Planning System at kuder.com. Published by Kuder, Inc., Adel, IA.

Measuring Progress or Change

In the third category of reasons to use assessment, instruments are used to measure some kind of change that is considered desirable in an individual or a group of individuals. For example, it is common to use a pretest and a posttest to measure change that should occur because of some kind of treatment—such as a career guidance curriculum, a series of workshops, or use of a Web-based system. In this case, the purpose of the assessment is to note the difference in the scores of an individual or a group before the treatment and after the treatment. The same instruments listed under category one (finding out the needs of clients) can be used to measure this progress or change.

WAYS IN WHICH ASSESSMENT INSTRUMENTS MAY BE ADMINISTERED

Traditionally, assessment instruments have been provided in print form. They are administered either by licensed or certified professional counselors or, more recently, by trained career development facilitators. In this mode, instructions are read by the administrator, and the examinee responds to the items of the instrument on a worksheet or optical scan form. The results may then be calculated by the examinee, by the test administrator, by computer software that has been acquired for that purpose, or by computer scoring at some central place. These different options for scoring also determine how soon the results will be available for interpretation to the client.

In recent years, the widespread availability of computers and access to the Internet have introduced additional ways in which administration and interpretation take place. Beginning in the late 1960s with the advent of computer-based career planning systems, some types of instruments—such as inventories of interests, skills, abilities, and values—became a part of such systems. In keeping with ethical standards, developers of computer-based systems engaged in research to ensure that instruments delivered in this way yielded the same results as if they were administered in print form. In this mode, it became possible for an inventory or test to be scored immediately and for the computer to provide a very standard report, though customized for the individual examinee, that could be viewed on the screen and/or printed. For the first time in this edition of this textbook, some assessments are now delivered to tablets and smartphones, which also display their interpretation. Reports provided from computers or smartphones are also made available electronically to a counselor or career advisor who can follow through with the client for more in-depth interpretation and application of the results to the client's specific needs.

Subsequent to their inclusion in computer-based career planning systems, many assessment instruments became available from their publishers in software form. In this mode, a site can purchase a computer disk that contains the instrument and the computer code required to administer and interpret it. This software may be installed on machines at the user site and is typically limited according to how much has been paid for it or for how many individual uses the site has been authorized.

The advent of the Internet and its ever-increasing use has introduced yet another venue for administration and interpretation of assessment. It has also made it more difficult to determine the quality of available assessments, especially those offered by sites that neither charge a fee nor provide a manual that describes the research and development work invested in the instrument. As trends continue in these areas, three different observations can be made: (a) many instruments and their results are available to the general public without charge and without opportunity to learn about the quality of the instrument; (b) well-known and researched instruments are being offered via the Internet for a fee, and their results are available immediately to the examinee; and (c) well-known and researched instruments are being offered via the Internet, and their results are electronically sent to a counselor specified by the examinee; the results are interpreted either face-to-face or via electronic exchange with the counselor.

Numerous inventories are available on the Internet—some without fees and others on a fee basis. Examples of formal and informal no-fee assessment Web sites are as follows:

- ACT's My Profile: act.org—This site, comprised of much of the content of the former fee-based *DISCOVER* career planning system, offers ACT's UNIACT interest inventory, skills inventory, and values inventory. Scores from these assessments are used to plot the user into ACT's World-of-Work Map, which identifies both occupations and postsecondary majors for further exploration. Information about colleges and universities is also provided.

- The Career Key: careerkey.org—A Web site that includes instruction on how to choose a career; an interest inventory for middle school students, high school students, or adults that yields a Holland code; instruction about how to choose a major or training program; instruction about skills; and listing of many career resources.
- iSeek Skills Assessment: iseek.org—This site has been developed by the Minnesota state colleges and universities. The site includes an interest assessment and a skills assessment, career planning tools, and extensive occupational information. Based on data from O*Net, the iSeek Skills Assessment allows the user to rate him- or herself on 35 different skills to see which occupations match those skills identified as being most important to the user. The entire tool takes 5 to 10 minutes to complete and the results are presented immediately upon completion, offering the user information on each career, how his or her skills match this profile, and the level of education or training usually required to perform this particular job.
- Motivational Assessment of Personal Potential: assessment.com—Offers an interest inventory that measures one's interest in working with people or things and other job characteristics; suggests occupations linked to their O*Net descriptions.
- MyNextMove: mynextmove.org—This site is sponsored by the U.S. Department of Labor Employment and Training Administration and provides the O*Net assessments described previously in this chapter. There is a Spanish version of the site as well as a customized version called My Next Move for Veterans. Besides the online O*Net Interest Profiler, these sites offer extensive occupational descriptions (from the O*Net database) accessed either by title or industry.

In some cases there is little or no available information about the developers of these instruments and sites. Counselors have the ethical responsibility to become knowledgeable about the quality of an instrument before recommending that students or clients take it.

Some of the inventories described previously are available as part of a comprehensive Web-based career planning system. These for-fee sites include the following:

- Kuder's *Navigator* and *Journey* career planning systems: kuder.com—Offer the *Kuder Career Interests Assessment (KCIA)*, the *Kuder Skills Confidence Assessment (KSCA)*, and the revised *Super's Work Values Inventory*. The first two inventories are based on the theory of John Holland and provide either a Holland code or a rank-ordered profile relating the user's interests to the 16 National career clusters. *Navigator* provides a complete career guidance system for students in grades 6–12, and *Journey* addresses the career planning needs of postsecondary students and adults. The assessments provide an interactive score report with linkage to occupational information, information about postsecondary majors, and their related schools. Includes a lifetime electronic portfolio.
- *SIGI3 (System for Interactive Guidance Information)*: sigi3.org—Offers assessment of values and academic capability and links results to occupations. The system assists users to assess the priority of each occupation based on the degree to which it may help them attain their important values. Published by Valpar International Corporation.

- *Choices:* bridges.com—Offers basic skills, interests, and values assessment whose results lead to identifying occupations, providing occupational descriptions. The system uses O*Net assessments and database and also offers a college and graduate school database and a scholarship database. Published by Xap Corporation.

The availability of an expanding plethora of instruments and their interpretation via the Internet poses a significant professional challenge. Counselors who prescribe the use of such instruments have an ethical responsibility to find out about and be professionally satisfied with the quality of the instrument before prescribing it.

Another trend of the 21st century is to administer many kinds of tests—such as tests that govern entrance to colleges, graduate schools, or licensure or certification for a given occupation—through secure test sites in addition to (or instead of) through the traditional paper-and-pencil approach. Because tests of this nature are used to make decisions that appreciably affect people's lives, their items must be kept secure; and it must be ensured that examinees do not use materials that will help them identify the correct responses. They must be administered in secure environments. That means that specific places are designated to which examinees must travel. These places have computer equipment that provides good service and response time. Monitors at these locations ensure that the persons taking the tests are those who registered to take them and that the test items themselves are sent to work stations from central computers where security is guarded. This method of administration also has the capability to immediately score the tests, electronically send the results to persons or organizations authorized to receive them, and use adaptive tests. *Adaptive tests* are those that include a large number of items that measure a specific content field. These items are arranged in hierarchical order related to their level of difficulty. Using formulas developed with scientific rigor, the computer software begins by presenting a few items that are easy. If the examinee answers these correctly, the software displays items of greater difficulty. This pattern continues until the general level of the examinee's knowledge is determined. Then, a greater number of items is presented from this category of items. The characteristics of this type of testing are (a) shorter testing time in general, (b) variable testing time for each examinee, (c) immediate scoring and feedback to authorized persons, and (d) potential capability to do a more thorough testing at the specific competency level of the examinee.

TYPES OF REPORTS

Reports of the result of a test or inventory typically come to a client in print form. If the instrument has been taken on a computer or from a Web site, the report may also appear on the screen but typically can also be sent to a printer. Counselors may receive reports in print form, on a computer disk from which they can be printed, or by electronic transfer via the Internet.

The results provided in the report may be idiosyncratic—that is, related only to the individual for whom the report was prepared—or may compare that person with one or more norm groups. If the report is idiosyncratic, the results are typically provided as raw scores and may also be represented in some graphic form. *Percentile scores* indicate a point or range on a normal distribution where the examinee's score falls compared with the scores of those in the norm group. A percentile score indicates the percent of the norm group that scored lower than the examinee and, by subtraction of the score from 100, provides the percentage of the norm group that scored higher.

Norm groups can vary widely, and the score reports of some instruments will report the examinee's position related to more than one norm group. Depending on the specific instrument, a norm group may be a large national sample representative of those for whom the instrument is suggested, including both genders, a variety of ages, racial-ethnic diversity, and a variety of educational levels. Other norm groups may be one gender; specific grade level; local school district, state, or national representation; or with some interest and abilities measures, by occupational group membership.

Raw scores report the number of items chosen or correct in a given category. Raw scores on Holland's *Self-Directed Search*, for example, would indicate the number of items "liked" by the examinee in each of the six Holland clusters—R, I, A, S, E, and C. A raw score on the Mathematics section of an achievement test, on the other hand, would indicate the number of items answered correctly in that section.

Further, scores for some instruments will be reported as a single-point score on a continuum or as a range, typically called a *band of confidence*. Reporting a band of confidence is an indication by a publisher that the examinee's score falls somewhere within that range, though an exact point is uncertain. Instruments have a property called a *standard error of measurement*, and the band of confidence shows what the range of this error of measurement may be.

Percentile scores are always on a range of 1 to 99. Another way of expressing a similar concept, but with less precision, is to report a *stanine*. By definition, a stanine is a prescribed range of percentile points, and that range is the same for all instruments and all populations to which they are administered. The nine stanines have the following definitions:

Stanine 1 = below 4% of a distribution

Stanine 2 = the next 7%, percentile values 4 to 10

Stanine 3 = the next 12%, percentile values 11 to 22

Stanine 4 = the next 17%, percentile values 23 to 39

Stanine 5 = the next 20%, percentile values 40 to 59

Stanine 6 = the next 17%, percentile values 60 to 76

Stanine 7 = the next 12%, percentile values 77 to 88

Stanine 8 = the next 7%, percentile values 89 to 95

Stanine 9 = the top 4%, percentile values above 95

In summary, stanines 1 through 3 represent the lowest quarter (called a *quartile*) of any distribution; stanines 4 through 6, the middle 50%; and stanines 7 through 9, the top quarter (*quartile*).

A third way of describing how an individual's score relates to that of a norm group is the concept of a *standard score* (also called a *T-score*). This term is related to the term *standard deviation*, which is a way of measuring how far an individual's score is from the middle (i.e., the 50th percentile) of the distribution. *Standard T-scores* range from 20 to 80, with 50 at the mean (50%), and each standard deviation is counted as 10 percentile points. Thus, an individual's score may be said to be two standard deviations above the mean (that is, at the 70th percentile), or 2.5 standard deviations below the mean (that is, at the 25th percentile).

Selection of Instruments

In summary, there is a wide variety of types and purposes for assessment, and the results emanating from assessment can take many forms. Instruments represent a wide variety of quality related to their psychometric properties and may be based on a wide range of theory or on none at all. Further, these instruments can be administered to individuals or groups and in multiple modes. Counselors may choose to administer only one assessment, a variety of different assessments, or a "package" of instruments placed together so that they can measure different but complementary attributes. These facts combined with the ethical standards that are cited in this chapter make the task of selecting instruments complex. When selecting an assessment instrument, counselors must be mindful of these guidelines:

- Determine the specific purpose(s) for assessment. Then, begin by identifying instruments that fit that purpose.
- Consider the characteristics of the person or group for whom the instrument is being selected. Determine if gender, racial or ethnic background, reading ability, intelligence level, or disability signals an alert to take special care in selection.
- Review the data about the groups used for testing and norming the instrument. Determine whether these groups are representative of those to whom the instrument will be administered or that they at least contain a reasonable number of persons similar to the population to be tested.
- For instruments that still qualify, search their technical manuals for data about reliability (.80 or above) and evidence of their validity.
- Read critical reviews of the instruments in reference books and/or Web sites. Talk with at least three other counselors who use the instrument.
- Purchase a sample copy of the instrument and take it. Study the score report, and consider whether its results seem appropriate. Read the manual to understand how the publisher suggests that the instrument be interpreted.
- Before adopting the instrument for wide use, administer it to a few individuals, and practice preparing them for taking it and providing an interpretation.
- If the instrument still qualifies, find out how much it costs, its various modes of administration and scoring, and adopt it.

SUMMARY

Assessment, in its many and varied forms, has been presented as one tool among many that counselors can use with students and clients for three specific purposes: to identify their needs, help them learn more about themselves, and monitor their progress. The responsibilities of the counselor were listed. A plea was made for using assessment in combination with many other tools and techniques, in harmony with where a client is in the career development process. Cautions were stated related to not overinterpreting the meaning of scores, and counselors were admonished to use the data from career planning instruments for exploration, guidance, and confirmation rather than for prediction. In this process the client is proposed as an active agent and is encouraged not to position the counselor in a role of superior knowledge.

The types, purposes, and characteristics of assessment instruments and their reports were reviewed. Some of the most common instruments were named and briefly described, and the counselor was encouraged to explore beyond this list. Finally, guidelines for selecting instruments for individuals or groups of clients were listed.

CASE STUDY

Georgina is a 45-year-old single mother with two teenage children. For the past 20 years she has worked as an accountant for a small company. In that role she has focused entirely on budgets, expenditures, cost analyses, and report writing. Her company was recently acquired by a much larger one, and she and everyone else in her department have been replaced by staff from that company. She has been terminated with three months of severance pay. She has come to your office in a community-based counseling center to ask for help in deciding what to do next.

In the first interview Georgina asks you to give her "one of those tests that tell you what to do." You temporarily bypass this request and ask her to describe her work over the past 20 years, indicating what she did and did not like about it. You learn that her primary dissatisfaction in her past job was that there was very little opportunity to interact with people. You also ask about her interest in getting additional education or training for the purpose of being able to enter an entirely different occupation. You learn that Georgina feels strongly that she cannot pursue more or different training at this time due to family responsibilities.

You then return to the subject of her request to take one or more assessments. What do you decide to tell her? And if you decide to give her access to any kinds of assessments, which do you choose, and why?

STUDENT ACTIVITIES

1. Jennifer, a college sophomore, encouraged by her parents and her academic advisor to choose a major, sought help from the career planning and placement center in making a career choice and selecting a related major. The counselor began by administering an interest inventory that summarizes interests related to the six ACT-Holland clusters. Jennifer's profile of interests was low and flat—that is, there was very little difference among the scores for the six occupational clusters, and all were below the 25th percentile related to those of a norm group of college students. The counselor appropriately concluded that Jennifer was not ready to make a selection of possible occupations or majors, so the counselor developed a plan for additional assessment

and counseling sessions before moving on with the specific goal stated by Jennifer.

2. Write a one-page, double-spaced response to the following questions about her case.

   a. Given the results of Jennifer's interest inventory (all six ACT/Holland groups below the 25th percentile), would you recommend additional assessment? Why or why not?

   b. If you answered "yes," what would you select as assessment tools? Defend your selection of each.

   c. What other approaches, in addition to or instead of assessment, would you take with Jennifer?

3. Refer to the MyCounselingLab® Video and Resource Library and select the video entitled *21st Century Application of Holland's Theory with a College Student: Dr. Janet Lenz*, in which the client's results from having taken the *Self-Directed Search* are interpreted. Then, write a short paper that provides responses to the following items:

   a. List and describe at least three things that the counselor did well in the interpretation of the *Self-Directed Search*.

   b. What additional things might you have done or said in this interview?

   c. In Holland terminology, explain the discrepancy that the counselor uncovered between the client's current major (Kinesiology) and the results of her SDS profile.

4. Refer to the MyCounselingLab® Video and Resource Library and select the video entitled *21st Century Career Assessment Interpretation with a College Student: Dr. David Reile,* which shows a professional counselor interpreting the results of the *Campbell Interest and Skill Survey (CISS)* with a student who is unsure about his selection of major. Then,

   a. List and describe at least five positive things that the counselor did as he interpreted the *Campbell Interest and Skill Survey*.

   b. List and describe at least two additional things that you would have done in this interview.

   c. Using this interview as a model, list at least five basic guidelines for the interpretation of an inventory or test.

CHAPTER 6

CAREER INFORMATION AND RESOURCES

Career information can be a dry topic to learn and teach. Labor market information (LMI) can appear cold and "unsexy" to counselors-in-training. The daily accountability of counselor educators may create gaps between understanding the changing school and workplace and providing current career information resources. Though entering counselor training to enjoy nurturing relationships, some counselors give little attention to the systems clients face as they move through career transitions. Moving immediately into "trait-factor" matching mode to provide just the right occupational or education information to gain the client's respect is also a common trap. Knowing how to integrate LMI into the career development intervention process is an essential skill for helping others move forward in their career development.

Dr. Rich Feller
Professor Emeritus, Colorado State University

Clarice is a 28-year-old single parent of three children who lives in a modest apartment and receives support from public aid. She dropped out of high school in her sophomore year after her first child was born. She has held part-time jobs at various fast-food restaurants since that time. Clarice goes to a no-fee community agency for assistance in determining if she can get any funding for additional training or education.

MyCounselingLab®

Visit the MyCounselingLab® site for *Career Development Interventions*, Fifth Edition, to enhance your understanding of chapter concepts. You will have the opportunity to practice applying what you learned in the chapter by completing the video- and case-based exercises in the MyLab. Taking the Licensure Quizzes will help you prepare for your certification exam.

Chapter 5 addressed assessment as a tool that counselors can use to help an individual make informed choices in the career planning process. Similarly, what is commonly called *career information* must be placed within this same context. As with assessment, counselors often make the mistake of viewing career information as an end in and of itself. Actually, it is another tool that the counselor can use to assist clients to make informed choices.

As suggested by the title of this chapter and its introductory paragraph, the common term for what will be presented is career *information*. We, however, prefer career *data*, meaning a collection of facts about occupational and educational opportunities. Borrowing from Tiedeman and O'Hara (1963), we endorse the perspective that students and clients, often with the assistance of counselors and technology, collect *data*. These data become *information* only when they are understood by clients and used to *inform* decision making—that is, to assist them to choose one alternative over another.

For the sake of making the linkage between data and an individual's career planning process, see Figure 6.1. Notice the centrality of the oval labeled Resources. This is a pool of data that

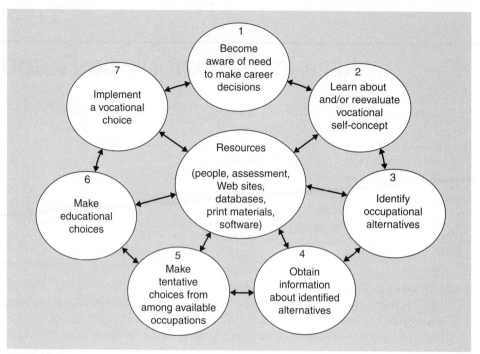

Figure 6.1
The career planning process.

Source: From *The Internet: A Tool for Career Planning,* 2nd edition, by JoAnn Harris-Bowlsbey, Margaret Riley Dikel, and James Sampson, p. 2, published by the National Career Development Association (2002). Used by permission.

should be available to a person who is in the process of career planning. Notice that at each of Steps 2 through 7, the person making a career choice needs to access data. These data may be contained in the results of assessment instruments, in print materials, in curricula, or in computer databases resident on Web sites. At Step 2, data gained from instruments measuring interests, skills, abilities, personality type, and/or values may be very useful.

At each step of the career planning process, the type, quantity, and depth of data needed may be different. This difference relates to the age of the persons going through the process. Middle school students may learn about themselves through informal assessment techniques; they may learn only about clusters of occupations (rather than individual occupations) and about possible ways of getting training and the importance of getting and maintaining satisfying jobs. Adults, on the other hand, may take formal assessment inventories and tests, and may seek the assistance of professional counselors in gaining self-information, may read highly specific occupational and educational information, and may need detailed information about companies and specific jobs. In other words, the process is common, whereas the level of specificity of the data required at each step changes with age and population.

At Step 3, search strategies that help students and clients find the titles of occupations that have or relate to the characteristics they have selected are most helpful. At Step 4, clients need to access databases or print materials that contain detailed descriptions of these identified occupations—including their work tasks, requirements for training, employment outlook, benefits and limitations, typical salary range, and sources for further information. At Step 5, which requires eliminating some of the identified occupations and keeping others, even more detailed data are needed about each. At this step, students and clients may seek data by talking with individuals who have experienced these occupations or by seeking some direct contact with the worksite as well as by reading and viewing videos.

At Step 6, students and clients need data about different ways (i.e., apprenticeship, two-year college, four-year college, vocational-technical school, etc.) to get training for occupations of their tentative choice and about options within the category they have chosen. At Step 7, students and clients need data about specific job openings and the companies or organizations that offer them.

THE COUNSELOR'S ROLE IN PROVIDING DATA

Counselors have three specific responsibilities related to career data. First, they have the responsibility to select high-quality print materials, computer-assisted career guidance systems, and Web sites—the most common sources of career data—that conform to the guidelines provided by professional associations. The most comprehensive set of guidelines is provided by the National Career Development Association (NCDA), and these are available in their entirety at ncda.org under the section titled "Guidelines." Counselors choosing resources should become familiar with this entire document.

Following are some of the salient points[1]:

- The source of the data should be clearly stated.
- Data should be updated on a regular schedule, and the date of last update should be displayed clearly.
- The material should be accurate and free from distortion caused by self-serving bias, sex stereotyping, or dated resources. Whenever possible, resources more than five years old should be avoided. Occupational descriptions should be written or at least reviewed by persons knowledgeable about each occupation.
- The data should be conveyed in a clear, concise, and interesting manner. A standard style and format for grammar should be adopted and used throughout the documents.
- The vocabulary and reading level should be appropriate for those who will be reading the material. Technical terminology or jargon should be fully explained or avoided, and use of nonsexist language is essential.
- Care should be taken to eliminate bias and stereotyping against persons with a disability or based on gender, race, social status, ethnicity, age, or religion.
- Any graphics or pictures should be current, should accurately depict the environment, and should represent without stereotype persons of both genders and of different races, ages, and physical abilities.
- If the data source deals with occupations, it should describe clearly the duties and nature of the work, work settings and conditions, preparation required for entry, special requirements or considerations, methods of entry, earnings and other benefits, usual advancement possibilities, employment outlook, opportunities for experience and exploration, related occupations, and sources of additional information.

---

[1] NCDA Policy Statements on Career Information. Copyrighted by the National Career Development Association. Reprinted with permission from NCDA.

A second responsibility of counselors is to make the availability of these high-quality resources known to students and clients and to make them as user-friendly as possible. A later section of this chapter will describe a *career center,* the usual repository for these resources and methods of organizing it. Counselors have the responsibility to acquaint students and clients with the resources, to illustrate how they can be accessed, and, even more important, to refer them to the specific ones that may be most helpful at a given point in their decision-making process. This statement underscores the fact that counselors must know these resources in detail in order to refer clients to them and to be able to discuss their content. For example, student and client use of a Web-based career planning system or of a Web site will be far less effective if counselors simply direct them to the system or site as opposed to providing a marked flowchart or site map accompanied with a statement such as "I'd like you to use *CareerOneStop,* selecting the option titled Occupation Information on the opening screen."

A third and more difficult responsibility of the counselor is to assist the client to process, or make meaningful use of, the data acquired. The goal is to turn the *data* into *information*—in other words, for the client to absorb and understand the data so that he or she can place some alternatives in high priority while discarding others. This is the most important of the counselor's roles. The counselor should have the following concerns:

- Is this client ready to receive data and deal with it effectively?
- What barriers does the client potentially have to using data effectively?
- What kinds of data, and how much, will be most helpful?
- What methods of receiving data—print material, Web sites, personal contact—will be most effective?
- What kind of decision style does the client use, and how will that affect his or her ability to use data effectively?

Barriers and Decision Styles

Students and clients may experience a variety of barriers as they search and use data. Some of these barriers may be physical, such as sight or hearing disabilities. Others may be intellectual, such as poor reading skill, poor comprehension skill, or low intelligence. Others may be cognitive, such as possession of irrational beliefs (Krumboltz, 1991) or negative thoughts (Sampson, Reardon, Lenz, & Peterson, 2003). Another barrier may be the lack of a strong self-concept or vocational identity, what some call a sense of self-efficacy. Sampson and his colleagues describe a condition of cognitive inability to understand or follow a logical information-processing model. They also underscore the premise that clients cannot make maximum use of data if they do not have the cognitive and emotional readiness to receive it.

Dinklage (1968) studied the way in which different individuals face the decision-making process. Little is known about how people acquire a specific decision-making style, but it is clear from the definitions of the eight types of "deciders" identified by Dinklage that the role of data, and therefore the work of the counselor, is different for each style. The eight types of deciders are as follows:

- *Planful.* One who approaches decision making in a systematic, step-by-step manner. Steps include setting a goal, identifying alternatives that will help reach the goal, collecting information about those alternatives, identifying one that is most likely to reach the goal, and taking action steps to implement that alternative. Persons with this decision-making style are likely to be able to make effective use of data with a minimum of assistance.

- *Agonizing.* One who attempts to engage in decision making in a systematic, step-by-step manner but becomes so engrossed in finding alternatives, collecting data about them, and trying to choose one over others that he or she is never able to reach a decision. For persons of this decision-making style, the more data that are available, the more difficult the decision becomes.
- *Impulsive.* One who does not know how to follow a systematic process or does not value it; rather, this type of decider selects an alternative quickly and does not spend the time to identify alternatives or collect data about them. Persons of this decision-making style do not recognize the need for or value of data.
- *Intuitive.* One who seems to be able to select one alternative over another (with good outcomes) without having to go through the steps of the planful process. This type of decider seems to be able to determine what his or her personal goals are quite quickly and then substitute experience and good judgment for extensive data collection. Persons of this decision-making style appear to need little data.
- *Compliant.* One who, either due to personal style or societal norms, allows others to make decisions for him or her. Persons of this decision-making style rely on the data that others may have collected.
- *Delaying.* One who recognizes that a decision needs to be made but continues to delay making it out of fear, lack of data, or lack of motivation. Persons of this decision-making style are not ready to collect or use data.
- *Fatalistic.* One who believes that he or she does not have control over the events of life and that they are largely determined by external forces. Persons of this decision-making style are not ready to collect or use data.
- *Paralytic.* One who recognizes the need to make a decision but is not able to move forward in the process because the process or the possible outcomes are very frightening. As with delaying and fatalistic types, these types of deciders are not ready to collect or use data. In fact, having a lot of data may cause them to be even more paralytic.

So students and clients present a variety of decision-making styles and levels of belief about their self-worth and self-efficacy. Many families in the White, non-Hispanic culture teach their children to follow a step-by-step, planful decision-making process in order to increase the probability of making informed decisions that yield *outcomes* or *consequences* that bring profit to the individual. On the other hand, putting the family or some other collaborative group's well-being first, ahead of personal interests and goals, is highly valued in many other cultures. Thus, the counselor should be aware that there is a cultural influence on how and why decisions are made, and these cultural differences must be respected.

Career Information and Diversity

Some students or clients who seek career information will need help that may include one-on-one assistance, special software or hardware, and/or language translation. Students with severe reading disabilities may need to have assessment items or occupational descriptions read to them. This service may be provided in Web-based systems by an on-screen character (called an avatar), by complementary audio files, or by a volunteer or paraprofessional.

Students or adults with visual disabilities will need the support of special equipment such as screen readers and related software. The sites they use will need to conform to the Web Content

Accessibility Guidelines 1.0 (w3.org/TR/WCAG10). Still others will have better understanding of the data available on the Internet if it can be displayed or described in their first language. Instructions or translation into another language can be done via an avatar or audio file. Because the software governing avatars can produce many different languages by reading a Word file of text in a given language, it is now relatively easy for developers to provide this opportunity.

THE CLIENT'S ROLE IN RECEIVING DATA

Although the counselor has a significant role in the data-gathering process, students and clients also have responsibilities: (a) to complete the assignments or suggestions provided by the counselor; (b) to work with the counselor to process the data—that is, to use them in ways that inform personal decision making; and (c) to assume responsibility for their own decision making.

The first responsibility of students and clients is to complete the data-gathering assignments that counselors give them. Unfortunately, many students and clients want quick and easy answers to their questions about career choice or change. Some expect a Web-based career planning system, a Web site, or a test to provide those answers. Others want counselors to advise them what to do and would like to shift the responsibility for decision making to them. The fact is, though, that the process of career choice and development is difficult and time consuming. It requires that one commit the time and energy to develop skill at data processing. Students and clients should be informed early in the counseling relationship about the need to spend considerable time doing the data-gathering homework that is assigned.

A second primary responsibility of students and clients is to engage in activities with the counselor that will help with the processing—that is, analyzing and making personal application—of the data that have been gathered. A student or client may, for example, read and print out the descriptions of 20 occupations identified by an interest inventory. The time required to complete that work may be wasted if the counselor and the client do not move from there to answer the question "So what?" Interests, abilities, and personality traits are very useful constructs to help students and clients identify possible occupations. Their use usually results in the identification of far more options than can be followed. The data-processing function occurs, then, when the counselor assists the client to identify and apply criteria that can be used to rank-order alternatives.

Criteria that guide decisions are typically called *values* or *characteristics*. Thus a counselor might use interviewing, a values inventory, or a card sort to help the client select several values and characteristics that can be used to eliminate and rank-order alternatives. Values are broader and deeper than characteristics. Examples of values are independence, altruism, high income, prestige, and authority. Examples of characteristics, applied to occupations, are working outside, being able to avoid overtime and night work, having longer-than-average vacations, and being able to enter the occupation without a college degree. Once preferred values and characteristics have been identified, it is possible to examine each identified alternative, using the data collected, for its potential to satisfy these. Doing so will provide a framework for eliminating some alternatives and rank-ordering the remainder, resulting in a short list of good alternatives.

A third responsibility of students and clients is to assume responsibility for their decisions. Some types of deciders—such as those described as compliant, paralytic, and agonizing—may attempt to relinquish to the counselor their right and responsibility to make decisions. It is wise to structure the expectations of the client early in the career planning process by reviewing the roles of the counselor and the client. There are times when counselors have to confront students and clients with the fact that they are not carrying out their responsibilities in the relationship.

TYPES OF DATA NEEDED BY CLIENTS

Career planning is defined as the sequential process of making educational and vocational choices based on knowledge of self and of the environment. Using this definition, it follows that, in addition to developing information about the self, students and clients need to learn about programs of study, occupations, schools and other types of training, financial aid opportunities, military service, and organizations offering jobs. Each of these databases will be considered separately.

Programs of Study

The term *programs of study* is used to describe sequences of high school courses; specialties in vocational-technical schools, apprenticeships, and the military; and majors in colleges and universities. Though it is highly desirable for individuals to have a broad base of knowledge in the liberal arts and a set of work skills like those described in the SCANS Report (U.S. Department of Labor, 1992), it is also highly desirable that individuals have coursework and training directed to the specific skills needed in the occupations of their choice. For that reason, it is very helpful to organize the courses in the high school curriculum, the specialties in on-the-job training opportunities, and the majors in college by the same organizational system used for occupations when these are presented to students. Further, the assessment used to identify interests, abilities, and/or values would also ideally be linked to the same organizational system.

Holland's typology has been applied to people through assessment instruments such as *The Self-Directed Search,* 5th edition (Holland & Messer, 2015), *Career Assessment Inventory* (Johansson, 1984), *Career Decision-Making System* (O'Shea & Feller, 2000), *UNIACT Interest Inventory* (ACT, 1989b), *Inventory of Work-Relevant Abilities* (ACT, 1989a), *Kuder Career Interests Assessment* (Kuder, 2013a), *Kuder Skills Confidence Assessment* (Kuder, 2013b), and *Campbell Interest and Skill Survey* (Campbell, 2000). The same system has been applied to occupations in *The Occupations Finder* (Psychological Assessment Resources, 2015a), *The Dictionary of Holland Occupational Codes* (Gottfredson & Holland, 1996), and the *O*NET* (U.S. Department of Labor, 2015) database. It has been applied to vocational-technical and college majors in *The Educational Opportunities Finder* (Psychological Assessment Resources, 2015b), in Web-based career planning systems such as the Kuder Career Planning System (Kuder, 2015c), and on Web sites such as careerkey.org.

The Holland codes have also been applied to leisure activities in *The Leisure Activities Finder* (Psychological Assessment Resources, 2015c); they could be used to describe job openings and company positions as well. Given this fact, one way to help students and clients process data that they collect about themselves, occupations, and educational opportunities is to organize all of this information—as well as school course offerings, career days, and data in the career center— within the same structural framework. Thus, a listing of courses offered at the high school level or majors/specialties offered at the postsecondary level, organized by the Holland typology, would be very useful in decision making.

Another system, described later in this chapter, that can be used to organize all of these pieces is ACT's World-of-Work Map (Prediger, 1981), based on the Holland typology. In this organizational scheme, ACT's assessment instruments (such as EXPLORE and PLAN) would be used, along with ACT's interactive online World-of-Work Map at act.org.

The most comprehensive source of general information about postsecondary majors and programs of study is the *Classification of Instructional Programs* (U.S. Department of Education, 2010). As suggested, high schools and colleges could easily provide a listing and descriptions of their courses and majors by Holland or World-of-Work Map categories, thus creating a local, organized database of descriptions of majors. Data about programs of study and how they relate to occupations are most relevant at Step 6 of the career planning process.

Extensive data about military programs of study are offered on Web sites such as todaysmilitary.com and armedforcescareers.com. In addition, each branch of the military also has its own Web site:

- U.S. Army: army.mil
- U.S. Navy: navy.mil
- U.S. Air Force: af.mil
- U.S. Marine Corps: marines.mil
- U.S. Coast Guard: uscg.mil

Data about military training programs are particularly relevant at Step 6 of the decision-making model as it may be possible to get the training needed for a chosen civilian occupation in the military. If not, serving in the military may provide the educational benefits needed to take coursework while serving or to continue education after leaving.

Data about apprenticeship programs in general and about programs offered in a given state are available from the U.S. Department of Labor Apprenticeship and Training Administration (doleta.gov) and from state apprenticeship offices. Such programs allow high school graduates to receive 144 hours of classroom instruction annually, typically provided without charge at the local community college, and the practical experience of learning a trade from an experienced worker while receiving a salary.

For college students, an internship program offers a valuable opportunity to learn about an occupation by experiencing it. Work-study programs allow students to work in a given occupation under supervision, receive pay for doing so, and typically earn college credit simultaneously. Data about apprenticeships and internships are relevant at Step 6 of the career planning process.

Print resources:

- *The Book of Majors 2015* (College Board, 2015b)
- *The Internship Bible, 10th ed.* (Princeton Review, 2005)
- *The Intern Files: How to Get, Keep, and Make the Most of Your Internship* (Fedorko & Allott, 2006)
- *The Back Door Guide to Short-Term Job Adventures: Internships, Extraordinary Experiences, Seasonal Jobs, Volunteering, Work Abroad* (Landes, 2004)

Web site for apprenticeships:

- Bureau of Apprenticeship and Training: doleta.gov

Web sites for internships:

- About.com: internships.about.com
- Internship Programs: internshipprograms.com
- MonsterCollege and MonsterTrak: college.monster.com

Occupations

The guidelines for occupational information provided by the National Career Development Association (1991) indicate that occupational descriptions should provide content in the following 11 areas: duties and nature of the work, work setting and conditions, preparation required, special requirements or considerations, methods of entry, earnings and other benefits, usual advancement possibilities, employment outlook, opportunities for experience and exploration, related occupations, and sources of additional information. The single most important source for data about occupations is the U.S. Department of Labor. In addition to providing descriptions of work tasks, work settings, entry methods and requirements, related occupations, and sources of additional information, the Department of Labor also conducts surveys about the labor market in general and its needs. The term *labor market* refers, on the one hand, to the supply of individuals who want and are able to work and, on the other hand, to the demand for workers from public and private employers. Surveys conducted at the state and federal level yield salaries for hundreds of occupations at the entry, median, and upper levels of experience. They also provide data about the expected growth or decline in the number of workers needed at both federal and state levels for hundreds of occupations. These data are reported in *CareerOneStop*, a Department of Labor Web site (acinet.org), under the menu item Occupation Profiles. These figures are based on estimates of the number of persons in an occupational group who will retire, number of students preparing for entry into the occupation, and number of openings expected due to growth. Labor market forecasts for different occupations are provided by the Department of Labor in the following standard categories:

If the Statement Reads:	Employment Is Projected to:
Grow much faster than average	Increase 27 percent or more
Grow faster than average	Increase 18 to 26 percent
Grow about as fast as average	Increase 9 to 17 percent
Grow more slowly than average	Increase 0 to 8 percent
Decline	Decrease any amount

Counselors need to remember that there is a great variance in the number of people in the hundreds of occupations about which the Department of Labor makes projections. Thus, the percentage of growth is meaningful only in combination with the number of people in the occupation. For example, growth of 14% in an occupation that has 130,000 incumbents represents more potential job openings than growth of 20% in an occupation that has 39,000 incumbents. The current state of demand for individuals in a given occupation is a powerful influence on the career choices of individuals.

Another comprehensive and definitive source of occupational information is O*NET, a database developed and maintained by the U.S. Department of Labor. It is within the prominent Web-based career information systems and on the Web site onetcenter.org. This database describes more than 1,100 occupations by hundreds of characteristics and is available in both English and Spanish. The organization of this database allows students and clients to relate information about themselves in many different ways, focusing on single characteristics or a combination of characteristics. It also provides a skills inventory; completion of this inventory identifies occupations in the database. Further, the site allows the download of three assessment instruments—the *O*NET Interest Profiler,* the *O*NET Ability Profiler,* and the *O*NET Work Importance Profiler*—either in print form or as executable code. Its latest development is the addition of a companion site called My Next Move (mynextmove.org). From this site users may take the *O*NET Interest Profiler,* whose results are provided in the form of a Holland code. Upon selection of a level of achieved or planned education, users receive a list of suggested occupations and can receive descriptions of these. There is a parallel site for veterans (accessible at mynextmove.org) that assists them to relate their military training to civilian jobs.

Another resource of the U.S. Department of Labor is *The Occupational Outlook Handbook* (OOH), available both in print form and on a Web site (bls.gov). This book, updated every two years, provides extensive data about the most common occupations. Lengthy descriptions include all of the topics included in the NCDA's guidelines. The content of this book is updated and expanded on a quarterly basis in *Career Outlook,* a publication available at bls.gov.

As indicated, the U.S. Department of Labor Web site *CareerOneStop* (acinet.org) is a very rich source of occupational information. The site offers a keyword-search capability for more than a thousand occupations (same titles as the O*NET database) as well as extensive descriptions of them, including detailed data about their employment outlook and salary range as a national average and by each state. There are also videos about the work tasks of most of the occupations. The site also provides a listing and data about the fastest-growing occupations, those with the largest employment, those that are declining, those that pay the highest salaries, and those related to the greening of America. The Resources section of the site offers linkages to a wide array of Web sites that provide assessment, occupational information, résumé-writing instruction, job-seeking instruction, and general career planning support. The site also provides a military-to-civilian occupation translator.

In addition to the publications, Web sites, and databases developed by the federal government, many private publishers offer high-quality material. Examples of these are listed here next. Searches for relevant occupational titles and detailed descriptions of them are most useful at Steps 3, 4, and 5 of the career planning process model.

Representative print resources include:

- *Encyclopedia of Careers and Vocational Guidance* (J. G. Ferguson Publishing, 2014)
- *The Occupational Outlook Handbook 2014–2015* (U.S. Department of Labor, 2014)

Representative Web-based systems include:

- ACT Profile (ACT, Inc., 2015)
- *CareerCruising* (Career Cruising, 2015)
- *CHOICES Explorer* and *CHOICES Planner* (Xap Corporation, 2015a, 2015b)
- *Galaxy* (Kuder, Inc., 2013c)
- *Journey* (Kuder, Inc., 2015a)
- *Navigator* (Kuder, Inc., 2015b)

Representative Web sites:

- U.S. Department of Labor sites:
  - acinet.org (*CareerOneStop*)
  - onetcenter.org (*O*NET*)

- bls.gov (*Occupational Outlook Handbook*)
- mynextmove.dol.gov (My Next Move)
- State of Arkansas: arkansasworks.kuder.com
- State of Indiana: indianacareerexplorer.com
- State of Nebraska: nebraskacareerconnections.org
- State of South Carolina sc.kuder.com
- State of Kansas: kansascareerpipeline.org
- State of Michigan: mitalent.org

Schools

Prior to seeking data about individual schools, students and clients need to understand the various types of schools, training, and degrees or certifications. These types include the following:

1. **Private (often called *proprietary*) vocational-technical schools.** These are for-profit schools that typically provide training for specific vocational fields within a three-month to two-year time frame. Though some offer associate degrees, most offer certificates that document the fact that students have successfully completed a program of study. There is a wide variation in the quality of these schools.

   Representative Web sites:

   - Guide to Career Education: collegesanddegrees.com
   - RWM Vocational Schools Database: rwm.org
   - Peterson's: petersons.com
   - College Surfing: collegesurfing.com
   - Search 4 Career Colleges: search04careercolleges.com

2. **Public community colleges.** These schools offer two categories of majors: transfer and career related. Students who enter the transfer program plan to continue at a four-year institution after two years at the community college where they typically receive an associate degree. Students in the career-related program expect to end formal education after completion of a career-technology program in fields such as electronics, information sciences, auto body repair, X-ray technology, and many more. These students receive either a certificate (in a program of less than two years in length) or an associate degree. Community colleges offer training in the same fields as private vocational-technical schools, often with much lower tuition fees and higher-quality teaching.

   Representative print resources:

   - *Peterson's Two-Year Colleges 2015* (Peterson's Publishing, 2015c)

   The representative Web-based systems and sites listed in the Occupations section of this chapter also include searches for and descriptions of community colleges.

3. **Four-year colleges and universities.** These come in many sizes and types. They may be funded by private or public funds, may be liberal arts colleges or universities, may be church related or not, and may have a wide range of admission

standards. They also have a wide variety of majors, and different schools have outstanding programs in specific areas.

Representative print resources:

- *Colleges That Change Lives: 40 Schools That Will Change the Way You Think About Colleges* (Pope & Oswald, 2012)
- *Fiske Guide to Colleges 2015*, Sourcebooks, Inc. (Fiske, 2015)
- *Profiles of American Colleges 2015* (Barron's Educational Publications, 2015)
- *Peterson's Four-Year Colleges 2015* (Peterson's Publishing, 2015b)
- *The Complete Guide to Colleges 2015* (Princeton Review, 2015a)

The representative career planning systems listed in the Occupations section of this chapter also provide searches and information about four-year colleges.

Representative Web sites:

- CollegeNET: cnsearch.collegenet.com
- College Navigator: nces.ed.gov/collegenavigator
- Go College: gocollege.com
- Peterson's Education Center: petersons.com
- *U.S. News and World Report:* usnews.com

4. **Graduate schools.** These include universities offering master's degrees, certificates of advanced study, and doctorates as well as schools of medicine, dentistry, veterinary science, and pharmacy.

Representative print resources:

- *ABA-LSAC Official Guide to ABA-Approved Law Schools: 2013 Edition* (Margolis, 2013)
- *Barron's Guide to Medical and Dental Schools* (Wischnitzer & Wischnitzer, 2012)
- *Best Graduate Schools 2015* (U.S. News and World Report, 2015)
- *Insider's Guide to Graduate Programs in Clinical and Counseling Psychology 2014–15* (Mayne, Norcross, & Sayette, 2014)
- *The Best 168 Medical Schools, 2013 Edition* (Princeton Review, 2013)
- *Peterson's Graduate Programs in Engineering and Applied Science* (Peterson's Publishing, 2015a)
- *The Official Guide to Medical School Admissions 2014: How to Prepare for and Apply to Medical School* (Association of American Medical Colleges, 2014)

Representative Web sites:

- Grad Schools: gradschools.us.com
- Peterson's Education Center: petersons.com
- *U.S. News and World Report*: usnews.com

The U.S. Department of Labor is predicting that, in the early 21st century, approximately 35% of jobs will require a bachelor's or advanced degree; 30% will require some college or an associate' degree; and the remaining 35% can be filled by high school graduates or dropouts (Carnevale, Smith, & Strohl, 2013). This information may help students and their parents make informed decisions about the levels of postsecondary education to pursue.

Financial Aid

Many students need financial aid in order to pursue the type of education they would like to have. Most schools use a federally established formula for determining whether a family or independent student needs financial assistance. This formula is embodied in the *Free Application for Federal Student Aid (FAFSA)*, a form that students and parents complete and submit for processing. It is available in print form from high school counselors or college financial aid officers and on the Internet at fafsa.ed.gov. Completing the form results in a number, called the *expected family contribution*, which reveals the dollar figure that a family (or an independent student not supported by family) is considered capable of contributing toward a year of college. The formula used in FAFSA can be summarized as follows:

Total cost of one year at college minus Expected Family Contribution for one year equals Unmet need.

Using this general formula, note these two examples:

$40,000 (expensive college)	$22,000 (less expensive college)
$14,600 (expected family contribution)	$14,600 (expected family contribution)
$25,400 (unmet need)	$ 7,400 (unmet need)

The college financial aid officer at the expensive college would try to provide financial assistance to the student who filed this application in the amount of the *unmet need*—that is, $25,400. This amount may be awarded from three kinds of resources: private, state, or federal grant funds; federal loan funds; and/or part-time work on campus. Money allocated from the first source would not have to be repaid. Loans, however, would have to be repaid. Typically, repayment starts after graduation and entry into a job, and the rate of interest is reasonable.

High school counselors and college financial aid officers know about many hidden sources of financial aid. These may be grants from community organizations, professional associations, companies, and individuals who have set up trust funds for this purpose. Further, many types of financial aid are provided by state and federal governments. In addition to learning about private sources on the job, counselors find the following resources to be valuable.

Representative print resources:

- *College Board Scholarship Handbook 2015* (College Board, 2015a)
- *Paying for College Without Going Broke 2015* (Princeton Review, 2015a)
- *The Ultimate Scholarship Book 2015: Billions of Dollars in Scholarships, Grants, and Prizes* (Tanabe & Tanabe, 2015)

Representative Web sites:

- CollegeBoard: bigfuture.collegeboard.org
- FastWeb: fastweb.com
- Scholarships.com: scholarships.com
- *U.S. News and World Report*: usnews.com
- U.S. Department of Education: studentaid.ed.gov
- National Association of Financial Aid Administrators: finaid.org

Information about financial aid is relevant at Step 6 of the career planning process.

Jobs

In many settings counselors assist students and clients in writing résumés, learning job inter-viewing skills, and identifying job openings, activities related to Step 7 of the career planning process. Adults can seek such services from their state job service offices (often called career centers or one-stop centers). The locations and services of these offices can be found at servicelo-cator.org. In addition, many good Web sites assist with this step.

Especially in times of economic downturn, counselors need to be prepared to assist clients with grieving job loss, and with learning how to survive while unemployed and how to find a job. Many adults who find themselves out of work have not had to face the job market for many years. They do not know how to prepare or update their résumés, how to apply their skills to other occupations, or how to present themselves in a job interview. Young people and adults do not know how to use social networking wisely in the job search, and indeed, many are never invited to an interview because of the kinds of public posting they have done on sites like Face-book. Chapter 7 provides more information about the power of the Web for creating and sustain-ing a social network that can be positive for job searching.

There are multiple books on all of these topics, but the Web is an abundant and rapidly updated source of information about jobs and job seeking. Two sites that offer a large amount of information on these topics as well as the capability to post résumés and see employer job listings are Riley's Guide (rileyguide.com) and Job Hunters Bible (jobhuntersbible.com).

Representative Web sites:

- Most states have a Web-based job bank, listing open positions in their state. Go to or call the nearest job service office (servicelocator.org) to use this job bank or get its URL for your state.
- CareerBuilder: careerbuilder.com
- Indeed: indeed.com
- NationJob: nationjob.com
- MonsterBoard: monsterboard.com
- Richard Bolles's site: jobhuntersbible.com
- The Riley Guide: rileyguide.com

OTHER METHODS OF COLLECTING DATA

The previous section focused on collecting data to inform the decision-making process through reading books, Web sites, or computer databases. Reading the resources listed in this chapter will be very helpful to support Steps 3 (identify occupational alternatives), 4 (collect data), 5 (make tentative choices), 6 (make educational choices), and 7 (implement a vocational choice). How-ever, it will be even more helpful at Step 5 (make tentative choices) to collect data from addi-tional sources, including career days, job shadowing, part-time jobs, and internships.

Career days, commonly offered in high schools, expose students to a wide variety of occu-pations through direct contact with people who work in those occupations. Speakers may be brought in to the school or students may be taken to workplaces. In either case the experience will have greater meaning if (a) the occupations are categorized in some meaningful way and (b) there has been some prior activity that suggests specific occupations for exploration. The occupations represented in the career fair may be organized by the six Holland or ACT clusters or by the 16 National industry-based clusters (see careertech.org). Assessment may have been administered to identify the students' preferred clusters. Students can then be scheduled to hear speakers or visit sites that represent those clusters.

Common ways for students to learn about occupations are mentoring (which may be e-mentoring) and job shadowing. In job shadowing, arrangements are made for students to spend a day with a person in an occupation they are considering. This firsthand experience allows students to view day-to-day activities of the occupation, experience a typical worksite, and ask questions of a person in the occupation. Part-time jobs, carefully chosen, can offer the same kind of experience for a longer period of time. At the college level, students may apply for an internship in an occupation of their choice. An internship allows students to take coursework and work part-time simultaneously. Students receive pay for the work and may also receive college credit.

These methods of providing on-site exploration of occupations can be very valuable when well supported. First, they must be well planned and organized so that students with specific interests are matched with people and sites that represent those interests. Second, students should be prepared for the experience in advance. Such preparation would include explaining the purpose of the experience and providing worksheets or guidelines for what the student should learn. It is as valuable to find out that interest in the occupation is not confirmed as it is to find out that there is interest in that occupation. Finally, as with all kinds of data collection, there should be a follow-through activity, either individual or group, that helps students analyze what they have learned and what the learning means for personal decision making or further exploration.

ORGANIZING OCCUPATIONS

In the former *Dictionary of Occupational Titles* (U.S. Department of Labor, 1991), nearly 13,000 occupations were described, and more than 1,100 groups of occupations are detailed in the *Dictionary*'s replacement, called *O*NET*. This vast difference in number of occupations exists because the *Dictionary of Occupational Titles (DOT)* breaks occupations into finer divisions; for example, the *DOT* describes multiple types of cooks (fast-food cook, pastry cook, pizza cook, etc.), whereas *O*NET* provides a general description of cook.

Even with the smaller number of 1,100 occupations, it is necessary to present these to career planners in some organized way. It is impossible to learn about all occupations individually, and providing information about groups of occupations allows students and clients to narrow their search to specific groups prior to getting into great detail. There are four common organizational systems used in schools and agencies: Holland's system (Holland, 1997), ACT's World-of-Work Map classification system (Prediger, 1981), the Department of Labor (2015) *O*NET* system, and the states' career clusters. Each is briefly described in the following sections.

The Holland System

Holland's theory (1997) proposes that work environments can be described as combinations of six different types: Realistic, Investigative, Artistic, Social, Enterprising, and Conventional. Definitions of these six types are provided in Chapter 2. Based on more than 40 years of research, Holland and his collaborators have provided three-letter Holland codes for most occupations.

The Occupations Finder (Psychological Assessment Resources, 2015a) provides codes for 1,224 occupations; the *Dictionary of Holland Occupational Codes* (Gottfredson & Holland, 1996) provides codes for 12,860 occupations. The *O*NET* database provides a two-letter Holland code for each of its occupations. As reviewed in Chapter 5, taking one of several inventories of interests and/or skills will provide a personal Holland code for a student or client. Use of such assessment will make it easy for counselors to recommend, or students to choose, speakers or sites that are most likely to be of interest to them.

The World-of-Work Map

Based on the research done by Holland while employed by ACT, the original hexagonal model was expanded to a circle called the World-of-Work Map (Figure 6.2). In addition to changing the hexagon to a circle, the six Holland personality types describing characteristics of people were changed to titles for six groups of occupations that provide work tasks and environments that the persons of a given Holland type would be likely to enjoy. Further, the concept of primary work tasks—that is, working with People, Data, Things, and/or Ideas—was added based on further research (Prediger, 1981). Thus, the Holland types have the following equivalents on the World-of-Work Map:

Holland type	ACT occupational cluster	Primary work tasks
Social	Social Service	Work with People
Enterprising	Administration/Sales	Work with People and Data
Conventional	Business Organization	Work with Data and Things
Realistic	Technical	Work with Things
Investigative	Science and Technology	Work with Things and Ideas
Artistic	Arts	Work with Ideas and People

Finally, ACT's research identified 26 families of occupations called *career areas*, groups of homogenous occupations, based on their work tasks. These 26 career areas were plotted on the World-of-Work Map based on the degree to which the occupations in the group require work with data, people, things, and/or ideas. On a horizontal continuum through the map, those groups that require relatively more contact with people are placed to the left of center, and those requiring more work with things/equipment are plotted to the right of center. On a vertical continuum through the map, those families that require relatively more work with data are plotted above the center line of the map, and those requiring relatively more work with ideas are plotted below the center line of the map.

Using ACT's Web site (actstudent.org), it is possible to find out where more than 500 common occupations and majors are plotted on the map. Using ACT's career planning assessments, it is possible to plot individuals on the map based on their interests and/or self-estimated abilities. High schools, vocational-technical schools, and colleges can assign their majors to the 26 career areas and thus to occupations. ACT's Web site at actstudent.org also offers exploration of postsecondary majors by clusters and career areas on the map. ACT's *Profile* (act.org) provides a free-of-charge systematic career guidance system based on the World-of-Work Map.

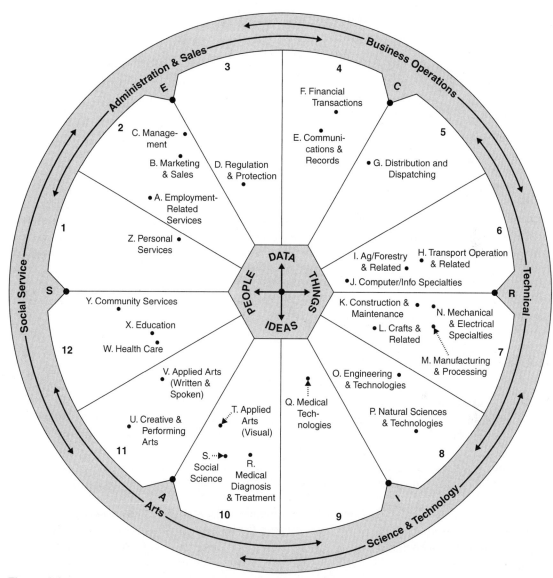

Figure 6.2
World-of-Work Map.

*O*NET* Classification System

O*NET has become the foundational source for occupational information, available at onet.center.org. As mentioned, it offers a very detailed description of more than 1,100 occupational groups related to the content and context of work. Occupations are described by more than 300 characteristics, including worker requirements, knowledge areas needed, basic and cross-functional skills needed, associated work values, Holland code, work tasks, education requirements, experience, and training. A skills search allows individuals to assess their own skills and to relate them to occupations in the database. The results of the *O*NET Interest Profiler*, *Ability Profiler*, and *Work Importance Locator* link individuals directly to occupations in this database. The My Next Move Web site (mynextmove.org) offers an online version of the *O*NET Interest Profiler* whose results suggest a list of occupations related to the user's interests and planned education level. Selecting any of the occupations on the list provides a short description of the occupation and offers a link to online *O*NET* for a more detailed description.

The National Career Clusters

The U.S. Department of Education established 16 broad career clusters. Each cluster consists of entry-level through professional-level occupations in a broad industry area. The cluster also includes the academic and technical skills and knowledge needed for further education and work in the occupations contained in the cluster. Occupations assigned to a cluster are divided into subgroups, or specialties called *career pathways*. Descriptions of these clusters are available atcareertech.org. The *Kuder Career Interests Assessment* (Kuder, Inc., 2013a) and the *Kuder Skills Confidence Assessment* (Kuder, Inc., 2013b) link individuals to the titles of occupations and postsecondary majors in these clusters through Kuder's career planning systems, *Navigator* (Kuder, Inc., 2013b) and *Journey* (Kuder, Inc., 2013a).

THE CAREER CENTER

The resources cited in this chapter and many others—including videos, journals, books, assessment instruments, and a variety of software programs—must be housed in some physical place, typically called a *career center*. This physical place should be of sufficient size to handle the collection, be an attractive place to read or use computers, be centrally located within the larger facility, and be well organized. Especially given the growing importance of Web sites as providers of career data, the center should contain computers both for the use of locally resident software and for linkage to the Internet. It also should contain equipment for viewing videos and taking assessment instruments.

There are various methods of organizing materials in a career center: (a) by type (print, video, software locally used, Internet access); (b) by content (self-information, occupational information, school information, financial aid information, etc.); (c) by step of the career planning process; or (d) by life role (student, worker, parent, leisurite, citizen, etc.).

Career centers should be staffed with one or more trained persons who have extensive content knowledge of all of their resources. In recognition of the need for trained personnel to work in career centers in support of counselors and clients, the National Occupational Information Coordinating Committee (NOICC) funded the development of a curriculum in the early 1990s for training paraprofessionals. This new occupation has been titled career development facilitator (CDF). The curriculum addresses 12 basic competencies that these paraprofessionals need, including basic helping skills, knowledge of labor market and occupational information, job-seeking skills, and ability to navigate computer-based systems and Web sites. Upon successful completion of this curriculum (for detailed information, see ncda.org) and application to the Center for Credentialing and Education (CCE), individuals can be certified. Trained CDFs can help students and clients acquire data to assist with career planning. Counselors need to assume responsibility for assisting students and clients in processing and making effective use of those data for personal decision making.

Virtual career centers are increasingly being developed on the Internet. Typically, these contain a combination of online assessments, locally developed databases (such as descriptions of majors available at a given institution), linkages to a selected and organized list of Web sites, and support from a counselor via the Internet. Such support may be by synchronous (both persons at the computer at the same time) or asynchronous (persons not at the machine at the same time) e-mail or video conferencing using a product such as Skype. With the rapidly expanding technology that allows images to be transmitted in real time, it has become feasible for counselors and clients to have real-time, face-to-face conversation via the Internet, removing the barrier of distance.

Tips from the Field

Despite a wealth and often an overload of data about occupations, majors, schools, and financial aid, counselors must assist their students/clients in processing these data through their own interests, skills, and values. In other words, the data only have meaning when they inform an individual's personal decision making.

HELPING CLIENTS TURN DATA INTO INFORMATION

The most difficult and also the most essential role of the counselor is to assist students and clients to make sense out of what can be an overload of data about occupations, schools and other training opportunities, financial aid, and so on. The goal is to use the data to make it clear which of the various alternatives (about occupational choice, type of training or school, scholarships available, and/or jobs to apply for) should be further explored and which should be removed from consideration. This chapter section illustrates how counselors can perform this essential work and offers two case studies.

Chris is a high school junior who feels pressured by both his counselor and his parents to state an occupational goal and have an educational plan. As a part of some special career guidance activities the counselors are doing in English classes, he spent two hours in the school's career center. While there he took an interest inventory included in a computer-based career planning system, which provided a printout with the titles of 48 occupations. At the direction of the paraprofessional in the center, he found many facts about 12 of these occupations through reading reference books, using the system's database, and linking to some sites on the Internet. As a result, he has 34 pages of printout and feels more confused about his possible choice of occupation than he did when he came into the center. Fortunately, he is going to have an interview with his counselor; he hopes that she can help him out of his confusion.

In this typical case, what can a counselor do to provide helpful assistance that will cut through this pile of paper and help the student move to some certainty about next career planning steps? Here are some suggestions:

- If the student has taken the interest inventory only in the Web-based system, the counselor should consider what other kind(s) of assessment, if any, might be helpful in this specific case. Since Chris is a high school junior, an assessment of values might be premature. A simple checklist of job characteristics, from which Chris is asked to select 5 to 10 items that are most important, would be one good approach.

- The counselor may ask Chris to tell about some of the most interesting courses, experiences, or leisure activities he has had and ask why he found these interesting, relating these reasons to characteristics of occupations.
- A review of Chris's high school record may help him identify some courses and abilities that surpass others. The counselor may also ask him about his plans or aspirations for education after high school.
- Chris may be asked to list occupations about which he has daydreamed in the past and tell what was attractive to him about these, even though he may not know the details of the work tasks or training. From this activity and previous ones, he can make a list of characteristics of importance to him (such as having a lot of independence, making more than the average amount of money, not having to travel long distances as a requirement of work, or not working with numbers and mathematics).
- Chris could share the list of occupations identified by the interest inventory he took, relating which, if any, of these occupational titles were attractive to him, and why. He could state which, if any, of these he would not consider and why, and compare the characteristics of occupations on the list with the personal list he has just developed.
- Using the list from the Web-based system and any others that may have been added during interviews, Chris might be asked to place the titles in three columns: those he would definitely not pursue, those that hold some promise, and those that he is favoring most.
- Chris should be given assignments designed to help him learn more about the list of occupations he is favoring most. This may initially include further research in the career center—using books, software, or Internet sites—depending on whether Chris has already adequately researched the favored occupations in this way. Additional activities may be designed to put Chris directly in touch with people who work in this occupation. This may be a job-shadowing assignment or an information interview with one or more persons who work in each of these occupations. He should be given a worksheet as part of the assignment to ensure that he collects the data that he needs. This worksheet should include questions that he suggests as well as the ordinary ones, such as benefits and limitations of the job, training required, opportunities for promotion, degree of independence, and what the person wishes he or she had known before entering the occupation.
- Following this assignment, Chris should be scheduled for another interview to discuss what he has learned from these assignments. He may further analyze each of the occupations he has researched by using the list of important characteristics developed in the previous session and writing down his current list of preferred occupations in priority order. He should be aware that he will make numerous career changes during his lifetime and that he should consider and be prepared for more than one occupation.
- With a short list of occupations in mind, Chris and his counselor should review the amount and type of education needed for these jobs and determine whether they all require the same level of education, such as community college or four-year college, or whether some could be entered through apprenticeship. Based on this review, Chris may be able to select a postsecondary educational goal. This might be an ideal time to include his parents in the discussion of his goals.

- Dependent on the postsecondary plans, Chris may be directed to other resources (computer searches, Web sites, books) that will assist with the selection of schools in which the needed training can be acquired. The counselor can provide a worksheet that lists the characteristics (such as geographic location, size of school, level of admission selectivity, type of school, cost range, student activities, etc.) that he and his parents can consider. He also needs to determine how various selections (such as how large the school is or how far away from home it is) will affect him and his parents.
- The counselor may help Chris to select the most relevant courses for his senior year and to make a timetable for coming back to talk about school selection, taking entrance tests, and filing applications for entry and financial aid.

This suggested approach combines good use of technology for acquiring data with counselor support for processing the data in a way that helps Chris and his parents make informed decisions.

As indicated at the beginning of this chapter, Clarice is a 28-year-old single parent of three children who lives in a modest apartment and receives support from public aid. Recent legislation, however, has mandated that she go to work within a year and has provided access to funding for some training. She dropped out of high school in her sophomore year after her first child was born. She has held part-time jobs at various fast-food restaurants since that time. Clarice goes to a no-fee community agency for assistance in determining what she can do to meet the requirements of the legislation.

What can a counselor do? Here are some suggestions:

- An extensive intake interview is a needed first step. During this interview, the counselor can learn about high school courses taken, expressed interests, motivational level, skills, details of part-time jobs, family situation, support system (network of friends and family), barriers (such as physical handicaps, need for child care, and lack of transportation), and goals.
- The counselor might decide to administer some assessment, such as an interest inventory (to broaden the options that the client may have expressed). From the list of occupations suggested by this inventory and the intake interview, the counselor and client can develop a list of reasonable (in terms of the amount of training needed) options. Clarice and the counselor make a list of five characteristics that are most important for the occupation to be selected: (a) does not require more than two years of training beyond high school completion, (b) does not require work during the evening or on weekends, (c) offers an opportunity to work directly with people and with equipment, (d) offers an opportunity for career growth when additional education can be attained when children are older, and (e) offers a beginning salary of at least $30,000 per year.
- The counselor asks Clarice to go to the local library and access *The Occupational Outlook Handbook* and *CareerOneStop* Web sites to learn details about the identified occupations. Clarice has not used the Internet before, so the counselor provides a worksheet with step-by-step instructions about how to access each of these sites and how to find the assigned information. Further, the counselor instructs the client to go to a specific person at the library to receive some general instruction about how to use the equipment and how to obtain assistance that may be needed in completing the assignment. The counselor asks Clarice to bring the printout to the next session or good, detailed notes if the library charges for printed pages and the cost of this is not feasible.

- Clarice completes the assignment and comes back the next week with printed descriptions of several occupations that require high school completion and training beyond that. The counselor helps Clarice evaluate each of the occupations in relation to the five criteria developed during the intake interview. Three occupations pass that review: radiation therapist, dental assistant, and dental hygienist. According to *CareerOneStop,* there is a high demand for workers in all three of these occupations in Clarice's state of residence, and beginning salaries for all three are above $30,000.
- The counselor suggests that Clarice complete two homework assignments before the next session: (a) have an informational interview with a person in each of these three occupations and (b) investigate sources of getting a high school diploma by taking the General Educational Development (GED) exam. The counselor explains what an information interview is and gives Clarice a list of suggested questions to which she can add others. The counselor makes some phone calls and sets up these three interviews at times when Clarice's mother will care for the youngest child. The counselor also gives Clarice the URL address of the Web site of the state labor department. One section of this site provides a list of opportunities for completing the GED exam.
- Clarice returns after completion of these assignments with enthusiasm about the opportunity to prepare for taking the GED exam through a course offered by the local community college. Her mother has agreed to stay with the children one night per week so that she can attend this course. Further, she indicates that, based on the visits she has made, she would like to pursue training to become an X-ray technician.
- The counselor works with Clarice, using a specific form, to develop an action plan and a time schedule designed to accomplish two primary goals: (a) getting a high school diploma by preparing to take the GED exam and (b) seeking entry into the X-ray technician program at the community college. The plan includes funding by the agency for the GED preparation course and coursework in the X-ray technician program at the community college. The plan also includes child care during class times and transportation to the community college. The counselor invites Clarice to call her at any time and indicates that she should call each month to make an appointment so that they can review progress in completion of the action plan.

MyCounselingLab®

Start with Topic 11—Information in Career Guidance.

SUMMARY

This chapter has described various types of resources available in print and electronic form that are critical sources of data as individuals engage in the career planning process. The responsibilities of counselors in selecting and using these resources wisely are reviewed. Similarly, the responsibilities of students and clients to spend the time and effort needed to acquire data are reviewed. Great emphasis is placed on the fact that providing good data to students and clients is not in and of itself sufficient to ensure that career decision making will be informed. The counselor's responsibility and role to help students and clients sort through a mass of data and transform elements of it into meaningful information is stressed. Finally, two cases have been presented with suggestions about how a counselor might deal with them.

CASE STUDY

Roel is a college sophomore, and he is faced with the need to declare a major. He comes to you in his college counseling center to ask for your assistance. You ask him how he has reached other major decisions in his life, such as which part-time jobs to accept, which car to buy, or which college to attend.

As Roel recounts how he has made these decisions and others, you begin to see the pattern that he typically is an impulsive decider, selecting an alternative that sounds good at the moment without seeking other alternatives or in-depth information.

Given this past history, how would you go about helping Roel to select one of more than one hundred majors available at your college?

STUDENT ACTIVITIES

The suggestions provided for Clarice on pages 177–178 are quite traditional and reflect a cognitive decision-making approach. This approach serves many clients well but is not helpful for others. Think about and write an answer to these two questions within one double-spaced page:

- For what kinds of clients might this approach *not* be helpful? Why?
- What alternate approaches might a counselor use to help Clarice reconstruct her life?

CHAPTER 7

USING INFORMATION AND COMMUNICATION TECHNOLOGIES TO SUPPORT CAREER COUNSELING AND PLANNING

Technology changes lives. For some, the changes are better; for others the changes are perceived as negative. In many ways career counselors have been at the forefront of changes in society and mental health. They have been among the first to use new tools and techniques in their work. Nowhere has this been truer than in the use of technology. The use of computers and, more recently, the Internet have changed the ways in which career counselors assist their clients. Though career counselors are, first and foremost, counselors, they are also providers of information. The provision of information when assisting clients with résumé writing, interview coaching, networking, and choosing education and training venues has been made better, faster, and more comprehensive through the Internet. Career counselors are now able to devote more time to counseling and coaching their clients while being able to quickly and easily locate information that supports their work. Popular Web sites have come and gone. However, in the years since becoming mainstream, the Internet has significantly changed the way career counselors do their work. Now there is no going back. We must learn to use technology to be effective and to provide our clients with the service they need and expect.

David M. Reile, Ph.D., NCCC
Career Development Alliance

MyCounselingLab®

Visit the MyCounselingLab® site for *Career Development Interventions*, Fifth Edition, to enhance your understanding of chapter concepts. You will have the opportunity to practice applying what you learned in the chapter by completing the video- and case-based exercises in the MyLab. Taking the Licensure Quizzes will help you prepare for your certification exam.

In Chapter 2 you learned about Juanita, a 17-year-old Hispanic student in the eleventh grade who appears to be struggling with poor self-concept, low motivation, low career maturity, lack of role models, and other factors related to making an informed vocational choice. Using one or more theoretical models presented earlier in this text, Juanita's counselor dealt with these factors through one-to-one and small-group interventions. After noting positive change in self-concept, motivation, and career maturity, the high school counselor decided to give Juanita some specific assignments related to the Web-based career planning system that the school has and use of several Web sites. You will note those assignments as you read this chapter.

The purposes of this chapter are to define and describe the various technologies that have an impact on the delivery of career planning services in the 21st century, to define the counselor's role as individuals use those technologies, and to propose how they can best be used to enhance the delivery of career planning services. There is an understandable tendency to confine our perception of technology to that provided by the computer or the Internet. Actually, the field of career planning has been impacted by technologies other than the computer—the test-scoring machine, the video camera, and the smartphone, for example. Computers, however, have exerted the most powerful impact on the field because of their capabilities to administer, score, and interpret tests and inventories; teach skills and concepts; facilitate interactive dialogue; store, search, and interrelate huge databases; store a record of the user's interaction; and prompt and monitor a user's interaction with the system. These computer capabilities have been progressively developed and applied to the field of career guidance since the late 1960s. Progress of computer-based technology can be viewed in the light of two different contexts. The first context relates to the ever-growing capability of computers progressing from early, stand-alone mainframe computers to networked mini- and personal computers, to the World Wide Web of computers, to expansion of services to smartphones and tablets, and finally to the incredible impact of social media. Each of these progressive steps has increased the potential to serve an increased number of individuals while also presenting an increasing variety of ethical concerns. With this expansion, what used to be called computer-assisted career information and guidance is now called information and communication technology (ICT).

The second context is the growing knowledge and body of research that informs counselors about the effectiveness of computer-delivered services for different populations and for different purposes. Many of these purposes have already been covered in Chapters 5 and 6 due to the fact that assessment, occupational information, educational information, and a host of other applications relevant to career planning are now almost exclusively accessed on the Web.

The results of a significant number of studies have provided evidence that use of computer-assisted career guidance systems deliver desirable outcomes. Here are a few of those outcomes:

- System users are consistently satisfied with their experiences (Fowkes & McWhirter, 2007).
- Computer-assisted systems appear to be most effective when used in conjunction with other career interventions that include some type of practitioner intervention (Fowkes & McWhirter, 2007; Gore & Leuwerke, 2008).
- Computer-assisted systems are most effective when users make in-depth, focused use of them, spending hours rather than minutes in absorbing their content (Gore, Bobek, Robbins, & Shayne, 2006).
- Users of computer-assisted systems had higher career decision-making self-efficacy (Betz & Borgen, 2010; Maples & Luzzo, 2005), a greater sense of control over decision making (Maples & Luzzo, 2005), and increased confidence in career decision making (Bobek et al., 2005).
- Students who entered occupations suggested by a computer-assisted system enjoyed higher job satisfaction years later than those who did not follow the system's suggestions. In a longitudinal study in Israel, Gati, Reuma, and Shemesh (2006) tested the predictive validity of Making Better Career Decisions (MBCD), a computer-assisted career planning system. The participants were divided into two groups: individuals whose chosen occupation was on the list of occupations recommended by MBCD and individuals whose

chosen occupation was not on the recommended list. In the first group, 84% were highly satisfied with their occupational choice and 16% were satisfied to a moderate extent while in the second group only 38% were highly satisfied with their chosen occupation, 44% were satisfied to a moderate extent, and 18% were dissatisfied with their choice.

- Use of a computer-assisted career guidance system increases the likelihood of secondary students transitioning to postsecondary education (D'Achiardi-Ressler, 2008).
- Use of a computer-assisted career guidance system to take an interest assessment, receive its interpretation, and choose a college major aligned with measured interests significantly increases the probability that students will remain in that major and complete their degrees (D'Achiardi-Ressler, 2008).
- Use of a computer-assisted career guidance system to take an interest assessment, receive its interpretation, and choose a college major aligned with measured interests predicts a higher grade point average for those users than for students who did not use such a system (Trusty, 2014).

INFORMATION AND COMMUNICATION TECHNOLOGIES: TRENDS OF THE 21ST CENTURY

Career guidance and information Web sites and systems of the 21st century are characterized by some new features, representing a synthesis of capabilities not possible in earlier versions. These include the following:

- Almost all systems and applications are Web based rather than installed on individual computers or networks.
- There is ever-expanding use of dynamic graphics, audio, and streaming video to enhance the message of the systems.
- There are multiple linkages to other sites on the Web and then back to the system itself for the purpose of expanding exponentially the amount of information a user can gain while still being "shepherded" within the confines of an integrated system.
- With more comprehensive systems, it is very common to offer the user the capability to start an e-portfolio at first sign-on and then to maintain and update that portfolio over the life span.
- With more comprehensive systems, there is a trend to include content for multiple audiences (i.e., students in grades 5–6, grades 7–8, high school, postsecondary level; adult workers; parents; administrators and counselors) within one system, and to direct the user to appropriate material based on information gained at sign-on.
- There is an increased capability to store documents (such as scanned certificates, transcripts, résumés, cover letters, and work samples) in the user's e-portfolio and then to send these to schools or employers as needed.
- There is a trend for the development of an integrated Web site for no-fee use by all citizens in a given state (such as in Alabama, Nebraska, Missouri, Kansas, South Carolina, and Arkansas) through cooperative development and funding by the departments of education, labor, economic development, and/or commerce. This trend is now expanding to countries—including Abu Dhabi, Qatar, and Rwanda—which have not previously offered career guidance services.

- There is an increasing trend to foster communication between and among users by sharing information (such as assessment results) generated within an integrated career guidance system with others via social media.
- There is an increasing trend to use social media sites for the purpose of creating electronic networks for job searching and learning about companies and jobs.
- There is an increasing trend to make career planning tools previously available only by computer access also available via tablets and smartphones.

THE INTERNET AS THE DELIVERER OF CAREER GUIDANCE

Most computer-based career planning systems are now delivered on the Internet. The Internet as a delivery tool—in contrast to a stand-alone or networked computer—has the following advantages:

- The system is available from home, the library, the coffee shop, and many other places on a 24/7 basis. It may also be available on a smartphone.
- There is a potential to serve an incredibly larger audience.
- E-portfolios can be developed and maintained on a Web site to which users may have lifelong access and from which documents (such as résumés, evidence of certifications, transcripts, etc.) can be sent electronically to employers or schools.
- Databases can be updated more frequently because they are developed and updated from one central source to which all end-user stations are connected.
- Linking to the resources of the Internet and to e-mail communication can be more seamlessly included in the system.
- Counselors can communicate with system users, also via the Internet, while they are online.

We now look at the state of use of technology for career guidance purposes in the early 21st century. Although this description is confined to what is happening in the United States, it is important to note that the use of Web-based services via computers, tablets, and smartphones is in common practice worldwide. Some developing countries appear to be jumping over the computer age to develop telephone-based applications, due to the fact that a larger proportion of their populations have Web access via a phone rather than by computer.

Stand-alone Web Sites

There are hundreds, if not thousands, of single-purpose Web sites that address some part of the career planning process. Many of these have already been listed in Chapters 5 and 6. These are sites that provide one or more of the following:

- A formal or informal assessment tool with interpretation
- A search for vocational-technical schools, colleges, or universities by multiple characteristics, providing a list and the capability to get in-depth information about each
- A search for grants and scholarships by multiple characteristics, providing a list and information about how and when to apply
- A search by title or industry for occupations, providing extensive information about each

- A search for job openings, using location, job type, and other characteristics, and access to a description of each opening and information about how to apply
- Tools and templates to develop a résumé or an electronic portfolio
- Instruction about how to find job openings, prepare appropriate documents, and participate in an effective job interview

Some of these types of sites have been developed and are being maintained by very reliable professional sources while others do not have this credibility.

Integrated Career Planning Systems

In contrast to the types of Web sites just described, the application described here is a Web site that incorporates tools and databases that assist users through a sequential process that includes multiple steps in the career planning process. The process is typically devised for a specific population such as elementary school students, middle school students, secondary school students, postsecondary students, unemployed adults, veterans, older unskilled adults, or unskilled youth in need of job skills. In other words, for each of these populations a developer has gone through the process of identifying the needs of some specific population and of creating content designed to address those needs. For elementary students, for example, those needs could be gaining some self-awareness as well as awareness of the breadth of the world-of-work and of the fact that there is a relationship between the two. For older, low-income, unskilled adults, as another example, the needs might be to assess current interests and work skills, provide training to improve skills, assist with developing a résumé, teach job interviewing skills, and provide a searchable database of jobs. In other words, integrated career planning systems offer a planned sequence of activities or resources specifically designed to meet the needs of a given target population. Typically, an electronic portfolio is developed for each user as a repository of choices made while using the system, résumés, cover letters, references, assessment results, and documents such as certificates of achievement or career readiness.

Integrated career planning systems are typically developed as a whole with many different content topics, each of which may be used independently, but all of which contribute to the interaction of the total system. In more specific terms, such systems may have an online interest assessment, a searchable occupational database, a searchable national postsecondary school database, a résumé writer, and a database of job openings. Some users may take only the interest assessment, use the searchable occupational database, and get occupational descriptions. Other users may go directly to the résumé writer and then to the searchable jobs database. Some systems are "intelligent" enough to identify the users' needs and to direct them to the specific parts of a large system that they need to use at a current decision point. An electronic portfolio that monitors and saves the results of use serves as the integrating piece of the system.

Most of the integrated career planning systems available in the United States have already been mentioned in Chapters 5 or 6, as they also offer assessment and provide educational and career information. Some companies that develop such systems offer only one version for all populations, while others offer different versions for persons of different age ranges. Some of these companies offer only a standard system while others offer a wide range of customization options, including developing totally customized systems for users in a specific state, agency, or country. As the developers of these systems often respond to competitive requests for proposals (RFPs) that require functionality beyond their usual offerings, there is also a growing tendency for them to partner with other companies that can offer additional services, such as electronic transfer of transcripts, online college applications, or preparation for taking college-entrance examinations. The following is a list of integrated systems in the United States and their contact information:

- ACT Profile – ACT, Inc., Box 168, Iowa City, IA., 42243-0168; act.org
- Career Information System (intoCareers) – 5258 University of Oregon, Eugene, OR 97403-1244; intocareers.com
  - Six products: CIS Junior, CIS High School, CIS College, CIS Workforce and Agency, CIS Corrections, and CIS Reality Check (financial literacy)
- FOCUS 2 – Career Dimensions, Inc., P.O. Box 998, Center Harbor, NH 03226; focuscareer2.com
  - Two products: FOCUS-2 (middle and high school students); My Golden Career (adults in transition)
- Hobson's – 1850 K Street NW, Suite 1000, Washington, DC 20006; hobsons.com
  - One online product: Naviance
- Kuder Career Planning Systems – 302 Visions Parkway, Adel, IA 50003; kuder.com
  - Three products: Kuder *Galaxy* (elementary school); Kuder *Navigator* (middle and high school); Kuder *Journey* (college students and adults)
- Valpar International Corporation – 2240 N. Coyote Drive, Tucson, AZ 85745; valparint.com
  - One product: System for Integrated Guidance Information (Sigi3)
- Xap Corporation – 3534 Hayden Avenue, Culver City, CA 90232-2413; xap.com
  - Eight products: Guidance Central, Transitions, *Choices Planner*, *Choices Explorer*, XAPlication, etranscript Xchange, *Choices Planner CT*, and *Your Mentor*

Virtual Career Centers

Another version of the integrated career planning system is a *virtual career center*. A virtual career center is a well-planned Web site that creates a master menu of existing no-fee sites that offer component pieces of an integrated career planning system. For example, one site may offer an interest inventory that yields a Holland code; a second site might allow a search for occupations and postsecondary majors by Holland code; a third site might offer a postsecondary school search; while a fourth site offers excellent instruction and tools for the job search. Thus, someone who understands the elements of an integrated career planning system may formulate a list of well-developed sites and put them all together under one menu that offers many or most of these components. In doing so, using a Google search to find such sites would be very helpful. Using the screened list maintained by Margaret Dikel and displayed on the Web site of the National Career Development Association at ncda.org would be an even better way to identify sites for use in a virtual career center.

The advantages of a virtual career center over licensing an integrated career planning system are lower cost and the ability to place local resources (such as parts of a university's own Web site or the site of a local state agency) into the menu. Important weaknesses of this approach are (a) the lack of the capability to guide a user to move from one activity to the next and (b) the inability to store assessment, information, choices made, notes, and a collection of valuable documents in an electronic portfolio that can be accessed and edited through life. Further, it is impossible to collect data about users and their progress in this type of system, and thus there is no reporting capability about use of the system or longitudinal research about its outcomes. Unlike integrated career planning systems, it is also impossible for counselors to communicate with the users of a virtual career center through e-mail, cell phone communication, or notes posted in their portfolios. The following sites are representative of the topics and appearance of virtual career centers: University of Maryland Career Center (careercenter.umd.edu) and U.S. Department of Labor's CareerOneStop (careerinfonet.org).

Mobile Phone Applications

The latest technology tool for delivery of career planning information and support is the smartphone. Due to the screen size on phones and the mobility of the person owning the phone, career guidance services must be delivered in small packages—quite the opposite of the content provided by the integrated career planning systems previously listed. For example, individuals might be able to recall their electronic portfolios and download a résumé to a wireless printer. A person on the way to a job interview might review a list of tips or likely interview questions. Another person might take a short interest assessment and receive a list of suggested occupations. Still another might retrieve the description of a college in preparation for a campus visit. One might consider these capabilities as a "just in time" approach to retrieving information needed in the career planning and job-seeking process. In some places, such as the United Kingdom, call centers have been established and staffed with people who are qualified to talk with individuals who contact them with questions that are prompted by the information provided in the mobile phone application.

In the past three years, many smartphone applications related to specific components of the career planning process have been developed. Most of these applications currently relate to the job-search process (Osborn, Kronholz, Finklea, & Cantonis, 2014) although ACT, Inc., has placed parts of the former *DISCOVER* integrated career planning system, now called My Profile, on a smartphone application, including its *UNIACT* interest inventory. Examples of job-searching applications include the following:

- *InterviewPro* – coaches users of job interview questions and how to answer them
- *JobMo* – gathers data of job openings from multiple job search sites simultaneously, based on multiple variables selected by user
- *LinkUp* – allows searches for jobs on company sites by keywords
- *VisualizeMe* – converts a text résumé into infographics (charts, graphics, timelines)
- *JibberJobber* – provides a format for organizing and keeping track of all aspects of an individual's job search

Most of these applications are available from the iTunes store. There is little to no information about the developers' credentials. It is extremely likely that this list will continue to grow rapidly given the worldwide acceptance of the smartphone.

Social Networking

The newest phenomenon related to the use of technology to support career planning is social networking. Networking, not of the electronic kind, has long been hailed as the most effective single approach to finding job openings. As of 2014 (Osborn et al., 2014), Facebook claimed over 1 billion active users, Twitter 255 million registered users (with 500 million tweets per day),

YouTube 1 billion unique visits per month, and LinkedIn more than 300 million members. This ever-growing involvement with social media by individuals is accompanied by the fact that most employers use social media for hiring purposes.

On Web-based social networking sites, such as LinkedIn, users can create a profile and provide as much personal and professional information as they wish. They may also upload photos, videos, and links. Members of online social networks invite individuals to join their network or to "friend" them. This process connects two individuals with the added benefit of allowing the newly linked members to see all the other "friends" in each other's network. LinkedIn screens acceptance of members and requires that contacts know each other or be introduced to each other from a common contact. This kind of social networking can be used to develop a job network as well. Here are some examples of how social networking sites can be used:

- On Twitter, followers can learn about companies and their job opportunities because the site serves as an informal job board. Users can have "tweetchats" with members of the network.
- LinkedIn offers company pages that provide descriptions of companies and their job openings. Through the formation of professional interest groups, members receive almost daily information about industry happenings, corporate cultures, and best practices for getting a job. Users can search job openings by job title, keyword, company name, and location. Through linkedin.com, users can identify alumni of their own college or university and seek to connect with them as one means of finding job openings.
- Facebook offers the capability to "broadcast" to a network of "friends" the fact that one is searching for a specific kind of job in a specific location, inviting friends to provide any information they may have about such job openings. Facebook ads advertise open positions. Members can find others connected with a given company who are in their network, or might be.

Regrettably, many young people today are posting messages and videos on their "walls" that are creating poor images of themselves as potential employees. Two researchers (Kolek & Saunders, 2008) found, in looking at Facebook profiles of students from a large public university, that the majority of students had profiles, and many contained large amounts of public personal information, including pictures of alcohol consumption. It is a known fact that employers are doing a social network search on job applicants prior to deciding whether to invite them to a job interview. Thus, any person who may be looking for a job should be very careful about the messages and postings that are associated with his or her name.

Two Types of Social Media Sites

Some social networking sites—such as Facebook and MySpace—are intended to be primarily vehicles for social communication. Others such as LinkedIn are professional social networks, and their purpose is to connect professionals for both social and business purposes. LinkedIn members can write endorsements for other members that serve as letters of recommendation and can be seen by employers. Members can use an advanced search function to find contacts related to a specific company or to browse through company profiles. LinkedIn also allows companies to post jobs and allows individuals to link their blogs to their profiles.

Given these two kinds of networks, clients need to learn how to use both, considering the increasing importance of such networks for job seeking and finding. A good plan is for job seekers to belong to both a carefully used social networking site and a professional networking site such as LinkedIn. A good strategy for using social networking to find a job might include these steps:

- Search for yourself on Google to see the links associated with your name. If some are undesirable, attempt to get them removed. Upload other documents (PowerPoint presentations, articles, book chapters, etc.) that would expand your Internet image (or "brand" as it is being called).
- Build two very professional profiles/résumés—one on LinkedIn as well as a video résumé.
- Make sure your postings are consistent in content—jobs held, skills, what you have to offer.
- Get as many connections and endorsements on LinkedIn as possible. Stay active in social networks such as Twitter and Facebook and in blogs in order to get your name known on the Internet with consistent branding.
- Focus on specific employers and jobs, and gain as much information about them as possible through communication with others who work for that company and through information interviews.
- Attempt to get in direct electronic contact with a hiring manager in a company that you want to work for, and cultivate that relationship.

Individuals can also easily create Web logs, also known as blogs, in which they can journal in a forum that can be joined by others. Users can establish specific topics to discuss and invite others to participate. Employers, including Microsoft, Pepsi, and Target, are using blogs to announce their available positions. Blogs can be accessed by a Google search with keywords, from company Web sites, or from job boards like Indeed.

Distance Counseling

The age of distance counseling is upon us. *Distance counseling* is the provision of counseling support to a client by a qualified professional via the Internet. Hardware and software exist to make such service possible, and indeed there are a few Web sites offering it; however, experience and research are insufficient at this time to allow an evaluation of its effectiveness. In such service delivery, a counselor or career advisor and a client may be physically located anywhere there is an Internet connection, and they can communicate with each other synchronously (i.e., at the same time) via interactive e-mail or video conferencing (i.e., being able to see each other because both have digital cameras and appropriate software on their machines). Although it is probably less effective, the interaction could take place asynchronously (i.e., the two are not at their machines at the same time). In such a relationship, the counselor and client may discuss any topics for which the Internet is a secure-enough platform, and the counselor may or may not assign the use of Web sites appropriate to those topics. Ethical guidelines for distance counseling have been developed by the National Board for Certified Counselors (nbcc.org).

COUNSELOR RESPONSIBILITIES RELATED TO ICT-SUPPORTED CAREER GUIDANCE AND COUNSELING

As the capabilities of ICT-supported career guidance and counseling tools have expanded since their initiation in the late 1960s, the role of counselors who support their use has changed. In the beginning, prior to the existence of ICT support, counselors played the role of a person with superior knowledge about the career planning process and the options it presents to students and clients. With the advent of integrated career planning systems, counselors' roles shifted to being viewed as having joint knowledge with these systems and, as needed, to provide support to their use. With the advent of social media and its widespread acceptance by students, clients, and employers, the counselor's role has shifted again more to that of a co-generator of information that will be helpful to students and clients who are playing an active role in the process (Hooley, 2012; Spivack, 2007).

We will turn now to a review of the responsibilities that counselors have related to student/client use of ICT as a career planning intervention. In a recent study conducted in Finland (Kettunena, Vuorinena, & Sampson, 2014), the researchers studied the attitudes of counselors about use of ICT in their work. They found a range of attitudes from total lack of acceptance and enthusiasm to high enthusiasm and desire to incorporate ICT into their daily work. Those who do wish to incorporate ICT need to be involved in the following kinds of tasks.

Know and Abide by Ethical Guidelines

Four professional organizations have developed guidelines for the use of ICT in career counseling and guidance. They are as follows:

- American Counseling Association (ACA) – counseling.org
- International Association for Educational and Vocational Guidance (IAEVG) – iaevg.org
- National Board for Certified Counselors (NBCC) – nbcc.org
- National Career Development Association (NCDA) – ncda.org

Counselors who want to use the Internet as a tool in their counseling or provide distance counseling should become thoroughly familiar with these codes of ethics.

Select Web Sites and Integrated Career Planning Systems

Counselors are typically included as part of a team that decides which of the integrated career guidance systems should be selected for use at their site or if the one presently being used should be replaced by another. In this event, it is necessary to gain in-depth knowledge of each system under consideration. Although presentations made by marketing representatives are helpful, the best ways to gain truly in-depth knowledge are to acquire and read the system's professional manual and then, or simultaneously, to use the entire system as a student or client would. The following are the critical topics to use as benchmarks while making an evaluation:

- *Theoretical base of the system.* Some systems, such as those that focus on file searches and data displays, are atheoretical—that is, they do not propose any process for career decision making, nor do they offer any content that is related to the work of any specific theorist. Other systems do both; they propose and offer a specific process for career decision making and use the theoretical work of one or more of the theorists included in this text as the basis for that process and/or other content. Clients need to follow an exploratory process. Counselors need to decide whether the computer will be the presenter and monitor of that process or whether the counselor will play a more active role, using the computer as a support system at points in the process.

- *Presence of online inventories and/or the capability to enter the results of assessment taken in print form.* For most clients and students, assessment of interests and skills/abilities—and perhaps also work values—is important. This being the case, counselors need to determine how such assessment will be administered. There are two possibilities, each of which can be used exclusively or combined with the other. First, assessment can be administered, scored, and interpreted online as a part of a Web-based career planning system, an Internet Web site, or by software licensed from a test publisher and resident on a local computer. Second, assessment may be administered in print form and either self scored (possible for some types of inventories) or sent elsewhere for scoring. In the latter case, the Web-based career guidance system may allow individual users to enter their own scores, or clerical support persons may enter the results for multiple individuals into the system so that they can be used to assist with their search for occupations.

- *Quality and comprehensiveness of databases.* Databases are an essential part of Web-based career guidance systems, and their quality is critical to the quality of the system. Such quality includes accuracy of descriptions of items in the databases (occupations, schools, financial aid sources, etc.), sources of data, and currency and frequency of update. Some systems contain only two databases—usually, occupations and schools. The school database may comprise four-year colleges only or may also include vocational-technical schools, two-year colleges, and graduate schools. These files could be only for the state of installation, for a geographic region, or for the entire nation. Some systems offer data about 200 to 300 occupations, whereas others include more than a thousand. Some have many databases in addition to occupations and schools, including financial aid, apprenticeships, internships, military occupations, and majors. Some vendors make maximum use of databases developed by reliable government sources, such as the U.S. Departments of Labor, Education, and Defense; others do not. Some vendors of systems update their files once annually; others perform a quarterly or biannual update. Another factor to consider is the style of writing used for the databases. Some systems use a factual, documentary writing style, whereas others describe an occupation in an informal "what I do on the job every day" kind of format. It is also important to note the reading level of these descriptions.

- *Ease of searches.* Being able to search databases by specific characteristics is a core function of Web-based systems. Searches can be intuitive and user-friendly, or they can be awkward. When you are reviewing a system, note how easy or difficult it is to remove an already selected search characteristic, or to add one or go back to the results of your last search and change only one or two variables.

- *Content of system.* The first item in this list addressed the matter of theoretical base, and the second dealt with assessment, both of which are elements of content. However, there can be other, vast differences in content. Some systems contain instructional material, such as how occupations can be organized, how to write a résumé, how to participate in a job interview, and how to find possible job openings through networking. The content desired in a system obviously relates both to the needs of the people served and to the elements of content provided in other ways.

- *User-friendliness and appeal.* The appearance of a Web-based system is determined by its graphics and icons, its color scheme, the availability of multimedia (video, still images, audio), the simplicity and attractiveness of screen layout, and the readability and attractiveness of the fonts used for text. Items that relate to user-friendliness include having a consistent way of navigating throughout the system, moving from one part to another, and integrating all materials needed within the system rather than having to rely on two or more media.

- *Multimedia capabilities.* Users of Web-based systems find them more appealing and are more motivated to use them if they have multimedia assets such as dynamic graphics, streaming video, and audio. The positive aspect of having multimedia is its motivational appeal and capability to give much more information to a user about occupations or schools, for example, than text alone. The challenging side of multimedia is the software and hardware requirements. These features may require specific software on users' machines as well as high-speed communication lines with significant bandwidth.
- *Quality and track record of vendor.* Some career planning systems and Web sites have been developed on a low budget by individuals who are not known in the career development field. Further, the support capabilities they offer related to training and technical support are sparse. Other systems are developed and maintained by large organizations that have a long history of high-quality support and product development. These organizations are able to invest a large portion of their revenue in enhancing systems, training, and keeping up with the next technological trend.

These same criteria can be used to evaluate individual Web sites that counselors may want to assign to clients or students and/or to include in a virtual career center.

The NCDA has a document titled *Software Review Guidelines*, which is available on its Web site at ncda.org. It lists 67 items that should be reviewed, and the worksheet allows the system reviewer to rate each item on a scale of 1 to 5, with 1 being unsatisfactory and 5 being outstanding.

Tips from the Field

Research consistently indicates that the most effective method of assisting individuals with career planning is a combination of Web-delivered service and counselor face-to-face support—either individually or in a group.

ADD HIGH TOUCH TO HIGH TECH

The list of capabilities of Web-based systems is impressive. At first glance, it might appear that such systems could provide career planning services without counselor support. There are at least three reasons why this is not the case. First, when students or clients say that they need help with career planning, their statement may mask a variety of other needs and concerns. As a counselor talks with a student or client, these other needs become apparent, if they exist. Obviously, a computer does not have this power of discernment. Second, not all individuals with a primary need for career planning can profit optimally from receiving these services by computer because everyone has a different learning style and personality type. Further, some clients are not ready to receive information because of a lack of readiness to process it effectively. Third, research (Taber & Luzzo, 1999; Whiston, Brecheisen, & Stephens, 2003) designed to determine the best way to deliver career planning services has consistently indicated that the optimal treatment for students/clients is the combination of human support services and computer services. In a recent study (Herman, 2010) using Career HOPES (an Internet-delivered group counseling intervention designed to facilitate occupational exploration and career decision making), experimental subjects showed greater gains than control group participants in career decidedness as measured by the Occupational Alternatives Questionnaire, occupationally relevant self-knowledge, and emission of career exploration behaviors. In the experimental group, the online group discussions were moderated by a psychologist with career counseling experience; in the control group, the discussions were unmoderated. Professional moderation resulted in better outcomes on several variables and greater overall satisfaction with the intervention.

Some of the most important counselor responsibilities related to adding high touch to high tech include the following:

- Determining the readiness of a person to receive information from a computer and apply it effectively. This determination may be made by use of assessments listed in Chapter 5 or through a skilled intake interview. Persons not ready to process information should be provided with individual counseling prior to using ICT tools.
- Expanding on the interpretation of tests and inventories so that they are more likely to inform the client's decision making appropriately.
- Assisting the client to identify the personal values that will guide the reduction of options provided by the computer.
- Providing motivation and emotional support for continued work related to career planning.
- Suggesting creative alternatives that the computer doesn't "know."

Counselor Competencies and Types of Support

As indicated previously in this chapter, research studies indicate that the most effective means of providing career planning assistance to students or clients is by a combination of ICT and counselor. The same studies indicate that receiving assistance from a computer-delivered system provides better outcomes than no assistance at all, but significantly greater gains are achieved when counselors can lend specific competencies to the picture. Pyle (2001) has identified the following list of needed counselor competencies:

- *Knowledge of computer-assisted software and Web sites.* Good content knowledge of valid and reliable Web-based guidance systems and Internet sites.
- *Capability to diagnose.* Ability to diagnose a client's needs effectively in order to determine whether use of a technology-assisted intervention is appropriate.
- *Capability to motivate.* Ability to explain the value of Web-based systems or sites in a way that will motivate the client to invest time in using them.
- *Capability to help the client process data.* Ability to assist a client to turn data into personally meaningful information.
- *Capability to move the client to an action plan.* Ability to assist a client to develop an action plan and then move forward on it.

These competencies may be applied in combination with different models of service delivery combining technology and counselor support, of which there are at least four: one-to-one counseling plus use of technology, group guidance plus use of technology, group counseling plus use of technology, and counselor support via the Internet plus use of Web sites.

In one-to-one counseling plus use of technology, the counselor gives the student or client specific assignments to use a Web-based system or sites between sessions. It is important that the assignments be specific instead of referring individuals to an integrated career guidance system or Web site without direction about which specific part(s) to use. For example, Juanita's counselor determined that she would profit from taking *The Self-Directed Search* (Holland & Messer, 2015). The counselor asked Juanita to take the instrument from its Web site, print out and read the extensive report, and return the next week. At the second session, the counselor expanded on the interpretation of the instrument and helped Juanita develop some guidelines for determining which of the many occupations suggested by the instrument to explore. Together, they developed a short list. The counselor asked Juanita to gather information about this list of occupations by using the *The Occupational Outlook Handbook* (U.S. Department of Labor, 2014) and *CareerOne-Stop* (acinet.org) online. At the third session, the counselor and Juanita discussed the information collected, and Juanita decided to learn more about training opportunities for Web designers. The counselor suggested that she search for such opportunities by using the National Center for Education Statistics site (nces.ed.gov) and to bring a printed list of information about each of the identified schools to the next session. This example illustrates how counselors can use either an integrated career planning system or a Web site as a valuable resource to help clients identify options and gain information about them.

The group guidance or classroom-plus-technology model is highly similar, though it may serve a group of 15 to 30 simultaneously. For example, a community college may offer a two-credit course in career planning, and its enrollment may be as many as 30 students. During class sessions, the instructor teaches basic concepts of career planning, using a curriculum such as *Take Hold of Your Future* (Harris-Bowlsbey, 2009) and leads the group in activities designed to apply those concepts to personal decision making. Further, the instructor may give specific assignments to use parts of *Journey* (Kuder, Inc., 2015), for example, between class sessions to take inventories online, to identify occupations, to get occupational descriptions, to select a major, to identify schools, and to learn job-seeking skills. This approach makes wise use of technology and gives the instructor class time to offer additional activities.

The group-counseling-plus-technology model is similar, but it serves students in groups not larger than eight and features counseling as opposed to guidance. Pyle (2001) has developed a model that requires three 1.5-hour group sessions and use of a Web-based system or site between the first and second and the second and third sessions.

ISSUES AND CONCERNS RELATED TO USE OF ICT

Although the prospect of providing good counseling and guidance services to a much larger audience than counselors can serve through one-on-one or small-group work through the Internet is bright, there are also issues and concerns that the profession must wrestle with and research. The most critical of these are counseling environment, content topics, client characteristics, security and confidentiality, quality of content, equality of access, counselor qualities and qualifications, and availability of supporting services. Each of these is addressed briefly here.

Counselors have been traditionally trained to create a nonpressured, accepting environment and to use specific relationship-building skills, including eye contact, attending behavior, immediate feedback through reflection, and intuitive questioning. Despite the use of digital cameras on workstations and videoconferencing software, achieving a psychologically warm environment and good facilitative skills for distance counseling in the medium of the Internet is challenging.

Responsiveness may be seriously impacted by the limitation of bandwidth or simply by the lack of synchronicity in the communication.

A second concern relates to the selection of presenting problems for attention via the Internet. Clients typically begin a counseling relationship by discussing topics that they believe will be acceptable, such as making a career choice or dealing with stress. However, it is typical that other concerns surface as the counseling relationship builds. The current guidelines indicate that counselors who do distance counseling should state on their Web sites the topics that they believe to be appropriate for distance counseling. This raises a concern as to whether the Internet should be used for counseling or only for the provision of guidance and information. It also raises the question of whether it is possible to stack presenting problems in hierarchical order and to divide them into the categories of "appropriate" and "inappropriate" for distance counseling or assignment of Web sites.

A third concern relates to determining which clients can profit from service via distance counseling, an integrated career planning system, assigned Web sites, or social media. The guidelines indicate that it is the responsibility of a counselor to determine whether a given client has the capability to maintain a relationship via the Internet and/or to profit from use of assigned Web sites. Yet, as a profession we have neither researched nor defined what the client characteristics are that would enhance their capability to profit from service in this mode or how a counselor may identify them, especially without a face-to-face interview.

A fourth concern relates to the fact that the Internet is an insecure environment. The counseling profession has always placed very high priority on the necessity to keep client communication and records secure and confidential. Encryption and other methods are being used to minimize the risk of having counselor case notes, client communication, and client records accessed by unauthorized persons; yet, these methods are not ironclad. The current guidelines indicate that counselors have the responsibility to inform their clients that the Internet is an insecure environment, but this may not be an adequate way to absolve counselors of this responsibility.

A fifth concern is quality of content (Sampson & Makala, 2014). The Internet houses many formal and informal assessments to measure interests, values, and personality traits. Some of these have been developed by qualified professionals, researched in regard to their validity and reliability, and marketed by responsible publishers who provide training in their use and interpretation. These statements do not apply to many assessments on the Internet. Those who take these assessments have no way to judge their quality either by lack of knowledge or because very few sites explain who developed the assessment and how it has been researched. The same concerns relate to databases found on the Internet. Many are released and maintained by reliable government agencies, such as the U.S. Department of Labor, Department of Education, and Department of Defense. Others are developed by other entities that may make some occupations and some colleges and universities to appear, for example, more attractive or of higher quality than they really are.

A sixth concern is inequality of access to ICT (Sampson & Makala, 2014). There is an increasing divide between the "haves" and the "have nots" economically, and the same applies to access to technology, even in the United States and especially in many Third World countries. Many, if not most, however, of those who do not have access to technology do not have access to human career counselors or advisors either.

A seventh concern is the lack of trained counselors or career paraprofessionals to support the use of any or all of the ICT tools described in this chapter. That fact is partly due to the lack of staff and time in schools, universities, and agencies where the people are who need assistance with career planning. It is further due to the fact that individuals can now take advantage of these ICT tools from anywhere, and thus supporting personnel are not available.

An eighth concern is how to identify and train counselors to work in this mode. It is likely that counselors who are effective in delivering service via the Internet and with ICT tools have characteristics that are different from those of their colleagues who prefer to work in a direct, face-to-face service mode. It is also very likely that counselors need to be trained differently for effective services with ICT tools than for traditional counseling. Research is needed to understand what those counselor personality and skill differences are so that appropriate people can be selected and taught appropriate skills.

THE PROMISE OF ICT

In a recent conference of the International Association for Educational and Vocational Guidance (IAEVG), several individuals reported on the use of ICT in their countries. From these reports, it is clear that there are immense benefits related to the fact that smartphones and the World Wide Web have become ever-increasing sources of career planning information, guidance, and support. The trends noted in this international symposium underscore the prediction that use of ICT for career guidance purposes will continue at a rapid pace and that most members of the world population will receive whatever career guidance assistance they are able to get either through a server on the World Wide Web, a mobile phone, or a combination of the two.

In New Zealand, career services have been delivered since 2000 to approximately 45,000 persons per year via telephone staffed by trained staff. Services offered by telephone include assistance with occupational choice and selection of appropriate postsecondary education, both university level and trade level. Individuals who are assessed as needing one-on-one services are referred to local career centers for face-to-face counseling. Access to the Internet is widespread, and career information is also provided in this mode via a government-supported Web site that offers extensive information to students, parents, and educators about such topics as choosing school subjects, selecting an occupation, entering tertiary education, getting a job, and options after leaving school. This service also offers the capability for the user to call, e-mail, or chat online for further information, or to share information with others by tweeting.

In Australia, there are many sources of Web-based information to assist youth and adults with career planning, Chief among them is the government-funded National Career Information System, a collaborative effort between state and Commonwealth governments to provide a comprehensive career exploration and information system for all Australians. Career information and guidance are also provided through a variety of telephone-based services and through career centers.

In Canada, a country long involved in the use of technology to support career planning, using Web-based activities plus human delivery of curriculum in classroom settings is widespread. Web-enabled versions of the *Real Game* have been developed, and these appear to hold promise as a mode of career service delivery. This series of games offers users the opportunity to experience life in an occupation much more realistically than simply reading its description. Users assume an occupational role, develop and modify a budget (which includes selection of a home, a vehicle, and leisure activities) based on the expected income in that occupation, and determine how they need to modify their career choices related to the lifestyle they hope to acquire. Filling a different need, Training Innovations, a government-funded initiative, assists adults with career management tasks and acquiring needed training through e-learning, often customized to an employer's needs. *Choices*, a well-known career information and guidance system, also continues to be strong. This system offers a user an electronic portfolio, extensive occupational information, assistance with selection of postsecondary majors, and guides for planning for high school and college.

At the University of Florence in Italy, a Web-based system is being developed for university students that, combined with distance counseling, seeks to move beyond the assessment and information-giving functions to assisting students to recognize that creating one's career is creating one's life. The system seeks to motivate students to have active engagement in designing this life, to develop the skills needed to implement such engagement, and to recognize the process as lifelong. The system also features the use of social networking as a part of the process.

The United Kingdom has a long history of development and delivery of computer-based and now Web-based and telephone-based systems. Systems such as CASCAiD and Prospect provide comprehensive educational and career guidance to students and adults via the Web, including Web chat and other social media capabilities. The government-funded expansive *LearnDirect* Web-based system provides hundreds of online courses to individuals who need to acquire new skills in order to enter the workplace. As in Australia and New Zealand, career services by telephone are also widely available.

Many other countries, including Egypt and India, are awakening to the need to assist their population with career planning services, largely centered at this time around the choice of majors and tertiary education options. Egypt has begun by training a cadre of career development facilitators. In India, the need and market for Web-based services is just now being recognized. The number of homes receiving Web service is rapidly increasing as is the use of the cellular phone with Web access. Connectivity to the Web is also increasingly available through small learning centers that have been established throughout the country. It is being recognized that students, their parents, and adults need assistance in finding their way through a complex educational system, identifying universities in other countries, and making realistic career choices that may be less influenced by parents than in the past. Given the current trends in India, it appears that the cellular phone may become a primary source of information and guidance.

The countries represented by the attendees at the IAEVG symposium illustrate a worldwide movement to provide career services to astoundingly more people through Web-based delivery. These services are wide ranging and include assessment, gaming, career information, job-seeking documents and instruction, and career advising. They are delivered via the conventional telephone, smartphones with Web access, and computers.

From the reports provided by the IAEVG attendees, it is obvious that the rapid expansion of worldwide Web capability as well as of the cellular phone has made it possible to provide career planning support services to an infinitely larger population at very reasonable cost. The content of these services is comprised of information about educational and occupational options, résumé-writing instruction and review, and skill-building courses; and content is sometimes accompanied by encouragement, coaching, and advising. In some systems, self-assessment is included as a precursor to the suggestion of career options and information about them. As needed, some modicum of human support is added to pure information delivery by phone conversation, online chat, participation in blogs, and videoconferencing.

Most past technology-driven services have been based on either the theory that information itself is sufficient to inform decision making or on a broader Parsonian (Parsons, 1909) model that involved learning about yourself (usually through formal assessment), learning about occupations, and then making a rational match between the two. Some of the more recent uses of technology are incorporating newer approaches to career counseling, such as the Savickas (2005) "career as story" approach. Students and clients are asked to choose one or more YouTube videos that have some specific meaning for them. The content of those selected videos are then used to assist individuals to identify themes that attracted them to the video.

What is the promise of these developments? First and foremost, these technologies are capable of reaching an almost infinite number of youth and adults as access to the Web, and especially to mobile telephone services, becomes more and more available and cost feasible, even in developing countries. Thus, this technological advancement creates a low-cost and efficient pipeline through which to deliver the content of career guidance.

Second, these services are available in all kinds of locations on a 24/7 basis. The barriers of distance, time, space, and disability are removed, making it possible for individuals in remote places, with handicapping conditions that would challenge their travel to a specific physical location, who might find it uncomfortable or impossible to meet with someone face to face, to receive assistance. Though the Web is still not accessible in many homes, it is increasingly accessible in public places such as libraries, community centers, and coffee shops.

Third, given that technology-based services are developed by a few for distribution to many, it is possible to determine and control their quality. Given that competent career professionals design the content and methods of service delivery and those who provide supportive services are well chosen and trained, high-quality services can be delivered in a standard way to a very large number of people. This is the promise of ICT.

MyCounselingLab®

Start with Topic 11—Information in Career Guidance.

SUMMARY

The computer has been used as a powerful tool in the delivery of career planning information and service since the late 1960s when such systems had their genesis. Delivered initially by stand-alone mainframe computers, these services have migrated to networked computers of all sizes and, more recently, to the World Wide Web. Although far more effective than no service at all, their function is optimally enhanced by the support of counselors in one-on-one counseling, group guidance, group counseling, or distance counseling. The advent and rapid growth of social media has added both significant opportunities and additional ethical challenges. ICT is being used increasingly in many countries of the world and holds promise to make career information and career guidance available to increased millions via computers, tablets, and smartphones.

CASE STUDY

Casio is a 32-year-old Hispanic male who has recently lost a job due to a reduction in state government employees. In his initial visit with you in a one-stop center, he indicates that he is very comfortable with using the Internet as one way to help in his job search.

Which sites would you recommend to Casio, and for what purposes?

STUDENT ACTIVITIES

1. In order to have firsthand experience with a Web-based integrated career planning system that was developed for middle school and high school students, sign on (without charge) to the Kuder career planning system called *Navigator* and use parts of it by following these steps:
   a. Access careerinterventions.kuder.com.
   b. Complete the brief form provided at that site, including your name, your instructor's name, and the name of the university where you are taking this course.
   c. Upon completion of the form and selection of Submit, an activation code will be displayed—a number that you can use when you register to use *Navigator*. This number will allow you to use the system and build an electronic portfolio without charge.
   d. Access the Kuder Web site at kuder.com.
   e. Move your cursor over the Login field at the upper right corner of the screen. The titles of three different systems will be displayed. Choose *Navigator* (the system for middle school and high school students) by clicking on Login.
   f. Under the Login box, select *New Users Register Here*. Complete the registration form, indicating that you are a student in grade 9. At the end of that process you will be asked to enter the activation code you have received. You will also create a unique user name and password. Record the user name and password because you will enter the same ones each time you return to the system.
   g. Use the following parts of the system. You may sign off at any time and return to the system by entering the user name and password that you created at first use.
      i. Under the tab titled *Learn About Myself*, choose *Take an Assessment*, and then the Kuder *Career Interests Assessment*. If you have time, come back to this menu later and take Donald Super's *Work Values Inventory*.
      ii. Under the tab titled *Explore Occupations*, select the option to *Explore Occupations by Assessment Results*. This option will give you a list of occupations suggested by the results of your interest inventory and values inventory. Look at the descriptions of at least three occupations, and save them to your portfolio. From your portfolio, compare the descriptions of the three occupations side by side. While you are in that section, notice the other ways in which students can explore and identify occupations.
      iii. Under the tab titled *Plan for Education*, search for a college, using at least four different characteristics. Look at the descriptions of at least three colleges, save them to your portfolio, and compare them. While in that section, note the other content that is available to students.
      iv. Choose the tab *Plan for Work* and look at the menu options to get an idea of the content of this module.
      v. Choose the tab *Find a Job* and look at the menu options to get an idea of the content of this module.
   h. After this review, write a brief report related to these three items:
      i. At the freshman level, your high school is looking for ways to meet a career guidance objective that reads, "Provide activities that are designed to expose students to a large number of career options and motivate them to explore these." Assuming that you had approval to assign students to a laboratory setting that offers the use of a Web-connected computer for each student, which specific part of Kuder *Navigator* would best meet this objective, and why?
      ii. You are a high school counselor with a responsibility for freshman students. A parent calls you and asks you to work

with her son in regard to a career choice and development of a high school plan of study that would support that choice. As a part of your assistance to this student, which parts of *Navigator* might you assign, and why?

    iii. Another counselor on your high school guidance staff works with college-bound juniors. Which parts of *Navigator* would you suggest that this counselor use with students, and why?

2. You are a high school counselor, and you have been asked to serve on a committee that will review three integrated Web-based career planning systems in order to choose one for your school. You have been asked to review the Kuder Career Planning System called *Navigator*. Your assignment is to sign on to *Navigator* (following the directions provided in Activity 1) and then to write a one- to two-page summary for the committee based on the criteria specified in this chapter, namely:

- Theoretical base
- Presence of online inventories and/or capability to enter assessment scores
- Quality and comprehensiveness of databases
- Ease of searches
- Content of system
- User-friendliness and appeal
- Multimedia capabilities
- Quality and track record of vendor

CHAPTER 8

CAREER COUNSELING STRATEGIES AND TECHNIQUES FOR THE 21ST CENTURY

Because we're human beings, career counselors can fall into the understandable trap of hearing and interpreting clients' stories from our own frame of reference. Developing the discipline to thoughtfully apply a range of theories in our work with clients enables us to push beyond our own perspectives in conceptualizing salient issues and interventions. By challenging ourselves to consider clients' career and life choices from different theoretical frameworks, we can view their worlds through a variety of lenses, each bringing a distinct focus to the work. Sometimes, when mulling over a first session with a client and reasoning through the presenting information, I push myself a bit by asking "How would Super—or Holland or Krumboltz or Schlossberg—view this client's situation, and what would each of them focus on in helping this client?" For me, the application of theory is a powerful tool that improves with frequent sharpening. It's a means for considering a series of possibilities and, thus, for keeping the work fresh and honoring the uniqueness of each client.

Barbara Hilton Suddarth, Ph.D., NCCC
Kensington Consulting

MyCounselingLab®

Visit the MyCounselingLab® site for *Career Development Interventions*, Fifth Edition, to enhance your understanding of chapter concepts. You will have the opportunity to practice applying what you learned in the chapter by completing the video- and case-based exercises in the MyLab. Taking the Licensure Quizzes will help you prepare for your certification exam.

Maggie, a 28-year-old, single, European American woman presented for career counseling. Maggie desperately wanted out of her current work situation because her retail sales position was simply not working out for her. However, Maggie had no clear sense of her career options. She also possessed very limited information about the career development process. At the first session, she was clearly distressed and anxious. She wondered whether there was any hope for her future, and she wanted to move on to something else as soon as possible. This was her first experience in career counseling.

Career development interventions provide the historical foundation for the counseling profession (Dorn, 1992). Herr, Cramer, and Niles (2004) point out that the counseling field emerged from three distinct movements: (a) vocational/career guidance, (b) psychological measurement, and (c) personality development. Despite the substantial influence of career development interventions on the counseling field and recent advances in career development theory, we know relatively little about the career counseling process (Anderson & Niles, 2000; Swanson, 1995; Whiston, 2003). Career counselors rarely study how career counseling actually "works" (Swanson). Rather, many career development researchers focus their efforts on career counseling outcomes (e.g., studying whether a career counseling intervention leads to less career indecision). Although career outcome research is obviously important, we also need to learn more about what happens within the career counseling process.

Is Career Counseling Effective?

The results of a small group of empirical studies account for much of what we know about the career counseling process. It is noteworthy that as we take a closer look at what happens in career counseling, we realize that career counseling and general counseling have much in common. This is not a new phenomenon. For example, Holland, Magoon, and Spokane (1981) reported that positive career counseling outcomes were related to techniques and strategies that included cognitive rehearsals of clients' career aspirations, providing clients with occupational information and social support, and cognitive structuring of clients' dysfunctional career beliefs. Heppner, Multon, Gysbers, Ellis, & Zook (1998) reported a positive relationship between career counselor confidence in establishing therapeutic relationships and client confidence in coping with career transitions. Heppner and Hendricks (1995) reported that both a career-indecisive client and a career-undecided client attached substantial importance to the development of a therapeutic relationship with their career counselor. Anderson and Niles (1995) reported that clients devoted considerable attention to noncareer concerns in career counseling sessions and often discussed family-of-origin and relationship concerns with their career counselors. Anderson and Niles (2000) reported that career counseling participants (i.e., counselors and clients) most frequently identified aspects of self-exploration, support, and educating as the most important and helpful career counseling interventions. One result from this small group of studies is the support for a close relationship between the processes of psychotherapy and career counseling. It is particularly evident that an effective working alliance is critical to positive outcomes in career counseling (Multon, Heppner, Gysbers, Zook, & Ellis-Kalton, 2001). Thus, many of the counseling skills used to establish rapport with clients (e.g., reflective listening, paraphrasing, demonstrating positive regard) also apply to effective career counseling.

Tips from the Field

Collaborate with your students and clients to co-construct career interventions that fit their life contexts. Remember that effective career counselors are, at their core, effective counselors.

Many researchers use meta-analyses to ascertain the effectiveness of career counseling. The majority of these analyses indicate that career counseling is effective in strengthening career decision-making confidence, lessening career indecision, bolstering secondary school student engagement, and increasing work satisfaction (Whiston & Blustein, 2013). The ripple effects of these outcomes have important societal implications (e.g., increased levels of education often relate to increased employment outcomes).

Career counseling outcome research indicates that career counseling is moderately to highly effective in helping clients resolve their career concerns (Oliver & Spokane, 1988). Whiston (2002) also states there is convincing evidence that career interventions without counseling are not as effective as career interventions with a counseling component. Brown, Ryan, and Krane (2000) note that career counseling is most effective when it contains individualized interpretation and feedback, occupational information, modeling opportunities, attention to building support for the client's choices within the client's social network, and written exercises. Despite more general evidence that career counseling is effective, we know less about the effectiveness of specific career counseling models (Whiston, 2003). This lack of information becomes more glaring when considering the question of which career counseling models work with which clients under what conditions. These issues expose the rather substantial gap that exists between career counseling research and practice. We agree with Whiston's (2003) call for a "surge in research that focuses on the process and outcome of career counseling" (p. 40).

EXPANDING THE LIMITED VIEW OF CAREER COUNSELING

Despite the need for more career counseling process and outcome research, it is possible to offer some summary statements regarding needed changes within career counseling practice. For example, over the past 30 years researchers have noted the close relationship that exists between the processes of psychotherapy and career counseling (Subich, 1993). Despite this relationship, many people still conceptualize the career counseling process as limited to measuring individual characteristics to identify congruent matches between people and prospective occupational environments. It is not surprising that this perception persists given the close connection between the development of interest inventories and aptitude tests during the early part of the 20th century and the use of these measures to help young people and veterans of the armed forces identify occupational preferences. Generations of people were exposed to this approach, and, thus, the predominant perception that this is the only approach to career counseling is pervasive and long-standing. Although this emphasis on finding the best occupational fit was crucial to the evolution of career development interventions and is an essential aspect of many current career counseling strategies, it does not describe the totality of career counseling interventions.

Clearly, there is a substantial body of evidence providing empirical support for career counseling strategies focused on person-environment fit; however, this limited view of career counseling is often accompanied by some less than desirable outcomes. For example, the widespread use of standardized tests in career counseling has led many clients to make the following request when presenting for career counseling: "I want to take a test that will tell me what I should do." Although no such test exists, many practitioners have been eager to comply with these requests, usually for a fairly steep financial fee.

The notion that career counseling is a process limited to test administration and interpretation also contributes to less than enthusiastic attitudes toward career counseling on the part of students in counselor training programs (Heppner, O'Brien, Hinkelman, & Flores, 1996). Students often conclude that career counseling is a rather mechanical process with a sequence of interventions that resembles the following:

Step 1   The client presents for career counseling.
Step 2   The counselor gathers client information and administers a test battery.
Step 3   The counselor interprets the tests and identifies a few appropriate occupational options for the client.

In this approach the counselor is in charge of the process. The counselor is directive and authoritative. Clients are passive recipients of a predetermined test battery. In this scenario the career counseling "process" is described as "test 'em and tell 'em" and "three interviews and a cloud of dust." Because some counselors use the same test battery over and over, regardless of the client's background and context, career counseling in these instances becomes something that is done to clients rather than something the counselor and client participate in collaboratively.

Many mental health practitioners also lack enthusiasm for the practice of career counseling (Spokane, 1991). Perhaps this is because practitioners also conceptualize career counseling as a process of administering tests and providing occupational information. Such views freeze career counseling at the middle of the 21st century and do not acknowledge the increased use of a variety of creative counseling strategies within career counseling (Amundson, Harris-Bowlsbey, & Niles, 2013).

Increasingly, career counselors infuse career counseling with general counseling strategies (Fouad et al., 2007; Multon et al., 2001; Savickas, 2012; Whiston & Blustein, 2013). There is a growing recognition on the part of practitioners that the perceived dichotomy between career and personal counseling is false and does not reflect life as most people live it. There is growing recognition that work and mental health are interwoven. Niles and Pate (1989) observe that:

> Given the relationship between work and mental health, it is perplexing that there has been an artificial distinction between career counseling and mental health counseling on the part of many clients and counselors. Career counseling and personal counseling are often referred to as if they were completely separate entities. In fact, there are few things more personal than a career choice. (p. 64)

Moreover, clients present with career concerns in virtually every setting in which counselors work. Accordingly, Niles and Pate (1989) argue for counselors to be systematically trained in both the career and noncareer intervention domains. Blustein and Spengler (1995) agree that a systematic and comprehensive integration of training experiences across career and noncareer domains is necessary to prepare competent counselors in the 21st century.

Although Brown and Brooks (1985) acknowledge that not all counselors can be skilled career counselors, they also encourage all counselors to at least become competent at recognizing situations in which career counseling is an appropriate intervention that warrants referral. To address the goals identified by career development scholars such as Brown and Brooks, we will now identify strategies for effective career counseling in the 21st century and offer a framework for conceptualizing the career counseling process.

CAREER COUNSELING IN THE 21ST CENTURY

Career counseling has evolved as both a counseling specialty and a core element of the general practice of counseling. The 2016 Standards for the Council for Accreditation of Counseling and Related Educational Programs (CACREP) continue to identify career development as a core area of counseling competence (see Appendix D). Thus, career counselors are professional counselors or psychologists with specialized training in the delivery of career development interventions. Career counselors possess the competencies required to provide multiculturally competent and general individual and group counseling interventions to their clients while also possessing knowledge, skills, and awareness particular to the career domain (e.g., career development theories; career counseling theories and techniques; occupational information resources; career concerns of diverse populations; career assessment, consultation, program management; and ethical issues related to career service delivery).

Career counseling can be classified within the general category of counseling because of the overlap in skills required to conduct general and career counseling (Sampson, Vacc, & Loesch, 1998). In this regard, Crites (1981) suggests that "career counseling often embraces personal counseling but it goes beyond this to explore and replicate the client's role in the main area of life—the world of work" (p. 11). Crites further contends that the need for career counseling is greater than the need for general counseling; that career counseling, in itself, is therapeutic for clients; and that career counseling is more effective and more difficult than general counseling.

Brown and Brooks (1991) suggest that career counseling clients must possess *cognitive clarity* to be able to benefit from career counseling. They define cognitive clarity loosely by referring to it as "the ability to objectively assess one's own strengths and weaknesses and relate the assessment to environmental situations" (p. 5). Brown and Brooks recommend that when counselors determine that their clients do not possess cognitive clarity, they should postpone addressing the client's career concerns until cognitive clarity is attained. Although on the surface this notion seems reasonable—and probably is applicable for clients with more severe psychological disorders—there is little empirical evidence to support this view for clients with normal developmental concerns. In fact, it is typical that career and general counseling concerns are so intertwined within career counseling that compartmentalizing them is not realistic for most clients (Kirschner, Hoffman, & Hill, 1994; Savickas, 2012; Subich, 1993). For example, Niles and Anderson (1995) examined the content of more than 250 career counseling sessions and investigated when clients discussed career and noncareer concerns within career counseling. They found no pattern for the presentation of career and noncareer concerns in the career counseling process. Thus, it may be more appropriate to view career counseling as a type of psychological intervention that, at times throughout the course of career counseling, may require the counselor and client to focus on noncareer concerns.

Rounds and Tinsley (1984) support this view, stating, "we believe that a conceptual shift in which career interventions are understood as psychological interventions (and career counseling as psychotherapy) would foster advances in the understanding of vocational behavior change and processes" (p. 139). In some instances, students and clients may simply need minimal self and/or occupational information to be able to cope with their career concerns. In other instances, more therapeutic interventions may be required to help students and clients move forward in their career development.

DESIGNING CAREER COUNSELING STRATEGIES

Such notions pertaining to career counseling reflect the widely recognized belief that career issues are contextual and that the context of the 21st century is not the same as the context of the early 20th century. Savickas (1993) argued for career counselors to respond to societal changes occurring in the new millennium by stating that "counseling for career development must keep pace with our society's movement to a postmodern era. Thus, counselors must innovate their career interventions to fit the new *zeitgeist*" (p. 205).

It should also be evident that the career counseling interventions used by professional counselors and psychologists must be guided by an understanding of how the current *zeitgeist* shapes the career tasks presented to students and workers. For instance, as we noted in

Chapter 1, career counselors must be cognizant of the fact that the hierarchical organizational pyramids, which once fostered the notion that career success is represented by climbing up the corporate career ladder, have been flattened. Career patterns now resemble roller coasters rather than gradual inclines, thereby requiring workers to redefine notions of what it means to be a success in one's career. Many adults present for career counseling with concerns that reflect unsuccessful attempts at coping with such changes. Adolescents worry about what they will experience in their careers as they watch their parents struggle to manage their career development. Brown et al. (2000) conclude from their meta-analysis of career counseling outcome studies that positive career counseling outcomes are likely to occur when career counselors have their clients compose written career goals, talk with the counselors about their future goals, become exposed to models of effective career decision making, assist in the search for and integration of occupational information, and establish a supportive network relative to achieving their future goals.

To respond to these issues effectively, we contend that professional counselors and psychologists must provide counseling-based career assistance and support to their students and clients (although these may at first glance appear to be obvious recommendations, we have too often observed career counselors who seem to blatantly disregard them in their work with clients). We view these recommendations as essential to providing career counseling that is sensitive to the career concerns young people and adults experience in the 21st century.

Providing Counseling-Based Career Assistance

Career counselors offering counseling-based career assistance do not view their clients as the problem and the counselor as the solution. Rather, they seek to empower clients to articulate their experiences, clarify their self-concepts, and construct their own lives. Accordingly, career counselors function as collaborators in this process and pay special attention to the therapeutic relationship. As we have noted, providing counseling-based career assistance requires counselors to possess multicultural competencies. These skills are essential in the career counseling process and every counseling relationship is cross-cultural (Leong, 1993). It is essential, therefore, that counselors understand how contextual factors such as gender, socioeconomic status, racial/ethnic identity, sexual orientation, and disability status influence each client's worldview, identity, and career goals.

To help counselors consider these factors in the career counseling process, Ward and Bingham (1993) devised a multicultural career counseling checklist that can be used to help counselors identify issues of race/ethnicity that may need to be addressed in career counseling. When necessary, counselors help their clients develop strategies for overcoming prejudice and discrimination in employment and training practices. Interventions such as cognitive-behavioral counseling techniques, mentoring, and advocacy are especially useful in this regard (Herr & Niles, 1998). Additional strategies for culturally appropriate career counseling (e.g., the Career-in-Culture Interview) were discussed in Chapter 4 and serve as foundational skills for effective career counseling.

Providing counseling-based career assistance to clients also requires the use of such basic skills as summarizing client statements, reflecting clients' feelings, paraphrasing, using indirect and/or open questions, expressing positive regard for the client, and empathic responding. These skills are essential for creating an effective working alliance with clients regardless of the theoretical perspective used by the counselor.

Establishing an effective working alliance with clients is fairly straightforward when clients are eager career counseling participants who are motivated to make changes. However, not all career counseling clients are eager and motivated. Some secondary school students, for example, present for career counseling because their parents have pressured them to make career choices, and these students do not yet see the importance of career planning in their lives. School systems expect all students to make curricular choices, which are essentially prevocational choices, at specific points in the educational process. Some students do not possess the readiness for making these choices and are not motivated to develop readiness, whereas others may be reluctant to identify career goals that run counter to their parents' plans for them. Adults who are victims of outplacement may experience resentment and bitterness toward their former employers. They may feel that what happens in their careers is out of their control and that it is useless to engage in career counseling. Other clients may be more comfortable dreaming about options than implementing them. Fears that they may fail or that the new options will not live up to the expectations they have for them may keep some clients stuck. Expressing the need to make a career change is much easier for most people than acting to implement a career change. Clients in each of these situations can be described as *resistant clients*. Although they recognize at some level that their career concerns need to be addressed, they are fearful of making changes in their lives.

Resistance represents a particularly interesting paradox in general counseling, and career counseling is no exception. People present for career counseling out of a desire to make changes in their career situations, yet, due to fear of changing, they resist making career changes. Because resistance exists, at some level, within all clients, career counselors must be competent at recognizing and dealing with resistance when it occurs. A starting point for working effectively with resistance involves understanding the different forms in which clients can express their resistance. To this end, Otani (1989) offers a taxonomy for classifying various forms of client resistance. Her taxonomy includes four categories: (a) response-quantity resistance (e.g., silence, minimum talk, verbosity); (b) response-content resistance (e.g., intellectualizing, symptom preoccupation, small talk, future/past preoccupation); (c) response-style resistance (e.g., discounting, thought censoring, second-guessing, last-minute disclosing, externalizing, forgetting, false promising); and (d) logistic management resistance (e.g., poor appointment keeping, personal favor asking). Otani notes that for client behaviors to be appropriately labeled as resistant, they need to occur repeatedly over several sessions. Thus, occasional silence, for example, may simply reflect the fact that the client is pondering a particular point rather than being resistant to change. Being alert to resistant behaviors can help counselors identify client concerns that may be important to explore within career counseling. Understanding the various ways in which clients can express their fear of changing, or resistance, also helps counselors to manage their countertransference when they encounter client expressions of resistance. Clearly, understanding the client's motivation for resistance (i.e., the affective experience the client hopes to avoid encountering) is critical to working effectively with resistant clients.

Spokane (1991) suggests guidelines that career counselors can use to cope with client resistance. (Spokane adapted these guidelines to career counseling from suggestions Meichenbaum and Turk [1987] offered to encourage compliance in therapy.) Specifically, Spokane recommends that career counselors should anticipate resistance from their clients (especially when it comes to putting plans into action). He also emphasizes the need for career counselors to take a collaborative, client-centered approach to the career intervention process. Finally, he encourages career counselors to take advantage of community resources (employers, job search banks, career groups, career planning classes, etc.) in creating a career counseling treatment plan with their clients.

Gysbers, Heppner, and Johnston (2014) also offer strategies for dealing with client resistance in career counseling. Specifically, they reinforce the importance of establishing an effective working alliance. There is a common saying that "Clients don't care how much you know until they know how much you care." This describes the foundational role that an effective working alliance can play in addressing resistance. Gysbers and his colleagues also note that by joining with the client (a skill that embraces and extends empathy as it calls on the career counselor to demonstrate accurate appreciation for the client's life struggles), career counselors can demonstrate that they are working with and for their clients. The use of metaphors can also help clients see their situations from different perspectives, thereby stimulating creativity, action, and hope (Amundson, 2009). These strategies obviously require career counselors to use general counseling techniques in the career counseling process. Providing counseling-based career assistance helps clients to engage in career exploration and cope effectively with the career-change process.

Providing Support in Career Counseling

Given the career development challenges confronting people today, professional counselors recognize that offering support to clients is essential to effective career counseling (Brehm, 1987; Holland et al., 1981; Kirschner, 1988). Counselor-initiated supportive acts engender feelings of hope, confidence, and purpose within clients (Highlen & Hill, 1984; Kalton, 2001). As Brammer (1993) notes, support "helps to counter feelings of 'falling apart,' 'being at loose ends,' or 'pulled in many directions at once'" (pp. 105–106). When clients acknowledge that they are unsure about their current and/or future career goals, it is common for them to experience feelings such as hopelessness, anxiety, confusion, and/or depression. Career counselors offering supportive acts help their clients to begin the process of coping more effectively with their career dilemmas.

Career counselors offer support to clients in a variety of ways. As noted, establishing an effective relationship between the counselor and the client is an essential first step in the career counseling process. However, the type of support clients need depends on the stage of career counseling and the specific career concerns being addressed. For example, Amundson (1995) discussed the importance of support in helping clients cope with unemployment. Specifically, he advocated connecting cognitive reframing interventions with the client's time perspective by focusing on the client's past (e.g., normalizing reactions to unemployment, recalling accomplishments, and identifying transferable skills), present (e.g., affirming the client's capacity to cope, externalizing the problem, limiting negative thinking), and future (e.g., identifying new cycles of activity, creating focused goal statements).

Support is also useful for highly self-conscious clients who are having difficulty making career decisions (Leong & Chervinko, 1996). Adolescents who have little work experience and limited self-knowledge to draw upon in their career planning may be tentative and insecure decision makers. Leong and Chervinko found that individuals who fear making a commitment and who internalize high standards from parents and significant others (i.e., socially prescribed perfectionism) also tend to have career decision-making difficulties. Career counselors can help these clients by encouraging them to examine the beliefs that stop them from making commitments and moving forward with their career decision making. In this regard, it may be useful to have clients first identify barriers to their career development and then focus on what clients have done in the past to overcome similar barriers (Luzzo, 1996). Counselors may need to take a more educative role in helping clients who have limited experience in coping with the barriers they are encountering (Krumboltz, 1996).

By offering support, career counselors help clients cope with the challenges they encounter as they attempt to manage their career development more effectively. Supportive acts in career counseling include all counselor-initiated interactions that involve one or more of the following key elements: affect, affirmation, and aid (Kahn & Antonucci, 1980). Supportive acts can be used to extend emotional support, informational support, and assessment support to clients (House, 1981).

Emotional support involves providing caring, trust, and empathy to clients. Informational support involves providing clients with information they can use in resolving their career concerns. Assessment support involves providing clients with information that is useful in making accurate self-evaluations (e.g., interest inventories, card sorts, measures related to career thoughts and beliefs). Although it is possible to make distinctions among the types of support that counselors provide to clients, the three types of support we have identified are not mutually exclusive (e.g., providing clients with assessment support can be an emotionally supportive act as well). Informational support and assessment support, however, focus on the transmission of information rather than the affect involved in emotional support (House, 1981).

Emotional Support in Career Counseling

The need to provide emotional support to clients is a basic presupposition of most forms of career counseling (Amundson, 1995; Crites, 1976; Salomone, 1982; Super, 1957). Caring and empathy are the essential supportive acts involved in extending emotional support to clients. These acts of emotional support are important throughout career counseling, but they are especially critical in the early phase of career counseling when an effective working alliance is being established (Amundson, 2009; Kirschner, 1988).

Offering emotional support requires career counselors to understand their clients' multiple perspectives and subjective experiences. Emotionally supportive acts, therefore, are grounded in multicultural counseling competencies (Pope-Davis & Dings, 1995; Sue et al., 1982). Although this seems to be a statement of the obvious, career counselors often act otherwise— that is, some career counselors demonstrate insufficient understanding of clients' multiple perspectives, as evidenced by the inappropriate use of assessment instruments (Fouad, 1993), the application of culturally inappropriate career counseling processes (Leong, 1993), and the lack of attention given to career concerns beyond the exploration stage of career development (Niles & Anderson, 1995).

To provide culturally appropriate career counseling assistance, Savickas (1993) recommends that career counselors move from acting as experts to acting as "cultural workers," from focusing on occupational choice to focusing on life design, and from focusing on test scores to focusing on clients' stories (pp. 210–214). Ignoring clients' perspectives and subjective experiences (at best) minimizes opportunities for providing effective emotional support to career counseling clients. The absence of an emotionally supportive relationship in career counseling increases the risk of poor goal clarification and the use of inappropriate career interventions (Leong, 1993).

Providing emotional support to clients in career counseling essentially helps clients feel as though they "matter." Schlossberg, Lynch and Chickering (1989) refer to *mattering*, which is the "beliefs people have, whether right or wrong, that they matter to someone else, that they are the object of someone else's attention, and that others care about them and appreciate them" (p. 7). Amundson et al. (2013) note that helping clients feel as though they matter requires skilled actions as well as good intentions on the part of career counselors. Amundson and his associates recommend that career counselors use the acronym PLEASE as an aid for expressing mattering to their clients.

> P—*protecting.* Providing a secure and safe haven for exploratory efforts. Ensuring that clients receive all of the benefits to which they are entitled.
>
> L—*listening.* Taking the time to hear all aspects of a person's story. Paying attention to underlying feelings in the telling of the story.
>
> E—*enquiring.* Expressing interest in the story through questions and requests for clarification. Being naturally curious and asking about events in the person's life.
>
> A—*acknowledging.* Noticing the other person and expressing greetings both verbally and nonverbally.
>
> S—*supporting.* Expressing encouragement and praise. Identifying positive attitudes and behaviors and providing specific feedback.
>
> E—*exchanging.* Sharing information about oneself. This self-disclosure should be genuine and appropriate to the situation. (p. 40)

Helping clients feel that they matter is clearly an effective way to extend emotional support and to establish a firm foundation for career counseling interventions. Although emotional support is a necessary condition for effective career counseling, it is usually not sufficient for supporting clients as they develop their careers.

Informational Support in Career Counseling

Informational support is an additional form of support that aids clients in their career development. Essentially, informational support empowers clients to help themselves. There are numerous examples of supportive acts that career counselors can use to extend informational support to their clients. Among these are teaching clients job search strategies, providing clients with access to lists of job openings, teaching decision-making strategies, examining clients' dysfunctional career beliefs, and providing clients with lists of reading materials that are relevant to their career concerns.

Informational support can also be provided to clients in the early phase of career counseling. Specifically, supportive acts can be used to provide information about the structure of career counseling. Because so many clients enter career counseling expecting counselors to use tests, it is important that career counselors discuss the career development process as well as the career counseling process with their clients. For instance, clients can be informed that career counseling is a collaborative process in which counselors offer feedback, affirmation, and support as clients interpret their needs and shape their lives. This information helps counteract clients' expectations to be tested by an expert who will then identify appropriate career options. Clarifying roles and responsibilities for career counseling helps clients understand that career counseling is a shared experience in which they are active participants. Informing a client that most people make career changes multiple times during their lives and that career change is often a very adaptive response to personal changes and/or changes in work helps normalize the client's career concerns.

Thus, extending informational support in the early phase of career counseling allows clients to take full advantage of the career counseling experience. Providing clients with emotional support and informational support in the early phase of career counseling helps to establish an effective working alliance and sets the stage for the incorporation of assessment support in the career counseling process.

Assessment Support in Career Counseling

Assessment support provides clients with opportunities to acquire information that is useful in making accurate self-evaluations. Assessment information can be used in the early phase of career counseling to support clients as they clarify their career concerns and identify their career counseling goals. Here again, exploring clients' multiple perspectives is an important step in providing culturally sensitive assessment support (Ibrahim, Ohnishi, & Wilson, 1994) because clients' patterns of career concerns are influenced by various personal and situational determinants that shape their life-role self-concepts (Super, 1980). Some individuals view work as the central role in life, whereas others see it as being on the periphery. Some view a career choice as the expression of personal fulfillment and others view it as the fulfillment of familial expectations. Thus, understanding the client's worldview, cultural identity, gender identity, sexual orientation, and disability status is a prerequisite for engaging in effective assessment activities.

Given the uncertainty related to career paths today, it should be clear that providing clients with information about themselves and the world-of-work through objective, standardized assessments is necessary, but often not sufficient, for empowering people to manage their careers effectively. To be sure, having information about how one's interests compare with others is helpful in the process of identifying viable career options. But, an overreliance on objective assessment ignores that "what exists for individuals is purpose, not positions on a normal curve" (Savickas, 1993, p. 213). Thus, two people with similar aptitude test and interest inventory results may select different occupations due to other factors influencing their decision making and sense of self. Our unique life experiences provide the clay out of which we sculpt our career decisions. To help people make meaning out of life experiences, career counselors pay attention to each client's subjective career (Carlsen, 1988). Most likely, the experiences that capture the most attention are those that have been the most painful (Adlerians call it "actively mastering what we at one time passively suffered" [Watkins & Savickas, 1990, p. 104]). Counselors can help clients sift through these experiences by augmenting traditional standardized assessment strategies with interventions that help clients translate their subjective experiences into purposeful career activities.

For example, in Savickas's (2013) career construction theory, he offers the career construction assessment model as a strategy for helping clients to identify subjective themes that guide their career development. In this approach, Savickas queries clients as to their early role models; early life recollections; favorite books, movies, and magazines; and life mottoes. The answers to these questions contain themes that clients use to guide their decisions as they work to turn their problems into opportunities. For example, one of our career counseling clients (Verneda) noted that her role model in early life was her high school principal because she "helped others overcome obstacles in their lives." Verneda, an African American woman, had experienced early life tragedies, serious chronic illness, and numerous instances of discriminatory treatment. Through the use of the Career Construction Inventory assessment, Verneda became aware of her life theme—"overcoming obstacles"—and decided to become a counselor to "help others overcome obstacles." She actively mastered what she had passively suffered early in her life and turned her preoccupation (overcoming obstacles) into an occupation (helping others overcome obstacles) through her work as a counselor. Savickas's approach focuses on working collaboratively with clients to translate their life themes into career goals. The use of projective techniques, autobiographies, laddering techniques, and card sorts are also useful, subjectively oriented strategies for incorporating life experiences into the career counseling process (Amundson, 2009; Neimeyer, 1992; Peavy, 1994).

Savickas (2012, 2013) offered a new paradigm for career intervention that acknowledges the impact that the digital revolution and the global economy have had on work and workers. Specifically, Savickas's life-design interventions are structured to (a) *construct* career through small stories, (b) *deconstruct* these stories and reconstruct them into an identity narrative or life portrait, and (c) *co-construct* intentions that lead to the next *action* episode in the real world.

Life-design intervention draws heavily on narrative and begins by having career counseling clients describe both (a) the incident that dislocates them from the current episode in their career story and (b) their goals for a new scenario that they want to co-construct with their counselor. Life-design intervention focuses on narrative stories because stories help clients build their identities and careers out of complex social interactions. As Savickas (2012) notes, "storytelling makes the self and crystallizes what clients think of themselves. The more stories they tell, the more they develop their identities and careers" (p. 19). Stories help people organize their life events into a sequence that describes their career development.

Desconstruction helps identify self-limiting thoughts and ideas that clients may adhere to, the cultural barriers they may experience, and the confining life roles in which they participate. Deconstruction seeks to make these factors more obvious so that they can be introduced into career counseling with the goal of considering strategies for rethinking limiting thoughts, addressing cultural barriers, and redefining unnecessarily limiting life-role participation—all with the intent of helping clients identify ways to move forward in their career development—to advance their career story.

As such, deconstruction of clients' career stories fosters the reconstruction process. Reconstruction involves the career counselor actively gathering "the story threads and weaving them together into one tapestry to craft a unified sense of individuality" (Savickas, 2013) so that a larger career story is constructed. This larger career story reflects the client's identity narrative. The larger career story contains the personal meaning and reveals life themes that the client uses to understand his/her past and present. This understanding then facilitates and guides future movement as the career counselor and the client co-construct a life portrait that portrays the client's story as accurately as possible relative to life themes, patterns, and personal meaning. "With new language, fresh perspectives, and expanded vistas clients may reorganize their meaning system and clarify what is at stake in the next episode of their career story" (Savickas). Essentially, the process fosters greater self-clarity relative to the client's career story and past, present, and future goals so that the client can take intentional actions to link a personal story with career possibilities.

Watkins and Savickas (1990) note that four types of clients tend to benefit the most from incorporating subjective assessment strategies into career counseling: (a) indecisive clients, (b) difficult cases, or clients who have received career counseling but have yet to resolve their career concerns, (c) mid-career changers, and (d) culturally diverse clients who may not be served adequately by objective-only interventions. To be of most use to clients, Savickas (1993) contends that counselors should augment, rather than replace, objective and standardized assessments focusing on congruence, developmental tasks, vocational identity, and career adaptability with subjective-oriented assessment strategies. Thus, career counselors must understand the purposes, strengths, and limitations of subjective and objective assessments. Specifically, subjective assessment strategies can be used to help clients address the following questions:

1. How do my life experiences connect to my career development?
2. What gives me meaning?

3. What sort of life do I want to construct?
4. What do I want to be able to express through my work?
5. Which work options will allow me to come the closest to expressing who I am?

Objective assessment strategies help clients address questions such as these:

1. How do my interests compare with others?
2. How much aptitude do I possess in specific areas?
3. How strong are my values in specific areas (e.g., economic rewards, aesthetics, ability utilization)?
4. What is my readiness for career decision making?

Of course, each approach has its own strengths and limitations that guide career counselors in decisions about which might be more useful to a client. The strengths of subjective assessments include the following:

1. They help clients understand themselves on a deep level.
2. They help clients consider the relevance of their life experiences to their career development.
3. They help clients attach a sense of purpose to their activities.
4. They are often inexpensive to use.
5. They actively engage clients in the career counseling process.
6. The assessment results are clearly connected to client responses to assessment questions.

The limitations of the subjective approach to assessment include the following:

1. They lack psychometric evidence related to the assessment activities.
2. They require substantial career counselor time within the career counseling process.
3. They typically have no clear interpretation guidelines for career counselors to follow.
4. They typically require more work on the part of the client than do objective assessments.

The strengths of objective assessments include these:

1. They allow the client to make comparisons with others.
2. They are outcome oriented.
3. They do not require as much in-session career counselor time as subjective assessments.
4. They often provide a useful starting point for subsequent consideration of career options.

The limitations of objective assessments include the following:

1. The results are not easily connected to specific responses.
2. They are counselor controlled.
3. They can be expensive.
4. Clients often have inappropriate expectations for what can be accomplished through the use of an objective assessment.
5. Measures do not always fit the client's context.

Career counselors need to adapt their assessment strategies to their clients' career concerns. Being skilled in incorporating objective and subjective assessments in career counseling helps counselors to more effectively serve their clients.

A FRAMEWORK FOR CAREER COUNSELING

Numerous frameworks exist for conducting career counseling. For example, Gysbers et al. (2014) view the career counseling process as typically progressing through several phases: (a) an opening phase in which the working alliance is established, (b) a gathering information phase in which the counselor and client gather data about the client's career situation, (c) a working phase in which the counselor and client use the information gathered to develop career goals and action plans, and (d) a final phase in which the counselor and client bring closure to career counseling.

Spokane (1991) proposes that career counseling consists of three overlapping and sequential phases labeled as a beginning phase, an activation phase, and a completion phase. During the beginning phase, career counselors provide clients with (a) structure concerning the career counseling process, (b) opportunities to rehearse their career aspirations either by themselves or in front of others, and (c) opportunities to uncover or identify conflicts engendered by their aspirations. During the activation phase, counselors provide support to clients as they process self-assessment data, test hypotheses about their career aspirations based on the new data they acquire, and begin formulating a commitment to a particular career option. During the completion phase, the career counselor helps the client implement and sustain a commitment to a career choice while also focusing on termination of the career counseling process.

Regardless of the framework used to conceptualize the career counseling process, most experts agree that career counseling typically involves a beginning or initial phase, a middle or working phase, and an ending or termination phase.

The Beginning or Initial Phase of Career Counseling

During the initial phase of career counseling, an effective career counseling relationship is developed, the counselor begins the process of gathering information about the client, and preliminary goals for career counseling are identified. Many career counselors begin sessions with their clients by asking them how they can be useful to the client. To clarify concerns, counselors encourage clients to identify individual and contextual factors contributing to their career dilemmas. Career counselors invite clients to discuss the strategies they have tried thus far to resolve their career dilemmas. Career counselors also seek to gather preliminary data concerning the clients' values, interests, and skills. Perhaps most important, career counselors work to establish rapport with their clients (Anderson & Niles, 2000; Fouad et al., 2007).

The initial phase of career counseling involves counselors providing clients with structure concerning the career counseling process. Career counselors work to clarify their clients' preferences and expectations for career counseling. Because clients seem clearer about what they prefer in career counseling than what they anticipate occurring, it is essential that counselors discuss with clients what they can expect to experience during the course of career counseling (Galassi, Crace, Martin, James, & Wallace 1992; Swanson, 1995). For example, Spokane (1991) recommends that counselors distribute to clients a brief handout describing the career counseling process and what is likely to occur in career counseling sessions. Informing clients about what they can anticipate within the process helps them to clarify the types of concerns that are appropriate to discuss in sessions. Additional structuring topics include the payment of fees, the length of sessions, confidentiality, counselor–client roles and responsibilities, and the career counselor's theoretical framework.

Theoretical frameworks help to organize the data that counselors collect from clients. For example, using Holland's theory, a career counselor could focus on collecting data to organize the counselor's understanding of the client's Holland types. This information helps counselors make initial assessments concerning the client's degree of congruence (What is the goodness of fit between the person's characteristics and the expectations of the person's current and/or most recent occupational environments?), consistency (How diverse or focused are the client's interests and competencies?), and aspirations (To which environments does the client aspire?).

A counselor relying on Super's (1990) life-span, life-space theory would be concerned with understanding the constellation of career development tasks confronting the client (e.g., Is the client an adolescent engaged in exploration stage tasks for the first time or an adult recycling through exploration stage tasks while also coping with tasks of other career stages?) and the client's life-role salience (e.g., What does the client hope to accomplish in each salient life role? To what degree is the client able to express important values in salient life roles?). Collecting this information in the initial phase of career counseling helps the counselor understand the client's life-role self-concepts (Super).

A career counselor operating from Krumboltz's (1996) learning theory of career counseling might organize the information collected from the client to understand the client's self-observation generalizations (How does the client describe himself or herself?), career beliefs (What does the client believe about the career development process? Are the client's beliefs functional or dysfunctional?), and which learning experiences have been most influential in the client's career development.

In these ways, career counseling theories provide the organizing structures used by career counselors to understand the information presented by their clients. Theories help shape the content of career counseling and provide a structure for conceptualizing clients' career concerns. Theories also provide a vocabulary the counselor and client can use to discuss the client's experiences.

Regardless of the theoretical perspectives used by career counselors, the following topics are addressed in the initial phase of career counseling:

1. The client's view of self; self-characteristics, worldview, racial/ethnic identity, view of the future; the client's health and physical status; the client's previous experiences in counseling (if any); and the client's presenting concerns and goals.
2. The client's family (e.g., Who are they? What has been their influence? What type of relationship does the client have with family members? What goals and aspirations do the family members have for the client? What is the client's attitude toward the family members?); the client's educational background (e.g., What type and level of education does the client have? Is the client open to considering additional education? What is the likelihood that the client could pursue additional education if desired?); and cultural influences (e.g., What cultural factors influence the client's attitudes, behavior, goals?).
3. The client's significant work and life experiences (e.g., How have these experiences influenced the client's attitudes, behavior, and goals? How has the client coped with difficulties in the past?); and significant individuals in the client's life (e.g., What role models does the client have? In what ways have the client's role models influenced the client's attitudes, behavior, and goals? What sources of support does the client have?).

At the onset of any career counseling relationship, career counselors should conduct a needs assessment to ascertain the client's concerns, expectations, and goals for career counseling. Goals for career counseling must achieve several criteria. Goals should be specific, observable, time specific, and achievable. Sometimes, goal identification can be facilitated by helping clients clarify the questions they are asking when they present for career counseling. For example, Maggie (the client introduced at the beginning of this chapter) presented for career counseling and declared in the first 10 minutes of her first session that her goal was "to get out of my miserable work situation" (she worked as a sales associate in a department store at the local mall). The counselor responded supportively to Maggie by reflecting her feelings of frustration and anger. This encouraged Maggie to tell more details about her work situation. When asked what occupations she had in mind, Maggie expressed in frustration that she didn't know but that "anything has to be better than what I am doing now." These statements provided the career counselor with a clear sense that Maggie wanted things to change and that she was not happy in her current job; however, it did little to provide the counselor and client with an indication as to what Maggie wanted to move toward in her career. Thus, the counselor clarified with Maggie that she already knew she wanted to stop doing what she was currently doing but that she did not know what she wanted to do next. The counselor provided Maggie with informational support by explaining the career development and career counseling process to her. The counselor was careful to emphasize the necessity of clarifying important self-information before attempting and acquiring relevant occupational information prior to making career decisions. To help Maggie clarify important self-information, the counselor asked Maggie for more information:

Counselor: Maggie, can you tell me some more about what you don't like about your current job?
Maggie: I work for a sexist creep who takes credit for my work and never has anything positive to say about what I do. I have no opportunities for advancement and the pay stinks.

After discussing with Maggie what specifically was wrong in her current situation and what she would like more of in her next situation, Maggie began to crystallize more specific, observable, time-specific, and achievable goals for career counseling. By clarifying the questions she was asking about her career situation, Maggie was able to state that her initial goal for career counseling was to identify occupational options that would allow her to engage in activities she enjoyed, use the skills she prized most, and express her important values. Maggie also felt that she was currently underemployed and hoped to get a job that would allow her to use her bachelor's degree in business administration. Thus, Maggie quickly acknowledged that her statement "anything would be better than what she was doing now" was not exactly accurate and did not reflect the questions she was asking about her career. There were certain things she wanted in a job and certain things she did not want to be part of her work.

To figure out what job she would like to pursue next, Maggie felt that focusing on clarifying her interests and values would be especially useful. After additional discussion of Maggie's interests, values, and skills, Maggie stated, "In the next few career counseling sessions, I would like to learn more about my interests and values. After we do that, I would like to identify some jobs that make sense for me." Articulating and clarifying goals provides the opportunity for the counselor and client to identify an initial plan of action for career counseling.

The initial phase of career counseling culminates in the establishment of an effective counselor–client relationship, a mutual understanding of the structure of the career counseling experience (e.g., roles, responsibilities, limits), and a shared understanding of the client's presenting issues and initial goals for career counseling. Providing emotional and informational support to clients also helps establish an effective working alliance in career counseling.

The Middle or Working Phase of Career Counseling

The middle or working phase of career counseling is the time when a client's concerns and goals are explored in depth and a specific plan of action for career counseling is more fully developed and implemented. Career counseling goals are often revised and/or refined in the middle phase of career counseling. For example, to help Maggie clarify her interests and values, she and her career counselor decided to use an interest inventory and values card sort exercise. Thus, assessment support became an important component of the middle phase of career counseling with Maggie. As Maggie proceeded to clarify important self-information, she was able to clarify a plan of action by stating, "In 6 months I would like to have a job that allows me to have more opportunities to use my verbal and computer skills. I want to work more independently and have more control over my success. I also want a job with more income potential that offers opportunities for advancement into higher levels of management."

Maggie and her counselor then began the process of identifying prospective occupational options related to her interests, values, and skills. Based on this exploration, Maggie came to the tentative conclusion that a career in computer sales offered her the opportunity to express her most important characteristics. To gather more information about computer sales positions, Maggie and her counselor decided that information interviewing would be useful. Maggie had never engaged in information interviewing, so she and her counselor decided that learning how to conduct an information interview would be a good first step in gathering additional occupational information. As they reviewed the steps involved in information interviewing, it became evident to the counselor that Maggie lacked assertiveness skills. Thus, the counselor and Maggie decided that it would be helpful to focus on developing assertiveness skills because these skills are essential for effective interviewing for occupational information (and interviewing for jobs). Maggie and her counselor engaged in assertiveness training.

Soon, Maggie was ready to begin information interviewing. A family friend actually worked in computer sales, and Maggie thought that this person would provide a good starting point for her information interviewing. They met for a 30-minute interview, during which Maggie received answers to many of her questions pertaining to work as a computer salesperson. At the end of the interview, Maggie asked for names of other computer salespeople with whom she could meet. Before she could schedule her second information interview, however, her interviewee learned of a vacancy in his company. He recommended Maggie for the position and she was offered an interview that resulted in her being hired as a computer salesperson.

Career counseling theories provide guideposts to direct the career counseling process. For example, interventions with Maggie focused on her information and skill deficits. Such interventions reflect a behavioral or social learning theory approach to career counseling. A developmental counselor working with Maggie might have encouraged her to clarify her life-role salience by constructing current and ideal life-career rainbows (Super, Savickas, & Super, 1996). This information would be useful in helping Maggie sort through occupational options (e.g., she could evaluate each option in light of the opportunity each option provided for participating in life roles that were important to her).

A counselor oriented toward using Holland's theory might have decided to teach Holland's typology to Maggie. Learning the Holland types would provide a structure and vocabulary that

Maggie could use to increase her self-understanding and sort through prospective occupational options. A counselor oriented toward Krumboltz's (1996) learning theory of career counseling might have encouraged Maggie to identify her career beliefs. The counselor may have administered the Career Beliefs Inventory (Krumboltz, 1988). Results from the Career Beliefs Inventory might have been used to highlight the specific beliefs causing Maggie difficulty and could have provided a starting point for forming more functional beliefs about the career development process.

Of course, how career counselors intervene depends not only on the counselor's theoretical framework but also on the type of decisional difficulty clients are experiencing. Decision-making difficulties occurring at the *beginning* of the decision-making process may be due to a lack of self- and/or occupational information, dysfunctional career beliefs, a lack of motivation, or more general indecisiveness within the client (Gati, Krausz, & Osipow, 1996). Decisional difficulties occurring *during* the career decision-making process could be due to insufficient information, conflicts related to personal characteristics and occupational options (e.g., skill levels insufficient for the occupation desired), and conflicts due to the influence of significant others (Gati et al.). Difficulties arising after decisions have been implemented may be the result of a poor choice of occupation, problems within the occupational environment, or the inability of the client to adjust to a particular work or educational situation.

When clients have made a poor occupational choice, they will need to recycle through Super's (1990) exploration-stage tasks. Maggie recycled through exploration-stage tasks as a more informed career explorer. She used information from her first sales position to help crystallize more appropriate occupational options.

Clients experiencing problems within the occupational environment may need to consider other jobs within the same occupation or may focus on strategies they can use to change their current work environment (e.g., clarifying with a supervisor one's roles and responsibilities, confronting a coworker). Maggie's situation was very limited in this regard. Her boss was not likely to change his attitudes and behaviors.

Clients having difficulty adjusting to their work environments may need to focus on developing important effective work competencies, such as developing interpersonal skills, assertiveness, and reliability. For example, an unassertive client experiencing ambiguity regarding work responsibilities may need assertiveness training to approach a supervisor to ask for more clarity concerning work tasks. Maggie decided that approaching her boss concerning his sexist attitudes was not as important to her as developing assertiveness skills to engage in information interviewing. These skills were essential to her in learning more about her new occupation and in succeeding in her job search.

It is interesting to note that career counseling research typically focuses on issues related to helping clients make and implement career choices. However, as implied by the previous discussion, career concerns continue after choices have been implemented (Carson, Carson, Phillips, & Roe, 1996). Indeed, many individuals have difficulty adjusting to the work they have chosen. Hershenson (1996) offers a systems model for career counselors to use in addressing work adjustment issues. Hershenson's system for work adjustment highlights the relationships among the subsystems of the person (work personality, work competencies, and work goals), the elements of the work setting (behavioral expectations, skill requirements, and rewards/opportunities), and the components of work adjustment (work-role behavior, task performance, and worker satisfaction). The formative influences of culture, family, school, and peer/reference group are also addressed in Hershenson's model of work adjustment. Thus, career counseling for work adjustment focuses on the relationship between the worker and the work environment.

Career counseling for work adjustment begins by assessing whether the problem is related to work-role behavior, task performance, worker satisfaction, or some combination of these three factors. If it is the former, then interventions focus on work personality. For issues of task performance, work competencies are addressed. Issues related to worker satisfaction require addressing work goals. Contextual factors (e.g., family, culture, and economics) are considered in all cases.

Thus, career counseling interventions are theory based and emerge from information gathered during the initial and middle phases of career counseling. When selecting interventions, the counselor provides the client with an explanation as to how the proposed intervention relates to the client's career concern and how the intervention might be useful to the client. The counselor and client discuss collaboratively whether the intervention seems appropriate. When it does, then there is a clear sense as to how career counseling will proceed. When the intervention does not make sense to the client, then there may be the need for the counselor to clarify his or her understanding of the client's concerns. Perhaps the counselor has missed important elements of the client's situation. For example, a client who is dissatisfied in his current job may be reluctant to engage in broad career exploration with the goal of entering a new and potentially more satisfying occupation when he has significant financial obligations that restrict his ability to sustain substantial periods of time without a paycheck. Although finding a more satisfying occupation may be an ideal goal from the counselor's perspective, in this instance it may not be realistic from the client's perspective.

When counselors discuss their understanding of clients' career concerns and propose interventions for addressing those concerns, they have the opportunity to receive important formative feedback from clients. Establishing an effective working alliance allows clients to feel comfortable discussing their perceptions of the career counseling process thus far. Working collaboratively in this fashion provides the opportunity for the client to take ownership of the career counseling process and outcome because the client has been actively involved in the entire career counseling experience.

Moreover, during the middle phase of career counseling, clients may become aware of important aspects of their career concerns that they were not aware of in the initial phase of career counseling. This new information may influence the client's goals for career counseling and result in the identification of alternative interventions that may be more appropriate for addressing the client's revised goals and concerns. In fact, Niles, Anderson, and Cover (2000) suggest that clients typically revise their concerns and goals during the course of career counseling, and counselors need to be alert to this phenomenon. Therefore, counselors should maintain flexibility in responding to clients' concerns as they emerge during the course of career counseling and, when necessary, should invite clients to consider revising their goals for career counseling.

Maggie and her counselor began by focusing on helping her to clarify the questions she was asking about her career. Maggie was also encouraged to learn more about her important self-characteristics. As she learned more about herself, especially her interests and values, she began to crystallize a career preference. As career counseling progressed, it became clear that Maggie would need to learn new skills to move forward in her career development. Thus, the counselor and Maggie revised their goals for career counseling to include training in information interviewing and assertiveness.

The Ending or Termination Phase of Career Counseling

In the ending or termination phase, career counselors connect the work done in the beginning and middle phases of career counseling by assessing the client's current status and relating that status to the client's goals for career counseling. If the client's goals have been achieved, then termination becomes the focus. Steps are taken to prepare for ending the career counseling relationship. The counselor and client review the progress the client has made, discuss what the client has learned as a result of career counseling, consider how the learning the client has experienced can be generalized into future scenarios, and review what the client can do if difficulties are encountered in the future.

In reflecting on where the client was initially and where the client is now in his or her career development, differences in cognitions, affect, and behavior can be highlighted. For example, when Maggie presented for career counseling she was confused, angry, and ready to quit her job for any job that she could get. As career counseling progressed, she became more focused on the specific questions she was asking. She became more focused on what she needed to do to move forward in her career. She systematically acquired new information and skills she needed to cope more effectively with her career concerns. As Maggie did this, she began to crystallize new options that connected more closely with important self-characteristics. In addition, Maggie became an active participant in her career planning. As she became more active (e.g., participating in information interviews), Maggie developed important skills for helping her acquire a job she wanted. The ultimate reward was that she eventually acquired a more satisfying job. This process would be important for Maggie and her counselor to review. By reviewing her progress, Maggie's counselor can take opportunities to reinforce important learning experiences in Maggie's career counseling:

Maggie:	When I think about how I felt when I first came to see you, I remember feeling anxious, frustrated, and even somewhat hopeless.
Counselor:	How does that compare to how you feel now?
Maggie:	I've come 180 degrees. I now feel more in control, confident, and satisfied.
Counselor:	What do you think has helped you to feel so good?
Maggie:	Obviously, having my new job helps! But, I think that I learned to approach my career more systematically. I never really thought that much about my interests and values. Career counseling helped me organize that information and connect it with career options. I think I am much more in control of my career now. I also know how good career decisions are made. I don't think I really understood that before.

Maggie and her counselor continued to discuss what Maggie learned in her career counseling. The counselor was careful to point out the many strengths that Maggie exhibited in her career counseling (e.g., she took control of her situation, she was willing to learn new skills, she was able to put her new skills to use in effective ways, she was able to communicate clearly to the counselor and others, she followed through on assignments the counselor gave to her). They also considered how Maggie could put her new learning to use in the future. However, the counselor invited Maggie to return for career counseling in the future if she felt the need. Finally, Maggie and her counselor discussed what was most useful to Maggie in her career counseling as well as what Maggie thought was not as useful to her. Acquiring this information from the client's perspective provides important evaluative data that the counselor can use to improve his or her career counseling skills. To help structure the feedback Maggie provided, she was given an evaluation form (see Figure 8.1) to complete. Finally, Maggie was encouraged to consider whether she would like to say anything to the counselor before terminating. As a result of her career counseling, not only did Maggie feel more satisfied with her new job; she also felt more confident about her ability to manage the career concerns she would encounter in the future.

CAREER COUNSELING EVALUATION

This evaluation of the Counseling Center's career counseling services will help us improve the quality of assistance to the students.

Use the rating scale below to indicate your response to each statement. Write the number that corresponds to your response in the blank.

0	1	2	3	4
Not Applicable	Strongly Disagree	Disagree	Agree	Strongly Agree

_____   1. The counselor understood what my noncareer concerns were.

_____   2. The counselor understood what my career concerns were.

_____   3. The counselor has helped me to identify effective ways to cope with my noncareer concerns.

_____   4. The counselor has helped me to identify effective ways to cope with my career concerns.

_____   5. The time and activities spent learning about my interests, skills, and values were helpful.

_____   6. The time and activities spent in learning about my different occupational and/or educational choices were helpful.

_____   7. The time and activities spent in learning about the career planning and decision making process were helpful.

_____   8. Career counseling is helping me to achieve personal and career goals.

_____   9. Career counseling is helping me to function more effectively as a student, worker, and as a human being.

_____ 10. Overall, my career counseling experience has been helpful to me.

Please describe below the most helpful activities and moments in career counseling.

Please describe below the least helpful activities and moments in career counseling.

Your social security number will allow us to connect your responses to demographic data to help understand our effectiveness with various populations. It will also identify you to your counselor and help him/her better understand your evaluation so your counselor can improve his/her effectiveness. Your reply, as well as all other information you provide to the Center, will be kept confidential. If you would prefer to respond anonymously, leave the social security number blank.

Social Security Number: _____   Date: _____

Counselor name: _____

Approximate number of counseling sessions: _____

Thank you for your assistance.

Figure 8.1
Sample career counseling evaluation.

Not all termination experiences are as positive as Maggie's, however. Termination can also occur when the client decides that now is not the time to take action. This decision can occur for a variety of reasons. For example, it may be that the client has decided to attend college but cannot do so at this time due to financial constraints. Or the client may decide that the current situation is simply preferable to a change and, therefore, may lack motivation for changing. In these instances, the counselor can discuss the steps the client can take if, in the future, making a change seems more reasonable.

There are also instances of *premature closure* that occur when clients end counseling before the counselor thinks the client is ready. Brown and Brooks (1991) suggest four possibilities as to why premature closure occurs: (a) clients believe that they have achieved their goals, (b) the career counseling experience does not meet clients' expectations, (c) clients fear what may be uncovered in career counseling, and (d) clients lack commitment to career counseling. When premature closure happens, it is essential that the career counselor try to understand the reasons for it occurring. In such instances supervision or consulting with a colleague can be very useful. For example, if the client terminated because the career counseling experience did not meet the client's expectations, the counselor and supervisor can explore what factors might have contributed to the client drawing this conclusion. Was the counselor sensitive to the client's concerns? Did the counselor establish an effective working relationship with the client? Were there factors associated with the client's background or concerns that were difficult for the counselor and therefore limited the counselor's effectiveness with this particular client?

Gysbers et al. (2014) note that when a client terminates prematurely by unexpectedly dropping out of career counseling, then the counselor must make a decision as to how this will be handled. What the counselor decides to do in these instances is based on the counselor's beliefs about how much responsibility he or she should take in encouraging a client to return to career counseling. Gysbers and his colleagues suggest that placing a phone call to the client has several advantages. For example, it provides the opportunity to express concern for the client's well-being. It also provides the opportunity for the career counselor to collect more data related to the client's reasons for termination and, if appropriate, to refer the client to a relevant helping professional. Finally, touching base with the client in this way can "keep the door open" for the client to return to career counseling in the future.

Although it is not a pleasant experience, premature closure provides opportunities for career counselors to learn about themselves and the career counseling process. Career counselors should take full advantage of these opportunities by consulting with other professionals and, when possible, communicating with clients.

Clearly, termination is an important phase of career counseling. It provides an opportunity for the career counselor and client to review the important work they have done together. It provides important feedback to the counselor and helps the client to consider what he or she can do to cope with future career concerns. Given the importance of termination, it clearly should be a career counseling phase for which the counselor and client prepare ahead of time. The counselor must alert the client to the fact that termination is approaching. The counselor can help the client prepare for termination by encouraging the client to consider what has been learned in the time they have spent together and how the client feels about termination. The counselor also needs to be in touch with his or her feelings about termination. Because career counseling is an interactive experience, counselors often learn a great deal about themselves as a result of any career counseling relationship. It is important that the counselor reflect on what has been learned as a result of working with each client.

To assess whether termination has been handled thoroughly, Gysbers, Heppner, and Johnston (2014) offer a seven-point checklist and recommend that the counselor ask:[1]

1. Did I review the content of what happened in counseling?
2. Did I review the process of what happened in counseling?
3. Did I reemphasize the client's strengths that were evident in counseling?
4. Did I evaluate what went well and what went poorly?
5. Did I explore things unsaid in counseling?
6. Did I discuss feelings related to the ending of the counseling relationship?
7. Did I provide clear and direct structure for the client's next steps? (p. 309)

Taking a planful approach to termination contributes to a positive career counseling experience and helps the client, and counselor, take full advantage of the career counseling process.

CAREER COUNSELING GROUPS

Group counseling offers a mode of service delivery that can be used instead of, or in addition to, individual career counseling. Pyle (2007) describes group counseling as an intervention for 5 to 15 members, with 5 to 8 members optimal. Structured career counseling groups address a specific issue that is a common concern to the group members (e.g., job search, outplacement, choosing a college major, career decision making, career planning). Activities in structured career counseling groups tend to resemble group career-guidance activities. Because structured groups focus on specific career development topics, there is often a teaching component provided by the group leader. Thus, structured groups tend to be more information oriented and didactic than less-structured groups. Structured career counseling groups typically meet for three to seven sessions.

An Example of a Structured Group Career Intervention

Teaching students and clients about job-search strategies represents an excellent topic for a structured group experience. For example, in *session one*, the career counselor can begin by providing an opportunity for introductions and an ice breaker (e.g., What is your occupational fantasy?). Then, an overview of job-search strategies can be provided. Active and passive job-search techniques could be described, résumé styles reviewed, job interview techniques highlighted, and strategies for managing a job search could be discussed.

Session two could address active versus passive job-search strategies in depth. Specifically, the career counselor could teach group participants about the importance of engaging in an active job-search campaign, noting that many people rely solely on a passive approach to job searching—they compose a general résumé and send it to employers who have placed advertisements for a specific job opening. This approach has a low probability of succeeding for a variety of reasons. First, because it is a common approach it is likely to result in a large number of applications being submitted for the same position. Second, employers favor hiring "known

---

[1] From Gysbers, N., Heppner, M., and Johnston, J. *Career counseling: Holism, diversity and strengths* (4th ed.). Alexandria, VA: American Counseling Association. Copyright © 2014 by American Counseling Association. Reprinted/adapted by permission of the publisher.

commodities"—that is, they are more comfortable employing a person with whom they have had previous contact or who has been highly recommended by a trusted associate. When employers have multiple applicants for a position, persons having had positive previous contacts with the employer have a decided edge over those without such contacts. Finally, when all a job searcher knows about a vacancy is what is listed in the job vacancy announcement, it is rather difficult to compose a cover letter and résumé that connects closely with the specific opening. Résumés composed in a general way are almost always poor ones. When employers read résumés they look for connections with the skills required for being successful in the position for which they are hiring. A general, or shotgun, approach to composing a résumé is likely to miss its target. Those candidates using a focused (rather than general) résumé that clearly connects with the responsibilities related to the job for which one is applying are the individuals most likely to be invited for an interview. Thus, describing relevant accomplishments in action-oriented terms (e.g., *managed, led, organized, developed, coordinated*) is key to an effective résumé.

Active job searchers do not rely on employers to announce job vacancies. Rather, they actively engage in meeting with those who may be most likely to employ people to do what it is that the job searcher wants to do. Active job searchers work diligently to activate and develop a *network* of persons who fit this description. They attend professional meetings and explore employment possibilities with friends, acquaintances, and relatives. They query others as to whether they know people who work in a job in which they are interested and/or whether they know people who hire people to work in a job in which they are interested. They rely on information interviewing to gather data about specific jobs and work environments as well as to expand their network of personal contacts within their field of interest. They activate a system of contacts that eventually helps them to connect with prospective employers in a personal way. After discussing the importance of networking, the career counselor could conclude session two by demonstrating effective information-interviewing skills and then having the group members engage in a role play using these skills (e.g., by asking questions related to what the person likes about his/her job, what sort of training is required, what the challenges of the job are, what a typical day is like, and whether the interviewee would be willing to provide a name of another person likely to be an information interview candidate).

Session three could address the different styles of résumés job searchers use and the pros and cons of each. For example, most people use (and employers tend to prefer) a chronological résumé. Chronological résumés contain important information related to the job searcher's educational and work experiences, listed in reverse chronological order. A useful strategy for composing a chronological résumé is to first itemize the essential skills required to succeed in the job in which the person is interested. Then, the job searcher should consider ways in which his or her experience can be described to match the requisite skills. As much as possible these skills should be described as achievements within each listing on the chronological résumé. The determination of whether particular information should be included on the résumé is based on whether the information is relevant to the job for which the person is applying. Although employers prefer a one-page résumé, workers with extensive experience may opt for two pages. In all cases, the résumé should be neat, professional in appearance, and error free. Many job searchers find it helpful to review many sample résumés as they seek to identify a format that they will use.

When job searchers do not have experiences that connect directly with the skills required for success in the job they are seeking, they often resort to using functional résumés, which rely on the use of functional skill categories (e.g., managerial skills, organizational skills, communication skills, computer skills) that are relevant to the job. The job searcher first identifies the essential skills for the job being pursued and then lists accomplishments/experiences within each of the functional skills categories. The most relevant and highest priority skill areas should be listed first on the résumé. Functional résumés become useful when a job searcher has developed relevant skill sets via activities such as volunteering and independent learning.

A final option for job searchers is a hybrid or chronological/functional résumé. Hybrid résumés can be used when a job searcher has some relevant employment experiences but also has developed relevant skills in nontraditional ways.

In all cases a résumé should convince prospective employers that the job searcher could do the job. If the résumé does not connect to the job the searcher is pursuing, then it will be viewed as weak and will not accomplish the goal of gaining an interview. At the conclusion of session three the career counselor could assign participants the task of developing a résumé. The career counselor could meet with the participants individually to provide ongoing feedback pertaining to the résumé being developed. The following resources provide résumé samples and useful information for this dimension of the job search process:

e-Résumés: Part I
Describes the purpose of résumés; provides tips:
susanireland.com
resumehelp.com

e-Résumés: Part II
Discusses privacy and confidentiality concerns:
gotthejob.com

Executive Résumé Preferences:
wendyenelow.com

References and Letters of Recommendation:
jobsearch.about.com

Résumé Styles
Examples of chronological, functional, and combination résumés;
distinctiveweb.com

Targeted Résumé:
jobsearch.about.com

After reviewing résumés with group participants, the career counselor could explore the essentials of job interview skills in *session four*. For example, the counselor could explain that all job interviews involve getting responses to three questions: Can you do the job? Will you do the job? Will you fit in? These are the essential questions employers have in mind when meeting with job candidates. A goal of the interviewee should be to address these three questions (whether the interviewer asks them or not). If the job searcher has engaged in a thorough process of self-assessment to decide which job(s) she or he wants to pursue, then the answers to these three questions should be apparent—that is, the job searcher should be clear about the relevant interests, skills, values, and other self-characteristics that predict a high probability for success in the job. Moreover, by identifying the requisite skills for success in the job when composing a résumé, the job searcher has already taken an important step in preparing for the job interview.

During the interview, the job searcher offers specific examples of relevant accomplishments that provide important data to the employer (the best predictor of success in the future is having been successful at a similar task in the past). For example, group participants can be told that rather than simply stating that they are confident in their organizational skills, they can also provide specific examples in which they successfully demonstrated organizational ability.

The question pertaining to whether the job searcher will "fit in" represents a key concern in the interview process. Perhaps more than anything else, employers want to know if a job candidate will demonstrate the sort of behaviors that contribute positively to the work climate. Skills such as getting along well with others, having effective communication skills, being reliable, being dependable, being stable in one's behavior, and staying on task represent the sort of self-management skills that employers strongly desire in their employees. Job interviewees must communicate that they possess these skills. This can be demonstrated in multiple ways (e.g., being on time for the interview, demonstrating effective interpersonal skills in the interview, dressing appropriately for the interview, discussing the fact that the job searcher possesses these skills—"I tend to be the sort of person who gets along well with others and works hard to contribute positively to my work environment, for example. ..."). Finally, the career counselor can demonstrate effective (and not-so-effective interview skills) in the group session and then have group members discuss the demonstration before practicing effective job interview role plays.

The final group session (*session five*) can address the activities required for managing a job search effectively (e.g., keeping records of all contacts, setting goals to make a particular number of contacts each week, the importance of engaging in good self-care and positive self-talk, connecting with others who can be supportive, joining a job search group). Last, but not least, the final session should involve collecting evaluative data to inform the career counselor about ways in which the experience can be improved in the future.

Typically, structured groups like the one we have just described blend didactic information with experiential information as career counselors seek to help their clients acquire pertinent knowledge, awareness, and skills connected to the purpose of the group. The career counselor should identify specific goals, objectives, and outcomes for each group session.

Less-Structured Career Groups

Career counseling groups can also be more process oriented and less structured. Less-structured groups tend to focus on the intrapersonal and interpersonal concerns clients experience in their career development. They also tend to be more affective oriented than structured group experiences. Spokane (1991) contends that less-structured career counseling groups will increase in popularity as career development interventions and general counseling interventions become more interwoven. Less-structured career counseling groups tend to meet over a longer period of time than structured groups. Pyle (2000, 2007) contends that less-structured groups are often useful for clients struggling with career choice or direction. Job searchers who are fully engaged in the job search process (i.e., they have already learned the skills described in the structured group) can also benefit from a process-oriented group experience. Riordan and Kahnweiler (1996) provide an excellent description of ways in which job search support groups can be beneficial to job seekers.

The skills required for group career counseling are the same as those required in any group counseling experience; however, the counselor also needs to possess the requisite career knowledge pertaining to career development theory and practice. Pyle (2000, pp. 122–127) identifies four stages in group career counseling:

1. **Opening Stage:** The group members meet, the counselor provides an overview of the content of the group program, and goals are established. The counselor uses basic counseling skills, such as attending, concreteness, and genuineness.
2. **Investigation Stage:** Members focus on discussing the issues and topics pertinent to the group's purpose. For example, they may explore self-information (e.g., values, skills, interests), barriers to career development, or understanding the world-of-work. The counselor uses skills such as facilitative responses, self-disclosure, and personalizing to encourage group discussion.
3. **Working Stage:** Members process, synthesize, and identify actions they can take to advance their career development. The counselor uses skills such as accurate empathy, confrontation, providing feedback, and information processing to help clients during this stage.
4. **Decision/Operational Stage:** Members take action and provide support to each other regarding their action steps. The counselor uses skills such as drawing conclusions, helping members articulate their action plans, and bringing closure to the group experience.

There is mixed research evidence related to the effectiveness of career counseling groups. However, most of this evidence focuses on the effectiveness of structured group experiences. Most experts agree that there are several advantages to group career counseling experiences. For example, group career counseling is an efficient mode of service delivery. It maximizes the use of the counselor's time. This is especially important in school settings in which counselors often have very high caseloads and cannot offer individual counseling to every student for whom they are responsible. Pyle (2007) identifies several advantages to conducting group rather than individual career counseling. According to Pyle, groups provide opportunities for trying out new interpersonal behaviors and also allow individuals to give, as well as receive, help from other group members. Career counselors can gain greater insight into client interpersonal behaviors with others when using a group format. These possibilities are not present in individual counseling. The interpersonal nature of group counseling can assist adolescents in gaining the necessary social skills needed to have a successful interview experience and provide instruction in new ways of relating to others that may help with networking opportunities and on-the-job interactions.

Kivlighan (1990) notes that career groups also provide opportunities for group members to (a) learn new information about themselves and others, (b) receive social and emotional support from other group members, and (c) learn from peers who are in similar situations. Group interventions also offer the opportunity for group members to share resources and ideas with each other, thereby maximizing opportunities for learning new strategies for coping with their career concerns. For example, Sullivan and Mahalik (2000) found that encouraging group members to focus on performance accomplishments, emotional arousal, vicarious experiences, and verbal persuasion was effective in helping group members increase career self-efficacy. Mawson and Kahn (1993) found that information-sharing aspects of the group process were helpful to group members in identifying stable career goals.

Group career counseling experiences are enhanced when the counselor is able to create a cooperative and inclusive group environment in which the members focus on commonly accepted goals. Hansen and Cramer (1971) note five additional criteria that contribute to successful groups:

1. There is open communication among group members.
2. There is a common goal for the group.
3. The group members set norms that direct and guide their activities and interactions.
4. The group members develop a set of roles to play within the group.
5. The group works toward the satisfaction of individual needs of the group members.

CAREER COUNSELING PROFESSIONAL DESIGNATIONS AND RELATED SERVICE PROVIDERS

Regardless of whether a career counselor provides individual and/or group career assistance, we encourage counselors to develop a professional disclosure statement describing their training, experience, services offered, and approach to service delivery. This is important for a variety of reasons. As we have noted, many clients have clear expectations for career counseling (i.e., that they will be tested and informed as to which occupations are appropriate for them), and these expectations often do not mesh with current approaches to career counseling. Moreover, career services providers differ substantially in their training and areas of expertise, thus making the process of selecting a service provider an overwhelming one for consumers. For example, a popular movement today is the emergence of career coaching (Chung & Gfroerer, 2003). Career coaches can range from persons with professional counseling degrees and expertise in career development interventions to persons who are essentially paraprofessionals with very little professional training. Generally, career coaches aspire to help people identify their skills, make better career choices, and become more productive and satisfied workers. Career coaches seek to help their clients identify strategies for accomplishing their goals in their work lives. We take the view that (because few things are more personal than a career choice) it is difficult to engage in career coaching without delving into issues/concerns that require professional training as a counselor or psychologist. We agree with the National Career Development Association (NCDA) whose view is that career coaching is an essential role for career counselors, as exemplified by the fact that it is one of the core career counseling competencies it identifies (NCDA, 2009).

Career counselors in many states must be licensed professional counselors to practice career counseling. The Council for Accreditation of Counseling and Related Educational Programs (CACREP) offers a master's program specialty in career counseling (CACREP, 2015). This training represents the gold standard for career counseling training at the master's level. Doctoral-level counseling psychologists and counselors also receive training that prepares them for career counseling.

A Career Development Facilitator is a person who has completed the Career Development Facilitator Training Program and works in a career development setting or who incorporates career development information or skills in his or her work with students, adults, clients, employees, or the public. A Career Development Facilitator has received 120 class/instructional hours, provided by a nationally trained and qualified instructor (ncda.org).

Regardless of one's professional background, it is important to inform clients of their rights and responsibilities relative to receiving career services. Toward this goal, the National Board of

Certified Counselors and Chi Sigma Iota, an honorary counseling social fraternity, have published the following statements:

Your Rights as a Consumer

- Be informed of the qualifications of your counselor: education, experience, professional counseling certifications, and license(s).
- Receive an explanation of services offered, your time commitments, fee scales, and billing policies prior to receipt of services.
- Be informed of the limitations of the counselor's practice to special areas of expertise (career development, ethnic groups, etc.) or age group (adolescents, older adults, etc.).
- Have all that you say treated confidentially and be informed of any state laws placing limitations on confidentiality in the counseling relationship.
- Ask questions about the counseling techniques and strategies and be informed of your progress.
- Participate in setting goals and evaluating progress toward meeting them.
- Be informed of how to contact the counselor in an emergency situation.
- Request referral for a second opinion at any time.
- Request copies of records and reports to be used by other counseling professionals.
- Receive a copy of the code of ethics to which your counselor adheres.
- Contact the appropriate professional organization if you have doubts or complaints relative to the counselor's conduct.
- Terminate the relationship at any time.

Your Responsibilities as a Client

- Set and keep appointments with your counselor. Let him or her know as soon as possible if you cannot keep an appointment.
- Pay your fees in accordance with the schedule you preestablished with the counselor.
- Help plan your goals.
- Follow through with agreed-upon goals.
- Keep your counselor informed of your progress toward meeting your goals.
- Terminate your counseling relationship before entering into arrangements with another counselor.

If You Are Dissatisfied with the Services of a Counselor

Remember that a counselor who meets the needs of one person may be wrong for another. If you are dissatisfied with the services of your counselor:

- Express your concern directly to the counselor, if possible.
- Seek the advice of the counselor's supervisor if the counselor is practicing in a setting where he or she receives direct supervision.
- Terminate the counseling relationship, if the situation remains unresolved.
- Contact the appropriate state licensing board, national certification organization, or professional association, if you believe the counselor's conduct to be unethical.

National Board for Certified Counselors:
nbcc.org

Chi Sigma Iota:
csi-net.org

MyCounselingLab®

Start with Topic 10—Helping Strategies.

SUMMARY

Career development interventions are the corner-stones of the counseling profession (Dorn, 1992). However, we know relatively little about the career counseling process. Many view career counseling from a perspective that is frozen in the past. Rounds and Tinsley (1984) suggest that conceptualizing career counseling as psychotherapy "would foster advances in the understanding of vocational behavior change and processes" (p. 139). Such notions pertaining to career counseling reflect the widely recognized belief that career issues are contextual and that the context of the 21st century is not the same as the context of the early 20th century. Savickas (1993) encourages career counselors to respond to the societal changes occurring in the new millennium by stating that "counselors must innovate their career interventions to fit the new *zeitgeist*" (p. 205).

It should also be evident that the career counseling interventions used by professional counselors and psychologists must be guided by an understanding of how the current *zeitgeist* shapes the career tasks presented to students and workers. To help clients address career tasks in contemporary society, career practitioners should provide counseling-based career assistance and support to their students and clients. By expanding their career interventions in these ways, career counselors provide assistance that is sensitive to the career concerns students and clients experience in the 21st century.

CASE STUDY

Hyung Kim is a 40-year-old, Asian American male who appears for his first session presenting as clean and neatly dressed in casual business wear. He is paraplegic, resulting from an automobile accident when he was age 27. He lives in a large city in California. He has been a househusband for approximately the past 13 years, but he has had a number of part-time jobs, primarily as a travel agent. He earned an associate' degree in business management 10 years ago.

Hyung Kim declared that he wanted help in deciding how to obtain work in which he can use the skills he learned in his business management degree program. He expressed very strongly that he does not want to be working as a travel agent for the rest of his life. He also expressed interest in obtaining additional education in the same area that he has begun in business management. He was fairly happy being a househusband but now feels a need to find employment, expand his work experience, and have more intellectual interaction in his life and work.

Hyung Kim has not expressed any unhappiness concerning his home life other than his desire for more intellectual stimulation in a job. He stated that his wife and family were supportive of his interests in pursuing a career at this time. Hyung Kim seemed happy with himself for achieving his associate' degree, yet he felt it was just "not enough."

Hyung Kim seems self-motivated to obtain information, support, and resources about what he wants to accomplish. He is not very knowledgeable about the range of opportunities and occupations that are available to him. He expressed his desire to expand his experiences and develop his skills. Hyung Kim stated that he liked a lot of variety in his work environment, and he disliked jobs that required him to do routine, monotonous tasks.

Which theories would guide you in your work with Hyung Kim? How do you conceptualize his career situation? In what ways might his disability impact his career development process? In what ways might his cultural background influence his career development at this point in his life? What career interventions are you likely to use in your work with him?

STUDENT ACTIVITIES

1. If you have never been a career counseling client, try to find someone who has (perhaps your course instructor can facilitate this). Ask if he or she would be willing to talk with you about what was helpful to him or her in this experience and what was not so helpful. If you have been a career counseling client, make a list of what was helpful to you in career counseling and what was not. Reflect on the ways in which what was helpful and what was not have implications for career counseling practice.

2. Consider what you think is helpful about the "test 'em and tell 'em" approach to career counseling. Make a list of the ways in which you think this approach can be helpful to clients. Now, consider and make a list of the limitations of this approach.

3. Consider what you think is helpful about the more expansive view of career counseling described in this chapter. Make a list of the ways in which you think this approach can be helpful to clients. Now, consider and make a list of the limitations of this approach.

4. What are the advantages of conducting career counseling groups? What are the disadvantages? Which career development concerns do you think might be most appropriate for a group career counseling experience? What career development concerns do you think might be inappropriate for a group career counseling experience?

5. How could you evaluate the effectiveness of career counseling?

DESIGNING, IMPLEMENTING, AND EVALUATING CAREER DEVELOPMENT PROGRAMS AND SERVICES

It is evident that career counseling embraces career/life-planning concerns. What is not as obvious is that providing career services demands structures that encompass business principles.

Those principles address such issues as strategic planning, program design, financial and marketing concerns, evaluation and review processes. Being exposed to the development of successful programs that deliver effective services strengthens the foundation of all we learn in our graduate programs.

Martha Russell, M.S. NCC
Russell Career Services

It has been reported that the majority of Americans who purchase a new car now consult one of several services that evaluate the quality of different cars being offered. The popularity of these services is attributable to the often stated view of car purchasers that a new car purchase is too important a decision to base on the unevaluated claims of the manufacturers.

If the choice of a new car is important enough for people to want a source that provides reliable evaluations of the cars offered, it only seems reasonable that career planning services that deal with potentially life-enhancing or life-damaging career advice and information should also be the object of responsible evaluation.

Careful reading of this chapter will enable you to design and plan your own evaluations. In addition, you will be able to assess if the evaluations undertaken by other services are adequate, a handy thing to know if you wish to refer people to quality programs and services. Specifically, you should be able to determine if the evaluation is formative (useful for improving an ongoing program) or summative (judging the overall worth of the program) or some of both. A useful skill to have, wouldn't you say?

Garry R. Walz, Ph.D., NCC
Counseling Outfitters, CEO
University of Michigan, Professor Emeritus (Past President of the American Counseling
Association and the National Career Development Association)

MyCounselingLab®

Visit the MyCounselingLab® site for *Career Development Interventions*, Fifth Edition, to enhance your understanding of chapter concepts. You will have the opportunity to practice applying what you learned in the chapter by completing the video- and case-based exercises in the MyLab. Taking the Licensure Quizzes will help you prepare for your certification exam.

P revious chapters, especially Chapters 4 through 8, have provided a great deal of information about the content of career planning services. This chapter focuses on the process of designing these programs and then delivering them to the students or clients for whom they are developed. The step-by-step process of design, development, delivery, and evaluation is described, and six sample programs are presented as examples.

There are important reasons for engaging in program design. The first is that it is impossible for counselors in any setting other than private practice to provide all of the assistance needed by the students or clients they serve on a one-to-one basis. Schools typically have counselor-student ratios ranging from 1:300 to 1:1,000, and among the mix of services provided by school counselors, attention to career concerns is low. Thus, without having a systematic program of career planning services that can be offered to groups of students, only a very small percentage of students would receive assistance.

Even if these services could be provided on a one-to-one basis, this would be a cost-ineffective way to provide them to all. The goal of career guidance services should be to provide the maximum benefit to students and clients at the lowest per-person cost. Clearly, given the workload and time restraints of counselors in schools and other settings, the goal should be to save one-on-one time for persons who need such specialized service while providing service to most students through a variety of methods, including classroom instruction, group guidance, group counseling, and Web-based career planning systems and sites.

A second rationale for careful program planning is to require that career services be carefully thought out before their delivery. Such thought, following a process detailed later in this chapter, results in much higher program quality. It also provides the basis for determining program content, methods of delivery, evaluation, and a clear description of the program for administrators, parents, and recipients of the program.

Counselors may play a variety of roles related to the design and implementation of career development programs and services in their work settings. These roles may include advocacy, coordination, participation, design, management, and evaluation. Let's look at each of those roles separately.

In the role of advocacy, counselors use their skills and influence to work with the various stakeholders, which may include faculty, administrators and managers, and, in some settings, parents, to achieve improved career planning services. This role may include serving on advisory boards or committees, making presentations, or exerting influence in a variety of other ways.

In the role of coordination, counselors collaborate with internal staff (such as other counselors, teachers, and managers) and external entities (such as employers, advisory board members, agencies, community organizations, and parents) to deliver parts of the program of services. They may work with teachers to develop a curriculum that includes career planning concepts, with managers to develop workshops, with community organizations to serve as mentors for students, with parents to raise money for some parts of the program, or with employers to offer job-shadowing experiences or internships.

In the role of participation, counselors personally deliver all or part of the program of service. They may do this through a combination of group work, one-to-one counseling, instruction, assessment, and support for the use of Web-based systems and sites.

Counselors may be the only people in schools or other organizations who are trained in career development theory and practice. Thus they are likely to be the people who are called on as designers, developers, and managers of services for students or clients. They may also be called on to provide evidence of the effectiveness of these services and to be instrumental in planning and carrying out their evaluation. For example, a counselor may be employed by a middle school, high school, or university that wishes to provide career development services for all of its students. Or, a counselor may work in a corporation as a personnel worker and be called on to develop services that meet immediate needs caused by corporate restructuring, downsizing, or other kinds of changes. A company undergoing such changes would likely ask a counselor to develop ways to help employees make these upsetting transitions with less stress and with a better image of the company.

If the school, university, or company has hundreds or thousands of students or employees who need to benefit from career planning services, it is impossible to meet this need by dealing with everyone on a face-to-face, interview basis. It is essential to design a program and then to deliver it in ways that will reach the largest number of people and will do so cost effectively. A process for accomplishing this is presented here in 10 steps, each explained in detail.

STEPS FOR DESIGNING AND IMPLEMENTING A CAREER DEVELOPMENT PROGRAM

Step 1: Define the Target Population and Its Characteristics

The purpose of this step of the program design process is to get a clear picture of the people whom the program will serve. It is necessary to describe the population with some clarity, as indicated in the following illustrations. This description might contain demographic data such as racial-ethnic background, mean and range of scores on achievement or aptitude tests, gender, age range, and types of diversity.

Elementary School

Morris Elementary School serves 750 students from kindergarten through fifth grade in a suburb of a large city in the Midwest. Most families in the community have an income exceeding $150,000 per year due to the fact that most fill professional positions and, in some families, both parents work. Eighty-seven percent of the students are Caucasian, and the remainder are of Asian descent. Parents' expectations are high that students will receive the quality of education that will allow them to enter prestigious colleges and universities. There is high parent involvement in the parent-teacher organization, and taxpayers are willing to pay for services they believe to be advantageous to their children.

High School

Midtown High School has 673 students who are fairly evenly divided over the four years (freshman, sophomore, junior, senior). They come from families in a small city and areas as far as 10 miles from the city. The student body is 61% male and 39% female; 70% are Caucasian, 14% African American, and 16% Hispanic. Most students come from middle-income families in which wage earners work in the area's tourist industry, or are retail merchants, or work as assembly workers in the local factories. In the past, no attention has been given to teaching students about planning for future jobs.

College/University

Upstate University, located in a rural area of the state, has approximately 14,000 full-time undergraduate students, 900 full-time graduate students, 1,700 part-time undergraduate students, and 2,500 part-time graduate students. It draws students from all over the state as well as 12% from other states and 5% from other countries. The mean age of undergraduate students is 19.4 years, and graduate students 29.4 years. Of the undergraduate students, 20% continue on to graduate school; the rest seek jobs immediately after graduation, most of them within the state. Job placement for those who complete the university's undergraduate and graduate programs has traditionally been very high, approaching 95% within three months after completion. Within the past three years, however, this figure has declined to approximately 90%, likely because major corporations in the state are reducing the number of new employees in order to be able to retain as many of their current employees as possible. In the past, no services have been provided to students to help them to seek employment or plan their careers.

Corporation

The Royal Corporation, located about 40 miles south of a large urban area, has almost 12,000 employees, ranging in age from 18 to 65. The corporation makes audio and video boards for computers. It offers positions in management, sales, advertising, and light factory-assembly work, in which manual dexterity and accuracy are critical to the quality of its products. The turnover rate of employees is 26% each year. In this company, no assistance has ever been provided with topics such as how to make transitions, how to conduct a successful job search, or how to analyze one's skills so that they can be transferred to another position.

Job Service Office

This office serves the northeast area of the city. Typical clients include adults in the age range of 35 to 65 who have been laid off or are displaced homemakers, veterans, ex-offenders from the local state prison, or persons receiving public aid. Most clients have very low skill levels in reading, mathematics, and language use and have no or little past work experience. Further, they have a mean educational level of sixth grade and have not acquired marketable job skills.

**

There are at least two ways to gather the information that will provide a description of a target population in some detail. One way that may yield sufficient details is to review the records that already exist in a school, agency, or company. The second way is to develop a questionnaire to administer to all potential students or clients—or at least to a group that has been selected as a random sample. A random sample is a small group taken from the whole group by using a computer program or by drawing specific numbers (which may be student- or employee-identification numbers) from a book of random numbers. Before using this approach, one should consult someone who knows research and sampling techniques or should read a chapter on this topic in a relevant book.

It is important to understand the nature of a target population before beginning to design a program of services. This information provides insight about the topics, reading level, methods, tools, time available, and level of sophistication for the material to be presented in the career planning program.

Step 2: Determine the Needs of the Target Population

Obviously, it is impossible for counselors to develop a program of services to meet student, client, or employee needs if they do not know in considerable detail what those needs are. If the target population consists of high school students, it is possible to infer from their age and stage in career planning that they have certain needs, such as deciding whether to attend a vocational-technical school, attend a university, or go directly to work. It is also safe to assume that they need assistance in selecting the occupation(s) they plan to enter. But, there may be other needs that cannot be identified by age or life stage alone—such as a need to have more information about the community colleges in the area—if needs are not assessed in a more formal way.

If the target population is in a college or university, it can be assumed, because of the age of these students and their stage in career planning, that they need to (a) understand the relationship between majors and specific occupations, (b) select one or more occupations, and (c) learn how to effectively find job openings and get a job. It cannot be known, however, without a needs assessment, if a large percentage of the students do not know how changes in the job market may affect their career planning significantly.

If the target population consists of employees in a corporation, then less is known from theory about their needs. One may surmise that those who will be laid off need to learn how to write a résumé and engage in job interviews, but program designers might not assume that a significant percentage would like to leave the corporation voluntarily because of job dissatisfaction without administering a questionnaire or working with focus groups.

There are at least four ways to identify the needs of any group. First, there may be some information already available from past questionnaires that can be used to identify some needs. Second, a short questionnaire can be made and administered in written form to everyone in the target group, potentially via the organization's intranet or in several small focus groups. A focus group is a group of 10 to 15 people who are selected for a specific purpose (in this case, to help identify needs) and are believed to be representative of the total population. Use of a focus group allows not only the completion of a questionnaire but also the opportunity to discuss the answers given by people in the group, thus gaining more in-depth information. Third, consultants may be hired to make recommendations based on their knowledge of normal developmental needs or of the needs of others in similar settings.

Finally, there are often needs in schools (such as a high percentage of dropouts) or corporations (such as unmotivated employees) that are related to poor or inadequate career planning. Thus in some settings it would be wise and helpful to ask administrators and managers to identify problems that need solutions. Then, services can be devised that address those particular problems. If solutions are found, it is likely that there will be support from management for the delivery of the career planning service. Following are examples of the kinds of needs that might be identified for different settings.

Elementary School

According to Super's (1980) theory, these are the years for developing self-concept, internal locus of control, decision-making skill, time perspective, and awareness of need to plan ahead.

Middle School

According to theory, these are the years for broad-based exploration of occupations and gaining awareness of the work world through becoming acquainted with clusters of occupations. It is also the time to motivate awareness on the part of the students that career choices must be made in the future and that there is a relationship between current schoolwork and future plans.

High School

Almost no students realize that there have been many changes in the past few years that will make their approach to career planning quite different from that of their parents. Students have no knowledge of how occupations are organized or how their work tasks vary. Few students can describe their interests or their best abilities, and those who can do not know how these may relate to their future work. Many students do not understand that different jobs require different amounts of education, and they cannot define the different paths of education (i.e., vocational-technical school, two-year college, university, apprenticeship, military service, etc.) that lead to work.

College/University

As with the high school students, few realize that there have been many changes in the past few years that should make their approach to career planning different from that of their parents. Further, they do not realize that they are likely to change occupations several times during their lifetime and that this will become the accepted pattern. Students on the whole do not understand how the world-of-work is organized, nor how specific subject-matter specialties relate to this organization and to jobs that they will be seeking. Many cannot state their personal interests, their best skills or abilities, nor the values that they would hope to attain through work. Many have had no instruction about how to decide what kinds of jobs they might like, how to find openings in these jobs, how to have successful job interviews, how to make effective use of social networking, or how to evaluate one job over another in accordance with personal preferences.

Corporation

Some workers still believe that the corporation should be responsible for their career planning or progression. Many have no knowledge about how to plan for a career change, leaving one company and going to another or to self-employment. Still others cannot identify their transferable skills or identify other jobs that will make use of those skills. Those who have been in one job for many years do not know how to write a résumé that can be transmitted electronically, to use face-to-face and social networking to identify job openings, or to feel comfortable in either a face-to-face or virtual job interview.

Step 3: Write Measurable Objectives to Meet Needs

A measurable objective is the clear statement of a goal, including how to determine whether or not the goal has been reached. There are at least two reasons for writing objectives for the career planning services. First, having to follow the discipline of writing objectives will require a counselor to think carefully about what he or she is trying to achieve and how to know if it has been achieved. Second, the objectives will become the basis for the content and evaluation of the services. It is almost universally true that management will not support a program, either psychologically or financially, that is not explained adequately and does not show evidence of being effective. So, in order to get and retain support for career planning services, it is necessary to define them clearly (via the objectives) and also to measure the outcomes of providing them (via evaluation).

The identified needs of the target population become the basis for writing measurable objectives. Many, if not most, sites will not have the resources to do a needs analysis. In that case, it will be prudent to base the local program on well-researched and tediously developed national models, such as those provided in such documents as the *National Career Development Guidelines*, funded by the U.S. Department of Education (2003), Office of Vocational and Adult

Education, and developed in collaboration with several professional organizations, and the more recent American School Counselor Association (2004) model. Most states and smaller entities have used one of these two sets of standards as the foundation for a customized local set of objectives.

Measurable objectives should always begin with the statement, "At the end of this (workshop, program of services, school year, course), students (employees, clients) will be able to. . . ." The statement of the objective, described in some way that makes it possible to measure its accomplishment, should follow this general statement. Some sample measurable objectives are listed next.

Elementary School

By the end of grade 5, students will be able to:

1. Describe themselves in terms of the areas of their strengths.
2. List the steps in making a good decision about something important.
3. State at least one goal they want to accomplish in the next year and at least two steps that will help them reach the goal.

High School

By the end of the second year of high school, students will be able to:

1. Describe changes in the U.S. workplace that will affect their own career planning.
2. State at least two areas of interest, using either Holland (1997) clusters or career areas on the World-of-Work Map (ACT, 2000) for future work.
3. Describe the courses or curricula available in their high schools to help prepare them for these areas of work.
4. Describe different paths of education or training that they might pursue after high school related to these areas of work.

By the end of the third year of high school, students will be able to:

1. State one or more tentative occupational choices.
2. List specific schools or ways in which they can get the postsecondary training needed for these occupations.
3. Complete an action plan that lists the steps needed to move from these choices through the education needed to enter the occupation.
4. Demonstrate job-seeking skills, such as completing a job application and engaging effectively in mock job interviews (for those not planning to seek further education).

College/University

By the end of the first year, students will be able to:

1. State at least two areas of their highest interest, using either Holland (1997) clusters or job families on the World-of-Work Map (ACT, 2000).
2. Describe in detail at least three occupations in each of these two areas, based on research through use of Web sites, Web-based career planning systems, and/or informational interviews.
3. Tentatively select an occupation or group of occupations.
4. Select a major that is related to the occupational choices.

By the end of the third year, students will be able to:

1. List at least three companies in the geographic area where they offer positions like those desired.
2. Describe each of these companies in terms of its products, number of employees, recent history related to reducing its workforce and/or restructuring, and potential for employees' further growth or training,
3. Write a high-quality résumé in at least two formats.
4. Exhibit skill, through participation in mock interviews, in the job-interviewing process.
5. State five personal criteria for identifying jobs or for selecting one job offer over another.

Corporation

At the end of this series of workshops, employees will be able to:

1. State how recent changes in the U.S. workplace are affecting their personal careers.
2. Describe the career planning process that they may need to use either because they choose to make career changes or because the company needs to make adjustments.
3. List their top 10 transferable skills should they need to make a career change.
4. Write a high-quality résumé that describes their education, work skills, and employment history.
5. State the type and length of training that would expand or update some of their job skills, making them more productive for the company or more marketable should they decide to leave the company.

Agency Serving Low-Income Adults

At the end of these three sessions, participants will be able to:

1. Identify skills learned in home management and state how to describe them in a résumé.
2. Identify jobs in which these identified skills can be used.
3. Write an attractive résumé that capitalizes on these skills.

As indicated, these objectives become the basis for the content of career planning services as well as the methods of evaluating them.

Step 4: Determine How to Deliver the Career Planning Services

In this step, the goal is to provide as rich an array of services to as many people as possible in the most cost-effective way. Providing service via one-to-one interviews is the most expensive and the most time-consuming way to deliver service. For this reason, it is desirable to do as much as possible through other methods that are effective but demand less time. Methods other than one-to-one interviewing include the following (of course, any of these could be combined with one-to-one interviewing):

- Offering special courses or units within existing courses about career planning topics (middle school, high school, and perhaps college/university) in face-to-face and/or Web-based delivery

- Offering workshops that serve 8 to 15 people (university and corporation)
- Creating a virtual career center that organizes high-quality Web sites that provide career planning content
- Assigning use of one of the comprehensive Web-based career planning systems listed in Chapter 7
- Providing self-help materials that may include assessment inventories and a companion workbook

The methods chosen to provide the career planning services will relate to available time, staff, budget, and resources (such as assessment inventories or self-help books) that fit the population's needs and objectives; the amount of time people have to spend on career planning needs at the school or worksite; and available technical resources (for use of Web-based career planning systems or Web sites).

Elementary School

In many schools the career guidance curriculum would be infused in the regular subject-matter curriculum. In elementary schools that have counselors, the guidance curriculum would be taught by counselors, using special advisory periods or segments of classroom instruction time.

Middle School and High School

Much of the content could be provided in the classroom by training teachers to include some of the topics in their curriculum or through a well-planned and staffed career center. Alternatively, a career planning course may be offered to students during designated class periods or through homeroom or advisement periods. This curriculum may be developed locally, or the site might use a curricular package such as *Direct Your Future* (Harris-Bowlsbey, 2010b). Individual interviews with counselors could be offered to students who need individualized help.

College/University

The content could be provided through a series of workshops, offered by a career counselor or certified career development facilitator, as part of the services of a well-equipped physical career center, through a virtual career center (i.e., a Web site), and/or through individual interviews with students who need them. Another viable method is offering a for-credit, one-semester career planning course. This course may be developed at the local level or may utilize an already developed course such as Take Hold of Your Future (Harris-Bowlsbey, 2010a).

Corporation

The content could be provided through a series of workshops provided by a career counselor or a certified career development facilitator, through workshops and individual interviews provided by a trained manager, or via the corporation's intranet or Web site. Many corporations have a career management center that provides a wealth of printed information, access to Web sites, and one-to-one counseling provided by a certified, professional counselor.

Community Agencies

The content may be provided through a series of workshops or through one-to-one interviews. Web sites may also be used for assessment, career information, and job searching. Individual counseling may also be available.

Step 5: Determine the Content of the Program

The content of the program is determined by its objectives, so it is necessary to look at each objective and imagine different ways it could be addressed. Here is one example for each of the populations.

Elementary

Objective: State at least one goal students want to accomplish in the next year and at least two steps that will help them reach the goal.

Methods of meeting objective: After a short lesson of what goals are and that they can be expressed as long-range goals and short-range goals, students are asked to think about something that they want to accomplish in any area of their life. They are then asked to write a goal that expresses what they want to accomplish and then divide it into mini-steps with some dates attached to each. The counselor or teacher reviews this written activity and makes suggestions for improvement, if necessary.

High School

Objective: Describe changes in the U.S. workplace that affect personal career planning.

Methods of meeting objective: Ask representatives from companies or government organizations to describe these changes in a scheduled meeting; ask students to read a book, use Web sites, or read several articles on this topic. Hold a group discussion after use of any of these methods of providing the basic information.

College/University

Objective: State at least two areas of students' highest interest, using either career areas on the World-of-Work Map or Holland clusters.

Methods of meeting objective: Administer one or a combination of instruments that measure interests and skills by Holland typology. Provide score reports to students, and interpret the results for them.

Corporation

Objective: Describe the career planning process employees may need to use either because they choose to make career changes or because the company must make adjustments.

Methods of meeting objective: Provide a workshop in which the career planning process is described; prepare a brochure for all employees; train managers in this process, and ask them, in turn, to provide this information and instruction in meetings that they have with employees; place this information on the corporate intranet or Web site.

Step 6: Determine the Cost of the Program

It is rare indeed that any project will be approved without knowledge of its cost. To calculate cost accurately, it is necessary that the objectives be defined, the method(s) of meeting each objective be detailed, and the content proposed for each objective be solidified. At that point, it should be possible to calculate a budget that includes all of the following components:

- Staff time for designing, developing, and evaluating the products and services
- Staff time needed either to deliver or to train others to deliver the program

- A Web-based career planning system that may be needed
- Equipment and materials needed, such as computers, reference books, or copies of assessment inventories
- Printing costs, if any
- Technical costs (e.g., if a virtual career center is being developed)
- Cost for using facilities, if any
- Cost of refreshments for participants, if any

A manager would want to know how much of the total cost requires spending additional money and how much represents the use of staff, equipment, and materials that already exist. In some settings, it may also be necessary to project expected gains from having delivered the program of services. For example, if it is offered in a university setting and the expectation is that the services will reduce the loss of enrolled students, the strategy of comparing the cost of delivering the service to one current student with that of recruiting and orienting one new student may be effective. If it is a corporate setting, the goal of a program of services is to improve the satisfaction of employees, resulting in higher productivity; cost may be justified by comparing the cost of delivering the service to one employee to the value of the increased productivity of that employee.

Because managers are always very busy, the budget should be presented in a very succinct way that summarizes the services, the benefits that are expected from the services, and the total or per client cost of delivering them.

Step 7: Begin to Promote and Explain Your Services

In any environment, there are always some who are willing to support career planning services and others who are ready to criticize them. It is important to build an understanding and supportive environment for the introduction of any new program. There are several ways to accomplish this:

- Early in the design process, invite or appoint a committee of people to help design the program or, at least, to provide feedback about preliminary plans. It is important to choose people who are respected by others and who are influential. When others see that the proposed program is being supported by these people, they will be more likely to do so as well.
- As soon as preliminary ideas are formed, begin to explain them to managers and ask for their input, either in individual meetings or through the circulation of a document to which they are invited to add their comments.
- Start with a small pilot test. Try to get some respected and visible students or employees to participate in the pilot test. Not only will a pilot test help to expand and refine ideas and procedures, but it will also begin to provide publicity by word of mouth. Capitalize on that by having short articles in the school or corporate newsletter in which someone talks about the new program and how it has benefited him or her.
- If the school or company is facing challenges or problems that might be alleviated by some part of the proposed career planning program, begin with that part. Ideally, the career planning assistance will help solve those problems and will thus be viewed positively when it is time for expansion.

Tips from the Field

The quality of the program of services, when it is delivered, will correspond directly to the time and energy put into the first seven steps of planning.

Step 8: Start Promoting and Delivering the Full-Blown Program of Services

It is important to notice that seven time-consuming planning steps have occurred before starting to deliver the services that have been designed and planned. Although this seems tedious, the time and energy spent in the long planning cycle will result in a higher quality end product.

No matter how good a product or service is, it will not meet its objectives if people do not avail themselves of it. It is very important, at the same time the content is being designed, to plan how the program will be promoted. Therefore, plans for promotion should be ready for implementation prior to the time the service itself is implemented.

Just as the first impression in a job interview is extremely critical, so is the impression that is created the first time new services are offered. Make sure that everything is ready for launching the program before beginning and that its first round of delivery is of very high quality, thereby ensuring that the program will gain an image of quality and usefulness from the outset.

Step 9: Evaluate the Program

Because evaluation is a time-consuming and expensive process, let us consider four reasons why evaluation is important. The predominant reason is to determine whether the program is helping people to achieve the objectives for which it was defined. Those objectives were written in order to meet the needs identified in the target population. If the program does not help people to achieve those objectives, it is not meeting needs.

Second, it is necessary to evaluate the services so that they can be improved. No matter how well the design and development stages have been accomplished, implementation of a new program will always identify additional needs, different possible approaches, and good ideas for enhancement. Program development and delivery comprise a cyclical process; new ideas should be included in the program at each subsequent delivery.

Third, evaluation provides ongoing information to supervisors and other stakeholders about the results of the program, meeting the requirement of accountability. Administrators typically want to know how many people are availing themselves of the program and about the effectiveness of the program in meeting identified needs.

Fourth, evaluation is sometimes done in order to determine whether the outcomes of delivering services are worth the money and other resources being invested. The focus of such evaluation is to make a decision to retain, expand, or discontinue services.

Evaluation is typically categorized as being *formative*, *summative*, or both. According to the Joint Committee on Standards for Educational Evaluation (2011), formative evaluation is done for the purpose of improving an ongoing program, whereas summative evaluation has the goal of drawing conclusions about the overall worth of a program in order to determine whether to retain it. Thus, the first three reasons just given for evaluation fall into the category of formative, whereas the fourth reason fits the category of summative. Evaluation can, of course, be designed to meet all four purposes.

Planning Evaluation

In planning evaluation it is necessary to follow several standard steps that will provide the structure for the implementation of the evaluation plan. The first step is to determine whether the evaluation is formative, summative, or both. The kinds of data collected depend on the answer to this question. For example, in formative evaluation, there will be questions about how the content of the program can be improved and about how the participants valued it. For summative evaluation, it is likely that there will be measurement of outcomes and cost, begging the question of whether or not the outcomes were worth the expenditures to accomplish them. This planning step may also include decision making about who will receive the data.

A second step is to determine what specific knowledge, skills, attitudes, or behaviors are to be evaluated. These may include global constructs, such as change in career maturity, decision-making skill, or self-concept; skills, such as job interviewing; or knowledge, such as how to research occupations. Longer-term behaviors, such as consistently getting to work on time or maintaining a job for a long period of time, may be measured. What is measured should relate directly to the statement of objectives for the program.

A third step is to determine what the source(s) of the evaluation data will be. In formative evaluation it is likely that the data will be sought from clients, program participants, or trained observers. In summative evaluation the data may be collected from records, budgets, and follow-up studies. For example, if a correctional system is doing a summative evaluation of a new program of vocational training and counseling services to offenders, the offenders themselves may never evaluate the program. Rather, data collection will focus on calculating the per offender cost of providing the service and comparing it to the change in job placement rate and, in turn, the effect on recidivism.

A fourth step is to determine how the data will be collected. There is a wide range of formal and informal methods from which to choose. Formal methods include the administration of standardized instruments, structured observation, and follow-up studies. Informal methods include group feedback, questionnaires, and interviews. This planning step will include review and selection of instruments (if these are to be used), development of questionnaires or observer checklists, and/or the design of follow-up studies. This step should also include decisions about who will administer these data-collection instruments and how the data will be collected, tallied or entered, and prepared for analysis.

Related to this step is the question of when the data will be collected. For formative evaluation, administrating a questionnaire or holding exit interviews may be sufficient to provide the feedback needed for program improvement. A higher level of evaluation may involve assessing—through instruments, observation, or changed behaviors—whether a specific knowledge or skill has been acquired. Such evaluation is likely to be done immediately after delivery of the program or treatment. If the focus of evaluation is to determine how skills, attitudes, or knowledge has changed as a result of the program, data may be collected both before and after the treatment.

A fifth step is to determine how the data will be analyzed. This step includes decisions about whether data will simply be tallied, providing the number of respondents and a breakdown of their responses, or whether specific statistical tests will be applied to it. Such tests would likely be selected to compare differences between experimental and control group results, or pretreatment and posttreatment results, and to determine their significance.

Stakeholders

Depending on the evaluation purpose, data may be sought from sources in addition to the persons who received the services. For example, when evaluating services provided to elementary students, a counselor would likely seek input from parents and school administrators as well as from the students themselves. At the middle school level, evaluation might be sought from students, parents, teachers, and administrators. At the high school level, these same audiences could be supplemented by colleges and employers who receive graduates. At the college level, evaluative input might be sought from students, administrators, and employers. At the community agency level, clients, employers, and organizations that fund the services could evaluate services.

Before designing evaluation, then, it is necessary to consider who the stakeholders are—that is, who is receiving the services and who cares about them, who profits from them, who needs to be informed, and who provides the approval and funding for their continuation. Ideally, representatives of all of these stakeholders would serve on a committee that drafts the evaluation plan.

Types of Data Collected

The term *evaluation* implies the collection of data. These data may either be *quantitative* or *qualitative*. Quantitative data reports numbers and these numbers would answer questions, such as the following, that are often posed by administrators:

- How many elementary school children received help with career awareness through the classroom units taught by the counselor?
- How many sixth-graders participated in the career fair?
- Of the seventh-graders who participated in the fair, what percentage made a tentative selection of a career cluster?
- How many eighth-graders brought their parents in for an interview to develop a four-year plan related to a selected career cluster?
- How many tenth-graders were served by the special series of homeroom programs about career planning?
- What percentage of seniors who went to full-time employment after graduation entered an occupation listed in their career portfolios or a highly related one?
- What percentage of college-bound seniors entered one of the majors selected in their career plans? What percentage of these students was still pursuing that major in the sophomore year?
- How many students at each high school grade level were interviewed by counselors specifically for career planning?
- What percentage of students who attended the job-seeking workshops found a job that was desirable to them within 60 days of graduation?
- How much does it cost each time a counselor spends an hour with a student?
- How many clients have been served this calendar year in the one-stop center?
- What is the breakdown of clients by problem presented?
- Of those seeking jobs, what percentage found a job within 60 days after receiving service?

Qualitative data provide information about the perceived value of the services and the extent to which predefined program outcomes were achieved. The indicators to measure quality may be different for different stakeholders. Let us imagine that a full-blown career guidance program was approved and funded for a large, urban high school. Different stakeholders may be interested in different outcomes of the intervention. Their different hoped-for outcomes might be as follows:

- Students—that they can decide on a major (those going on to postsecondary education) and an occupation
- Counselor delivering the program—that the students will experience growth in career maturity, including decision making
- Principal—that the school dropout rate will be reduced because students become aware of the relationship between school and work
- Parents—that students will be directed to occupations and postsecondary education that are "good" for them so that money will not be wasted on further education
- Employers—that students will learn soft skills that will contribute to their job retention
- Teachers—that the program is worth the class time that they and the students give up

This list illustrates why individuals representing a range of stakeholders need to be involved in evaluation design.

Benchmarks for Evaluation

The word *evaluation* implies that outcomes will be compared with a desired standard. Thus, evaluation is impossible unless a standard has been set for desirable outcomes. Because there are different types of career planning services, each with different expected outcomes and stakeholders, the standard used for evaluation may be different for each.

One primary mode of delivering career services is through one-on-one, face-to-face interviewing. It is customary in such a relationship for clients, assisted by counselors, to set goals for the relationship. Examples of such goals are as follows:

- To identify and discard the irrational beliefs the client holds that are preventing him or her from being able to formulate career goals and move ahead with them
- To develop a clearer and more positive self-concept
- To identify skills learned from past work experience and to determine how to transfer them to at least three occupations that are different from the ones already pursued
- To learn how to market oneself in a job interview

In the case of individual counseling, then, the standard for evaluation for the counselor and the client is whether or *to what extent the relationship results in accomplishment of the client's goal(s)*. It is likely that such accomplishment can be measured only by two people—the client and the counselor. Qualitative evaluation of accomplishment with this mode of service delivery may be as simple as these three steps:

- Early in the counseling relationship, specific goals are set by the client and the counselor, and these are placed in writing.
- At the end of the counseling relationship, the client and the counselor separately rate, on a scale of 1 to 5, the degree to which each goal has been accomplished.
- These ratings are shared and discussed.

An administrator in this setting is likely to want to know the number of individual clients served in a year by counselors, the mean number of sessions per client, and the hourly cost of counseling service. Data to answer these questions may be collected by requiring that counselors keep log sheets on paper or electronically or by setting up a system by which a clerical support person logs these data for everyone in the counseling or career planning center.

In group counseling, group guidance, or a career planning class, the goals are typically set for the participants by the facilitator or instructor. As described previously in this chapter, these goals are stated in the form of *measurable objectives* that begin with the phrase "At the end of this series of _____, participants will be able to _____," a second kind of benchmark for program evaluation. Accomplishment of these types of objectives can typically be measured by a questionnaire developed by the counselor or program administrator. Such a questionnaire could provide both quantitative and qualitative data. The following illustrate statements that include both qualitative and quantitative data:

After completion of the program,

- 87% of elementary students who participated in it were able to match appropriate work tasks with the four dimensions of the World-of-Work Map—People, Data, Things, and Ideas.
- 92% of middle school students were able to sort a list of 30 occupations into the correct Holland clusters.
- 96% of high school students were able to list two or three career areas by name in which they have interest, including the titles of specific occupations in those families.

Administrators may value additional data, including the following:

- The number of students, clients, or employees served by the program (quantitative)
- The per person cost of providing the service (quantitative)
- Participant satisfaction with the program measured by a questionnaire in which participants are asked to rate the quality or value of the program (qualitative)
- Feedback from parents about the program (qualitative)

Parent evaluation could be assessed by a questionnaire sent to homes, including questions similar to the following:

- Did your child talk about the career exploration program at home? If so, what kinds of things did he or she say?
- Did this program trigger any conversations at home about your child's career planning? If so, what were the topics of those conversations?
- To what extent, if any, do you think that this program helped your son or daughter to determine what work he or she either does or does not want to do?

A third benchmark for evaluation of individuals' progress related to career planning is *national* or *local guidelines* that have been adopted. The latest version of the National Career Development Guidelines, developed by the U.S. Department of Education (2003), address desired competencies and behaviors in three domains, eleven goals, and multiple indicators. These have been adopted by many school districts across the United States. The following are a few sample behavioral indicators from the high school version of these guidelines, accompanied by an example of how the existence of the indicator might be assessed.

Indicator	One Way to Assess
Identify your interests, likes, and dislikes.	After appropriate interventions, ask students to list three occupational fields/clusters of their primary interest.
Identify your abilities, strengths, skills, and talents.	After completion of a skills bombardment activity, during which all members of a group are asked to tell each person what his or her primary strengths are, ask students to indicate what they have learned from the activity and how their view of self has been modified.
Identify your positive personal characteristics (e.g., honesty, dependability, responsibility, integrity, and loyalty).	Ask students to write a short essay about the positive personal characteristics that they believe they have, how they acquired these characteristics, and how they believe that they exhibit them.
Identify your work values/needs.	Using the results of a recent work values inventory, ask students to share the most important ones with others in a small group and indicate how they think they can attain these values in work.
Describe aspects of your self-concept.	Ask students to bring three pictures of themselves to class, each of which demonstrates some part of their self-concept. In a small group, have them show each other the pictures and describe what they say about themselves.

Developmental Tasks (Super, 1957)	Possible Methods of Evaluation
Crystallization: shortening a list of occupations to a small number that have the highest potential to implement the self-concept.	After having offered interventions that assist students to develop a list of preferred occupations, ask them to circle three to five that they are considering most seriously. Ask students to write or talk about why they have kept these on the list while discarding others.
Specification: one occupation is selected from the short list of occupations.	Ask students to indicate the occupation that they will plan to enter, what training they will need to complete in high school and thereafter, what the typical duties of this occupation are, what the future employment outlook is, what the beginning salary range will be, which other occupations are closely related (using the same or a similar set of skills), and how they will learn more about this occupation and test it out in reality before further commitment.
Implementation: engaging in the coursework that is desirable or required for the occupation.	Ask students to make a four-year plan, listing courses available at their high school that will best prepare them for the occupation. Also ask them to describe the post–high school training needed, where it is available, and how they plan to take advantage of it.

Local school districts or state educational systems often develop their own guidelines for career interventions, modeled after this national set of guidelines or the more recent American School Counselor Association (2004) model. When schools adopt or develop guidelines, these should become the basis for both program content and evaluation.

A fourth kind of standard for evaluation is *theory*. Think, for example, about the first three of Super's (1957) five developmental tasks. These could be used as the basis for both program content development and evaluation at the secondary level.

Methods of Evaluation

As indicated at the beginning of this chapter, the primary purposes of evaluation are to determine whether specified outcomes are being achieved, to improve services, to provide data to supervisors and other stakeholders, and to make decisions about continuation of services related to cost-effectiveness. Evaluation is possible only through collection and organization of data. The data collected must be directly relevant to answering the evaluation questions, and evaluation questions are possible only when clear objectives for services have been identified. Thus, the evaluation cycle is as follows:

- Determine the specific measurable objectives (desired outcomes) of the program or service.
- Determine the *indicators* or *behaviors* that will be telltale signs of having reached the stated objectives.
- Identify the best way(s) to observe or measure these indicators or behaviors.
- Collect data using these methods.
- Organize the data in ways that will answer the specific evaluative questions posed by different stakeholders.
- Deliver the data to these stakeholders.
- Use relevant data for the various purposes of evaluation: to determine whether the program achieved its objectives, to improve the services for future delivery, to serve public relations purposes, and/or to make decisions about program retention.

There are several common ways of collecting the data needed for evaluation. One is through a carefully planned *questionnaire* or *interview*. In either case the same standard questions would be asked, either in written form or in a face-to-face interview. Examples of such questionnaire items have been provided throughout this chapter. Following are general guidelines for writing items (which may either be questions or statements, such as "List the three best sources of information about job openings"):

- Make sure that the items relate directly to the indicators, behaviors, or outcomes you are trying to evaluate.
- Avoid questions that can be answered with *yes* or *no*.
- Make sure that the items are written clearly, without ambiguity.
- Make sure that the items are at an appropriate reading level for their audience.
- Make sure that the items cover all of the indicators or topics you need to cover in the evaluation.
- Modify the items as needed for different stakeholders.
- Make the questionnaire or interview as short and succinct as possible while still getting the core data that you need.

In most cases, questionnaires are administered to all persons who received a service (the subjects) immediately or within a relatively short time (one week to one month) after service completion. Sometimes, for the sake of documenting change, the same questionnaire is administered prior to receiving the service (called the *treatment*) and again after receiving the service.

This type of evaluation allows a comparison of data before and after, leading to evaluative statements such as "Before the career planning unit was taught to all sophomores, 85% of them indicated that they had no idea about their future vocational choice. After the completion of the unit, only 24% indicated that they had no idea."

A second method of evaluation is the *administration of more formal instruments* developed by test publishers, some of which are described in Chapter 5. Such instruments measure global constructs (career maturity, decision-making skill, career decidedness, career concerns, and career beliefs) rather than the accomplishment of specific objectives. If the goal of offering a specific service were to increase or modify one or more of these global constructs, use of such instruments could be helpful. These are listed and described in detail in *A Counselor's Guide to Career Assessments*, 6th edition (Wood & Hays, 2013), published by the National Career Development Association (NCDA) and updated periodically.

As with questionnaires, these instruments may be administered to the same group or individual, both before and after the career planning service has been provided, or only after. Typically, the before-after administration is used when the study is nonscientific—that is, when there is no *control group* (denied the service at the time of evaluation) considered equivalent to the *experimental group*. The use of randomly selected groups is typically required in *research studies*. However, in *evaluation studies* this design is not typically used because it is very difficult to achieve in day-to-day operational settings.

Another common method of collecting data is the *follow-up study*. In such a study, those who have participated in some form of treatment are contacted by phone, e-mail, regular mail, or in person at one or more intervals of time after completion of the program. The purpose of this contact, of course, is to determine whether specific predefined outcomes have been or are being experienced as a result of the treatment. As an example, suppose that an instructional unit was provided to high school seniors who are not planning to enter any kind of postsecondary education. The unit provides extensive instruction about job-seeking skills. A primary objective was stated as follows: "Upon completion of this unit and graduation from high school, at least 85% of students will get a job within a month after graduation." In this case, a counselor might conduct a follow-up study by either sending a questionnaire to graduates, sending an e-mail, or placing a phone call, any of which would be designed to find out if the graduate had found a job and begun work. Thus, it would be easy to determine whether the objective set for the instructional unit had been met.

Using the Results of Evaluation

The reason for which evaluation is done determines how the results will be used. Imagine that evaluative results—both qualitative and quantitative—have been collected for the delivery of a unit of career planning instruction to middle school students. Briefly stated, the results are as follows:

From *administrators* (based on receipt of a content outline of the program): This program looks exceptionally good, and its content is needed by all students. Be careful not to take too much class time for the program, however, especially from the core subjects.

From *parents* (based on a short questionnaire included with report cards for students who participated in the program):

- 99% indicated that their students need this instruction;
- 76% indicated that their child talked about the program at home;
- 32% indicated that their child formed a tentative career goal as a result of the instruction;

- 45% indicated that their child would use what was learned in the instructional unit to help with the development of a four-year plan; and
- 90% indicated that they thought the school should continue the program.

From the *students* (based on an end-of-unit questionnaire):

- 88% of students, when given a list of 30 occupational titles with short descriptions, could place each title in the correct Holland cluster;
- 95% of students selected one of the six Holland clusters as a "first-choice" cluster; and
- The same 95% of students drafted a mock four-year plan for selection of high school courses related to the cluster of their first choice.

When asked what they learned during the unit,

- 81% indicated that they learned how occupations can be organized;
- 92% indicated that they learned more about their own interests; and
- 73% indicated that they learned about the relationship between school subjects and work.

When asked what they liked best about the unit (listing the five top choices):

- 97% selected the field trips;
- 94% selected the use of a Web site that explains the six clusters and gives titles and descriptions of occupations;
- 85% selected the guest speakers;
- 76% selected the videos about the six clusters; and
- 74% selected the use of a Web-based system that provides titles and occupational descriptions by cluster.

When asked what they liked least about the instructional unit,

- 94% selected the requirement to write a short paper about the cluster of occupations they liked best;
- 90% selected the requirement to interview someone who works in the cluster selected as favorite;
- 85% selected having to complete a four-year high school plan for the cluster selected;
- 61% selected having to memorize a definition of each of the six clusters; and
- 25% selected having to miss English class for three days.

From *classroom teachers who gave their classrooms and class time to make the unit possible* (based on a short interview with each):

- The counselor should have made arrangements for this unit no later than September 15 so that lessons and assignments for the English class could have been modified earlier.
- Students seemed to have more freedom while the counselor was teaching this unit. As a result, the room was more disorderly than usual.
- The bus that took students on the field trip returned to school late, resulting in a need for the teacher to write a late pass for every student before he or she went to the next class period.
- In casual conversation, students showed a lot of enthusiasm for the unit.
- Students need to know this content, but it would be better if it could take less time away from the English class.

Assuming this evaluative feedback, how will the counselor use it to improve the unit the next time it is delivered? These conclusions could be drawn from the data:

- The basic methods of presenting the content (field trip, speakers, videos, Web sites) are well received by the students.
- Specific assignments, though disliked by the students, should be kept because of their value.
- Based on administrator, teacher, and student feedback, the length of the program should be cut without losing its valuable outcomes.
- Great care should be taken to work with English teachers very early in the semester, or even at the end of the previous semester, so that their lesson plans can be modified both to reflect the content being taught in this special guidance unit and to accommodate for the time loss it causes.
- The schedule for field trips must be very carefully monitored so that students never return to the school building late.

How could a counselor use the same results to determine whether program objectives have been met? Although not stated here, let us imagine that the counselor had several clearly written and measurable objectives for this program and that data listed at the beginning of the previous list indicated that the objectives had been met at an even higher level than indicated in the objectives. Such data would confirm that program objectives had been met.

How would a counselor use these results to promote and explain the program as well as to ensure that it continues? Here are some ideas in that regard:

- A short executive summary of the results could be sent to the administrator, along with a memo that thanks him or her for continued support for the program and indicates that its length, now six hours, has been reduced to four hours for the next year in order to ensure that the amount of time taken away from English classes is not excessive. The report might contain not only the basic data but also several positive quotes from parents, teachers, and/or students. The cover memo might also include a summary of the plans for the next semester or year.
- A short summary of the results could be included in the school newsletter to parents, along with some student quotes. Further details might be presented at a PTA meeting.
- An article about the program could be written and sent to the local newspaper. A cover letter might state when the program will be offered again and invite a reporter to cover one or more of the main events (such as the field trip to show the different kinds of work tasks included in the six clusters of occupations) next time.
- A report about the success of the program could be sent, along with a thank-you letter, to the English teachers who gave up class time for the program and to their department chair. The letter might include a paragraph indicating that some time has been cut from the program in order to use as little English-class time as possible and that greater care will be taken in the future about the condition of classrooms and the prompt arrival of buses from field trips.

How might an administrator use the data to determine whether to retain the program of services or to discontinue it? An analysis of the number of hours spent by the counselor and the number of students served reveals that the cost of delivery was $2.45 per student. Based on the strong parent and student feedback, the principal decides to retain the program in spite of some faculty resistance about the fact that class time is taken for its delivery.

Roadblocks to Evaluation

It is not easy to find the time or the motivation to do evaluation of career counseling and career planning services. Most counselors work in settings in which there are many conflicting demands on their time and priorities. The crisis situations—such as dealing with violence, drugs, excessive absence, and a variety of behavioral problems—receive first priority. In high school settings, planning and changing course schedules often demands second priority; making or finding time to provide career planning services receives, at best, third priority; and designing or evaluating any of these services falls near the bottom of the priority list. Patrick and Niles (1988) identified three additional roadblocks, as follows:

- Because evaluation is designed to reveal the quality of services as perceived by those who receive them, the potential for negative results is threatening. If evaluation did result in negative findings, funding, staff, and program approval could be in jeopardy.
- Unless the services of a guidance or student affairs office have been designed in the way described in this chapter, its offerings may be so nonsystematic—that is, without defined objectives—that it is difficult or impossible to evaluate them.
- Many counselors believe that the kind of work they do cannot be objectively evaluated because it is not quantifiable or definable. Thus, they resist any method of evaluation.

In addition to these roadblocks, counselors may not have the financial resources to purchase instruments that would be helpful in evaluation or in conducting a follow-up study. Further, they may not have the time or expertise to develop questionnaires, observer checklists, or exit interviews to be used. In cases in which better data would be acquired if there could be an experimental-control group design, the realities of the work setting may not support such a design.

Step 10: Revise the Program as Needed

In this step of the process, developers use the results of evaluation of the previous delivery of the program, feedback from managers, and additional creative ideas in order to revise the program and prepare for its next delivery. Revisions are a very normal part of the process because it is never possible to anticipate how students or clients will react to interventions until they have been tested with members of the target population. Revisions may include changes to content, time allocated to different activities, facilities, personnel, and methods of evaluation. The number of changes will decrease as the number of times the program is delivered is increased.

SOME SAMPLE PROGRAMS

A wealth of information about career development theory and practice has been covered in this book. The purpose of this content, of course, is to enable counselors to create programs to serve different kinds of clients in a variety of settings by using curricular, group, and one-to-one approaches, all enhanced by the use of Web-based career planning systems and sites. This section of the chapter provides examples of the program design process in six different settings. These are merely illustrations provided for the purpose of offering further clarity about the development process.

Example 1: An Elementary School

You have just been hired as a counselor at an elementary school that has not previously had the services of a counselor. Your principal asks you to plan some career development activities for the students in grade 3. You decide to go to the American School Counselor Association (2004) standards for career development. You find these listed on the organization's website:

> Standard A: Students will acquire the skills to investigate the world of work in relation to knowledge of self and to make informed career decisions.
>
> **C:A1 Develop Career Awareness**
> C:A1.1 Develop skills to locate, evaluate and interpret career information
> C:A1.2 Learn about the variety of traditional and nontraditional occupations
> C:A1.3 Develop an awareness of personal abilities, skills, interests and motivations
> C:A1.4 Learn how to interact and work cooperatively in teams
> C:A1.5 Learn to make decisions
> C:A1.6 Learn how to set goals
> C:A1.7 Understand the importance of planning

You decide to build your program around these first seven objectives under Standard A.

Executive Summary

The American School Counselor Association (ASCA) has gathered many consultants in the field of guidance and counseling to assist them to develop a sequence of life and career development objectives for students in grades K–12. These objectives are organized into three categories: Academic, Personal/Social, and Career Development. Further, ASCA has suggested that, at the elementary level, these objectives are best met through curriculum that is developed by counselors and teachers and delivered by them.

This document provides seven general objectives proposed by the ASCA model for elementary students in the category of Career Development and explains how curriculum will be developed and delivered in pursuit of those seven objectives.

Needs

The developmental needs of students are well stated in the ASCA National Model, so the first seven objectives under Standard A will be used as the basis for developing curricular content that third-grade teachers can use to help students meet these objectives. The general purpose of this curriculum is to raise awareness, not to precipitate any kinds of career decisions at this age level. This awareness will be the basis for guided exploration during the middle school years and, eventually, for selection of course work and establishment of career goals.

Specific Objectives

By the end of grade 3, students will be able to:

1. State the titles of John Holland's six clusters and describe the kind of work that is done in each.
2. State the titles of at least three occupations in each of these six career clusters and give a brief description of what workers in those occupations do.
3. State which two of those career clusters they have the most interest in and why.
4. Using a graphic provided, describe the steps in the process of making a first career choice.

Proposed Plan

In order to achieve the preceding objectives, the counselor will work with the three third-grade teachers to develop lesson plans that can be included in their classroom work, student assignments that follow these lessons, and related field trips. Samples of classroom activities to address these objectives include the following:

- Create six bulletin board areas within the classroom for the Holland six clusters of occupations: Social Service, Administration and Sales, Business Operations, Technical, Science and Technology, and Arts. The bulletin board would include pictures of people working in occupations in each career cluster.
- Make a list of all the kinds of jobs found in the school building or district (principal, superintendent, teachers, counselor, school nurse, cafeteria cook, bus driver, maintenance mechanic, groundskeeper, etc.). Ask students to place each position within a circle containing the titles of the six clusters listed above.
- Play the Holland Party Game. In this game, a description of the kind of work that takes place in each of the six areas of the World-of-Work would be read for each of the six clusters. Then students are asked to move to that part of the room (near the bulletin board) that has occupations that appeal to them most. Next, they are asked to move to the area of the bulletin board that has the kind of work tasks (occupations) that they like next best.
- Using a worksheet provided, describe two occupations from each of these two clusters. Get the information by using the Internet, using a book in the library, or talking to someone who works in these chosen occupations.
- Using a worksheet provided, list the steps needed from the present to completion of education or training for one selected occupation.

Resources Needed

The following will be needed in order to develop and deliver the proposed curriculum:

1. Time for three third-grade teachers and counselors to meet for planning and further development of lesson plans and related activities
2. Six bulletin boards per third-grade classroom
3. Duplication of worksheets needed to do the classroom activities

Expected Outcomes

1. Students will begin to understand that there is a way to organize (and later explore) the more than 1,000 occupations in the United States.
2. Students will have a foundation for learning to categorize occupations as they explore them in much more detail in the future and recognize their similarities and differences.
3. Students will have a foundation for beginning to associate their personal interests and abilities with those related to each of these six clusters.
4. Students will have a foundation for developing four-year high school course plans as, or if, this organizational scheme is carried on into the middle and high school years.

Methods of Evaluation

1. Give a brief quiz after each lesson or activity that tests the content, such as:

   a. Ask students to match the titles and brief descriptions of 12 occupations to the six clusters.

      b. If students have access to the Internet, direct them to the Occupation Finder at bls.gov, a U.S. Department of Labor site that describes all occupations in the United States. Assign 12 (or more) occupational titles to students, ask them to read the description of the occupations, and then to assign each to one of the six career clusters.

      c. Provide six brief case studies that describe how a young person went about making a career choice (some following the steps taught and some not). Ask students to indicate whether the process used by the person in the case study followed the suggested process, or if not, what was not done well.

Example 2: A Middle School

You have been a teacher in a middle school (grades 6 to 8) of approximately 400 students. You recently completed a master's degree in counseling, and your principal has asked you to work with a task force of teachers to figure out how to incorporate career guidance objectives and content into the curriculum. Your team used the National Career Development guidelines for the middle school years (see Chapter 11) as the basis for this work. Although individual teachers have provided some content and activities related to occupational choice, there has been no integrated plan for providing career exploration for the students. For that reason, under your leadership, the task force begins by writing a document for the principal, briefly describing your proposal.

Executive Summary

Career development is a lifelong process. Within the context of this process, students at the middle school level should be encouraged to engage in career exploration—that is, to become aware of their personal characteristics (self-awareness), occupations and their similarities and differences (occupational exploration), and career preparation (curricular choices). The U.S. Department of Education (2003), in collaboration with appropriate professional organizations, has developed detailed guidelines. The committee has used the middle school guidelines as the basis for its own development of specific objectives for our school.

Needs

The needs of middle school students are well defined by the National Career Development Guidelines. The specific objectives included are drawn both from theory (especially that of Donald E. Super) and from the demands of their transition to high school. Thus, the needs are to develop a strong base of self- and occupational knowledge during these years and to accomplish the following objectives.

Specific Objectives

By the time students transition to high school, they will be able to:

1. Describe the world-of-work as six clusters of occupations and differentiate the work tasks, work settings, skills, and educational levels unique to each cluster;
2. Select one or two clusters of highest interest;
3. Develop a tentative four-year high school plan that would prepare them for work in or further educational preparation for work in the selected cluster(s); and
4. Describe work as one significant role among others that make up one's personal career.

Proposed Plan

In order to accomplish the preceding objectives, the following steps are suggested:

1. It is proposed that the World-of-Work Map (ACT, 2000) be taught in social studies classes at the sixth-grade level as a way to help students understand how occupations are organized and the different roles that workers play in our society in order to make it function economically with sufficient production of goods and services. Also, Super's (1980) definition of career as a combination of life roles being played at any point in life will be used and explained.

2. At the seventh-grade level, a concerted effort would be made to provide information to students about the work tasks, work setting, and academic preparation needed for work in each of these six clusters. To facilitate this, school subjects would be assigned to each of the six clusters, and teachers of those subjects would be provided with a list of occupations (at various educational entry levels) that belong to the cluster to which their subject matter is related. Teachers would be asked to make linkages as often as possible between subject matter being taught and tasks of occupations in the cluster. They would also be encouraged to invite speakers into the class to talk about occupations in the cluster and how the subject matter being taught relates to their work. Further, the school counselor will coordinate a career day that is organized by the six clusters, inviting representatives of many occupations to the school so that students can talk with them. The counselor will also increase the resources of the career center and organize all occupational information by the same six clusters.

3. The counselor will work with the high school to organize the high school curriculum by the same six clusters. During the eighth grade, the counselor will work with students and their parents in groups to draft a four-year high school plan related to each student's selected cluster(s) and future educational plans.

Resources Needed

To implement the proposed program, the following resources will be needed:

1. Time for students to use the World-of-Work Map on the Internet at actstudent.org
2. One to two hours of time in department or faculty meetings during which the counselor can explain these materials to teachers and suggest ways in which they may be used as a part of their course
3. A budget of $500 to be used for expenses related to planning for, advertising, and sponsoring the career day
4. Time allocated to the counselor to organize and be in charge of the career day
5. Time allocated to the counselor to meet with members of the high school guidance department to plan and complete the work related to organizing the high school courses by the World-of-Work Map organizational system

Expected Outcomes

The following outcomes are expected as a result of program delivery:

1. Students will be able to make meaningful relationships between schoolwork and later work.
2. Students will gain broad awareness of the meaning of *career* and of how the world-of-work is organized.

3. Students will make informed occupational choices and take high school courses that will validate and/or prepare them for those choices.

Methods of Evaluation

The following methods are suggested for the purpose of evaluation:

1. Students will have a quiz after instruction on the World-of-Work Map. They will be asked to place occupational titles (which include short descriptions) into the six clusters.
2. Students will be asked to select one or two clusters of their preference and to list at least five occupations in each of these clusters in which they might have interest.
3. Students will develop a four-year high school plan related to the cluster(s) they have selected.

Example 3: A High School

Suppose that you have just been hired as a counselor in a local high school that has approximately 1,500 students. The first thing you did was to request space and funds for a career center equipped with computers and Web access so that students could access the resources described in Chapter 6. This request was granted, and the equipment has been ordered.

In the past there has been no service of any kind for helping students plan for future occupational choices. Some time can be made available during the school day for sophomores, so you decide to begin your program at this level. Further, you decide to develop a program that provides service to all sophomores in a cost-effective manner, though you are willing to see those with special needs individually. The school principal asks you to provide a short document that describes what you have in mind and what your needs are. Your document might look like the following executive summary.

Executive Summary

This brief document describes the needs, objectives, content, expected outcomes, and requested resources for a career guidance program proposed for all sophomores. The needs listed can be assumed from our knowledge of career development theory and of the context in which the young people of the United States find themselves. Based on these needs, several specific objectives for the program are listed, and content and activities are proposed. Finally, the document summarizes expected outcomes, resources needed, and methods of evaluation.

Needs

Given the age of these students and the contextual changes occurring in the United States, sophomore students have the following needs:

1. To understand the changes in the workplace and how these changes will affect their personal career planning;
2. To learn the process of career planning that they can apply now and will need to apply again and again throughout their lives;
3. To identify their personal interests and abilities;
4. To relate these interests and abilities to possible occupations;

  5. To learn about these occupations; and
  6. To select courses in high school that will lay the academic basis for further education and entry into one or more of these occupations.

Specific Objectives

At the end of the proposed program, at least 80% of the students who complete the program will be able to:

  1. Describe in detail three significant trends in the United States that are changing employers and jobs and include the implications of these for personal career planning;
  2. Describe the steps of a planful process for making career decisions;
  3. State three to five groups (families) of occupations that relate to their personal interests and abilities;
  4. Make a list of occupational titles from those groups;
  5. Describe in detail at least five occupations from that list;
  6. Select at least three occupations of highest interest; and
  7. State the educational implications of preparing for those three occupations.

Proposed Plan

It is proposed that the following sessions be held with sophomores:

Session 1: Learn about changes that are occurring in the workplace.

Three speakers will be invited from three different companies. Each will talk about changes that have occurred in the past five years and what the projected changes are for the future, including what these may mean for young people entering the job market.

All sophomores will be assembled in the auditorium. A one-page worksheet will be given to each student on which he or she can record the main points of each speaker as well as a summary that includes at least three implications of what speakers said for personal career planning.

Projected time: 1½ hours

Session 2: Learn a process for making personal career decisions.

The career planning process (copy of a graphic enclosed for your information) will be described by the counselor to sophomores in groups of 40 using a PowerPoint presentation. Students will receive a short handout that provides a graphic of the career decision-making process and an explanation of each of its steps.

An interest inventory (copy enclosed for your information) will be administered to each group of 40 students. Answer sheets will be scored and results printed, using the computer program licensed with the instrument.

Proposed time: 2 hours—1 hour for presentation of the career planning model (including answering student questions) and 1 hour for describing the purpose and administering the interest inventory. Because there are 400 students in the sophomore class, this will require 20 hours of counselor time plus another 3 hours for preparation of visual materials and handout.

Session 3: Interpret the results of the interest inventory to students in groups of 40.

Give each student his or her score report. Describe the score report by use of a sample (for some fictitious student) score report projected on the screen, and explain each section of the report. Then ask the students to look at their own reports. Answer as many questions as possible in the group sessions. If students have additional questions, invite them to make an appointment for an interview. Ask students to circle the names of three clusters that interest them on the material provided with the score report.

Projected time: 1 hour for each of 10 groups of students, requiring 10 hours of counselor time for presentations, an additional 2 hours for preparation, and an estimated 10 hours for individual interviews requested by students or invited by the counselor because of the pattern of results.

> Session 4: Assist students to identify occupations that belong in the three career clusters they have selected and to get information about those occupations.

Schedule students in groups of 20 to come to the career center. Provide brief instruction about the materials in the center that contain occupational descriptions, including two specific Web sites. Also, explain what an information interview is and how students can find people who are willing to talk with them. Provide students with a worksheet that will guide their use of materials so that they can record the titles of occupations and information gained about each. Assign an information interview for each of three occupations, and provide a worksheet for students' use in summarizing their learning.

Projected time: 2 hours each for 20 groups of students—a total of 40 hours of counselor time.

> Session 5: Offer opportunities for students to discuss their learning from the research in the career center and from informational interviews, and give students time to complete a personal Career Action Plan.

Students will come to the center in groups of 20. Students will be asked to share with the group some of the things they learned by doing the research and by interviewing individuals who work in occupations that interest them. Ask students to complete a one-page career action plan that lists (a) three occupations of highest interest at this time, (b) the level and kind of education needed for entering each occupation, and (c) next steps. These steps may include taking courses that are needed in high school, researching the occupation further, or requesting an interview with the counselor.

Projected time: 40 hours of counselor time for the group sessions plus an estimated 10 additional hours for individual interviews.

Resources Needed

It is anticipated that the following resources will be needed in order to deliver this program:

1. Use of the auditorium and audiovisual equipment for Session 1
2. 400 copies of the interest inventory
3. Permission to duplicate handouts for students that will total about 20 pages per student

Expected Outcomes

As a result of the delivery of this program, the following outcomes are expected:

1. High student motivation because of the school's concern for their future planning.
2. Improved student choice of curriculum while in high school.

3. Knowledge of decision-making and research skills that will be needed many times later in life.
4. Support and involvement of parents.

Methods of Evaluation

The following are suggested as methods of evaluation:

1. Review work forms completed by students to ensure that they have been able to complete assigned tasks.
2. Provide questionnaire that each student completes at the end of the five sessions.
3. Interview 20 randomly selected students to ask them how they rate the effectiveness of the program and to capture ideas they have for improvement.

Another idea related to this program is to have an evening meeting with parents prior to beginning the program. If this is not feasible, then it may be possible to send a letter from the principal to each student's home. Either of these approaches would explain the purpose of these meetings with students, describe the general content, and offer parents a chance to talk with a counselor if they have questions.

Example 4: A University

Imagine that you have just been hired as a career counselor at a major university. Other than the assistance that faculty mentors may give to students, there has previously been no staff or program to assist students with the selection of majors, occupations, or jobs. One of the conditions you stated when you considered the job was that the university would invest in the facilities and resources needed to establish a career center for students and alumni. This request was granted, and you are in the process of drawing a layout for the center and of ordering the furnishings and resource material. You are anxious to get permission for a program of services for students, but because this is a new idea, your dean asks you to provide a short proposal, which you do, as follows.

Executive Summary

This document describes a voluntary program of services for seniors at the university that will assist them to prepare the documents needed for searching for jobs and will provide them with skills to identify job openings, secure job interviews, conduct themselves effectively in job interviews, and select a good place of employment.

Needs

The needs stated here have been identified both by a review of the career development literature and by a random survey of alumni who graduated from the university last year. Based on these sources, graduates of this university have the following needs:

1. To understand how the workplace they are about to enter has changed;
2. To learn a process for career decision making that they can use now and in the future;
3. To develop an effective résumé for today's job market;
4. To know how to find or create job openings;
5. To know how to identify personal skills and relate them to job openings; and
6. To know how to participate in an effective interview.

Objectives

Based on these identified needs, students who participate in the program of services described next will be able to:

1. Describe at least three trends in the United States today that affect their personal careers and what they should expect of their future employers;
2. Describe a process for making career choices;
3. Show a personal résumé, in at least two formats (e.g., chronological and functional), that can be used for a job search; and
4. In mock interviews, demonstrate an ability to participate effectively in job interviews, including relating personal skills to a job opening.

Content

The content described next will be presented in a series of three workshops to be presented four times throughout the academic year.

> Session 1 (1 hour): A presentation by the counselor, using audiovisual aids, about the systemic changes in the workplace, how these will affect personal careers, and how individuals will need to take responsibility for their own career choices; presentation (with handout) of a career decision-making model.

> Session 2 (1 hour): Presentation about the purpose of a résumé and of two different formats for preparing one. Via a handout, show good examples of sample résumés, and provide worksheets that each student can use to write his or her own résumé in both formats. Ask students to prepare these sample résumés by the next session. Invite students who wish to come for an individual interview to do so. Offer to review and make suggestions about their résumés. Show good examples of Web-based e-portfolios and how a résumé is used as a central part of that portfolio.

> Session 3 (2 hours): Presentation about the characteristics and stages of an effective interview, with handout. Following that, do a mock interview with one student. Then hand out descriptions of a job opening and an applicant; ask students to form triads, with one playing the role of an employer, one the role of an applicant, and the third the role of an observer who is noting whether the characteristics of a successful interview are present. Videotape the job interviews, and use these videos as a basis for discussion of effective and ineffective interview behaviors.

Expected Outcomes

As a result of delivery of this program, the following outcomes are anticipated:

1. Students will learn about changes in the U.S. job market that affect their careers and what their expectations of employers should be in the future.
2. Students will learn a decision-making model that they can use to assume personal responsibility for their own career decisions again and again.
3. Students will be able to prepare an effective résumé and post it for review by employers.
4. Students will be more comfortable and more effective in job interviews.

Resources Needed

The following resources will be needed:

1. Capability to advertise these workshops in all university media
2. Permission to duplicate handouts to support these workshops
3. Use of a larger facility if the number of students who wish to attend exceeds the capacity of the career center
4. Postage and time for follow-up study

Methods of Evaluation

The program will be evaluated in the following ways:

1. Ask students who attended all three workshops to complete a questionnaire at the end of the sequence.
2. Tally the number of students who attend each workshop and the number who attend all three.
3. Do a follow-up survey by mail of 100 students one year after the workshop series to determine what percentage have jobs, their degree of satisfaction with these jobs, and how they believe the workshops helped them to find and acquire employment.

Example 5: A Corporation

Imagine that you have just been hired as a career counselor by a large corporation that needs to reduce the size of its workforce. It is doing this by offering older employees an early retirement financial package and terminating 456 middle managers. When you were hired, you were told that your services were desperately needed to help these two specific target populations. You asked for the physical space and the funds to set up a career management center, and these requests were granted. You are asked to provide a proposal for serving one of these two target populations as soon as possible. You decide to initiate a program for the 456 mid-level managers first because their needs are more immediate than those of the early retirees who have six more months of employment left. You submit the following proposal.

Executive Summary

This document describes a program of services that will be initiated with 456 middle managers who are to be terminated in two weeks. The program focuses on assisting them to learn and practice job-search skills so that they can find another job quickly.

Needs

These employees are understandably in a state of shock, anger, and denial. They need an opportunity to talk about the present situation, with the hope that they will be able to get through the anger and denial stages and move quickly to being able to formulate an action plan for reemployment. Also, because these employees are in the age range of 42 to 50 and most have worked for this company for many years, it is assumed that they need to review the latest job-search techniques and to practice these until they are comfortable.

Objectives

At the end of this series of workshops, employees who are going to be terminated will be able to:

1. Recognize that the situation they are facing is a result of economic conditions and resultant corporate decisions and that it has no relationship to their work performance;
2. Accept that, though the situation is unfortunate and stressful, it is not catastrophic and that they can find a way to make a successful transition;
3. Write an effective résumé in multiple formats that adequately expresses their skills and experience;
4. Participate effectively in mock job interviews;
5. Describe three effective ways of finding job openings; and
6. Using Schlossberg's model, develop a plan for coping successfully with this transition.

Content

Employees will be allowed to use normal working hours to attend a series of workshops, have individual interviews with the counselor, and use the Career Management Center. There will be a series of four two-hour workshops, which these employees will be encouraged to attend. Because 30 people would be a maximum number for each workshop, multiple sequences of these workshops will be scheduled.

Workshop 1 (2 hours): This workshop will be less structured than the remaining three. Because employees are unlikely to be able to focus on action planning until they have been able to express their anger and grief about job loss, this session will allow individuals to talk about their feelings. Several people from top management will be invited to attend, and, when appropriate, they may answer questions or provide information about the events that led the corporation to make the decision about termination of these employees.

Workshop 2 (2 hours): This session will focus on the preparation of a good résumé, in at least two formats, that expresses the skills and experience of each employee. A presentation will be made about how to develop such a résumé, and good examples will be provided as handouts. Individuals will spend the remaining time preparing a first draft of their own résumés. They will be invited to make individual interviews with the counselor, if they wish, and/or to leave their résumés in the counselor's office for review and feedback.

Workshop 3 (2 hours): This session will focus on a review of good interviewing skills. The various stages of the job interview will be described. Particular emphasis will be placed on teaching individuals how to research companies via the Internet and other means so that when they have interviews, they are able to relate their skills and experience to the particular job for which they are applying. Two good interviews will be role-played for the group. A checklist will be provided that outlines the characteristics of a good interview. Then, members of the group will be asked to divide into triads. One will play the role of interviewer, one the role of job seeker, and the third the role of observer, evaluating the interview using the checklist of characteristics.

Workshop 4 (2 hours): This session will focus on how to find job openings (including use of placement agencies, Web searching, social networking, and direct application to companies) and on learning how to network with others to identify job openings that are never publicly listed. Schlossberg's model for coping with transition will be described, and a worksheet will be provided on which individuals in the group can list ways they will cope with the transition by planning specific action steps. Members of the group will share these plans with others in the group.

Expected Outcomes

As a result of delivery of the program, the following outcomes are anticipated:

1. Terminated employees will be able to get rid of some of their anger and frustration and may leave the company with a more positive attitude.
2. Terminated employees will have improved chances of finding another job within a reasonable time because of instruction on job-seeking documents and skills.

Resources Needed

To deliver the program effectively, the following resources will be needed:

1. Permission to invite people to come to the workshops on company time
2. Cooperation from division heads to help publicize and promote the workshops through newsletters and other communications
3. A budget for refreshments
4. Use of audiovisual equipment and printing facilities
5. Permission to use Survey Monkey to conduct a follow-up study

Methods of Evaluation

The following methods of evaluation are planned:

1. Provide a questionnaire that participants will complete at the end of the four sessions.
2. Follow up with a random sample of participants 90 days after completion of the workshop to determine if they have found a job and if the content of the workshop helped them to do so.

Example 6: A Community Agency

Imagine that you have accepted a position as a counselor in a one-stop center. Your manager asks you to develop a service to assist community adults who, for whatever reason, want to pursue a different occupation from the one in which they are currently engaged.

Executive Summary

This document describes a proposed program of service for adult men and women who come to the agency seeking assistance with making a new career choice. Given the restraints of time, these individuals will be offered three group sessions with the requirement of an intake interview prior to the first session and an opportunity for a counseling interview following the three group sessions. The content of these sessions has been determined by the counselors' past experience with similar clients as well as through work with a randomly selected focus group of members of the target population. The intake interview, workshop sessions, and potential content of the counseling interview are described. Further, a summary of needed resources and the plan for evaluation are provided.

Needs

The needs identified for this population are as follows:

1. To understand the implications of career change
2. To assess the resources and barriers related to making the change

3. To consider possible choices and to define one
4. To draft a realistic action plan for making the change

Objectives

By the end of the sequence of activities, clients will be able to:

1. Describe realistically the transition they have chosen to make;
2. Identify forces for and forces against accomplishing the change; and
3. State a definite career goal and how they plan to reach it.

Content

Each client who expresses a desire to make a career change (that is, select and pursue a different occupation) will be asked to participate in an intake interview. The format of intake interviews will be the same for all clients. Questions asked by the interviewer will address the following topics:

- Past work history
- Client's view of his or her best skills and greatest work-related accomplishments
- Client's reasons for desiring to make an occupational change
- Ideas the client has about what this change might be
- How much the client knows about the occupation or field he or she now wants to enter
- Resources that support the client's ability to make a change (such as financial situation, persons who will be supportive, children grown and independent, etc.)
- Barriers the client will need to surmount (such as lack of support from some important persons, need for retraining, etc.)
- Willingness to make a commitment to the three group sessions and the follow-up counseling session

The three group sessions will be scheduled for two hours on the same night in three consecutive weeks. Their content will be as follows:

Session 1: Sharing within the group in regard to the kinds of changes they are seeking to make and the supports and barriers they confront for the transition. Following this, individuals will take three assessment inventories contained in a Web-based career planning system: an interest inventory, a skills inventory, and a values inventory. They will receive their results from these inventories immediately and can print them out.

Session 2: The counselor will provide a group interpretation of the three assessments, using a fictitious composite score report and a PowerPoint presentation. Group members will have an opportunity to ask questions in general or about their own reports. Members of the group will then share their specific occupational goals or dreams and indicate whether or not the results of the assessment support those ideas. The counselor will facilitate discussion. If individuals in the group need individual assistance in identifying possible occupational alternatives, they may make an appointment with the counselor for an individual interview before Session 3.

Session 3: Using worksheets based on the Schlossberg model for transition, clients will draft a plan to pursue a goal they have set for themselves. In this process they will identify specific steps they need to take (such as getting some training or having an information interview), assign a feasible timeline for completion of each step, and identify barriers and methods of dealing with these.

Following the three sessions, each participant will have an individual interview with the counselor. The purpose is to review the action plan together so that the counselor may be able to provide further information or suggest strategies for following the plan.

Expected Outcomes

As a result of this sequence of activities, it is expected that clients will:

1. Have a specific plan for making a career change.
2. Have a realistic career goal in keeping with self-information that has been gained.
3. Experience the support of the counselor and the group for moving forward with this plan.

Resources Needed

Delivery of the program as designed will require the following resources:

1. For the first session, a meeting room equipped with computers and Web access that will hold 15 people. Meeting room space, but without computers, will also be needed for an additional two consecutive weeks
2. Equipment to display a PowerPoint presentation at each session
3. Fifteen copies of the Schlossberg model worksheet
4. Use of the center's career development facilitator to conduct the intake interviews
5. Counselor time for preparing PowerPoint presentations, facilitating the three workshop sessions, and conducting individual counseling sessions

Methods of Evaluation

The following methods of evaluation will be used:

1. Ask each client to complete a questionnaire, either in print form or via Survey Monkey on the Web, at the end of the entire sequence.
2. Contact participants by phone or e-mail three months after the sequence of activities to assess the degree to which they have followed, or are following, the action plan they developed.

MyCounselingLab®

Start with Topic 5—Systematic Planning.

Watch the video *21st Century Career Development Interventions in the Schools: Dr. Carol Dahir* and complete Student Activity #1 at the end of this chapter.

Watch the video *Structured Activities*.

Watch the video *Use of Metaphor*.

SUMMARY

After building a rationale for program development and defining the roles counselors may play in it, this chapter has described a 10-step process for developing a program of career planning services for a specific target population. This process begins with understanding the characteristics of the target population, assessing its needs, and writing clear, measurable objectives focused on meeting those needs. It then includes developing program content, determining a combination of ways in which the program will be delivered, and determining how to promote and evaluate the program. Significant attention is given to the purposes and methods of evaluation and to ways in which its results can be used.

To make this process more practical, six sample programs for different target populations are described in some detail. They are proposed only as examples of the many different approaches to providing career planning service.

CASE STUDY

Your high school has a dropout rate of 19%, far higher than desired by the faculty and members of the school board. As director of guidance, you are asked by your principal to develop an initiative that would (a) identify students who are at risk of dropping out, (b) provide special services that may reduce that risk, and (c) evaluate the success of one year of delivery of these services.

How would you go about meeting the request of your principal?

STUDENT ACTIVITIES

1. Refer to the MyCounselingLab® Video and Resource Library and select the video entitled *21st Century Career Development Interventions in the Schools: Dr. Carol Dahir*, which is an interview between Dr. Spencer Niles, the lead author of this text, and Dr. Dahir, who was the lead author of the ASCA national model, which includes career development. Then, write a short paper that provides responses to these questions:
   a. List and describe at least two trends in the career development field that these two professionals talked about.
   b. From the many ideas that Dr. Dahir shared, did you get any ideas for a program of services that you would like to develop in a setting where you expect to work?
   c. Based on what you learned in this video, what are some of the barriers that school counselors have as they attempt to provide career planning services to students?

2. By this time in the course, you may have watched videos of several clients who participated in one-on-one counseling with professional counselors in a community counseling center. Suppose that you are the director of this center and you are told that it must serve more clients than can be dealt with in one-on-one mode with the allocated budget. Write a one- or

two-page, double-spaced paper that addresses the following questions:

- What kinds of programs of service could you develop within the same budget to serve the needs of more clients who need career counseling?
- What are some of the first steps you would take in developing these programs, and why?

3. Choose a setting where you hope to work as a counselor after you complete your training.

Then, write a short paragraph about each of the following:

- Some basic facts about the students or clients (target population) with whom you hope to work
- What you believe their career (vocational and educational) development needs may be
- The kinds of interventions you would provide to meet these needs

CHAPTER 10

CAREER DEVELOPMENT INTERVENTIONS IN THE ELEMENTARY SCHOOLS

As an elementary school counselor, I've found few guidance subjects to be more engaging for students in kindergarten through fifth grades than the topic of careers. At its most basic level, career lessons provide students with an understanding of the community and world around them. For all ages, talk of careers allows for deeper insight into self—a popular and valuable point of discussion for the egocentric phase of childhood development. Children enjoy discussing themselves, especially in regard to the question "What might you like to be when you grow up?" Elementary students explore careers through play and imagination. For upper elementary grades, I've found career discussions lend well to the linking between current education and future success. Students learn to view school as their important work as opposed to an irrelevant chore. Students begin to link their actions and choices to "having a job someday." In fifth grade, I explain to my students that they are beginning to have an active hand in their educational development and subsequently their career development when they make their elective choices for sixth grade. Discussions of career topics and relevant skills help to promote students' feelings of confidence, self-efficacy and motivation, each necessary to the development of successful citizens in the 21st century.

Jennifer Niles-Orefice,
Professional School Counselor, Brunson Elementary School, Winston-Salem, NC

MyCounselingLab®

Visit the MyCounselingLab® site for *Career Development Interventions*, Fifth Edition, to enhance your understanding of chapter concepts. You will have the opportunity to practice applying what you learned in the chapter by completing the video- and case-based exercises in the MyLab. Taking the Licensure Quizzes will help you prepare for your certification exam.

Rosita was only five years old, but she had already experienced many difficult situations in her life. Her father, Enrique, left home before she was born. Her mother, Rosa, struggled with substance abuse problems. Rosa's lack of education (she never completed high school) severely limited her employment opportunities. She was able to find occasional employment as a waitress; however, she had a pattern of absenteeism and tardiness. These behaviors typically resulted in her termination from work. During her periods of unemployment, Rosa often turned to drugs to numb the pain. Rosa loved Rosita, but did not know how to extricate herself from this self-defeating behavioral pattern. Fortunately, Rosa's mother lived nearby and provided much needed emotional support to her daughter and granddaughter. Despite this support, Rosita struggled with her father's absence and her mother's frequent bouts with substance abuse and unemployment. Today, however, Rosita had other thoughts. It was her first day of school. She felt scared and anxious as she wondered what school would be like. She took comfort in the fact that her best friend, Melissa, was also starting kindergarten today.

In this chapter (as well as in Chapters 12 and 13), we provide ideas for helping students like Rosita acquire developmentally appropriate career development skills. We also set the context for providing career development interventions in the schools by discussing important national models of career development standards, important topics to consider in creating career development interventions in the schools, specific steps for creating systematic and coordinated career development programs, and relevant research literature that provides useful theories and models constructing career interventions.

OVERVIEW OF CAREER DEVELOPMENT STANDARDS FOR CONSTRUCTING CAREER INTERVENTIONS IN THE SCHOOLS

Throughout their history, professional school counselors have been engaged in helping students, such as Rosita, advance in their career and educational planning. It is likely that Rosita is not concerned about her future work options on her first day of school, but her total school experience, even at this early age, will serve as a major influence in the eventual career goals Rosita identified. The American School Counselor Association (ASCA) creates standards to guide professional school counselors in their work with students. The most recent standards are entitled the ASCA *Mindsets and Behaviors for Student Success* (ASCA, 2014). These standards are organized into three domains relating to academic, career, and social/emotional development. The career domain highlights standards emphasizing the school and work connection and transition planning relative to moving from high school to postsecondary school or work. The *Mindsets and Behaviors* standards were preceded by the National Standards for School Counseling Programs (Campbell & Dahir, 1997) and the ASCA National Model for School Counseling (ASCA, 2003, 2012). The earlier standards also emphasize the importance of career development as an essential element in effective school counseling programs (Dimmitt & Carey, 2007).

The National Standards (ASCA, 2012), which were developed to address the growing need for standardization and accountability in school counseling programs, consist of four components (foundation, delivery system, management system, and accountability system). The foundation consists of program philosophy statements; it connects with the mission of the school and contains information regarding expected student competencies in the three domains (academic, career, and personal/social development). There are also nine standards (three per domain) that, in turn, are each connected to student competencies linked to specific knowledge and skills that students will develop as outcomes of their exposure to school counseling programs.

At the elementary school level, the career development domain in the National Standards (ASCA, 2012) contains the standards, competencies, and indicators that highlight the importance of helping students acquire basic information about work and occupations; identify a beginning sense of self-awareness pertaining to their interests, abilities, etc.; and begin to understand how to make decisions effectively. The major theme of career development at the elementary school level is awareness. Because much information that children receive about work can be stereotypical (e.g., women working as nurses, men working as carpenters), a major emphasis in helping elementary school students develop career awareness is to provide non-stereotypical information. Children need to be exposed to non-traditional workers to begin to understand that a fuller range of options is possible for them in the future than what they may perceive to be the case based on gender, racial, ethnic and other stereotypes.

Clearly, the National Standards represent a comprehensive and holistic view of career development. By themselves, however, the standards could seem overwhelming to the novice professional school counselor seeking to use the standards as a developmental framework from which specific career development programs can be designed and implemented. Fortunately, the ASCA National Model for School Counseling Programs links with other national standards such as the National Career Development Guidelines (National Occupational Information Coordinating Committee, 1992). Essentially, the current guidelines update those developed in 1989. More specifically, in 2003 the U.S. Department of Education's Office of Vocational and Adult Education (OVAE) embarked upon an effort to revise the National Career Development Guidelines (NCDG). The specific goals of the revision project were to update and revise the framework of competencies and indicators to align with the goals of No Child Left Behind (2001); expand the target audiences to include K–12 students and their parents, teachers, counselors and administrators, postsecondary students, and other adults and the business community; provide the target audiences with accessible career development information, learning activities, and strategies that lead to informed career decision making; and create a career development Web site to deliver career development information, learning activities, and strategies. (Extensive links to multiple resources professional school counselors will find helpful are available at cte.ed.gov.)

The revision of the National Career Development Guidelines resulted in a new framework that is organized into three domains. In addition, there are goals for each domain and mastery indicators for each goal. The indicators are further grouped by learning stage. The domains for the Guidelines are Personal Social Development (PS), Educational Achievement and Lifelong Learning (ED), and Career Management (CM). Interestingly, the three domains provide a parallel to the National School Counseling Model. Each domain contains goals that define broad areas of career development competency. Under each goal in the framework are mastery indicators that highlight the knowledge and skills needed to achieve that goal. Each indicator is presented in three learning stages based on *Bloom's Taxonomy* (Bloom, Engelhart, Furst, Hill, & Krathwohl, 1956): knowledge acquisition, application, and reflection. Unlike the previous guidelines, the current ones are not tied to an individual's age or level of education. This change acknowledges both the heterogeneity in career development and the fact that people recycle through career development tasks.

The NCDG framework coding system (PS–Personal Social Development; ED–Educational Achievement and Lifelong Learning; CM–Career Management) can be used to identify domains, goals, indicators, and learning stages (see ncda.org). The coding system is intended to makes it easy to use the NCDG for program development and to track activities by goal, learning stage, and indicator. Thus, goals are coded as PS, ED, or CM and then listed numerically under the respective domains. For example, under the Personal Social Development domain:

Goal PS1: Develop understanding of yourself to build and maintain a positive self-concept.

Goal PS2: Develop positive interpersonal skills including respect for diversity.

Indicators and Learning Stages (K–Knowledge Acquisition; A–Application; R–Reflection) are coded numerically by domain, goal, and learning stage. For example, the second indicator under the first goal of the Personal Social Development domain:

PS1.K2: Identify your abilities, strengths, skills, and talents.

PS1.A2: Demonstrate use of your abilities, strengths, skills, and talents.

PS1.R2: Assess the impact of your abilities, strengths, skills, and talents on your career development.

The NCDG framework can be used in various ways to inform the creation, implementation, and evaluation of career intervention programs. For example:

Youth and adults can use the goals and indicators as an informal checklist to determine areas of competency and gaps that need attention.

Parents, guardians, spouses, or family members can use the framework to better understand how to help someone with career development questions.

Teachers can use the framework to review their curriculum and existing lessons for career development connections.

Teachers can use the framework to write new lessons that enhance academic rigor by infusing career development concepts.

Counselors, career practitioners, and administrators can use the framework to review an existing career development program for students or adults to see what competencies are covered and where the gaps are.

Counselors, career practitioners, and administrators can use the framework to craft needs assessments for youth and adults.

Counselors, career practitioners, and administrators can use the framework to craft a new competency-based career development program for youth or adults.

Counselors, career practitioners, and administrators can use the framework to develop a program evaluation and accountability plan.

Counselors, career practitioners, and media specialists can use the framework to review materials and resources on hand or those being considered for purchase.

The framework can serve as the basis for staff development workshops offered locally, statewide, or regionally (e.g., American School Counselor Association workshops).

The framework can inform the development of professional standards, accreditation, certification, and legislation and policy at both the national and state levels.

Product developers can use the framework to target their materials to meet specific career development needs of potential customers. (U.S. Department of Education, 2007)

We contend that the ASCA (2012) standards and the National Career Development Guidelines represent two national models that provide an outstanding structure that professional school counselors can use to construct career development interventions.

When constructing career development interventions, we think it is especially important for professional school counselors to be cognizant of the ways in which environmental constraints (e.g., sexism, racism, heterosexism, discrimination experienced by students with disabilities) negatively affect students' career development. Clearly, career development interventions must be designed to address these experiences (Holcomb-McCoy, 2007; Jackson & Grant, 2004).

> **Tips from the Field**
>
> Career development is alive and often not doing so well in childhood. Media and stereotypes influence what children think is possible. Challenge this process!

IMPORTANT CONSIDERATIONS IN DEVELOPING CAREER DEVELOPMENT INTERVENTIONS IN THE SCHOOLS

Several authors (e.g., Gysbers & Henderson, 2001; Lapan, 2004; Schmidt, 2003) advocate for making career development programs an integral part of the school curriculum rather than an ancillary service. Niles, Trusty, and Mitchell (2004) take a systems perspective to designing career development interventions and emphasize that professional school counselors must communicate effectively with important subsystems (students, teachers, administrators, parents, and families) regarding the goals and objectives of the career development program. Effective communication with students includes conducting a needs assessment to guide professional school counselors in the construction of career development programs and to serve as a basis for evaluation of program effectiveness. Effective communication with parents and families includes helping parents understand how they can positively influence their children's career development.

Teachers need assistance connecting academic content to career and educational planning. Providing and/or delivering classroom career guidance activities assists teachers in making such connections. Professional school counselors can also help teachers become aware of research data that indicate the positive correlation between career planning and school success (Herr, Cramer, & Niles, 2004). Educating administrators regarding these data also helps increase the probability that the career development program will be an integral part of the school curriculum. The critical point here is that, in a very real sense, professional school counselors operate within a political context that does not always understand and support the need for career services. Therefore, professional school counselors must work as advocates for career development as they deliver systematic and coordinated career services to students (Perusse & Goodnough, 2004).

Those questioning the usefulness of career development interventions assume that career-related activities take students away from time spent focusing on core academic subjects. In addition, career education critics assume that career education programs pressure students to pursue work immediately after high school rather than pursuing a college education. Many people who are unfamiliar with how careers develop do not understand why career development interventions are important at the elementary and secondary school levels. The fact that career education initiatives were funded with monies external to school districts and that, in many instances, career education proponents had not generated local support for career education were also factors contributing to negative attitudes toward the career education movement (Herr et al., 2004). Thus, career education initiatives often become entangled in the political issues common to education today (e.g., the "back-to-basics" movement, the push to eliminate teaching of values in education, and the misconception that career education is the same as vocational education).

Those questioning the usefulness of career interventions in the schools are often even more adamant about their opinion that career interventions are not necessary for elementary school students. Those arguing against career interventions for elementary school students often view career decision making as events that occur at particular points during the course of secondary school education (e.g., when students must select a curriculum of study, when they leave high school). Such perspectives lack an appreciation of the precursors to effective career decision making. Viewing career development as an event rather than a process sets up students for failure as many students have not developed the developmental precursors required for effective educational and career planning. Expecting such students to make career decisions when they are not prepared is no different than asking a student to solve a math problem when that student lacks the necessary skills and knowledge to do so.

Another issue related to the implementation of career education programs relates to the fact that many school districts do not provide career development programs in a systematic and coordinated fashion (Herr et al., 2004; Walz & Benjamin, 1984). The piecemeal implementation of career development interventions obviously limits the degree to which such interventions can positively influence students. Moreover, such an approach often creates confusion as to the meaning and purpose of career development programs by those not directly involved in their creation and implementation. Thus, it is essential that school counselors at the elementary and secondary school levels engage in systematic and coordinated planning prior to implementing career development programs (Gysbers & Henderson, 1998; Myrick, 1993).

Tips from the Field

If you plan your career interventions developmentally, students will develop more planfully.

SYSTEMATIC AND COORDINATED PLANNING FOR CAREER DEVELOPMENT PROGRAMS IN THE SCHOOLS

Herr et al. (2004) recommend using a five-stage planning model for facilitating the implementation of systematic career development intervention programs. The stages are:

Stage 1:   Develop a program rationale and philosophy.
Stage 2:   State program goals and behavioral objectives.
Stage 3:   Select program processes.
Stage 4:   Develop an evaluation design.
Stage 5:   Identify program milestones.

An important component of Stage 1 involves conducting a needs assessment to determine appropriate program rationales, goals, and interventions (Niles et al., 2004). As we have noted, the needs assessment provides benchmarks against which program outcomes can be assessed. Herr et al. (2004) emphasize the importance of incorporating teachers, students, parents, and community participants in the needs assessment to increase understanding of, and involvement in, career development programs. Clearly, a properly conducted needs assessment provides a firm foundation upon which effective career development intervention programs can be constructed.

Walz and Benjamin (1984) also provide important recommendations for developing systematic career development intervention programs. Their recommendations include the following:

1. Involve a team of knowledgeable professionals, parents, and representatives from the community in all phases of program planning.
2. Use developmentally appropriate interventions.
3. Be sure that the program goals and objectives are clearly communicated to all involved in the program.
4. Make sure the program is based on student needs.
5. Have an evaluation component to determine the degree to which the program goals and objectives have been achieved.
6. Make sure that those involved in program delivery are highly competent.

Once again, the implicit theme in both sets of recommendations is that professional school counselors need to be sensitive to the political climate in which they operate. For example, in some locations, not clearly connecting career development interventions to student academic achievement will significantly decrease the chances of program success. Also, not adequately communicating successful program outcomes will result in the program resources being vulnerable to funding cuts. If school personnel view the program as an additional burden to their already heavy workloads, then there is little chance that the program will succeed. Thus, the "marketing" of the program to all stakeholders becomes an important aspect of program development and implementation. Having clearly defined behavioral objectives that address the specific needs of program participants will be useful in marketing the program and providing outcome data demonstrating program benefits.

Similar to the systems approach advocated by Niles et al. (2004), these recommendations highlight the importance of taking a team approach to service delivery. Although there is no one prescription for how the roles and responsibilities for delivering career development interventions should be distributed, it is logical that counselors take the lead role (not the sole role) in developing and implementing career development programs. Counselors are often the only professionals in the school system with specific training in career development. Therefore, counselors possess the knowledge of career development theory and practice necessary for formulating appropriate career development program interventions. Moreover, the processes typically used in program delivery relate to counselors' primary areas of expertise. These processes are counseling, assessment, career information services, placement services, consultation procedures, and referrals. Professional school counselors can use their knowledge and skills related to career development to empower teachers and parents/guardians to function as collaborators in career services delivery.

The development of a systematic and coordinated career development program across grades K–12 requires an understanding of the developmental tasks confronting students as they progress through school. Having an awareness of the tasks students deal with at all levels of schooling prepares school personnel to work collaboratively in program development and implementation. A comprehensive understanding of the career development process also sets the stage for developing program interventions that are sequential and cohesive. Thus, the following sections of this chapter (and the primary topics of the following chapters) focus on career development tasks, program goals, and recommended interventions for elementary, middle/junior high school, and high school students, respectively.

CAREER DEVELOPMENT IN THE ELEMENTARY SCHOOLS

Careers unfold and develop throughout the life course. Ignoring the process of career development occurring in childhood is similar to a gardener disregarding the quality of the soil in which a garden will be planted. For children, school and leisure activities represent their work. These activities provide essential learning experiences that shape self-perceptions and understandings of the world-of-work. They form the seedbed from which children begin to identify their preferences and connect themselves to their futures as workers.

One approach addressing career development in childhood is the children's conceptions of career choice and attainment model (CCCA) developed by Howard and Walsh (2010, 2011). This innovative model is based on principles of cognitive development and emphasizes the dynamic interaction between children and their respective environments. The model includes six levels of reasoning, with each level involving increasingly complex formulations of career choices and attainment. More specifically, CCCA proceeds from a focus on external, observable objects or activities of an occupation, to the steps taken to choose and enter an occupation, to the dynamic consideration of multiple factors involved in pursuing a career (Howard & Walsh, 2011). The CCCA model organizes children's concepts of career choice and attainment around three approaches (Association, Sequence, and Interaction) children use to reason about career-related processes.

In the first category of career reasoning in the CCCA model, Association, the child uses external objects, activities, and/or experiences associated with a job. For example, Rosita at age 5 may become fascinated with the job of firefighter. She might wear the work clothes of a firefighter and desire to visit fire stations in order to play out her occupational fantasy. A child at this level cannot differentiate between how jobs are chosen and how jobs are secured. Level 1 of Association is Pure Association in which the job or career simply exists for the child. Children in Level 2 of Association, Magical Thinking, can describe a method for a job choice and attainment but cannot explain a process by which the method they associate with the job or career leads to the actual choice or attainment of a job/career (Howard & Walsh, 2011).

As children continue their cognitive development, they move to the Sequence level in the CCCA model. Sequence involves the level in which children shift from fantasy or imagination to the types of activities and tasks that are of interest to them (Howard & Walsh, 2011). Careers not connected to interests are excluded. Using interests to conceptualize career choice and attainment leads to the child's consideration of his/her strengths and weaknesses relative to occupational requirements (e.g., I like math and get good grades in that subject, which is a requirement of becoming an engineer). This more engaged, but still limited, self-reflection is heavily influenced by factors such as perceived gender appropriateness followed by prestige and social class. The Sequence approach can be characterized by children being able to identity an activity, event, situations and/or condition that leads to the choice and attainment of a job or career. Children understand choice and attainment as separate processes and can explain the relationship between them (Howard & Walsh, 2010). Level 3, External Activities, involves children being able to describe a process of learning about jobs and then choosing one that they like. Children at Level 3 can also describe the external, observable, and learnable skills that can lead to securing a job (Howard & Walsh, 2010). For example, when Rosita achieves this level, she might explain that she likes science, is good at it, and, because those are required for being a scientist, might declare that becoming a scientist is a job she wants to do. To become a scientist, Rosita might further explain that she must complete high school, go to college, study science, graduate from college, and get a job as a scientist. In this example, Rosita also exemplifies Level 4, Internal Processes and Capacities, in which she can match herself to a job.

The Interaction approach in the CCCA model occurs when children are able to define the act of choosing a job or career as a process involving a dynamic interaction of self-knowledge and personal attributes with environmental opportunities. In Level 5 (Interaction), adolescents describe a dynamic interaction of multiple causes at the individual, relational, and immediate environmental levels (Howard & Walsh, 2011). Level 6, the final level, is Systemic Interaction, in which dynamic interactions of multiple causes at the individual, relational, and immediate environmental levels and systemic levels are identified.

The CCCA model provides useful information for considering how a child or adolescent's cognitive development interacts with environmental factors to influence career development processes. It also provides a more current explanation that stands alongside classic developmental models, such as Erikson's (1963).

Prior to entering elementary school, children have moved through the first two of Erikson's (1963) eight stages of development. Those who have coped successfully with these stages have developed a sense of trust and autonomy. Thus, children ideally enter school believing they can trust the adults in their world and that they will be able to cope successfully with challenges they will encounter. Children operating from a perspective of trust and self-sufficiency are likely to approach school tasks with a positive and enthusiastic attitude. Children who have not been as successful in developing trust and autonomy will operate from a different attitudinal stance. These children will be more likely to question whether they can trust others. They may also lack confidence concerning their ability to master the tasks they confront. Erikson notes that when trust and autonomy are not achieved, children experience the emotional consequences of mistrust, doubt, and shame. To overcome these negative consequences, it is critical that children experience success and support.

Havighurst (1972) notes that during infancy and early childhood (ages 0 to 5), children encounter a series of critical developmental tasks. For example, during this developmental stage children:

1. Learn to walk
2. Learn to eat solid foods
3. Learn to talk
4. Learn to control elimination of bodily wastes
5. Learn sex differences and modesty
6. Learn to relate emotionally to family members
7. Prepare to read
8. Learn to identify the difference between right and wrong

Havighurst notes that to progress to subsequent stages of development, children must be successful in coping with these tasks. Failure to cope with these tasks successfully "leads to unhappiness in the individual, disapproval of society, and difficulty with later tasks" (p. 2).

Rosita, introduced at the beginning of this chapter, had experienced events in her life that did not foster the acquisition of many of the skills identified by Havighurst (1972). Her father's absence and her mother's drug-induced emotional absences also made it difficult for Rosita to believe that she could count on adults being there for her. She also wondered about her own self-worth and capabilities. She hoped that she would do okay at school, but deep down she was convinced that she would not do well. What she needed most as she entered school was to encounter adults who consistently supported her. She would also need remedial assistance to enhance her interpersonal and academic skills, especially in the area of reading.

During the elementary school years, children begin formulating a sense of identity through greater interaction with the world beyond their immediate families. Interactions with peers, teachers, parents, and community members shape the child's self-perceptions. Through exposure to adult life patterns via observations in schools, community activities, home, and the media, children draw conclusions about their lives. The conclusions children draw include assumptions about their current and future place in the world.

Porfeli, Hartung, and Vondracek (2008, p. 28) summarize their review of the literature pertaining to career development in childhood and note that (a) children know much more about the world-of-work than many people believe, (b) career aspirations of children are influenced by gender-based stereotypes, and these aspirations tend to be stable across the elementary school years, (c) career aspirations are influenced by occupational stereotypes that move girls away from science, technology, engineering, and math-related occupations and boys away from female-dominated occupations, (d) children from economically challenged situations as well as Hispanic and African American children tend to identify less prestigious career aspirations than do their more affluent and Caucasian peers, and (e) children tend to relinquish more glamorous aspirations for more realistic ones that are in line with their skills and interests as they progress through elementary school.

Erikson (1963) proposes that during elementary school, children encounter developmental stages related to developing initiative (ages 4 to 6) and industry (ages 6 to 12). These qualities are essential to the career development process. If they are not developed, then children experience guilt and inferiority. These negative consequences do not foster the sort of active and broad-based exploration that is necessary for children to advance in their career development. When a sense of initiative and industry are achieved, then children use their curiosity as a stimulus for exploring and gathering information about themselves and their worlds. Moreover, children experience feelings of personal effectiveness when they begin to do things on their own and experience positive outcomes associated with their self-initiated activities.

Havighurst (1972) suggests that during middle childhood (ages 6 to 11), children encounter an array of developmental tasks related to motor coordination, emotional development, and attitudinal perspectives related to self and others. Specifically, he notes that children during this stage must:

1. Develop physical skills for participating in games
2. Build positive attitudes toward themselves
3. Develop interpersonal skills
4. Become more tolerant
5. Learn appropriate gender social roles
6. Develop academic skills in reading, writing, and mathematics
7. Achieve a greater sense of independence
8. Develop attitudes toward groups and institutions

Applying these tasks to Rosita, it is clear that to advance in her career development Rosita would need continued support and assistance. Positive reinforcement for her accomplishments, encouragement to engage in new activities that interest her, and guidance in helping her identify tasks and chores that would foster a sense of industry are all important developmental interventions for Rosita. Although some interventions would require Rosita to work independently, it would also be important for her to engage in some group-oriented activities. Group activities would provide Rosita with opportunities to develop her interpersonal skills while also increasing her circle of friends. Thus, Rosita provides an excellent example of how general statements of developmental tasks must be contextualized for the individual student.

GOALS OF CAREER DEVELOPMENT INTERVENTIONS AT THE ELEMENTARY SCHOOL LEVEL

Obviously, there is tremendous variability in the quality of the life patterns to which children are exposed. Television, for example, often provides children with examples of men and women in gender-stereotyped roles and occupations (e.g., only women working as nurses, only men working as auto mechanics, women taking the primary or sole responsibility for homemaking and parenting). Children use this information to draw conclusions about the life patterns that are appropriate for them. As children are increasingly exposed to stereotypical behaviors and expectations, they begin to eliminate nontraditional life patterns and occupations from further consideration. Gottfredson (2002) contends that this gender-based elimination process begins as early as age 6. Gottfredson also suggests that between the ages of 9 and 13, children begin to eliminate those occupations from further consideration that they perceive to be less prestigious for their social class. Such variables as sex typing and prestige rankings interact with self-perceptions of abilities and interests, as well as with family and community expectations, to shape the decisions young people make about potential occupational options. Geography also factors into this equation because children in rural areas tend to be exposed to different (and often fewer) occupational options than children in more urban locations (Lee, 1984). Because elementary school children have not yet had the opportunity to fully explore their options and potentialities, an important goal of career development interventions in elementary school is to counteract environmental factors that pressure students to prematurely commit to educational and occupational options (Marcia, 1966). The use of nontraditional role models (e.g., male nurses, male secretaries, female physicians, female engineers) and exposure to a broad range of occupational environments in career development interventions is encouraged during the elementary school years. The same is true for any assessments used at this level. Relatedly, Tracey and Caulum (2015) report their successful efforts in minimizing gender bias in the development of the Inventory of Children's Activities, an instrument used to assess Holland types in children.

Rosita could benefit from being exposed to women working in a wide variety of occupational environments. Because the women in her immediate and extended families have worked in traditional occupations, it would be useful for Rosita to learn about women working in nontraditional occupations. Having the opportunity to be mentored by a woman in an occupation of interest to her might also help Rosita develop a sense of trust, autonomy, initiative, and industry.

Another goal of career development interventions with elementary school children is to provide an environment in which each student's natural sense of curiosity can flourish (Super, 1990). Curiosity provides the foundation for exploring. Children naturally express curiosity through fantasy and play. For example, children often engage intensely in fantasy-based play related to occupations such as physician, firefighter, teacher, professional athlete, and nurse. Curiosity can be guided to help students learn accurate information about themselves and their environments. For example, field trips to occupational environments related to a child's fantasy-based occupational interests reinforce the child's sense of curiosity and stimulate further exploring and the gradual crystallization of interests (Super, 1957).

It obviously would be useful for Rosita if her counselor would encourage her to identify and explore activities of high interest and then work with Rosita to help her process what she learns about herself as a result of participating in exploratory activities. Fostering a sense of curiosity related to herself and the world-of-work will help to increase Rosita's sense of what might be possible and to counteract environmental limitations she may be experiencing. In other words, it is a way to begin empowering Rosita.

Encouraging students to participate in activities relating to their interests nurtures a sense of autonomy, the anticipation of future opportunities for exploring, and the beginning of planful behaviors (Watts, Super, & Kidd, 1981). When interests connect with skills and capacities, a positive self-concept emerges which, in turn, provides the foundation for coping with the career development tasks of adolescence (Super, 1994). As children move toward adolescence, they must accomplish four major career development tasks. Specifically, they must (a) become concerned about the future, (b) increase personal control over their lives, (c) convince themselves to achieve in school and at work, and (d) develop competent work habits and attitudes (Super, Savickas, & Super, 1996, p. 131).

Unfortunately, when these four tasks are compared with data from the National Assessment of Educational Progress's Career and Occupational Development Project (a survey of approximately 28,000 9-year-old children), one might conclude that elementary school students have been only marginally successful in accomplishing these tasks. Results from this survey indicate that children have limited self-knowledge and limited occupational information and take limited responsibility for their behavior and future career decision-making (Miller, 1977). Clearly, these results provide cause for concern because children who are not able to accomplish the career development tasks they encounter in the elementary school are at risk for even more difficulty when they encounter the career development tasks presented to them during their secondary school experience. Thus, there is the need to consider how career development interventions might be provided to elementary school students in a more systematic and effective fashion.

Based on the counseling and developmental literature, career development goals for elementary school children should be directed toward helping children develop basic skills and awareness in the following areas:

Self-knowledge

Skills to interact with others

Basic skills in educational and occupational exploration

Awareness of the benefits of educational achievement

Awareness of the relationship between work and learning

Basic skills to understand and use career information

Awareness of the importance of personal responsibility and good work habits

Awareness of how work relates to the needs and functions of society

An understanding of how to make decisions

Awareness of the interrelationship of life roles

Awareness of different occupations and changing male/female roles

Awareness of the career planning process

CAREER DEVELOPMENT INTERVENTIONS IN THE ELEMENTARY SCHOOLS

When combined with the ASCA National Model and the National Career Development Guidelines (see Appendix E), these goals provide a framework for establishing career development goals and interventions. Because self-awareness provides the foundation for processing career information, career development interventions in the primary grades can focus first on helping students develop more sophisticated self-knowledge. For example, in grades K and 1, students can increase their self-knowledge by describing themselves through drawings, writing sentences describing the things they like and the things that are important to them, and bringing some of their favorite things to school to show to their classmates. Sharing their self-descriptions with others helps students to clarify their self-concepts. Each of these activities can also emphasize the importance of appreciating the similarities and differences that exist among students in the classroom. Differences among students can be described as valuable contributions to the learning process because we often learn more from students who are different from us than from those who are like us in our interests, skills, or backgrounds. Activities that encourage students to focus on clarifying their global self-concepts can be emphasized and can be easily infused into the curriculum during the first years of school. Differences in cultural traditions among students can be highlighted and celebrated.

In clarifying her self-concept, it is likely that Rosita would benefit from understanding that her family situation is not something that she caused. Emphasizing her positive relationship with her grandmother may be useful as well. In processing the contextual differences among students, it would be important for Rosita's teacher to discuss the different ways to define family. This may help Rosita focus on what she has rather than what she has lost regarding her family structure.

Activities that help students learn more about themselves can be supplemented with activities that focus on educational and occupational exploration as children progress through the primary and intermediate grades. For example, in the primary grades students can identify the occupations of their family members (e.g., parents, grandparents, aunts, and uncles) as well as the level and type of education each family member attained. As students share this information, the relationship between education and work can be stressed (e.g., some jobs require a college education, and others may require a different type of training such as trade school or an apprenticeship). Differences in family members' occupations can be discussed as strengths (e.g., it takes people working in a wide variety of occupations to make our society function effectively). To counteract occupational sex-typing, men and women working in nontraditional occupations can be invited to school to discuss their work. (To expand Rosita's awareness of occupational options, it would be useful for Rosita to be exposed to Latinas working in professional occupations.)

Beale and Williams (2000) discuss the "anatomy of a school-wide career day" (p. 205) in an elementary school setting. Specifically, they point out that much planning goes into making the career day successful. They note that successful career days provide opportunities to break down occupational stereotypes, to involve parents/guardians as well as community and business representatives in the school counseling curriculum, and to help students begin making positive connections between themselves and their futures.

To prepare for the career day, Beale and Williams (2000) suggest that a planning committee (involving the counselor, teachers, administrators, community representatives, and parents) be established. The first step of the planning committee is to establish goals and objectives for the career day (e.g., expand students' awareness of the school-work connection, increase students' understanding of workers in the community, increase students' understanding of the interrelatedness of workers, increase students' awareness of traditional and nontraditional careers).

Next, the planning committee should identify a timeline for completing specific tasks (e.g., writing and mailing letters informing parents and teachers of the date, time, place, goals, and objectives of the career day). Concerning the timing of the career day, counselors may want to connect the career day to the NCDA's Career Development Month (usually in November). The NCDA sponsors a poetry and picture contest during National Career Development Month and offers resources that counselors can use to prepare for activities such as a school-wide career day. Clearly, the planning committee must systematically select speakers for career day. Using Holland's occupational categories (i.e., Realistic, Investigative, Artistic, Social, Enterprising, and Conventional) as a guide for identifying representative occupations may be useful. Surveying teachers and parents, contacting the local chamber of commerce, and soliciting suggestions from the planning committee members are ways to identify potential career-day speakers. When inviting potential speakers to participate, it helps to identify the time and place of the event, the purpose of the career day, the specific topics to be discussed, and the format (e.g., "show and tell" versus lecture) for discussing the work-related topics. Once workers agree to participate, Beale and Williams (2000) recommend sending speakers a confirmation letter containing the vital information for their participation. As the day approaches, school announcements reminding students and school personnel of the event should be made.

Additional issues to be addressed by the planning committee include deciding on the format to be used during the career day (e.g., whether a central location will be used, whether students will rotate from classroom to classroom to meet with speakers, or whether speakers will rotate from classroom to classroom). Once the plans for the career day are finalized, counselors should construct a detailed schedule to distribute to all participants.

Student preparation for the career day can include creating a mural of all workers in the school, having students interview their parents/guardians to gain information about their work, having students create poster presentations of workers using pictures in magazines and newspapers, and having students generate a list of possible interview questions to be used during the career day.

On career day, volunteers should be assigned to meet speakers when they arrive and help them get oriented. Speakers should also be asked to complete an evaluation of their experience that can be turned in at the end of the day. Evaluating the effectiveness of the day is important for improving future career days. Thank-you notes should be sent to all involved. After the career day, counselors can engage in classroom guidance activities to help students assimilate the information they learned, discuss their perceptions of the jobs they learned about, and identify next steps to take to learn more about the world-of-work.

Students in grades K and 1 can begin the process of learning about work by focusing on occupations with which they have the most immediate relationship (e.g., occupations of family members, occupations in the school setting, occupations in their neighborhoods). Then, elementary school students can gradually learn about occupations that are more remote (e.g., occupations in the community, occupations in the state, occupations in the nation, and occupations throughout the world) as they progress from grades 2 to 5. Using a proximity-distance scheme to guide students in the acquisition of occupational information helps students understand the relevance of work in their lives and the ways in which various workers contribute to society. At each level of proximity, the relationship between work and the educational requirements for performing specific occupations can be highlighted. Students can also discuss what is required to perform occupations successfully. Job-content skills (the specific skill requirements for each occupation), functional skills (the skills that are transferable across occupations), and self-management skills (e.g., being reliable, getting along with coworkers, being trustworthy, completing assignments on time) can be integrated into these discussions as well.

Beale (2000) provides an excellent example as to how a well-conceived field trip can enhance career awareness in elementary school students. Using a field trip to a hospital as an illustrative example, Beale notes that for this sort of activity to be useful it must be carefully planned and implemented. For example, in planning for a career awareness field trip, counselors need to involve teachers, students, workplace personnel, and parents. In addition to identifying specific objectives of the trip and securing consent from administrators, parents, and teachers, counselors should also engage in a dry run through the worksite prior to the trip. During the preliminary worksite visit, the counselor should meet with worksite representatives (e.g., administrators and workers with whom the students will interact) to clarify the purpose and duration of the visit and what opportunities will be made available to the students. Copies of any interview questions the students will be asking should be provided to all relevant employees. Eliminating surprises during the visit and helping employees to be prepared will help to maximize the effectiveness of the trip.

It is important to note, however, that students also need to be well prepared for the field trip. Strengthening the pre-visit interest and motivation of students will increase the chances of the trip being successful. Ways to accomplish this involve engaging students in pre-trip classroom career activities. For example, in preparing bulletin boards related to the field trip, students can bring in pictures of workers and services provided in the worksite. Students can engage in classroom discussions on what to look for during the field trip. Preparing sample questions (e.g., How long have you been doing this kind of work? What do you like best/least about your job? How long did you have to go to school to do what you do?) that students can ask of workers helps to guide student learning for the field trip. (It is also important to let students know that questions such as "How much money do you make?" are inappropriate.) Having workers come to the classroom (in their work clothes) can also raise student interest and motivation for the field trip. Here, counselors should keep in mind the importance of providing examples of non-stereotypical workers (e.g., a female physician, a male nurse, an African American female CEO). Additional preparatory activities can include drawing pictures of the worksite, looking in the Yellow Pages or surfing the Web to identify the number of related worksites in the area, and talking about whether students have ever visited a similar worksite.

Beale (2000) also recommends that counselors use the time en route to the worksite as an opportunity for preparing students. For example, giving each student a list of specific occupations to look for in the worksite is one way to focus student thinking en route to the worksite, as are providing students with scrambled work sheets; hidden word puzzles; or crossword puzzles using words related to the different occupations, work materials, and equipment that they will see on the tour.

After the visit, Beale (2000) recommends activities that reinforce student learning and career awareness. For example, class discussions related to student reactions to the visit that focus on listing the occupations observed, identifying school subjects related to the occupations the students observed, and discussing the interrelationship of various occupations (e.g., "What would happen if there were no nurses, custodians, receptionists, orderlies, etc.?") represent useful follow-up activities. Having students prepare a scrapbook containing information related to the field trip and/or developing a slide presentation of the visit (in which students compose and narrate the script) also represent important activities that can be connected to the curriculum. Conducting an evaluation of the activity (e.g., asking students to identify whether they learned more about work in the worksite visited and whether they enjoyed the activities before, during, and after the visit) is an important final step in the process.

Educational and occupational exploration activities can be infused into the curriculum in a variety of additional ways. For example, assignments highlighting the various types of work required in different geographic locations can be integrated into the social studies curriculum. Language arts assignments (e.g., short-story writing) can also be constructed to help students learn more about what workers do in different occupations and to express their important self-characteristics (e.g., writing an autobiography). The art curriculum can include drawing, painting, and photographing workers in various occupations.

Activities to help students learn about the career planning and decision-making process could include having students read biographies and then discussing the important career decisions made by the people whose biographies they read. Students can be encouraged to consider what constitutes a "good" rather than a "bad" career decision as they discuss the biographies they read. In addition, students can use a timeline to chart the important events that influenced the decisions that the people they read about made in their lives.

Encouraging students to read stories about people working in nontraditional occupations can contribute to counteracting the effects of occupational sex-typing. Discussions can include the ways in which culture, gender, and social class may have influenced the career development of the person in the biography.

Another key focus in providing career development interventions at the elementary school level is that of increasing students' awareness. Interventions that increase students' self-awareness, occupational awareness, awareness of the relationship between work and education, and awareness of how career decisions are made are all important topics to address with elementary school students. Students should be encouraged to engage in activities that foster broad self- and career exploration to arouse interest in the future. A sense of internal control (e.g., "I can influence my direction"), the belief that it is important to be concerned about the future (e.g., "What happens to me is important to me"), and an attitude of personal competence or self-efficacy (e.g., "I am able to do what I am expected to do") should also be outcomes of career development interventions at the elementary school level (Super et al., 1996). Armed with these beliefs, students are prepared to cope with the career development tasks they will confront at the middle/junior high school level.

Magnuson and Starr (2000) offer the following thoughts to guide the planning of career development interventions:

1. Become a constant observer of children:

   Notice how children approach tasks.

   Notice the activities in which children choose to participate.

   Observe and encourage the child's initiative taking.

   Notice the thematic patterns emerging in each child's activities.

2. Consider the processing of an activity as important as the activity itself.

   To help children develop a sense of industry rather than inferiority, focus feedback on the specifics of children's efforts.

   Accompany career awareness and career exploration activities with opportunities for students to express their beliefs about themselves in relation to various occupations. (p. 100)

All of these suggestions must be viewed within the context of reality, however. One dimension of that reality is that elementary school counselors receive little support for delivering career services to their students. For example, Perkins (2012) examined school counselors' perceptions of elementary school counselor roles related to the three content areas of work focus (Personal/Social, Academic, Career Development) identified by the National Standards for School Counseling Programs (Campbell & Dahir, 1997). Participants (124 elementary school counselors and 65 elementary school teachers) completed the School Counselor Role Survey, which assessed their perceptions of the importance of school counselor roles, specifically those related to the content areas advocated by ASCA. Two primary research questions were addressed: (a) "What value do stakeholders place on elementary school counselor roles?" and (b) "Do stakeholders' perceptions differ on the values placed on elementary school counselor roles?" Of the three content areas, Career Development received the lowest overall mean score. Essentially, elementary school counselors and teachers were neutral concerning the value of elementary counselors engaging in the delivery of career services to their students. Participants also indicated that they do not view career roles for elementary school counselors to be as important as personal/social and academic roles. This is discouraging and ignores another important reality: that students in elementary school are already forming beliefs about their future possibilities. When students are encouraged to view school as their important work as opposed to an irrelevant chore and begin to link their actions and choices to "having a job someday" (as our elementary school counselor stated at the beginning of this chapter), then their motivation and level of school engagement increase. Unfortunately, the opposite is also true and more likely when school counselors are not engaged in career development.

PARENTAL INVOLVEMENT

Parents have substantial influence over the career development of their children. Parents provide the greatest amount of indirect and direct exposure to work for their children. Most adults can recount numerous instances in which they recall their parents conveying positive and negative expressions of their work experiences. These expressions influence children vicariously as they formulate their understanding of an area of life they have yet to encounter directly. Thus, children rely on adults and peers for information. As has been noted, children use the information they receive to make preliminary decisions about the appropriateness of the occupational options of which they are aware.

Young (1994) suggests that the influence parents exert on the career development process is most effective when it is planned, intentional, and goal oriented. However, many parents possess minimal knowledge regarding career development theory and how environmental factors influence the career development process of children. Thus, it is important that counselors help parents to learn ways to contribute positively to the career development of their children. Counselors can begin by providing parents with information about the career development process (e.g., during elementary school, children are encouraged to expand their awareness related to self and the world-of-work). Counselors can also explain to parents how the environment affects options children are willing to consider. For example, the influence of occupational stereotyping within the media and gender-role stereotyping can be discussed with parents. Finally, counselors can help parents identify specific strategies they can use to facilitate career development in their children. Engaging in conversations in which parents provide accurate occupational information and challenge occupational stereotyping represents an obvious, yet important, way that parents can foster positive career development in their children. Parent-child career conversations regarding career development should foster a sense of curiosity, openness to possibilities, awareness of options, and a positive attitude toward the world-of-work.

Herr et al. (2004) identify eight ways parents can help children advance in their careers. These strategies include the following:

1. Parents can encourage children to analyze important self-characteristics (e.g., interests, capacities, and values).
2. When parents are familiar with specific work requirements for jobs, they can communicate these to their children.
3. Parents can discuss the importance of work values in work behavior.
4. Parents can explain the relationship between work, pay, and the economic condition of the family.
5. Parents can connect children with informational resources (e.g., other workers, books, films) for acquiring accurate career information.
6. Parents can be careful to avoid stereotyping occupational alternatives and workers.
7. Parents can provide children with opportunities for work in the home and community.
8. Parents can provide children with opportunities to learn and practice decision-making skills. (p. 364)

Helping parents become aware of their own attitudes toward work and occupations, exposing children to work opportunities in the home and community, and providing support to children as they engage in career decision-making tasks are all ways to help children cope effectively with the career development process. By empowering parents with knowledge and information that can be used to help their children cope effectively with career development tasks, counselors make an important contribution to the career development of the students with whom they work.

Both Rosita and her mother could benefit from learning more about the career development process. Helping Rosa understand how careers develop would give her information that she could use to manage her own career development more effectively. Coaching Rosa as to the ways she could help Rosita with her career development would not only help Rosita but would also help Rosa feel more effective as a parent. Strengthening the bond between Rosa and Rosita would help Rosita develop the trust and autonomy she needs to move forward in her development.

MyCounselingLab®

Start with Topic 6—Career Counseling in Schools.

Watch the video *21st Century Career Development Interventions in the Schools: Dr. Carol Dahir* and complete Student Activity #7 on page 288.

SUMMARY

New parents often wonder which occupations their children will select later in life. What many parents do not realize is that children begin charting courses toward specific occupations early in life. Occupational selection represents the confluence of genetic and environmental influences that shape the career course. Like any developmental task, the career development process can be approached systematically and intentionally, or it can be approached haphazardly and passively. Most parents would prefer that their children receive systematic career development assistance oriented toward providing children with the competencies required for managing their careers effectively. For elementary school children, the task is to learn more about themselves and the educational/occupational options that are available. By providing support, dispelling bias in occupational perceptions, and helping children acquire accurate information about themselves and the world-of-work, counselors provide children with the foundation for effective career planning and decision-making.

CASE STUDY

Robert is a nine-year-old African American male in the fifth grade at a local urban elementary school. Robert is a below-average student. Although he is at the top of his class in science, his reading and writing skills are below grade level. His teacher describes Robert as a likable, outgoing child who causes too many disruptions in the classroom. Although Robert responds well to the adults in the school, he has been referred to the principal several times for bullying other students.

Robert's life outside of school is challenging. His biological father left home after a divorce when Robert was age six and is now incarcerated for dealing drugs. His mother remarried and moved to another state when he was seven years old, and he has lived with his legal guardians, his paternal grandparents, since his mother left. Although he visits his father in prison, he has seen his mother infrequently since she left. Robert's grandfather is a retired police officer who is not involved much with Robert (he says he already raised his kids). Robert's grandmother is the primary caregiver and has met with school administrators and you (school counselor) expressing her concerns about Robert (low achievement, referrals, and lack of friends).

When prompted, Robert identifies sports as his main interest. He cannot identify anything in school that he really likes besides gym class. In casual conversation, Robert talks about being a professional athlete when he gets older. In three meetings with you at school, Robert has talked excitedly about rejoining his father when he is released from prison but resists any discussion about his mother. He seems ambivalent about his grandparents and struggles to identify any friends in school. Robert explains that he spends most of his time outside of school at the park with boys from the middle school.

If you were Robert's school counselor, how would you address Robert's career development needs? Who would you involve in your career work with him? Which theories do you think would be helpful to you in understanding his situation? How might you foster a stronger sense of self-esteem and motivation in him?

STUDENT ACTIVITIES

1. What career development tasks do you think are most important to help elementary school–age children address?

2. What factors do you think could negatively influence the career development of children?

3. What are three strategies you could use to foster positive career development in children?

4. Why do you think there is resistance to providing career interventions with elementary school children?

5. How could you help parents/guardians to help their children experience positive career development?

6. Interview an elementary school student about his or her career development. Ask this student what occupations s/he thinks are possible for him/her. Ask whether the student thinks there are any occupations that are not possible. Ask your interviewee to discuss why s/he thinks certain occupations may not be possible. Ask what occupation s/he would choose if s/he could choose anything. Then, explore with your interviewee what s/he thinks is attractive about that occupation.

7. Refer to the MyCounselingLab® Video and Resource Library and select the video entitled *21st Century Career Development Interventions in the School: An Interview with Dr. Carol Dahir*. How would you use Dr. Dahir's comments to convince your principal and school board of the importance of career development interventions in elementary schools?

Sample Career Development Activities for Elementary School Students

Interesting Activities

NOICC CAREER DEVELOPMENT GUIDELINES: Self-Knowledge

ASCA STANDARDS: Standard A—Students will acquire the skills to investigate the world-of-work in relation to knowledge of self and to make informed career decisions.

PURPOSE: To discuss interests related to various activities.

OBJECTIVE: Students will learn to connect interests to activities.

MATERIALS: Magazines and scissors

INTRODUCTION: Discuss the importance of participating in activities that we find enjoyable. All activities, including work, can be fun when we participate in activities that we enjoy. The opposite is also true, however. When we participate in activities, including work, that we do not enjoy, we experience different reactions. Ask students to discuss how they feel when they participate in activities they like versus activities they do not like.

ACTIVITIES: Have each student cut out pictures from magazines demonstrating people engaged in activities that the student enjoys. Students will share the pictures with the class and tell what the activity is and what they like about it using the following phrase: "What I find interesting about this activity is. . . ."

DISCUSSION: Discuss the different activities and interests revealed. Ask students if any of them liked the activities that were shared by any of the other students. Have the students identify which activities they like and say what they find interesting about that activity. Ask students if they disliked any of the activities shared. Have the students identify which activities they do not like and what they do not like about that activity.

CLOSURE: Emphasize that there is no "right or wrong" associated with the likes and dislikes expressed by students. What really matters is that the students are clear about what they find interesting. Discuss how students' interests can be linked to vocational and avocational activities. Emphasize the importance of both types of activities for providing outlets for expressing interests.

TIME: 45 minutes

EVALUATION/ASSIGNMENT: Have students construct a list of the activities they find interesting and the activities that they do not find interesting.

Skills I Have

NOICC CAREER DEVELOPMENT GUIDELINES: Self-Knowledge

ASCA STANDARDS: Standard A—Students will acquire the skills to investigate the world-of-work in relation to knowledge of self and to make informed career decisions.

PURPOSE: To discuss the skills students have developed.

OBJECTIVE: Students will be able to identify the skills they possess.

MATERIALS: Skills list handout, paper, and pencils

INTRODUCTION: Discuss the fact that all people have many skills. Some skills are learned in school, some are learned at home or in play, and others seem to be "natural" skills. Distribute a list of skills to the students. Review the list to be sure that the students understand the skills listed.

ACTIVITIES: Have students list three activities they participate in that they enjoy. Divide students into groups of four. Assign each student one of the following roles: interviewer (two students), interviewee, and recorder. The interviewee must identify one activity that he or she enjoys. The interviewers must try to identify as many skills as possible that the interviewee uses when participating in the activity. The interviewee must say either "yes" or "no" to the skills the interviewers identify. The recorder lists the skills that the interviewee uses in the activity. After 10 minutes, the leader should stop the activity and ask students to rotate their roles. At the conclusion of each interview, give the recorder's list to the interviewee.

DISCUSSION: Discuss the importance of recognizing the skills we possess. Indicate the reasons why it is useful to identify the skills we use when we participate in activities that we enjoy. Review how identifying these skills can be useful in career planning.

CLOSURE: Repeat the activity until the students have a skills list for all three activities (it is recommended that this activity take place over multiple sessions; e.g., three 30-minute sessions). Have students review their skills lists. Ask them to circle the skills that appear on more than one list. Discuss the importance of focusing on these skills in career exploration.

TIME: 60–90 minutes

EVALUATION/ASSIGNMENT: Ask students to identify occupations relating to the skills appearing on more than one list.

Feelings

NOICC CAREER DEVELOPMENT GUIDELINES: Self-Knowledge

ASCA STANDARDS: Standard A—Students will acquire the skills to investigate the world-of-work in relation to knowledge of self and to make informed career decisions.

PURPOSE: To discuss the importance of understanding the feelings of others.

OBJECTIVE: Students will identify feelings from non-verbal cues and identify ways to respond to the feelings of others.

MATERIALS: Pictures of persons expressing various emotions, chalkboard, and chalk

INTRODUCTION: Explain the importance of being sensitive to the feelings of others. Talk with students about how they feel when others are insensitive to their feelings. Contrast these situations with those in which others are sensitive to students' feelings. Begin by brainstorming feelings. List the feelings students identify on the board.

ACTIVITIES: Brainstorm feelings and list them on the board. Then show students pictures of persons expressing various emotions. Have students guess the feelings being expressed. List the feelings on the board.

DISCUSSION: Discuss with students how they could respond to each of the feelings listed. Role play various responses (noneffective responses and effective responses). Have students react to each response by identifying how they might feel if someone responded to them in that way.

CLOSURE: Emphasize that being able to recognize and respond to the feelings of others is very important in effective interpersonal communication.

TIME: 45 minutes

EVALUATION/ASSIGNMENT: Give students three statements, each of which expresses different feelings (e.g., happiness, sadness, anger). For example, "It hurt my feelings when the teacher yelled at me for something I did not do." Instruct the students to write how they would respond to each statement if it were expressed by one of their friends (e.g., "You sound sad that the teacher yelled at you.").

What Is a Friend?

NOICC CAREER DEVELOPMENT GUIDELINES: Self-Knowledge

ASCA STANDARDS: Standard A—Students will acquire the skills to investigate the world-of-work in relation to knowledge of self and to make informed career decisions.

PURPOSE: To identify what is valued in friendships with others.

OBJECTIVE: To enhance self-awareness and the awareness of others; to determine valued attributes in a friend.

MATERIALS: Paper, pencils, poster board or chalkboard and chalk

INTRODUCTION: Ask students, "What is a friend?"

ACTIVITIES: Students will answer individually or divide into groups to answer the question "What is a friend?" The leader will write on the chalkboard or poster board words that describe a friend. Students may then draw an illustration of "what a friend is."

DISCUSSION: Discuss students' definitions of what a friend is; ask students to prioritize these definitions (e.g., number them from 1 to 10); ask students if they have followed their own guidelines of "friendship" and why or why not; ask, "Is it important and why?" Focus on how friends can provide a source of support that helps one achieve goals or on how they can influence a person in ways that are counterproductive to goal achievement.

CLOSURE: Discuss how true friends help each other to achieve their goals.

TIME: 30–45 minutes

EVALUATION/ASSIGNMENT: Have students list five characteristics they want in a friend.

The "Problem Bucket"

NOICC CAREER DEVELOPMENT GUIDELINES: Self-Knowledge

ASCA STANDARDS: Standard A—Students will acquire the skills to investigate the world-of-work in relation to knowledge of self and to make informed career decisions.

PURPOSE: To discuss a range of problems that individuals are experiencing and possible solutions.

OBJECTIVE: Students will assist one another in thinking about problems that each is experiencing and possible solutions.

MATERIALS: Pencils, container ("bucket"), and note cards

INTRODUCTION: Explain to students the purpose of the "problem bucket": Individuals anonymously contribute, into the bucket, problems facing them. The problems will then be discussed and solutions explored.

ACTIVITIES: Ask students to write down on note cards the problems they are experiencing. Put these note cards into the bucket. Move students into small groups to discuss the problems and possible solutions. Ask students to handle information seriously and confidentially and to respect the anonymity of contributors.

DISCUSSION: Allow small groups to present problems they were discussing, as well as any solutions they developed, to the larger group. Encourage other groups to offer solutions as well.

CLOSURE: Discuss how many students share similar problems. Focus additional discussion on how it

feels to talk with others about problems and on how almost all problems have solutions.

TIME: 30–45 minutes

EVALUATION/ASSIGNMENT: Ask students to write a response to the following question: "As a result of this activity, what did you learn about 'problems' and how to solve them?" Answers should focus on the topics discussed in the activity, especially on the closure segment of the activity.

Comic Strips

NOICC CAREER DEVELOPMENT GUIDELINES:
Self-Knowledge; Educational and Occupational Exploration

ASCA STANDARDS: Standard A—Students will acquire the skills to investigate the world-of-work in relation to knowledge of self and to make informed career decisions; Standard C—Students will understand the relationship between personal qualities, education, training, and the world-of-work.

PURPOSE: To explore the ways in which comic strips reflect human behavior, personality, lifestyle, and so on.

OBJECTIVE: Students will be able to identify and discuss the ways in which comic strips reflect real people and society.

MATERIALS: A newspaper comic strip, comic books, books with collections of comic strips, etc.; pencil, paper, chalk, and a chalkboard

INTRODUCTION: Students will be asked to look through the newspaper comic section or comic books to find the ways in which comics reflect truth about life.

ACTIVITIES: Ask students to list the ways in which characters in the comics reflect human behavior and personality. Ask students to find examples in the comics of a family crisis, a conflict, a human value, a social problem, a prejudice, stereotypes (particularly about work-related issues, if desired), and a problem

at work. Then ask students to draw their own comic strips about a particular aspect of their own lives, such as school, a sport they play, or their choice of occupations.

DISCUSSION: Ask students how these comics reflect or fail to reflect real life in U.S. culture. Discuss how the comics are humorous and why students think others laugh at the situations in comics. Ask students to choose a comic character whom they would like to be and why. Ask students if they feel comics are purposeful or if the influence of comics is somehow negative (e.g., violence in a comic might be seen as a negative influence on children).

CLOSURE: Comics tell us about both common experiences in our culture and culture-specific problems people encounter. They often reveal how culture influences our responses to the problems we encounter. Finally, the main theme of comics is the importance of keeping perspective in dealing with problems and of maintaining a sense of humor. By developing effective coping strategies, one can manage all problem situations more effectively and the situations are less stressful.

TIME: 1 hour, but this activity can also be used over multiple meetings, especially if students are assigned to draw their own comic strip

EVALUATION/ASSIGNMENT: Students can respond to the following question: "How does humor help you handle the problems you encounter?"

Workers I Know

NOICC CAREER DEVELOPMENT GUIDELINES: Educational and Occupational Exploration

ASCA STANDARDS: Standard A—Students will acquire the skills to investigate the world-of-work in relation to knowledge of self and to make informed career decisions; Standard B—Students will employ strategies to achieve future career goals with success and satisfaction.

PURPOSE: To introduce students to occupations that they encounter each day.

OBJECTIVE: Students will identify the workers that they see every day in their lives.

MATERIALS: Chalkboard, chalk

INTRODUCTION: Discuss the fact that there are many types of workers that students encounter each day. Emphasize the point that each of these workers plays an important role in keeping our society functioning.

ACTIVITIES: List the workers that students see each day. Identify the role that each worker plays in helping the community function.

DISCUSSION: Discuss the importance of each occupation listed, the training required for each occupation, and the benefits associated with each occupation. Be sure to address gender stereotyping with each occupational selection (i.e., challenge students who assume that only members of one gender can perform a particular occupation).

CLOSURE: Reinforce the importance of learning more about occupations. Encourage students to continue listing occupations that they observe for the next two days.

TIME: 30–45 minutes

EVALUATION/ASSIGNMENT: Ask students to list the workers and their occupations that they observe in their school and community for the next two days.

Women and Men at Work

NOICC CAREER DEVELOPMENT GUIDELINES: Self-Knowledge; Educational and Occupational Exploration

ASCA STANDARDS: Standard A—Students will acquire the skills to investigate the world-of-work in relation to knowledge of self and to make informed career decisions; Standard C—Students will understand the relationship between personal qualities, education, training, and the world-of-work.

PURPOSE: To discuss gender-role stereotyping in work.

OBJECTIVE: Students will recognize that occupational selection does not have to be gender based.

MATERIALS: Two flip charts, markers

INTRODUCTION: Ask students to think about the workers that they see each day.

ACTIVITIES: Ask students to list on a sheet of paper at their desks the workers they see each day and whether they are male or female (e.g., principal—female; custodian—male; bus driver—female). Then, using two flip charts, label one "women" and the other one "men." Have students call out occupations that they have noticed. List the occupation under either "women" or "men," depending on the

gender of the worker in the occupation the student noticed.

DISCUSSION: Discuss the overlap of occupations on the "women" and the "men" charts. Ask students what conclusions they draw from the overlap. For occupations listed only on one chart, ask students to discuss whether they think a person of the opposite sex could perform those jobs. Challenge gender-based assumptions expressed by students.

CLOSURE: Emphasize the importance of not assuming that an occupation is for "women only" or for "men only" just because a particular occupation may be more populated by members of one gender than another.

TIME: 30–45 minutes

EVALUATION/ASSIGNMENT: Ask students to identify two people who are opposite in gender from the workers they listed originally. For example, if on the original list students noted a principal who was female, instruct them to identify a male who is a principal. If they cannot identify someone in their immediate environment, they can ask their family members if they know anyone who works in a particular occupation and is opposite in gender from the person on the original list.

Future Skills

NOICC CAREER DEVELOPMENT GUIDELINES: Self-Knowledge; Educational and Occupational Exploration; Career Planning

ASCA STANDARDS: Standard A—Students will acquire the skills to investigate the world-of-work in relation to knowledge of self and to make informed career decisions; Standard B—Students will employ strategies to achieve future career goals with success and satisfaction; Standard C—Students will understand the relationship between personal qualities, education, training, and the world-of-work.

PURPOSE: To discuss the future and the impact of technology on our daily lives.

OBJECTIVE: Students will become aware of the impact of technology on their future lives.

MATERIALS: Chalkboard and chalk

INTRODUCTION: Discuss how many of the things we do today are influenced by technology. For example, communication via e-mail, satellite television, microwave ovens, computers in cars, facsimile machines, and car phones all allow us to do things in ways that are very different from when our parents were growing up. Discuss the jobs that exist now because of technology. Compare how things are accomplished today with how things were done 100 years ago.

ACTIVITIES: Divide students into groups. Have each group work collaboratively on creating posters in which they make drawings of "life in the future."

DISCUSSION: Have students share their drawings and discuss the pictures they drew. Discuss what the pictures suggest regarding jobs in the future. Discuss what jobs might not exist in the future due to technology.

CLOSURE: Emphasize the implications of life in the future for career planning. For example, students can discuss the skills that will be needed to work in the future.

TIME: 45 minutes

EVALUATION/ASSIGNMENT: Have students write a short report identifying what they think will be fun about work in the future and what they think will be scary about work in the future.

Picture This!

NOICC CAREER DEVELOPMENT GUIDELINES: Self-Knowledge; Educational and Occupational Exploration; Career Planning

ASCA STANDARDS: Standard B—Students will employ strategies to achieve future career goals with success and satisfaction; Standard C—Students will understand the relationship between personal qualities, education, training, and the world-of-work.

PURPOSE: To discuss assumptions students make about workers based on race/ethnicity and gender.

OBJECTIVE: Students will recognize that race/ethnicity and gender are not occupational requirements.

MATERIALS: Magazines and scissors

INTRODUCTION: Explain to students that many people draw conclusions about occupational requirements based on false assumptions and factors that have nothing to do with the tasks of the job.

ACTIVITIES: Show students pictures of persons employed in different occupations (be sure to use a diverse sample of persons at work). Ask students to guess each person's occupation.

DISCUSSION: Discuss the assumptions students made in guessing each person's occupation. Discuss why it is not appropriate to relate demographic information to occupations. Discuss ways in which students' assumptions may be counterproductive in their own career development (e.g., because it can lead to eliminating occupations that might be very appropriate for the student).

CLOSURE: Encourage students to identify reasons that they might eliminate nontraditional occupations from consideration in their own career planning. Discuss whether these reasons are a good basis for career decision making.

TIME: 45 minutes

EVALUATION/ASSIGNMENT: Have students interview one person employed in a nontraditional occupation and ask the person to respond to questions such as:

1. What do you like about your occupation?
2. Was it difficult to choose a nontraditional occupation?
3. What are the challenges you face working in a nontraditional occupation?
4. Would you encourage others to consider working in a nontraditional occupation?

ABC List of Occupations

NOICC CAREER DEVELOPMENT GUIDELINES: Educational and Occupational Exploration

ASCA STANDARDS: Standard B—Students will employ strategies to achieve future career goals with success and satisfaction; Standard C—Students will understand the relationship between personal qualities, education, training, and the world-of-work.

PURPOSE: To have students list as many occupations as they can think of alphabetically and determine which require the most work from the worker.

OBJECTIVE: To identify occupations and consider which ones students think would require the most energy to perform.

MATERIALS: Chalkboard and chalk, pencils, and paper

INTRODUCTION: Ask students to construct an ABC list of occupations so that you have one job listed for each letter of the alphabet. Ask students which three jobs they think require the most work from the worker and why (be sure to have them discuss the criteria they used for defining the "most work"—manual labor, hours worked per day, etc.).

A variation of this activity is to divide the group into two and have each group compete against each other in constructing an alphabetical list of occupations within a pre-specified amount of time (e.g., 2 minutes). The leader can time the activity.

ACTIVITIES: Students will list occupations on the board or on paper.

DISCUSSION: Discuss how the students perceive the definition of work and the energy required in performing specific occupations. Discuss whether the jobs with the least or the most energy requirements are the least or the most desirable to the students and why. Ask students which jobs they feel earn the most money. Do they feel energy expended always leads to higher pay?

CLOSURE: Discuss the importance of knowing about jobs and job requirements. Emphasizing how our personal preferences influence our opinions about jobs is also an important part of this activity. The latter point also reinforces the notion that there is no one way to list preferred jobs. Each person will have his or her own list and reasons for preferring certain jobs and particular types of jobs.

TIME: 30–45 minutes

EVALUATION/ASSIGNMENT: Ask each student to write responses to the following question: "What type of 'work' do I prefer?" Next, have students complete this sentence: "After this activity, I think I know (choose 1): (a) a lot about jobs, (b) an average amount about jobs, or (c) a little about jobs." Then ask students to identify three jobs they would like to learn more about based on this activity.

School and Work

NOICC CAREER DEVELOPMENT GUIDELINES: Career Planning; Self-Knowledge; Educational and Occupational Exploration

ASCA STANDARDS: Standard B—Students will employ strategies to achieve future career goals with

success and satisfaction; Standard C—Students will understand the relationship between personal qualities, education, training, and the world-of-work.

PURPOSE: To discuss the relationship between school and work.

OBJECTIVE: Students will identify occupations that relate to specific school subjects.

MATERIALS: Chalkboard and chalk, pencils, and paper

INTRODUCTION: Begin by discussing the relationship between school and work.

ACTIVITIES: List school subjects (e.g., math, science, language arts, music, physical education) on the chalkboard. Divide students into small groups. Ask students to list occupations under each school subject that require the use of that subject (e.g., math—accounting, bank teller, cashier). Have each group write its list on the board.

DISCUSSION: Review the list from each group. Have students identify how they think the subject matter is used in each occupation. Discuss what would happen if a person in each occupation didn't have a background in a relevant subject matter.

CLOSURE: Reinforce the connection between school subjects and work.

TIME: 30–45 minutes

EVALUATION/ASSIGNMENT: Have students interview their family members to identify the subject areas that are important for performing their jobs.

Leaders and Followers

NOICC CAREER DEVELOPMENT GUIDELINES: Self-Knowledge; Educational and Occupational Exploration

ASCA STANDARDS: Standard A—Students will acquire the skills to investigate the world-of-work in relation to knowledge of self and to make informed career decisions; Standard B—Students will employ strategies to achieve future career goals with success and satisfaction; Standard C—Students will understand the relationship between personal qualities, education, training, and the world-of-work.

PURPOSE: To discuss the attributes of individuals considered to be "leaders."

OBJECTIVE: Students will be able to identify characteristics of a "leader" and compare them with the characteristics of a "hero."

MATERIALS: Chalkboard and chalk, pencils, and paper

INTRODUCTION: Begin by brainstorming the words that come to their minds when students think of the words *leader* and *follower*. List the words on the chalkboard under each term.

ACTIVITIES: Students should make a list of persons they consider to be great leaders, including artists, athletes, politicians, scientists, writers, pioneers, businesspersons, and entertainers. Write down the major achievements of these leaders and five common traits these individuals share (e.g., hard worker, natural talent, etc.). Ask students to name someone they know that has these leadership qualities (from home, school, etc.). Discuss the difference between a leader and a follower. What are the positive traits of both?

DISCUSSION: Review the characteristics of a leader. Ask if being a leader is always a good thing, and why or why not. Ask students to discuss if they prefer being a leader or a follower and to identify reasons for their preferences. Note that they may have preferences for leading in certain situations. When this latter situation occurs, ask students to discuss why they may prefer leading in certain situations but not in others. They should focus on the activities they are engaged in, how they feel about their abilities to complete these particular activities, and so on. Finally, discuss how people become leaders (e.g., Are they "born leaders" or can these skills be developed?). A parallel discussion can take place for "followers."

CLOSURE: Discussion should focus on the importance of leaders and followers in the workplace. Emphasize the importance of both. What would happen if everyone wanted to be a leader? What would happen if everyone wanted to be a follower?

TIME: 30–45 minutes

EVALUATION/ASSIGNMENT: Have students write down what skills they need to develop to become better leaders and better followers.

School: The Good and the Bad

NOICC CAREER DEVELOPMENT GUIDELINES: Self-Knowledge; Educational and Occupational Exploration

ASCA STANDARDS: Standard A—Students will acquire the skills to investigate the world-of-work in relation to knowledge of self and to make informed career decisions; Standard C—Students will understand the relationship between personal qualities, education, training, and the world-of-work.

PURPOSE: To have students explore their feelings about school in general.

OBJECTIVE: Students will think about what they like about school as well as their complaints about school.

MATERIALS: Chalkboard and chalk

INTRODUCTION: Make two lists on the board with headings "good" and "bad."

ACTIVITIES: Ask students to take turns writing something under a list of good or bad things about school. If the first student writes under the "bad" list, the next student must write under the "good" list, and vice versa. Examples might be, "I get to see my friends" or "I hate the school lunches."

DISCUSSION: Have students discuss the items on the lists. Encourage them to think of the ways school enhances their lives. Students will then brainstorm ideas for turning "bad" items into "good" items. For example, if a bad item is "homework," then participants can discuss what might be useful about homework. Students could also share strategies they use for making homework better or more enjoyable. Students can also talk about how and when they do their homework. Different strategies can be discussed. The same approach can be used for other "bad" items. Note that it is likely that all "bad" items may not be converted into "good" items. The leader will need to select which items to focus on in this exercise.

CLOSURE: Center the discussion on whether anything in life is all good. Emphasize the importance of turning "bad" into "good."

TIME: 30–45 minutes

EVALUATION/ASSIGNMENT: Students can list three items in their "bad" category that they could change into "good." Strategies for converting these items from bad to good should be identified.

Changes

NOICC CAREER DEVELOPMENT GUIDELINES: Self-Knowledge; Educational and Occupational Exploration; Career Planning

ASCA STANDARDS: Standard A—Students will acquire the skills to investigate the world-of-work in relation to knowledge of self and to make informed career decisions; Standard C—Students will understand the relationship between personal qualities, education, training, and the world-of-work.

PURPOSE: To explore the ways people change.

OBJECTIVE: Students will be able to discuss ways in which they have experienced change as individuals and changes that may likely occur in the future.

MATERIALS: Pencils, paper

INTRODUCTION: Ask students to list or name something about themselves that has changed.

ACTIVITIES: Ask students to name something about themselves that has changed (a) in the past 24 hours (such as clothes), (b) in the past week (something new learned in school), (c) in the past year (joined a sports team, changed grades), and (d) since birth. Then ask students to predict changes that are likely to occur in the future (next year, in 5 years, in 10 years, etc.).

DISCUSSION: Discuss the changes that each student has experienced and whether he or she considers these changes positive or negative. Discuss which changes students feel have had the greatest impact on who they are today. Discuss fears about changes likely to occur in the future and how individuals successfully deal with change in their lives. Ask what students might like to change about themselves or their environment and what impedes these changes from occurring.

CLOSURE: Review the discussion and ask students to write down things they notice about themselves that are changing in the next week or month. Request that students each choose something

they would like to work on changing in the next few weeks, and ask that they keep a journal of their progress regarding this change (e.g., get homework done on time, get up 10 minutes earlier, help with household chores, change looks somehow, etc.).

TIME: 45 minutes to 1 hour

EVALUATION/ASSIGNMENT: Share the journal with the leader.

■ ■

Career Investigators

NATIONAL CAREER DEVELOPMENT GUIDELINES: Educational and Occupational Exploration

ASCA STANDARDS: Standard C—Students will understand the relationship between personal qualities, education, training, and the world-of-work.

PURPOSE: Knowing where and how to obtain information about the world-of-work and postsecondary training/education.

OBJECTIVES: Students will be able to identify roles and responsibilities of individuals in the world-of-work.

MATERIALS: A big magnifying glass (paper or real); "tool box": a collection of tools that workers use

INTRODUCTION: Have or make an oversized faux magnifying glass (you can easily make one by duct-taping a roll of masking tape to a magic marker). Tell the students that you are investigating the work people do. Ask the students to help you in the investigation.

ACTIVITY:

1. Walk around classroom using the magnifying glass to get a closer look at various people and things in the room—act like a detective, without talking directly to students.
   - Make comments like "Hmmmm," "This is interesting," "I can use this as evidence."
   - As you're walking around, gather "evidence" of a teacher's work role and responsibilities.
2. Explain to students that they will help you investigate what people do while they are working. Ask three or four students to tell the class their definition of *investigate*, *work*, and *workers*.

3. Reveal the "tool box." Pull out one or two tools; ask individual students to help you by holding the tools.
4. Use questions to prompt student discussion/participation such as:
   - "Hmmm. . . . I wonder who would use this tool at work?"
   - "Who will demonstrate how a worker uses this tool?"
   - "What skills does someone need to use this tool at work?"
   - "Does anyone have a family member who uses this tool at work?"

Follow the same procedure with three or four more tools (depending upon students' attention span).

DISCUSSION: As you close this lesson, ask students to tell one thing they have discovered about workers.

CLOSURE: Ask students to help you learn more about what people do at work by observing workers at home or wherever they go:

   - "When you go home, look at your parents or grandparents or older sister or brother, or whoever else might live in your house with you. Try and notice the things that they do for work. Maybe you'll even want to ask them what they do at their work or what tools they get to use!"
   - "During our next lesson together, we will talk about your observations and you will get to see more of the tools in the tool box."

TIME: 30 minutes

EVALUATION/ASSIGNMENT: Students will demonstrate their engagement by following with their eyes and will contribute to the discussion by helping the investigators to identify occupations. Students may also volunteer definitions of *investigate*, *work*, and *workers*.

VOCABULARY:

- tool
- job title
- role
- responsibility
- investigate
- worker
- work

Possible "Tools" and Corresponding Occupations

Tool	Job Title	Role	Responsibility
Hammer	Carpenter	Build/repair houses	Follow plans/directions from homeowner
Wrench	Mechanic	Repair vehicles	Repair what the owner asks
Paintbrush	Painter (Could also be an artist)	Paint rooms/houses	Change color to satisfy the owner
Pencil	Writer	Write books	Meet deadlines
Hair Dryer	Beautician	Fix people's hair	Talk with people about what they want done with their hair
Bowl and Spoon	Chef	Cook meals	Follow recipe
Stethoscope	Doctor	Help people who are sick	Listen to patient
Ruler	Architect	Design buildings	Make sure the building is safe
Books	Librarian	Provide information and resources	Help people find books
Telephone	Receptionist	Answer questions	Provide accurate information
Calculator	Banker/Teller	Manage accounts	Accurately count money
Needle and Thread	Seamstress	Construct/repair garments	Create or repair clothing to meet the interests of people
Tractor	Farmer	Plant/grow crops	Take care of the crops/soil

A Few of My Favorite—And Not So Favorite!—Things

NATIONAL CAREER DEVELOPMENT GUIDELINES: Self-Knowledge

ASCA STANDARDS: Standard C—Students will understand the relationship between personal qualities, education, training, and the world-of-work.

PURPOSE: To develop awareness of self, work, and workers.

OBJECTIVE: Students will be able to identify likes and dislikes at home and at school.

MATERIALS: Puppet and activity sheet

INTRODUCTION: Puppet and counselor will facilitate a discussion with students including the following questions:

- "Is it important to have things you like to do? Why?"
- "What if I don't like everything I do? Is that okay?
- "What are some favorite things you like to do at home? At school?"

- "What are some things you don't like to do at home? At school?"

ACTIVITY:

1. Acting as both yourself and as a the puppet, use the previous questions to conduct a discussion of students' favorite and least favorite things to do at school and at home. Feel free to be silly and energetic as the puppet! Because students will be excited to share their ideas with the puppet, it will be extra necessary to encourage students to raise a quiet hand, take turns, and help them to focus their responses.
2. As the puppet, ask three or four students what their favorite subjects are at school. The puppet can share his/her favorite subject as well.
3. As the puppet, continue the discussion by asking what activities the students like and dislike when they are at home. Ask three or four more students to share their least favorite things at home. Be sure to include all students by using questions like "Who else feels this way?" or "Who else likes/dislikes to do that, too?" Encourage quiet hands instead of calling out.
4. As counselor and puppet, hand out *My Favorite/Least Favorite Things Activity Sheet*. In the first column, students will draw one thing they like to do at school and one thing they like to do at home. In the second column, students will draw something they dislike doing at school and one for at home.
5. Once students have completed their drawings on the activity sheet, encourage them to share their drawings. In large classes, you may want to divide the class in half—one side sharing what they like best, and the other side sharing what they like least.
6. As the counselor, ask, "How do you know what you don't like?" "How do you know what you do like?" Students' responses will indicate an early awareness of influences in their lives—such as "I don't like getting dirty" or "My brother likes drawing, but I like playing outside."

DISCUSSION: Puppet and counselor will conduct a summarizing discussion. Include:

a. Everyone had great ideas!
b. There were so many different ideas.
c. Everyone has different and similar ideas of what are his or her favorite and not-so-favorite things to do—and that is okay because that's what makes you YOU!
d. Some of our favorite and not-so-favorite things will stay the same as we grow up, and some of them will change as we grow up and change, too.
e. We make choices based on what we like and what we don't like.

Students will respond to and discuss these topics to show that they understand the concepts, especially that each person has favorite and not-so-favorite things he or she does, such as "Jayden likes math, and I like music!"

CLOSURE: As counselor, tell the puppet it's time to go. The puppet is at first sad to leave but then remembers how much fun he/she and the students had together and praises the students for their hard work. The puppet then thanks the students for letting him/her come to their classroom and promises to come back again soon.

EVALUATION/ASSIGNMENT: Students' drawings pertain to their likes and dislikes. Students are able to differentiate between the feelings they have when they are doing something they like and the feelings they have when they are doing something they dislike. Students will contribute to the discussion and listen to their peers.

TIME: 30 minutes

VOCABULARY:

- Favorite
- Least favorite/Not-so-favorite

WORKSHEET

My Favorite Things . . . Draw a picture of one or more of your favorite things.
at school . . .
at home . . .

My Least Favorite Things . . . Draw a picture of one or more of your least favorite things.
at school . . .
at home . . .

■ ■

Let's Play Dress-Up!

NATIONAL CAREER DEVELOPMENT GUIDELINES: Educational and Occupational Exploration

ASCA STANDARDS: Standard A—Students will acquire the skills to investigate the world-of-work in relation to knowledge of self and to make informed career decisions.

PURPOSE: Learning about the variety that exists in the world-of-work; explore specific occupations and their tasks and responsibilities.

OBJECTIVES: Students will identify a worker that they see or interact with regularly in their daily lives. Students will then dress like that specific worker, and role-play with the class. Have students provide a brief summary about the responsibilities and tasks of a worker in that profession.

MATERIALS: For this activity, students will mainly be bringing their own materials from home. In case students have limited materials available to them, be sure to have extra hats, jackets, and props for each student's occupation.

INTRODUCTION: Tell students to think about workers they see every day. Help remind them about all the different people they interact with throughout their day. This can include their parents/guardians, siblings, neighbors, bus drivers, crossing guards, teachers, administrators, and so on. Have students brainstorm a list and write down what they come up with.

ACTIVITY:

1. In the initial guidance lesson with students after brainstorming a list of workers, explain to students that for next time they will need to come prepared to class dressed like one of the people they see working on a daily basis. This can include teacher, homemaker, businessman/-woman, artist, bus driver, and so on—the possibilities are endless! Each student will then sign up for a specific occupation. It is okay if two or three (but no more than three) students choose the same occupation, as there may be some variation within that occupation (e.g., one might choose a kindergarten teacher, and another might choose a fifth-grade teacher; business employees

might also have similar but different tasks and responsibilities).

2. Have students use the Internet to research the tasks and responsibilities of a worker in that profession.

3. Students present to the class what they learned about the worker. You may invite parents to hear their child's presentation!

4. After presentations, students can have a "party" in which they mingle with one another and role-play as their worker. Snacks are optional based on budget or how much time is available. Most important, students should be able to tell other students about their "job" and what they have learned through their research.

DISCUSSION: To close the session, ask students how it felt to be someone else for a day. Encourage students to tell you what they liked or disliked about the job that they chose.

CLOSURE: In your next visit to the class, spend one guidance lesson conducting a follow-up discussion with students. Ask them what it was like to interview the worker they imitated or to research their occupation:

- "What things surprised you about the worker and his or her job?"
- "What do you like about the kind of work you explored? What do you dislike?"
- "Do you think when you grow up that you will want to do the work you chose now?"
- "Tell me some new things that you learned from your classmates." (Make a brainstorm list together.)

After discussing as a class, provide children with paper and crayons, markers, or colored pencils. Have students draw a picture of themselves as the workers they presented. Post them on the wall or bulletin board under a career-themed title. This will be a fun way to conclude the project and for kids to proudly demonstrate what they presented and learned!

TIME: 30–45 minutes

EVALUATION/ASSIGNMENT: Students will research their chosen occupation (help from grown-ups is permitted). Type of research (interview, Internet searches, or library) is up to grade level, ability, and availability. After researching, students will be able to "teach" what they have learned about their chosen occupations to their peers with the use of role play.

VOCABULARY:

- explore
- interview
- worker
- occupation
- role play

Career Collage Comic Strip

NATIONAL CAREER DEVELOPMENT GUIDELINES: Career Planning

ASCA STANDARDS: Standard B—Students will employ strategies to achieve future career goals with success and satisfaction.

PURPOSE: Being able to picture a future career goal and then be able to identify steps to achieving that goal. Students will demonstrate goals and steps through pictures and collage.

OBJECTIVE: Students will identify a career that interests them or one that they can see themselves participating in. Using this image as a goal, students will then identify specific steps in order to move from where they are today toward their goals. Each step and goal will be demonstrated in comic strip form using drawing, painting, written dialogue, or collage.

MATERIALS: Newspapers and magazines, poster boards, watercolor paints, crayons, markers, colored pencils, glue sticks, and scissors. Before the lesson, cut poster boards in half (students will not need full poster boards for this activity; a half is the perfect size for each student to map out his or her goal and steps).

INTRODUCTION: Ask students to share some of the things they might like to be when they grow up. Go around the room and let a few students tell the class their ideas. You can even share some of the things that you wanted to be when you were a kid. Ask students, "What does it take for someone to get to do his or her dream job?" On the board, make a list of what the students tell you (answers can include *education, working hard, doing a lot of jobs, going to college, meeting people*, etc.). Emphasize that we do not wake up one day and magically get to be what we dreamed of but, rather, that it takes a

lot of hard work, planning, and time. To get there, it takes many small and big steps.

ACTIVITY:

1. After sharing, tell the students to close their eyes and imagine themselves in their dream career. (If some students have more than one dream career, tell them to pick one for today. It's okay if it changes later on.) Prompts include:
   a. "Imagine what you would be doing at your job."
   b. "Think about who you would be working with. How old are the people you would be working with?"
   c. "How much money would you get paid at your job?"
   d. "What do you wear to your job?"
   If it helps, students can write down the ideas that come to mind as they are imagining themselves in their dream job.

2. After the students have solidified an idea of their dream job, tell them that this will be their goal. Then, talk with them about some of the steps that might help them get to their dream job. Students can share their goals for examples. As the steps become clearer, students can write these down on a sheet of paper as well. Have students number their steps. Students should have about 5 to 6 steps each (no more than 10).

3. Once students have identified their goals and steps, hand out the poster boards to each student. Tell students to divide their poster into enough boxes or spaces so that each of their steps and their goal can have one space each (you may want to demonstrate this on the board or on your own sheet of poster board). Then, tell students to number their boxes per

number of steps and write "My Goal" in the box where their goal will be. It should look something like this:

Step 1:	Step 2:	Step 3:	Step 4:	My Goal!:

4. If there is time, students may title their steps (i.e., Step 1: Practice a lot, Step 2: Do all my homework, etc.). After mapping out their posters, pass around the materials. Tell students that now they can look for pictures that demonstrate what their steps or goals look like. If they can't find a picture, they can draw things instead. Students may use words, but encourage them to demonstrate their goals through pictures as much as possible. Students can take time drawing, flipping through magazines, cutting out pictures, and gluing pictures to their comic strip collage. Note: This may take more than one guidance lesson to complete.

5. After day one, collect what the students have started and encourage them to continue thinking about their posters. On day two, students can pick up where they left off and complete their posters. After finishing, close day two with a discussion about goals and steps.

DISCUSSION: Have students explain the difference between long- and short-term goals. Talk about what it takes to reach a long-term goal. Ask students what kinds of things came up for them when they were planning for their long-term goal. Ask students, "Do you like every single one of your steps? Is it okay if we like some of our steps but not others?"

CLOSURE: Remind students that things that they are doing now will impact them in the future and that is why it is so important for them to work hard now. Encourage students to recognize when one of their steps is successful and that each day they are getting closer and closer to their goals. Students can then take home their comic strip collages or, if there is space, can hang the collages on a bulletin board, in the hallway, or around the room.

TIME: Two 45-minute lessons (total of 90 minutes)

EVALUATION/ASSIGNMENT: Students will visualize their goals and steps through pictures. Students will show the counselor and the class that they can see and explain their goals and what goes into planning and reaching their goals. Students' pictures will demonstrate an understanding of career planning and short- and long-term goals.

His Job or Her Job?

NATIONAL CAREER DEVELOPMENT GUIDELINES: Career Planning: Awareness of different occupations and changing male/female roles

ASCA STANDARDS: Standard B—Students will employ strategies to achieve future career goals with success and satisfaction.

PURPOSE: To describe traditional and nontraditional careers and how they relate to career choice.

OBJECTIVE: Students will learn about the challenges and benefits of pursuing a non traditional career.

MATERIALS: White board, paper, and coloring materials for each student

INTRODUCTION: Tell students that they'll be doing some drawing that relates to careers.

ACTIVITY:

1. Help students fold paper into three sections (like a brochure). Tell students these are three separate sections. If it helps them to visualize the sections, they can draw a line down each fold.

2. Explain that in each section they'll draw an image of a person in a particular career—no talking or looking at other students' papers. Give 3 to 5 minutes for each drawing.

3. Tell students to draw the following three occupations. Give students time between each occupation.
   a. First, tell students to draw what a NURSE looks like.
   b. Second, an AIRPLANE PILOT.
   c. Third, a MUSICAL PERFORMER.

4. Circulate around the room to make sure students are drawing independently and have enough time to complete three detailed drawings. Instruct them to put their drawing utensils down after the third drawing.

5. Make a chart on the board to document the gender of the people drawn for each job. Ask how many students drew a male nurse and then how many drew a female. Next ask how many drew a female pilot and then how many drew a male. The order is not important for the musical performer—it should be rather even.

DISCUSSION: Discuss why their images of nurses are primarily female and pilots primarily male. Offer statistics (dol.gov) about how many men are nurses (5.7%) and how many females are pilots (3.4%). Challenge students to think of a career that can only be performed by one gender. (Be prepared to prove them wrong!) Then lead students through a brainstorm about the benefits and challenges of pursuing a nontraditional career.

CLOSURE: Remind students to think about careers in terms of their interests instead of gender traditions.

EVALUATION/ASSIGNMENT: Students will challenge gender traditions in careers. In discussion, students will identify reasons to pursue nontraditional careers. If time allows, have students write a five-minute reflection.

- -

What Subjects Do Workers Like?

NATIONAL CAREER DEVELOPMENT GUIDELINES: Educational and Occupational Exploration: Awareness of the relationship between work and learning

ASCA STANDARDS: Standard C—Students will understand the relationship between personal qualities, training, education, and the world-of-work.

PURPOSE: To discuss the relationship between subjects at school and the world-of-work.

OBJECTIVE: Students will identify occupations related to specific school subjects. Subjects will include core subjects as well as specials such as music, art, physical education, and so on.

MATERIALS: Chalkboard and chalk (or butcher paper and markers), paper, pencils

INTRODUCTION: Talk with students about the connection between school and work. Ask students to share some examples of similarities between school and work, as well as some of the differences. "What are some things that you do at school that you will need for working?" (Answers can include reading, writing, knowing how to do math, reading music, knowing about science, etc.)

ACTIVITY: List school subjects along the top of the chalkboard or on butcher paper. Ask a few students to give examples of jobs that use things from the school subjects (e.g., a banker uses math, and a journalist uses language arts). You can ask students to share and record their answers or allow students to come up one at a time and write their ideas. After a few ideas have been written on the board, divide students into small groups to brainstorm their own ideas. Circulate throughout the room to make sure students understand. After 10 to 15 minutes, have each group write on the board under each subject the jobs it came up with.

DISCUSSION: Go over each group's list. Have the students give examples of how the school subject might be used in each occupation. Be sure to point out some ways that a job might use a subject that students might not guess at first (Musicians use counting and numbers—that's math!). Talk with students about why it is important that each worker in a certain occupation has a background in his or her specific subject.

CLOSURE: Remind students how we decided school and work are similar and are closely related.

TIME: 45 minutes

EVALUATION/ASSIGNMENT: Students will talk to other workers they see on a daily basis to learn more about which subjects are important for doing their jobs.

- -

Guess Who: Careers

NATIONAL CAREER DEVELOPMENT GUIDELINES: Educational and Occupational Exploration

ASCA STANDARDS: Standard A—Students will acquire the skills to investigate the world-of-work in relation to knowledge of self and to make informed career decisions.

PURPOSE: To be able to describe elements, responsibilities, and tasks of specific careers. To expand students' vocabulary related to occupations.

OBJECTIVE: Students will be able to use clues to describe occupations to their classmates. Students will also be able to guess specific occupations based on the clues they are given.

MATERIALS: Note cards (one for each student and yourself), a marker, masking tape

INTRODUCTION:

a. Before visiting the class, create a list of occupations including a variety of occupational types. The list should include occupations that students will be familiar with but also some that are more challenging. After the list is finalized, use a marker to write one occupation on each note card. Students should be able to read the note card from across the room.

b. Take occupation note cards and masking tape to the classroom. Before starting, have the students make a circle with their desks or sit in a circle on the floor.

c. Explain to the students, "I want to see how much each of you knows about different occupations. In this activity, show me what you know by giving your classmates clues about specific occupations. If you're not sure you know what clues to give about an occupation, ask me or someone else, and we can help each other out."

ACTIVITY:

1. With the teacher or a helper, go around the room and tape one note card to each student's forehead. The student should not look at or be able to see what is written on his or her note card. "Do not look at your note card. You are going to have to guess what is written on it based on the clues your classmates give you!"

2. Once each student has a note card, tape the remaining note card to your forehead in order to participate with the students. You can start the activity or take a volunteer to be the first guesser. Ask three or four students to raise their hand and have each give one clue about what is written on the guesser's forehead note card. Help students to stay relevant with their clues. For example, clues can include:

    a. "You work in a school."
    b. "You use your hands to work."
    c. "You use tools to fix things."
    d. "You like people/animals."

    Students may not use a part of the word on the note card in their clue (e.g., if the word is *Teacher*, students cannot say, "You teach kids"). Encourage students to use clues relating to context, environment, tasks, tools implemented, and so on.

3. Go around the room until each student has guessed his or her occupation note card. Encourage all students to give clues.

DISCUSSION: Ask students, "What was it like to give your classmates clues? To receive clues?" Talk with students about any words that came up that were unfamiliar to them. Help students to understand that there are many different titles of occupations and that usually there are many different parts to an occupation. For example, a school counselor has to know how to give classroom guidance but also needs to know how to talk with people one on one.

CLOSURE: Encourage students by telling them the positive things you noticed about the clues they gave each other. Reiterate that there are many different job titles and many different things that workers do.

TIME: 30 minutes

EVALUATION/ASSIGNMENT: Students will participate in the activity and give appropriate and relevant clues. Students will then go home and ask parents/guardians, siblings, or other workers they see about the many different aspects of their work.

■ ■ ■ ■ ■ ■ ■ ■ ■ ■ ■ ■ ■ ■ ■ ■ ■ ■

How Do I Get There from Here?

NATIONAL CAREER DEVELOPMENT GUIDELINES: Career Planning

ASCA STANDARDS: Standard C—Students will understand the relationship between personal qualities, education, training, and the world-of-work.

PURPOSE: To acquire knowledge to achieve career goals.

OBJECTIVE: Students will understand the relationship between educational achievement and career success.

MATERIALS: Computer with Internet access for each student or pair of students. Worksheets—one for each student, markers and large poster board or butcher paper for the class

INTRODUCTION: Discuss how school subjects are related to careers and career choices. Introduce the activity and go through the directions, explaining that only a small number of careers will be listed for each subject area on the Web site ("Your fantasy job may not be listed. If it's not, try and find a different one to learn about"). Encourage students to look for a job that they don't already know a great deal about.

ACTIVITY: Assist each student in accessing the Bureau of Labor Statistics Web site for kids (bls.gov/k12) and monitor their browsing. When each student has completed the chart on the worksheet, record the data from the whole class on a large chart for students to compare findings. Note which careers require the most/least training, are growing/shrinking in demand, and earn the highest/lowest salaries.

CLOSURE: Emphasize that students' performance in school has a significant influence on their readiness to enter a training program, educational program, or career. Help students understand that they do *not* need to know right now what they want to do when they grow up but, instead, that trying out different classes and putting in their best effort can help them to learn more about what they like or dislike. Stress the importance of working hard and encourage students to keep an eye out for and to celebrate the results and successes.

TIME: 30 minutes

EVALUATION/ASSIGNMENT: Students will turn in the worksheet with data completed. Evaluate for participation and completion. Students will then be able to share their findings with the class on a chart (each student will be able to share at least one finding and put it on the chart).

WORKSHEET

Choose one of the areas that interest you, select it, and then choose one career from those listed and select it. For that job, read, "What is this job like?" and "How do you get ready?" Then complete the following chart by finding the information you need from "How much does this job pay?" "How many jobs are there?" and "What about the future?"

CAREER DEVELOPMENT INTERVENTIONS IN THE ELEMENTARY SCHOOLS

Job Title _____

Number of jobs	Available	Preparation	The future	Pay $$

CHAPTER 11

CAREER DEVELOPMENT INTERVENTIONS IN MIDDLE SCHOOLS

Providing career development interventions in my work as a middle school counselor is important because students need to learn how to explore their interests and strengths. By offering career guidance at this level, counselors help middle school students build the foundation necessary for understanding career possibilities and world-of-work expectations.

Many of the work habits that students develop at this level are carried over to high school and beyond. It is crucial that educators provide the assistance students need to form healthy habits and make informed decisions. The earlier students learn about careers and occupations, the better prepared they are to explore the pathways leading toward their own future goals.

Through interest inventories, career fairs, mock job interviews, visits from community business members, and numerous other middle school activities, students are introduced to career development. Ideally, teachers from all disciplines combine to provide a full-circle approach to educating students on the importance of career exploration.

Self-awareness is critical at the middle school level. Self-awareness activities provide a realistic view of potential career paths and opportunities for students to match them with their likes and abilities. Our middle school also offers numerous clubs and activities so students can try out new ideas and experiences to further define their future aspirations.

Overall, the more we encourage our students to pursue interests and new experiences, the more we help them to form good work habits and positive life skills. These skills highlight the importance of using sound judgment when exploring careers and planning for the future.

Michael J. Brannigan
Professional School Counselor
Queensbury Middle School
Queensbury, NY

MyCounselingLab®

Visit the MyCounselingLab® site for *Career Development Interventions*, Fifth Edition, to enhance your understanding of chapter concepts. You will have the opportunity to practice applying what you learned in the chapter by completing the video- and case-based exercises in the MyLab. Taking the Licensure Quizzes will help you prepare for your certification exam.

Antonio was new to the school. He and his parents had recently moved from Los Angeles to rural Pennsylvania. As a seventh grader in L.A., Antonio had lots of friends, knew most of his teachers, and was one of the star players on the soccer team. In Belltoona, Pennsylvania, Antonio was new, disoriented, and unsure of himself. He was angry about moving; he felt alone, and he was depressed. Antonio's parents noticed that he had become apathetic and uninvolved in many of the activities that once gave him a sense of satisfaction and pride.

> **Tips from the Field**
>
> Adolescents in middle school need to engage in broad exploration to begin clarifying which educational and career paths make the most sense for them. This does not imply that the emphasis on self-awareness and career awareness in elementary school is complete. In fact, school counselors must help students develop more sophisticated awareness in these areas as they encourage students to explore future possibilities. More specifically, school counselors can begin by helping students explore possibilities through the lens of accurate self-understanding, starting with their interests.

MIDDLE/JUNIOR HIGH SCHOOL

Antonio's situation represents what many middle school students experience. Students at the middle school level are confronted with a more sophisticated set of developmental tasks than they experienced during their elementary school years. Erikson (1963) notes that between the ages of 12 and 18 adolescents must clarify their identities. If identity clarification is not achieved, then adolescents will experience confusion as they attempt to negotiate the tasks presented to them. Specifically, Havighurst (1972) suggests that adolescents must accomplish the following developmental tasks:

1. Achieve new and more sophisticated relations with peers
2. Achieve emotional independence from parents and other adults
3. Set vocational goals
4. Prepare for marriage and family life
5. Develop skills for civic competence
6. Acquire a set of values and an ethical system as a guide to behavior
7. Set realistic goals and make plans for achieving these goals

These tasks present a daunting challenge to young people as they move from childhood to adolescence and early adulthood. The often stormy experience of transitioning from childhood to adolescence not only presents a challenge to the young person experiencing this transition but also to those who are part of the young person's social network. Social development expectations encourage the preadolescent to take strides toward independence. Strides toward independence, however, are often accompanied by feelings of insecurity, conflict, fear, and anxiety; as Vernon (1993) states, "Dramatic changes in cognition and the intensification of affect contribute to a fluctuating sense of self" (p. 10). Bireley and Genshaft (1991) describe early adolescence as the process of "struggling toward maturity" (p. 1). As a result of their advancing development, middle school students are preoccupied with belonging and are influenced significantly by their same-sex peers. Thus, counselors providing career interventions for middle school students need to challenge students to become active agents in the career development process while at the same time offering supportive assistance as students acquire additional self- and career information (American School Counselor Association, 2004).

Antonio's parents asked his school counselor to meet with Antonio. They wanted Antonio to become more connected with the school and to begin working harder at making new friends. During their meeting, Antonio's counselor convinced him to join a school activity. Together, they explored the wide range of activities available at Antonio's school. The school counselor also encouraged Antonio to explore the various options with his parents. After these discussions, Antonio reluctantly agreed to join a community service group at the school. The counselor also asked the captain of the middle school's soccer team to "mentor" Antonio and help him to become more familiar with the school and other students. Antonio met with his counselor on a regular basis for the first half of the school year and was clearly becoming more connected with the school and making new friends. Antonio and his counselor discussed a variety of topics, including Antonio's experience in the community service group. These discussions also focused on other areas of interest for Antonio. A seemingly natural leader, Antonio's counselor encouraged him to assume a leadership role within the community service group. Antonio liked "being in charge" and at the next election of group officers, he was voted in as the president. Because Antonio had not thought much about life after high school, his counselor suggested that they spend some time discussing his career plans. Soon, Antonio and his counselor began to explore how his interests related to various occupational options.

To provide a broader context for Antonio's career development experiences, it is important to note that 93% of middle school students report that their goal is to attend college. Only 44%, however, eventually do, and only 26% graduate with a college diploma within six years of enrolling (Conley, 2012). This aspiration and completion disparity underscores the need for college and career support for students, beginning in middle school (Berardi-Demo, 2012). As a seventh-grader, Antonio is at a critical career transition. His parents may sense this, and that may be what propelled them to seek assistance for Antonio.

Understanding the career development status of middle school students is crucial for developing goals for career development interventions. As is true at the elementary school level, counselors in middle school settings should view providing career assistance to students as central to their work (American School Counselor Association, 2003; Campbell & Dahir, 1997). Career assistance provided to middle school students must be sensitive to the contextual, physical, and emotional transitions that students experience. Akos (2004) highlights the shifts occurring from elementary to middle school, noting that rising middle school students encounter "multiple teachers, larger school buildings, block scheduling, lockers, and new and different peers" (p. 881). These contextual changes occur concurrently with significant physical and emotional development changes during puberty. Researchers have found that students making the transition to middle school often experience decreases in self-esteem, increases in psychological distress, and decreases in academic achievement (Akos).

Akos, Konold, and Niles (2004) found that middle school students exhibit distinct patterns of needs regarding developing their readiness for career decision making. Some students reflect developmentally appropriate career indecision or moratorium status, some indicate the need for more focused and intense personal and career counseling interventions, whereas others may highlight premature career identity foreclosure and are disengaged from the career decision-making process. Understanding a student's career decision-making needs helps counselors to identify specific career development interventions that may be most useful in fostering a student's career development. Here again, data from the National Assessment of Educational Progress's Project on Career and Occupational Development provide useful information for understanding the career development status of middle school students. For example, survey results from a

influenced by puts

national sample of 38,000 13-year-olds indicate that young people at this age have made progress in crystallizing their self-concepts, as exemplified by the fact that they tend to be able to identify their strengths and weaknesses. Students at this age also evidence a growing understanding of the world-of-work. Often this progress is the result of students participating in school activities, hobbies, and/or part-time work. Boys and girls at age 13 tend to be equally knowledgeable about highly visible occupations and can link at least one school subject to a job. Most students at this age indicate that they have at least started the process of thinking about a future job. Interestingly, their choices for future jobs tend to be occupations requiring college degrees or lengthy training periods beyond high school, rather than jobs now held by the majority of the workforce (i.e., those not requiring a college degree). Of most concern in the data provided by the National Assessment of Educational Progress's Project on Career and Occupational Development is the fact that racial minority students and students living in economic poverty tend to lag behind other students in their career development. Thus, the effectiveness of current career development interventions provided to middle school students is variable.

This variability points to the importance of being clear about the societal expectations placed on students in middle school. As these students transition between Super's growth and exploration stages, they encounter the task of crystallizing occupational preferences. They are expected by teachers, counselors, and designers of the school curriculum to develop a realistic self-concept and to acquire additional information about more opportunities (Super, 1984). Specifically, middle school students are required to learn about themselves and the world-of-work and then translate this learning into an educational plan for the remainder of their secondary school education. Super, Savickas, and Super (1996) refer to the crystallization process by noting that "when habits of industriousness, achievement, and foresight coalesce, individuals turn to daydreaming about possible selves they may construct. Eventually, these occupational daydreams crystallize into a publicly recognized vocational identity with corresponding preferences for a group of occupations at a particular ability level" (p. 132). Thus, to establish an appropriate course of action for high school and beyond, career development interventions during middle school must be directed toward helping students cope successfully with the tasks of crystallizing and specifying occupational preferences (Super et al., 1996).

The ASCA National Standards (ASCA, 2003, 2012) also provide direction for professional school counselors as they construct career development interventions for middle school students. Specifically, the standards indicate that middle school students should "(a) acquire the skills to investigate the world-of-work in relation to knowledge of self and to make informal career decisions, (b) employ strategies to achieve future success and satisfaction, and (c) understand the relationship between personal qualities, education and training, and the world-of-work" (p. 17).

During his meetings with his counselor, Antonio discussed how working in the community service group helped him feel less lonely and better about himself in general. Antonio enjoyed planning and organizing the group's service activities. He had quickly become a leader in this group and enjoyed this role as well. Antonio confided to his counselor that he had often dreamed about being a CEO for a company that does something to help others. He stated that "being in charge" and "helping others" were two things that were fun and important to him. Antonio's counselor carefully listened to Antonio's important self-referent statements. The counselor helped underscore for Antonio how this self-knowledge could be used to direct Antonio's further exploration of career options. Specifically, Antonio's counselor suggested that he use the computer information delivery system available at the school to find out which occupations would provide him with opportunities to "be in charge" and "help others." After generating a list from the computer, Antonio met with his counselor to discuss the options on the list and determine where he could get more information about the options that interested him the most.

CAREER DEVELOPMENT GOALS FOR MIDDLE SCHOOL STUDENTS

Based on the career development literature and the National Career Development Guidelines, the following career development goals can be identified for middle school students: increase self-awareness, foster a positive self-concept, increase understanding of the school-to-work transition, strengthen interpersonal skills, learn how to acquire educational and career information, develop an understanding of the different life roles that people play, and learn about the career planning process.

A variety of career development interventions can be constructed systematically by using the ASCA Standards and National Career Development Guidelines. Prior to discussing possible interventions, however, it is useful to examine the career planning considerations offered by Herr, Cramer, and Niles (2004):

1. Because middle school is a transitional experience from the structured and general education of the elementary school to the less structured but more specialized education of the secondary school, students must be provided with a broad opportunity to explore their personal characteristics as well as those of the educational options from which they must choose. Opportunities to relate curricular options to the possible and subsequent educational and occupational outcomes seem highly desirable.

2. Because wide ranges in career maturity, interests, values, and abilities characterize middle school students, a variety of methods are needed to accommodate the range of individual differences. Students whose parents have not completed high school frequently have not had the developmental experience or occupational knowledge enjoyed by students from homes in which the parents are well educated.

3. Although students in middle school are capable of verbal and abstract behavior, exploration will be enhanced if they are given concrete, hands-on, direct experiences as well.

4. Fundamental to the rapid changes that students experience in middle school is a search for personal identity. Therefore, career guidance programs must encourage students to explore feelings, needs, and uncertainties as a base for evaluating educational and vocational options. Values clarification and other similar processes are helpful in this regard. (p. 392)

In addition to these important considerations, professional school counselors need to remain cognizant of the ways in which gender and racial stereotyping related to occupational options can artificially constrict the range of options students are considering. Clearly, counselors must deliver career development interventions that aggressively attack these discriminatory influences.

CAREER DEVELOPMENT INTERVENTIONS IN MIDDLE SCHOOL

Thematic consideration of middle school–level career development competencies reveals the importance of students acquiring the necessary knowledge, skills, and understanding to advance in their career development. Interventions that combine psychoeducational activities and experiential tasks are useful in helping students cope with the career development tasks confronting them. Examples of the former include teaching students about the relationship between education and work (e.g., by interviewing workers of their choice and asking the workers how academic subjects connect their work tasks); the importance and interaction of life roles (e.g., by asking students to identify how they spend their time in the course of a typical week and then to identify the values they express in how they spend their time). It is also important to help students understand issues related to equity and access in career choice (e.g., by sponsoring a career fair comprised of nontraditional workers representing a wide range of occupations, such as female carpenters, African American female engineers, etc.). Finally, helping students develop awareness regarding the career development tasks they will confront now and in the future (e.g., by having students construct their ideal future life and then discuss how prepared they feel for taking on those future tasks, what they can do between now and then to become better prepared for them, etc.) and the ways in which they can access and evaluate occupational information (e.g., by educating students about ways to identify bias in occupational information) are central to effective educational and career planning in secondary school. These interventions can easily occur in group and/or classroom guidance activities. The ASCA National Model (ASCA, 2003) provides an excellent guide for identifying topics to incorporate in psychoeducational activities with students. Examples of experiential tasks include job shadowing, attending career fairs, conducting occupational information interviews, and engaging in activities to clarify interests, values, and skills. Both psychoeducational and experiential activities help students acquire the knowledge, skills, and understanding needed to develop the attitudes and skills of readiness for educational and career decision making (Super, 1990).

With the help of his counselor, Antonio decided that it would be helpful to him to speak with a local hospital administrator, the executive director of a local social service agency, and the minister of his church. The purpose of the meetings was to learn more about each of these occupations (e.g., what each person liked and did not like about his or her occupation, training required for each of the occupations, and the academic subjects that were more important for doing the work well). After conducting these occupational information interviews, Antonio expressed an interest in job shadowing with the hospital administrator. He also stated that after he finished high school, it would be important for him to attend college.

It is also important at this developmental level that career interventions continue to stimulate curiosity in students. Students who are curious about their emerging self-concepts (e.g., their avocational and vocational interests, skills, and values) are more likely to engage in exploratory behavior to acquire the information they need for self-concept clarification (Super, 1981). Helping students identify and connect with role models can also facilitate a sense of internal control and future time perspective, which can, in turn, lead to planful behaviors and the development of effective problem-solving skills (Super, 1990). Stott and Jackson (2005) found that a service learning approach with middle school students was very useful in helping them make stronger connections between academics and career possibilities.

To help guide students in their exploration, counselors can administer career assessments. In selecting career assessments, it is important that the reading level, language, and normative samples are appropriate for the school population with which the assessments will be used. Interest inventory results can foster more systematic thinking about the activities in which students enjoy participating. Aptitude tests can also help students acquire accurate estimates of their abilities. Interest and aptitude assessments are often administered to students during the middle school grades. The combination of interest inventory results and aptitude test results provides a useful foundation for the exploration process. Students will find it useful to explore occupational areas for which they have high interest and high aptitude. When the results of an interest inventory suggest that a student has no area of above average or high interest, it may be that he or she needs exposure to activities across several interest areas to determine what will interest the student. Thus, a key to making assessments (especially interest inventories) useful is that students must have the experiential base to draw upon to respond to assessment items. Students with limited exposure to a variety of activities will be forced to guess at appropriate responses to questions requiring them to identify their likes and dislikes. (One counselor shared with us that he attempted to administer an interest inventory to his daughter when she was in sixth grade. Her reading level at that time far exceeded the reading level of the inventory, but her experiential base was such that she did not understand many of the items presented to her on the inventory. It very quickly became evident that the inventory results would not serve to foster her career development!) When school systems have a systematic career development intervention program in place for all grades, it is safer to assume that middle school students have been exposed to activities that have addressed bias in occupational choices and that have fostered student self- and career exploration. When no such programs exist, counselors must be especially cognizant of the possibility that many students will need more remedial career development interventions prior to being administered career assessments.

Providing middle school students with exposure to work facilitates the acquisition of knowledge, skills, and awareness related to the career development domains within the National Career Development Guidelines. These activities also connect to Standards C:A1 (Develop Career Awareness) and C:B1 (Acquire Career Information) of ASCA's National Standards. Teaching students how families of occupations can be clustered according to factors such as skill requirements, interests, and/or training helps students organize the world-of-work and connect their characteristics to occupational options (ASCA's Develop Career Awareness and Identify Career Goals standards). For example, Holland's classification system links the six personality types, described in Chapter 2, to group occupations. *Realistic* occupations include skilled trades and technical occupations. *Investigative* occupations include scientific and technical occupations. *Artistic* occupations include creative occupations in the expressive arts. *Social* occupations include the helping professions. *Enterprising* occupations involve managerial and sales occupations. *Conventional* occupations include office and clerical occupations. Occupations are classified according to the degree to which the activities of the occupation draw upon the Holland types. The three most dominant types reflected in the occupation are used to classify each occupation. (The Inventory of Children's Activities [ICA-3]) described in Chapter 10 is very useful in assessing Holland types in a way that minimizes gender bias.)

Antonio was administered ICA-3 and obtained the Holland code of Enterprising, Social, and Artistic. He met with other students and the counselor to discuss the inventory results. They talked about their Holland codes and whether they thought the codes were accurate. With the counselor's assistance, they also brainstormed a list of occupations for each Holland type. Antonio decided that it made sense for him to continue to explore the occupations of hospital administrator and social service director.

The National Association of State Directors of Career Technical Education Consortium (2015) organizes occupations according to whether they involve producing goods or providing services. These two broad categories are then subdivided into 16 career clusters as follows:

1. Agriculture, Food, and Natural Resources
2. Architecture and Construction

3. Arts, A/V Technology, and Communications
4. Business Management and Administration
5. Education and Training
6. Finance
7. Government and Public Administration
8. Health Science
9. Hospitality and Tourism
10. Human Services
11. Information Technology
12. Law, Public Safety, Corrections, and Security
13. Manufacturing
14. Marketing
15. Science, Technology, Engineering, and Mathematics
16. Transportation, Distribution, and Logistics

The National Career Clusters Framework groups occupations based on similar skill sets, interests, abilities, and activities (National Association of State Directors of Career Technical Education Consortium, 2015). The clusters contain subgroupings called Career Pathways. The pathways identify the knowledge and skills required for a particular career field. The pathways link academics with career fields. Career pathways can help students understand the vital connection between the courses they take in high school and particular career fields that interest them. Students can explore career clusters based on their interests and then examine a variety of postsecondary options—higher education, training, or apprenticeship—that will help them succeed in those career fields.

Clustering systems such as the career clusters and Holland's system can be used to guide career exploration by using the types to organize career information resources, career fairs, curricula experiences (e.g., students can be assigned the task of writing an essay about occupations that fall within their dominant Holland type), job-shadowing experiences, participation in extracurricular activities, avocational pursuits, college exploration, and part-time employment experiences. Specific educational plans can be developed for specific career pathways (e.g., careertech.org).

To develop effective interpersonal skills related to the work environment (ASCA's Develop Employment Readiness competency, C:A2), students can be provided with difficult interpersonal interactions (e.g., a coworker who interacts angrily for no apparent reason, an angry boss who places unreasonable demands on workers), and students can brainstorm ways of coping with the situation. Students can then role-play solutions to handling difficult interpersonal interactions at work.

The use of group interventions is also an effective approach to helping students develop career development competencies. For example, Hutchinson (2013) recommends the use of small groups focused on STEM (science, technology, engineering, and math) occupations, especially for those students who might not typically consider these career pathways. Girls in middle school, in particular, can be encouraged to consider ways in which their interests and strengths can connect to STEM careers (Goal CM3 in the National Career Development Guidelines). The Council of Chief State School Officers (2014) recommends exposing students to real-world work experiences while in secondary school, noting that students who receive such exposure are more likely to graduate from high school and then persist in and complete postsecondary education. Strategies such as regular monthly group meetings expose students to workers from different career fields. It is always important to attend to the need to expose students to nontraditional workers (e.g., a male nurse, female carpenter, female engineer).

To increase students' thinking about the interrelationship of life roles (ASCA's Acquire Knowledge to Achieve Career Goals competency, C:C1, and NCDG's Personal Social Development domain), counselors can use a group guidance format to help middle school students examine their current life-role salience by responding to such questions as "How do you spend your time during a typical week?" "How important are the different roles of life to you?" "What do you like about participating in each of the life roles?" "What life roles do you think will be important to you in the future?" "What do you hope to accomplish in each of the life roles that will be important to you in the future?" "What life roles do members of your family play?" "What do your family members expect you to accomplish in each of the life roles?"

Obviously, patterns of life-role salience are significantly influenced by immediate (e.g., family, cultural heritage, level of acculturation) and distal (e.g., economics, environmental opportunities for life-role participation) contextual factors (Blustein, 1994). Contextual factors, therefore, contribute to patterns of life-role salience. However, many middle school students lack an awareness of the ways in which contextual factors (such as the dominant culture and the student's culture of origin) interact with identity development to shape life-role salience. Group discussions pertaining to these topics can help middle school students develop their sense of which life roles are important to them now, which life roles will be important to them in the future, and how life roles can interact to influence life satisfaction.

An effective tool for helping middle school students engage in purposeful planning, exploring, information gathering, decision making, and reality testing related to two prominent life roles (i.e., student and worker) is an educational and career planning portfolio. Educational and career planning portfolios are typically used to help students chart their academic and career decision making. This charting process can begin in middle school and continue until the student leaves high school. By making at least annual entries into the portfolio, the student and counselor can track the student's career development progress. They can also make systematic educational and career plans that build upon the growing base of self- and occupational knowledge the student is developing. In essence, the portfolio provides a vehicle for the student and counselor to discuss what the student has done and what the student will do next to advance his or her career development. There are several very useful portfolios available (e.g., "Get a Life" developed by the American School Counselor Association), and portfolios are fairly easy to develop locally (see the portfolio developed by Niles for the Virginia Department of Education in Appendix B).

By completing the educational and career planning portfolio on a regular basis, students, their parents, and school counselors can trace students' academic, co-curricular, extracurricular, and career exploration activities. When portfolios are completed at least annually, they provide the focus for goal identification and further intentional educational and career planning. We encourage you to examine the portfolio in Appendix B as well as the portfolio available through your access to Navigator (Kuder, 2015), a career planning system for middle and high school students. Using the most recently completed portfolio, the student, his/her counselor, and his/her parents can review past career goals and determine whether they continue to make sense, and whether there are ways they may need to be revised based on new experiences the student has had. The latter, in particular, can be used to set goals for the forthcoming year. Using a career and educational planning portfolio in this way helps the student learn how to make career decisions systematically.

To help students focus on the interrelationship of life roles and to engage in planning related to their salient life roles, the educational and career planning portfolio can be expanded to a *life-role portfolio* by addressing students' readiness for life roles beyond those of student and worker. Students can be encouraged to plan, explore, and gather information for each of the major roles of life. For example, students who anticipate being parents in the future can plan for this role by considering how parenting interacts with other roles. Students can explore different styles of parenting by interviewing parents about their parenting practices and philosophies. Students can also gather information about the skills required for effective parenting (perhaps by taking a class). Through these activities they can learn the things that are important to consider in making decisions about parenting. Finally, students can reality-test their interest through participating in child-care activities. Thus, the life-role portfolio serves as a stimulus for counselor and student meetings focused on planning, exploring, information gathering, decision making, and reality testing vis-à-vis the major life roles. When the portfolio is used over successive years, it also provides developmental documentation of activities and decisions related to major life roles.

This expanded use of the planning portfolio is an example of a counseling activity that is intended to help students address the developmental task of identity formation within the context of developing life-role readiness. It also provides additional opportunities for discussing contextual influences on life-role salience. Regardless of the life role, it is important that counselors are sensitive to how students' culture of origin influences their perceptions of future possibilities.

MyCounselingLab®

Start with Topic 6—Career Counseling in Schools.

Watch the video *21st Century Career Development Interventions in the Schools: Dr. Carol Dahir* and complete Student Activity #13 on page 317.

SUMMARY

Middle school represents a transition point at which students must become actively engaged in preparing for the significant educational choices they will make as they enter high school. Thus, professional school counselors at the middle-school level empower students to become active agents in the career development process through activities that foster greater self-understanding, occupational knowledge, stronger decision-making skills, and a more sophisticated understanding of the interrelationship of life roles. Concurrently, school counselors must offer supportive assistance to help middle school students cope with the myriad academic, career, social, and emotional challenges they experience. As middle school students develop more advanced self-awareness and career awareness than they possessed in elementary school, they use their advanced knowledge to consider future possibilities and prepare to enter high school.

CASE STUDY

James is a 13-year-old African American boy in the eighth grade. His parents were divorced when he was in the first grade. Since then, James has had sporadic contact with his father (although his father seems to genuinely care about him). After the divorce, James's mother relocated to an upper-class suburban town in New Jersey. James lives with his mother and older sister (age 18). James's father lives in the town where James was born, which is two hours away. James's other sister (age 16) lives with her father and his second family. Although his parents' divorce was very difficult, no one in the family has received any counseling relative to this event.

James's parents are college graduates. James's father has a master's degree in educational leadership and has worked as a middle school teacher. However, he is currently employed as the head of the personnel department for the National Guard. He changed occupations to increase his salary ("You can't pay the bills on what they pay you as a teacher"). James's mother is employed as a high school Spanish teacher. James's older sister is an airline ticket agent. His younger sister is a successful athlete and good student in the eleventh grade.

Until now, James has given very little attention to his career. His major interests revolve around sports. He plays baseball, basketball, and football. He follows the local sports teams as well as the professional sports teams in his area. His heroes are all professional athletes and James dreams of being a professional athlete one day. He has no other hobbies.

Interpersonally, James is a friendly, but shy, boy. Lately, he has started to associate with a group of boys in his neighborhood who tend to get into trouble at school. A few have even gotten into minor problems (e.g., vandalism) with the law. James has not been a disciplinary problem.

In school, James has been an average to above average student. He finds history and English to be interesting but struggles with mathematics. Not surprisingly, his favorite class is physical education. James has a general lack of confidence when it comes to his academic ability. He likes school because it is where he gets to play sports with his friends. His mother would like you to help him identify some career goals. Ideally, James's mother thinks he should be a lawyer because they "earn a good living and it is a prestigious occupation." But James thinks it would be "fun" to be a coach. James's mother dismisses this as an appropriate occupation, telling James that he will "never make any money as a coach" and that one day he will be "too old" to be involved in sports. James and his father have never discussed what James might do "when he grows up." His mother has spoken with the school principal about having the school counselor give James some sort of test that will identify appropriate career options for him. The principal has asked you (the school counselor) to help out.

What are James's career development needs? What other issues does James present? What career tasks must he complete to begin to engage in effective educational and career planning? How will you work with James to help him move forward?

STUDENT ACTIVITIES

1. What career development tasks do you think are most important to help middle school students address?

2. What factors do you think could negatively influence the career development of middle school students?

3. What are three strategies you could use to foster positive career development in middle school students?

4. What do you think is the most common type of career assistance provided to middle school students? Do you think this type of assistance is helpful? If so, why? If not, why not?

5. How could you help parents/guardians to help their middle school students experience positive career development?

6. Interview a middle school student about his or her career development. Ask this person what occupations s/he thinks are possible for him/her. Ask your interviewee whether there are any occupations that are not possible for him/her. Ask the person to discuss why certain occupations may not be possible. Ask what occupation your interviewee would choose if s/he could choose anything. Then, explore with your interviewee what s/he thinks is attractive about that occupation.

7. What career development tasks do you think are most important to help middle school students address?

8. What factors do you think could negatively influence the career development of middle school students?

9. What are three strategies you could use to foster positive career development in middle school students?

10. What do you think is the most common type of career assistance provided to middle school students? Do you think this type of assistance is helpful? If so, why? If not, why not?

11. How could you help parents/guardians to help their middle school students experience positive career development?

12. Ask a group of middle school students (or one student if a group is not available) what life roles they hope to play when they are adults (you will need to provide examples of life roles). Then, ask if they think they will be able to perform well in each of those life roles. Ask how they think they will learn the skills required for successful performance in each of those life roles.

13. Refer to the MyCounselingLab® Video and Resource Library and select the video entitled *21st Century Career Development Interventions in the School: An Interview with Dr. Carol Dahir*. How would you draw upon Dr. Dahir's comments to convince your principal and school board of the importance of career development interventions in middle school settings?

Sample Career Development Activities for Middle School Students

Note: Please note that most of these activities are readily adaptable to high school students.

An Interesting Journal

NATIONAL CAREER DEVELOPMENT GUIDELINES: Personal Social Domain: PS1.K1; PS1.A1; PS1.R1

ASCA STANDARDS: Standard A—Students will acquire the skills to investigate the world-of-work in relation to knowledge of self and to make informed career decisions; Standard C—students will understand the relationship between personal qualities, education, training, and the world-of-work.

PURPOSE: This activity encourages students to identify their interests and to consider how their interests can inform their career decisions.

OBJECTIVE: To help students identify their interests and connect their interests to career possibilities.

MATERIALS: Notebook or journal

INTRODUCTION: Discuss how our interests should guide career plans: "Do what you enjoy and you will never work a day in your life." By focusing on the things that we find most enjoyable, we can begin to clarify those activities that we should incorporate into our career plans.

ACTIVITIES: Instruct students to keep a log of how they spend their out-of-school time over the course of one week. As they enter the activity in their journals, they should give the activity a rating from 1 ("hated it") to 5 ("loved it"). The time frame can be lengthened to get a better sense of the activities students liked and disliked.

DISCUSSION: Students can discuss the activities they liked and did not like. They can also identify reasons for their reactions to their activities.

CLOSURE: The leader can help students understand how they can use their interests to guide their career exploration. For example, if a student enjoys working with animals, then the group can brainstorm additional activities that can provide that

student with the opportunity to work with animals. The group can also brainstorm career opportunities that provide people with the opportunity to work with animals. As each student discusses his or her likes, the group can brainstorm in a similar fashion.

TIME: 45–60 minutes

EVALUATION/ASSIGNMENT: At the end of the activity, students should identify two activities in which they are interested and two things they can do to gain additional exposure to their interests.

- -

Values Sorting

NATIONAL CAREER DEVELOPMENT GUIDELINES: Personal Social Domain: PS1.K4; PS1.A4; PS1.R4; Career Management Domain: CM2.K5; CM2.A5; CM2.R5

ASCA STANDARDS: Standard A—Students will acquire the skills to investigate the world-of-work in relation to knowledge of self and to make informed career decisions.

PURPOSE: Good career decisions are values based. However, few career options provide individuals with the opportunity to express all of their important values. Thus, we must prioritize values and identify those that are most important to us. We must be clear as to which values we are willing to part with, if necessary. Each decision we make requires us to sort our values and make choices accordingly. Being able to select career options that provide us with maximal opportunities for values expression requires us to subjectively define our important values. For example, although many people value "financial rewards," this value is defined somewhat differently across individuals. Understanding how we define the most important values in our lives helps us to determine which options fit best. Finally, it is important to understand how values are connected to our participation in the life roles we play.

OBJECTIVES: As a result of participating in this activity, participants will (a) learn the importance of values clarification, (b) become aware of their most important values, and (c) understand the importance of considering values in career decision making and career planning.

MATERIALS: Handouts of the values list and five slips of paper per participant

INTRODUCTION: Introduce this activity as an exercise that helps participants identify and define important values in their lives.

ACTIVITY: To start this activity, give participants a list of values such as this one:

VALUES LIST
_____ Financial security
_____ Job security
_____ Good family relationships
_____ A world that is free of discrimination
_____ Creativity
_____ Having a set routine
_____ Time by myself
_____ Community activities
_____ Physical activities
_____ An attractive physical appearance
_____ Variety
_____ Power
_____ Recognition
_____ Prestige
_____ Freedom from stress
_____ Associating with people I like
_____ Success
_____ Freedom to live where I choose

_____ Leisure time

_____ Fame

_____ Strong religious faith

_____ Adventure

_____ World peace

_____ Helping others

_____ Having children

_____ Good health

_____ A beautiful home

_____ Autonomy

_____ Other

_____ Other

Instruct students to identify their top 10 values from this list by putting an X next to the values that are most important to them (the values chosen are not ranked at this point). Then, after discussing their experience of conducting this initial values sort, provide participants with five slips of paper. Ask them to identify their top 5 values from the list of their top 10 and to write one value on each slip of paper (again these values are not ranked). Participants are then informed that the activity leader will be taking a value from them, one at a time. Thus, participants must now decide which of their top 5 values they are willing to part with first. At this point, the activity leader actually goes around the room taking a value from each participant.

Immediately after students give a value to the leader, instruct the participants to record and define what that value means to them (e.g., "financial rewards: having an income of more than $45,000/year with good health and retirement benefits"). Continue this process for each of the remaining values. At the conclusion of the exercise, participants have a list of their top 5 values, with definitions, in descending order. For example, here are five value definitions:

1. Financial rewards: having an income of more than $45,000/year with good health and retirement benefits
2. Autonomy: being able to make my own decisions as to how to best accomplish my job duties but having a colleague who can give me advice when I need it
3. Associating with people I like: being friends with my coworkers and doing things together outside of work
4. Good health: eating right and exercising three times per week
5. Strong religious faith: going to church on a regular basis and volunteering at a soup kitchen

DISCUSSION: After completing the exercise, explain how the activity relates to career decision making. Explain that in every decision there is the promise of gain and the threat of loss (otherwise, one could simply choose the "perfect" option in every instance). The risk involved in decision making is lessened when options are selected based on the individual's key values.

CLOSURE: Encourage participants to consider how they spend their time in the course of a typical week and if they spend time in activities reflecting their top values. If the answer is no, then encourage participants to identify strategies for increasing their participation in activities reflecting their values (e.g., agreeing to a moderate exercise program, identifying opportunities for volunteering).

TIME: Approximately 30 minutes

EVALUATION/ASSIGNMENT: Students will list their five most important values and identify three jobs in which they could express these values.

The Pie of Life

NATIONAL CAREER DEVELOPMENT GUIDELINES: Personal Social Domain: PS1.K4; PS1.A4; PS1.R4; Career Management Domain: CM2.K5; CM2.A5; CM2.R5

ASCA STANDARDS: Standard A—Students will acquire the skills to investigate the world-of-work in relation to knowledge of self and to make informed career decisions; Standard B—Students will employ strategies to achieve future career goals with success and satisfaction; Standard C—Students will understand the relationship between personal qualities, education, training, and the world-of-work.

PURPOSE: To focus on how students spend their time now and how they hope to spend their time in the future.

OBJECTIVE: To enhance self-awareness regarding values and life-role participation.

MATERIALS: Paper, pencils

INTRODUCTION: Encourage students to consider a typical week in their lives and ask them how they spend their time. Emphasize with students the importance of spending time in activities that reflect their interests and values.

ACTIVITIES: Ask each student to draw a circle on a piece of paper. Encourage students to consider the circle as if it were a "pie of life." Instruct them to consider how they spend their time over the course of a typical week (24 hours a day, 7 days a week). Tell them to divide the circle or pie into "slices" according to how much of their time is spent in each activity over the course of a week. Once they have divided their pies into slices, ask students to write answers to the following question: "What conclusions could someone draw from your 'pie of life' about what you like to do and what you value?"

DISCUSSION: Divide students into small groups. Encourage them to share their "pies of life" with each other. Then encourage students to share with the entire class any reactions they had to dividing their "pies of life" into slices as well as any reactions they had to hearing how their peers divided their pies.

CLOSURE: Emphasize the importance of having a "pie of life" that reflects your interests and values as much as possible. If students do not have a pie that reflects their interests and values, then encourage them to consider what changes they can make to increase the degree to which their "pie of life" reflects their values and interests.

TIME: 45 minutes

EVALUATION/ASSIGNMENT: Have students draw a second circle that reflects their lives as an adult (choose a specific age, such as 35 years old). Instruct them to divide their "pie of life" into slices according to how they hope to spend their time in the future. Ask them to identify how their slice relates to their interests and values. Ask them to identify the life roles reflected in their future slice of life. Finally, ask students to identify five things they can do between now and when they turn age 35 to increase the chances that their future "pie of life" will come true.

Time Capsule

NATIONAL CAREER DEVELOPMENT GUIDELINES: Personal Social Domain: PS1.K4; PS1.A4; PS1.R4; Career Management Domain: CM2.K5; CM2.A5; CM2.R5

ASCA STANDARDS: Standard A—Students will acquire the skills to investigate the world-of-work in relation to knowledge of self and to make informed career decisions; Standard B—Students will employ strategies to achieve future career goals with success and satisfaction; Standard C—Students will understand the relationship between personal qualities, education, training, and the world-of-work.

PURPOSE: To explore what possessions are valuable to students and why.

OBJECTIVE: Students will learn about themselves and others by examining a valued possession; students will explore what they would like future generations of people to know about them. Students will also discuss how the possessions they value are influenced by the culture in which they live.

MATERIALS: Ask students to bring a valued object from home that tells something about them that they might leave behind in an imaginary time capsule for future generations of middle school students.

INTRODUCTION: Ask students to bring an item from home to show other participants. Students should be prepared to explain what the item is and why it is important to them.

ACTIVITIES: Each student will describe the possession, explain why it is important to him or her, how it reflects something about the student, and what he or she would like to communicate to future middle school students by placing this item in an imaginary time capsule.

DISCUSSION: Students may discuss the items, any common concerns/messages for future generations, what they would like others to know about them, what is valued and why, and so on. Students will also discuss the group similarities and differences in the items they chose as valuable. Students can discuss how these items might be different if they lived in another country.

CLOSURE: Students can discuss the fact that the things we value are reflected in the things that are valuable to us. They are, in essence, symbolic representations of things that are important to us due to a variety of reasons (e.g., what the objects represent, because a person who is important to us gave us the object). The uniqueness of the objects selected tells us something important about ourselves.

TIME: 45 minutes to 1 hour

EVALUATION/ASSIGNMENT: Students will complete the following sentences: "Three things that are important to me are _____." and "These objects are important to me because _____."

Becoming a Member of Another Culture: A Fantasy

NATIONAL CAREER DEVELOPMENT GUIDELINES: Career Management Domain: CM2.A5; Personal Social Domain: PS2.K9; PS2.A9; PS2.R9

ASCA STANDARDS: Standard A—Students will acquire the skills to investigate the world-of-work in relation to knowledge of self and to make informed career decisions; Standard B—Students will employ strategies to achieve future career goals with success and satisfaction; Standard C—Students will understand the relationship between personal qualities, education, training, and the world-of-work.

PURPOSE: For students to learn what it would be like to suddenly find themselves as members of another culture.

OBJECTIVES:

1. For students to think about what privileges go along with certain cultures.
2. For students to recognize how they perceive their culture and others' cultures.

MATERIALS: None

INTRODUCTION: Say to students, "I am going to need everyone to relax and close his or her eyes. We are going to use our imaginations in this exercise to think about what it would be like to be a member of another culture."

ACTIVITIES: (Read aloud) "You're feeling relaxed now; you're very calm; it's the middle of the week, just prior to bedtime. You find yourself sitting in your comfortable chair, very relaxed. Your eyes are closed. . . . You are tired, very tired, and decide to go to bed. You enter a very restful sleep, very restful sleep. (Pause 10 seconds.) Now, visualize yourself awakening the next morning. You see yourself entering your bathroom. Take a careful look in the mirror; you see there's been a rather startling transformation during the night. . . . You woke up as a member of another culture with physical characteristics typical of those from that culture. . . . You went to bed a member of one culture and you woke up a member of another! (Pause.) How does it feel? (Pause.) Now you find yourself walking outside and meeting your best friend. How does your friend react? (Pause.) Now, visualize yourself walking across the campus. How do people react to you? You meet your favorite teacher—what happens? How do you feel? What is the overall reaction toward you? (Pause.) Okay. Open your eyes now."

DISCUSSION: Place students in small groups to take turns sharing their fantasies. Ask members to ask each other open-ended questions about what they share (what, how, when, or where). Request that they do not "interpret" another's fantasy.

CLOSURE: Discuss some of the themes in the students' fantasies and their specific reactions to suddenly being a member of a different culture.

TIME: 20–30 minutes

EVALUATION/ASSIGNMENT: Ask students to write two paragraphs describing how it felt to be a member of a culture different from their own.

Who Am I?

NATIONAL CAREER DEVELOPMENT GUIDELINES: Career Management Domain: CM2.A5; Personal Social Domain: PS2.K9; PS2.A9; PS2.R9

ASCA STANDARDS: Standard A—Students will acquire the skills to investigate the world-of-work in relation to knowledge of self and to make informed career decisions; Standard B—Students will employ strategies to achieve future career goals with success and satisfaction; Standard C—Students will understand the relationship between personal qualities, education, training, and the world-of-work.

PURPOSE: To help members learn more about themselves and each other in the group.

OBJECTIVE: Students will have an increased level of understanding among students about what makes each of them uniquely different and also what are some of their similarities.

MATERIALS: Pins, 4 × 6 cards for each student

INTRODUCTION: Tell students "We will be learning a lot about who we are. It is important to understand yourself and what has influenced who you are today. The activity we will be starting with is a great way to remind us about what things are unique to each of us and help us to recognize the differences in others."

ACTIVITIES: Give each student a 4 × 6 card and read aloud the following instructions:

a. Print your first name in the center of the index card. Write large enough so other people can read it.
b. In the upper left-hand corner, write or put a symbol for:
   1. Where you were born
   2. A favorite place you would like to visit on a vacation
c. In the upper right-hand corner, put a symbol or write words that depict something you like to do to have fun.

d. In the lower left-hand corner, write three words your best friend might use to describe you if you were not present.
e. In the lower right-hand corner, describe one characteristic about the specific culture to which you belong (Anglo, African American, etc.) that you value and appreciate.
f. Finally, somewhere on your card put another symbol that tells something you are really looking forward to doing in the future.

After completing their "Who Am I" card, have students fasten the cards to the fronts of their shirts or blouses. Then ask them to find an individual they do not know very well, preferably of a different culture or gender, someone with whom they can pair up. Each pair should interview one another concerning the data on the cards for 10 minutes.

DISCUSSION: Next, form a large circle with pairs standing together. Each pair should in turn step forward and introduce one another to the group. Afterward, have students share something they have learned regarding a student and what they would like to know more about.

CLOSURE: Ask the participants to wear their name tags to subsequent sessions until everyone knows everyone else.

TIME: 1 hour

EVALUATION/ASSIGNMENT: Have students follow through on the activity by instructing them to learn more about one person in the group.

Responding to Labels

NATIONAL CAREER DEVELOPMENT GUIDELINES: Career Management Domain: CM1.K1; CM1.R1; Personal Social Domain: PS2.K9; PS2.A9; PS2.R9

ASCA STANDARDS: Standard A—Students will acquire the skills to investigate the world-of-work in relation to knowledge of self and to make informed career decisions; Standard B—Students will employ strategies to achieve future career goals with success and satisfaction; Standard C—Students will understand the relationship between personal qualities, education, training, and the world-of-work.

PURPOSE: For students to think about some of the ways society labels people and how they can sometimes use some of the conflict resolution techniques when they feel like they are possibly being labeled.

OBJECTIVES:

1. Let the students experience what it is like when society labels certain individuals.
2. Help students to decide how to handle labeling, such as peer-group labels.

MATERIALS: Sheets of paper, tape, and a marker

INTRODUCTION: Place labels on certain individuals' backs. People in the room will respond to these individuals according to the labels they have on their backs. The individuals with labels will not know what they are and should pay close attention to how others in the room are treating them. While doing this activity, think about other labels that society gives people. For example, there are probably labels that your peers give to people in school.

ACTIVITIES: Write one of the following labels on separate sheets of paper and tape them on a few of the students' backs. Have the students without the labels walk around and react to the students as if they actually were what they are labeled.

- Famous movie star
- Person with HIV
- Mental patient
- Deaf person
- Criminal
- Drug addict
- Famous athlete

DISCUSSION:

1. Have the students who had labels talk about what it felt like to wear the labels. Have

each guess what they think his or her label might be.
2. Next, have the students who did not have labels talk about how it felt to treat people according to their labels.

Ask the students if they think this happens in our society. What are some of the labels people attach to others? Have students consider how damaging these labels can be to the individuals assigned the labels by society.

Ask the students what they can do to deal with labeling. Have them refer back to some of the skills they learned in the conflict resolution activities. List their answers on the board.

CLOSURE: Ask students to think about how knowledge gained from this activity can make us more aware of labeling in our society and ways of handling situations in which someone is being labeled.

TIME: 30 minutes

EVALUATION/ASSIGNMENT: Ask students to list ways in which they encounter labeling each day (e.g., television, music, newspapers, family, and friends).

The Rocket Kid's Story

NATIONAL CAREER DEVELOPMENT GUIDELINES: Career Management Domain: CM2.R4; CM3.K2; CM3.A2; CM3.R2; CM3.K4; CM3.A4; CM3.R4; CM3.K5; CM3.A5; CM3.R5; CM3.K6; CM3.A6; CM4.A5; CM4.R5; CM4.A6; CM4.R6

ASCA STANDARDS: Standard A—Students will acquire the skills to investigate the world-of-work in relation to knowledge of self and to make informed career decisions; Standard C—Students will understand the relationship between personal qualities, education, training, and the world-of-work.

PURPOSE: To learn about the life of a real scientist and explore the manner in which a boy achieved his career goal despite numerous obstacles.

OBJECTIVE: Students will be able to identify the goals of the movie characters in the film they are about to watch. They will also be able to identify the risks taken to achieve those goals and the role of teamwork in achieving goals.

MATERIALS: The movie *October Sky*, paper, pencils, a blackboard and chalk, rocket-making kit (if desired)

INTRODUCTION: Develop a list of questions for students to respond to such as "Do you know anyone like the movie characters?" "How did teamwork play a role in the success of the 'rocket boys'?" "What was the father's attitude toward college and the son's career interests?" "What was the family's attitude toward sports, and what role did sports play in the lives of the young people?" "What was Homer's original destiny, and how and why did that change?" "What risks did Homer take to implement his career goal?"

ACTIVITIES:

1. Ask students to watch the video *October Sky* or, if preferred, to read the book *Rocket Boys* by Homer Hickam. (Note: Parents may need to give permission to see this movie, as its rating is PG-13, and there is some language

that may be offensive to some individuals.) After watching the movie, students will respond to the questions in the Introduction section or others you develop. Follow this by actually building and/or setting off a rocket (kits to simplify the rocket building can be purchased at toy and crafts stores), if circumstances allow.

2. Students can then list their "dream" jobs or "occupational fantasies."

3. To provide examples of people who have overcome obstacles and achieved their goals, invite past program participants to the session. The past participants could share their stories and discuss what obstacles they overcame to achieve their goals. If it is not possible to have past participants, consider videotaping interviews from past participants. In the interviews the past participants could share their stories and identify the obstacles they overcame to achieve their goals.

DISCUSSION: Review the questions in the Introduction section and others that arise as students watch the movie. Ask students to take notes or write down a list of questions that arise as they watch this video. Emphasize the risks taken by the characters in the story and the role of teamwork in creating success in one's career. Students should list the obstacles the movie characters overcame to achieve their goals. Feelings may also be discussed, such as "Do you feel as if success similar to that of the movie characters is within your reach?" Share stories of past students who have achieved their goals (e.g., being admitted to college, graduating from college, attaining a job with a college degree).

CLOSURE: Discuss the fact that people must overcome obstacles to achieve their goals in life. Obstacles can be viewed as opportunities rather than reasons not to pursue a goal.

TIME: 2–3 hours

EVALUATION: Students can list the obstacles they have already overcome in their lives.

CHAPTER 12

CAREER DEVELOPMENT INTERVENTIONS IN HIGH SCHOOLS

Including career development interventions in my work as a high school counselor is important because high school counselors prepare students to go into the working world. At the high school level, career development involves teaching students how to plan and prepare for the workforce. Many teenagers have no idea what direction they want to head into and need help sorting through their interests and abilities. This is important because self-information can dictate everything from how students choose their postsecondary education to what jobs they search for while in school. As such, they need to know how to create résumés, fill out applications, and prepare for interviews. Counselors must also teach students life management skills and how career choice can affect your ability to support yourself and others. An additional aspect of career development for counselors can be job placement, more unique to the high school level. Students of all levels are looking for various types of employment. Some students need help finding part-time positions to help pay for expenses or save for college. Other students need training and basic skills for full-time employment that will begin as soon as they graduate. High school counselors must be in contact with community resources and businesses to find out what positions are available to students and sometimes to monitor a student's on-the-job performance. These contacts may employ students as well as provide opportunities for apprenticeships or internships, job shadowing experiences, and coming into the schools for presentations or recruitment. Career development interventions serve as the bridge between students' current experiences and future possibilities.

Megan Martin, M.Ed.
Professional School Counselor
Orange County High School
Hillsboro, NC

MyCounselingLab®

Visit the MyCounselingLab® site for *Career Development Interventions*, Fifth Edition, to enhance your understanding of chapter concepts. You will have the opportunity to practice applying what you learned in the chapter by completing the video- and case-based exercises in the MyLab. Taking the Licensure Quizzes will help you prepare for your certification exam.

Elly was a 16-year-old junior in high school when she came to see you for help with her career choice. The oldest of three children, Elly is shy but friendly. She is a "B" student and currently her plans are to attend college after high school graduation. Elly would be the first person in her family to attend college. Her tentative plan is to major in sociology or psychology because they involve learning about people. She volunteered at a children's camp the past two summers, and on Sunday mornings Elly is a volunteer at the day care in her church. She reports feeling "worried" because she thinks she is "behind her friends" in knowing what career she wants to pursue. "They have better grades and more work experience than I have. I'm not even sure that I can get into a college," Elly shared. She also stated that when she talks with these friends, she feels "stupid" and loses her confidence. Elly wants help deciding what she wants to do so she can feel more confident about herself and her future. If you were her counselor, how would you help her?

Tips from the Field

High school students often feel pressure to be more clear and confident about their futures. Being engaged in career exploration while also being open to future possibilities is a much more realistic and appropriate goal.

lthough the developmental shifts and contextual changes between middle and high school are not as dramatic as those between elementary and middle school, the educational stakes rise relative to their long-term implications for each student's future academic and career success. As students rise through middle school and into high school, so too does the intensity of the academic expectations they encounter. This intensity is evident in Elly's story. Likewise, the need for high school students to engage systematically in educational and career planning also increases during this educational period. "Students often choose academic tracks that impact not only the next four years of high school, but also their future post-secondary and work options" (Akos, 2004, p. 883). As with all developmental transitions, the transition to high school offers opportunities for actively engaging students in career development interventions that can strengthen their academic motivation, bolster their self-esteem, and help them to make connections between their school experiences and their future academic and career opportunities. Elly is hoping to gain strength in each of these ways.

More specifically, as students transition to high school, they focus more directly on the tasks of identifying occupational preferences and clarifying career/lifestyle choices (these tasks build upon all of the American School Counselor Association [ASCA] competencies within the Career Development domain as well as all of the tasks within the National Career Development Guidelines). According to Super (1957), the tasks of crystallizing, specifying, and implementing tentative career choices occur during early (ages 12 to 15), middle (ages 16 to 18), and late (ages 18 to 24) adolescence. Ultimately, specifying and implementing become critical goals for high school students. Super, Savickas, and Super (1996) describe specifying as follows: "Through broad exploration of the occupations, individuals eventually complete the task of specifying an occupational choice by translating the privately experienced occupational self-concept into educational/vocational choices" (p. 132). Simply put, implementing involves taking action toward achieving the specified goal.

In many ways, Elly's concerns are, in fact, in line with developmental expectations. Elly has acquired experience through volunteering at summer camps and the day care center located in her church. These are important experiences that Elly seems to be minimizing as she describes her angst relative to future possibilities. Such activities provide the foundation for greater self-understanding (crystallizing), which, in turn, provides important information for specifying.

There is little doubt that these experiences have added to Elly's self and world-of-work information. Perhaps one thing she could benefit from now is a conversation with her counselor about what she has learned from engaging in these activities thus far. Her counselor could help reinforce the important learning she has acquired from her volunteering.

In this regard, it is important to note that a substantial portion (though still the minority) of secondary school students in the United States enters work immediately upon leaving high school. According to Casselman (2014), in 2013, 68.4% of female high school graduates enrolled in college, versus 63.5% of male grads. Less than 60% of African American and Hispanic members of the class of 2013 were enrolled in college in the fall of 2014, compared to 67% of white graduates. Moreover, young black and Hispanic Americans also have a higher unemployment rate than whites, indicating that they are not choosing to forgo college because of excellent job opportunities. High school graduates who do not enroll in college face challenging, at best, job prospects. The unemployment rate for recent graduates who do not attend college was 30.9% in October 2013—more than four times the rate for the population as a whole (Casselman).

These figures stand in contrast to the 84% of high school seniors who plan to get a two- or four-year college degree. However, only 41% of high school graduates ages 30 to 34 actually have college degrees (Rosenbaum & Person, 2003). Feller (2003) reports that over 70% of high school seniors expect to hold professional jobs (i.e., those requiring a college degree). Many school counselors, Feller notes, hesitate to confront this "silent dream" of obtaining a college degree. Perhaps this hesitation relates to the findings of Anctil, Smith, Schenck, and Dahir (2012) in which they report that the school counselors they surveyed gave lower prioritization to, and provision of, career services to their students than they did academic development and personal-social development. This is a perplexing result given the critical nature of career development in high school. School counselors must do a better job remaining engaged in career service delivery and use information from relevant research studies to support this engagement. For example, Lapan, Whitcomb, and Aleman (2012) found that the inclusion of college/career counseling services and lower counselor-to-students ratios led to a reduction in suspension rates and disciplinary incidents for the high school students they studied. Anctil, Smith, Schenck, and Dahir (2012) also implore school counselors to advocate on behalf of their students' career development. Abdicating this responsibility is not a benign action as the evidence in the next chapter indicates.

Many students default to enrolling in college while possessing no clear goal and, often, lacking in the academic readiness to succeed. This is a dangerous combination of deficiencies. The trend toward "college for all" aspirations emerged from three revolutionary changes (Rosenbaum & Person, 2003, p. 252). First, the labor market dramatically increased its skill demands and augmented the earnings advantages for college graduates. Second, college enrollment became dramatically more accessible in recent decades. Third, community colleges instituted an open admissions policy. Although there has been a popular concern about school counselors being too restrictive by encouraging some students not to attend college, now the opposite may be true. The point here is that school counselors need to do a better job of informing students, parents, and school personnel that jobs leading to rewarding careers exist in a wide variety of fields, including technical specialties, financial services, construction, and trades. Unfortunately, too little is known about jobs in these areas. Moreover, because 31% of college entrants (52% of whom are students with high school grades of C or lower) actually earn no college credits (Rosenbaum, 2001), these students are in reality work bound, and they do not benefit from the "college for all" approach. Thus, we believe that professional school counselors should help students make choices from a full range of options, including those occupations not requiring a college degree. Rosenbaum and Person recommend that professional school counselors also help others become aware of the following new rules regarding the labor market and college:

- All students can attend college, but low-achieving students should be cautioned about the need to take remedial courses once they enter college.
- Even if high school students have college plans, they must prepare for work.
- College plans require substantial effort and good academic planning in high school.
- Many good jobs do not require a college degree.
- High school students improve their chances for obtaining good jobs by having better academic achievement, taking vocational courses, getting job-placement assistance from teachers, and developing "soft skills" such as interpersonal competence and good work habits.

These points highlight the importance of developing workforce readiness to cope successfully with the school-to-work transition. The definition of *workforce readiness* changes with the times. Until recently this term may have focused solely on helping adolescents acquire training for a specific job, but now employers are more concerned with "finding youth who can read and write, have a good attitude, are motivated, are dependable, follow directions, and can be good team members" (Krumboltz & Worthington, 1999, p. 316). Academic skills, interpersonal skills, and engaging in lifelong learning have emerged as important skills for youth to acquire if they are to be successful workers. In this regard, Hansen (1999) argues for expanding school-to-work career development interventions to include student development in addition to the more traditional emphasis on workforce development. Hansen points to curricula such as the Missouri Life Career Development System, the Minnesota Career Development Curriculum, and a model development by the Florida Department of Education titled "A Framework for Developing Comprehensive Guidance and Counseling Programs for a School-to-Work System" as excellent examples of comprehensive career development interventions to help youth prepare for the transition from secondary school to work.

Baker and Gerler (2008) emphasize the importance of school counselors providing "transition enhancement" assistance to secondary school students as they progress toward further education, training, or employment. Because such transitions are a regular part of high school students' development, Baker recommends that counselors view transitions as a process rather than as events or a sequence of events. The basic needs of students coping with the transition process can be classified into the categories of support, awareness, and skills.

Students need emotional support to lessen the anticipatory anxiety they may experience as they consider the transitions they will encounter. Moving from the familiar to the unknown creates anxiety in all people. However, it is reasonable to expect this anxiety to be fairly high among adolescents who have lived their lives primarily in the arenas of home and school. Postsecondary work, training, and education present new challenges and experiences. Although some of these challenges may seem somewhat intimidating, counselors can remind students that the competencies they have developed thus far in their lives will also be helpful to them as they negotiate the postsecondary transition experience. Reassuring students that it is "normal" to feel a bit anxious during a transition also provides emotional support to students as they move forward in their career development plans. In many respects, school counselors are the human development specialists in the schools. Educating stakeholders about the developmental process that students will experience as they move through school helps students, teachers, administrators, and parents develop the awareness to think proactively about the tasks students will encounter. Thus, infusing the academic and school counseling curricula with developmental concepts helps students acquire the awareness that fosters a planful approach to coping with career development tasks.

When conceptualized as a process, the skills required for coping with the school-to-work and school-to-school transition are linked to the elementary and middle school career development competencies discussed previously—that is, transition skills build upon the self-awareness, occupational awareness, and decision-making skills students have developed throughout their educational experience. Transition skills also build upon the basic educational competencies related to reading, writing, and arithmetic (Baker, 2000). For example, composing a resumé and cover letter requires writing skills. Performing effectively in a job or college interview requires skills in oral communication and interpersonal communication. Acquiring information about jobs, colleges, and training programs requires research, technology, and reading skills. Transition skills can also be expanded to include those related to stress and anxiety management. The American School Counseling Association (2003, 2012) takes the position that counselors in the schools must assume the primary (but not the sole) responsibility for fostering these skills in students noting that career guidance is one of the most important contributions a school counselor can make. Likewise, counselors must be competent in strategies to help students who encounter difficulty in mastering career development tasks.

Much of Super's research focused on understanding how adolescents can develop their readiness to address the various career development tasks confronting them. The term initially used by Super (1955) to describe career readiness in adolescence was *career maturity*. Because the career development tasks confronting adolescents emerge from expectations inherent in academic curricula and society (e.g., family, teachers), the career development process during this life stage is more homogeneous than in adulthood. The school system expects students to make career decisions at specific points in the curriculum (e.g., eighth-graders choosing an academic program that they will study in high school). Because the timing of these career development tasks can be predicted, career development practitioners can provide a systematic set of interventions to foster adolescent career development. Super et al. (1996) reinforced this point in stating that adolescent career development can be guided "partly by facilitating the maturing of abilities, interests, and coping resources and partly by aiding in reality testing and in the development of self-concepts" (p. 125).

Other influential researchers such as Marcia (1966) have also identified important variables for adolescent career development. Specifically, Marcia focuses on two variables—crisis/exploration and commitment—as central to the career development process during adolescence. Crisis/exploration refers to the process of sorting through identity issues; questioning parentally defined goals, values, and beliefs; and identifying personally appropriate alternatives regarding career options, goals, values, and beliefs. Commitment refers to the extent that the individual is personally involved in, and expresses allegiance to, self-chosen aspirations, goals, values, beliefs, and career options (Muuss, 1998). The degree to which adolescents resolve the tasks associated with crisis/exploration and commitment provides the conceptual structure for Marcia's taxonomy of adolescent identity (Marcia, 1980). This taxonomy comprises four identity statuses: identity diffused (or identity confused), foreclosed, moratorium, and identity achieved.

1. The *identity-diffused* person has yet to experience an identity crisis or exploration and has not made any personal commitment to an occupation, much less to a set of goals, values, and beliefs.

2. The *foreclosed* person has yet to experience an identity crisis or exploration but has committed to an occupation and to a set of goals, values, and beliefs (usually due to indoctrination or social pressure by parents and/or significant others). This type of foreclosure is premature because it has occurred without exploring and struggling with the basic existential questions related to identifying one's values, beliefs, goals, and so on.

3. The *moratorium* person is engaged in an active struggle to clarify personally meaningful values, goals, and beliefs. Committing to a particular set of values, goals, and beliefs has been placed "on hold" until the process of identity clarification is more complete.

4. The *identity-achieved* person has sorted through the process of identity clarification and resolved these issues in a personally meaningful way. Moreover, as a result of exploring and resolving identity issues, the identity-achieved person commits to an occupation and a personal value system.

Rather than being a singular process of exploring and committing to a set of values, goals, and beliefs, identity formation occurs across several domains, such as occupation, religion, politics, and sexuality. In many respects, these domains parallel Super's (1980) notion of life-role self-concepts (e.g., worker, leisurite, student, and homemaker) and reinforce Hansen's (1999) call for holistic career development interventions in the schools.

In addition, the individual's identity status within each domain is not static but rather an ongoing process involving back-and-forth movement across stages (Muuss, 1998). Marcia (1980) notes that although any of the identity statuses can become terminal, the foreclosed person experiences the greatest risk of closed development.

Thus, career development interventions for preadolescents and adolescents (who by definition enter into these life stages with a relatively diffused identity) should be carefully designed to foster exploration and identity development related to the career domain. For example, Kolodinsky et al. (2006) described the ways in which a career fair designed to expose students to nontraditional workers resulted in both greater exploration and a broader understanding of potential occupational options for student participants. Specifically, these researchers designed a one-day fair with 11 females employed in nontraditional occupations such as border patrol officer, emergency medical technician, computer repair technician, cable technician, firefighter, military officer, and water treatment technician, and 4 males employed as hair stylist, nurse, respiratory therapist, and receptionist, respectively. Each discussed and demonstrated his or her experiences with nontraditional careers. After listening to and interacting with the presenters, students demonstrated increased occupational self-efficacy and relinquished stereotypical beliefs about what is "women's work" and what is "men's work." They also demonstrated increased interest in specific occupations represented by the workers.

Given survey results such as those obtained by Gibbons, Borders, Wiles, Stephan, and Davis (2006) indicating that ninth-graders expressed a desire for additional career information as it relates to developing their career and educational plans, the provision of interventions such as a career fair comprised of nontraditional workers can be an important intervention that offers students accurate information about potential career options.

CAREER DEVELOPMENT GOALS FOR HIGH SCHOOL STUDENTS _____

The extensive body of literature related to adolescent career development helps counselors identify appropriate career development goals and interventions for high school students. The specific career development competencies identified as being appropriate for high school students are:

1. Develop more advanced self-knowledge:

   a. Develop skills to interact positively with others
   b. Understand the implications of continued growth and development for career planning

2. Develop skills for engaging in educational and occupational exploration:

   a. Understand the relationship between educational achievement and career planning
   b. Understand the need for positive attitudes toward work and learning
   c. Develop the skills to locate, evaluate, and interpret career information
   d. Develop more sophisticated job-search skills
   e. Understand how societal needs and functions influence the nature and structure of work

3. Strengthen the skills to make decisions:

   a. Understand the interrelationship of life roles
   b. Understand the continuous changes in male/female roles
   c. Develop skills in career planning

In constructing interventions to foster the development of these competencies, Herr, Cramer, and Niles (2004) recommend attending to several potential issues confronting high school students. For example, it is essential that students construct and know how to implement a career plan. School counselors must also address the fact that students differ in their readiness to address career and educational planning tasks. Thus, career interventions need to be flexible enough to account for these student differences in readiness for career decision making. Finally, students must develop awareness related to postsecondary options, specifically the pros and cons of each option under consideration (e.g., joining the military, enrolling in community college, attending a four-year university).

CAREER DEVELOPMENT INTERVENTIONS IN HIGH SCHOOLS _____

The emphasis on knowledge, skills, and understanding that emerged in the middle school level competencies is continued in the high school competencies. The high school competencies, however, challenge students to become more focused on making career plans by translating their self- and career information into career goals. Savickas (1999) proposed career development interventions that foster the sort of self-knowledge, educational and occupational exploration, and career planning described in the high school competencies. Specifically, these interventions focus on (a) orienting students' comprehension of careers, (b) developing students' planning and exploring competencies, (c) coaching students to develop effective career management techniques, and (d) guiding students in behavioral rehearsals to become prepared for coping with job problems. Interventions that focus on these areas address the American School Counselor Association (ASCA) standards in the Career Development domain.

To orient ninth-grade students to the planning tasks they will encounter as they move through high school, Savickas (1999) recommends using a group guidance format to discuss items on career development inventories, such as the Career Maturity Inventory (Crites, 1978) or the Adult Career Concerns Inventory (Super, Thompson, Lindeman, Jordaan, & Myers, 1988). Using inventory items to orient students to the tasks they need to address to manage their career development effectively helps provide a stimulus for planning and exploring behaviors (Savickas, 1990). For example, the Adult Career Concerns Inventory (ACCI) (Super et al., 1988) measures developmental task concern for the career stages of Exploration, Establishment, Maintenance, and Disengagement. Reviewing the career stages and tasks within the ACCI teaches high school students about the general process of career development. Using ACCI items, adolescents can identify those career development tasks they are likely to encounter in the near future. Strategies for coping with current and near-future career development tasks can be identified. In this way, high school students' understanding of time perspective or "planfulness" can be enhanced (Savickas, Stilling, & Schwartz, 1984). These activities connect with Standards A, B, and C in the Career Development domain of the National Standards for School Counseling.

Antonio's counselor used a group guidance format to discuss students' scores on Holland's Self-Directed Search. They brainstormed occupational options for each type and then discussed what sort of education would be required to enter each occupation. The group members also discussed which school subjects they thought would be most important for each occupation.

Sharing this information with parents and guardians helps foster parental awareness of the career development tasks confronting their children. Keller and Whiston (2008) found a significant relationship between parental behaviors and middle school students' career decision-making self-efficacy. To foster parental awareness of, and involvement in, the career development process, evening informational sessions and newsletters provide opportunities to orient parents and guardians to the career development tasks they can expect high school students to encounter. These activities also provide opportunities to advise parents as to how they can help their children manage these career development tasks more effectively (Turner & Lapan, 2002).

Antonio's counselor sent materials home that described the Holland types and the Self-Directed Search. The counselor invited parents to an evening meeting in which they were given an informal assessment of their Holland types. In a fashion similar to what the counselor had done with the students, parents were then encouraged to brainstorm occupations for each type, identify educational requirements for each occupation, and then list the academic subjects they thought were most important for each occupation. After this activity, the counselor identified ways in which the parents could help their children use the information they had acquired in their career planning.

To help increase self-knowledge and to encourage educational and occupational exploration (ASCA Standards A and C in the Career Development domain), counselors can facilitate student participation in informational interviews. To prepare for these experiences, counselors and teachers guide students in composing interview questions that relate to the high school–level career development competencies. For example, questions pertaining to the importance of interpersonal communication, positive work attitudes, and the relationship between educational achievement and career planning can be identified.

Results from interest and abilities measures administered at the end of middle school or at the beginning of high school provide direction as to which occupational environments offer the best potential for fruitful exploration. As noted, the range of career assessment possibilities that can be used systematically with youth is substantial. To measure interests, counselors can use instruments that provide information related to students' Holland types, such as the Self-Directed Search (Holland, 1985) and the Career Assessment Inventory (Johansson, 1986). Ability measures include the Differential Aptitude Test (Bennett, Seashore, & Wesman, 1992), the Ability Explorer (Harrington, 1996), and assessments of functional skills from school transcripts or educational and career planning portfolios. Areas of high interest and ability can be matched to occupational clusters, and students can identify specific occupations for in-depth exploration (C:B2 in the National Standards).

Although interest and ability assessment results provide important data pertaining to career choice content (i.e., relating students' abilities and interests to occupational options), these data fail to address whether students have developed readiness for career decision making (Super, 1983). Approaches to career assessment must attend to both content and process variables in order to adequately address the needs of youth (Savickas, 1993). Specifically, interests and abilities can be considered as career choice content data that must be viewed in light of career choice process data such as readiness for career decision making, life-role salience, and values—which can be labeled as moderator variables (Super, Osborne, Walsh, Brown, & Niles, 1992). To be ready to effectively choose, and adapt to, an occupation, it is important for high school students to "see themselves as coping with certain developmental tasks, at a stage in life at which they are expected, and may expect themselves to make certain decisions and acquire certain competencies" (Super, 1983, p. 559). Students who have not successfully accomplished the career development tasks presented to them at previous educational levels will need remedial interventions (e.g., additional opportunities for self-concept clarification, training in acquiring occupational information) prior to focusing on career decision making.

From this perspective, addressing career choice readiness (Super, 1990) becomes a necessary precursor to the effective use of ability- and interest-assessment data. According to Super, career choice readiness involves five dimensions: "(a) having a planful attitude toward coping with career stages and tasks, (b) gathering information about educational and occupational opportunities, (c) exploring the world-of-work, (d) knowing how to make good career decisions, and (e) being able to make realistic judgments about potential occupations" (p. 231). These dimensions (which relate to Standards A–C in the National Standards) are important because, if an adolescent knows little about the world-of-work, his or her interest inventories that use occupational titles or activities may produce misleading scores and the student may make poor choices (Super et al., 1996). Likewise, when adolescents do not engage in appropriate career planning, they often encounter career tasks for which they are not prepared (Herr et al., 2004). Thus, assessing high school students' resources for choosing, and adapting to, an occupation requires conducting appraisals of career choice content (e.g., abilities, interests, values) and process (e.g., life-role salience, career choice readiness) variables. When a student is lacking in any of the five dimensions that make up career choice readiness, then the counselor should focus on interventions to help the student progress in that particular domain prior to focusing on career choice content.

It is important to note that traditional assessment approaches focusing only on career choice content variables assume that all individuals place a high value on work and that all individuals view work as the prime means of values realization. It can be argued that this is a Western, middle-class, male view of career development and, thus, is a culturally encapsulated view of life-role salience. Different patterns of life-role salience exist, and they must be considered in helping high school students clarify and articulate their career goals (Niles & Goodnough, 1996). For example, when salience for the work role is high, youths view work as providing meaningful opportunities for self-expression. In such cases, high school students are often motivated to develop the career maturity necessary (e.g., to be planful, to explore opportunities, to gather information) for making good career decisions. When work-role salience is low, however, adolescents often lack motivation and career maturity. In the latter instances, counselors need to begin the career development intervention process by arousing the individual's sense of importance for the worker role (Super, 1990). Disputing irrational beliefs, exposing young people to effective role models, and providing mentors are examples of activities that foster career arousal (Krumboltz & Worthington, 1999).

To help young people further clarify their life-role self-concepts, counselors can encourage high school students to revisit life-role salience questions posed during the middle school years (e.g., How do I spend my time during the course of a typical week? What changes would I like to make in how I spend my time? How important is each life role to me? How important is each life role to my family? What do I like about participating in each life role? What do I hope to accomplish in each life role? What does my family expect me to accomplish in each life role? What life roles do I think will be important to me in the future? What must I do to become more prepared for the life roles that will be important to me in the future?). Discussing these questions helps high school students clarify and articulate their life-role self-concepts. Specifically, by discussing these questions during the first years of high school, adolescents can become clearer as to the values they seek to express in each life role. This information is vital not only for guiding high school students in the selection and pursuit of appropriate educational and occupational options but also in developing appropriate expectations for values satisfaction within the respective life roles.

These discussion questions also provide opportunities for exploring the individual's level of acculturation, cultural identity, and worldview. For example, high school students can discuss family expectations and other cultural factors influencing their life-role participation. Finally, discussing these questions helps counselors become aware of potential barriers, as well as potential sources of support, for students as they move closer to negotiating the school-to-work or school-to-school transition. These discussions also foster the acquisition of the high school–level career development competencies related to understanding the interrelationship of life roles and understanding the changing nature of male/female roles. This information also helps high school students identify those roles in which they spend most of their time, those to which they are emotionally committed, and those that they expect to be important to them in the future. By clarifying information concerning life-role salience (and the cultural factors influencing role salience), high school students establish the foundation for making accurate self-evaluations and for developing career choice readiness.

An important task in acquiring adequate self-knowledge for effective educational and occupational exploration is clarifying values. Clarifying values is important because values are indications of the qualities people desire and seek in "the activities in which they engage, in the situations in which they live, and in the objects which they make or acquire" (Super, 1970, p. 4). Because values reflect the individual's goals, they provide a sense of purpose and direction in the career planning process. However, though many agree that values clarification is critical to choosing an occupation, relatively few put forth the effort to examine their values in a systematic way (Harrington, 1996). Values card sorts (e.g., Career Values Card Sort Kit, Nonsexist Vocational Card Sort) and instruments such as the Career Orientation Placement and Evaluation Survey (COPES) are instruments that are useful in values clarification. Interest inventory results can also be used to identify work-related activities that provide opportunities for values expression.

Regarding parental involvement in the career intervention process, Amundson and Penner (1998) recommend that professional school counselors consider involving parents/guardians directly in the career counseling experience. To this end, Amundson and Penner devised an innovative, parent-involved career exploration (PICE) process that includes five steps. In step one (Introduction), two students and at least one parent, or guardian, for each student are invited to participate in an innovative career exploration activity. The participants' roles are explained (it is the student's career counseling session and parents are invited as observers), and the participants are introduced. The next step is labeled as the Pattern Identification Exercise (PIE) activity and requires the students to each identify a leisure activity and specify an instance when their participation in the activity went very well and an instance when it was less than positive. The counselor works with each student to elaborate regarding the people involved in both instances and the student's feelings, thoughts, challenges, successes, and motivation. The purpose of this discussion is to elucidate each student's strengths and weaknesses. Once a full description is outlined, each student is asked to consider the types of patterns suggested in the information presented. Specifically, students are asked to consider the various goals, values, aptitudes, personality traits, and interests revealed in the information. The final step in the PIE activity links the identified patterns to the career choices the student is facing. Then, the counselor invites input from the students' parents. Parents can confirm what has been discussed and add their perspectives. The next step in PICE is to examine the academic experience. Specifically, students discuss what courses they are taking, how they are performing in each of their courses, and what their feelings are about each of the courses. As before, parents are then asked to provide their perspective of the information the student has shared. Next, students discuss the options under consideration in light of the current labor market situation (e.g., current labor market trends, the need for flexibility, information interviewing, anxiety about the future, admissions to postsecondary opportunities, etc.). Parents are also asked to contribute to this discussion and offer their perspectives about labor market trends and strategies for coping with the current nature of work. The final step in PICE involves action planning. Students and parents are provided with information about school and community career resources. Students are asked to identify what step(s) they will take next in their career planning.

Collectively, these interventions represent examples of ways in which secondary school counselors can help students prepare for a successful school-to-work or school-to-school transition. When counselors at all grade levels work collaboratively to develop systematic career development interventions, then there is the likelihood that high school students will be prepared for the career development tasks they will encounter as they move through secondary school. Two more recent publications provide additional examples of effective strategies for fostering career development in students. Specifically, Perusse and Goodnough (2004) and Erford (2003) are excellent resources for professional school counselors. Both publications contain chapters that address career development with recommended activities, which, in the case of Perusse and Goodnough, are connected to the National Standards.

Although we realize that group and classroom career interventions represent the most reasonable way for school counselors (who, on average nationally experience student-counselor ratios of 476:1) to provide career assistance to students, overreliance on group approaches can foster a one-size-fits-all mentality. Clearly, such a mentality does not lend itself to addressing individual and group differences in career development processes. As we have noted in previous chapters, students from collectivistic cultures approach the career development process differently from those who adhere to more of an individualistic worldview. Due to prejudice, students who are ethnic/racial minorities, disabled, sexual minorities, members of economically challenged groups, and so on, must cope with the career development challenges they experience as a result of discrimination. School counselors must empower students to address these challenges constructively. Thus, effective school counselors understand the processes and the potential effects of discrimination and contribute to helping students develop the knowledge, skills, and awareness necessary for managing their careers in a world in which some people try to limit the opportunities available to others. Surely, individual career assistance and targeted group interventions addressing topics such as the importance of offering and receiving emotional and informational support, challenging occupational stereotypes, and empowering students to acquire the skills/attitudes essential for confronting discrimination are necessary but addressing such issues also requires school counselors to be actively engaged in advocating with employers, school personnel, and community members in efforts to eradicate discrimination in workplace, school, community, and family settings.

CAREER DEVELOPMENT INTERVENTIONS FOR AT-RISK STUDENTS

Successfully completing high school is critical for each student's future success. A male high school graduate who works until age 65 will earn, on average, nearly $333,000 more than a student who leaves school without graduating, and a worker with some college will earn $538,000 more (National High School Center, 2008). In 1964, a high school dropout earned 64 cents for every dollar earned by an individual with at least a high school diploma. In 2004, students who dropped out of high school earned only 37 cents for each dollar earned by an individual with more education (Wise, 2007). Yet, every school day 7,000 U.S. students leave high school, never to return. In 2004, approximately 3.8 million 16- through 24-year-olds were not enrolled in high school and had not earned a high school diploma or alternative credential, such as a GED. Based on calculations per school day (180 days of school, seven hours each day), one high school student drops out every nine seconds. Male students are consistently 8% less likely to graduate than female students, and the gap is as large as 14% between male and female African American students (National High School Center).

The benefits of earning a secondary degree are clear, but our educational system performs poorly relative to preparing minority students and students with disabilities to enter and succeed in higher education. For instance, while 65% of White high school graduates entered college immediately upon graduation in 2001, only 56% and 53% of African American and Latino graduates did the same, respectively (Haycock, 2004). Among White students graduating from high school in 2002, 40% were considered "college-ready," compared to 23% of African American students, and 20% of Latino students (Greene & Winters, 2005). Among students with disabilities, 9% have attended a four-year college after leaving high school, with 6% doing so in 2003, and although this figure is up from previous years, it is still significantly lower than the general population (Wagner, Newman, Cameto, Garza, & Levine, 2005).

Jerald (2006) notes that the three secondary school requirements for postsecondary school success are (a) high expectations and rigorous instruction for all students, (b) equal access to rigorous coursework, and (c) adequate support for student success. As such, it is reasonable to expect in a democratic society that all students will have access to these requirements. However, while 65% of high-income and nearly half of middle-income students are participating in a college preparatory curriculum, only 28% of low-income students are enrolled in a similar program (Pathways to College Network, 2004). African American students are half as likely to be enrolled in "gifted" programs and three times more likely to be enrolled in special education than their White classmates (Pathways to College Network). African American students make up 17% of the public high school population, yet represent 4% of AP Exam test takers. The statistics are similar for Latino students (Barton, 2003).

Such disparities reflect serious deficiencies in the educational system within the United States. In addition, ensuring equal access to the three requirements identified by Jerald (2006), helping students make connections between their academic experiences and future educational and career opportunities fosters academic motivation and achievement. For example, McLaughlin, Sum, and Fogg (2006) report that exposure to work experiences in high school is linked to greater success both in the workforce and in postsecondary education. Given the current lack of job opportunities for young people, however, school counselors need to be actively engaged in advocating on behalf of their students in order to help them gain access to work experiences during high school. Creating volunteer opportunities, job-shadowing experiences, internship experiences, and so on represent ways in which school counselors can help their students bridge the school-to-work connection. Here again, disparities exist as more White teens—sometimes twice as many—held summer jobs in 2006 than non-White teens; further, teens with higher family annual incomes engage more in summer employment opportunities than students from lower-income families (Sum, McLaughlin, & Khatiwada, 2006). When school counselors help create workplace opportunities for students from lower-income families, they help address the fact that high school students from low-income families (the lowest 20%) are six times more likely to drop out than students from higher-income families. The Alliance for Excellent Education (2006) has estimated that the more than 12 million students who will drop out over the next decade will cost the nation $3 trillion. Thus, when school counselors develop and deliver effective career guidance programs to address school retention, they provide important data for policy makers regarding the essential nature of career development services in education.

Froeschle (2009) provides an excellent example of a career development program that was created to influence dropout rates for at-risk students. The program consists of four distinct components: (a) mentorship, (b) small-group solution-focused counseling sessions, (c) psychoeducational career lessons led by counselors and mentors, and (d) implementation of solution-focused skills within the classroom.

Mentors should be individuals who are committed to participating in training sessions, who are willing to meet students on a weekly basis, and who should pass a background check (per local or state district policy). Mentors listen to student concerns and offer empathy, support, and advocacy while modeling good behaviors and decision making (Froeschle, 2009). Being consistently engaged with the student is crucial for the program's success. Mentors are also encouraged to consult with the school counselor after each student meeting to provide updates and solicit advice regarding the mentor's work with the student. The school counselor should also offer students an opportunity to discuss mentoring sessions before, during, or after small-group counseling sessions.

The small-group component of the program uses solution-focused counseling strategies to encourage students to share positive accomplishments, and to refocus thoughts on positive personal traits that led to past successes, exceptions to problems, and leadership skills (Froeschle, 2009). Using solution-focused techniques such as the miracle question, exception questions, complimenting, and scaling questions connected to school performance and career development, small-group meetings seek to empower at-risk students to develop skills to address barriers to achieving career adaptability and school success.

To provide solution-focused strategies in the classroom, school counselors train teachers to focus on students' positive attributes to create an encouraging classroom atmosphere. For example, teachers are trained to notice and record times when students are performing well or have shown improvement. These success lists are provided to the school counselor to share with students in small-group counseling sessions, and/or teachers can share the list privately with students (Froeschle, 2009).

Psychoeducational sessions focus on teaching social skills, providing career information to facilitate goal setting, and creating social support for the students (Froeschle, 2009). Social skills training is linked with positive classroom behavior, developing a career goal is a protective factor connected to positive youth development, and social support provides a coping resource for persevering through challenging times. These groups meet monthly and alternate between being resource focused (e.g., having a guest speaker who provides career information relevant to the participants' interests) and fun activities (field trips to educational and workplace settings; attending events such as sporting activities, plays, movies, which provide the basis for group discussions related to important topics such as teamwork, discipline, overcoming challenges, etc.).

Froeschle (2009) concludes that programs such as this one, which are strengths based and solution focused, "form a school based career counseling program with the potential to reduce dropout rates among minority students. Advocacy for policy changes along with the implementation of this program will result in a better educated class of minority students with greater academic and career potential, maturity, and choices" (p. 18).

MyCounselingLab®

Start with Topic 6—Career Counseling in Schools.

Watch the video *21st Century Career Development Interventions in the Schools: Dr. Carol Dahir* and complete Student Activity #9 on page 340.

SUMMARY

Today, perhaps more than ever, systematic career development interventions are needed to help young people advance in their career development. The nature of work is changing dramatically, requiring new skills sets (e.g., transition skills, stress manage-ment, the ability to engage in lifelong learning, personal flexibility, computer skills) that suggest that change, rather than constancy, will be the norm. Workers in the 21st century will experience multiple career changes that will bring associated levels of stress that must be managed effectively. It is naive to expect parents, many of whom are struggling to manage their own careers effectively, to provide children and adolescents with the competencies they need to advance in their careers. Career development interventions help students prepare for the tasks they will encounter as adults. Moreover, career development interventions help students connect current school activities with their futures. This connection is key to increasing school involvement and school success. Clearly, "when professional school counselors provide career and educational guidance to their students, they influence the future by helping clarify developmental decisions that often last a lifetime" (Erford, 2003, p. 153).

CASE STUDY

When Natasha was 9 years old, her mother was killed in an automobile accident. Prior to this, her father had been incarcerated for armed robbery. As a result, Natasha has been in foster care since that time. Now in 11th grade, Natasha's plans are to find some sort of job or maybe attend community college after high school. In the meantime, moving from a succession of foster homes has taken its toll on her. Her shifts from family to family and school to school have always kept her "off balance" academically. Natasha has always felt out of step and behind her peers. She is, however, a student who takes school seriously. In fact, she is typically a "B" student. She seems to know that doing well academically could be a real boost to her future and she wants a better future for herself.

Natasha has lived with her current foster parents for three years (a long time given her much briefer stints in other foster homes). Her foster parents are focused on supporting and encouraging her in any way that they can. Lately, they have been encouraging her to consider going to college after high school. This is a new consideration for Natasha and she is intrigued by it.

Natasha's interests revolve around music and science. Regarding the latter, she does well in science courses but has not enrolled in the more academically rigorous courses that are part of the college preparatory program of study. Interpersonally, Natasha is a humble and gentle person. Her foster parents have encouraged her to meet with you (the school counselor) to explore the idea of attending college after high school.

What are Natasha's career development needs? What other issues does Natasha present? What career tasks must she complete to begin to engage in effective educational and career planning? How will you work with Natasha to help her move forward?

STUDENT ACTIVITIES

1. What career development tasks do you think are most important to help high school students address?

2. What factors do you think could negatively influence the career development of high school students?

3. What are three strategies you could use to foster positive career development in high school students?

4. What do you think is the most common type of career assistance provided to high school students? Do you think this type of assistance is helpful? If so, why? If not, why not?

5. How could you help parents/guardians to help their high school students experience positive career development?

6. Interview a high school student about his or her career development. Ask this person what

occupations s/he thinks are possible for him/her. Ask your interviewee whether there are any occupations that are not possible for him/her. Ask the person to discuss why certain occupations may not be possible. Ask what occupation your interviewee would choose if s/he could choose anything. Then, explore with your interviewee what s/he thinks is attractive about that occupation. Finally, ask your interviewee what additional information he or she needs to take a next step in career and educational planning.

7. What do you think is the most common type of career assistance provided to high school students? Do you think this type of assistance is helpful? If so, why? If not, why not?

8. How could you help parents/guardians to help their high school students experience positive career development?

9. Refer to the MyCounselingLab® Video and Resource Library and select the video entitled *Career Development Interventions in the School: An Interview with Dr. Carol Dahir.* How would you draw upon Dr. Dahir's comments to convince your principal and school board of the importance of career development interventions in high school settings?

Sample Career Development Activities for High School Students

An Interesting Journal

NATIONAL CAREER DEVELOPMENT GUIDELINES: Personal Social Domain: PS1.K1; PS1.A1; PS1.R1

ASCA STANDARDS: Standard A—Students will acquire the skills to investigate the world-of-work in relation to knowledge of self and to make informed career decisions; Standard C—Students will understand the relationship between personal qualities, education, training, and the world-of-work.

PURPOSE: This activity encourages students to identify their interests and to consider how their interests can inform their career decisions.

OBJECTIVE: To help students identify their interests and connect their interests to career possibilities.

MATERIALS: Notebook or journal

INTRODUCTION: Discuss how our interests should guide career plans: "Do what you enjoy and you will never work a day in your life." By focusing on the things that we find most enjoyable, we can begin to clarify those activities that we should incorporate into our career plans.

ACTIVITIES: Instruct students to keep a log of how they spend their out-of-school time over the course of 1 week. As they enter the activity in their journals, they should give the activity a rating from 1 ("hated it") to 5 ("loved it"). The time frame can be lengthened to get a better sense of the activities students liked and disliked.

DISCUSSION: Students can discuss the activities they liked and did not like. They can also identify reasons for their reactions to their activities.

CLOSURE: The leader can help students understand how they can use their interests to guide their career exploration. For example, if a student enjoys working with animals, then the group can brainstorm additional activities that can provide that student with the opportunity to work with animals. The group can also brainstorm career opportunities that provide people with the opportunity to work with animals. As each student discusses his or her likes, the group can brainstorm in a similar fashion.

TIME: 45–60 minutes

EVALUATION/ASSIGNMENT: At the end of the activity, students should identify two activities in which they are interested and two things they can do to gain additional exposure to their interests.

- -

Values Sorting

NATIONAL CAREER DEVELOPMENT GUIDELINES: Personal Social Domain: PS1.K4; PS1.A4; PS1.R4; Career Management Domain: CM2.K5; CM2.A5; CM2.R5

ASCA STANDARDS: Standard A—Students will acquire the skills to investigate the world-of-work in relation to knowledge of self and to make informed career decisions.

PURPOSE: Good career decisions are values based. However, few career options provide individuals with the opportunity to express all of their important values. Thus, we must prioritize values and identify those that are most important to us. We must be clear as to which values we are willing to part with, if necessary. Each decision we make requires us to sort our values and make choices accordingly. Being able to select career options that provide us with maximal opportunities for values expression requires us to subjectively define our important values. For example, although many people value "financial rewards," this value is defined somewhat definitely across individuals. Understanding how we define the most important values in our lives helps us to determine which options fit best. Finally, it is important to understand how values are connected to our participation in the life roles we play.

OBJECTIVES: As a result of participating in this activity, participants will (a) learn the importance of values clarification, (b) become aware of their most important values, and (c) understand the importance of considering values in career decision making and career planning.

MATERIALS: Handouts of the values list and five slips of paper per participant

INTRODUCTION: Introduce this activity as an exercise that helps participants identify and define important values in their lives.

ACTIVITY: To start this activity, give participants a list of values such as this one:

VALUES LIST

_____ Financial rewards

_____ Job security

_____ Good family relationships

_____ A world that is free of discrimination

_____ Creativity

_____ Having a set routine

_____ Time by myself

_____ Community activities

_____ Physical activities

_____ An attractive physical appearance

_____ Variety

_____ Power

_____ Recognition

_____ Prestige

_____ Freedom from stress

_____ Associating with people I like

_____ Success

_____ Freedom to live where I choose

_____ Leisure time

_____ Fame

_____ Strong religious faith

_____ Adventure

_____ World peace

_____ Helping others

_____ Having children

_____ Good health

_____ A beautiful home

_____ Autonomy

_____ Other

_____ Other

Instruct students to identify their top 10 values from this list by putting an X next to the values that are most important to them (the values chosen are not ranked at this point). Then, after discussing their experience of conducting this initial values sort, provide participants with five slips of paper. Ask them to identify their top 5 values from the list of their top 10 and to write one value on each slip of paper (again these values are not ranked). Participants are then informed that the activity leader will be taking a value from them, one at a time. Thus, participants must now decide which of their top 5 values they are willing to part with first. At this point, the activity leader actually goes around the room taking a value from each participant.

Immediately after students give a value to the leader, instruct the participants to record and define what that value means to them (e.g., "financial rewards: having an income of more than $45,000/year with good health and retirement benefits"). Continue this process for each of the remaining values. At the conclusion of the exercise, participants have a list of their top 5 values, with definitions, in descending order. For example, here are five value definitions:

5. Financial rewards: having an income of more than $45,000/year with good health and retirement benefits
4. Autonomy: being able to make my own decisions as to how to best accomplish my job duties but having a colleague who can give me advice when I need it
3. Associating with people I like: being friends with my coworkers and doing things together outside of work
2. Good health: eating right and exercising three times per week

1. Strong religious faith: going to church on a regular basis and volunteering at a soup kitchen

DISCUSSION: After completing the exercise, explain how the activity relates to career decision making. Explain that in every decision there is the promise of gain and the threat of loss (otherwise, one could simply choose the "perfect" option in every instance). The risk involved in decision making is lessened when options are selected based on the individual's key values.

CLOSURE: Encourage participants to consider how they spend their time in the course of a typical week and if they spend time in activities reflecting their top values. If the answer is no, then encourage participants to identify strategies for increasing their participation in activities reflecting their values (e.g., agreeing to a moderate exercise program, identifying opportunities for volunteering).

TIME: Approximately 30 minutes

EVALUATION/ASSIGNMENT: Students will list their five most important values and identify three jobs in which they could express these values.

The Pie of Life

NATIONAL CAREER DEVELOPMENT GUIDELINES: Personal Social Domain: PS1.K4; PS1.A4; PS1.R4; Career Management Domain: CM2.K5; CM2.A5; CM2.R5

ASCA STANDARDS: Standard A—Students will acquire the skills to investigate the world-of-work in relation to knowledge of self and to make informed career decisions; Standard B—Students will employ strategies to achieve future career goals with success and satisfaction; Standard C—Students will understand the relationship between personal qualities, education, training, and the world-of-work.

PURPOSE: To focus on how students spend their time now and how they hope to spend their time in the future.

OBJECTIVE: To enhance self-awareness regarding values and life-role participation.

MATERIALS: Paper, pencils

INTRODUCTION: Encourage students to consider a typical week in their lives and ask them how they spend their time. Emphasize with students the importance of spending time in activities that reflect their interests and values.

ACTIVITIES: Ask each student to draw a circle on a piece of paper. Encourage students to consider the circle as if it were a "pie of life." Instruct them to consider how they spend their time over the course of a typical week (24 hours a day, 7 days a week). Tell them to divide the circle or pie into "slices" according to how much of their time is spent in each activity over the course of a week. Once they have divided their pies into slices, ask students to write answers to the following question: "What conclusions could someone draw from your 'pie of life' about what you like to do and what you value?"

DISCUSSION: Divide students into small groups. Encourage them to share their "pies of life" with each other. Then encourage students to share with the entire class any reactions they had to dividing their "pies of life" into slices as well as any reactions they had to hearing how their peers divided their pies.

CLOSURE: Emphasize the importance of having a "pie of life" that reflects your interests and values as much as possible. If students do not have a pie that reflects their interests and values, then encourage them to consider what changes they can make to increase the degree to which their "pies of life" reflect their values and interests.

TIME: 45 minutes

EVALUATION/ASSIGNMENT: Have students draw a second circle that reflects their lives as an adult (choose a specific age, such as 35 years old).

Instruct them to divide their "pies of life" into slices according to how they hope to spend their time in the future. Ask them to identify how their slices relate to their interests and values. Ask them to identify the life roles reflected in their future slices of life. Finally, ask students to identify five things they can do between now and when they turn age 35 to increase the chances that their future "pies of life" will come true.

Time Capsule

NATIONAL CAREER DEVELOPMENT GUIDELINES: Personal Social Domain: PS1.K4; PS1.A4; PS1.R4; Career Management Domain: CM2.K5; CM2.A5; CM2.R5

ASCA STANDARDS: Standard A—Students will acquire the skills to investigate the world-of-work in relation to knowledge of self and to make informed career decisions; Standard B—Students will employ strategies to achieve future career goals with success and satisfaction; Standard C—Students will understand the relationship between personal qualities, education, training, and the world-of-work.

PURPOSE: To explore what possessions are valuable to students and why.

OBJECTIVE: Students will learn about themselves and others by examining a valued possession; students will explore what they would like future generations of people to know about them. Students will also discuss how the possessions they value are influenced by the culture in which they live.

MATERIALS: Ask students to bring a valued object from home, something that tells something about them that they might leave behind in an imaginary time capsule for future generations of high school students.

INTRODUCTION: Ask students to bring an item from home to show other participants; students should be prepared to explain what the item is and why it is important to them.

ACTIVITIES: Each student will describe the possession, explain why it is important to him or her, how it reflects something about the student, and what he or she would like to communicate to future high school students by placing this item in an imaginary time capsule.

DISCUSSION: Students may discuss the items, any common concerns/messages for future generations, what they would like others to know about them, what is valued and why, and so on. Students will also discuss the group similarities and differences in the items they chose as valuable. Students can discuss how these items might be different if they lived in another country.

CLOSURE: Students can discuss the fact that the things we value are reflected in the things that are valuable to us. They are, in essence, symbolic representations of things that are important to us due to a variety of reasons (e.g., what the objects represent, because a person who is important to us gave us the object). The uniqueness of the objects selected tells us something important about ourselves.

TIME: 45 minutes to 1 hour

EVALUATION/ASSIGNMENT: Students will complete the following sentences: "Three things that are important to me are _____." and "These objects are important to me because _____."

Becoming a Member of Another Culture: A Fantasy

NATIONAL CAREER DEVELOPMENT GUIDELINES: Career Management Domain: CM2.A5; Personal Social Domain: PS2.K9; PS2.A9; PS2.R9

ASCA STANDARDS: Standard A—Students will acquire the skills to investigate the world-of-work in relation to knowledge of self and to make informed career decisions; Standard B—Students will employ strategies to achieve future career goals with success and satisfaction; Standard C—Students will understand the relationship between personal qualities, education, training, and the world-of-work.

PURPOSE: For students to learn what it would be like to suddenly find themselves as members of another culture.

OBJECTIVES:

1. For students to think about what privileges go along with certain cultures.
2. For students to recognize how they perceive their culture and others' cultures.

MATERIALS: None

INTRODUCTION: Say to students, "I am going to need everyone to relax and close his or her eyes. We are going to use our imaginations in this exercise to think about what it would be like to be a member of another culture."

ACTIVITY: (Read aloud) "You're feeling relaxed now; you're very calm; it's the middle of the week, just prior to bedtime. You find yourself sitting in your comfortable chair, very relaxed. Your eyes are closed. . . . You are tired, very tired, and decide to go to bed. You enter a very restful sleep, very restful sleep. (Pause 10 seconds.) Now, visualize yourself

awakening the next morning. You see yourself entering your bathroom. Take a careful look in the mirror; you see there's been a rather startling transformation during the night. . . . You woke up as a member of another culture with physical characteristics typical of those from that culture. . . . You went to bed a member of one culture and you woke up a member of another! (Pause.) How does it feel? (Pause.) Now you find yourself walking outside and meeting your best friend. How does your friend react? (Pause.) Now, visualize yourself walking across the campus. How do people react to you? You meet your favorite teacher—what happens? How do you feel? What is the overall reaction toward you? (Pause.) Okay. Open your eyes now."

DISCUSSION: Place students in small groups to take turns sharing their fantasies. Ask members to ask each other open-ended questions about what they share (what, how, when, or where). Request that they do not "interpret" another's fantasy.

CLOSURE: Discuss some of the themes in the students' fantasies and their specific reactions to suddenly being a member of a different culture.

TIME: 20–30 minutes

EVALUATION/ASSIGNMENT: Ask students to write two paragraphs describing how it felt to be a member of a culture different from their own.

Who Am I?

NATIONAL CAREER DEVELOPMENT GUIDELINES: Career Management Domain: CM2.A5; Personal Social Domain: PS2.K9; PS2.A9; PS2.R9

ASCA STANDARDS: Standard A—Students will acquire the skills to investigate the world-of-work in relation to knowledge of self and to make informed career decisions; Standard B—Students will employ strategies to achieve future career goals with success and satisfaction; Standard C—Students will understand the relationship between personal qualities, education, training, and the world-of-work.

PURPOSE: To help members learn more about themselves and each other in the group.

OBJECTIVE: Students will have an increased level of understanding about what makes each of them

uniquely different and also what are some of their similarities.

MATERIALS: Pins, 4 × 6 cards for each student

INTRODUCTION: Tell students, "We will be learning a lot about who we are. It is important to understand yourself and what has influenced who you are today. The activity we will be starting with is a great way to remind us about what things are unique to each of us and help us to recognize the differences in others."

ACTIVITIES: Give each student a 4 × 6 card and read aloud the following instructions.

a. Print your first name in the center of the index card. Write large enough so other people can read it.

b. In the upper left-hand corner, write or put a symbol for:
   1. Where you were born
   2. A favorite place you would like to visit on a vacation
c. In the upper right-hand corner, put a symbol or write words that depict something you like to do to have fun.
d. In the lower left-hand corner, write three words your best friend might use to describe you if you were not present.
e. In the lower right-hand corner, describe one characteristic about the specific culture to which you belong (Anglo, African American, etc.) that you value and appreciate.
f. Finally, somewhere on your card put another symbol that tells something you are really looking forward to doing in the future.

After they have completed their "Who Am I" card, have students fasten the cards to the fronts of their shirts or blouses. Then ask them to find an individual they do not know very well, preferably of a different culture or gender, someone with whom they can pair up. Each pair should interview one another for 10 minutes concerning the data on the cards.

DISCUSSION: Next, form a large circle with pairs standing together. Each pair should in turn step forward and introduce one another to the group. Afterward, have students share something they have learned regarding a student and what they would like to know more about.

CLOSURE: Ask the participants to wear their name tags to subsequent sessions until everyone knows everyone else.

TIME: 1 hour

EVALUATION/ASSIGNMENT: Have students follow through on the activity by instructing them to learn more about one person in the group.

Responding to Labels

NATIONAL CAREER DEVELOPMENT GUIDELINES: Career Management Domain: CM1.K1; CM1.R1; Personal Social Domain: PS2.K9; PS2.A9; PS2.R9

ASCA STANDARDS: Standard A—Students will acquire the skills to investigate the world-of-work in relation to knowledge of self and to make informed career decisions; Standard B—Students will employ strategies to achieve future career goals with success and satisfaction; Standard C—Students will understand the relationship between personal qualities, education, training, and the world-of-work.

PURPOSE: For students to think about some of the ways society labels people and how they can sometimes use some of the conflict resolution techniques when they feel like they are possibly being labeled.

OBJECTIVES:

1. Let the students experience what it is like when society labels certain individuals.
2. Help students to decide how to handle labeling, such as peer-group labels.

MATERIALS: Sheets of paper, tape, and a marker

INTRODUCTION: Place labels on certain individuals' backs. People in the room will respond to these individuals according to the labels they have on their backs. The individuals with labels will not know what they are and should pay close attention to how others in the room are treating them. While doing this activity, think about other labels that society gives people. For example, there are probably labels that your peers give to people in school.

ACTIVITIES: Write the following labels on separate sheets of paper and tape them on a few of the students' backs. Have the students without the labels walk around and react to the students as if they actually were what they are labeled.

- Famous movie star
- Person with HIV
- Mental patient
- Deaf person
- Criminal
- Drug addict
- Famous athlete

DISCUSSION:

1. Have the students who had labels talk about what it felt like to wear the labels. Have each guess what he or she thinks his or her label might be.
2. Next, have the students who did not have labels talk about how it felt to treat people according to their labels.

Ask the students if they think this happens in U.S. society. What are some of the labels people attach to others? Have students consider how damaging these labels can be to the individuals assigned the labels by society.

Ask the students what they can do to deal with labeling. Have them refer back to some of the skills they learned in the conflict resolution activities. List their answers on the board.

CLOSURE: Ask students to think about how knowledge gained from this activity can make us more aware of labeling in our society and ways of handling situations in which someone is being labeled.

TIME: 30 minutes

EVALUATION/ASSIGNMENT: Ask students to list ways in which they encounter labeling each day (e.g., television, music, newspapers, family, and friends).

Educational and Occupational Exploration Informational Interviewing

NATIONAL CAREER DEVELOPMENT GUIDELINES: Personal Social Domain: PS2.K9; PS2.A9; PS2.R9; Career Management Domain: CM2; CM3.K2; CM3.A2; CM3.R2; CM3.K4; CM3.A4; CM3.R4; CM3.K5; CM3.A5; CM3.R5; CM3.K6; CM3.A6; CM4.A5; CM4.R5; CM4.A6; CM4.R6

ASCA STANDARDS: Standard A—Students will acquire the skills to investigate the world-of-work in relation to knowledge of self and to make informed career decisions; Standard B—Students will employ strategies to achieve future career goals with success and satisfaction; Standard C—Students will understand the relationship between personal qualities, education, training, and the world-of-work.

PURPOSE: To provide students with information concerning their possible career goals.

OBJECTIVE: Students will learn about specific occupations. Students will gather information pertaining to occupational requirements, training requirements, occupational conditions, and so on, for occupations that interest them.

MATERIALS: Writing materials and interview guide

INTRODUCTION: Tell students, "To get real-life information about jobs, it is useful to interview people working in a job in which you are interested. Workers can provide important information concerning what they like about their work and what they do not like. They can also tell you about the training requirements involved in preparing for the job."

ACTIVITIES: Students will interview workers who enjoy doing their jobs and are good at them. In other words, the interviewees will need to be screened to ensure that they meet these two requirements (the first requirement being more important than the second). Students will conduct a structured interview asking the following questions:

1. What do you like most about your job?
2. How did you decide that this job was a good choice for you?
3. What type of training is required for this job?
4. What types of benefits are provided in a job like this?
5. How many hours do you usually work each week?
6. How much vacation time do you have each year?
7. What are the most important things for doing this job well?
8. What things do you not like about your job?
9. What is the most important piece of advice you would give to someone interested in doing this job?
10. Is there anything else you think I should know?

DISCUSSION: Have students review the responses to these questions and share them with the group. Have them respond (in writing and/or verbally) to the following question: "This job would or would not (select one) be a good match for me because _____."

CLOSURE: Encourage students to compare the information they learned about the job with the information they have learned about themselves (e.g., their interests, values, skills, etc.). Students can eliminate jobs that do not seem like a good fit after further consideration. Students can identify next steps for additional exploration of jobs that seem like a good fit, such as participating in job shadowing and engaging in additional research to learn more about the job.

TIME: Varies depending on the number of interviews; each interview should take 20–30 minutes

EVALUATION/ASSIGNMENT: Students will complete the questions listed in the Discussion section.

Work Lessons

NATIONAL CAREER DEVELOPMENT GUIDELINES: Career Management Domain: CM2.R4; CM3.K2; CM3.A2; CM3.R2; CM3.K4; CM3.A4; CM3.R4; CM3.K5; CM3.A5; CM3.R5; CM3.K6; CM3.A6; CM4.A5; CM4.R5; CM4.A6; CM4.R6

ASCA STANDARDS: Standard A—Students will acquire the skills to investigate the world-of-work in relation to knowledge of self and to make informed career decisions; Standard B—Students will employ strategies to achieve future career goals with success and satisfaction; Standard C—Students will understand the relationship between personal qualities, education, training, and the world-of-work.

PURPOSE: To provide students with information concerning the jobs their family members have held.

OBJECTIVE: Students will link their family's history with the world-of-work.

MATERIALS: Interview guide

INTRODUCTION: Remind students that we learn a lot about work from our family members. Often, family members pass on to their children and grandchildren the lessons they have learned from their work experiences.

ACTIVITIES: Students will interview immediate and extended family members concerning their work experiences. Students will conduct a structured interview asking the following questions:

1. What jobs have you held in your life?
2. How did you choose each of these jobs?
3. Which job did you like the most and why?
4. What type of training is required to do the job you liked most?
5. What are the most important skills and interests for doing this job well?
6. What did you learn about working as a result of doing this job?
7. Would you recommend this job to me? Why or why not?
8. What job did you like least and why?
9. What did you learn about working as a result of doing this job?
10. What is the most important piece of advice you could give to me about making a career choice?

DISCUSSION: Students can review the responses to these questions and share them with the group. They can also respond (in writing and/or verbally) to the following question: "The job that one of my family members has held that is most interesting to me is _____. This job is interesting to me because _____."

CLOSURE: Encourage students to discuss what they learned about work as a result of interviewing their family members. Encourage students to talk about what they like or dislike about what they learned. Finally, encourage students to discuss how they can use what they learned in their own career planning.

TIME: Varies depending on the number of interviews; each interview should take 20–30 minutes

EVALUATION/ASSIGNMENT:

1. Students will complete the questions listed in the Discussion section.
2. Students can gather information about the job that they liked most.

Family Meeting Role Play

NATIONAL CAREER DEVELOPMENT GUIDELINES: Career Management Domain: CM2.R4; CM3.K2; CM3.A2; CM3.R2; CM3.K4; CM3.A4; CM3.R4; CM3.K5, CM3.A5; CM3.R5; CM3.K6; CM3.A6; CM4.A5; CM4.R5; CM4.A6; CM4.R6

ASCA STANDARDS: Standard A—Students will acquire the skills to investigate the world-of-work in relation to knowledge of self and to make informed career decisions; Standard B—Students will employ strategies to achieve future career goals with success and satisfaction; Standard C—Students will understand the relationship between personal qualities, education, training, and the world-of-work.

PURPOSE: To explore the pros and cons of, and concerns about, college attendance, from the points of view of a range of family members.

OBJECTIVE: To clarify values in and identify obstacles to going to college (real, imagined, attitudes, etc.).

MATERIALS: Students may role-play family members and/or bring in family members for this activity; use hats or costumes if desired.

INTRODUCTION: Explain to students the role-play task: Each student must role-play a family member other than himself or herself. Then students switch roles to see different points of view or concerns of all family members. Encourage real family members to participate when possible. Identify questions to ponder, such as "Where will the money for college come from?" "Will a parent/sibling be okay when the college student leaves home?" "Why do you want to go to college when there are jobs here at home you can do?"

ACTIVITIES: Conduct the role plays and follow-up questions. Monitor group discussions and identify a note taker to list barriers, concerns, and general attitudes.

DISCUSSION: Review concerns and barriers, discuss solutions, and identify feelings that arise and the impact of those feelings upon college decisions.

CLOSURE: Focus on sorting out which concerns are real and which are imagined. Identify solutions (via brainstorming) to the real concerns. Encourage students to let go of the imagined concerns.

TIME: 30 minutes–1 hour

EVALUATION/ASSIGNMENT: Have students complete a table with two columns in which they list the real concerns about attending college in one column and the imagined concerns about attending college in the other column.

What Can I Buy? Comparing Incomes: College or No College

NATIONAL CAREER DEVELOPMENT GUIDELINES: Educational Achievement and Lifelong Learning Domain: ED1.R2; ED1.R3; ED1.K5; ED1.A5; ED1.R5; Career Management Domain: CM1.A1; CM1.A2; CM1.K5; CM1.A5; CM1.R5

ASCA STANDARDS: Standard A—Students will acquire the skills to investigate the world-of-work in relation to knowledge of self and to make informed career decisions; Standard B—Students will employ strategies to achieve future career goals with success and satisfaction; Standard C—Students will understand the relationship between personal qualities, education, training, and the world-of-work.

PURPOSE: To compare an average college graduate's income with the income of a high school graduate, and give examples of what extra income might be used for in a given period of time.

OBJECTIVE: Students will be able to visually compare the purchasing power a college degree income has over that of a high school degree.

MATERIALS: Store catalogs with pictures, car brochures, newspaper photos (e.g., houses for sale), and so on

INTRODUCTION: Ask students if they would rather earn more money or less money in their lives. Then tell students that there is a way to increase significantly the probability that they will be able to achieve their goals of earning more money. Use the chart that follows to explain to students that a man or woman with a college degree may earn from 82% to 96% more than a person with a high school diploma. Show examples of annual differences in income, five-year differences, and ten-year differences on the blackboard.

Activities: Have students draw, cut out pictures, or describe verbally what the differences in incomes could purchase for an individual with a college degree (e.g., first year—number of pairs of sneakers, basketballs, a small car; fifth year—two medium-size cars; tenth year—a home). Ask students to construct a weekly budget based on a high school degree versus a college degree.

Discussion: Review income differences and examples of the purchasing power of college versus no college incomes. Ask students, "Is this important?" "Why?"

Closure: Discuss how extra effort (e.g., staying in school four years longer) can make a significant difference in one's life. Emphasize that the decisions we make, especially about education, have real and long-term effects in our lives.

Time: 30–40 minutes

Evaluation/Assignment: Have students respond to the following question: "What is meant by the phrase 'The more you learn, the more you earn'?"

The Value of Work

National Career Development Guidelines: Educational Achievement and Lifelong Learning Domain: ED1.R2; ED1.R3; ED1.K5; ED1.A5; ED1.R5; Career Management Domain: CM1.A1; CM1.A2; CM1.K5; CM1.A5; CM1.R5; CM3.K1; CM3.A1; CM3.R1; CM3. R3; CM3.K4; CM5.K1

ASCA Standards: Standard A—Students will acquire the skills to investigate the world-of-work in relation to knowledge of self and to make informed career decisions; Standard B—Students will employ strategies to achieve future career goals with success and satisfaction; Standard C—Students will understand the relationship between personal qualities, education, training, and the world-of-work.

Purpose: To learn that the compensation for work is not always equal to the value of a particular service provided by workers.

Objective: Students will be able to state which occupations they feel are the most valuable and/or which they feel should be compensated at a higher rate for the work performed.

	High School Graduate	College Graduate	Difference
In 1 year	$10,000	$19,000 (90% more)	$9,000
In 5 years	$50,000	$95,000	$45,000
In 10 years	$100,000	$190,000	$90,000

Materials: Pencils, paper, chalkboard and chalk

Introduction: Give students a list of jobs and services, including teacher, police officer, garbage collector, professional athlete, firefighter, secretary, computer programmer, doctor, writer, bus or cab driver, rock musician.

Activities: Have students rank the jobs according to the amounts they feel they should be paid, from lowest to highest salary.

Discussion: Have students compare their lists and discuss the reasons for ranking each as they did.

Closure: Discuss with the students the difference between the economic value of a job (i.e., the salary of a job determined by the economic principles of supply and demand) and the social value of a job (i.e., the degree to which the job contributes to society and others).

Time: 30 minutes

Evaluation/Assignment: Each participant will be able to list three jobs with high economic value (i.e., those that pay well but do not necessarily contribute to society, such as athlete and performer). Each participant will be able to list three jobs with high social value (i.e., those that contribute to the betterment of society).

People and Things

NATIONAL CAREER DEVELOPMENT GUIDELINES: Educational Achievement and Lifelong Learning Domain: ED1.R2; ED1.R3; ED1.K5; ED1.A5; ED1.R5; Career Management Domain: CM1.A1; CM1.A2; CM1.K5; CM1.A5

ASCA STANDARDS: Standard A—Students will acquire the skills to investigate the world-of-work in relation to knowledge of self and to make informed career decisions; Standard B—Students will employ strategies to achieve future career goals with success and satisfaction; Standard C—Students will understand the relationship between personal qualities, education, training, and the world-of-work.

PURPOSE: To explore tasks that require interpersonal skills and those that do not.

OBJECTIVE: Students will be able to identify activities that require interpersonal skills and differentiate between tasks that do or do not require interpersonal skills.

MATERIALS: Paper; pencils; lists of activities, such as hobbies, pet care, sports, clubs, going to school, and so on

INTRODUCTION: Ask students to list activities that they or others might do in any given day.

ACTIVITIES: Ask students to differentiate between the activities requiring interpersonal skills and those that do not. Write these lists on the blackboard.

DISCUSSION: Review and compare the lists of activities. Ask students to determine which of these activities are their favorites, which they'd like to avoid, which are particularly difficult due to the need for compromise with others, and so on.

CLOSURE: Emphasize the importance of focusing on the category of activities (those relying on a high level of interpersonal skills vs. those that do not) to which students seem most drawn in their career planning. Encourage students to identify occupations within each category.

TIME: 30–45 minutes

EVALUATION/ASSIGNMENT: Ask students to list occupations that fall within two categories: (a) those that rely heavily on interpersonal skills and (b) those that do not rely heavily on interpersonal skills.

Career Planning: Map of My Life

NATIONAL CAREER DEVELOPMENT GUIDELINES: Personal Social Domain: PS1.K4; PS1.A4; PS1.R4; Career Management Domain: CM1.A1, CM1.A2, CM1.K5, CM1.A5, CM1.R5, CM3.K1, CM3.A1, CM3.R1, CM3.R3, CM3.K4, CM5.K1

ASCA STANDARDS: Standard A—Students will acquire the skills to investigate the world-of-work in relation to knowledge of self and to make informed career decisions; Standard C—Students will understand the relationship between personal qualities, education, training, and the world-of-work.

PURPOSE: Students will recognize how different events and people have changed their lives.

OBJECTIVE: Each student will construct a personal road map with dates and his or her birthplace, family, schools, friends, significant influences, accomplishments, setbacks, interests, and short- and long-term goals.

MATERIALS: Large piece of art paper and colored markers

INTRODUCTION: Tell students, "You will be making a map of your life on a large piece of art paper. To learn more about ourselves and events and people who have influenced who we are today, you are going to make a personal road map."

ACTIVITIES: Have students complete their maps using words and illustrations and then pair off to discuss their maps.

DISCUSSION: Ask the class to discuss these questions: "Did anyone learn something new about himself or herself?" "Was it difficult to think of future goals?" "Were some people surprised by how much they had on their maps?"

CLOSURE: Tell students, "I hope this activity helped you understand some of the things that have influenced you. It is important to have self-understanding before making decisions. We will be looking at our goals in some later activities."

TIME: 35 minutes

EVALUATION/ASSIGNMENT: Have students identify one long-term goal and three things they can do to achieve that goal.

My Roles in Life

NATIONAL CAREER DEVELOPMENT GUIDELINES: Personal Social Domain: PS4.K1; PS4.A1; PS4.R1; PS4.K2; PS4.A2; PS4.R2; PS4.K3; PS4.A3; PS4.R3; PS4.K4; PS4.A4; PS4.R4

ASCA STANDARDS: Standard A—Students will acquire the skills to investigate the world-of-work in relation to knowledge of self and to make informed career decisions; Standard B—Students will employ strategies to achieve future career goals with success and satisfaction; Standard C—Students will understand the relationship between personal qualities, education, training, and the world-of-work.

PURPOSE: To provide students with the opportunity to consider life roles that are and will be important to them.

OBJECTIVE: Students will engage in life-role planning.

MATERIALS: Writing materials, chalkboard and chalk

INTRODUCTION: Tell students, "While busy making livings, people are busy living their lives. All the things we do can contribute to our life satisfaction. We can describe our activities in life in terms of 'life roles.' For example, one life role most adults play is the role of 'worker.' Many adults are also parents. All young people play the life role of 'student.'" Discuss additional life-role possibilities for young people and adults. Write them on the chalkboard under either the heading of "young people" and/or "adults" according to which category or categories are most appropriate. Emphasize that participating effectively in the life roles we play (e.g., being a good worker, being a good parent, being a good student) has much to do with our life satisfaction, and we need

to give serious consideration to what life roles we want to play and how we want to play them.

ACTIVITIES: Have students respond to the following questions:

1. What life roles are important to me now?
2. What life roles will be important to me when I am an adult?
3. What can I do to prepare for the life roles that will be important to me in the future?

DISCUSSION: Divide students into small groups. Encourage students to share their responses to the first two questions listed in the Activities section. Then have the students brainstorm responses to the third question for each student.

CLOSURE: Discuss the importance of planning for future life-role participation. Ask each student to list the life roles s/he plans to participate in as an adult. Have each list two things to do between now and then to prepare for participating in that life role.

TIME: 45–60 minutes

EVALUATION/ASSIGNMENT: Have students discuss with their parents/guardians the following questions:

1. What life roles do you play?
2. What do you like about each life role you play?
3. What life roles do you expect me to play when I am an adult?
4. What do you expect me to accomplish in the life roles I will play as an adult?

Have students discuss in small groups the results of the interviews with their parents/guardians. Encourage them to consider how the results of their interviews may influence their career planning.

My Life as a Book

NATIONAL CAREER DEVELOPMENT GUIDELINES: Educational Achievement and Lifelong Learning Domain: ED1.R2; ED1.R3; ED1.K5; ED1.A5; ED1.R5; Career Management Domain: CM1.A1; CM1.A2; CM1.K5; CM1.A5; CM1.R5; CM3.K1; CM3.A1; CM3.R1; CM3. R3; CM3.K4; CM5.K1

ASCA STANDARDS: Standard A—Students will acquire the skills to investigate the world-of-work in relation to knowledge of self and to make informed career decisions; Standard B—Students will employ strategies to achieve future career goals with success and satisfaction; Standard C—Students will understand the relationship between personal qualities, education, training, and the world-of-work.

PURPOSE: To help students see the themes or patterns in their lives and to encourage students to consider their future "stories."

OBJECTIVE: Students will identify activities that they find meaningful and discuss ways to gain additional exposure to these activities. Students will identify goals toward which they would like to strive.

MATERIALS: Writing materials

INTRODUCTION: Explain to the student that a person's career is like a story. Each story has a beginning, middle, and end. Each person can take an active role in writing his or her own story or autobiography. Students should consider their lives as if they were books. Just as there are happy stories and sad stories, we can work hard to write the types of stories about our lives that we would like. By understanding our story or life as we have lived it thus far, each of us can decide if we want to continue in the same direction or make changes. By considering the direction we would like our lives to take, we can establish goals for our futures.

ACTIVITIES: Ask students to consider their lives as if they were books. They should give titles to their

books or lives as they have lived them thus far (e.g., *The Baseball Player, The Dancer, The Next Bill Gates*). Then ask students to divide the lives they have lived thus far into chapters. Their chapters may reflect developmental stages (e.g., infancy, preschool, primary grades, intermediate grades) and/or they may reflect important life events (moving from home, parents divorcing, having a new sibling). Encourage the students to give titles to their life chapters. Next, have the students consider their futures. What do they want these chapters to be like? What goals can they identify in their future chapters?

DISCUSSION: Students can discuss their lives thus far and share the titles of their books. They can also discuss what future chapters they would like to live. In discussing future chapters, students can identify goals they would like to achieve and the group can help each student brainstorm strategies for achieving his or her goals.

CLOSURE: Tell students that each of them can take an active role in writing his or her own destiny. Our pasts can help us to make decisions about what we would like to achieve in the future. By identifying what we would like our futures to look like, we can identify goals toward which to strive. We can also then begin to develop a plan for achieving our goals.

TIME: 60–90 minutes

EVALUATION/ASSIGNMENT: At the conclusion of the activity, students should be able to identify two or three goals they would like to achieve in their lives and strategies that they can use to help them achieve their goals.

The Rocket Kid's Story

NATIONAL CAREER DEVELOPMENT GUIDELINES: Career Management Domain: CM2.R4; CM3.K2; CM3.A2; CM3.R2; CM3.K4; CM3.A4; CM3.R4; CM3.K5; CM3.A5; CM3.R5; CM3.K6; CM3.A6; CM4.A5; CM4.R5; CM4.A6; CM4.R6

ASCA STANDARDS: Standard A—Students will acquire the skills to investigate the world-of-work in relation to knowledge of self and to make informed career decisions; Standard C—Students will understand the relationship between personal qualities, education, training, and the world-of-work.

PURPOSE: To learn about the life of a real scientist and explore the manner in which a boy achieved his career goal despite numerous obstacles.

OBJECTIVE: Students will be able to identify the goals of the movie characters in the film they are about to watch. They will also be able to identify the risks taken to achieve those goals and the role of teamwork in achieving goals.

MATERIALS: The movie *October Sky*, paper, pencils, chalkboard and chalk, rocket-making kit (if desired)

INTRODUCTION: Develop a list of questions for students to respond to, such as "Do you know anyone like the movie characters?" "How did teamwork play a role in the success of the 'rocket boys'?" "What was the father's attitude toward college and the son's career interests?" "What was the family's attitude toward sports, and what role did sports play in the lives of the young people?" "What was Homer's original destiny, and how and why did that change?" "What risks did Homer take to implement his career goal?"

ACTIVITIES:

1. Ask students to watch the video *October Sky* or, if preferred, to read the book *Rocket Boys* by Homer Hickam. (Note: Parents may need to give permission to see this movie, as its rating is PG-13, and there is some language that may be offensive to some individuals.) After watching the movie, students will respond to the questions in the Introduction section or others you develop. Follow this by actually building and/or setting off a rocket (kits to simplify the building can be purchased at toy and crafts stores), if circumstances allow.
2. Students can then list their "dream" jobs or "occupational fantasies."
3. To provide examples of people who have overcome obstacles and achieved their goals, invite past program participants to the session. The past participants could share their stories

and discuss what obstacles they overcame to achieve their goals. If it is not possible to have past participants, consider videotaping interviews from past participants. In the interviews, the past participants could share their stories and identify the obstacles they overcame to achieve their goals.

DISCUSSION: Review the questions in the Introduction section and others that arise as students watch the movie. Ask students to take notes or write down a list of questions that arise as they watch this video. Emphasize the risks taken by the characters in the story and the role of teamwork in creating success in one's career. Students should list the obstacles the movie characters overcame to achieve their goals. Feelings may also be discussed, such as "Do you feel as if success similar to that of the movie characters is within your reach?" Share stories of past students who have achieved their goals (e.g., being admitted to college, graduating from college, attaining a job with a college degree).

CLOSURE: Discuss the fact that people must overcome obstacles to achieve their goals in life. Obstacles can be viewed as opportunities rather than reasons not to pursue a goal.

TIME: 2–3 hours

EVALUATION/ASSIGNMENT: Students can list the obstacles they have already overcome in their lives.

Resources for Information on Colleges

NATIONAL CAREER DEVELOPMENT GUIDELINES: Personal Social Domain: PS1.K4; PS1.A4; PS1.R4; Career Management Domain: CM1.A1; CM1.A2; CM1.K5; CM1.A5; CM1.R5; CM3.K1; CM3.A1; CM3.R1; CM3.R3; CM3.K4; CM5.K1

ASCA STANDARDS: Standard A—Students will acquire the skills to investigate the world-of-work in relation to knowledge of self and to make informed career decisions; Standard B—Students will employ strategies to achieve future career goals with success and satisfaction; Standard C—Students will understand the relationship between personal qualities, education, training, and the world-of-work.

PURPOSE: To provide students with information about colleges.

INTRODUCTION: Tell students, "There are many college resources available to you. Here are some ideas to get you started. Your school counselor should be your most valuable resource in your college search. Your counselor can provide you with help on testing, college requirements, choosing colleges to apply to, academic programs, the application process, and financial aid. You should visit your counselor as soon as possible to discuss your plans for after high school."

THE INTERNET

General College Sites

College Board Online: collegeboard.org

Connects to a tremendous range of college materials.

Adventures in Education: tgslc.org

Includes a wide array of college and career information to help students and parents.

CollegeNET: collegenet.com

Lets students search for institutions by geography, tuition, enrollment, and college major. Provides separate databases for four-year colleges and community, technical, and junior colleges; lists colleges by category; and links to sources of financial aid information.

Peterson's Education Center: petersons.com

Peterson's Education Center includes information about educational programs at all levels and provides searchable databases of colleges and academic programs. All college/university sites provide basic information, and many provide extensive descriptive material, online viewbooks, and applications.

Financial Aid Sites

Fastweb: fastweb.com

Includes a database of 375,000 scholarships; plug in your name for a free scholarship search.

FinAid: finaid.org

The Internet's most complete financial aid site, with links to other key college sites. It also includes a Scholarship Scam Alert with information about scams and how to avoid them.

The Federal Government's Sites

Federal Student Aid: studentaid.ed.gov

Offers information about the U.S. Department of Education's federal student financial aid programs.

Federal Student Aid: fafsa.ed.gov

Provides an online form you must complete in order to receive federal student aid. You can submit it by regular mail or at this site over the Internet.

College Loan Sites

Mapping Your Future: mappingyourfuture.org

Sponsored by agencies that take part in the Federal Family Education Loan Program (FFELP).

Sallie Mae Bank: salliemae.com

A financial services corporation that funds education.

College and University Home Pages

At individual college Web sites, you can read catalogs and admission requirements, check activities, and learn more about the school.

CHAPTER 13

CAREER DEVELOPMENT INTERVENTIONS IN HIGHER EDUCATION

It is now fairly universally acknowledged that career development is a complex, lifelong process—a process that many college students are ill prepared to negotiate effectively and that many find supremely challenging. It is further acknowledged that the career development needs of our increasingly heterogeneous, multicultural society do not lend themselves to one-size-fits-all, recipe-driven career interventions or service-delivery models. In response to these acknowledged conditions and the recent societal trend away from institutional/corporate responsibility for career development and toward greater individual responsibility, institutions of higher education are struggling to implement career services, programs, and interventions that meet the ever-changing needs of today's college student. In an era of unprecedented accountability, college and university career services professionals must choose from a complex array of career interventions and career service–delivery models. This chapter provides the reader with exposure to the career development needs of higher education students, a discussion of the evolution of career development interventions in higher education, and some models, services, and standards for career development interventions in higher education. It is a "must read" for those charged with setting the future course for the delivery of career services in our nation's institutions of higher learning.

Jack Rayman, Ph.D.
Senior Director (Emeritus) of Career Services
Pennsylvania State University

Presently, almost all colleges and universities provide a variety of career interventions. Career guidance services have roots in counseling and testing centers established in the early 20th century to assist college students in clarifying career goals. Also, colleges routinely established placement offices to assist graduates in securing employment. During the later portion of the 20th century, many higher education institutions merged the missions for career guidance and employment and established career development and placement offices. These offices evolved to 21st-century career centers that hold the university-wide mission for career guidance, experiential education, and employer relations. Typically, comprehensive career centers today offer a variety of services ranging from career counseling, assessment, and programming through employment recruitment.

Technological innovations to career services have exploded during recent years to include many Web-based applications. Today's career centers continue to offer personal and group-based career interventions in addition to technologically driven services. Career services have gained considerable respect from higher education administrators and are viewed as important offices that support recruitment, retention, and fundraising efforts in facilitating the career preparation of graduates. As a result, career centers are often located in centralized, highly visible campus locations. Career development interventions are at the heart of the counseling profession. Today's comprehensive career centers boast services assisting thousands of clients annually, including college recruits, freshmen, seniors, and graduate students as well as alumni representing all career fields ranging from the liberal arts to business and engineering. This chapter reflects the dynamic and exciting nature as well as the significance of higher education career development interventions in the 21st century.

Jeff W. Garis, Ph.D.
Senior Director (Emeritus) of Career Services
Florida State University

MyCounselingLab®

Visit the MyCounselingLab® site for *Career Development Interventions*, Fifth Edition, to enhance your understanding of chapter concepts. You will have the opportunity to practice applying what you learned in the chapter by completing the video- and case-based exercises in the MyLab. Taking the Licensure Quizzes will help you prepare for your certification exam.

Robert had experienced substantial success in his career since graduating with an associate degree in business from the local community college. Over the past 15 years, he had worked his way up to a middle-management position with a medium-size manufacturing firm. His success has come at a price, however. He has consistently worked long hours and weekends. He was increasingly uneasy with the time he was spending on the job. His two children were both in middle school, and he realized that he had already missed important moments in their lives due to his involvement at work. Moreover, he had come to feel that his work was "not contributing anything positive to the world." A series of layoffs within his company heightened his sense that it was time to make a change. His precarious employment situation, combined with his desire to spend more time with his family and engage in work that he felt was meaningful, led him to decide to explore his career and educational options. After several sessions with a career counselor in the community, Robert decided he would like to return to college to earn a four-year degree. However, he was anxious about returning to school. Among other things, he wondered if he would be "smart enough" to finish his degree, if he would be able to cover the tuition costs, if his family would support his decision, and if, at age 35, he would be the "old man" in his classes. Because his desire to make a change was stronger than his anxieties about changing, he decided to meet with a career counselor at the local college. He hoped this person would help him sort through his educational and career options in a way that would turn his desire for change into a concrete plan.

L ike Robert, a substantial portion of people in the United States view postsecondary education (i.e., four-year colleges, community colleges, career and technical education) as essential to their career development. As of 2011, 21 million students (nearly 5.7% of the total population) were enrolled in one of the 4,599 degree-granting institutions of higher education in the United States (National Center for Education Statistics, 2014a). According to the Bureau of Labor Statistics (2014), in October 2013, 65.9% (approximately 2 million) of 2013 high school graduates were enrolled in colleges and universities. The college enrollment rate in 2013 for young women was 68.4% compared to 63.5% for young men. The college enrollment rate of Asians (79.1%) was higher than for recent White (67.1%), Black (59.3%), and Hispanic (59.9%) graduates. About 6 in 10 recent high school graduates who were enrolled in college attended four-year institutions. Of these students, 27.8% participated in the labor force, compared with 45.2% of recent graduates enrolled in two-year colleges. The unemployment rate for high school graduates not enrolled in college was 30.9%.

THE CHANGING LANDSCAPE OF HIGHER EDUCATION

The Pew Research Center (2009) reported that some 3.1 million young adults, or 10.9% of all 18- to 24-year-olds, had chosen, like Robert, to enroll in a community college. A year later, that figure had risen to 3.4 million students, or 11.8% of all 18- to 24-year-olds. Community college enrollments have long been considered somewhat countercyclical—that is, they tend to rise as the economy worsens. One reason is that community colleges are less expensive than four-year institutions—they average $6,750 per year (including tuition, fees, and room and board) for full-time students, compared with $9,800 for four-year public colleges and $21,240 for four-year private colleges. Community colleges offer university transfer programs, technical programs, job training programs, basic skills programs, and special interest programs of study, and, therefore, appeal to an ever-increasing broad spectrum of students. Moreover, in his State of the Union address in January 2015, President Barack Obama proposed that community colleges should be "as free and universal in America as high school," noting that 40% of college students in the United States choose to enroll in a community college.

Approximately 14 million students participated in secondary and postsecondary career and technical education (CTE) programs during the 2007–2008 school year (Association of Career and Technical Education, 2011). One-third of college students are involved in CTE programs, and as many as 40 million adults engage in short-term, postsecondary occupational training. Career and technical education in the United States evolved from a relatively small number of vocationally oriented programs at the beginning of the 20th century into a much more comprehensive postsecondary system. Today's CTE educational options include a broad array of diverse subject areas that reflect the constantly changing global economy (ACTE, 2011).

The number of young students has been growing more steadily than the number of older students. Between 1995 and 2006, the enrollment of students under age 25 increased by 33%. Enrollment of people 25 and over rose by 13% during the same period. From 2006 to 2017, the National Center for Education Statistics (2014a) projects a rise of 10% in enrollments of people under 25, and a rise of 19% in enrollments of people 25 and over. (Robert clearly would not be alone as an "older" student should he decide to enroll in a four-year college.)

Many students enrolled in postsecondary education emerge from high school experiences in which they received minimal career development assistance. For those students, who may also have diffuse vocational identities, negotiating the tasks of selecting a college major and identifying potential occupations is daunting at best. Statistics support this contention since only 19% of students enrolled in 4-year bachelor's degrees at nonflagship colleges; 36% from flagship or very high research universities, graduate in four years (Complete College America, 2014). Only 59% of students (56% for males and 61% for females) who enter colleges and universities graduate in six years (NCES, 2014b), and according to Marklein (2009), only 63% of students who enroll in a four-year university will earn a degree. Clearly, many students are not prepared for what they encounter when they step onto a college or university campus. Moreover, the high costs of college attendance are made even higher when the graduation target becomes three years for an associate degree (instead of two years) and six years for a bachelor's degree (instead of four). More specifically, the cost for each additional year of enrollment in a two-year college is nearly

$16,000 and for a public four-year college nearly $23,000 (Complete College America). So, why do so many people choose to enroll in postsecondary education?

Survey results from the Higher Education Research Institute (2012) indicate that 87% of first-year college students attend college to "be able to get a better job." This is up from 77% in 1999 (American Council on Education, 1999) and 67.8% in 1976 (HERI, 2012). In addition, 75% report that they choose to attend college "to make more money" (HERI). Finally, 83.4% of students entering a four-year college expect to graduate in four years (HERI). Clearly, there is a mismatch between student expectations and the reality related to time-to-degree completion. Perhaps this mismatch provides a partial explanation for the finding that 30.4% of the students (40.5% of the females and 18.3% of the males) in the HERI survey report that they frequently felt overwhelmed during their senior year of high school. It is also obvious that many students view higher education as a means for advancing their careers. Helping students crystallize and implement their career identities is a critical role of career services professionals in higher education.

It is important to note, however, that students enrolled in higher education today represent a vast array of cultural and ethnic backgrounds. Many students are, like Robert, returning adult students. Other students have disabilities that require accommodations. Still others represent the first generation in their families to attend higher education. Finally, a growing trend for students graduating from postsecondary education in the United States is that they are graduating having incurred substantial debt to pay for their education.

The Project on Student Debt (Kingkade, 2014) reports that 69% of students graduating in 2013 from four-year colleges and universities had student-loan debt. This reflects a disturbing trend. In 2008, 62% of graduates from public universities had student loans; 72% of graduates from private nonprofit universities had student loans; 96% of graduates from private for-profit universities had student loans (a major increase from 2004, when 85% of these graduates had student loans). Average debt levels for graduating seniors with student loans rose to $28,400 in 2013 up from $23,200 in 2008. In 2008, 36% of enrolled students graduated from college in four years. Not surprisingly, coinciding with increased student debt and time to graduation is an increase in pressure from parents, politicians, and students themselves to decrease the amount of time spent in postsecondary education, in order to reduce loan indebtedness. Career professionals in higher education can play a vital role in helping students achieve this goal. Thus, in this chapter we discuss the career needs of those enrolled in higher education today; the evolution of career services in higher education; the competencies students in higher education must develop to cope effectively with career development in adulthood; models, services, and standards for career services; and issues that must be considered in managing career services.

Tips from the Field

Students in higher education often think that career decision making occurs in the following manner: You must first know what you want to do before you can take action. Actually, just the opposite is true: In order to know what you want to do, you must first take action. Doing leads to knowing. Therefore, students in higher education need help in engaging in experiential career activities (e.g., volunteering, externships, internships) so they can make effective career decisions.

Although a large number of students enroll in higher education immediately following their high school graduation, increasingly, these students do not fit the traditional stereotype of the American college student (i.e., age 18 to 22, enrolled full-time, and living on campus). In fact, fewer than one in six students in higher education fit this traditional stereotype (Colozzi, 2000). More than ever in the history of higher education, today's students represent a diverse mix in terms of their backgrounds, characteristics, developmental levels, and career development needs.

The exact definition of a nontraditional student has been the source of much discussion. Age (over age 24) is the most frequently used defining characteristic for this group and is a surrogate variable for what is really a large, diverse population of students. Some observers contend that the increase of nontraditional students in higher education is the most significant trend in higher education (Hess, 2011). For example, 38% of those enrolled in higher education are age 25 or older, with 25% being over the age of 30. This proportion is predicted to grow by another 23% by 2019. Of the 17.6 million undergraduate students, only 15% attend four-year colleges and live on campus. The majority of adults returning to higher education do so primarily to enhance their career opportunities (Luzzo, 2000). However, many adult students must balance their pursuit of higher education with child rearing and other life-role responsibilities. Moreover, many adult students experience insecurity over their decision to return to school; they are uncertain about their ability to succeed academically and are anxious about whether they will be able to convert their academic experience into new career opportunities (Marron & Rayman, 2002). Thus, it is not surprising that nontraditional students also tend to have more specific career/educational needs reflecting their life circumstances (e.g., specialized certificate programs, evening and/or weekend courses, wanting to take online courses).

International students also represent a substantial and growing percentage of those enrolled in higher education within the United States. For instance, Herr, Cramer, and Niles (2004) reported that approximately 500,000 international students were enrolled in higher education in 2001. In 2013, this number had increased to 886,052 (Institute of International Education, 2014). This latter number is almost double the number hosted by the second leading host country: the United Kingdom. Moreover, it represents an increase of 66,408 over the previous year (Institute of International Education). Interestingly, 289,408 American students studied abroad during the 2013–2014 academic year. Thus, the realization that international education is crucial to developing positive relationships between people and communities in the United States and around the world appears to be strengthening.

Historically, however, international students have not received sufficient assistance with their career development. Specifically, international students tend to receive inadequate information concerning employment opportunities in their home countries; they often receive inadequate academic advice from advisors who are not sensitive to concerns of international students; and they frequently experience difficulty in self-expression in an unfamiliar culture. Since September 11, 2001, many international students from the Middle East have experienced undeserved hostility. These experiences do not foster career development, and they reflect special needs that career practitioners must address to provide comprehensive career services to international students.

Within the past two decades, higher education institutions have also experienced a surge in enrollment of people with disabilities (Conyers & Szymanski, 1998). For example, more than 11% of undergraduate students reported having a disability in 2008 (National Center for Education Statistics, 2014a). In any large undergraduate class, there is a good chance that 2 out of every 100 students will have a learning disability (Vickers, 2010). According to the Americans with Disabilities Act (1990), *disability* is defined as physical or mental impairment that substantially limits one or more of the major life activities of such individual" who is disabled. Of the types of student disabilities reported by institutions for students enrolled in the 2008–2009 academic year, 31% were specific learning disabilities, 18% were ADD/ADHD, 15% were mental illness, 11% were health impairment/condition (National Center for Education Statistics, 2014a).

Two federal laws have opened the doors to higher education for many Americans with disabilities. Specifically, section 504 of the Rehabilitation Act of 1973 and the Americans with Disabilities Act (1990) (and the ADA Amendments Act of 2008) created an environment of increased access to higher education for persons with disabilities. Despite increased access to higher education, people with disabilities have not fared well in the labor market (Hitchings & Retish, 2000). Thus, students with disabilities need assistance during their higher education experience to increase their chances of being successful in their careers following graduation. For example, Ohler, Levinson, and Barker (1996) report that students with learning disabilities who require many accommodations demonstrate lower levels of career maturity when compared with students with learning disabilities. Despite the need for career assistance, Friehe, Aune, and Leuenberger (1996) report that college students with disabilities use career services at a significantly lower rate than nondisabled students. Clearly, career practitioners in higher education must do a better job of meeting the career development needs of students with disabilities.

Students in the early centuries of higher education were predominantly European American men; however, women now constitute the majority of students enrolled in higher education. The percentage of women attending postsecondary education is also increasing at a rapid rate. From 2001 to 2011, the percentage of women attending four-year colleges full-time increased 56%, whereas for men it increased 36% (NCES, 2014a). Women made up 57% (about 12 million) of the undergraduate student population in 2014, with just over 9 million men enrolled (NCES). Fassinger and O'Brien (2000) contend that the career development needs of female students are considerably different from those of college males. Specifically, Fassinger and O'Brien note that two themes characterize the differences between female and male college students' career development: (a) women experience a pervasive and persistent underutilization of their abilities and talents, resulting in occupationally segregating women into jobs that are typically lower in pay and status than jobs held by the majority of men, and (b) women experience a higher level of participation in family roles than men. This results in a higher frequency of role overload issues that women experience as their career aspirations are juxtaposed with family responsibilities. Career practitioners must address these themes to foster the career development of women enrolled in higher education.

The percentage of students enrolled in higher education who are members of racial/ethnic minority groups has also increased in recent years. Herr et al. (2004) point out that the total enrollment for racial/ethnic minorities represented 32% of all students in higher education in 2007. From 1976 to 2011, the percentage of Hispanic students rose from 4% to 14%, the percentage of Asian/Pacific Islander students rose from 2% to 6%, the percentage of Black students rose from 10% to 15%, and the percentage of American Indian/Alaska Native students rose from 0.7 to 0.9%. During the same period, the percentage of White students fell from 84% to 61%. Despite this level of enrollment within higher education, and despite these increases, ethnic minorities are still less likely than European Americans to attend college, complete college degrees, and enter professional training programs. Historically, occupational stereotyping by high school counselors, lack of role models, and few perceived opportunities have led to restricted career choice patterns among ethnic minority students. The discriminatory treatment experienced by students of color presents a wide range of issues that must be addressed in the career development process.

Lesbian, bisexual, gay, transgendered, and questioning students also encounter numerous contextual barriers in their career development. In a recent survey of 90,000 college students conducted by the American College Health Association (2012), 3% of the students surveyed identified as gay/lesbian, 3% as bisexual, 1.9% as unsure, and when asked about gender 0.2% identified as transgender (ACHA). Sexual minorities are more likely to be bullied, less likely to feel like they fit in, and less likely to report having an adult that they can turn to for support than straight students.

Unfortunately, the career development needs of LGBTQ students have long been ignored by career services in higher education. Pope, Prince, and Mitchell (2000) urge career professionals to work to change this by providing a safe and welcoming environment on college campuses for gay and lesbian students. One way to contribute to creating an environment that is more responsive to the needs of lesbian and gay students is to offer career services that more thoroughly address their career development needs. Pope et al. (2000) note that lesbian and gay students are likely to have encountered biased career information, may be reluctant to consider certain career options because of concerns about discrimination or negative stereotyping, and may need help in considering the advantages and disadvantages of coming out in the workplace. Career services can be provided to help lesbian and gay students cope with these and other career concerns related to their sexual orientation. For example, (a) providing students with information on employment antidiscrimination laws and policies and with lists of gay and lesbian resources and community agencies, (b) encouraging gay and lesbian students to attend workshops addressing complex career/relationship issues, (c) providing names of gay and lesbian alumni who are willing to provide mentoring and networking opportunities, (d) and making sure that career development interventions are appropriate/relevant to lesbian and gay students are some of the ways in which career services can be made more responsive to this substantial population of students in higher education (Pope et al., 2000).

This sampling of students enrolled in higher education clearly paints a landscape that is very different from that of previous centuries. What was once an environment populated by European American men of privileged socioeconomic status is now characterized by heterogeneity at all levels. This increased diversity suggests that career development interventions in higher education must be comprehensive and planned systematically to meet the myriad career development needs of students today. The current scenario is very different from the one out of which career services in higher education emerged early in the 20th century.

THE EVOLUTION OF CAREER DEVELOPMENT INTERVENTIONS IN HIGHER EDUCATION

Career development interventions have a long history in higher education. Comprehensive career services, ranging from helping students select a major to helping students find a job, are relatively recent in higher education. Current approaches to career services were preceded by a "system" of service delivery that primarily depended on the efforts of professors who provided mentoring and placement assistance to selected students. Herr, Rayman, and Garis (1993) note that:

> "career services" were essentially confined to how a professor or a don advocated for or mentored a student prodigy as part of his induction into a profession. This was a male-dominated activity, an "old boy's network" by which a faculty member would speak in behalf of a student to persons of importance who might employ him as a favor to, or out of respect for, the professor. (p. 1)

Job placement was the focus of this sort of career assistance. The rate of success for this placement activity depended on the professor's contacts and stature within the field as well as the professor's degree of regard for a particular student. In other words, this system probably worked well for some students but not as well for other students.

In the early 1800s, commercial employment agencies offered placement services to graduates from teacher training programs. By the late 1800s there were nearly 200 employment agencies in the United States (Herr et al., 1993). As enrollments in higher education increased and student services emerged in university settings, placement offices were created to provide all students with placement assistance. For example, Yale University established a placement office in 1919 to provide vocational guidance to students and to match them with employment positions during the academic year, the summer months, and after graduation (Herr et al., 1993).

From prototypical efforts such as those initiated at Yale, the influence of the emerging vocational guidance movement being pioneered by the concepts of Frank Parsons in the early 1900s, and the growing interest of students and employers in placement assistance, employment offices or placement bureaus were instituted on campuses throughout the United States. Often these offices were combined with efforts of faculty, other college and university student personnel officials, and alumni who sought to identify employment opportunities and match students to them.

The focus on placement services resulted in the separation of placement offices from other student affairs functions that were more focused on student development. Rather than training in areas such as counseling and psychology, career placement "officers" tended to have a variety of backgrounds, but they were often linked to business. Placement was a process by which the students were matched to the requirements of commerce, industry, and the professions based on the careers they had developed through their college experiences (Herr et al., 1993). Services provided by placement officials emphasized job-search skills (e.g., interviewing and résumé writing). Typically, these services tended to be in more demand as students approached graduation. In contrast, counseling centers were more likely to be concerned with student development (e.g., the remediation of emotional or academic distress), and services were provided at any time during the student's collegiate experience.

A shift occurred in career services in higher education beginning in the late 1950s and early 1960s. Career planning activities that had been a part of many counseling centers were relocated to placement offices and combined with placement services: "In essence, in many colleges and universities, an organizational entity frequently known as the career planning and placement office or the career development and placement center or service was formed" (Herr et al., 1993, p. 4). This shift reflected an expanded perspective of career services that moved beyond a singular focus on placement to a developmental perspective of career planning. The developmental perspective included the use of interventions to help students engage in systematic career planning. Placement was now viewed as the culminating activity, rather than the only activity, in the career development of students enrolled in higher education.

Herr et al. (1993) note that currently "there is no single type of counseling center or career development and placement center. Each of these evolves from different institutional histories. In some cases, college and university counseling centers embrace the full range of career services; in others, they have essentially none" (p. 3). Survey results from 963 institutions participating in a study conducted by Whiteley, Mahaffey, and Geer (1987) led these researchers to identify five major approaches used in higher education for delivering career services:

1. **Macrocenter:** broad range of services, including career and personal counseling, testing, and special functions such as training and consultation with some advising services offered
2. **Counseling orientation:** similar to macrocenters except with fewer career services
3. **General-level service:** broader functions, including some "dean of students"–type functions; more services to more students than a conventional counseling center
4. **Career planning and placement:** career-oriented services with minimal counseling and other functions
5. **Minimal service:** characterized by providing minimal services in all areas

It is unfortunate that some institutions of higher education are unwilling or unable to provide a full range of career services to students. For example, had Robert (the returning student mentioned at the beginning of this chapter) presented for assistance at a career services office focused exclusively on placement, he would have received limited assistance. The career placement officer may have provided him with placement statistics and information on job openings and job search strategies. But Robert was clearly at a place in his career development where he needed other assistance. He needed help clarifying his vocational identity and learning about the options available to him. He also needed information about financial aid. Finally, it would have been very useful for him to speak with someone knowledgeable about the concerns confronting returning students. In many ways, Robert's career situation reflects the variety of contextual and intrapersonal challenges students confront in their career development. Given this complexity, it is not surprising that most major surveys examining the needs of students enrolled in higher education reveal the fact that students express a strong desire for help with a variety of career-related concerns (Healy & Reilly, 1989; Normyle, 2014; Weissberg, Berenstein, Cote, Cravey, & Heath, 1982). For example, Normyle conducted a survey of 100,727 incoming first-year college students at 338 colleges and universities in the United States in 2013. The majority of the respondents were women (56.1%), and the average age of the respondents was 20.1 years old. Fifty-four percent were White, 19.7% were Black/African American, 14.5% Hispanic or Latino, 3.8% Asian or Pacific Islander, 0.8% American Indian or Alaskan Native, and the remainder were unidentified. Nearly half of the respondents indicated that they wanted career counseling assistance, noting that they would like some help selecting an occupation that is well suited for their interests and abilities. In addition, 67.3% wanted help selecting an educational plan that would prepare them to get a good job, and 63.7% indicated a desire to talk with someone about the qualifications needed for certain occupations. One in five freshmen reported being very confused about their future occupational choice. The same needs were expressed by racial/ethnic minority students. For example, 62.6% of the respondents who were Asian or Pacific Islander indicated that they would like help selecting an occupation that is well suited to their interests and abilities, 55.4% of the Hispanic or Latino respondents indicated the same need, and 52.9% of the Black/African American students expressed a need for this type of assistance. With regard to receiving help in selecting an occupation that would prepare them to get a good job, 78.2% of the Asian or

Pacific Islander students, 74.5% of the Hispanic or Latino respondents, and 75.5% of the Black/ African American students were seeking this assistance. The same patterns were found with regard to the need to talk with someone about the qualifications required for specific occupations. Finally, 41% of those students age 25 or older expressed a need for career counseling. The need for receiving career assistance has been a consistent finding for decades.

Healy and Reilly (1989) reported that the students in their study of 1,540 women and 1,386 men enrolled in 10 community colleges in California desired assistance in knowing more about themselves, identifying career goals, becoming more certain of their career plans, exploring career options, educational planning, and learning job-search skills. Such consistent survey results provide evidence that students enrolled in higher education, regardless of their backgrounds and characteristics, are very concerned about their ability to make and implement career choices. It seems reasonable to expect institutions of higher education to provide assistance to students as they attempt to translate their life and academic experiences into career choices. The Office of Postsecondary Education within the U.S. Department of Education offers a program guide that identifies excellent resources to helping postsecondary students manage their educational experience (mappingyourfuture.org). In addition to being aware of useful resources such as this one, providing career assistance effectively requires understanding the career development tasks that students confront while they are enrolled in higher education and as they move forward in their career development beyond higher education.

CAREER DEVELOPMENT COMPETENCIES IN ADULTHOOD

The National Career Development Guidelines (NCDG) were originally developed by the National Occupation Information Coordinating Committee (1989) and were updated and revised in 2003 by the U.S. Department of Education. The guidelines are very useful for identifying the competencies that postsecondary school students need to manage their careers effectively. These guidelines provide the target skills toward which comprehensive and systematic career services in higher education must be directed. Like the NCDG competencies identified for students in grades K–12, the adult-level competencies are categorized within three domains: (a) personal social development, (b) educational achievement and lifelong learning, and (c) career management. These domains provide target goals for those engaged in designing and delivering career services in higher education.

Personal Social Development

Personal social development goals include the following:

1. Develop understanding of self to build and maintain a positive self-concept.
2. Develop positive interpersonal skills, including respect for diversity.
3. Integrate growth and change into your career development.
4. Balance personal, leisure, community, learner, family, and work roles.

Postsecondary school students need to develop self-understanding to build and maintain a positive self-concept that encompasses an accurate understanding of their strengths, interests, abilities, and values. Moreover, college students need to understand how these important self-characteristics influence their career decisions. A holistic understanding of one's self-concepts across life roles provides the foundation for educational and career exploration. Skills related to interpersonal communication, stress management (e.g., engaging in positive self-care activities, identifying resources for social support, and overcoming self-defeating behaviors), and an understanding of life-span development are essential for helping adults manage their career development (NOICC, 2003).

Most often, career services providers help students in higher education to develop an accurate understanding of their self-characteristics through the use of self-assessment activities. Assessment results can be reviewed in individual career counseling or small-group counseling sessions. Career counselors provide a variety of standardized assessments, such as interest inventories, personality measures, and career maturity measures. Career counselors in higher education also expose students to computer-assisted career guidance systems that provide opportunities for engaging in self-exploration. To develop an understanding of life-span development and to enhance skills in areas such as stress management, practitioners encourage students to enroll in career planning courses. In these courses students receive career development assistance in large- and small-group interactions. Thus, skills in interpersonal communication are also enhanced. Students also learn about various approaches to career decision making (Niles, Erford, Hunt, & Watts, 1997). Reed, Reardon, Lenz, and Leirer (2001) describe a career planning course based on the cognitive information-processing theory. Reed and her colleagues divide their course into three units. Unit I covers career concepts and applications focusing on self-knowledge, knowledge of options, and decision making. Unit II addresses social conditions affecting career development, focusing on current social, economic, family, and organizational changes affecting the career planning process. Finally, Unit III focuses on employability skills and strategies for implementing academic and career plans. To gain a fuller understanding of the range of material typically covered in career planning courses, we refer readers to the career planning course syllabus presented at the end of this chapter.

Educational Achievement and Lifelong Learning

Goals within this domain involve:

1. Attaining educational achievement and performance levels needed to reach your personal and career goals.
2. Participating in ongoing, lifelong learning experiences to enhance your ability to function effectively in a diverse and changing economy.

Self-concepts evolve over time, making career choice and adjustment a continuous process (Super, 1984). Thus, students in postsecondary education must know how to access and use the information they gather in their educational and occupational exploration. Using self-knowledge and career information effectively requires the ability to identify short- and long-range career goals. Goals emerge from connecting self-knowledge with accurate career information. Making this connection requires the ability to locate relevant career information, identify relevant educational opportunities, understand training requirements related to jobs, and demonstrate a general understanding of the nature of work in a diverse, changing, and global economy.

Inevitably, postsecondary students will need to develop strategies for overcoming obstacles in their career paths (e.g., finding adequate child care, obtaining financial resources to cover educational costs). Because engaging in lifelong learning is a common requirement for most career options, students need to possess the requisite skills for experiencing academic success (e.g., skills related to taking tests, studying, and taking lecture notes) and, when necessary, accessing academic support services.

Career practitioners in higher education use a variety of interventions to help students develop knowledge, skills, and awareness in educational and occupational exploration. Career planning courses contain units to help students learn goal-setting skills. Instructors encourage students to identify short- and long-range career plans based on the occupational and self-information they have acquired. Career services centers in higher education contain resources related to educational and occupational information. Career information libraries provide students with printed materials describing educational programs, occupational options, and prospective employers. Career information delivery systems offer students state-specific information describing various educational and occupational opportunities. To access information online, career services centers provide students with listings of Web sites that provide useful occupational information. Career planning courses, workshops, and small groups give students opportunities to learn about the process of locating, evaluating, and interpreting career information. Externships provide students with opportunities to acquire hands-on exposure to specific occupational environments. Students are assigned to job shadow a person employed in an occupation that is of interest to the student. Typically, these assignments last from three to five days and provide students with important information they can use in their educational and career planning.

Career Management

Career management goals include:

1. Create and manage a career plan that meets your career goals.
2. Use a process of decision making as one component of career development.
3. Use accurate, current, and unbiased career information during career planning and management.
4. Master academic, occupational, and general employability skills in order to obtain, create, maintain, and/or advance your employment.
5. Integrate changing employment trends, societal needs, and economic conditions into your career plans.

Like the goals emanating from the two previous domains, effective career management for students in higher education involves a variety of skill sets. For example, students need to possess sufficient self-understanding for making effective plans about training, education, and work. Such understanding encompasses intra-individual characteristics (e.g., skills, values, interests, personality traits) and extra-individual factors (e.g., demands from nonwork life roles, accessibility of training opportunities, financial resources, family support). Because choosing and adjusting to choices are continual processes in career development, skills to manage transitions from one circumstance to another are also essential to effective career management. Skills in stress management and interpersonal communication and engaging in positive self-talk all contribute to coping with transitions. Because work activity occurs amid demands from other nonwork life roles, being able to balance demands from multiple life roles is imperative for reducing the stress associated with making transitions. Thus, career management involves not only planning for work but also planning for the sort of life one hopes to live. Because we live within a social system, planning is often a collective activity encompassing the needs and hopes of the individual and other prominent people in the individual's social network (e.g., partner, children, and parents).

Career practitioners help students in higher education develop career planning skills via individual and/or small-group counseling, workshops, and career planning courses. To develop decision-making skills, researchers suggest that it is important for students to understand multiple approaches that can be used for making decisions. For example, Johnson (1978) identified systematic, spontaneous, internal, and external decision-making styles. Individuals using the systematic decision-making style approach decisions in a rational and logical fashion. They actively seek all relevant information and accept personal responsibility for their decision making. Spontaneous decision makers make decisions holistically and quickly. Internal decision makers process information privately and quietly. External deciders think out loud and talk to others about decisions. Niles et al. (1997) found that students who rely on a systematic/internal decision-making style tend to be less advanced in their career development and less confident in their ability to complete career development tasks than students who rely on a systematic/external style. Moreover, the students in the Niles et al. study who had the highest career decision-making self-efficacy and the lowest career indecision were those who preferred a systematic/external decision-making style, had clarified their values, and had acquired occupational information. The students with the lowest career decision-making self-efficacy preferred a systematic/internal decision-making style and were not clear about how to make career decisions. Thus, it seems important to provide career assistance that is sensitive to students' preferences for gathering and analyzing data in the decision-making process. For example, students who prefer to analyze data internally may benefit from maintaining career decision-making journals and writing career autobiographies. In addition, to analyze data effectively, internalizers need accurate information about how career decisions are made. Students who prefer to analyze data externally are likely to find participating in career counseling groups and career planning classes to be a useful form of career assistance.

The goals of interventions directed toward helping students develop career management skills include the following:

1. Helping students learn to identify and transfer career interests to a plan of action
2. Helping students to relate interests and goals to opportunities
3. Helping students to relate their career plans to life goals and opportunities
4. Helping students learn how to evaluate their progress toward career goals through academic preparation

Career planning courses contain content to help students understand life-structure issues and to help students formulate plans that provide opportunities for participating in their most salient life roles (Halasz & Kempton, 2000). Computer-assisted career guidance systems, such as *Kuder Journey* (Kuder, 2015), provide students with opportunities to clarify their salient life roles and consider which roles they think will be important to them in their futures. Standardized and nonstandardized assessment opportunities can be provided to help students consider the impact of work on individual and family life. Group discussions in career planning courses can focus on the continuing changes in male/female roles. By incorporating activities directed toward enhancing stress-management skills, counselors help students acquire skills that are essential to managing career transitions effectively.

Clearly, this list of competencies required for successful career management is daunting. Moreover, one could analyze the National Career Development Guidelines at the micro level and expand the list of knowledge, skills, and behaviors exponentially. It is unrealistic to expect students to develop all of these skills while they are enrolled in higher education. However, career services practitioners in higher education can strive to help sensitize students to the challenges they are likely to encounter as their careers develop. Career practitioners in higher education can also foster students' career development by providing comprehensive and systematic interventions directed toward developing basic competencies in the three domains of personal social development, educational achievement and lifelong learning, and career management. Although our returning student, Robert, probably needs assistance across all three domains, he first needs help enhancing his personal social development, understanding the transition process, and bolstering his self-esteem.

MODELS, SERVICES, AND STANDARDS FOR CAREER DEVELOPMENT INTERVENTIONS IN HIGHER EDUCATION

Models, services, and standards for career development interventions in higher education have evolved greatly over the past 50 years. In part, this evolution results from evolving priorities in college and university settings. As student populations get older, for example, the time when services are delivered (e.g., evenings and weekends), the method of delivery (online), and the interventions themselves are adapted to meet the current needs of students in higher education. A consistent theme, however, has been the ongoing emphasis on placement following graduation. That said, we begin by examining models of service delivery.

Models

To deliver career services systematically and comprehensively, practitioners are required to operate from models of service delivery that are also systematic and comprehensive. There is a variety of models for career services that can be used to develop the competencies that are essential for effectively managing one's career in adulthood (e.g., Colozzi, 2000; Reardon, Lenz, Sampson, & Peterson, 2000; Sampson, 2008). As students progress through higher education, they need assistance in narrowing the range of occupational options under consideration. Typically, students begin the career development process in higher education by (a) exploring a variety of options, (b) then crystallizing a narrow range of specific options, (c) at which point the student makes a commitment to a particular choice and specifies a college major, (d) which leads to implementing the option selected. Career development professionals can help students progress through this process by first assessing each student's career development needs and then offering group and individual career development interventions based on the needs identified for each student. (Interventions with Robert must begin with a comprehensive assessment of his needs; however, it seems clear he will need to begin at the beginning—that is, exploring.) To further assess students' development, we recommend readministering the needs assessment to students at regular intervals (e.g., every six months). Data from the subsequent assessments can be used to identify further interventions needed to foster each student's career development.

Powell and Kirts (1980) propose a systems approach to career services in higher education. Their approach focuses on providing awareness programming to new students. Awareness programming involves giving all new students an overview of career services. In large-group meetings, career services staff members and upper-level students describe the career development process and the services available to help students advance in their careers. Voluntary small-group meetings of fewer than 30 students then follow these large-group meetings. In the small-group meetings career counselors and student peer counselors describe in greater detail the career services available and respond to students' specific questions and concerns. Students needing additional assistance are then referred to the appropriate career service (e.g., individual career counseling, career planning courses).

The second component in the Powell and Kirts (1980) model involves self-assessment activities. Powell and Kirts recommend offering small groups in which students first view a videotape of upper-class students who discuss the ways in which various career services have been useful to them. Students use information provided via the videotape to identify resources that they think might help them learn more about themselves (e.g., workshops, individual counseling, and groups).

The next phase in the Powell and Kirts model focuses on exposure as students engage actively in career exploration. Career exploration activities are offered to help students integrate self-assessment information and occupational information. Powell and Kirts note that, in this phase of their model, career counseling and traditional placement functions merge. They recommend using career courses in which alumni and local business leaders link educational and career information (i.e., they identify how academic subjects are relevant for various occupations). Alumni and local business leaders can also serve as resources for creating externship and internship opportunities to expose students to career opportunities.

The final phase of the Powell and Kirts (1980) model is training, which involves providing students who are approaching graduation with training in job-search skills. This phase of the model involves an approach similar to the one used in the awareness phase. Specifically, career services staff members provide students in their last year of study with a large-group (convocation-like) overview of placement services. Students are then invited to participate in small-group sessions according to their academic majors. These sessions focus on the specifics of job searching using videotapes of recent graduates discussing the requisite skills and attitudes for effective job searching. Subsequent group meetings focus on résumé writing, mock interviewing, accessing information about job opportunities, and so on.

Awareness programming would be especially useful to Robert. As a returning student, Robert needs to learn about the range of services available to him. The inclusion of returning students in the videotapes focused on how students have found career services useful would be very important to Robert. Because Robert is experiencing many of the fears typically experienced by returning students, it would be beneficial for him to hear other returning students expressing similar concerns and discussing how they coped with them. As he moves through career exploration and placement activities, career counselors will need to be sensitive to Robert's life situation as a returning student with family responsibilities and, most likely, limited geographical mobility.

Reardon (1996) also describes a comprehensive career services model in use at Florida State University. The Florida State model is a curricular career information service (CCIS) model with five modules. In the CCIS model, career services focus on providing students with an introduction to the service, orienting students to the career decision-making process, helping students engage in self-assessment, helping students locate career information, and helping students match majors and jobs. A unique aspect of the CCIS model is that it is self-help oriented and uses paraprofessionals, instructional models, and multimedia resources in service delivery. The CCIS model is a comprehensive and efficient approach to career services. It also allows students to direct their learning about career planning and manage their own career development.

Sampson (2008) recommended that career programs in higher education use an eight-step model, which begins with evaluating and assessing current career resources and services and then, based on the initial assessment, revising and adapting career resources and services. Then the revised and improved resources and services are integrated into the existing career services with appropriate staff training. Sampson notes the importance of conducting a pilot study to evaluate the new program. Data from the pilot test are used to further revise and develop the program prior to final implementation with ongoing training and evaluation.

Models for service delivery such as the ones discussed reflect not only the expanded and developmental perspective within career services but also expanded modes of service delivery. They clearly demonstrate the variety of ways in which career services in higher education have gone beyond their initial focus on placement to help students develop the knowledge, skills, and awareness required to manage their career development effectively.

For example, results from a survey by the National Association of Colleges and Employers (NACE) indicate that roughly four out of every five career centers provided group-oriented career counseling interventions and workshops (Collins, 1998). Of the institutions participating in the NACE survey, 52% offered career planning courses. Hardesty (1991) conducted a meta-analysis focusing on the effectiveness of career planning courses and found that students completing career courses were "40% more capable of making career decisions than students who did not complete these courses" (p. 185). For students completing career planning courses, Hardesty found that they were 48% more certain about their career choices at completion of the course than they were at the beginning.

A recent meta-analysis conducted by Whiston, Sexton, and Lasoff (1998) compared the effectiveness of workshops, career planning courses, computer programs, and individual counseling and found that individual career counseling was the most effective. However, when one considers the range of needs that must be addressed by career centers and the number of career counselors available, it becomes readily apparent that providing individual career counseling to all students is not possible. Moreover, some students may benefit from the peer support that is often experienced in group-oriented career interventions. Rayman (1996) contends that though individual career counseling is at the core of the profession, comprehensive career centers should use a wide range of approaches in delivering career services to students.

Services

The models discussed also reflect the fact that career services are delivered to students by a variety of people in a wide range of venues. Herr et al. (2004) identify four major approaches used for delivering career services to students in higher education: (1) courses, workshops, and seminars that offer structured group experiences in topics such as career decision making, career planning, and job-search skills; (2) group counseling activities directed toward students experiencing such issues as career indecision, career indecisiveness, and job-search anxiety; (3) individual career counseling; and (4) placement programs such as on-campus and/or online job interviewing. Obviously, the use of Internet-based career planning systems and computer information delivery systems offers vehicles for service delivery that range from career decision making to placement. Computer-assisted career guidance systems have existed for some time; more recent placement-oriented computer services include virtual job fairs, online résumés, and chat rooms for job seekers (Miller & McDaniels, 2001). Social networking Web sites such as Facebook, LinkedIn, and videoconferencing options provide opportunities for online career services delivery that many college and university students (and alumni) find appealing.

Davidson (2001) stresses that as career services professionals increase their reliance on technology in career services delivery, they also need to address the wide range of ethical issues associated with increased use of technology. For example, researchers suggest that it is important to balance high-tech with high-touch. Students need access to humans as well as computer-based services. One does not replace the other. Computer-based services are not yet effective at providing empathy, addressing individual student needs, and responding to subtle nonverbal expressions in client statements. Moreover, many online services have not been constructed according to the ethical and professional standards to which career services professionals adhere.

These multiple approaches for services delivery provide the means by which students receive a wide array of career-related services. For example, Reardon, Zunker, and Dyal (1979) identified 31 categories of career services delivered by 302 institutions of higher education. These services include, but are not limited to, providing occupational information via computerized and printed resources, job-search skills training, educational information, standardized and nonstandardized assessment opportunities, referrals to campus and community resources, self-help materials, training in decision making, assertiveness training, communications skills training, career planning courses, externships, internships, on-campus and off-campus job interview opportunities, and job interview training via videotaped role-play practice.

Herr (1989) observes that, in addition to individual career counseling of students, there are at least nine categories of career services in higher education. These categories affirm the comprehensiveness of career services and include approaches such as:

1. Infusing academic subject matter systematically with information pertinent to career development
2. Providing courses for academic credit that focus on career development
3. Using external resources (e.g., speakers, externships, and internships) to provide direct communication of career-related information
4. Integrating placement and transfer processes in support of career planning
5. Offering opportunities for work-study/cooperative education
6. Providing decentralized counseling using academic departments as the location for counselors who, among other responsibilities, coordinate the career and academic advisement of students
7. Providing seminars in residence halls, student unions, and so on, that focus on college life and educational and career planning
8. Providing group counseling focused on self-awareness and career planning
9. Providing interactive, computer-based career guidance and information systems

From the perspective of the broad goals to be met in career services in higher education, Herr et al. (2004) contend that services such as these are offered to achieve the following goals:

1. Provide students with assistance in the selection of a major field of study
2. Provide students with assistance in self-assessment and self-analysis
3. Provide students with assistance in understanding the world-of-work
4. Provide students with assistance in decision making
5. Provide assistance that addresses the unique needs of various subpopulations of students
6. Provide students with assistance with access to the world-of-work

When working with incoming students, Normyle (2014) highlights the importance of understanding the full range of student needs/concerns as they pertain to career planning assistance. She recommends a student needs inventory be used to facilitate this. Career professionals should connect with students early in their first year to implement an effective college-to-career model. Using engaging career assessment instruments may be one way to build this connection. Finally, providing services in a decentralized manner, for example in residence halls, helps increase student involvement with career services.

Chan and Derry (2013) suggest a more radical reimagining of career services in higher education. In their crowdsourced report entitled *Rethinking Success: From Liberal Arts to Careers in the 21st Century*, they summarize the major findings from a 2012 conference addressing the need for transforming the college-to-career experience for college students. Among other findings, they note the essential requirement for top-level institutional support and leadership for creating an environment that values career development. Such support should include upper echelon administrators and boards of trustees while also extending to academic departments, alumni, employers, and parents. University-wide engagement in valuing and prioritizing career development creates greater opportunities for connecting with students. The likelihood that their careers will be influenced by broad-based engagement increases exponentially when compared to traditional centralized career services units.

Vision statements from innovative career development offices can be used to communicate the perspective that career development links to human development and should be viewed holistically. For example, the vision statement for career services at Washington University (n.d.) in St. Louis is "We support students and alumni as they transform their passions, education, and skills into purposeful career paths by teaching lifelong career development strategies and by connecting our diverse students, alumni, and employers." The Wake Forest University vision statement reads as follows: "To inspire, challenge and prepare all students to find careers that reflect their values and lead to lives of connection and meaning" (Chan & Derry, 2013, p. 8). Reinforcing these innovative vision statements, Chan and Derry contend that the title "career services" is no longer adequate. Career services, they contend, is too intertwined with placement services only, which represents a narrow portion of the services students need to become career ready. Chan and Derry suggest that this means that career offices in higher education must prioritize the "developmental processes to teach, engage and equip students to find the unique intersection between who each student is and where they fit in the world of work" (p. 9).

Chan and Derry (2013) also emphasize the importance of career professionals addressing the value proposition involved in pursuing a college degree. Proving that it is worth the investment of money and time expended is a legitimate question for parents and students to ask—and a legitimate answer should be provided. A partial answer is found in the strong interest among employers for graduates able to think critically, articulate concepts clearly, learn readily, cope with change effectively, and interact with others sensitively, which represent some of the skill sets that students should acquire in postsecondary education. Partnerships with alumni and employers providing experiential worksite opportunities for students represent unique opportunities for acquiring exposure and experience for future employment opportunities. Tracking alumni relative to their employment experiences provides outcome data that connect directly to the value proposition question. Rather than being particularly revolutionary, most of the suggestions reported from this conference reflect a nudge toward a more innovative and expansive vision of career services that shares responsibility across multiple stakeholders who can serve as influencers in students' career development. These are exactly the sort of services that could help Robert.

As Robert progressed through career counseling addressing his developmental needs, he increased his self- and career awareness through self-assessment exercises. He became aware of his passions and how he might be able to translate these into career opportunities. He also participated in a career planning group consisting of returning students focused on crystallizing their career choices after being employed in the labor force for substantial periods of time. Employers representing a university-employment partnership also participated in this group at strategic times in order to share their perspective of the added value that nontraditional students bring to the workplace. These activities helped Robert decide to pursue a career in education. Specifically, he decided to become a social studies teacher at the secondary school level. He thought this career option would provide him with opportunities to help others in meaningful ways while also spending more time with his family than he had in his previous jobs.

Standards

Because various models and approaches to career development interventions in higher education exist, there is the need for the professional community to identify the essential components of career services programs. Standards provide useful guides for delivering career development interventions in higher education. The comprehensive career models and services discussed thus far are similar to the perspectives advocated by the Council for the Advancement of Standards for Student Services/Development Programs (CAS) (Council for the Advancement of Standards in Higher Education, 2010). The council is a consortium of professional associations in higher education that collectively devised and published *Standards and Guidelines*, a document that recommends criteria for student services in colleges and universities. One of these student services is career planning and placement. In the CAS Standards, the mission for career services centers is described as "assisting students and other designated clients in developing, evaluating, and implementing career, education, and employment plans" (CAS, 2010, p. 6). The CAS Standards and Guidelines also stipulate that career services programs in higher education should be institutional resources regarding career issues and employment data. Career services professionals in higher education should also develop positive connections with academic units and external constituents. Career services should be directed toward helping students to develop self-understanding and knowledge of occupational information and trends; to identify academic programs of study that match the student's interests and abilities; to increase each student's sense of ownership and responsibility related to coping effectively with career development tasks; to gain relevant career-related experiences (co-curricular, extracurricular, and experiential); to develop job-search skills and networking skills with alumni, prospective employers, and potential future academic programs; and to learn how to use technology to manage their career development.

To accomplish its goals, career services in higher education must provide the following services: career advising, counseling, education, information and resources on careers and further study, opportunities for career exploration through experiential education, job-search services, graduate and professional school or further education planning, employer relations and recruitment services, and consultation services to faculty and administrators.

The CAS Standards (CAS, 2010) also address topics that are essential for the day-to-day operation of career services in higher education. These topics include the following:

- *Leadership* (e.g., leaders of career services programs must have appropriate training; be able to articulate a clear vision for career services; set goals and objectives; prescribe and practice ethical behavior; and manage, plan, budget, and evaluate services/personnel)

- *Organization and Management* (e.g., policies and procedures must be current and accessible, there must be written performance expectations for all staff members, and processes for resolving grievances must be clearly stated)
- *Human Resources* (e.g., there must be adequate staffing, selection training and staffing procedures must be established, support staff must be adequate, affirmative action policies must be followed, and professional development opportunities must be encouraged and supported)
- *Financial Resources* (e.g., career services must have adequate funding)
- *Technology* (e.g., Internet-based resources providing current information regarding the mission, location, staffing, programs, and services available; computer-assisted career guidance systems; online recruiting and employment systems)
- *Facilities and Equipment* (e.g., facilities and equipment must be adequate and suitably located; facilities, technology, and equipment must comply with federal, state, and local requirements for access and safety)
- *Legal Responsibilities* (e.g., staff members must be knowledgeable about laws and regulations pertaining to service delivery)
- *Equity and Access* (e.g., staff members and services must not discriminate on the basis of age, color, disability, gender, national origin, race, religious creed, sexual orientation, and/or veteran status)
- *Campus and External Relations* (e.g., career services programs establish, maintain, and promote effective relations with relevant campus offices and external agencies)
- *Diversity* (e.g., career services staff members and programs must nurture environments in which similarities and differences among people are recognized and honored)
- *Ethics* (e.g., relevant ethical standards must be adhered to in all career services practices)
- *Assessment and Evaluation* (e.g., regular and systematic quantitative and qualitative evaluations must occur to determine program quality)

The CAS (2010) Standards reflect the fact that career services in higher education extend throughout the campus and beyond. Comprehensive career services interact with other student services units (e.g., counseling, residential life), academic units, and community resources. The Standards also provide career practitioners with a useful list of topics and issues that must be addressed in the overall operation of career services in higher education. In these ways, the Standards can be used as benchmarks against which quality and effectiveness of career services can be assessed.

The Professional Standards for College and University Career Services developed by the National Association of Colleges and Employers (NACE, 2010) overlap with the CAS Standards and Guidelines (CAS, 2010). According to the NACE Standards, key program components for career services in higher education must be defined clearly, designed in alignment with student needs, and based on contemporary career services practices. There is also the expectation that career services providers will work collaboratively with academic units, faculty members, and prospective employers. Drawing on resources such as college newspapers, Web sites, and other electronic media helps to increase the reach of the career services provided. Specific program components include (a) career advising/counseling, (b) career information, (c) employment services, (d) graduate school planning, and (e) experiential education.

Career advising and career counseling can occur through individual career counseling appointments, group programs, career planning courses, outreach programs, and via information technology. The primary intent of each of these services is to empower students to make informed educational and career choices based in accurate self-, educational, and occupational information. Career advising and career counseling services are sensitive to a student's cultural contexts as well as the developmental and personal contexts each student must address when constructing career and educational plans. Integrating experiential activities (e.g., job shadowing, volunteering, internships, externships, part-time employment) into career advising and career counseling helps students develop short- and long-term career plans.

Career information includes helping students acquire accurate self-assessment activities, current occupational and labor market information, effective job-search strategies, and accurate employer information (NACE, 2010).

Employment services include helping students engage in exploration related to career possibilities that match their career goals, developing job-search competencies, obtaining employer information, making connections with prospective employers, and developing relevant job search networks (NACE, 2010).

Graduate school planning activities include helping students to identify graduate school opportunities that match their interests, skills, and goals; acquire information regarding prospective programs; learn how to apply to graduate school programs; and develop the skills to connect effectively with potential graduate school programs (NACE, 2010).

Experiential education activities include working with employers and academic units to help students experience career-related learning via job shadowing, volunteering, internships, externships, cooperative education, and apprenticeships. When necessary, career services should also include helping students identify potential funding sources for engaging in experiential education opportunities (NACE, 2010).

The comprehensive NACE (2010) Professional Standards for College and University Career Services also address other important topics for developing and delivering career services in colleges and universities. Specifically, the standards address the following topics: program management, office organization, job descriptions for career services professionals, job responsibilities for career services directors, professional positions, pre-professional positions, professional student employee and volunteer positions, support staff and technical positions, financial resources, facilities and equipment, technology considerations, campus and external relations, employer relations and recruitment services, legal responsibilities, equal opportunity, access, affirmative action, diversity, ethics, program evaluation, assessment, and research.

MANAGING CAREER SERVICES IN HIGHER EDUCATION

The NACE (2010) and CAS (2010) Standards highlight important topics for the management of career services in higher education. Although a full discussion of topics pertaining to managing career services in higher education is beyond the scope of this chapter, there are a few topics that are important to review. For example, it is important to consider the organizational structure of the career services operation because it substantially influences the planning and delivery of career services.

A prominent issue influencing the delivery of career services in higher education is whether career services should be centralized or decentralized. A centralized structure is the most common one for organizing career services in higher education (Powell & Kirts, 1980). Centralized services have clear advantages. Because services are located primarily in one place, it is clear to faculty, students, and employers where career services are provided on campus.

Herr et al. (1993) note additional advantages of a centralized, rather than decentralized, career services structure:

1. Centralized services are more likely to achieve a critical mass in terms of professional staff.
2. There are substantial efficiencies and economies of scale that occur in terms of interview room use, career information resources, and support staff.
3. Because a centralized career services structure draws a very heterogeneous student population, it creates a more vibrant, challenging, and interesting environment for students and staff. (p. 57)

Herr et al. (1993) are quick to point out, however, that there are also advantages to decentralized career services (e.g., the service may be viewed as more personalized, and the services are likely to be more accessible because they are located closer to where students spend a substantial portion of their time). Some institutions provide a combination of centralized and decentralized career services. For example, career counseling services can be decentralized and placement services centralized. There is some logic to this approach due to the fact that in decentralized structures, career counselors often have more direct contact with students and, thereby, find it easier to establish relationships with the students with whom they work. Providing centralized placement services is likely to be less confusing to employers as it is clear to everyone where this activity occurs on campus.

Another issue pertaining to managing career services in higher education relates to the place of career services within the institutional structure. Career service units in higher education typically report to the chief administrator responsible for student services or the chief academic administrator. The results of a survey conducted by the College Placement Council (1991) indicate that nearly three fourths of career services offices report to the vice president of student services. Reporting to the vice president of student services has several advantages. For example, in this administrative structure career services are likely to be viewed as an integral aspect of student services. Because in this structure career services personnel meet regularly with professionals representing other student services units, communication among career services staff members and other student services providers (e.g., counselors, residence life directors) will probably be enhanced. This facilitates service delivery in various ways (e.g., referrals, programming, collaboration among student services professionals). There is a strong possibility that the vice president of student services will have a good understanding of, and appreciation for, the complete range of career services provided by the unit. When career services offices report to the chief academic administrator, they are better aligned with the primary enterprise of the institution. This also provides benefits to career services, such as facilitating relationships with faculty.

The ways in which these administrative issues are resolved in specific institutions will most likely depend on the structure of the overall student services operation and the university itself. Although Herr et al. (1993) view this issue as important for career services delivery, they are careful not to overstate the case, noting that "clearly, the structure of career services must be compatible with the institution in which it operates. Our experience has been that excellent career services often exist despite, rather than because of, a particular organizational structure" (pp. 106–107).

Rayman (1999) identified 10 imperatives for career services in higher education for the next millennium. These imperatives provide college and university career practitioners with useful guidelines as they plan and evaluate the career assistance they provide to students.

- *Imperative 1:* We must acknowledge the lifelong nature of career development and initiate programs and services that enable and encourage students to take responsibility for their own career destinies.
- *Imperative 2:* We must accept and embrace technology as our ally and shape its use to free staff time for those tasks that require human sensitivity.
- *Imperative 3:* We must continue to refine and strengthen our professional identity and that of career services within the academy.
- *Imperative 4:* We must acknowledge and accept that individual career counseling is at the core of our profession and endeavor to maintain and enhance the centrality of individual career counseling in the career development process.
- *Imperative 5:* We must forge cooperative relationships with faculty, advising professionals, other student affairs professionals, administrators, parents, and student groups to take advantage of the "multiplier effect" that such collaborative relationships can have in furthering our goal of enhanced student career development.
- *Imperative 6:* We must redouble our efforts to meet the changing career development needs of an increasingly diverse student body.
- *Imperative 7:* We must accept our position as the most obvious and continuing link between corporate America and the academy, but we also must maintain our focus on career development and not allow ourselves to be seduced into institutional fundraising at the expense of quality career services.
- *Imperative 8:* We must acknowledge and accept that on-campus recruiting as we have known it is a thing of the past and develop alternative means of facilitating the transition from college to work.
- *Imperative 9:* We must resolve the ambiguities that exist about our role in delivering alumni career services and solicit from our alumni associations the resource support necessary to provide these services.
- *Imperative 10:* We must advocate more effectively for resources to maintain and increase our role in facilitating student career development within the academy, and we must become more efficient and innovative in our use of existing resources.

Rayman's imperatives reveal both the challenges and opportunities for career practitioners in higher education in the 21st century. Clearly, the challenges focus on dwindling resources within the context of a growing need to help students in higher education move forward in their career development. The growing need for career services represents a tremendous opportunity to equip students with the knowledge, awareness, and skills to manage their careers effectively in the emerging workplace.

MyCounselingLab®

Start with Topic 7—Higher Education.

Watch the videos *21st Century Application of Career Construction Theory with Student 1* and *21st Century Application of Career Construction Theory with Student 2* and complete Student Activity #7 on page 379.

Watch the video *21st Century Application of Holland's Theory with a College Student: Dr. Janet Lenz* and complete Student Activity #8 on page 379.

SUMMARY

Career services in higher education have a long and venerable history. In many ways, the evolution of these services reflects the evolution of the field in general as services evolved from an orientation toward job placement to a full range of career planning services being offered to meet the needs of diverse student populations. Increasingly, career services providers in higher education enlist a broad range of resources to deliver comprehensive career assistance to students. Alumni, faculty, peers, and community and business representatives are among those participating in the delivery of career services in higher education. Coordinating and providing comprehensive services requires careful and systematic planning, a familiarity with the career development competencies toward which services must be directed, knowledge of current standards for service delivery, awareness of the current literature identifying efficacious career development interventions, and skills in conducting formative and summative evaluations of career services. It is our hope that comprehensive career services, staffed by an adequate cadre of career professionals committed to meeting the career development needs of diverse student populations, will become the norm in higher education. Given survey results in which students identify career planning as their greatest concern, it would seem difficult, at best, for higher education institutions to justify anything less.

CASE STUDY

Allison is a 21-year-old junior at a large Midwestern university. She was the youngest of four children and was raised by her mother and father who lived in New Orleans until Hurricane Katrina destroyed their home and they were forced to move in with her father's parents in Alabama. Allison lost all of her possessions in the devastation caused by Katrina (which occurred when Allison was in her first year of college). During high school, she attended an urban parochial high school in New Orleans.

She has come to the university's career center to get some help in making a career decision. During her first session with the career counselor, Allison talks about a number of occupations she has considered. She likes to write and has thought about working as a journalist or a researcher. She is also very concerned about the environment, but she is not aware of any occupations that would allow her to be involved in environmental issues. She also likes working with children and elderly people and wants to know how she can tie these interests into her career. She has considered the possibility of going to law school because it seems like a "smart thing to do." She is clear that her experience with Katrina has changed her, and she wants to make a difference in the lives of others, especially those who are in "difficult situations" like she was.

Her struggle to make a career decision is also reflected in the difficulty she has experienced in selecting an academic major. After "trying out" several possibilities, Allison decided to major in history and French. These majors seem a bit meaningless to her now. She is not involved in any extracurricular or community activities.

Allison presents herself in a confident way. She is very talkative and animated and seems at ease throughout the session. Her primary concern is identifying what career would be best for her "given all that has happened" in her life. Toward the end of the first session, she asks you about how you got into counseling because it is another occupation that interests her.

What are Allison's career development needs? Which career theories help you understand her situation? Are there any challenges you would experience in trying to understand her situation? What steps would you take to help her?

STUDENT ACTIVITIES

1. What career development tasks do you think are most important for students enrolled in higher education to address?

2. What factors do you think could negatively influence the career development of these students?

3. What are three strategies you could use to foster positive career development in these students?

4. What do you think is the most common type of career assistance provided to students enrolled in higher education? Do you think this type of assistance is helpful? If so, why? If not, why not?

5. What career development challenges did you experience in higher education? What would have helped you address these challenges effectively?

6. Why do you think so few students enrolled in higher education seek career planning assistance from their career services office? What are some strategies that you think could be effective in helping more students get more actively engaged in their career planning?

7. Refer to the MyCounselingLab® Video and Resource Library and select the video entitled, *21st Century Application of Career Construction Theory with a College Student: Dr. Mark Savickas*. What are the benefits of using this model in a postsecondary school career center? What are the limitations of using this model in a career center?

8. Refer to the MyCounselingLab® Video and Resource Library and select the video entitled *21st Century Application of Holland's Theory with a College Student: Dr. Janet Lenz*. What are the benefits of using this model in a postsecondary school career center? What are the limitations of using this model in a career center?

■ ▬ ■

COURSE SYLLABUS FOR A CAREER PLANNING CLASS

Effective Career Decision Making
Fall 2011
Tuesday and Thursday, 11:15 AM–12:30 PM
202 Rackley

Office: Career Services
Office Hours: 2:00–3:00 p.m., Tuesday and Wednesday, and by appointment

Text: *The Career Fitness Program: Exercising Your Options (9th ed.)*
Handout packet provided by the instructor

PURPOSE

This course is designed for students who are undecided about their major and career selection. This course is not appropriate for students who have already chosen a major and developed career goals. It does not cover topics such as job-search strategies, résumé writing, cover letters, and interviewing skills. One of the other career courses offered by Career Services would be more appropriate for these students than this course.

COURSE OBJECTIVES

1. Engage in a variety of activities and experiences that are useful in building knowledge about yourself, careers, academic majors, and the world-of-work.
2. Know the core concepts and applications of basic career theories.
3. Identify and integrate personal history, interests, values, skills, and abilities.
4. Understand how career assessments (e.g., the Self-Directed Search and the Myers-Briggs Type Indicator) are used to facilitate career decision making.
5. Gain information and support through the use of the university's academic advising and career resources.
6. Learn how to use workplace trends to enhance current and future career decisions.

Students with disabilities who require accommodations should consult with the instructor within the first two weeks of class to address modifications that are needed to complete course requirements. Consistent with university policy, any student requesting an accommodation must provide documentation from the Office for Disability Services.

GRADING SCALE

A = 279–300	B = 249–260	Miscellaneous 15%
A− = 270–278	B− = 240–248	Lifeline and Brief Paper 5%
B+ = 261–269	C+ = 231–239	Occupation Informational

C = 210–230   F = Below 180   Interview Paper 20%

D = 180–209   Career Autobiography Paper 20%

Exams 20%

Group Presentation 10%

Attendance and Participation 10%

LATE ASSIGNMENT POLICY

Assignments: Lose one point per late class period. Career Autobiography Paper and Occupation Informational Interview Paper: lose five points per late class period.

If you will be absent on a day the assignment is due, you are expected to turn the assignment in prior to your absence if possible.

Course Schedule

Date	Class Topic	Reading	Assignment Due
Tues., August 22	Introduction. Review of course syllabus and requirements. Discussion of student and instructor expectations. (Introduce Introductory Assessments.)		
Thurs., August 24	Effective career decision making. Career planning issues. Orientation to career services.		Introductory Assessments
Tues., August 29	Career development theories. (Introduce Lifeline assignment.)		
Thurs., August 31	Career development theories continued. (Hand out semester packets.)	Chapter 1, "Taking Stock"	
Tues., September 5	Career assessment strategies. The career counseling process. Orientation to academic majors. (Assign DISCOVER.) (Receive group assignments.) (Sign up for tour of Career Information Center.)		
Thurs., September 7	Small Group Workshop 1— Sharing and discussion of Lifelines		
Tues., September 12	Personal and career decision-making strategies. (Administer the Myers-Briggs Type Indicator.)	Chapter 8, "Making Decisions"	Exercises 8.1 and 8.15
Thurs., September 14	Values decisions in career and life planning. Values and work satisfaction. Lifeline Brief "Values Paper."	Chapter 3, "Values Clarification"	Lifeline Brief Paper Exercises 3.1 and 3.2

(Continued)

Date	Class Topic	Reading	Assignment Due
Tues., September 19	Interests. Holland's typology of personality and career interests. (Assign Self-Directed Search.)	"Focusing on You: Personality and Interests"	Interest Checklist for Worker Trait Groups pages 65–69
Thurs., September 21	Interpretation of the Self-Directed Search.		Self-Directed Search
Tues., September 26	Personality characteristics and workplace preferences. Interpretation of the Myers-Briggs Type Indicator.		
Thurs., September 28	Abilities and their role in academic and career planning. Synthesis–integration of internal information. (Introduce Career Autobiography.)	Chapter 5, "Skills Assessment"	Assessing Your Skills, pages 85–86 and Exercise 5.8
Tues., October 3	Exam 1		
Thurs., October 5	Small-Group Workshop 2—Review of assessment results. Bring results from Self-Directed Search, Myers-Briggs Type Indicator, Values and Skills exercises, Majors Checklist, DISCOVER, and Self-Assessment Summary.		Majors Checklist and Self-Assessment Summary
Tues., October 10	FALL BREAK		
Thurs., October 12	World-of-work work sectors; relationship between basic work tasks, academic majors, and career choice. (Assign Advising Interviews.)	Chapter 7, "Information Integration." Review pages 72–73.	DISCOVER Reaction Paper
Tues., October 17 or Wed., October 18	Career information resources at Career Services. Class meets in room 410 Boucke at 5:00 PM		
Thurs., October 19	Small-Group Workshop 3—Planning for group presentation. Decision-making style and personal issues effect on major/career decision making.		Career Autobiography Paper
Tues., October 24	Interviewing for occupational information. (Introduce Occupation Informational Interview paper.)		
Thurs., October 26	Experiential Learning: Internships, externships, summer jobs, education abroad, activities, and volunteer work. Collegiate and community involvement and its role in career development.		Exercise 7.6
Tues., October 31	Guest speakers.		

Date	Class Topic	Reading	Assignment Due
Thurs., November 2	Discuss academic advising interviews.		Summaries of Advising Interview Experiences
Tues., November 7	Cultural Diversity: personal and career issues related to gender, race/ethnicity, and disability status.	Chapter 6, "The World and You"	
Thurs., November 9	Small-Group Workshop 4—Cultural Diversity. Discuss the impact of the culturally diverse workplace on career decisions.		Multicultural Me
Tues., November 14	Group Presentations.		
Thurs., November 16	Group Presentations.		
Tues., November 21	Workplace trends and issues.		Article from popular literature about a current workplace trend or issue for group discussion
Thurs., November 23	Thanksgiving		
Tues., November 28	Discuss Informational Interviews.		Occupation Informational Interview Paper
Thurs., November 30	Exam 2. Continue discussion of Informational Interviews.		
Tues., December 5	Course wrap-up and evaluations.		
Thurs., December 7	Small-Group Workshop 5—Putting it all together. Discussion of course learning as it applies to personal career situations. Next steps for career planning.		Putting It All Together

ASSIGNMENT DESCRIPTIONS

Assessments

You will be required to take three formal assessments: the Self-Directed Search, the Myers-Briggs Type Indicator, and DISCOVER.

Myers-Briggs Type Indicator (to be completed in class on September 12)

Self-Directed Search   *Due: September 21*

The Myers-Briggs and the Self-Directed Search are popular assessment tools that measure personality and interests, respectively. As we will discuss in class, personality preferences and tendencies and personal interests are important contributors to the career development process.

The instruments will be administered in class. It is your responsibility to attend class and complete the assessments as instructed.

DISCOVER   *Reaction Paper Due: October 12*

DISCOVER is a computer-assisted career guidance system (CACGS) housed in Career Services, 410 Boucke, which can assist you with making career decisions. You will need to schedule a one-hour appointment between September 6 and October 11. Appointments can be scheduled by going to 412 Boucke between the hours of 8:00 AM and 5:00 PM. More details on this assignment will be provided in class on September 5.

Lifeline and Paper   *Lifeline Due: September 7*
                                                                Paper Due: September 14

The lifeline is a collection of important events in your personal development. There are two parts to this assignment. First, you will create the lifeline in any format you choose and present your project to your small-group members. Second, you will prepare a two-page written statement about your lifeline.

1. The lifeline can be presented in any format you choose. Previous lifelines have included the following:
   - Drawn, painted, or cartooned pictures of scenes throughout a lifetime
   - A poem describing feelings and/or major events (If you choose this format, make sure the content is substantial.)
   - A physical object representing a person's life, attitude, or an event (Include a written explanation.)
   - A recording of various relevant songs
   - Clip art, sculptures, collages, or creative writing

   Although there are no formal requirements for length or content, grades will be determined by the amount of work, thought, or creativity evident through the presentation and the ability to express important events in a person's life.

   You will present your lifeline at the first small-group session on September 7. Please be aware that you will have about 10 minutes to share your lifeline, so plan accordingly! If you have more to say, you can write about it in your summary.

   Your project is to be turned in to your group leader.

2. A two-page summary of your lifeline should include your reactions to the presentations, thoughts that were triggered, the benefits of the assignment, and so on. Consider the following questions for group discussion and your paper:

   Who are/were some of the significant people in your life?

   Who has influenced you the most in terms of your educational and/or career planning?

   What were some of the highs and lows or significant events in your life?

   What accomplishments are you proudest of?

   How did you decide to attend college, and why did you choose _____?

   What major(s)/career(s) were you considering when you first decided to attend _____?

   Are you completely unsure of what you want to major in or what occupation you might enjoy?

   How does it feel to be uncertain?

First Paper: Career Autobiography   Due: October 19

The Career Autobiography is meant to help you synthesize and process the information you have gained about yourself from class through various assessments, exercises, and discussions. The paper must be typed, approximately five to seven pages long, and should include the following:

- A discussion of your background and significant life events. Include family background, careers you thought about as a child, how and why you decided to attend _____, and so on.
- Consideration of how your experiences to date, including work experience and extracurricular activities, have influenced your past or present educational and career plans.
- A review of the relationship between your life/career plans and information from the course. Discuss how well your assessment results from the SDS and Myers-Briggs "fit" you. Do you agree with your results? Why or why not? What did you learn about yourself from the values and abilities exercises? What is your decision-making style and how does it affect your choice of major? Which career theories apply to you? How? Be sure to cite some content from lectures, class discussion, assignments, and/or the text.
- A brief review of your present situation concerning your academic and career plans. Also, review possible future directions, including possible majors.

Please include a cover page. (Your cover page should include your name, course title, title of your paper, and the date.)

The following criteria will be used in grading your paper:

1. Integration of course concepts   20 pts.
2. Effect of your life experience on educational and career decisions   15 pts.
3. Present and future career issues   10 pts.
4. Overall presentation organization, grammar, and spelling   15 pts.
   Total   60 pts.

Second Paper: Occupation Informational Interview   Due: November 28

Researching a career is essential to the career decision-making process.

The paper must be typed, double-spaced, approximately five to seven pages in length, and should include the following:

- A review and discussion of an informational interview conducted with someone employed in a career area that may be of interest to you. Preferably, the person will not be a relative and will be employed outside of _____. (The instructor before the interview must approve relatives and _____ employees.) Include the reason you chose to interview somebody in this particular field. Consider:
  - The nature of the work (duties, responsibilities)
  - Qualifications necessary (education and/or experience)
  - Typical lines of advancement in this field
  - Typical hiring organizations for this kind of job
- A summary of the nature of the organization in which the professional is employed. Consider:
  - The organization's structure
  - Profits or funding sources
  - Services or products

- Work environment
- Types of entry-level positions for college graduates
- If available, any handout information, such as an annual report or organizational brochure. This would be included in an appendix.
- A review of your reaction to your interview with the professional.
- How similar or different was the information you obtained compared with your previous knowledge of the career field?
- What effect has this information had on your interest in the field and your decision to pursue it?
- What information do you still need about this career?
- What are your next steps or plans of action?
- A cover sheet with the name of the person you interviewed, name of the organization, date of the interview, and the interviewee's full mailing address and telephone number.

You will also be required to make a brief presentation about your informational interview on the day that it is due. You will not be graded on your presentation. The purpose is to share information about occupations with your fellow classmates.

Refer to the handout on "Occupational Information Interviewing" in your packet for ideas on questions to ask.

The following criteria will be used in grading your paper:

1. Information about the interviewee   15 pts.
2. Information about the organization   10 pts.
3. Your reaction and thoughts   20 pts.
4. Overall presentation organization, grammar, and spelling   15 pts.
   Total   60 pts.

Group Report and Presentation   *Due: November 14 and 16*

Each discussion group will select a major and related occupation (or occupations) to research. It may not be possible to find a major and career that all group members would personally consider pursuing, so try to choose one that most members are curious to learn about. The group should review the following information for the selected major:

1. General nature of the program
2. Course and program requirements
3. Entrance requirements
4. Type and ranges of occupations associated with the major as well as opportunities for graduate/professional school
5. Sources of information and relevant student organizations

Information regarding the selected occupation(s) related to the major should include the following:

1. Nature of the work and typical responsibilities
2. Appropriate academic preparation and training; identify a range of undergraduate majors that could lead to the occupation(s)
3. Types and range of organizations/settings in which the occupation is performed
4. Job outlook and earnings
5. Sources of information and relevant student organizations

This presentation should be fun and informative for you and your classmates! Small skits, television shows, takeoffs on movies, game-show-style presentations, and other creative ideas are encouraged! Your group will have a time range of 15 to 20 minutes.

The purpose of this assignment is to become familiar with the kinds of information necessary to make informed career choices and ways to research this information.

A few suggested resources: Academic Advising Centers, Student Organization Directory, Career Information Center, college/university library, and the Internet.

Each group will turn in a one-page, typed summary or outline of their presentation on or before the day of the presentation.

ASSIGNMENT DUE DATES AND COURSE GRADING CRITERIA

Date	Assignment	Points
August 24	Introductory Assessments	3 pts.
September 7	Lifeline	15 pts.
September 12	Myers-Briggs Type Indicator	2 pts.
September 12	Decision-Making Exercises 8.1 & 8.15	2 pts.
September 14	Values Exercises 3.1 & 3.2	2 pts.
September 14	Brief Paper	
September 19	Interest Exercise, pages 65–69	2 pts.
September 21	Self-Directed Search	3 pts.
September 28	Skills Exercise, pages 85–86 and Exercise 5.8	2 pts.
October 3	Exam 1	30 pts.
October 5	Majors Checklist	3 pts.
	Self-Assessment Summary	3 pts.
October 12	DISCOVER Reaction Paper	5 pts.
October 19	Career Autobiography Paper	60 pts.
October 26	Gathering the Facts, Exercise 7.6	6 pts.
November 2	Academic Advising Summaries	6 pts.
November 9	Multicultural Me	2 pts.
November 14 & 16	Group Presentation	30 pts.
November 21	Work Trend Article	2 pts.
November 28	Occupation Info. Interview Paper	60 pts.
November 30	Exam 2	30 pts.
December 7	Putting It All Together	2 pts.
	Class Attendance & Participation	30 pts.
	Total	300 pts.

CHAPTER 14

CAREER DEVELOPMENT INTERVENTIONS IN COMMUNITY SETTINGS

So much

"To continue its good work in the next decade, the career counseling profession must intensify efforts to serve a diverse clientele in new settings … construct new tools that exploit the potential of informational technology … and assist counselors worldwide who seek to internationalize the profession of career counseling" (The Career Development Quarterly, 2004). These lofty aspirations suggest that never before has a profession expected so much of itself.

So many

A recent Gallup Organization survey conducted for the National Career Development Association reported that a significant number of adult workers seek assistance from professionals in the careers field. The broadening list of presenting issues includes career dissatisfaction, work-life imbalance, job-loss grief, as well as the traditional job-search training. Will the dawn of the next decade witness increased public demand for professional career services? If so, then it may well be true that never before has so much been owed by so many individuals and their families.

So few

Some employers and professional organizations bemoan that there are so few highly trained professionals providing preventative (i.e., primary, secondary, and tertiary) career services. Small but growing is the demand for evidence-based career interventions that are deliverable in multiple formats (i.e., individual, couple/family, and group services), with returns on investment (ROI) that are measurable, sustainable, and replicable.

A retrospective at decade's-end may prove whether the words of Prime Minister Winston Churchill during WWII's Battle of Britain characterize the 21st-century workforce: "Never in the field of human conflict was so much owed by so many to so few" (Churchill, 1940).

Michael E. Hall, Ph.D., LPC, C.M.F.
Principal of a solo career-, marital-, and leadership-development
practice in Charlotte, North Carolina

MyCounselingLab®

Visit the MyCounselingLab® site for *Career Development Interventions*, Fifth Edition, to enhance your understanding of chapter concepts. You will have the opportunity to practice applying what you learned in the chapter by completing the video- and case-based exercises in the MyLab. Taking the Licensure Quizzes will help you prepare for your certification exam.

Alexa is a 30-year-old woman with a bachelor's degree in accounting. She has been working as an accountant for seven years and is greatly dissatisfied with her choice of occupation, one strongly suggested by her father. Not knowing how to get assistance in developing other occupational alternatives, she went to the local one-stop center. The counselor there was very helpful in teaching her how to use the state's electronic job bank to identify jobs that were available in her state and how to use other Web sites that would help her with labor market information and job seeking. She was, however, confused by the amount of information on these Web sites and realized that she needed extensive assistance in determining what her interests and values are in relation to work before being immersed in information and job possibilities. She called her former high school counselor, who was able to refer her to a local certified career counselor in private practice.

Although the profession of counseling had its genesis in 1908 in Frank Parsons's Vocation Bureau in Boston, which was a community-based setting, this specialty of career counseling has experienced a long struggle for recognition. Counseling was first recognized as a necessary function in public high schools; and the National Defense Education Act of 1958, which provided government funds for the training of counselors for placement in high schools, had a tremendous impact on institutionalizing high school counselors. Chapters 10, 11, and 12 of this textbook describe the role and function of counselors in school settings, including elementary, middle, and high schools. Counseling in postsecondary educational settings, as described in Chapter 13, has become a recognized and essential component of the student services provided by two- and four-year colleges.

In addition, the need to provide career counseling to adult populations has been recognized. Responding to a need to have a professional organization for all counseling specialties, the American Personnel and Guidance Association (APGA), now the American Counseling Association (ACA), was formed in 1952 by the four professional associations—for career counselors, school counselors, college student personnel, and counselor educators and supervisors—then in existence. Since its founding, ACA has recognized the following specialties in counseling, which have become divisions within the main body of ACA:

- Association for Assessment in Counseling (AAC)
- Association for Adult Development and Aging (AADA)
- Association for Assessment and Research in Counseling (AARC)
- Association for Child and Adolescent Counseling (ACAC)
- Association for Creativity in Counseling (ACC)
- American College Counseling Association (ACCA)
- Association for Counselors and Educators in Government (ACEG)
- Association for Counselor Education and Supervision (ACES)
- Association for Humanistic Counseling (AHC)
- Association for Lesbian, Gay, Bisexual and Transgender Issues in Counseling (ALGBTIC)
- Association for Multicultural Counseling and Development (AMCD)
- American Mental Health Counselors Association (AMHCA)
- American Rehabilitation Counseling Association (ARCA)

- American School Counselor Association (ASCA)
- Association for Spiritual, Ethical, and Religious Values in Counseling (ASERVIC)
- Association for Specialists in Group Work (ASGW)
- Counselors for Social Justice (CSJ)
- International Association of Addictions and Offender Counselors (IAAOC)
- International Association of Marriage and Family Counselors (IAMFC)
- National Career Development Association (NCDA)
- National Employment Counseling Association (NECA)

Note that the names of these divisions vary in that some focus on the setting in which the counseling takes place (such as the American School Counselor Association); some, the population (Adult Development and Aging); and some, the primary concern of the counseling (such as the National Career Development Association). However, none of these specifically recognize the community as a setting for providing counseling and career development services. Further, though the members of the NCDA might have the highest degree of interest in providing career counseling and development services, the fact is that counselors who work in all of the specialties and settings represented by other divisions also inevitably work with clients who have major concerns with career choice and development. In addition to membership in these divisions of ACA, counselors specializing in career planning services in any setting might belong to a division of the American Psychological Association (APA), namely Division 17, comprised of members who specialize in vocational psychology.

TRAINING, CERTIFICATION, AND LICENSURE

The basic training for counselors in all specialties is a master's degree in a counseling curriculum that includes training in eight core areas and a supervised practicum. This training may be acquired in a graduate institution that is approved by the Council for Accreditation of Counseling and Related Educational Programs (CACREP) or one that is not CACREP approved. CACREP-approved programs now require 48 semester hours for most counseling specialties (but 60 hours for addiction, mental health, and marital counseling) of graduate work in the field and 100 clock hours of supervised practicum followed by 600 hours of supervised internship. CACREP standards recognize specialties in both community and career counseling. There are 10 graduate institutions with a specialty in career counseling, and 235 that meet the requirements for training as a community counselor or clinical mental health counselor (now combined as one category).

The standards referred to in the previous paragraph are standards for graduate school programs; doubtless, these standards result in better preparation of those who attend schools that meet these standards. Other standards, notably those of the National Board for Certifed Counselors (NBCC) and of state licensure boards, apply directly to the qualifications of individual counselors. NBCC offers certification to counselors who meet its requirements (48 semester hours of coursework, two academic terms of supervised field experience, and two years of post-master's counseling experience); persons who qualify for certification may use the title National Certified Counselor (NCC). In addition to voluntarily applying for and maintaining certification, counselors must meet the requirements for licensure as defined in their own state's law. In addition to all of this, many career counselors (especially those who want to practice in higher education or in private practice) earn a Certificate of Advanced Study (CAS) or doctoral degree (Ed.D. or Ph.D.) with a specialty in career development theory and practice.

COMPETENCIES

It is easy to view community-based counseling as that which occurs in any setting other than education. This definition appears to be insufficient. A common definition (Hershenson, Power, & Waldo, 1996) of community-based counseling is "the application of counseling principles and practices in agency, organizational, or individual practice settings that are located in and interact with their surrounding community" (p. 26). The AllPsychology Web site describes the work of a community counselor as follows: "Community counselors analyze problems on an individual level and then determine what it takes to solve those problems on a larger, community level. Similar to repairing a bumpy road before it causes more problems for people, community counselors work to prevent problems before they occur" (AllPsychologyCareers, n.d.). This difference in approach implies that community career counselors need and use additional competencies beyond those needed in educational settings. These competencies include coordination, consultation, advocacy, and case management.

Coordination

Coordinating is the process whereby a counselor brings together the needs of a client and the resources of the community. A first step in being able to coordinate is to assess thoroughly the client's strengths and barriers and to investigate and become knowledgeable of the resources that the community has. A client's strengths and barriers are typically identified through informal and formal assessment techniques. The most common informal assessment technique is the interview. The first of such interviews is called an intake interview. It is a structured interview in which the counselor uses some predetermined questions to collect the information needed to understand the client's strengths and barriers. One model used for this process is based on Schlossberg's transition theory.

Schlossberg (1989) defines a transition as an event or nonevent that results in change that is significant enough to cause disruption in one's usual roles, relationships, and/or routines. Many of the concerns that send clients to community-based career counselors fit this definition.

Schlossberg proposes that the severity of such transitions can be controlled by use of a four-step process:

- Define the *situation* clearly. This step includes finding out how the client perceives the situation or problem, what its timing is, how long the client has had to absorb it, and how much control the client believes he or she can exert to resolve or manage the situation.
- Learn about the *self* or inner resources the client has. This step includes learning about how the client has dealt with past transitions; what his or her dominant goals, interests, and skills are; and what emotional and spiritual strengths lie in the personal reservoir.
- Learn about the *support system* that does or does not surround the client in this transition. This system includes the support of family, friends, agencies, and material goods that can assist with the transition.
- From the knowledge gained in these three areas, the counselor and the client can develop a *strategy* for coping with the present need or transition.

If a counselor were, for example, using this kind of theoretical base as a guide for asking open-ended questions (those that cannot be answered with a single word), this could be a valuable informal assessment technique for the identification of the client's strengths, barriers, and coping mechanisms.

In this technological age, Web-based integrated career guidance systems, such as Kuder's *Journey* (Kuder, Inc., 2015), may also ask users to identify needs or barriers that they have as they face the job market. In this system, users may identify any of the following as significant needs or barriers:

Needs	Barriers
Housing	Insufficient past work experience
Child care	Lack of enough education or training
Knowledge of job-seeking skills	Mental or physical health problems
Clothing	Addiction
Better reading skills	Inability to speak English well
Better math skills	
Completion of high school	

The system then provides a state-specific list of Web sites that identify community-based sources of assistance in each of the areas identified by the user. Further, the system provides individual reports for users that community-based counselors can access in order to develop a support plan for a given client.

As indicated with the preceding example, the other side of the equation is the identification of resources in the community that can meet the identified needs of the client or assist in removing barriers. In this process the career counselor spends significant time finding and cataloging community resources related to specific categories of need—such as job placement, shelter, vocational training, clothing, legal assistance, and other areas. Because resources of this kind come and go, there is a need for an ongoing scan of the environment to identify new resources and resources that may no longer be available.

Identification of services is only the first step. The second step is to become knowledgeable about them: visiting the organization that provides the service; establishing and maintaining a personal contact; and getting detailed information about services provided, criteria for those who can access the services, length and cost of services provided, and the best way to access the services.

The third step is to make an informed linkage between the client and available services. One method is to organize client needs by the same descriptors as services provided by organizations. Given that client profiles and resource profiles are entered into a database, a counselor could easily relate the two by a simple computer search. Lacking this capability, counselors may maintain up-to-date print files or notebooks that describe community referral resources.

So, the process of coordination involves the steps of (a) identifying client needs, (b) matching client needs with community resources, (c) introducing the client to these resources through personal contact, (d) referring the client to the resource, and (e) following through with both the client and the resource to determine the effectiveness of the referral and what the next steps should be.

As an example of the task of coordinating, suppose that a counselor working in a prison setting identified vocational training as one of the primary needs of an ex-offender. The client is particularly interested in learning to cook, and the Salvation Army has a training program for cooks. The counselor follows all of the steps previously listed, including making a personal contact with the Salvation Army and setting an appointment for the client. The client presents himself effectively in the interview and is accepted in the culinary training program. The counselor is not yet finished; he or she needs to monitor the client's continuation and success in the program, especially during the first three to six months.

Consultation

Consultation is a second important competency for community-based career counselors (Dougherty, 1990). AllAboutKids.com (n.d.) defines *consultation* as "the seeking and giving of advice, information, and/or opinion." Consultation should not be confused with supervision, which implies that one person has the responsibility for directing the activities of another and for corrective action if performance does not meet expectations. Consultation, on the other hand, is the work of one professional with another in an attempt to find ways to identify interventions that will address the needs of a third party (the client).

As an example, suppose that a 45-year-old single mother who comes to a community mental health center for career counseling has a heart condition that is potentially significant enough to affect the kind of work that she can do. As the counselor discusses the possible ways that she could afford additional training, he learns that she has always had a goal to attend college but does not believe it is possible considering her age and financial condition. The counselor describes the services of the Division of Vocational Rehabilitation and explains that there may be an opportunity for her to receive funds through this agency to attend the local community college or a state-supported university.

With the client's enthusiastic permission, the counselor makes an appointment with a staff member at the local office of the Division of Vocational Rehabilitation (DVR). During that meeting, the counselor describes his client and her needs. The DVR staff member and counselor compare the client's characteristics with the current policies of DVR and jointly conclude that the client is eligible for a service that would pay for tuition at a publicly supported institution of higher education. The counselor formally refers the client to the contact person at DVR, who proceeds to work with her to develop a formal application for services.

Many clients who receive services from community-based counselors lack the skills that are needed to overcome the barriers they face and reach the goals they seek. These skills may be social, academic, or psychological. In other words, there may be deficits in ability to communicate effectively with others, in specific skills needed to perform in a job, or in personal coping skills such as decision making or goal setting. As the counselor identifies these needs, he or she may seek ways to meet these deficits through consultation with persons in community agencies.

Advocacy

A third competency that Hershenson et al. (1996) attribute to community-based counselors is *advocacy*. This term describes a role that counselors may play to exert pressure on some aspect of the community in order to improve the resources available for clients. Advocacy may be exercised through representation on boards of referral agencies, pressing for specific legislation, writing newspaper columns, joining protests of various kinds, writing to legislators, exerting individual influence, or making presentations to groups that can have influence.

Suppose that you worked as a career counselor in a rehabilitation agency. A local community college offers an excellent program in desktop publishing, and five of your clients with disabilities are enrolled in it. However, it is very difficult for your clients to get a job, no matter how well they do in this program, because of the prejudice against persons with disabilities. You identify four major employers of persons trained in desktop publishing and make an appointment with the director of human resources in each of the four sites. When you visit, you take a copy of the performance-based curriculum that the community college offers. You also take some work samples and letters written by employers of past graduates of the program. Finally, you show pictures of your five clients and ask the director of human resources to grant an interview to these clients for the next desktop publishing job available. You commit to careful follow-through with your clients who become employees to increase the probability that they will be productive employees. Advocacy includes performance of all of the kinds of activities included in this example.

More than those in any other counseling specialty, community counselors must orchestrate a variety of people, resources, and services in order to meet the needs of their clients. This process of orchestration is called *case management*. In large agencies, the persons involved in case management may be different from those who provide counseling. More typically, however, the community counselor plays a multifaceted role that includes both counselor and case manager. This dual role demands diverse skills, ranging from the facilitative skills of a good counselor to the coordinating, consulting, and advocacy skills just described.

Case Management

The goal of case management is to ensure that clients receive the sequence of services they need in a timely and coordinated fashion. Thus, one of the most critical roles of a community-based counselor is to develop a comprehensive case plan, which might be called an action plan, and then to monitor it continually. For some clients, services may be provided by the counselor and the agency that he or she represents with only one external service provider. For other clients, whose needs are complex and include needs outside the scope of the agency such as physical problems, housing needs, financial needs, and job needs, there may be several service providers external to the counselor's home site.

Tips from the Field

The services of coordination, consultation, and advocacy are delivered through the development and implementation of an effective case management plan.

The role of case manager demands skill in assessment (to determine needs), coordination with referral resources, evaluation of services provided, advocacy for the client, and continual follow-through with the client and the external service providers. Case management requires the development of a sound plan at the outset, establishment and maintenance of excellent relationships with specific persons within referral agencies, tact in communication and evaluation, ongoing instructional and emotional support to the client and perhaps the client's family, and wisdom about when to make a change in service provider or to terminate service to the client. The types of resources that may be included in a case plan are as varied as the needs of clients for whom plans are developed.

It is common for community-based centers to have differentiated staffing. A counselor addressing career concerns may be on a team with psychologists, social workers, nurses, medical doctors, and perhaps career development facilitators (CDFs). A career development facilitator is a paraprofessional trained to work under the supervision of a professional counselor to assist with a number of duties most directly related to career planning and job placement.

SIMILARITIES AND DIFFERENCES IN COMMUNITY-BASED SETTINGS

Career counseling provided to individuals or groups in community-based settings is both similar to and different from career counseling provided in other settings. It is similar to work in educational settings in that it draws on the same counseling and career development theories for many of its tools and techniques and requires the same facilitative skills when working with clients. In addition, its clients may be dealing with career choice and development problems that in many ways parallel those of students.

Conversely, providing career development services in community-based settings differs from doing so in educational settings in the following ways:

- Clients who seek career counseling in community-based settings are typically adults who have major responsibilities in several life roles, such as spouse, parent, and citizen in addition to worker. They are typically facing one of the following areas of concern: (a) reentry into the workforce after child rearing or loss of job; (b) dealing with being plateaued and wanting to find greater job satisfaction through job change, upward mobility, or job enrichment; or (c) dissatisfaction with an occupation or job or a change in an occupation's requirements that necessitates significant retraining.
- The options they have for career choice or change are intimately tied to availability of resources and/or dilution of barriers in the community. *Community* is defined as all of that which surrounds the individual—that is, community may be the family, the neighborhood, and/or the organization in which one is imbedded.
- Based on this assumption, the counselor may spend as much time and effort in working with the community to make resources available as with the individual client.
- Work with the community may take the forms of finding training opportunities to augment the individual's current skills, advocating for additional or modified resources, removing barriers to those resources, consulting with appropriate persons or agencies, and/or coordinating between and among the client and community resources.
- The skills of coordination, consultation, advocacy, and case management—though also necessary in educational settings—may be needed and used more often in community-based settings than in school settings.
- These counselors work in the community in settings such as private practice, government agencies, mental health centers, drug and abuse centers, and corporations. They may also work in the global community by delivering services via the Internet.

SETTINGS FOR COMMUNITY-BASED CAREER COUNSELORS

There is an increasingly wide variety of settings in which community-based counselors work—some devoting full time to career-related concerns and others dealing with such concerns in the context of a much broader array. The most common of these community-based settings and the typical tasks of counselors who work in them are summarized next.

Private Practice

The term *private practice* implies that a trained counselor, who may have taken additional course-work related to career development, has chosen to form a company, market career development services, and identify clients who can and are willing to pay for services. Such a person would likely rent facilities or work from home and acquire clients through such approaches as newspaper ads, a Web site, listing in the Yellow Pages, referrals, and word of mouth. Such a counselor might join a private practice made up of a group of counselors and, within that group, be the specialist in working with clients for whom career issues appear to be the leading ones.

Because this professional focuses his or her services on career concerns, clients are likely to state a career problem as the reason for seeking assistance. It may be stated as a need to find a different job (because of recent loss of a job or dissatisfaction with a current one), as a desire to get additional training in order to have new skills to use in a different kind of job, or as a desire to analyze the reasons why a recent potential for promotion has not been realized. It is rare, however, that the presenting problem is the only problem that needs to be addressed in the counseling sessions, because a career choice or change issue is likely to affect other life roles, such as spouse and parent. Further, the career problem presented may be affected by other problems, such as drug abuse, alcoholism, inability to sustain relationships, or poor self-concept. Thus, it is impossible to speak of "career counseling" with adults in community settings as purely related to career choices; presenting problems are almost inevitably entwined with a host of others.

At Alexa's first visit to a career counselor in private practice, she indicated that she was bored with her work as an accountant and was seeking assistance in identifying a different occupation, one in which she could work with people instead of numbers. As her story unfolded, however, she revealed that her father was a prominent figure in her life and that he had continually encouraged her to become an accountant, despite her lack of interest in detail. He thought that it was a high-paying occupation for a woman, one without significant emotional or physical stress. Through interviewing and assessment, the counselor helped Alexa to become aware of her interests and values related to working with people in some way. She also helped Alexa to delve deeply into her relationship with her father and the reasons she was still letting his influence affect major decisions in her life.

Alexa decided that she did not want to spend significant time in retraining because she had purchased a home and established a lifestyle that required continuation of her present level of income. Further, she realized that it would be very difficult for her to go against her father's wishes and advice about her occupational choice. Thus, the counselor suggested that Alexa explore other occupations related to accounting that would give her more opportunity to work with people on a face-to-face basis. After using print resources and Web sites to gather information about such specialties, Alexa had several information interviews with accountants who worked in entirely different settings—helping people with financial planning, providing service to professionals about retirement plans and options, and teaching accounting in a community college. This experience gave her perspectives on how she could use her accounting background in ways she had never thought of before, and she terminated her relationship with the counselor with a one-year action plan.

Career counselors in private practice typically work with their clients on a one-to-one basis through a sequence of interviews. As in other one-to-one settings, the counselor is likely to begin the sequence by assessing the client's needs and barriers, establishing goals with the client for the counseling relationship, working with the client to reach those goals, and ultimately terminating when the two agree that goals have been reached or that further work together will not be beneficial.

As in other settings, private practitioners, in addition to skilled interviewing, use the tools of assessment, technology (Web-based systems and Web sites), career information, referral, and advocacy to assist their clients to meet established goals. Their services may be short term, as would be the case if the goals are to write an effective résumé, practice job interviewing, identify desirable job openings, and get a job. Conversely, the services may be long term, as would be the case if there are underlying problems of dysfunctional career beliefs, poor self-concept, drug abuse, or role conflict.

Counselors who work as private practitioners should have at least a master's degree in counseling with additional coursework in career development theory and practice. Many have doctorates and, through this additional study, have been able to acquire more background in career development theory than a master's-degree counselor would have. They may and should be National Certified Counselors (NCCs) and preferably National Certified Career Counselors (NCCC). Unfortunately, the latter certification has been discontinued. However, the NCDA has established categories of membership that can be helpful to the consumer; those who qualify by educational background and experience to hold NCDA membership as a Master Career Counselor are likely to have the theoretical underpinnings and experience to work as private practitioners. In addition to these academic and experiential qualifications, counselors in private practice need business skills in order to market their services and to do the financial accounting required of small businesses. Further, as suggested in a previous section, they may need additional skills in coordination, consultation, advocacy, and case management.

The World Wide Web: Online Counseling and Career Advising

The year 2000 signaled the beginning of counseling services via the Internet. To date, these services are being offered by certified counselors, career development facilitators, or career advisors working from their homes or offices. Their clients are self-selected on the Internet, and provision of service is brokered through a Web site that has the appropriate infrastructure to handle synchronous (both the client and the counselor are at a computer at the same time) text-based or video-based communication, appointment scheduling, and billing. Although initial sets of ethical guidelines have been developed by professional associations (described in Chapter 7), at this time there are many unknowns about this form of counseling. These relate to lack of knowledge about the types of clients and issues that may be addressed in this way, how to know when to refer clients for face-to-face counseling, and what counselor characteristics may predict counselor satisfaction and effectiveness in this mode of intervention. Further, at this time most insurance companies will not pay for services delivered in this mode. Nonetheless, it is likely that online counseling or advising will become a specialized version of private practice in the 21st century.

Mental Health Centers

Funded by both public and private organizations, community mental health centers assist citizens, regardless of their ability to pay, with concerns that may affect the quality of their lives and the community. These concerns include career-related problems. A major goal of mental health centers is early intervention, in an attempt to alleviate problems before they have greater impact on the individual and the community. Services for clients include individual counseling, assessment, referral, career information, skill building, and perhaps job placement. Counselors use the techniques of group and individual counseling, instruction, consultation, referral, and advocacy.

The problems encountered and approaches used do not vary significantly from those encountered and used by a career counselor in private practice. A counselor in this setting may have a larger caseload than one in private practice, may spend less time per client, may have the advantages of a wider network for consultation and referral, and may have reduced responsibility related to promotion, marketing, and management.

Substance Abuse Centers

Counselors in substance abuse centers work with clients who have come voluntarily or have been referred by other organizations, including the courts. The centers may be located in a hospital, in a community mental health center, or in a separate organization. Typical services include individual and group counseling, support groups, educational programs about substance abuse, career counseling and assessment, referral for acquisition of job skills, and perhaps job placement. There may also be follow-through with employers for a period of time for the purpose of assisting substance-abuse offenders to develop job-keeping skills.

Rehabilitation Settings

Rehabilitation counselors deal with a variety of client concerns, including career counseling and job placement. They have more specialized training and certification than do counselors in more general settings, because of the additional knowledge and competency that are required.

The Division of Vocational Rehabilitation (DVR) is a government agency whose mission is to remove the barriers to satisfying and productive work that exist for persons with disabilities. Any person with a physical or mental disability that could affect employability may be eligible for the services of DVR. These services include counseling, vocational assessment, vocational training, on-the-job training, work adjustment training, funding for postsecondary education, job site modification, and purchase of equipment or technological devices that will assist the disabled person to perform work duties and maintain employment. Many rehabilitation counselors are employed in the nationwide network of offices of the DVR. Others are employed by private rehabilitation facilities.

Counselors who work with persons with disabilities use the same techniques and tools as other career counselors—including interviewing, assessment, career information, and technology—in assisting their clients. Because of their disabilities, clients are likely to have a restricted number of career options; they are likely to need a high level of support in accomplishing action plans, counseling in areas such as self-concept and self-efficacy, and career counseling. Further, counselors working with this population will use coordinating, consulting, advocacy, and case-management skills at a high level in helping their clients with job readiness and placement.

Corrections and Probation

The pendulum swings from time to time with regard to public opinion about the services that offenders and ex-offenders should receive. Currently, given the known relationship between getting and keeping a job upon release and recidivism, there is emphasis from the federal level on providing career planning and job placement services to offenders. These services are designed to contribute to offenders' capability to select, be trained for, and enter jobs in keeping with their interests and/or skills and to know how to retain those jobs.

The range of services available to offenders and the resources available to deliver them are limited. Work tasks in this setting include one-to-one interviewing, group instruction about career-related concerns, assessment, provision of career information, and job placement. This is a particularly difficult setting in which to work because the nature of the helping relationship, as traditionally defined by counselors, has to be substantially modified and, further, counselors can feel a continual pull between the client's needs and the needs of the prison and the larger society. Goals for career services in correctional facilities are also limited. They focus on acquiring some type of job training, getting a job, and being able to keep the job.

In the past few years there has been a national focus on training corrections staff in their environment as career development facilitators, also called Offender Workforce Development Specialists (OWDSs). Teams from many states have been trained to develop programs of service for offenders prior to release or to ex-offenders after release. The goal is to assist ex-offenders to gain some work skills, learn how to behave in the work environment, get a job, and especially to keep a job. Research underscores the fact that there is a high correlation between getting and keeping a job and reduced recidivism.

Military Settings

Civilian counselors are common on military bases, and they work both with military personnel and members of their families. Counselors may engage in assessment, educational advisement, individual counseling related to career and personal issues, and referrals. In recent years, because of the significant downsizing of the military, counselors in this setting have focused on assisting military personnel with the transition from military to civilian occupations for which they have transferable skills and on the use of funding available to them to acquire additional education.

In times like the present, when large numbers of military personnel are coming home from long and stressful combat, there is an increase in services offered to veterans and designed to assist with the transition to civilian life. Some of these services are offered virtually on sites such as Military.com, which offer searches through job banks, assistance with résumés, information about job fairs, and the opportunity to network with other veterans. Another site, MilitaryOneSource.mil, is the official site of the U.S. Departments of Defense, Labor, and Veterans Affairs and was developed to support the Transition Assistance Program. The site offers a wealth of information about services available to veterans and provides many resources for making a successful transition, including a search for physical transition centers. Professional counselors are available at Transition Assistance offices to assist those separating from the military to plan for education or training funded by the GI Bill of Rights, to identify career options, to prepare for the job search, and to get a job. Mental health services are also provided by means of referral to appropriate professional personnel.

Job Service Offices and One-Stop Centers

By far, the largest proportion of community-based career guidance and support is provided by One-Stop Career Centers, of which there are more than 2,500 in the United States. Funded under the 1998 Workforce Investment Act (WIA), these centers represent a government initiative to place under one roof a variety of services needed by job seekers: unemployment compensation, access to the services of the Division of Vocational Rehabilitation, and access to a wide variety of services offered by One-Stop Career Centers. Individuals can find the center closest to their homes by accessing servicelocator.org.

These services include all of the following:

- Job-search and job-placement assistance
- Free access to computers, Internet, fax machines, and printers for job-search purposes
- Access to millions of job listings
- Labor market information for clients' state and regions within the state
- Assistance preparing résumés
- Comprehensive assessment of job skills, abilities, aptitudes, and needs
- Career counseling
- Workshops on topics such as interviewing skills
- Case management
- Prevocational support services (such as learning English, improving basic skills)
- Information on unemployment insurance
- Development of individual employment plans
- Training in literacy skills
- Rehabilitative services
- Referrals to training, education, and related supportive services (such as transportation and child care)
- Outreach and recruitment for business (job development)

Many of the job-search and labor market information services that One-Stop Career Centers offer are also available on the Internet at careeronestop.org. Typically, persons who staff One-Stop Career Centers are not trained as professional career counselors. Many have considerable experience in dealing with the challenges that One-Stop Career Centers tackle; and increasingly, centers are employing people who have become certified as Career Development Facilitators (CDFs), a paraprofessional level in the field.

One-Stop Career Centers serve a wide variety of clients, from Ph.D.s who have been laid off by NASA to the unskilled homeless. Other categories of clients include ex-offenders, high-risk youth, unemployed adults, displaced homemakers, veterans, older Americans, and persons with disabilities. In times like the 2009–2012 recession, when unemployment rates approached 10% (or more in some states), both the number and the diversity of clients who seek these free services increase significantly. As stated by the *New York Times* (Goodman, 2010), "Call them the new poor: people long accustomed to the comforts of middle-class life who are now relying on public assistance for the first time in their lives—potentially for years to come" (p. A1).

The principles that guide the One-Stop Career Centers include the following:

- Streamline services through an integration of multiple programs, including Wagner-Peyser and Workforce Investment Act, at the service level.
- Empower individuals with information and resources they need to manage their own careers.
- Provide employer services that recognize business as a customer as well as a source for jobs leading to meaningful employment.

- Provide universal access for all job seekers to a core set of career decision-making and job-search tools.
- Increase accountability of the delivery system to achieve improved results regarding skill gains, credentials earned, job placement rates, earnings, and retention in employment.
- Offer state and local flexibility to ensure that delivery systems are responsive to the needs of individual communities.
- Offer the opportunity for local boards and the private sector to impact the design and operation of delivery systems.

In difficult economic times, One-Stop Career Centers may receive increased funding, as was the case with the American Recovery and Reinvestment Act (ARRA), which provided $1.25 billion for dislocated adult workers, such as those laid off or who have received advanced notice of a factory closing; $1.2 billion for dislocated youth workers; $500 million in state grants to provide assistance to low-income adults; and $500 million to fund training for sustainable energy jobs.

Besides the array of services listed earlier, One-Stop Career Centers are also the pipeline for providing assistance that may be required for diminishing barriers that low-skilled and low-income adults may have. This assistance may include USDA Food Stamps (in October 2008, this program was renamed Supplemental Nutrition Assistance Program [SNAP]), financial support for child care and/or transportation, the opportunity to learn English and other basic skills, and grants to underwrite a learning plan designed to provide education or training that develops marketable skills.

One-Stop Career Centers also provide employers with a variety of services to meet workforce needs. Electronic job banks provide the needed link between employers and qualified job seekers. These offices also provide employers with reemployment services for dislocated workers, labor market information for planning business expansion, and focused recruitment for specialized workers needed due to new business ventures.

Faith-Based Organizations

Legislation enacted under the George W. Bush administration provided funding to faith-based organizations and other nonprofit organizations that would devise programs to support the unskilled or low skilled, ex-offenders, and/or homeless. Typical support services offered by faith-based organizations include housing and food for the homeless, vocational training, mentorship, clothing, and sponsorship for job fairs. In fact, more than half of the job fairs offered across the nation are organized by faith-based organizations that make a tremendous contribution both in dollars and in volunteer support.

An outstanding example of the work of a nonprofit organization is that of Goodwill Industries. Its mission is stated as "Goodwill Industries International strives to enhance the dignity and quality of life of individuals and families by helping people reach their full potential through education, skills training, and the power of work" (Goodwill, 2015). In 2010, Goodwill was ranked sixth out of 121 nonprofit organizations that provide workforce development services related to both quantity and quality of its services (Philanthropedia, 2010). In 2013 alone, Goodwill International served 9.8 million individuals with employment and training programs; assisted 261,875 individuals to get jobs that earned them, in total, $4.4 billion; and provided personal and family support services to 44 million individuals (Goodwill).

The American Association of Retired Persons (AARP) is a second outstanding example of a nonprofit organization that is providing a wide range of career support services, using federal funding made available for older workers in need of employment. AARP offers no-fee services through hundreds of offices throughout the United States. These services include assessment (measurement of interests and skills), funding of training, and placement of low-income older adults who, especially in this depressed economy, need to continue to work in order to survive. Training is provided online for over 80 different certifications through the WorkSearch system, jointly developed by AARP and the National Business Services Alliance (NBSA). The certifications were created by NBSA in collaboration with a consortium of accredited universities. At the completion of the NBSA Certification Program, clients earn a certificate from a nationally known accredited state university. Participating universities not only validate NBSA's system of self-assessments; they create and deliver course content to ensure that holders of an NBSA Skills Certificate are well prepared to do the job. All users of the WorkSearch system are offered free access to 17 essential skill courses. NBSA Certification Programs are geared toward jobs that are in high demand in the U.S. economy. This Certification Program also includes one-on-one assistance from a personal training advisor who helps to customize the learning experience for individuals. At aarpworksearch.org, an immense amount of content about the job search can be accessed, including a search for job openings by zip code.

There are some obvious differences in the services provided by U.S. Department of Labor One-Stop Career Centers and nonprofit organizations compared to those provided in schools, universities, and private practice. First, the range of education, needs, and past experience possessed by clients is far wider than in other settings. Second, the treatment provided to these clients has to be all encompassing, ranging much farther than simply helping them get a job. Third, to be successful, the support provided must start with the initial interview and continue through at least the first six months after getting a job. Fourth, the array of services—which may include child care, transportation, training, résumé preparation, and more—is offered through the collaboration of agencies and the merging of public and private funding.

Corporations and Other Organizations

Many organizations—such as the World Bank and the Federal Deposit Insurance Corporation—as well as private corporations, hire career counselors. They are typically housed in a facility that includes a well-furnished career center. Typical centers provide individual career counseling, assessment, use of the Internet or software, and group instruction.

Career counselors working in such settings deal with client concerns about career mobility within the organization or, in the case of downsizing, with client plans to move out of the organization. They may offer workshops on topics such as keeping one's résumé updated, how to facilitate one's promotion, or how to profit from mentoring. They may also deal with plans for upgrading skills or acquiring new skills and with issues related to conflicts between supervisors and employees or between employees. Their job descriptions may also include the provision of counseling services that are unrelated to career progression.

In these diverse settings, fees for service may be nonexistent to clients, may be shared by clients in proportion to their ability to pay, or may be at full rate per session. For some clients in some settings (such as mental health agencies and private practice), the counselor may receive third-party payment, the counselor's services having been approved for coverage under an insurance plan.

MyCounselingLab®

Start with Topic 8—Career Development in the Workplace and Topic 9—Special Adult Career Concerns.

Watch the video *21st Century Counseling with an Unemployed Adult: Dr. Barbara Suddarth* and complete Student Activity #1 on page 404.

Watch the video *21st Century Job-Seeking Intervention with an Unemployed Adult: Dr. Michael Hall* and complete Student Activity #2 on page 404.

SUMMARY

This chapter has addressed the specialty of community-based career counseling that is practiced in a variety of noneducational settings. Not only is the setting for this career counseling specialty different from that of others, but the client characteristics, reasons for intervention, and the roles and functions of the counselor may also be different. Clients are typically adults who face career choice problems as a part of a much larger complex of issues and thus do not have as many options available to them as students do.

Intervention may be the free choice of individuals or may be forced due to layoffs, legislation, separation from the military or from prison, or some life event. Counselor functions extend beyond counseling to coordination, consultation, advocacy, and case management. Further, the counselor providing career assistance may work as part of a team that includes psychologists, social workers, medical specialists, and career development facilitators.

CASE STUDY

Frank is a 25-year-old veteran who has served two tours of duty in Iraq. While there, he lost his right arm while removing wounded soldiers from the combat zone. He is suffering from posttraumatic stress disorder. His military specialty is artillery maintenance specialist. Now he faces the need to get housing and a civilian job that provides enough income to support himself, his wife, and their two children. While he has been away, his wife and children have lived with her parents, but now Frank and his wife would like to have their own home.

Frank has a high school diploma but has not pursued any education beyond that. Before entering the military, he drove a florist delivery truck. Linda, his wife, has completed an associate degree in paralegal studies at the local community college while Frank has been away. She is willing to work if they could find a way to acquire good child care services.

What kinds of next steps would you investigate with Frank as you work with him on an action plan? To what agencies and resources might you refer Frank? What kinds of support services does this family need?

STUDENT ACTIVITIES

1. Refer to the MyCounselingLab® Video and Resource Library and select the video entitled *21st Century Counseling with an Unemployed Adult: Dr. Barbara Suddarth*. Then write a short paper that responds to the following items:
    a. What practical suggestions was the counselor able to give this client?
    b. In what ways did the counselor provide emotional support to this client?
    c. What barriers to a successful job search does this client have?
    d. What are this client's strengths as he faces the job search?

2. Refer to the MyCounselingLab® Video and Resource Library and select the video entitled *21st Century Job-Seeking Intervention with an Unemployed Adult: Dr. Michael Hall*. This counselor used a large number of techniques with this client. List and describe at least six of them.

3. Using the Web site servicelocator.org, find a One-Stop Career Center near you. Visit that center and learn about the services offered and the populations served.

4. Find a nonprofit organization (such as a church-sponsored program, Goodwill Industries, or Salvation Army) near you. Make an appointment and visit in order to learn about the services offered and the populations served.

5. Interview a mental health counselor who works in a community agency in order to learn how that counselor works with the community (schools, employers, agencies) as well as with the clients.

■ ■

GUIDELINES FOR DEVELOPING PROGRAMS FOR ADULTS

Community agencies may provide services to adults by means of small group workshops. When they do, the National Career Development Guidelines (National Occupational Information Coordinating Committee, 1989) can serve as a useful foundation on which to build the content of those workshops or group sessions. Some guidelines that are most relevant to work in the community are provided here, also found at http://acrn.ovae.org/ncdg/ncdg_what.htm.

NCDG INDICATORS

This chart identifies indicators of skill mastery for this goal at three learning stages: knowledge acquisition, application, and reflection.

Career Management

Goal: Create and manage a career plan that meets your career goals.

Indicators		
Knowledge	**Application**	**Reflection**
Recognize that career planning to attain your career goals is a lifelong process. [CM1.K1]	Give examples of how you use career-planning strategies to attain your career goals. [CM1.A1]	Assess how well your career planning strategies facilitate reaching your career goals. [CM1.R1]
Describe how to develop a career plan (e.g., steps and content). [CM1.K2]	Develop a career plan to meet your career goals. [CM1.A2]	Analyze your career plan and make adjustments to reflect ongoing career management needs. [CM1.R2]
Identify your short-term and long-term career goals (e.g., education, employment, and lifestyle goals). [CM1.K3]	Demonstrate actions taken to attain your short-term and long-term career goals (e.g., education, employment, and lifestyle goals). [CM1.A3]	Reexamine your career goals and adjust as needed. [CM1.R3]
Identify skills and personal traits needed to manage your career (e.g., resiliency, self-efficacy, ability to identify trends and changes, and flexibility). [CM1.K4]	Demonstrate career management skills and personal traits (e.g., resiliency, self-efficacy, ability to identify trends and changes, and flexibility). [CM1.A4]	Evaluate your career management skills and personal traits (e.g., resiliency, self-efficacy, ability to identify trends and changes, and flexibility). [CM1.R4]
Recognize that changes in you and the world of work can affect your career plans. [CM1.K5]	Give examples of how changes in you and the world of work have caused you to adjust your career plans. [CM1.A5]	Evaluate how well you integrate changes in you and the world of work into your career plans. [CM1.R5]

NCDG INDICATORS

This chart identifies indicators of skill mastery for this goal at three learning stages: knowledge acquisition, application, and reflection.

Personal Social Development

Goal: Balance personal, leisure, community, learner, family, and work roles.

	Indicators	
Knowledge	**Application**	**Reflection**
Recognize that you have many life roles (e.g., personal, leisure, community, learner, family, and work roles). [PS4.K1]	Give examples that demonstrate your life roles including personal, leisure, community, learner, family, and work roles. [PS4.A1]	Assess the impact of your life roles on career goals. [PS4.R1]
Recognize that you must balance life roles and that there are many ways to do it. [PS4.K2]	Show how you are balancing your life roles. [PS4.A2]	Analyze how specific life-role changes would affect the attainment of your career goals. [PS4.R2]
Describe the concept of lifestyle. [PS4.K3]	Give examples of decisions, factors, and circumstances that affect your current lifestyle. [PS4.A3]	Analyze how specific lifestyle changes would affect the attainment of your career goals. [PS4.R3]
Recognize that your life roles and your lifestyle are connected. [PS4.K4]	Show how your life roles and your lifestyle are connected. [PS4.A4]	Assess how changes in your life roles would affect your lifestyle. [PS4.R4]

NCDG INDICATORS

This chart identifies indicators of skill mastery for this goal at three learning stages: knowledge acquisition, application, and reflection.

Career Management

Goal: Use a process of decision making as one component of career development.

	Indicators	
Knowledge	**Application**	**Reflection**
Describe your decision-making style (e.g., risk taker, cautious). [CM2.K1]	Give examples of past decisions that demonstrate your decision-making style. [CM2.A1]	Evaluate the effectiveness of your decision-making style. [CM2.R1]

Indicators		
Knowledge	**Application**	**Reflection**
Identify the steps in one model of decision making. [CM2.K2]	Demonstrate the use of a decision-making model. [CM2.A2]	Assess what decision-making model(s) work best for you. [CM2.R2]
Describe how information (e.g., about you, the economy, and education programs) can improve your decision making. [CM2.K3]	Demonstrate use of information (e.g., about you, the economy, and education programs) in making decisions. [CM2.A3]	Assess how well you use information (e.g., about you, the economy, and education programs) to make decisions. [CM2.R3]
Identify alternative options and potential consequences for a specific decision. [CM2.K4]	Show how exploring options affected a decision you made. [CM2.A4]	Assess how well you explore options when making decisions. [CM2.R4]
Recognize that your personal priorities, culture, beliefs, and work values can affect your decision making. [CM2.K5]	Show how personal priorities, culture, beliefs, and work values are reflected in your decisions. [CM2.A5]	Evaluate the effect of personal priorities, culture, beliefs, and work values on your decision making. [CM2.R5]
Describe how education, work, and family experiences might impact your decisions. [CM2.K6]	Give specific examples of how your education, work, and family experiences have influenced your decisions. [CM2.A6]	Assess the impact of your education, work, and family experiences on decisions. [CM2.R6]
Describe how biases and stereotypes can limit decisions. [CM2.K7]	Give specific examples of how biases and stereotypes affected your decisions. [CM2.A7]	Analyze the ways you could manage biases and stereotypes when making decisions. [CM2.R7]
Recognize that chance can play a role in decision making. [CM2.K8]	Give examples of times when chance played a role in your decision making. [CM2.A8]	Evaluate the impact of chance on past decisions. [CM2.R8]
Recognize that decision making often involves compromise. [CM2.K9]	Give examples of compromises you might have to make in career decision making. [CM2.A9]	Analyze the effectiveness of your approach to making compromises. [CM2.R9]

CHAPTER 15

ETHICAL ISSUES IN CAREER DEVELOPMENT INTERVENTIONS

Though not always evident, ethics is a constant of our daily lives. Although frequently unconscious or professionally intuitive, some aspects of ethical decision making are readily evident and require careful attention and deliberation by all people. Vigilant adherence and commitment to ethics, ethical standards, and ethical principles are hallmarks of all professions, and all professionals are ethically accountable and liable. It may surprise many counselors and counselor educators to see the universality of many ethical principles manifest in ethical standards for professions as varied as computer associations, multinational corporations, and the U.S. military. Ethical principles common to the ethical standards of many professions center on respect for human beings; respect for privacy, accountability, responsibility, and truth; and crediting one's sources, among other principles.

Typically in counselor preparation and practice, ethics and ethical standards and principles are considered along with legal principles and practices, yet ethics is different from law in terms of the origins of ethics in philosophy and in terms of legality being far more explicitly definitive than ethics. In law, there is close attention to legal precedent and nuance refining principles of justice in guiding legal behavior and adjudication of perceived illegalities. In ethics, there is attention to more general ethical standards and principles guiding ethical practice and adjudication. In the history of mental health professions, ethical principles and standards frequently are at risk of being lost in attention to the negative reinforcers of law and legal rules for practice. In fact, there is healthy room for attention and adherence to law and ethics, and this chapter does both with some enlightening points of view and examples.

Probably the most vital aspect of ethics in counselor preparation is close and deliberate attention to, and discussion of, ethics, ethical issues, and ethical standards within the quiet calm of a noncrisis classroom environment. Though one might typically think of legal and ethical standards as negative reinforcers highlighting what to avoid, a closer look at ethical standards and principles might help one see the fuller context of ethics as inspiring and empowering. One might sense this uplifting aspect of ethics in the preamble to the American Counseling Association's Ethical Standards, noting counselors' dedication to human worth, dignity, uniqueness, and potential and similar perspectives at points in the Ethical Standards of the American Psychological Association. Finally, as one notes that standards are minimal—the least one must do—career counselors and aspiring counselors can begin to ponder and commit to maxima, to aspirational standards focused on the most one can ethically do for one's client.

With these thoughts in mind, welcome to a chapter of considerable breadth and depth and welcome to what may be new perspectives in professional growth for readers, who should find much to ponder and much potential for growth. Read, learn, ponder, and enjoy.

Dennis Engels, Ph.D., LPC, NCC, NCCC
Regents Professor Emeritus, Counseling Program
President, National Career Development Association (1995–1996)
University of North Texas

The authors of this text, like others who teach and work in the area of career counseling, often deal with questions or statements that suggest that career counseling is not "real" counseling and question whether professional concepts such as ethical standards apply to those who are involved in career development interventions. We believe that all career practitioners (not just counselors) are subject to ethical standards. Likewise, those who work for or who are employed or supervised by counseling professionals in providing career counseling services must be aware of and in most instances adhere to the same standards. We have elected to follow the National Career Development Association (NCDA) *Code of Ethics* (National Career Development Association, 2015) and use the term *career counseling professional* to refer to all those covered by that code. As you know by now, we also view career counseling as "real" counseling that is quite central to a person's life. This chapter is our attempt to provide an orientation to the ethical standards of the counseling profession, with emphasis and examples relevant for career counseling professionals. Ethical, professional behavior requires adherence to applicable laws and regulations, and in some instances we suggest that those faced with certain dilemmas not only seek ethical consultation from a supervisor or respected colleague but also seek legal advice. Before we begin our exploration of ethical issues, however, we would like you to meet a counselee, José.

José, a 16-year-old student in the ninth grade, was asked to come into the school counselor's office to review his interest inventory results (the inventory had been administered to all ninth-grade students). José's academic record throughout his school years has been mixed. He was held back twice in elementary school and was often absent from school. His absences were mostly the result of José working with his father in the fields during harvest season. Lately, he has shown some interest in developing his career plans. A frequent computer user, José has gone online at the local library to explore career options in the computer field. He found a Web site that offered free "vocational aptitude testing." He took the test and was excited that the results seemed to suggest that he had the aptitude necessary for working as a computer programmer. He was eager to receive the information about becoming a computer programmer that the Web site offered to send everyone who took the online test. José was not sure what a computer programmer's job involved, but he knew that he loved playing computer games.

José's father was "dead set against" this type of work. A blue-collar worker all his life with no computer experience and only a ninth-grade education, José's father felt strongly that José should acquire training in a more traditional trade, such as carpentry. José's grandfather had been a carpenter in his home country, Guatemala. When the family relocated to the southeastern United States, the only work José's father could acquire was in agriculture. He thought that he had not been given serious consideration, due to being Guatemalan, for a number of jobs for which he was qualified. José's father thought that becoming a carpenter would be in line with the family tradition and would provide an income that would be sufficient for raising a family (something that was a constant struggle for him). José told his counselor that his father wanted to speak with the counselor about José attending vocational school. His father was also interested in exploring options that José might have in the military. In fact, he wanted José to meet with military recruiters when they visited José's school. José had no interest in becoming a carpenter and was not enthusiastic about the prospect of military service.

If you were José's counselor you would probable have several concerns about his situation. For example, you might be concerned about the quality of the online test José had taken. You might also be uneasy about "bursting José's bubble" and deflating the interest he had shown in making career plans. However, the results of the interest inventory administered at school gave no indication that José had high interest in computer-related occupations. His interests were more focused on artistic and helping occupations. If you were his counselor, you might also wonder about the strong, clear vision José's father had for what occupation and career path José would choose. In fact, the counselor wondered whether José's father's encounter with discriminatory hiring practices influenced the career goals he had identified for his son. Finally, the counselor was reluctant to encourage José to meet with the military recruiters but was not sure how to communicate this reluctance to José's father.

You may remember that when we introduced José, his counselor was introduced as a school counselor and not a career counselor. Yet his presenting concern was certainly career related, if not explicitly a career counseling concern per se. A number of ethical issues and concerns are apparent in the brief scenario. For example, some of the ethical questions embedded in José's case include the quality of the assessment he took online, and even whether the assessment instrument the counselor administered to José was appropriate for a person from José's background; the ethics of the online service suggesting a specific career option as if it were the result of career counseling rather than a blatant marketing ploy; the ethical dilemma confronting the school counselor regarding José's father's wishes and José's wishes; and the always present ethical issue of the counselor's competence in dealing with the concerns and issues presented by José.

These are complex issues. To help career counseling professionals practice ethically, professional columns, publications, and workshops on ethics abound. Despite the increased attention to ethical practice in career services delivery, there are often no clear answers to many career practitioners' most difficult questions about proper practice. Given the frequency of litigation in the helping professions, it is perplexing that career development textbooks, at best, pay minimal attention to ethical issues confronting career counseling practitioners. The NCDA's *Code of Ethics* (NCDA, 2015) states that a code of ethics "helps to define professional behavior and serves to protect the public, the profession, and those who practice within the profession" (p. 1). Thus, in this chapter we hope to heighten the awareness of career counseling professionals to ethical issues and provide guidance for career development practitioners as they consider ethical issues. Because readers will have varied backgrounds in the ethical concepts that affect career counselors, we offer a primer on basic principles.

A good starting point for addressing ethical issues in career development interventions is to consider the following question: How can it be that career counseling practitioners have multiple ethics codes to guide their practice and yet ethical violations continue? Even when practitioners are well trained and conscientious, situations can arise in which determining proper practice is a complex task. The following chart provides a useful framework for examining behaviors within the career counseling relationship.[1] This matrix can be used to classify career counseling practitioners' behaviors into one of four categories.

Ethical and Legal	Unethical and Legal
Ethical and Illegal	Unethical and Illegal

Tips from the Field

At all times regarding ethical practice in career interventions, remember: "When in doubt, check it out!" If you are not sure whether ethical issues exist in your work with students and clients, refer to the ethical standards of practice and consult with other counseling professionals.

The obvious goal for career counseling professionals is to function ethically and legally and to avoid any activity that would be acknowledged as illegal and/or unethical. Although this goal seems straightforward, in some instances achieving this goal is not so simple. A career client might disclose his or her frustration with an unsuccessful job search by saying "I was so upset over my layoff that when my daughter asked me a question I snapped and hit her. I have never done anything like that before." Some career counselors would suggest an ethical (and legal) obligation to report the possible child abuse. Others might cite the circumstances of one episode without evidence of harm and the primacy of client confidentiality as a reason to oppose reporting. Some career counseling professionals would include a counselor's "Miranda warning" about the limits of confidentiality and required disclosures in the initial discussion of counseling expectations, as part of informed consent, which some view as off-putting to clients. However, without such an orientation to the limits of confidentiality, the counselor who received the information might be reluctant to even consider reporting it.

Ethical issues can arise in which practices common outside the career counseling professional's helping relationship deviate from what is ethically appropriate. For example, a business relationship between a career counseling professional and a client is considered unethical because it constitutes a dual relationship that could impair objectivity. A career counseling professional helping a friend, relative, or the child of a friend might cause a strain on objectivity, which could also occur for any other professional, yet the recognition is not so apparent to the person who asks for "a small personal favor." For example, if in the earlier scenario José's father and José's counselor were friends, then how should the counselor proceed to help José in this instance? The situation could become even more complicated if José's counselor were the only counselor in José's high school.

Career counseling professionals are also likely to face dilemmas that could be labeled as "business ethics." Examples of such dilemmas are when clients ask career counselors awkward questions, such as how much to tell potential employers about other job options they have, or how to deal with multiple offers. Likewise, potential employers can ask the career counselors

---

[1] Because we have seen this chart attributed to various authors, and thus its origin is somewhat ambiguous, we simply acknowledge that the concept of this 2 × 2 matrix is not ours.

about their clients. Those who work in settings having a placement function often deal with inquiries from potential employers of their clients. The career counseling professional, in ways not so common in other types of counseling, is often asked to assist clients in dealing with workplace issues such as unethical behavior on the part of supervisors, sexual harassment, and unfair hiring and promotion practices. Career counseling professionals might have access to nonpublic information that could be used unethically. For example, should a placement counselor tell a client that he or she overheard a recruiter say the client was the top choice for a position? What about information that might lead to a financial gain to the professional, such as information about the plans of a business that might have implications for noncounseling-related investments of the counselor? Career counseling professionals often need guidance in dealing with ethical situations that are not covered in current ethical codes.

Chapters and sections of chapters throughout this text recognize the role of school counselors in developmental career interventions for both individuals and groups. There is one area of ethical concern that troubles many secondary school counselors, and which we believe deserves special mention. That is the role of the secondary school counselor in assisting students with determining appropriate educational and/or training plans and the role of the same counselor as a provider of recommendations for their counselees to the institutions at which they might pursue postsecondary education. Many colleges have a specific expectation that secondary school counselors provide a recommendation for applicants. The simultaneous role of helping the students determine an appropriate institution and providing a recommendation to the institution could be considered a dual relationship. These issues are complicated by the role of parents who, in addition to sometimes expecting counselors to help them realize their hopes and dreams for their children's educational and career plans, often want to review recommendations written for college admission. There are complex ethical and legal issues involved in such activities, and we advise school counselors to become well versed in their school systems' policies pertaining to student records and recommendations and to become familiar with the provisions of the Family Educational Rights and Privacy Act (1974). The National Association for College Admission Counseling (NACAC) has produced a *Statement of Principles of Good Practice* (2007). We suggest that secondary school counselors who provide required recommendations for their students study the statement and consult, when questions and issues arise, with supervisors and, when necessary, with the legal advisor for their school.

Although studying the *Code of Ethics* of the American Counseling Association (2014) is important and effective for career practitioners who are career counselors, more is needed. That "more" is an understanding of the bases and intention of the standards. It is not possible for an ethical code or standard to provide an unambiguous answer to every potential ethical question. There will inevitably be occasions when career counselors and other career professional practitioners will need the assistance of trusted professional colleagues to provide an assessment of the proper action in response to an ethical dilemma. Thus, a useful rule of thumb for career counseling professionals whenever they are unsure about the proper action to take to resolve an ethical dilemma is to consult with professional colleagues who understand career interventions.

ETHICAL DILEMMAS VERSUS MORAL TEMPTATIONS

Clearly, resolving ethical dilemmas can be a complex task for career counseling professionals. It is important to note, however, that not all issues involving ethics or proper behaviors deserve the title "dilemma." Kidder (1995) contends that an ethical dilemma occurs only in instances in which there are competing "rights" or there is a struggle to determine the "least bad" course of action. Instead of dilemmas, Kidder labels situations in which the struggle is between right and wrong as *moral temptations*. Unfortunately, some counseling professionals struggle with moral temptations and may take actions that most peers would categorize as unethical. For example, a career counselor might become interested in a noncounseling business or personal relationship with a client and be tempted to prematurely end a formal career counseling relationship to start the "clock" or deny that a relationship was counseling. The involved professional might not be the best judge of whether the relationship meets the ethical standards to change from career counseling to a personal relationship. Attempting to judge the propriety of one's own actions might be the ultimate dual relationship.

Sometimes the career counseling practitioner faces choices between actions that may help the client but have some risk to the counselor. For example, the ACA (2014), NCDA (2015), and American Psychological Association (APA) (2010) ethics statements address the topic of bartering (as a means of paying for services) as a specific of dual relationships, and they discourage the practice. Many bartering relationships begin innocently, and bartering may even be based on the career counselor's desire to provide a way for a client to invest in counseling and be motivated by clinical, rather than financial, reasons. However, if problems develop in either the counseling or the bartering aspect of the relationship, the potential for the client to raise ethical issues *ex post facto* exists.

To guide career counseling professionals in resolving ethical dilemmas, we will review the principles on which ethical codes are based. We will then examine the basic ethical concepts included in all counseling ethical codes. It is important to note again, however, that no ethics code and certainly no book or chapter can provide answers to all the questions that will arise in the delivery of career counseling services. The following excerpt from the "Purpose" section of the National Association of Social Workers (NASW) *Code of Ethics* (2008) eloquently states and reinforces this point:

> A code of ethics cannot guarantee ethical behavior. Moreover, a code of ethics cannot resolve all ethical issues or disputes, or capture the richness and complexity involved in striving to make responsible choices within a moral community. Rather a code of ethics sets forth values, ethical principles, and ethical standards to which professionals aspire and by which their actions can be judged. (p. 2)

The NCDA *Code of Ethics* (2015) requires all career counseling professionals who believe an ethical violation has occurred to take action. We hope that your exploration of the topic will heighten your awareness of potential ethical problems and the multiple considerations involved in addressing those problems.

USING PRINCIPLES TO RESOLVE ETHICAL DECISIONS

VanHoose (1986), a pioneer in the study of counseling ethics, observed that "ethical principles provide a more solid framework for decision making than do ethical codes or statutes" (p. 168). VanHoose recommended that counselors use the following five principles, which Herlihy and Corey (2006) continue to consider foundational and essential to counseling practice and the basis of the ACA ethical standards:

1. *Autonomy* refers to independence and self-determination. Under this principle, counselors respect the freedom of clients to choose their own directions, make their own

choices, and control their own lives. We have an ethical obligation to decrease client dependency and foster independent decision making. We refrain from setting imposing goals, avoid being judgmental, and are accepting of different values.

2. *Nonmaleficence* means do no harm. Counselors must take care that their actions do not risk hurting clients, even inadvertently. We have a responsibility to avoid engaging in practices that cause harm or have the potential to result in harm.

3. *Beneficence* means to promote good, or mental health and wellness. This principle mandates that counselors actively promote the growth and welfare of those they serve.

4. *Justice* is the foundation of our commitment to fairness in professional relationships. Justice includes consideration of such factors as quality of services, allocation of time and resources, establishment of fees, and access to counseling services. This principle also refers to the fair treatment of an individual when his or her interests need to be considered in the context of the rights and interests of others.

5. *Fidelity* means counselors make honest promises and honor their commitments to clients, students, and supervisees. This principle involves creating a trusting and therapeutic climate in which people can search for their own solutions and taking care not to deceive or exploit clients. (pp. 9–10)

The principles are similar to those suggested by Beauchamp and Childress (2001) in their classic text on medical ethics. They also identified the following additional principles as relevant for professional-patient relationships:

1. *Veracity*—Tell the truth and do not lie or deceive others.
2. *Privacy*—Allow individuals to limit access to information about themselves.
3. *Confidentiality*—Allow individuals to control access to information they have shared.

Collectively, the ACA principles and those offered by Beauchamp and Childress (2001), including their suggestions for professional-patient relationships, provide guidelines for ethical behavior in career counseling services. The principles are the basis for mandatory ethical standards, those behaviors of the counselor that can be enforced, whereas aspirational ethics refer to the highest standards of conduct to which career counseling professionals can aspire (Herlihy & Corey, 2006). Herlihy and Watson (2006) suggest that virtue ethics as contrasted with principle ethics are necessary to produce a culturally sensitive approach to making ethical decisions. Herlihy and Corey offer the following as virtue ethics distilled from the literature on virtue ethics:

- Discernment or prudence
- Respectfulness
- Integrity
- Self-awareness
- Acknowledgement of the role of emotion
- Connectedness with the community

When questions arise pertaining to proper practice, these principles can be used to help career counseling professionals identify appropriate behaviors. Career counselors should feel especially comfortable with the principles of autonomy and beneficence because they represent the hallmarks of career counseling at its best. Finally, it is worth noting that despite the various purposes and audiences to which ethical codes and principles are addressed, ethical codes and statements for the major psychologically based helping professions (counseling, psychology, and clinical social work) are remarkably similar. According to the ethical standards for the American School Counselor Association (ASCA) (2010), the following steps should be taken when there is doubt about the ethical behavior of a colleague(s): (a) consult confidentially with a professional colleague, (b) when possible, confront the colleague whose behavior is in question, (c) document all action steps taken, (d) utilize the established channels for addressing ethical concerns (e.g., within the school, agency, or school district, and relevant state ethics board), and (e) if the matter remains unresolved, contact the relevant state professional association (e.g., state school counselor association) and/or national association (e.g., American School Counselor Association, National Career Development Association, American Psychological Association).

However, some ethical questions and decisions related to career interventions cannot be easily resolved by reference to ethical codes that were written to address interventions that were likely to be therapeutic in nature. Some of those issues in career interventions have their basis in values that are often the basis of aspirational and virtue ethics.

THE ROLE OF VALUES IN DEFINING CAREER DEVELOPMENT INTERVENTIONS

Values assumptions underlie all questions (and answers) related to ethical behavior in career development interventions. Values assumptions are particularly relevant regarding the counselor's and the client's understanding, and definition, of the career counseling relationship. Bergin (1985) suggests, "values are orienting beliefs about what is good for the clients and how that good should be achieved" (p. 99). As such, value issues permeate the career development intervention process. Any intervention in the life space or lifestyle of people carries with it values implications (London, 1964). The need for practitioners to clearly understand their own values represents an essential starting point for career services delivery and is an ethical issue within career services. Because value-free career interventions do not exist, career practitioners must be cognizant of how their personal values influence their work with clients.

Tjeltveit (1986, pp. 515–537) suggests the following strategies for minimizing the likelihood of counselors behaving in ways that are insensitive to clients' values:

1. Become informed about the variety of values held in society.
2. Be aware of your own values.
3. Present value options to clients in an unbiased manner.
4. Be committed to clients' freedom of choice.
5. Respect clients with values that differ from your own.
6. Consult with others when necessary.
7. Consider referring clients to another counselor when substantial moral, religious, or political value differences exist.

When career counseling professionals incorporate Tjeltveit's strategies into their daily practice, they go a long way toward ensuring that their interventions will be ethical. Career counselors must constantly monitor their own values and how those values affect their career interventions.

Tjeltveit's suggestions to consult with professional colleagues and to refer clients to more appropriate service providers when necessary also apply to instances in which the client's concerns extend beyond the traditional issues of clarifying, specifying, and implementing a career choice. For example, it is increasingly evident that adults in career transition experience ego dystonic emotions that must be addressed within the career counseling process (Anderson & Niles, 1995; Subich, 1993). When clients' concerns include depressive feelings, low self-esteem, low self-efficacy, and so on, career practitioners need to evaluate whether they are competent to address such issues. In this regard, Niles and Pate (1989) argue that a career practitioner must, at the minimum, be able to identify mental health issues presented by a client. Once such issues are identified, the career practitioner must determine whether it is appropriate to refer the client to a mental health practitioner (if the career practitioner does not feel competent to deal with these issues, then a referral is the ethical decision) or address the client's mental health issues within the context of career counseling.

The ACA *Code of Ethics* (ACA, 2014) requires that counseling including career development interventions also requires counselors to be aware of the client's values and the values embedded in career development intervention models. Each of these value sets (i.e., the counselor's, the client's, and the values embedded in interventions) interacts. Personal values influence such dynamics as the client behaviors the practitioner attends to in the career counseling process and the intervention strategies selected by the practitioner. Career practitioners communicate personal values through nonverbal and verbal behavior. Thus, the counselor's values can inadvertently influence the client's behavior. For example, if a client seeks to earn the counselor's approval, the client may opt for career options that the client perceives will please the counselor and disregard other factors in the career decision-making process. In such instances, a career practitioner can unknowingly convert a client to the counselor's values.

Referring to counseling and psychotherapy, Herr and Niles (1988) noted that:

> Western therapies have a particular way of looking at and processing human behavior; Eastern therapies have a different way of defining such behavior and planning interventions. One is not a substitute for the other because value sets, assumptions, and cultural artifacts make some forms of counseling and psychotherapy unacceptable or ineffective in cultures different from those in which such interventions were invented. (p. 14)

This statement applies to career interventions as well. Career intervention models based on European American values emphasizing individualism do not mesh with family expectations or traditions found in societies in which group decisions are the norm and the family is the principle arbiter of appropriate occupational choices. Thus, a career counseling professional adhering to European American career intervention models steeped in individual action runs the risk of violating clients' values when those values reflect a collectivistic orientation. An illustration of this point is provided by the career counseling case of Kenji.

Having recently relocated to the United States from China, Kenji came to the guidance office during his senior year in high school with the concern of whether poor performance in his physics and math courses would prevent him from being able to major in engineering in college. In the course of meeting with Kenji, it became obvious to the counselor that, although his concerns were projected toward a college major in engineering, his interests and abilities pointed toward a program of study in a nonscience area. In fact, he had failed physics and just barely passed several math courses. He thoroughly enjoyed the social sciences and had performed well in classes related to this area. When asked to discuss his tentative decision to pursue a college major in engineering, it quickly became apparent that his decision was based on the plans his father had made for him. When asked about the appropriateness of this goal, given his prior academic performance and his interests, it was clear that Kenji was not about to enlarge the range of options under consideration.

A counselor who believes Kenji should adhere to the need for students to develop traditional European American career development values of individual action and an internal locus of control may decide to use a counseling strategy that would challenge Kenji's tendency to adhere to the wishes of others (his father in this case) in his career decision making. The projected treatment plan may even include assertiveness training with the goal of having Kenji confront his father about his career development goals. Unfortunately, this type of career counseling strategy is not sensitive to Kenji's culture of origin in which it is not uncommon for fathers to dominate the career decision making of their sons. Any attempts to influence Kenji's career direction would need to include sensitivity to this very important cultural dynamic. (Interestingly, after the case of Kenji was developed from a composite of the authors' experiences, one of the authors discovered a novel with a plot strikingly similar in many ways to the case [Lee, 1994]. We believe the case of Kenji is based on experiences that are, unfortunately, too common.)

The case of José, presented at the beginning of this chapter, also illustrates the potential for value conflicts between the counselor, José's family, and José. If José becomes acculturated into European American values of individualistic action but his father maintains a collectivistic orientation toward José's career development, then, as with Kenji, the counselor will need to be sensitive to these culturally based values interactions. Such value conflicts illustrate that career development practitioners must be sensitive to the interaction between their personal values, the values prized by the client, and the value sets embedded within specific career counseling models. The latter often reflect the values promulgated at the national level.

Because career development interventions promote specific values, national governments vary in their support and expectations of career interventions. Super (1983) notes that countries that are relatively prosperous and free from the threat of outside interventions tend to view career development interventions as vehicles for fostering the individual's abilities, personal values, and interests. Conversely, countries experiencing economic hardships or the possible threat of outside intervention tend to view career development interventions as vehicles for channeling people into occupations deemed as being crucial for national survival. In the United States, the Soviet Union's *Sputnik* program provides an example of the latter. Feeling threatened by the apparent superiority of Soviet space technology in the late 1950s, the U.S. government focused funding and legislative efforts on directing young people into science-related occupations. More recently, the shifting winds of the political climate in the United States have resulted in funding support at the national level for increasing the talent pipeline into science/technology/engineering/math (STEM) occupations. Often, career development programs, initiatives, and interventions "follow the money" or the financial support that government provides for such initiatives.

In summary, avoiding unethical practice in career development interventions requires career development practitioners to be sensitive to the assumptions underlying their personal values, their clients' values, career interventions models, and the values being prioritized at the national level at any point in time (Herr & Niles, 1988). Practicing only within one's area of training and competence is an additional requirement for ethical practice in the career development intervention process. Again, we offer the suggestion of consultation with professional colleagues because counselors may need help to objectively judge their competence. When professional career practitioners possess value awareness, use ethical principles in their professional decision making, and adhere to the relevant ethical codes, they increase the likelihood that they will function ethically in providing career development interventions to their clients.

USING ETHICAL CODES

Many believe that there are too many ethical codes and that we should move toward a unified ethics code for the counseling profession (Herlihy & Remley, 1995). Most readers of this chapter are, or will be, subject to the ethical codes of the ACA (2014), the NCDA (2015), the APA (2010), the International Association for Educational and Vocational Guidance (1995), and/or the ASCA (2010).

We agree with the position that too many ethical codes exist, and we hope that at some future time the counseling profession will move toward a model of a single ethics code with annotations or appendices for special situations and areas of practice. However, we doubt that the multiple codes themselves are the source of ethics violations. There are many situations that are unique to specialized areas of counseling practice, such as career counseling. The authors commend those responsible for the NCDA *Code of Ethics* and for structuring the code to be compatible with the ACA code while making the code profession specific for NCDA members. Likewise, the authors of the NCDA code recognized that many career practitioners are associated with professional associations in addition to or instead of ACA. This effort is an important step in addressing the problems of multiple codes identified by Herlihy and Remley (1995).

In our previous edition we discussed three areas for which we found the then-current ethical codes inadequate to provide direction for career counseling professionals: (a) the definition of a career counseling relationship, given the fact that not all career interventions constitute therapy; (b) ethical standards for the appropriate and proper role of those who provide career counseling services but are not professionally trained counselors; and (c) the ethical use of the Internet to provide or enhance services. These three areas demand greater attention in professional training and workshops. They also present important challenges to be addressed by the profession.

Progress on Ethical Challenges Facing Career Counselors

This section reviews and explores recent progress on the three challenges that we identified in our previous edition. The issues are: (a) whether all career interventions are counseling relationships subject to the ethical standards of counseling, (b) what the proper role is of those who have training and experience in career interventions but do not have the training, education, and experience that are accepted as essential for one to be a professional counselor, and (c) how to determine the proper use of Internet technology in career interventions. We have considered the existing ethical codes lacking in adequate guidance for career counselors in these areas, and we have been bold enough to offer suggestions about needed clarifications. We are happy to report that progress has been made in each of the areas, and we offer the following progress report, which demonstrates that ethical codes are as they should be: dynamic and responsive to current situations.

Are All Individual Career Interventions Governed by the Same Ethical Standards?

An area of continuing ethical concern is personal relationships with clients. Confidentiality, counseling relationships, professional responsibility, and relationships with other professionals consistently remain at the top of the list of inquiries received by the American Counseling

Association (ACA) Ethics Committee (Glosoff & Freeman, 2007). Some ethical requirements are clear and unambiguous. For example, sexual relationships between career counselors and their clients are unethical. The ethical requirements are clear and unambiguous. However, situations exist in which the expected ethical behavior is not so clearly defined. For example, the psychologically based helping professions are not uniform in their view of how much time must elapse before a "helper" might make a case that an intimate relationship with a former client was not exploitative. We believe that career counselors are professional counselors with specialized education and experience in career interventions (Niles & Pate, 1989). However, there are many questions about the nature of helping relationships that focus on career issues. Career counseling professionals within and outside of educational settings often provide services that are typically not considered therapy. For example, consider the case of a career counseling professional in a university career center who reviews a résumé for a graduate student of the same age. Some weeks later they meet at a social event and begin a social relationship. Is that relationship subject to the same ethical scrutiny as a relationship that involved multiple sessions of counseling in a university counseling center and complex career issues? Reasonable counseling professionals might offer different answers.

Additional complications in determining proper action can arise because the specific requirements of many laws governing counselor behavior are far from clear, and the standards of practice incorporated in the regulations of many states are inconsistent with the ethical codes they resemble. For example, the regulations of the Commonwealth of Virginia Board of Counseling (2007) contain a standards of practice section. Included in that section is a statement about sexual relationships, which states:

> Counselors shall not engage in any type of sexual intimacies with clients or those included in a collateral relationship with the client and not counsel persons with whom they have had a sexual relationship. Counselors shall not engage in sexual intimacies with former clients within a minimum of five years after terminating the counseling relationship. Counselors who engage in such relationship after five years following termination shall have the responsibility to examine and document thoroughly that such relations do not have an exploitive nature, based on factors such as duration of counseling, amount of time since counseling, termination circumstances, client's personal history and mental status, or adverse impact on the client. A client's consent to, initiation of or participation in sexual behavior or involvement with a counselor does not change the nature of the conduct nor lift the regulatory prohibition. (p.15)

The ACA *Code of Ethics* (2014) similarly addresses sexual relationships between counselors and clients:

A.5. Roles and Relationships with Clients
(See F.3., F.10., G.3.)

A.5.a. Current Clients
Sexual or romantic counselor–client interactions or relationships with current clients, their romantic partners, or their family members are prohibited.

A.5.b. Former Clients
Sexual or romantic counselor–client interactions or relationships with former clients, their romantic partners, or their family members are prohibited for a period of 5 years following the last professional contact.

Counselors, before engaging in sexual or romantic interactions or relationships with clients, their romantic partners, or client family members after 5 years following the last professional contact, demonstrate forethought and document (in written form) whether the interactions or relationship can be viewed as exploitive in some way and/or whether there is still potential to harm the former client; in cases of potential exploitation and/or harm, the counselor avoids entering such an interaction or relationship.

A.5.c. Nonprofessional Interactions or Relationships (Other Than Sexual or Romantic Interactions or Relationships)

Counselor–client nonprofessional relationships with clients, former clients, their romantic partners, or their family members should be avoided, except when the interaction is potentially beneficial to the client. *(See A.5.d.)*

A career practitioner might have previously believed or asserted that engaging in an intimate personal relationship with a former client was permissible because, as in the previous résumé critique example, the professional service was not counseling. However, the same career counselor (who would be required to be licensed if he or she practiced privately in Virginia and called himself or herself a counselor) might be judged to have behaved unethically by those with different interpretations of the ethical requirements. Likewise, a career counseling professional might have believed that the two-year standard could apply to begin to make a case that an intimate relationship was nonexploitive (APA, 2010).

The NCDA *Code of Ethics* (2015) recognizes in section A.1.b. that career counseling professionals provide different types of services. The responsibility of all career counseling professionals to provide only those services within the scope of their competence and qualifications is made explicit. Although the discrepancy between the APA (2010) "two-year standard" and the ACA and NCDA five-year standard for sexual intimacy to even be defended as other than exploitive continues, section A.5.b of the NCDA code makes the five-year limitation applicable to all career counseling professionals. The issue has been addressed clearly and explicitly. All career counseling professionals are subject to the code in their professional activities.

Should Those Without Traditional Training and Credentials as Professional Career Counselors Provide Career Counseling Services?

The issue of the proper role of those providing career counseling services (e.g., providing career information, career advising) without the customary training and credentials for professional counseling relates to managed care and third-party payers because many professional counselors depend on those sources for their livelihood. These counselors are understandably concerned about anything that would make the competence of those delivering counseling services subject to question. However, many consider prohibiting persons with appropriate talents and skills from providing the services for which they are qualified as itself an unethical and unnecessary restraint. Still others contend that having any person other than a fully qualified counselor provide any career counseling services is a threat to client welfare and the reputation of the counseling profession. These are contentious issues within the profession. Regardless of one's opinion, the reality is that many individuals engage in providing career counseling services with little or no formal training in career development theory and practice. Moreover, many of these individuals have no training in the helping professions. Counselor and psychology licensure laws typically do not prohibit unlicensed individuals from providing training in job-search skills, résumé writing, and so on.

Section A.1.b. of the NCDA *Code of Ethics* (2015), mentioned above, recognizes that career counseling professionals provide different types of services. That same section makes it obligatory for career counseling professionals to make explicit the limits of the services for which they are competent and qualified and which they can offer. As explained, the section that addresses sexual intimacy with former clients also makes explicit the obligation of all career counseling professionals to follow the *Code of Ethics*. Likewise, section A.1.c. makes clear the obligation of all career counseling professionals to engage only in nonprofessional interactions that are beneficial to their clients.

Great progress has been made. NCDA has recognized, by supporting training and credentialing for Global Career Development Facilitators (GCDF), that there are persons who, although they are not trained as professional counselors, can provide career counseling services. The NCDA *Code of Ethics* (2015) has made those who are recognized as career counseling professionals subject to the code. The basic question has been answered; but the challenge of the many who provide career counseling services who are not subject to the NCDA, or any other, ethical code remains as a concern to all career counseling professionals and a potential threat to the clients who are unaware of the distinctions among those offering career counseling services.

How Should the Internet Be Used in Career Development Interventions?

The dimensions of the Internet counseling controversy are in many ways similar to the issues in endorsing career interventions by the untrained or undertrained professional counselor. Most counselors acknowledge the potential of the Internet as a source of information that can be accessed by people who might not have access to other sources of the information. They also recognize the superiority, breadth, depth, and currency of the information available through the Internet. Although some copyright issues about information and assessment are provided through the Internet, ethical issues most often arise when the services are considered to be professional counseling. Many career counselors define counseling as face-to-face contact and that ends the consideration. Others allow the possibility that some career counseling services (e.g., information) might be provided through the Internet, but they wonder about regulation. How can service providers potentially thousands of miles from the person helped be accountable? The questions are many. NCDA developed guidelines for the use of the Internet for providing career information and planning services (NCDA, 1997). In addition, NCDA published a guide to using the Internet in career planning (Sampson, Dikel, & Osborn, 2012). These guidelines acknowledge that the Internet can be used in four ways for the purpose of providing career counseling services to clients:

1. To deliver occupational information
2. To provide online searches of occupational databases for the purpose of identifying occupational options
3. To deliver interactive career counseling and career planning services
4. To provide online job searches

These four purposes are subject to guidelines that address a variety of ethical issues. For example, the qualifications of the Web site developer or provider must be clearly stated on the site. Clients have the right to be informed about the expertise and experience of the career counseling professional. Moreover, the career counseling professional must not use a false e-mail identity when interacting with clients. The provider must clearly state the appropriate uses (and limitations) of the Web site. The career counseling professional must appropriately screen clients to determine whether the client can benefit from using the online services provided. The career counseling professional must also provide adequate support for the client via periodic telephone contact or videoconferencing.

Providing career counseling services to clients in other geographical locations presents a variety of challenges to the service provider. For instance, the career counseling professional has the obligation to be aware of local conditions, cultures, and events that may have an impact on the client using the online services. The career counseling professional must also be able to refer clients to local practitioners when the client is in need of additional services. Internet providers of career counseling services must also ensure that the content of the Web site is current and appropriate for use in electronic form. Current online information is especially critical when the service includes online job searching. The costs of all services provided must be clearly stated. When the services include assessment instruments, only assessments with adequate psychometric evidence of their reliability and validity may be used. The issues of confidentiality and storage of client data must be clearly addressed on the Web site.

The use of the Internet to provide career counseling services increases each day. With its increased use, career counseling practitioners are consistently presented with new ethical issues in services delivery. Adhering to guidelines offered by NCDA, consulting with others, and having external consultants evaluate online services are some strategies career counseling practitioners can use to ensure that their online services are ethical. Clearly, this mode of services delivery will continue to present practitioners with ethical dilemmas as its use increases in the future.

THE ETHICAL STANDARDS OF NCDA

Last, but certainly not least important, we focus directly on the ethical standards of NCDA (2015) and offer what we hope will be a summary of ethics for career counseling professionals. We have included the introduction to each of the nine main sections of the NCDA code, and we urge careful reading of the entire code included as Appendix A.

Section A: The Professional Relationship

Career professionals facilitate client growth and development in ways that foster the interest and welfare of clients and promote formation of healthy relationships. Trust is the cornerstone of the professional relationship and career professionals have the responsibility to respect and safeguard the client's right to privacy and confidentiality. Career professionals actively attempt to understand the diverse cultural backgrounds of the individuals they serve. Career professionals also explore their own cultural identities and how these affect their values and beliefs about the working relationship. Career professionals are encouraged to contribute to society by devoting a portion of their professional activity to services for which there is little or no financial return (*pro bono publico*).

Section B: Confidentiality, Privileged Communication, and Privacy

Career professionals recognize that trust is a cornerstone of the professional relationship. Career professionals work to earn the trust of clients by creating an ongoing partnership, establishing and upholding appropriate boundaries, and maintaining confidentiality. Career professionals communicate the parameters of confidentiality in a culturally competent manner.

Section C: Professional Responsibility

Career professionals provide open, honest, and accurate communication in dealing with the public and other professionals. They practice in a nondiscriminatory manner within the boundaries of professional and personal competence and have a responsibility to abide by the NCDA *Code of Ethics* (2015). Career professionals actively participate in local, state, and national associations that foster the development and improvement of the provision of career services. Career professionals are encouraged to promote change at the individual, group, institutional, and societal levels in ways that improve the quality of life for individuals and groups and remove potential barriers to the provision or access of appropriate services being offered. Career professionals have a responsibility to the public to engage in ethical practice. Career professionals engage in professional practices that are based on rigorous research methodologies. Career professionals are encouraged to contribute to society by devoting a portion of their professional activity to services for which there is little or no financial return (*pro bono publico*). In addition, career professionals engage in self-care activities to maintain and promote their emotional, physical, mental, and spiritual well-being to best meet their professional responsibilities.

Section D: Relationships with Other Professionals

Career professionals recognize that the quality of their interactions with colleagues can influence the quality of services provided to clients. They work to become knowledgeable about colleagues within and outside the profession. Career professionals develop positive working relationships and systems of communication with colleagues to enhance services to clients. Career professionals may provide coaching and/or consultation to individuals, groups, or organizations. If career professionals perform such services, they must provide only the services that are within the scope of their professional competence and qualifications.

Section E: Evaluation, Assessment, and Interpretation

Career professionals use assessment instruments as one component of the career services process, taking into account the client's personal and cultural context. Career professionals promote the well-being of individual clients or groups of clients by developing and using appropriate career, educational, and psychological assessment instruments.

Section F: Providing Career Services Online, Technology, and Social Media

Career professionals actively attempt to understand the evolving nature of the profession with regard to providing career services online using technology and/or social media, and how such resources may be used to better serve their clients. Career professionals strive to become knowledgeable about these resources, recognizing that periodic training is needed to develop necessary technical and professional competencies. Career professionals understand the additional concerns related to providing career services online and using technology and/or social media, and make every attempt to protect confidentiality and data security, ensure transparency and equitable treatment of clients, and meet any legal and ethical requirements for the use of such resources.

Section G: Supervision, Training, and Teaching

Career professionals foster meaningful and respectful professional relationships and maintain appropriate boundaries with supervisees and students. Career professionals have theoretical and pedagogical foundations for their work and aim to be fair, accurate, and honest in their assessments of other career professionals, students, and supervisees.

Section H: Research and Publication

Career professionals who conduct research are encouraged to contribute to the knowledge base of the profession and promote a clearer understanding of the conditions that lead to a healthy and more just society. Career professionals support efforts of researchers by participating fully and willingly whenever possible. Career professionals minimize bias and respect diversity in designing and implementing research programs.

Section I: Resolving Ethical Issues

Career professionals behave in a legal, ethical, and moral manner in the conduct of their professional work. They are aware that client protection and trust in the profession depend on a high level of professional conduct. They hold other career professionals to the same standards and are willing to take appropriate action to ensure that these standards are upheld. Career professionals work to resolve ethical dilemmas with direct and open communication among all parties involved and seek consultation with colleagues and supervisors when necessary. Career professionals incorporate ethical practice into their daily work. They engage in ongoing learning and development regarding current topics in ethical and legal issues in the profession.

If you have not read the NCDA *Code of Ethics* (2015), please stop now and read the code in Appendix A before you proceed. As you read these standards, it is important to be aware of the fact that ethical statements contain both mandatory and aspirational standards. The authors' reading of the NCDA, IAEVG, APA, ACA, ASCA, GCDF, and other ethical statements suggests variation primarily among the aspirational standards (i.e., standards that reflect the philosophy of the profession but are not easily enforceable). There is, in our interpretation, more consistency across ethical codes regarding the mandatory standards.

Based on our interpretation of multiple ethical codes, we offer standards that are central to ethical standards and ethical practice. These standards are each based on an overriding principle of concern for the welfare of the client. Maintaining an overriding concern for client welfare means that career counselors must constantly test all potential actions they take against the principles of promoting client autonomy, promoting client good, never acting to harm a client, promoting equal treatment of those similarly situated and adapting services based on client needs, and keeping promises to clients. As a result of the enhanced emphasis on advocacy and social justice in the ACA and NCDA codes of ethics, we offer the following as critical ethical concepts for career professionals:

1. Career professionals offer only services they are competent to offer. Competence includes training, supervised experience, and some external validation of that competence. This includes all counseling techniques and strategies, assessment devices, and technology-assisted counseling.

2. Career professionals respect and value individual differences among clients and potential clients. To respect and value these differences, it is necessary for counselors to study ways to serve diverse populations.

3. Career professionals treat information received from and about clients as owned by the client and held in trust by the counselor. Such information is revealed only with the consent of the client, when required by law, or to protect the client or others from harm. The basis of career professionals' relationships with clients is the assumption that their communications will be respected as confidential.

4. The career professional does not engage in any professional relationship in which the counselor's objectivity and ability to work solely for the welfare of the client might be impaired. This includes but is not limited to intimate emotional and physical relationships. Professionals must anticipate how potential nonprofessional relationships could possibly lead to future ethical conflicts and take action to avoid future problems.

5. Career professionals assume professional responsibility for clients, and if they are unable to assist, they help the client to obtain alternative services. This requirement extends to assisting clients who cannot, or do not, pay for services as agreed, and for providing services when the career counselor is not available.

6. Career professionals recognize that they have obligations to other members of the profession and to society to act in responsible ways and to consider the effects of their behavior on others. This requirement extends to research and publication, to online services, and to business relationships, so that counselors do not use their profession for inappropriate financial gain (e.g., diverting clients from a provided service to a private practice).

Career professionals are advocates for their clients and for social justice. The latest revision of the NCDA (2015) ethical standards recognizes career professionals' responsibility for advocacy on behalf of their clients and for social justice. The chapters of this book leave no doubt that work is a vital component of the ability of people to achieve their potential to contribute to society. Advocacy for career professionals can range from appropriate advocacy for individual clients to advocacy for changes that expand the opportunities for all and remove barriers to employment. The ethical principle of justice suggests that career professionals have a special obligation to work to ensure that those who are equal on criteria related to any selection are treated equally, and that those who have potential that might not be recognized without encouragement and assistance receive the appropriate encouragement and assistance from career professionals. This is a statement of aspirational and virtue ethics that is difficult, if not impossible, to mandate for enforcement. However, we believe career professionals not only have the unique expertise to advocate for expanded and equal access to meaningful and rewarding work, but that they also have an ethical obligation to do so.

Using an Ethical Decision-Making Model

The information we have provided in this chapter thus far provides useful information for you to use in understanding the various dilemmas that career practitioners often confront. Integrating this information into an ethical decision-making model will also guide you in determining a specific course of action to take when you encounter such dilemmas. Forester-Miller and Davis (1996) provide an ethical decision-making model for professional counselors that can be applied to career counseling. Specifically, they identify the following steps in ethical decision making:

1. Identify the problem.
2. Apply the NCDA *Code of Ethics*.
3. Determine the nature and dimensions of the dilemma.
4. Generate possible courses of action.
5. Consider the potential consequences of all options and choose a course of action.
6. Evaluate the selected course of action.
7. Implement the course of action selected.

In identifying the problem, career counseling practitioners should gather extensive information to clarify the ethical concern. Being specific, objective, and factual will help remove bias and opinion from the problem being identified. Forester-Miller and Davis (1996) recommend considering the following questions: Is it an ethical, legal, professional, or clinical problem? Is it a combination of more than one of these? Is the issue related to me and what I am or am not doing? Is it related to a client and/or the client's significant others and what they are or are not doing? Is it related to the institution or agency and its policies and procedures?

After you have clarified the problem, refer to the NCDA *Code of Ethics* (2015) to see if the issue is addressed there. If so, then follow the course of action described by the standard. "If the problem is more complex and a resolution does not seem apparent, then you probably have a true ethical dilemma and need to proceed with further steps in the ethical decision making process" (Forester-Miller & Davis, 1996). In the latter case, consider the moral principles described previously in this chapter (e.g., autonomy, nonmaleficence, etc.) to determine if any apply to the current dilemma. Draw upon the professional literature for guidance in deciding a course of action.

To determine the nature of the dilemma and to generate possible courses of action, it is helpful to consult with experienced professional colleagues and/or supervisors. They may be able to provide alternative viewpoints, or they may identify additional dimensions regarding the situation. Consulting with the ethics professional within the relevant professional association (e.g., ASCA, ACA, APA) is also an important consultative step.

Use the information gathered through this process to generate several potential courses of action. It may also be helpful to involve a colleague in this process. Brainstorm as many courses of action as possible and consider the potential consequences of each action. Evaluate each potential course of action relative to its impact on your client, you, and others. Consider whether the course of action creates any additional ethical concerns. Review whether the course of action is fair, whether it is the sort of action that you would recommend to others in a similar situation, and whether you would be comfortable if the public knew about the course of action should you take it (Forester-Miller & Davis, 1996).

Once an appropriate course of action has been identified, it should be implemented. Forester-Miller and Davis (1996) recommend that, after implementing your course of action, it is important to assess whether your actions had the anticipated effect and consequences.

SUMMARY

The need for career counseling professionals to be vigilant in providing interventions that are ethical is, perhaps, obvious. Unfortunately, ethical practice itself is not always obvious. Career development practitioners and, most important, their clients, will be best served when practitioners use multiple strategies to guide their ethical decision making. Using ethical principles, possessing values awareness, and adhering to the relevant ethical codes (e.g., those published by the NCDA, ACA, APA, ASCA, GCDF, and IAEVG) are strategies that career counseling professionals can use to increase the probability that they will engage in proper practice. We recommend the use of the strategies for ethical practice that are discussed in this chapter. Whenever possible, we also encourage readers to discuss their questions and concerns with trusted and respected consultants. Discussion of these issues will provide multiple perspectives related to each issue presented.

What do you think would be proper behavior of the career counselor faced with the following challenges?

1. A school counselor has reservations about military service. The father of the client, whom the counselor knows to be caring and concerned, asks the counselor about giving his child information about military service as a means to help the child become more mature and live up to his/her high potential. The counselor knows the child has high potential but lacks self-discipline. The counselor tends to agree with the father but questions the military as the source of that discipline.

2. A small career counseling services office counselor helps a second-year, 32-year-old college student write a résumé and then has no further contact with the student until the counselor enrolls in a yoga class in which the student is also enrolled. The student asks the counselor to go for coffee after class.

3. A career counselor in private practice is counseling an executive about her career plans. She shares information about her excitement concerning an offer she will accept and tells the counselor about the IPO Corporation and her anticipation of a position with stock options. The client believes the stock options will multiply over a short term. The counseling is terminated, and the counselor wonders about an investment in IPO. The counselor does not think there is a counseling dilemma because the gain or loss could not affect the terminated counseling relationship.

4. A high school counselor meets with a student who is excited about military service due to recent advertisements about the military service providing resources for higher education. The student has no resources for further study and no potential family support. The student has great potential, but the counselor is concerned about recent press information about the military attitude toward gays and lesbians in the military. Rumors about the young person's sexual orientation abound in the school, but the counselor has no information that the student has ever mentioned his/her sexuality.

5. An elementary school counselor is planning career-related activities and has arranged a class trip to a large, nearby dairy that has supported the school. A parent objects not only to his child's participation but also to any participation of the school because the parent believes dairy farming is an unethical exploitation of animals. The parent has written the local press and has been on call-in radio objecting to the school serving milk, in spite of meetings with officials that have demonstrated legal requirements for serving milk in lunch programs.

CASE STUDY

Molly is an 18-year-old college freshman experiencing substantial stress related to her inability to identify a college major. Her father, a CEO of a large pharmaceutical company, has told her to major in business to prepare for working within his company when she graduates. Molly's mother, a painter, has been silent about her expectations for Molly. Molly feels that her father is overbearing and her mother is nonsupportive. Molly's struggles have resulted in her experiencing depression and a sense of urgency about how to resolve her dilemma. She lacks academic motivation and has been spending afternoons smoking pot and listening to music. Recently, she and her younger sister, Susan, have concocted a plan to leave school and home to travel throughout Europe. They have already saved money for this experience and plan on simply leaving without informing their parents. At the same time, you have recently received an e-mail from Molly's father, who would like to meet with you during the upcoming Parents' Weekend.

Molly's father wants to discuss Molly's career plans. Molly wants your advice about her trip to Europe. What potential ethical issues do you foresee?

STUDENT ACTIVITIES

1. Identify which of the following topics could present personal ethical/moral issues for you in your work as a career counselor:
   - A student who wants to explore a career in the military
   - A client whose religious beliefs lead him to conclude that a "woman's place is in the home"
   - A parent who wants you to convince her child to pursue a career in engineering because the student is good at math
   - An Asian student who firmly believes she should choose the occupation her parents have identified for her, despite the fact that she has no interest in this occupation
   - An acquaintance that is out of work but asks you to provide career counseling in exchange for him performing some light maintenance work around your home
   - A mother of a student for whom you are a school counselor who asks you to tell her which educational options her daughter is considering
   - An adult college student for whom you once provided a résumé critique who (unbeknownst to you) has been asked to play on your YMCA volleyball team

2. What are the similarities and differences between the ethical standards for the International Association for Educational and Vocational Guidance (1995) and the ethical standards for the National Career Development Association (2015)?

NCDA CODE OF ETHICS PREAMBLE

Introduction

A code of ethics helps to define professional behavior and serves to protect the public, the profession, and those who practice within the profession. Ethical behavior involves incorporating the principles espoused in the code of ethics into your personal and professional life and using the code to help determine a course of action. At the same time, ethical behavior is about transparency. Can your behavior withstand the scrutiny of others? Will you be embarrassed, ashamed, or concerned if someone else knew that you did or said something?

The *NCDA Code of Ethics* (Code) has been designed as a guide and resource for career practitioners. While it offers a set of principles that can be applied to a wide range of settings and situations, it is not (nor can it be) comprehensive. If you are concerned about whether or not a particular practice is ethical, then you should not engage in that behavior without getting competent advice. More succinctly, when in doubt—don't; at least not without professional consultation. Peer review isn't always going to give you perfect advice; but you can take comfort in knowing that you questioned your behavior before proceeding and allowed others to comment before taking action. There is safety and strength in the depth and breadth of opinions you seek before engaging in activity that may be untried or questionable.

SECTION A: THE PROFESSIONAL RELATIONSHIP

Introduction

Career professionals facilitate client growth and development in ways that foster the interest and welfare of clients and promote formation of healthy relationships. Trust is the cornerstone of the professional relationship and career professionals have the responsibility to respect and safeguard the client's right to privacy and confidentiality. Career professionals actively attempt to understand the diverse cultural backgrounds of the individuals they serve. Career professionals also explore their own cultural identities and how these affect their values and beliefs about the working relationship. Career professionals are encouraged to contribute to society by devoting a portion of their professional activity to services for which there is little or no financial return (*pro bono publico*).

Section A.1: Welfare of Those Served by Career Professionals

Section A.1.a: Primary Responsibility

The primary responsibility of career professionals is to respect the dignity and to promote the welfare of the individuals to whom they provide service.

Section A.1.b: Differentiation Between Types of Services Provided

"Career planning" services are differentiated from "career counseling" services. Career planning services include an active provision of information designed to help a client with a specific need, such as review of a résumé; assistance in networking strategies; identification of occupations based on values, interests, skills, prior work experience, and/or other characteristics; support in the job-seeking process; and assessment by means of paper-based and/or online inventories of interest, abilities, personality, work-related values, and/or other characteristics. In addition to providing these informational services, "career counseling" provides the opportunity for a deeper level of involvement with the client, based on the establishment of a professional counseling relationship and the potential for assisting clients with career and personal development concerns beyond those included in career planning. All career professionals, whether engaging in "career planning" or "career counseling", provide only the services that are within the scope of their professional competence and qualifications.

Section A.1.c: Records and Documentation

Career professionals maintain records necessary for rendering professional services as required by laws, regulations, or agency/institution procedures. Career professionals include sufficient and timely documentation in their records to facilitate delivery and continuity of services. Career professionals take reasonable steps to ensure that documentation in records accurately reflects client progress and the services provided. If amendments are made in records, career professionals take steps to properly note the amendment according to applicable policies. Career professionals are encouraged to purge their files according to the time frame required by federal, state, local, and/or institutional statute, law, regulation, or procedure, particularly when there is no reasonable expectation that a client will benefit from maintaining the records any longer than required. Career professionals are expected to know and abide by all applicable federal, state, local, and/or institutional statutes, laws, regulations, and procedures regarding record keeping.

Section A.1.d: Career Services Plans

Career professionals and their clients work jointly in devising integrated career services plans (in writing or orally) that offer reasonable promise of success and are consistent with the abilities and circumstances of clients. Career professionals and clients regularly review career plans to assess their continued viability and effectiveness, respecting the freedom of choice of clients.

Section A.1.e: Support Network Involvement

Career professionals recognize that support networks hold various meanings in the lives of clients and consider enlisting the support, understanding, and involvement of others (e.g., family members, friends, and religious/spiritual/community leaders) as positive resources, when appropriate and with client consent.

Section A.2: Informed Consent in the Professional Relationship

Section A.2.a: Informed Consent

Clients have the freedom to choose whether to enter into or remain in a professional relationship. To make informed choices, clients need adequate information about the working relationship and the career professional. Career professionals have an obligation to review in writing and orally the rights and responsibilities of both the career professional and the recipient of services prior to the beginning of the working relationship. Further, informed consent is an ongoing part of the professional relationship, and career professionals appropriately document discussions of informed consent throughout the working relationship.

Section A.2.b: Types of Information Needed

Career professionals clearly explain to clients the nature of all services provided. They inform clients about issues such as, but not limited to, the following: the purposes, goals, techniques, procedures, limitations, potential risks, and benefits of services; the career professional's qualifications, credentials, and relevant experience; the role of technology, continuation of services upon the incapacitation or death of the career professional; and other pertinent information. Career professionals take

steps to ensure that clients understand the implications of diagnosis (if applicable), the intended use of tests/assessments and reports, fees, and billing arrangements (including procedures regarding nonpayment of fees). Clients have the right to confidentiality and to be provided with an explanation of its limitations (including how supervisors and/or treatment team professionals are involved); to obtain clear information about their records; to participate in the ongoing career services plans; and to refuse any services or modality change and to be advised of the consequences of such refusal.

Section A.2.c: Developmental and Cultural Sensitivity

Career professionals communicate information in ways that are both developmentally and culturally appropriate. Career professionals use clear and understandable language when discussing issues related to informed consent. When clients have difficulty understanding the language used by career professionals, arrangements may be made (e.g., helping to locate a qualified interpreter or translator) to ensure comprehension by clients. The cost for such services, however, may be passed onto clients in accordance with federal, state, local, and/or institutional statute, law, regulation, or procedure. Thus clients should be given the opportunity to seek another career professional or to employ an interpreter or translator of their own choosing. In collaboration with clients, career professionals consider cultural implications of informed consent procedures and, where possible and appropriate, career professionals adjust their practices accordingly.

Section A.2.d: Inability to Give Consent

When providing career services to minors or persons unable to give voluntary consent, career professionals seek the assent of clients to services, and include them in decision making as appropriate. Career professionals recognize the need to balance the ethical rights of clients to make choices, their capacity to give consent or assent to receive services, and parental or familial legal rights and responsibilities to protect these clients and make decisions on their behalf.

Section A.2.e: Mandated Clients

Career professionals discuss the required limitations to confidentiality when working with clients who have been mandated for services. Career professionals also explain what type of information and with whom that information is shared prior to the beginning of providing services. The client may choose to refuse services. In this case, Career professionals will, to the best of their ability, discuss with the client the potential consequences of refusing services.

Section A.3: Clients Served by Others

When career professionals learn that their clients are in a professional relationship with another mental health professional, if appropriate, they request a written release from clients to inform the other professionals and always strive to establish positive and collaborative professional relationships, when necessary and appropriate.

Section A.4: Avoiding Harm and Imposing Values

Section A.4.a: Avoiding Harm

Career professionals act to avoid harming their clients, students, trainees, and research participants and to minimize or to remedy unavoidable or unanticipated harm.

Section A.4.b: Personal Values

Career professionals are aware of their own values, attitudes, beliefs, and behaviors and avoid imposing values that are inconsistent with clients' goals. Career professionals respect the diversity of clients, students, trainees, and research participants.

Section A.5: Roles and Relationships with Clients

Section A.5.a: Current Clients

Sexual or romantic interactions or relationships with current clients, their romantic partners, or their family members are prohibited.

Section A.5.b: Former Clients

Sexual or romantic interactions or relationships with former clients, their romantic partners, or their family members are prohibited for a period of 5 years following the last professional contact or longer as required by all applicable federal, state, local, and/or institutional statutes, laws, regulations, and procedures. Career professionals, before engaging in sexual or romantic interactions or relationships with clients, their romantic partners, or client family members after 5 years following the last professional contact, demonstrate forethought and document (in written form) whether the interactions or relationship can be viewed as exploitive in some way and/or whether there is still potential to harm the former client. In cases of potential exploitation and/or harm, the career professional does not enter into such an interaction or relationship.

Section A.5.c: Nonprofessional Interactions or Relationships (Other Than Sexual or Romantic Interactions or Relationships)

Nonprofessional relationships with clients, former clients, their romantic partners, or their family members should be avoided by career professionals, except when the interaction is potentially beneficial to the client.

Section A.5.d: Potentially Beneficial Interactions

When a nonprofessional interaction with a client or former client may be potentially beneficial to the client or former client, the career professional must document in case records, prior to the interaction (or as soon as feasible), the rationale for such an interaction, the potential benefit, and anticipated consequences for the client or former client and other individuals significantly involved with the client or former client. Such interactions should be initiated with appropriate client consent. Where unintentional harm occurs to the client or former client, or to an individual significantly involved with the client or former client, due to the nonprofessional interaction, the career professional must show evidence of an attempt to remedy such harm. Examples of potentially beneficial interactions include, but are not limited to, attending a formal ceremony (e.g., a wedding/commitment ceremony or graduation); purchasing a service or product provided by a client or former client (excepting unrestricted bartering); hospital visits to an ill family member; and mutual membership in a professional association, organization, or community.

Section A.5.e: Role Changes in the Professional Relationship

When a career professional changes a role from the original or most recent contracted relationship, s/he obtains informed consent from the client and explains the right of the client to refuse services related to the change. Examples of role changes include, but are not limited to:

1. changing from providing individual career services to therapy, relationship or family counseling, or vice versa;
2. changing from a non-forensic evaluative role to a therapeutic role, or vice versa;
3. changing from a career professional to a researcher role (i.e., enlisting clients as research participants), or vice versa; and/or
4. changing from a career professional to a mediator role, or vice versa.

Clients must be fully informed of any anticipated consequences (e.g., financial, legal, personal, or therapeutic) of role changes with a career professional.

Section A.5.f: Other Relationships

Career professionals avoid providing services to individuals with whom they have had a previous romantic or sexual relationship. They also avoid providing services to friends or family members with whom they have an inability to remain objective. If career professionals engage in providing services to any of these individuals, they must consult with another career professional and document their reasons for not referring the client to someone else.

Section A.6: Roles and Relationships at Individual, Group, Institutional, and Societal Levels

Section A.6.a: Advocacy

When appropriate, career professionals advocate at individual, group, institutional, and societal levels to examine potential barriers and obstacles that inhibit access and/or the growth and development of clients. A.6.b. Confidentiality and Advocacy Career professionals obtain consent prior to engaging in advocacy efforts on behalf of a client to improve the provision of services and to work toward removal of systemic barriers or obstacles that inhibit client access, growth, and development.

Section A.7: Multiple Clients

When a career professional agrees to provide career services to two or more persons who have a relationship, the career professional clarifies at the outset which person or persons are clients and the nature of the relationships the career professional will have with each involved person. If it becomes apparent that the career professional may be called upon to perform potentially conflicting roles, the career professional will clarify, adjust, or withdraw appropriately from one or more roles.

Section A.8: Group Work

Section A.8.a: Screening

Career professionals screen prospective group participants. To the extent possible, career professionals select members whose needs and goals are compatible with goals of the group, who will not impede the group process, and whose well-being will not be jeopardized by the group experience.

Section A.8.b: Protecting Clients

In a group setting, career professionals take reasonable precautions to protect clients from physical, emotional, or psychological trauma.

Section A.9: Fees and Business Practices

Section A.9.a: Self-Referrals and Unacceptable Business Practices

Career professionals working in an organization (e.g., school, agency, institution) that provides career services do not refer clients to their private practice unless the policies of a particular organization make explicit provisions for self-referrals. In such instances, clients must be informed of other options open to them should they seek private career services. Career professionals also do not participate in fee splitting, nor do they give or receive commissions, rebates, or any other form of remuneration when referring clients for professional services.

Section A.9.b: Establishing Fees

In establishing fees for professional career services, career professionals consider the financial status of clients and the locality in which they practice. In the event that the established fee structure is inappropriate for a client, career professionals assist clients in attempting to find comparable services of acceptable cost.

Section A.9.c: Nonpayment of Fees

If career professionals intend to use collection agencies or take legal measures to collect fees from clients who do not pay for services as agreed upon, they include such information in their informed consent documents and also inform clients in a timely fashion of intended actions and offer clients the opportunity to make payment.

Section A.9.d: Bartering

Career professionals may barter only if the relationship is not exploitive or harmful and does not place the career professional in an unfair advantage, if the client requests it, and if such arrangements are an accepted practice among professionals in the community. Career professionals consider the cultural implications of bartering and discuss relevant concerns with clients and document such agreements in a clear written contract. Career professionals must also be aware of local, state, and/or federal laws, including the tax implications of such an arrangement. Further, career professionals must make the recipients of their services aware of all applicable federal, state, local, and/or institutional statutes, laws, regulations, and procedures and should direct them to seek qualified counsel (i.e., attorney and/or accountant) in determining if such an arrangement is in their best interest.

Section A.9.e: Receiving Gifts

Career professionals understand the challenges of accepting gifts from clients and recognize that in some cultures, small gifts are a token of respect and a way of showing gratitude. When determining whether or not to accept a gift from clients, career professionals take into account the nature of their relationship, the monetary value of the gift, a client's motivation for giving the gift, the career professional's motivation for wanting to accept or decline the gift, and all applicable federal, state, local, and/or institutional statutes, laws, regulations, and procedures.

Section A.10: Termination and Referral

Section A.10.a: Abandonment Prohibited

Career professionals do not abandon or neglect clients to whom they provide career services. Career professionals assist in making appropriate arrangements for the continuation of treatment, when necessary, during interruptions such as vacations, illness, and following termination.

Section A.10.b: Inability to Assist Clients

If career professionals determine an inability to be of professional assistance to clients, they avoid entering into or continuing the relationship. Career professionals are knowledgeable about culturally and clinically appropriate referral resources and suggest these alternatives. If clients decline the suggested referrals, career professionals may discontinue the relationship.

Section A.10.c: Appropriate Termination

Career professionals terminate a professional relationship when it becomes reasonably apparent that the client no longer needs assistance, is not likely to benefit from, or is being harmed by continued service provision. Career professionals may terminate the working relationship when in jeopardy of harm by the client, or another person with whom the client has a relationship, or when clients do not pay agreed upon fees. Career professionals provide pre-termination career services and recommend other providers when feasible and necessary.

Section A.10.d: Appropriate Transfer of Services

When career professionals transfer or refer clients to other practitioners, they ensure that appropriate clinical and administrative processes are completed and open communication is maintained with both clients and practitioners.

SECTION B: CONFIDENTIALITY, PRIVILEGED COMMUNICATION, AND PRIVACY _____

Introduction

Career professionals recognize that trust is a cornerstone of the professional relationship. Career professionals work to earn the trust of clients by creating an ongoing partnership, establishing and upholding appropriate boundaries, and maintaining confidentiality. Career professionals communicate the parameters of confidentiality in a culturally competent manner.

Section B.1: Respecting Client Rights

Section B.1.a: Multicultural/Diversity Considerations

Career professionals maintain awareness and sensitivity regarding cultural meanings of confidentiality and privacy. Career professionals respect differing views toward disclosure of information. Career professionals hold ongoing discussions with clients as to how, when, and with whom information is to be shared.

Section B.1.b: Respect for Privacy

Career professionals respect client rights to privacy. Career professionals solicit private information from clients only when it is beneficial to the working relationship.

Section B.1.c: Respect for Confidentiality

Career professionals protect the confidential information of prospective and current clients. Career professionals do not share confidential information without client consent or without sound legal or ethical justification.

Section B.1.d: Explanation of Limitations

At initiation and throughout the professional relationship, career professionals inform clients of the limitations of confidentiality and seek to identify foreseeable situations in which confidentiality must be breached.

Section B.2: Exceptions

Section B.2.a: Danger and Legal Requirements

The general requirement that career professionals keep information confidential does not apply when disclosure is required to protect clients or identified others from serious and foreseeable harm or when legal requirements demand that confidential information must be revealed. Examples of when career professionals may divulge confidential information may include, but not be limited to, mandated reporting in cases of suspected or actual child or elder abuse, when a client has a communicable and life threatening disease or condition and may infect an identifiable third party, or when notifying a collection agency to recover unpaid fees from a client. Career professionals consult with other professionals, include attorneys, when in doubt as to the validity of an exception.

Section B.2.b: Contagious, Life-Threatening Diseases

When clients disclose that they have a disease commonly known to be both communicable and life threatening, career professionals may be justified in disclosing information to identifiable third parties, if they are known to be at demonstrable and high risk of contracting the disease. Prior to making a disclosure, career professionals assess the intent of clients to inform the third parties about their disease or to engage in any behaviors that may be harmful to an identifiable third party. Career professionals adhere to relevant state laws concerning disclosure about disease status.

Section B.2.c: Court-Ordered Disclosure

When ordered by a court to release confidential or privileged information, career professionals endeavor to inform the client and to obtain written consent from the client or take steps to prohibit the disclosure, or have it limited as narrowly as possible, to minimize potential harm to the client.

Section B.2.d: Minimal Disclosure

To the extent possible, clients are informed before confidential information is disclosed and are involved in the disclosure decision-making process. When circumstances require the disclosure of confidential information, only essential information is revealed.

Section B.3: Information Shared With Others

Section B.3.a: Subordinates

Career professionals make every effort to ensure that privacy and confidentiality of clients are maintained by subordinates, including employees, supervisees, students, clerical assistants, and volunteers.

Section B.3.b: Treatment Teams

When client treatment involves a continued review or participation by a treatment team, the client will be informed of the team's existence and composition, information being shared, and the purposes of sharing such information.

Section B.3.c: Confidential Settings

When providing services to clients, career professionals strive to work only in settings where they can reasonably ensure client privacy. When such a setting is not possible, career professionals discuss the limitations of the setting and seek the client's consent to proceed. If the client does not wish to proceed with service in that setting, the career professional offers (where possible and available) alternative options and/or a referral to another career professional. When conferring with another professional, career professionals discuss confidential information only in settings in which they can reasonably ensure client privacy.

Section B.3.d: Third-Party Payers

Career professionals disclose information to third-party payers only when clients have authorized such disclosure and in accordance with federal, state, local, and/or institutional statute, law, regulation, or procedure.

Section B.3.e: Transmitting Confidential Information

Career professionals take precautions to ensure the confidentiality of information transmitted through the use of any medium.

Section B.3.f: Deceased Clients

Career professionals protect the confidentiality of deceased clients, consistent with legal requirements and agency or institutional policies.

Section B.4: Groups and Families

Section B.4.a: Group Work

When working with groups, career professionals clearly explain the importance and parameters of confidentiality for the specific group.

Section B.4.b: Providing Career Services to Multiple Family Members

When providing career services to multiple family members (e.g., spouses/partners, parent and child, etc.), career professionals clearly define who is considered "the client" and discuss expectations and limitations of confidentiality. Career professionals seek agreement and document in writing such agreement among all involved parties having capacity to give consent concerning each individual's right to confidentiality and any obligation to preserve the confidentiality of information known.

Section B.5: Clients Lacking Capacity to Give Informed Consent

Section B.5.a: Responsibility to Clients

When providing career services to minor clients or adult clients who lack the capacity to give voluntary, informed consent, career professionals protect the confidentiality of information received in the professional relationship as specified by federal and state laws, written policies, and applicable ethical standards.

Section B.5.b: Responsibility to Parents and Legal Guardians

Career professionals inform parents and legal guardians about the role of career professionals and the confidential nature of the professional relationship. Career professionals are sensitive to the cultural diversity of families and respect the inherent rights and responsibilities of parents/guardians over the welfare of their children/charges according to law. Career professionals work to establish, as appropriate, collaborative relationships with parents/guardians to best serve the needs and welfare of their clients.

Section B.5.c: Release of Confidential Information

When providing career services to minor clients or adult clients who lack the capacity to give voluntary consent to release confidential information, career professionals seek permission from an appropriate third party to disclose information. In such instances, career professionals inform clients consistent with their level of understanding and take culturally appropriate measures to safeguard client confidentiality.

Section B.6: Records and Documentation

Section B.6.a: Creating and Maintaining Confidential Records and Documentation

Career professionals create and maintain records and documentation necessary for rendering professional services. Career professionals ensure that records and documentation kept in any medium are secure and that only authorized persons have access to records.

Section B.6.b: Permission to Record

Career professionals obtain permission from clients prior to recording sessions through electronic or other means.

Section B.6.c: Permission to Observe

Career professionals obtain permission from clients prior to allowing observation of sessions, review of session transcripts, or viewing recordings of sessions with supervisors, subordinates, faculty, peers, or others within a training environment.

Section B.6.d: Client Access

Career professionals provide reasonable access to records and copies of records when requested by competent clients. Career professionals limit the access of clients to their records, or portions of their records, only when there is compelling evidence that such access would cause harm to the client and in accordance with federal, state, local, and/or institutional statute, law, regulation, or procedure. Career professionals document the request of clients and the rationale for withholding some or all of the record in the files of clients. In situations involving multiple clients, career professionals provide individual clients with only those parts of records that related directly to them and do not include confidential information related to any other client.

Section B.6.e: Assistance with Records

When clients request access to their records, career professionals provide assistance and consultation in interpreting such records.

Section B.6.f: Disclosure or Transfer

Unless exceptions to confidentiality exist, career professionals obtain written permission from clients to disclose or transfer records to legitimate third parties. Steps are taken to ensure that receivers of career services records are sensitive to their confidential nature.

Section B.6.g: Storage and Disposal After Termination

Career professionals store records following termination of services to ensure reasonable future access, maintain records in accordance with all applicable federal, state, local, and/or institutional statutes, laws, regulations, and procedures governing records, and dispose of client records and other sensitive materials in a manner that protects client confidentiality. Career professionals are encouraged to purge their files according to time frames acceptable to federal, state, local, and/or institutional statute, law, regulation, or procedure, particularly when there is no reasonable expectation that a client will benefit from maintaining the records any longer. Career professionals are expected to know and abide by all applicable federal, state, local, and/or institutional statutes, laws, regulations, and procedures regarding record keeping and disposal.

Section B.6.h: Reasonable Precautions

Career professionals take reasonable precautions to protect client confidentiality in the event of the career professional's termination of practice, incapacity, or death and appoint a records custodian when deemed appropriate.

Section B.7: Research and Training

Section B.7.a: Institutional Approval

When institutional approval is required, career professionals provide accurate information about their research proposals and obtain approval prior to conducting their research. They conduct research in accordance with the approved research protocol.

Section B.7.b: Adherence to Guidelines

Career professionals are responsible for understanding and adhering to state, federal, agency, or institutional policies or applicable guidelines regarding confidentiality in their research practices.

Section B.7.c: Confidentiality of Information Obtained in Research

Violations of participant privacy and confidentiality are risks of participation in research involving human participants, however, investigators maintain all research records in a secure manner. They explain to participants the risks of violations of privacy and confidentiality and disclose to participants any limits of confidentiality that can reasonably be expected. Regardless of the degree to which confidentiality will be maintained, investigators must disclose to participants any limits of confidentiality that can reasonably be expected.

Section B.7.d: Disclosure of Research Information

Career professionals do not disclose confidential information that reasonably could lead to the identification of a research participant unless they have obtained prior consent of the person. Use of data derived from professional relationships for purposes of training, research, or publication is confined to content that is disguised to ensure the anonymity of the individuals involved.

Section B.7.e: Agreement for Identification

Identification of clients, students, or supervisees in a presentation or publication is permissible only when they have reviewed the material and agreed to its presentation or publication.

Section B.8: Consultation

Section B.8.a: Agreements

When acting as consultants, career professionals seek agreements among all parties involved concerning each individual's rights to confidentiality, the obligation of each individual to preserve confidential information, and the limits of confidentiality of information shared by others.

Section B.8.b: Respect for Privacy

Information obtained in a consulting relationship is discussed for professional purposes only with persons directly involved with the case. Written and oral reports present only data germane to the purposes of the consultation, and every effort is made to protect client identity and to avoid undue invasion of privacy.

Section B.8.c: Disclosure of Confidential Information

When consulting with colleagues, career professionals do not disclose confidential information that reasonably could lead to the identification of a client or other person or organization with whom they have a confidential relationship unless they have obtained the prior consent of the person or organization or the disclosure cannot be avoided. They disclose information only to the extent necessary to achieve the purposes of the consultation.

SECTION C: PROFESSIONAL RESPONSIBILITY INTRODUCTION

Introduction

Career professionals provide open, honest, and accurate communication in dealing with the public and other professionals. They practice in a nondiscriminatory manner within the boundaries of professional and personal competence and have a responsibility to abide by the *NCDA Code of Ethics.* Career professionals actively participate in local, state, and national associations that foster the development and improvement of the provision of career services. Career professionals are encouraged to promote change at the individual, group, institutional, and societal levels in ways that improve the quality of life for individuals and groups and removes potential barriers to the provision or access of appropriate services being offered. Career professionals have a responsibility to the public to engage in ethical practice. Career Professionals have a responsibility to the public to engage in professional practices that are based on rigorous research methodologies. Career professionals are encouraged to contribute to society by devoting a portion of their professional activity to services for which there is little or no financial return (*pro bono publico*). In addition, career professionals engage in self-care activities to maintain and promote their emotional, physical, mental, and spiritual well-being to best meet their professional responsibilities.

Section C.1: Knowledge of and Compliance with Standards

Career professionals have a responsibility to read, understand, and follow the *NCDA Code of Ethics* and adhere to all applicable federal, state, local, and/or institutional statutes, laws, regulations, and procedures.

Section C.2: Professional Competence

Section C.2.a: Boundaries of Competence

Career professionals practice only within the boundaries of their competence, based on their education, training, supervised experience, state and national professional credentials, and appropriate professional experience. Whereas multicultural counseling competency is required across all counseling specialties, career professionals gain knowledge, personal awareness, sensitivity, dispositions, and skills pertinent to being a culturally competent career professional.

Section C.2.b: New Specialty Areas of Practice

Career professionals practice in specialty areas new to them only after obtaining appropriate education, training, and supervised experience. While developing skills in new specialty areas, career professionals take steps to ensure the competence of their work and to protect others from possible harm.

Section C.2.c: Qualified for Employment

Career professionals accept employment only for positions for which they are qualified by education, training, supervised experience, state and national professional credentials, and appropriate professional experience. Career professionals hire for professional positions only individuals who are qualified and competent for those positions.

Section C.2.d: Monitor Effectiveness

Career professionals continually monitor their effectiveness as professionals and take steps to improve when necessary. Career professionals take reasonable steps to seek peer supervision, as needed, to evaluate their efficacy as career professionals.

Section C.2.e: Consultation on Ethical Obligations

Career professionals take reasonable steps to consult with other career professionals, the NCDA Ethics Committee, and/or related practitioners when they have questions regarding their ethical obligations or professional activities.

Section C.2.f: Continuing Education

Career professionals recognize the need for continuing education to acquire and maintain a reasonable level of awareness of current scientific and professional information in their fields of activity. They take steps to maintain competence in the skills they use, are open to new proce-dures, and keep current with the populations with whom they work.

Section C.2.g: Impairment

Career professionals are alert to the signs of impairment from their own physical, mental, or emotional problems and refrain from offering or providing professional services when such impairment is likely to harm a client or others. They seek assistance for problems that reach the level of professional impairment, and, if necessary, they limit, suspend, or terminate their professional responsibilities until such time as it is determined that they may safely resume their work. Career professionals assist colleagues or supervisors in recognizing their own professional impairment. They provide consultation and assistance, when warranted, with colleagues or supervisors showing signs of impairment and intervene as appropriate to prevent imminent harm to clients.

Section C.2.h: Incapacitation, Death, or Termination of Practice

Career professionals prepare and plan for transfer of clients and files and disseminate to an identified colleague or "records custodian" a plan for the transfer of clients and files in case of their incapacitation, death, or termination of practice.

Section C.3: Advertising and Soliciting Clients

Section C.3.a: Accurate Advertising

When advertising or otherwise representing their services to the public, career professionals identify their credentials in an accurate manner that is not false, misleading, deceptive, or fraudulent.

Section C.3.b: Testimonials

Career professionals who use testimonials do not solicit them from individuals who may be vulnerable to undue influence. Career professionals discuss with clients the implications of and obtain permission for the use of any testimonial.

Section C.3.c: Statements by Others

Career professionals make reasonable efforts to ensure that statements made by others about them or the services they provide are accurate.

Section C.3.d: Recruiting Through Employment

Career professionals do not use their places of employment or institutional affiliations to recruit or gain clients, supervisees, or consultees for their private practices, unless they have permission. If permitted to solicit for their private practices, career professionals must make potential clients, supervisees, or consultees aware of the free or low-cost services already provided by them or others through their place of employment or institutional affiliation.

Section C.3.e: Products and Training Advertisements

Career professionals who develop products related to their profession or conduct workshops or training events ensure that the advertisements concerning these products or events are accurate and disclose adequate information for consumers to make informed choices.

Section C.3.f: Promoting to Those Served

Career professionals do not use individual consultation, teaching, training, or supervisory relationships to promote their products or training events in a manner that is deceptive or would exert undue influence on individuals who may be vulnerable. However, educators may adopt textbooks and/or other materials they have authored or developed for instructional purposes.

Section C.4: Professional Qualifications

Section C.4.a: Accurate Representation

Career professionals claim or imply only professional qualifications actually completed, use professional titles accurately, and correct any known misrepresentations of their qualifications by others. Career professionals truthfully represent the qualifications of their professional colleagues. Career professionals clearly distinguish between paid and volunteer work experience and accurately describe their continuing education and specialized training.

Section C.4.b: Credentials

Career professionals claim only licenses or certifications that are current and in good standing.

Section C.4.c: Educational Degrees

Career professionals clearly differentiate between earned and honorary degrees.

Section C.4.d: Implying Doctoral-Level Competence

Career professionals clearly state their highest earned degree in counseling or a closely related field. Career professionals do not imply doctoral-level competence when possessing only a master's degree in counseling or a related field. Career professionals do not use the title "Dr." nor refer to themselves as "Dr." in a counseling or career services context when their doctorate is not in counseling or a related field. Career professionals do not use "ABD" (all but dissertation) or other such terms to imply competency.

Section C.4.e: Program Accreditation Status

Career professionals accurately represent the accreditation status of their degree program at the time the degree was earned.

Section C.4.f: Professional Membership

Career professionals clearly differentiate between current, active memberships and former memberships in associations. Career professionals only claim a membership designation in NCDA for which their education and experience entitles them.

Section C.5: Nondiscrimination

Career professionals do not condone or engage in discrimination against any individual based on age, culture, mental/physical disability, ethnicity, race, religion/spirituality, creed, gender, gender identity, sexual orientation, marital/partnership status, language preference, socioeconomic status, any other characteristics not specifically relevant to job performance, or any basis prohibited by law. Career professionals do not discriminate against clients, students, employees, supervisees, or research participants in a manner that has a negative impact on these persons.

Section C.6: Public Responsibility

Section C.6.a: Sexual Harassment

Career professionals do not engage in or condone sexual harassment. Sexual harassment is defined as sexual solicitation, physical advances, or verbal or nonverbal conduct that is sexual in nature, that occurs in connection with professional activities or roles, and that is either

1. unwelcome, offensive, or creates a hostile workplace or learning environment, and career professionals know or are told this; or
2. sufficiently severe or intense to be perceived as harassment to a reasonable person in the context in which the behavior occurred. Sexual harassment can consist of a single intense or severe act or multiple persistent or pervasive acts.

Section C.6.b: *Reports to Third Parties*

Career professionals are accurate, honest, and objective in reporting their professional activities and judgments to appropriate third parties, including courts, health insurance companies, those who are the recipients of evaluation reports, and others.

Section C.6.c: *Media Presentations*

When career professionals provide advice or comment by means of public lectures, demonstrations, radio or television programs, prerecorded tapes, technology-based applications, printed articles, mailed material, or other media, they take reasonable precautions to ensure that

1. the statements are based on appropriate professional literature and practice,
2. the statements are otherwise consistent with the *NCDA Code of Ethics,* and
3. the recipients of the information are informed that a professional relationship has not been established.

Section C.6.d: *Exploitation of Others*

Career professionals do not exploit others in their professional relationships.

Section C.6.e: *Scientific Bases for Treatment Modalities*

Career professionals use techniques/procedures/modalities that are grounded in theory, are generally considered to be established professional practice in the fields of counseling and career development, and/or have an empirical or scientific foundation. Career professionals who do not must define the techniques/procedures as "unproven" or "developing" and explain the potential risks and ethical considerations of using such techniques/procedures and take steps to protect clients from possible harm.

Section C.6.f: *Contributing to the Public Good* (Pro Bono Publico)

Career professionals make a reasonable effort to provide services to the public for which there is little or no financial return (e.g., speaking to groups, sharing professional information, offering reduced fees).

Section C.7: Responsibility to Other Professionals

Section C.7.a: *Personal Public Statements*

When making personal statements in a public context, career professionals clarify that they are speaking from their personal perspectives and that they are not speaking on behalf of all career professionals or the profession.

Section C.8: Policies and Guidelines

Section C.8.a: *Creating and Maintaining Policy Statements and Guidelines*

As part of informed consent, policy statements and guidelines assist in anticipating questions and concerns and serve as part of an ongoing dialogue with clients. Career professionals are encouraged to create policy statements and guidelines for use in their practice. Career professionals ensure that clients are fully informed, understand, and agree to the parameters and limitations of receiving career services. Policy statements and guidelines may include, but are not limited to, all areas of informed consent, such as incorporating the use of social media and electronic communication in professional practice, privacy and confidentiality (e.g., limits of confidentiality, documentation, and records maintenance), boundaries and multiple relationships, collection of fees, termination of services, etc.

Career professionals are expected to review their policy statements and guidelines annually and to update them as needed.

SECTION D: RELATIONSHIPS WITH OTHER PROFESSIONALS

Introduction

Career professionals recognize that the quality of their interactions with colleagues can influence the quality of services provided to clients. They work to become knowledgeable about colleagues within and outside the profession. Career professionals develop positive working relationships and systems of communication with colleagues to enhance services to clients. Career professionals may provide coaching and/or consultation to individuals, groups, or organizations. If career professionals perform such services, they must provide only the services that are within the scope of their professional competence and qualifications.

Section D.1. Relationships with Colleagues, Employers, and Employees

Section D.1.a: *Different Approaches*

Career professionals are respectful of approaches to career services that differ from their own. Career professionals are respectful of traditions and practices of other professional groups with which they work.

Section D.1.b: Forming Relationships

Career professionals work to develop and strengthen interdisciplinary relations with colleagues from other disciplines to best serve clients.

Section D.1.c: Interdisciplinary Teamwork

Career professionals who are members of interdisciplinary teams delivering multifaceted services to clients keep the focus on how to best serve the clients. They participate in and contribute to decisions that affect the well-being of clients by drawing on the perspectives, values, and experiences of the profession and those of colleagues from other disciplines.

Section D.1.d: Confidentiality

When career professionals are required by law, institutional policy, or extraordinary circumstances to serve in more than one role in judicial or administrative proceedings, they clarify role expectations and the parameters of confidentiality with their colleagues.

Section D.1.e: Establishing Professional and Ethical Obligations

Career professionals who are members of interdisciplinary teams clarify professional and ethical obligations of the team as a whole and of its individual members. When a team decision raises ethical concerns, career professionals first attempt to resolve the concern within the team. If they cannot reach resolution among team members, career professionals pursue other avenues to address their concerns consistent with client well-being.

Section D.1.f: Personnel Selection and Assignment

Career professionals select competent staff and assign responsibilities compatible with their knowledge, skills, and experiences.

Section D.1.g: Employer Policies

The acceptance of employment in an agency or institution implies that career professionals are in agreement with its general policies and principles. Career professionals strive to reach agreement with employers as to acceptable standards of conduct that allow for changes in institutional policy conducive to the growth and development of clients.

Section D.1.h: Negative Conditions

Career professionals alert their employers of inappropriate policies and practices. They attempt to effect changes in such policies or procedures through constructive action within the organization. When such policies are potentially disruptive or damaging to clients or may limit the effectiveness of services provided and change cannot be achieved, career professionals take appropriate further action. Such action may include referral to appropriate certification, accreditation, or state licensure organizations, or voluntary termination of employment.

Section D.1.i: Protection from Punitive Action

Career professionals take care not to harass or dismiss an employee who has acted in a responsible and ethical manner to expose inappropriate employer policies or practices.

Section D.2: Coaching and Consultation

Section D.2.a: Coaching and Consultant Competency

Career professionals take reasonable steps to ensure that they have the appropriate resources and competencies when providing coaching and/or consultation services. Career professionals provide appropriate referral resources when requested or needed.

Section D.2.b: Understanding Consultees

When providing coaching or consultation, career professionals attempt to develop with their consultees a clear understanding of problem definition, goals for change, and predicted consequences of interventions selected.

Section D.2.c: Coach/Consultant Goals

The coaching/consulting relationship is one in which consultee adaptability and growth toward self-direction are consistently encouraged and cultivated.

Section D.2.d: Informed Consent in Coaching and Consultation

When providing consultation, career professionals have an obligation to review, in writing and orally, the rights and responsibilities of career professionals and consultees. Career professionals use clear and understandable language to inform all parties involved about the purpose of the services to be provided, relevant costs, potential risks and benefits, and the limits of confidentiality. Working in conjunction with the consultee, career professionals attempt to develop a clear definition of the problem, goals for change, and predicted consequences of interventions that are culturally responsive and appropriate to the needs of consultees.

SECTION E: EVALUATION, ASSESSMENT, AND INTERPRETATION _____

Introduction

Career professionals use assessment instruments as one component of the career services process, taking into account the client's personal and cultural context. Career professionals promote the well-being of individual clients or groups of clients by developing and using appropriate career, educational, and psychological assessment instruments.

Section E.1: General

Section E.1.a: Assessment

The primary purpose of educational, psychological, and career assessments is to provide measurements that are valid and reliable in either comparative or absolute terms. These include, but are not limited to, measurements of ability, personality, interest, intelligence, achievement, skills, values, and performance. Career professionals recognize the need to interpret the statements in this section as applying to both quantitative and qualitative assessments.

Section E.1.b: Client Welfare

Career professionals do not misuse assessment results and interpretations, and they take reasonable steps to prevent others from misusing the information these tools provide. They respect the client's right to know the results, the interpretations made, and the bases for career professionals' conclusions and recommendations.

Section E.2: Competence to Use and Interpret Assessment Instruments

Section E.2.a: Limits of Competence

Career professionals utilize only those testing and assessment services for which they have been trained and are competent in administering and interpreting. Career professionals using technology-assisted test interpretations are trained in the construct being measured and the specific instrument being used prior to using its technology-based application. Career professionals take reasonable measures to ensure the proper use of psychological and career assessment techniques by persons under their supervision.

Section E.2.b: Appropriate Use

Career professionals are responsible for the appropriate application, scoring, interpretation, and use of assessment instruments relevant to the needs of the client, whether they score and interpret such assessments themselves or use technology or other services.

Section E.2.c: Decisions Based on Results

Career professionals responsible for decisions involving individuals or policies that are based on assessment results have a thorough understanding of psychometrics involving educational, psychological, and career measurement, including validation criteria, assessment research, and guidelines for assessment development and use.

Section E.3: Informed Consent in Assessment

Section E.3.a: Explanation to Clients

Prior to assessment, career professionals explain the nature and purposes of assessment and the specific use of results by potential recipients. The explanation will be given in the language of the client (or other legally authorized person on behalf of the client), unless an explicit exception has been agreed upon in advance. Career professionals consider the client's personal or cultural context, the level of the client's understanding of the results, and the impact of the results on the client.

Section E.3.b: Recipients of Results

Career professionals consider the examinee's welfare, explicit understandings, and prior agreements in determining who receives the assessment results. Career professionals include accurate and appropriate interpretations with any release of individual or group assessment results.

Section E.4: Release of Data to Qualified Professionals

Career professionals release assessment data in which the client is identified only with the consent of the client or the client's legal representative. Such data are released only to persons recognized by career professionals as qualified to interpret the data.

Section E.5: Diagnosis and Recommendations

Section E.5.a: Proper Diagnosis and Recommendations

Career professionals take special care to provide proper diagnosis and recommendations and do so only when making a diagnosis is appropriate and when properly trained. Assessment techniques (including personal interviews) used to determine client care (e.g., locus of treatment, type of treatment/services, or recommended follow-up) are carefully selected and appropriately used.

Section E.5.b: Cultural Sensitivity

Career professionals recognize that culture affects the manner in which clients' issues are defined. Clients' socioeconomic and cultural experiences are considered when making a diagnosis.

Section E.5.c: Historical and Social Prejudices in Diagnosis

Career professionals recognize historical and social prejudices in the misdiagnosis and pathologizing of certain individuals and groups and the role career professionals can play in avoiding the perpetuation of these prejudices through proper diagnosis, recommendations, and provision of services.

Section E.5.d: Refraining From Diagnosis

Career professionals may refrain from making and/or reporting a diagnosis or recommendation if they believe it would cause harm to the client or others. Career professionals carefully consider both the positive and negative implications of a diagnosis/recommendation.

Section E.6: Instrument Selection

Section E.6.a: Appropriateness of Instruments

Career professionals carefully consider the validity, reliability, psychometric limitations, and appropriateness of instruments when selecting assessments and, when possible, use multiple forms of assessment, data, and/or instruments in forming conclusions, diagnoses, or recommendations.

Section E.6.b: Referral Information

If a client is referred to a third party for assessment, the career professional provides specific referral questions and sufficient objective data about the client to ensure that appropriate assessment instruments are utilized.

Section E.7: Conditions of Assessment Administration

Section E.7.a: Administration Conditions

Career professionals administer assessments under the same conditions that were established in their standard-

ization. When assessments are not administered under standard conditions, as may be necessary to accommodate clients with disabilities, or when unusual behavior or irregularities occur during the administration, those conditions are noted in interpretation, and the results may be designated as invalid or of questionable validity.

Section E.7.b: Technological Administration

Career professionals ensure that administration programs function properly and provide clients with accurate results.

Section E.7.c: Unsupervised Assessments

Unless the assessment instrument is designed, intended, and validated for self-administration and/or scoring, career professionals do not permit inadequately supervised use of any assessment.

Section E.7.d: Provision of Favorable Conditions

Career professionals provide an appropriate environment for the administration of assessments (e.g., privacy, comfort, freedom from distraction).

Section E.8: Multicultural Issues/ Diversity in Assessment

Career professionals use, with caution, assessment techniques that were normed on populations other than that of the client. Career professionals recognize the possible effects of age, color, culture, disability, ethnic group, gender, race, language preference, religion, spirituality, sexual orientation, and socioeconomic status on test administration and interpretation, and place test results in proper perspective with other relevant factors. Career professionals use caution when selecting assessments for culturally diverse populations to avoid the use of instruments that lack appropriate psychometric properties for the client population.

Section E.9: Scoring and Interpretation of Assessments

Section E.9.a: Reporting

When career professionals report assessment results, they consider the client's personal and cultural background, the level of the client's understanding of the results, and the impact of the results on the client. In reporting assessment results, career professionals indicate reservations that exist regarding validity or reliability due to circumstances of the assessment or the inappropriate-ness of the norms for the person tested.

Section E.9.b: Research Instruments

Career professionals exercise caution when interpreting the results of research instruments not having sufficient technical data to support respondent results. The specific purposes for the use of such instruments are stated explicitly to the examinee. Career professionals qualify any conclusions, diagnoses, or recommendations made that are based on assessments or instruments with questionable validity or reliability.

Section E.9.c: Assessment Services

Career professionals who provide assessment scoring and interpretation services to support the assessment process confirm the validity of such interpretations. They understand and accurately describe the purpose, norms, validity, reliability, and applications of the procedures and any special qualifications applicable to their use. The public offering of an automated test interpretation service is considered a professional-to-professional consultation. The formal responsibility of the career professional is to the individual/organization requesting the assessment, but the ultimate and overriding responsibility is to the client.

Section E.10: Assessment Security

Career professionals maintain the integrity and security of tests and other assessment techniques consistent with legal and contractual obligations. Career professionals do not appropriate, reproduce, or modify published assessments or parts thereof without acknowledgment and permission from the publisher.

Section E.11: Obsolete Assessments and Outdated Results

Career professionals do not use data or results from assessments that are obsolete or outdated for the current purpose. Career professionals make every effort to prevent the misuse of obsolete measures and assessment data by others.

Section E.12: Assessment Construction

Career professionals use established scientific procedures, relevant standards, and current professional knowledge for assessment design in the development, publication, and utilization of educational and psychological assessment techniques.

Section E.13: Forensic Evaluation: Evaluation for Legal Proceedings

Section E.13.a: Primary Obligations

When providing forensic evaluations, the primary obligation of career professionals is to produce objective findings that can be substantiated based on information and techniques appropriate to the evaluation, which may include examination of the individual and/or review of records. Career professionals form professional opinions based on their professional knowledge and expertise that can be supported by the data gathered in evaluations. Career professionals define the limits of their reports or testimony, especially when an examination of the individual has not been conducted.

Section E.13.b: Consent for Evaluation

Individuals being evaluated are informed in writing that the relationship is for the purposes of an evaluation, not to provide career services. Entities or individuals who will receive the evaluation report are identified. Written consent to be evaluated is obtained from those being evaluated unless a court orders evaluations to be conducted without the written consent of individuals being evaluated. When children or vulnerable adults are being evaluated, informed written consent is obtained from a parent or guardian.

Section E.13.c: Client Evaluation Prohibited

Career professionals do not evaluate current or former clients, clients' romantic partners, or clients' family members for forensic purposes. Career professionals do not counsel individuals they are evaluating.

Section E.13.d: Avoid Potentially Harmful Relationships

Career professionals who provide forensic evaluations avoid potentially harmful professional or personal relationships with family members, romantic partners, and close friends of individuals they are evaluating or have evaluated in the past.

SECTION F: PROVIDING CAREER SERVICES ONLINE, TECHNOLOGY, AND SOCIAL MEDIA

Introduction

Career professionals actively attempt to understand the evolving nature of the profession with regard to providing career services online, using technology and/or social media, and how such resources may be used to better serve their clients. Career professionals strive to become knowledgeable about these resources, recognizing that periodic training is needed to develop necessary technical and professional competencies. Career professionals understand the additional concerns related to providing career services online and using technology and/or social media, and make every attempt to protect confidentiality and data security, ensure transparency and equitable treatment of clients, and meet any legal and ethical requirements for the use of such resources.

Section F.1: Knowledge and Legal Considerations

Section F.1.a: Knowledge and Competency

Career professionals who engage in providing career services online and using technology and/or social media develop knowledge and skills regarding related technical, ethical, and legal considerations. Career professionals understand and follow the terms of service of any technology or social media platform employed.

Section F.1.b: Laws and Statutes

Career professionals who engage in providing career services online and using technology and/or social media within their practice understand that they may be subject to laws and regulations of both the career professional's practicing location and the client's place of work/residence. Career professionals ensure that use of technology services with clients is in accordance with all applicable federal, state, local, and/or institutional statutes, laws, regulations, and procedures, particularly when the services are offered via technology across state lines and/or international boundaries.

Section F.1.c: Outside Assistance

When necessary and appropriate, career professionals seek business, legal, and technical assistance when using technical applications, particularly when the use of such applications crosses state lines and/or international boundaries.

Section F.2: Informed Consent and Security

Section F.2.a: Informed Consent and Disclosure

Clients have the freedom to choose whether to access career services online or to engage in the use of technol-

ogy and/or social media within the career development process. In addition to the usual and customary protocol of informed consent between career professional and client for face-to-face services, the following issues, unique to the use of career services online, and the use of technology and/or social media, should be addressed in the informed consent process:

- professional credentials, physical location of practice, and contact information;
- risks and benefits of engaging in the use of career services online, technology and/or social media;
- possibility of technology failure and alternate methods of service delivery;
- anticipated response time;
- emergency procedures to follow when the career professional is not available;
- time zone differences, local customs, and cultural and/or language differences that may affect delivery of services;
- where applicable, pertinent legal rights and limitations governing the practice of a profession over state lines or international boundaries; and
- social media policy.

Section F.2.b: Confidentiality and Limitations

Career professionals inform clients about the inherent limits of confidentiality when using technology and acknowledge the limitations of maintaining the confidentiality of electronic records and transmissions. Where feasible, career professionals inform clients of anyone who may have access to such records or transmissions. Career professionals urge clients to be aware of those to whom they give access to information disclosed using this medium during the professional relationship.

Section F.2.c: Security

Career professionals take reasonable precautions to ensure the confidentiality of information transmitted through any electronic means, including using current encryption standards within their websites and/or technology-based communications where appropriate to meet applicable legal requirements.

Section F.3: Client Verification

Career professionals who engage in providing career services online, and use technology and/or social media to interact with clients take steps to verify the client's identity at the beginning and throughout the working relationship. Verification can include, but is not limited to, using code words, numbers, graphics, or other nonde-script identifiers.

Section F.4: Providing Career Services Online

Section F.4.a: Benefits and Limitations

Career professionals inform clients of the benefits and limitations of using technology applications in the provision of career services. Such technologies include, but are not limited to, computer hardware and/or software, telephones and applications, social media and Internet-based applications and other audio and/or video communication, or data storage devices or media.

Section F.4.b: Professional Boundaries in Providing Career Services Online

Career professionals understand the necessity of maintaining a professional relationship with their clients. Career professionals discuss and establish professional boundaries with clients regarding the appropriate use and application of technology and the limitations of its use (e.g., lack of confidentiality, times when not appropriate to use). When technology-assisted career services are deemed inappropriate by the career professional or client, career professionals provide appropriate alternatives, including face-to-face service. If the career professional is not able to provide face-to-face services (e.g., lives in another state), the career professional assists the client in identifying appropriate services.

Section F.4.c: Technology-Assisted Services

When providing technology-assisted services, career professionals make reasonable efforts to determine that clients are fully capable of using the application and that the application is appropriate for the needs of the client. Career professionals verify that clients understand the purpose and operation of technology applications and follow up with clients to address any issues that may arise.

Section F.4.d: Access

Career professionals provide information to clients regarding reasonable access to pertinent applications when providing technology-assisted services. This access may include being aware of free and/or low cost public access points to technology resources and the Internet within the community, so that a lack of financial resources does not create a significant barrier to clients accessing career services or information, assessment, or instructional resources. If career professionals are unable to provide access to technology resources, they provide an alternative method of service delivery.

Section F.4.e: Communication Differences in Electronic Media

Career professionals consider the differences between face-to-face and electronic communication (nonverbal and verbal cues) and how these may affect the career development process. Career professionals educate clients on how to prevent and address potential misunderstandings arising from the lack of visual cues and voice intonations when communicating electronically.

Section F.4.f: Use of Assessments via Electronic Media

When using assessments carried out via electronic media, career professionals are responsible for knowing and abiding by other standard ethical practices related to client assessment, such as those outlined in Section E of this *NCDA Code of Ethics*. In addition, where applicable, career professionals should:

- determine if the assessments have been tested for online delivery and ensure that their psychometric properties are the same as in print form; or the client must be informed that the assessments have not yet been tested for this mode of delivery;
- determine if the assessments have been validated for self-help use or that appropriate intervention is provided before and after completion of the assessment resource if the resource has not been validated for self-help use;
- make every effort to protect the confidentiality of client results; and
- refer clients to qualified career professionals in his or her geographic area, if there is evidence that the client does not understand the assessment results.

Section F.5: Records

Career professionals create and maintain electronic documents and records in accordance with relevant laws and statutes and all other relevant aspects of this *NCDA Code of Ethics*. Career professionals inform clients on how records are maintained electronically. This includes, but is not limited to, the type of encryption and security assigned to the records, and if/for how long archival storage of transaction records is maintained.

Section F.6: Web Maintenance and Technology Development

Section F.6.a: Maintaining Websites and Technology Resources

Career professionals who maintain websites or other technology resources do the following:

- Regularly ensure that electronic links are working and are professionally appropriate.
- Provide electronic links to relevant licensure and professional certification boards to protect consumer rights and facilitate addressing ethical concerns.
- Assist clients in determining the validity and reliability of information found on websites and in other technology applications.
- If a website includes links to other websites, the career professional who creates this linkage is responsible for ensuring that the services to which the site is linked meet all applicable ethical standards. If this is not possible, career professionals should post a disclaimer explaining that the linked site may not meet all applicable ethical standards and (if known) which standards are not met by the site.

Section F.6.b: Multicultural and Disability Considerations

Career professionals who maintain websites and other technology resources provide accessibility or inform persons with disabilities of assistive devices that will make the content accessible, when feasible. They provide access to translation capabilities for clients who have a different primary language, when feasible. Career professionals acknowledge the imperfect nature of such translations and accessibilities.

Section F.6.c: Qualifications of the Developer or Provider

Websites and other services designed to assist clients with career planning and job searching should be developed with content input from career professionals. The service should clearly state the qualifications and credentials of the developers.

Section F.6.d: Managing Job Posting and Searching Websites or Databases

All job postings must represent a valid opening for which those searching have an opportunity to apply. It is encouraged that job postings be removed from the database once application acceptance deadlines have passed or shortly after positions have been filled. Names, addresses, résumés, and other information that may be gained about individuals should not be used for any purposes other than provision of further information about job openings.

Section F.7: Social Media

Section F.7.a: Creating and Maintaining a Virtual Professional Presence

When creating a virtual professional presence, career professionals carefully reflect on the goals and objectives for using available social media tools. Career professionals who maintain a professional virtual presence commit the necessary time and effort to ensure a continual presence, avoiding extended gaps in involvement or communication with clients that could have negative effects.

Section F.7.b: Separating Professional Presence from Personal Presence

When career professionals maintain a professional and personal presence on social media, separate professional and personal web pages and profiles are created to clearly distinguish between the two kinds of virtual presence.

Section F.7.c: Identifying Professional Roles and Expertise

When using social media, career professionals clearly identify their names, training and expertise, and affiliation to an organization or employer. Career professionals only post information and address questions that are within the scope of their professional competence and qualifications.

Section F.7.d: Maintaining Confidentiality in Virtual Spaces

Career professionals act judiciously to protect the privacy, confidentiality, and reputation of clients, colleagues, organizations, and others. Applicable federal guidelines (such as HIPAA and FERPA) provide guidance on protecting confidential and proprietary information. Career professionals must avoid posting identifiable images (without obtaining permission of those identified) or any personally identifiable information that could be used to locate someone offline (e.g., phone numbers or addresses). In no circumstance, should protected or highly-sensitive information be shared via social media platforms (e.g., Social Security number, financial information, credit card or payment information, counseling or health records, information subject to nondisclosure agreements, etc.).

Section F.7.e: Respect Privacy of Clients' Virtual Presence

Career professionals respect the privacy of their clients' presence on social media, and avoid searching clients' virtual presence unless given consent to view such information.

Section F.7.f: Social Media as Part of Informed Consent

As a part of the informed consent procedure, career professionals clearly explain to their clients the benefits, limitations, and boundaries of the use of social media.

Section F.7.g: Social Media Policies and Fair and Equitable Treatment

Career professionals develop social media strategies and guidelines that provide fair and equitable treatment to all clients. For clients who may lack access or have limited technical knowledge, fair and equitable treatment may mean providing alternative service delivery methods.

Additionally, fair and equitable treatment means creating an approach to using social media that is consistently applied and clearly communicated to all clients. For example, some organizations may choose a policy of not linking to any current clients, while another organization allows career professionals to link to current clients only when the client makes a request and agrees to a social media informed consent. Still another organization may find it more favorable to "link" all clients to an organization page rather than to link clients to a career professional's individual social media account. Career professionals work within their organizations to develop and clearly communicate an approach so that the social media practice is transparent, consistent, and easily understood by clients.

Section F.7.h: Permanence of Information, Accuracy, and Audience

Career professionals recognize that information posted on social media sites are largely permanent and easily shared beyond the privacy settings of any particular site. Postings should be respectful and appropriate for broad audiences. Postings should also be regularly checked to ensure accuracy of information shared.

Section F.7.i: Respect Copyright and Original Sources

Career professionals post information, photos, videos, etc. only in compliance with copyright, trademark, and fair use laws. When others' content is posted, sources are clearly identified, with links to original materials if applicable.

Section F.7.j: Educating Clients about the Role of Social Media in the Career Development Process

Career professionals educate their clients about the role of social media platforms in the career development and job search process. This includes encouraging both knowledge of the potential impact that social media use may have on the professional relationship between the client and career professional, and promoting an understanding of the benefits and risks of using social media within the career exploration, job search, and career management process.

SECTION G: SUPERVISION, TRAINING, AND TEACHING _____

Introduction

Career professionals foster meaningful and respectful professional relationships and maintain appropriate boundaries with supervisees and students. Career professionals have theoretical and pedagogical foundations for their work and aim to be fair, accurate, and honest in their assessments of other career professionals, students, and supervisees.

Section G.1: Client Welfare

Section G.1.a: Client Welfare

A primary obligation of supervisors and educators is to monitor the services provided by other career professionals or students for whom they have responsibility. Supervisors and educators also monitor client welfare and supervisee/student performance and professional development. To fulfill these obligations, supervisors and educators meet regularly with supervisees/students. Supervisees and students have a responsibility to understand and follow the *NCDA Code of Ethics*.

Section G.1.b: Credentials

Supervisors and educators work to ensure that supervisees/students communicate their qualifications to render services to their clients.

Section G.1.c: Informed Consent and Client Rights

Supervisors and educators make supervisees/students aware of client rights including the protection of client privacy and confidentiality in the professional relationship. Supervisees/students provide clients with professional disclosure information and inform them of how the supervision process influences the limits of confidentiality. Supervisees/students make clients aware of who will have access to records of the professional relationship and how these records will be utilized.

Section G.2: Supervisor Competence

Section G.2.a: Supervisor Preparation

Prior to offering supervision services, career professionals are trained in supervision methods and techniques.

Career professionals who offer supervision services regularly pursue continuing education activities including both career services and supervision topics and skills.

Section G.2.b: Multicultural Issues/ Diversity in Supervision

Supervisors are aware of and address the role of multiculturalism/diversity in the supervisory relationship.

Section G.2.c: Online Supervision

When using technology in supervision, supervisors are competent in the use of those technologies. Supervisors take the necessary precautions to protect the confidentiality of all information transmitted through any electronic means.

Section G.3: Multiple Relationships

Section G.3.a: Relationship Boundaries

Supervisors and educators clearly define and maintain ethical professional, personal, and social relationships with their supervisees/students, and they avoid or keep to a minimum nonprofessional relationships with current supervisees/students. If supervisors and educators must assume other professional roles (e.g., clinical and administrative supervisor, instructor, etc.) with supervisees/students, they work to minimize potential conflicts and explain to supervisees/students the expectations and responsibilities associated with each role. They do not engage in any form of nonprofessional interaction in which there is a risk of potential harm to the supervisee/ student or that may compromise the supervisory/training relationship, experience or grades assigned.

Section G.3.b: Sexual Relationships

Any form of sexual or romantic interactions or relationships with current students or supervisees is prohibited.

Section G.3.c: Harassment

Supervisors and educators do not condone or subject students or supervisees to harassment, sexual or otherwise.

Section G.3.d: Close Relatives and Friends

Supervisors and educators avoid accepting close relatives, romantic partners, or friends as students/supervisees and are prohibited from engaging in supervisory or training relationships with individual with whom they have an inability to remain objective.

Section G.3.e: Potentially Beneficial Relationships

Supervisors and educators are aware of the power differential in their relationships with supervisees/students. If they believe nonprofessional relationships with a supervisee/ student may be potentially beneficial to the supervisee/student, they take precautions similar to those taken by career professionals when working with clients. Examples of potentially beneficial interactions or relationships include attending a formal ceremony; hospital visits; providing support during a stressful event; or mutual membership in a professional association, organization, or community. Supervisors and educators engage in open discussions with supervisees/students when they consider entering into relationships with them outside of their supervisory or training roles. Before engaging in nonprofessional relationships, supervisors and educators discuss with supervisees/students and document the rationale for such interactions, potential benefits or drawbacks, and anticipated consequences for the supervisee. Supervisors and educators clarify the specific nature and limitations of the additional role(s) they will have with the supervisee/student.

Section G.3.f: Relationships with Former Supervisees/Students

Supervisors and educators are aware of the power differential in the relationship between supervisors and educators and supervisees/students. Supervisors and educators foster open discussions with former supervisees/students when considering engaging in a social, sexual, or other intimate relationship. Supervisors and educators discuss with the former supervisee/student how their former relationship may affect the change in relationship.

Section G.4: Supervisor Responsibilities

Section G.4.a: Informed Consent for Supervision

Supervisors are responsible for incorporating into their supervision the principles of informed consent and participation. Supervisors inform supervisees of the policies and procedures to which they are to adhere and the mechanisms for due process appeal of individual supervisory actions.

Section G.4.b: Emergencies and Absences

Supervisors establish and communicate to supervisees procedures for contacting them or, in their absence, alternative on-call supervisors to assist in handling crises.

Section G.4.c: Standards for Supervisees

Supervisors make their supervisees aware of professional and ethical standards and legal responsibilities.

Section G.4.d: Termination of the Supervisory Relationship

Supervisors or supervisees have the right to terminate the supervisory relationship with adequate notice. Reasons for withdrawal are provided to the other party. When cultural, professional, or other issues are crucial to the viability of the supervisory relationship, both parties make efforts to resolve differences. When termination is warranted, supervisors make appropriate referrals to possible alternative supervisors.

Section G.5: Student Responsibilities and Evaluation, Remediation, and Endorsement

Section G.5.a: Ethical Responsibilities

Students/supervisees have a responsibility to understand and follow the *NCDA Code of Ethics*. Students/supervisees have the same obligation to clients as those required of other career professionals.

Section G.5.b: Impairment

Students/supervisees monitor themselves for signs of impairment from their own physical, mental, or emotional problems and refrain from offering or providing professional services when such impairment is likely to harm a client or others. They notify their faculty and/or supervisors and seek assistance for problems that reach the level of professional impairment, and, if necessary, they limit, suspend, or terminate their professional responsibilities until it is determined that they may safely resume their work.

Section G.5.c: Professional Disclosure

Before providing services, students/supervisees disclose their status and explain how this status affects the limits of confidentiality. Supervisors and educators ensure that clients are aware of the services rendered and the qualifications of the students/supervisees rendering those services. Students/supervisees obtain client permission before they use any information concerning the counseling relationship in the training process.

Section G.5.d: Evaluation

Supervisors and educators clearly state to students/supervisees, prior to and throughout the training program, the levels of competency expected, appraisal methods, and timing of evaluations for all areas of competency. Supervisors and educators document and provide students/supervisees with ongoing performance appraisal and evaluation feedback throughout the training program.

Section G.5.e: Limitations and Remediation

Through ongoing evaluation and appraisal, supervisors and educators are aware of the limitations of students/supervisees that might impede performance. Supervisors and educators assist students/supervisees in securing remedial assistance when needed. If students/supervisees request counseling or if counseling services are required as part of a remediation process, educators and supervisors provide acceptable referrals. Supervisors and educators recommend dismissal from training programs, applied practice settings, or state or voluntary professional credentialing processes when those students/supervisees are unable to provide competent professional services. Supervisors and educators seek consultation and document their decisions to dismiss or refer students/supervisees for assistance. They ensure that students/supervisees are aware of options available to them to address such decisions and ensure that students/supervisees have recourse in a timely manner to address decisions to require them to seek assistance or to dismiss them and provide them with due process according to institutional policies and procedures.

Section G.5.f: Multiple Roles/Relationships with Students and Supervisees

If students/supervisees request counseling, career services, or any other professional service which a supervisor or educator may ordinarily offer, the supervisor or educator will provide the student/supervisee with acceptable referrals. Supervisors and educators do not typically engage in multiple roles/relationships with students/supervisees. If supervisors or educators must provide a service to a student or supervisee in addition to providing supervision, they work to minimize potential conflicts and explain to students/supervisees the expectations and responsibilities associated with each role. In addition, the supervisor or educator must address participation in multiple roles/relationships with the students/supervisees in terms of the impact of these issues on clients, the supervisory relationship, and professional functioning.

Section G.5.g: Endorsement

Supervisors and educators endorse students/supervisees for certification, licensure, employment, or completion of an academic or training program only when they believe the students/supervisees are qualified for the endorsement. In addition, supervisors and educators do not withhold endorsement of qualified students/supervisees for certification, licensure, employment, or completion of an academic or training program for any reason unrelated to their fitness as a student or professional. Regardless of qualifications, supervisors and educators do not endorse students/supervisees whom they believe to be impaired in any way that would interfere with the performance of the duties associated with the endorsement.

Section G.6: Responsibilities of Educators

Section G.6.a: Educators

Educators who are responsible for developing, implementing, and supervising educational programs are skilled as teachers and practitioners. They are knowledgeable regarding the ethical, legal, and regulatory aspects of the profession, are skilled in applying that knowledge, and make students and supervisees aware of their responsibilities. Educators conduct education and training programs in an ethical manner and serve as role models for professional behavior. Career professionals who function as educators or supervisors provide instruction within their areas of knowledge and competence and provide instruction based on current information and knowledge available in the profession. When using technology to deliver instruction, educators develop competence in the use of the technology.

Section G.6.b: Integration of Study and Practice

Educators establish education and training programs that integrate academic study and supervised practice.

Section G.6.c: Teaching Ethics

Educators make students and supervisees aware of the ethical responsibilities and standards of the profession and the ethical responsibilities of students to the profession. Educators infuse ethical considerations throughout the curriculum.

Section G.6.d: Peer Relationships

Educators make every effort to ensure that the rights of peers are not compromised when students or supervisees lead career groups or provide supervision. Educators take steps to ensure that students and supervisees understand they have the same ethical obligations as educators, trainers, and supervisors.

Section G.6.e: Innovative Theories and Techniques

When educators teach techniques/procedures that are innovative, without an empirical foundation, or without a well-grounded theoretical foundation, they define the techniques/procedures as "unproven" or "developing" and explain to students the potential risks and ethical considerations of using such techniques/procedures.

Section G.6.f: Field Placements

Educators develop clear policies within their training programs regarding field placement and other practical experiences. Educators provide clearly stated roles and responsibilities for the student or supervisee, the site supervisor, and the program supervisor. They confirm that site supervisors are qualified to provide supervision and inform site supervisors of their professional and ethical responsibilities in this role. In addition, educators do not accept any form of professional services, fees, commissions, reimbursement, or remuneration from a site for student or supervisee placement.

Section G.7: Student Welfare

Section G.7.a: Orientation

Educators recognize that orientation is a developmental process that continues throughout the education and training of students. Faculty provide prospective and current students with information about the educational program's expectations including but not necessarily limited to:

1. the type and level of skill and knowledge acquisition required for successful completion of the training;
2. training program goals, objectives, and mission, and subject matter to be covered, including technology requirements;
3. bases for evaluation;
4. training components that encourage self-growth or self-disclosure as part of the training process;
5. the type of supervision settings and requirements of the sites for required clinical field experiences;
6. student and supervisee evaluation and dismissal policies and procedures; and
7. up-to-date employment prospects for graduates and career advisement, including making them aware of opportunities in the field.

Section G.7.b: Self-Growth Experiences

Education programs delineate requirements for self-disclosure or self-growth experiences in their admission and program materials. Educators use professional judgment when designing training experiences they conduct that require student and supervisee self-growth or self-disclosure. Students and supervisees are made aware of the ramifications their self-disclosure may have when career professionals whose primary role as teacher, trainer, or supervisor requires acting on ethical obligations to the profession. Evaluative components of experiential training activities explicitly delineate predetermined academic standards that are separate from and do not depend on the student's level of self-disclosure. Educators and supervisors may require students/supervisees to seek professional help to address any personal concerns that may be affecting their competency.

Section G.8: Multicultural/Diversity Competence in Education and Training Programs

Section G.8.a: Faculty Diversity

Educators are committed to recruiting and retaining a diverse faculty.

Section G.8.b: Student Diversity

Educators actively attempt to recruit and retain a diverse student body. Educators demonstrate commitment to multicultural/diversity competence by recognizing and valuing diverse cultures and types of abilities students bring to the training experience. Educators provide appropriate accommodations that enhance and support diverse student well-being and academic performance.

Section G.8.c: Multicultural/Diversity Competence

Educators actively infuse multicultural/diversity competency in their training and supervision practices. They actively train students to gain awareness, knowledge, and skills in the competencies of multicultural practice.

SECTION H: RESEARCH AND PUBLICATION

Introduction

Career professionals who conduct research are encouraged to contribute to the knowledge base of the profession and promote a clearer understanding of the conditions that lead to a healthy and more just society. Career professionals support efforts of researchers by participating fully and willingly whenever possible. Career professionals minimize bias and respect diversity in designing and implementing research.

Section H.1: Research Responsibilities

Section H.1.a: Use of Human Research Participants

Career professionals plan, design, conduct, and report research in a manner that is consistent with pertinent ethical principles, all applicable federal, state, and local statutes, laws, regulations, and/or procedures, host institutional regulations, and scientific standards governing research with human research participants.

Section H.1.b: Need for Research and Review

Career professionals have an obligation to contribute to periodic evaluations of the services they provide to their clients. The interventions, techniques, and methods of service delivery they use should be evaluated to establish evidence-based practice. Career professionals also have an obligation to periodically review the evaluation and research literature in their area of expertise so that the career services they provide to their clients reflect established best practice.

Section H.1.c: Deviation from Standard Practice

Career professionals seek consultation and observe stringent safeguards to protect the rights of research participants when a research problem suggests a deviation from standard or acceptable practices.

Section H.1.d: Independent Researchers

When career professionals conduct independent research and do not have access to an Institutional Review Board (IRB), they are bound to the same ethical principles and federal and state laws pertaining to the review of their plan, design, conduct and reporting of research. When independent researchers do not have access to an IRB, they should consult with researchers who are familiar with IRB procedures to provide appropriate safeguards.

Section H.1.e: Precautions to Avoid Injury

Career professionals who conduct research with human participants are responsible for the welfare of participants throughout the research process and should take reasonable precautions to avoid causing injurious psychological, emotional, physical, or social effects to participants.

Section H.1.f: Principal Researcher Responsibility

The ultimate responsibility for ethical research practice lies with the principal researcher. All others involved in the research activities share ethical obligations and responsibility for their own actions.

Section H.1.g: Minimal Interference

Career professionals take reasonable precautions to avoid causing disruptions in the lives of research participants that could be caused by their involvement in research.

Section H.1.h: Multicultural/Diversity Considerations in Research

When appropriate to research goals, career professionals are sensitive to incorporating research procedures that take into account cultural considerations. They seek consultation when appropriate.

Section H.2: Rights of Research Participants

Section H.2.a: Informed Consent in Research

Individuals have the right to decline requests to become research participants. In seeking consent, career professionals use language that

1. accurately explains the purpose and procedures to be followed;
2. identifies any procedures that are experimental or relatively untried;
3. describes any attendant discomforts, risks, and potential power differentials between researchers and participants;
4. describes any benefits or changes in individuals or organizations that might be reasonably expected;
5. discloses appropriate alternative procedures that would be advantageous for participants;
6. offers to answer any inquiries concerning the procedures;
7. describes any limitations on confidentiality;
8. describes the format and potential target audiences for the dissemination of research findings; and
9. instructs participants that they are free to withdraw their consent and to discontinue participation in the project at any time without penalty.

Section H.2.b: Deception

Career professionals do not conduct research involving deception unless alternative procedures are not feasible and the prospective value of the research justifies the deception. If such deception has the potential to cause physical or emotional harm to research participants, the research is not conducted, regardless of prospective value. When the methodological requirements of a study necessitate concealment or deception, the investigator explains the reasons for this action as soon as possible during the debriefing.

Section H.2.c: Student/Supervisee Participation

Researchers who involve students or supervisees in research make clear to them that the decision regarding whether or not to participate in research activities does not affect one's academic standing or supervisory relationship.

Students or supervisees who choose not to participate in educational research are provided with an appropriate alternative to fulfill their academic or other requirements.

Section H.2.d: Client Participation

Career professionals conducting research involving clients make clear in the informed consent process that clients are free to choose whether or not to participate in research activities. Career professionals take necessary precautions to protect clients from adverse consequences of declining or withdrawing from participation.

Section H.2.e: Confidentiality of Information

Information obtained about research participants during the course of an investigation is confidential. Procedures are implemented to protect confidentiality.

Section H.2.f: Persons Not Capable of Giving Informed Consent

When a person is not capable of giving informed consent, career professionals provide an appropriate explanation to, obtain agreement for participation from, and obtain the appropriate consent of a legally authorized person.

Section H.2.g: Commitments to Participants

Career professionals take reasonable measures to honor all commitments to research participants.

Section H.2.h: Explanations After Data Collection

After data are collected, career professionals provide participants with full clarification of the nature of the study to remove any misconceptions participants might have regarding the research. Where scientific or human values justify delaying or withholding information, career professionals take reasonable measures to avoid causing harm.

Section H.2.i: Informing Sponsors

Career professionals inform sponsors, institutions, and publication channels regarding research procedures and outcomes. Career professionals ensure that appropriate bodies and authorities are given pertinent information and acknowledgment.

Section H.2.j: Disposal of Research Documents and Records

Within a reasonable period of time following the completion of a research project or study, career professionals take steps to destroy records or documents (audio, video, digital, and written) containing confidential data or information that identifies research participants in accordance with all applicable federal, state, local, and/or institutional statutes, laws, regulations, and procedures. When records are of an artistic nature, researchers obtain participant consent with regard to handling of such records or documents. Career professionals are encouraged to purge their files according to the time frame required by federal, state, local, and/or institutional statute, law, regulation, or procedure, particularly when there is no reasonable expectation that anyone will benefit from maintaining the records any longer.

Section H.3: Relationships with Research Participants (When Research Involves Intensive or Extended Interactions)

Section H.3.a: Nonprofessional Relationships

Nonprofessional relationships with research participants should be avoided as these interactions may set up dual relationships and role confusion that may be harmful to the emotional health of participants.

Section H.3.b: Relationships with Research Participants

Sexual or romantic interactions or relationships between career professionals/researchers and current research participants are prohibited.

Section H.3.c: Harassment and Research Participants

Researchers do not condone or subject research participants to harassment, sexual or otherwise.

Section H.3.d: Potentially Beneficial Interactions

When a nonprofessional interaction between the researcher and the research participant may be potentially beneficial, the researcher must document, prior to the interaction (when feasible), the rationale for such an interaction, the potential benefit, and anticipated consequences for the research participant. Such interactions should be initiated with appropriate consent of the research participant. Where unintentional harm occurs to the research participant due to the nonprofessional interaction, the researcher must show evidence of an attempt to remedy such harm.

Section H.4: Reporting Results

Section H.4.a: Accurate Results

Career professionals plan, conduct, and report research accurately. They provide thorough discussions of the limitations of their data and alternative hypotheses. Career professionals do not engage in misleading or fraudulent research, distort data, misrepresent data, or deliberately bias their results. They explicitly mention all variables and conditions known to the investigator that may have affected the outcome of a study or the interpretation of data. They describe the extent to which results are applicable for diverse populations.

Section H.4.b: Obligation to Report Unfavorable Results

Career professionals report the results of any research of professional value. Results that reflect unfavorably on institutions, programs, services, prevailing opinions, or vested interests are not withheld.

Section H.4.c: Reporting Errors

If career professionals discover significant errors in their published research, they take reasonable steps to correct such errors in a correction erratum, or through other appropriate publication means.

Section H.4.d: Identity of Participants

Career professionals who supply data, aid in the research of another person, report research results, or make original data available take due care to disguise the identity of respective participants in the absence of specific authorization from the participants to do otherwise. In situations where participants self-identify their involvement in research studies, researchers take active steps to ensure that data is adapted/changed to protect the identity and welfare of all parties and that discussion of results does not cause harm to participants.

Section H.4.e: Replication Studies

Career professionals are obligated to make available sufficient original research data to qualified professionals who may wish to replicate a study.

Section H.5: Publication

Section H.5.a: Recognizing Contributions

When conducting and reporting research, career professionals are familiar with and give recognition to previous work on the topic, observe copyright laws, and give full credit to those to whom credit is due.

Section H.5.b: Plagiarism

Career professionals do not plagiarize; that is, they do not present another person's work as their own.

Section H.5.c: Review/Republication of Data or Ideas

Career professionals fully acknowledge and make editorial reviewers aware of prior publication of ideas or data where such ideas or data are submitted for review or publication.

Section H.5.d: Contributors

Career professionals give credit through joint authorship, acknowledgment, footnote statements, or other appropriate means to those who have contributed significantly to research or concept development in accordance with such contributions. The principal contributor is listed first, and minor technical or professional contributions are acknowledged in notes or introductory statements.

Section H.5.e: Agreement of Contributors

Career professionals who conduct joint research with colleagues or students/supervisees establish agreements in advance regarding allocation of tasks, publication credit, and types of acknowledgment that will be received.

Section H.5.f: Student Research

Manuscripts or professional presentations in any medium that are substantially based on a student's course papers, projects, dissertations, or theses are used only with the student's permission and list the student as lead author.

Section H.5.g: Duplicate Submission

Career professionals submit manuscripts for consideration to only one journal at a time. Manuscripts that are published in whole or in substantial part in another journal or published work are not submitted for publication without acknowledgment and permission from the previous publication.

Section H.5.h: Professional Review

Career professionals who review material submitted for publication, research, or other scholarly purposes respect the confidentiality and proprietary rights of those who submitted it. Career professionals use care to make publication decisions based on valid and defensible standards. Career professionals review article submissions in a timely manner and based on their scope and competency in research methodologies. Career professionals who serve as reviewers at the request of editors or publishers make every effort to review only materials that are within their scope of competency and use care to avoid personal biases.

SECTION I: RESOLVING ETHICAL ISSUES

Introduction

Career professionals behave in a legal, ethical, and moral manner in the conduct of their professional work. They are aware that client protection and trust in the profession depend on a high level of professional conduct. They hold other career professionals to the same standards and are willing to take appropriate action to ensure that these standards are upheld. Career professionals work to resolve ethical dilemmas with direct and open communication among all parties involved and seek consultation with colleagues and supervisors when necessary. Career professionals incorporate ethical practice into their daily work. They engage in ongoing learning and development regarding current topics in ethical and legal issues in the profession.

Section I.1: Standards and the Law

Section I.1.a: Knowledge

Career professionals understand the *NCDA Code of Ethics* and other applicable ethics codes from professional organizations or from certification and licensure bodies of which they are members and/or which regulate practice in a state or territory. Career professionals ensure that they are knowledgeable of and follow all applicable federal, state, local, and/or institutional statutes, laws, regulations, and procedures. Lack of knowledge or misunderstanding of an ethical responsibility is not a defense against a charge of unethical conduct.

Section I.1.b: Conflicts Between Ethics and Laws

If ethical responsibilities conflict with laws, regulations, or other governing legal authorities, career professionals make known their commitment to the *NCDA Code of Ethics* and take steps to resolve the conflict. If the conflict cannot be resolved by acknowledging and discussing the pertinent principles in the *NCDA Code of Ethics*, career professionals must adhere to the requirements of all applicable federal, state, local, and/or institutional statutes, laws, regulations, and procedures.

I.2. Suspected Violations

I.2.a. Ethical Behavior Expected

Career professionals expect colleagues to adhere to the *NCDA Code of Ethics*. When career professionals possess knowledge that raises doubts as to whether another career professional is acting in an ethical manner, they take appropriate action, as noted in I.2.b-I.2.g.

I.2.b. Informal Resolution

When career professionals have reason to believe that another career professional is violating or has violated an ethical standard, they attempt first to resolve the issue informally with the other career professional if feasible, provided such action does not violate confidentiality rights that may be involved.

I.2.c. Reporting Ethical Violations

If an apparent violation has substantially harmed, or is likely to substantially harm, a person or organization and is not appropriate for informal resolution or is not resolved properly, career professionals take further action appropriate to the situation. Such action might include referral to state or national committees on professional ethics, voluntary national certification bodies, state licensing boards, law enforcement or other appropriate institutional authorities. This standard does not apply when an intervention would violate confidentiality rights or when career professionals have been retained to review the work of another career professional whose conduct is in question.

I.2.d. Consultation

When uncertain as to whether a particular situation or course of action may be in violation of the *NCDA Code of Ethics*, career professionals consult with others who are knowledgeable about ethics and the *NCDA Code of Ethics*, with colleagues, and/or with appropriate authorities.

I.2.e. Organizational Conflicts

If the demands of an organization with which career professionals are affiliated pose a conflict with the *NCDA Code of Ethics*, career professionals specify the nature of such conflicts and express to their supervisors or other responsible officials their commitment to the *NCDA Code of Ethics*. When possible, career professionals work toward change within the organization to allow full adherence to the *NCDA Code of Ethics*. In doing so, they are mindful of and address any confidentiality issues.

I.2.f. Unwarranted Complaints

Career professionals do not initiate, participate in, or encourage the filing of ethics complaints that are made with reckless disregard or willful ignorance of facts that would disprove the allegation.

I.2.g. Unfair Discrimination Against Complainants and Respondents

Career professionals do not deny employment, advancement, admission to academic or other programs, tenure, or promotion to anyone based solely upon their having made or their being the subject of an ethics complaint. This does not preclude taking action based upon the outcome of such proceedings or considering other appropriate information.

I.3. Cooperation with Ethics Committees

Career professionals assist in the process of enforcing the *NCDA Code of Ethics*. Career professionals cooperate with investigations, proceedings, and requirements of the NCDA Ethics Committee or ethics committees of other duly constituted associations or licensing/certifications boards having jurisdiction over those charged with a violation. Career professionals are familiar with the NCDA Policy and Procedures for Processing Complaints of Ethical Violations and use it as a reference for assisting in the enforcement of the *NCDA Code of Ethics*.

APPENDIX B

EDUCATIONAL AND CAREER PLANNING PORTFOLIO

Name _____ _____ _____
        (Last)   (First)   (Middle)

Name of School/Division _____ Predominant Language Used at Home _____

Dates Contacts Made, Name, and Relationship to Student

Date of Contact	Name	Relationship to Student	Date of Contact	Name	Relationship to Student

Curriculum Emphasis:
- ☐ Apprenticeship
- ☐ Technical Education
- ☐ College Preparatory
- ☐ Youth Work-Study
- ☐ Tech Prep
- ☐ Cooperative Education
- ☐ Occupational & Technical Education
- ☐ Other (Please Specify) _____

Required and Elective Courses

(If this information is available elsewhere, please place a copy of the student's record of required and elective courses in the portfolio.)

School Year: _____

Required Courses	Grade	Credit
_____	____	____
_____	____	____
_____	____	____
_____	____	____

Elective Courses
_____	____	____
_____	____	____
_____	____	____

School Year: _____

Required Courses	Grade	Credit
_____	____	____
_____	____	____
_____	____	____
_____	____	____

Elective Courses
_____	____	____
_____	____	____
_____	____	____

School Year: _____

Required Courses	Grade	Credit
_____	____	____
_____	____	____
_____	____	____
_____	____	____

Elective Courses
_____	____	____
_____	____	____
_____	____	____

School Year: _____

Required Courses	Grade	Credit
_____	____	____
_____	____	____
_____	____	____
_____	____	____

Elective Courses
_____	____	____
_____	____	____
_____	____	____

Planning Future Assessments/Examinations

(Circle if needed and indicate anticipated dates of examinations)

Literacy Passport Test ____	Interest Inventory ____
ACT ____	PSAT ____
ASVAB ____	SAT ____
Achievement ____	Vocational Assessment ____
Aptitude ____	Virginia VIEW ____
Other _____	

Counselor/Student Review of Assessment/Examinations

(Circle when completed and indicate date of review)

Literacy Passport Test ____	Interest Inventory ____
ACT ____	PSAT ____
ASVAB ____	SAT ____
Achievement ____	Vocational Assessment ____
Aptitude ____	Virginia VIEW ____
Other _____	

Extracurricular or Co-curricular Activities

School Year: _____

Activity _____

Student's Role or Responsibility _____

_____

School Year: _____

Activity _____

Student's Role or Responsibility _____

_____

School Year: _____

Activity _____

Student's Role or Responsibility _____

_____

School Year: _____

Activity _____

Student's Role or Responsibility _____

_____

School Year: _____

Activity _____

Student's Role or Responsibility _____

_____

School Year: _____

Activity _____

Student's Role or Responsibility _____

_____

Career Exploration Activities

School Year: _____

Activity: (e.g., volunteering, job shadowing, work-study, cooperative education, other)

Career(s) Explored _____

_____

School Year: _____

Activity: (e.g., volunteering, job shadowing, work-study, cooperative education, other)

Career(s) Explored _____

_____

School Year: _____

Activity: (e.g., volunteering, job shadowing, work-study, cooperative education, other)

Career(s) Explored _____

_____

School Year: _____

Activity: (e.g., volunteering, job shadowing, work-study, cooperative education, other)

Career(s) Explored _____

_____

School Year: _____

Activity: (e.g., volunteering, job shadowing, work-study, cooperative education, other)

Career(s) Explored _____

_____

School Year: _____

Activity: (e.g., volunteering, job shadowing, work-study, cooperative education, other)

Career(s) Explored _____

_____

Special Prizes, Honors, Offices, and Recognition

School Year: _____
_____
_____

School Year: _____
_____
_____

School Year: _____
_____
_____

School Year: _____
_____
_____

School Year: _____
_____
_____

School Year: _____
_____
_____

Transition Plan (Complete as appropriate)

Services Provided	Activity Completed	Date Completed
Vocational Assessment		
Career Counseling		
Employability Skills		
Work-Based Learning		
Social Skills		
Continuing Ed. Support		
Postsecondary Transition Plan		
Vocational Rehab.		
Employment Services		
Job Placement		
Ongoing Job Support		
Financial Aid Info		
Reference Letters		
Other		

PART II

INDIVIDUAL CAREER PLAN (ICP)–ADOLESCENT EDUCATION

SCHOOL YEAR _____

(ICP to be completed annually)

NAME _____

      Last   First   Middle

SCHOOL _____

1. My interests are:

    _____

    _____

    _____

2. My abilities are:

    _____

    _____

    _____

3. My hobby and recreational/leisure activities are as follows:

    _____

    _____

    _____

4. I do best in these school subjects:

    _____

    _____

    _____

5. I have explored the following careers:

    _____

    _____

    _____

6. I have worked part-time or had some experience with the following jobs or work tasks:

    _____

    _____

    _____

7. My tentative career goal(s) is (are) the following:

    _____

    _____

    _____

8. In order to achieve my career goal(s):

a. I need to develop the following habits or behaviors: (Check the item when it has been successfully accomplished.)

_____

_____

_____

b. I plan to develop the following knowledge, skills, or attitudes: (Check the item when it has been accomplished successfully.)

_____

_____

_____

c. I plan to participate in the following home, school, and community activities to help me develop the knowledge, skills, and attitudes I want: (Check the item when accomplished successfully).

_____

_____

_____

d. I plan to pursue further education beyond high school in the following programs, schools, colleges, or military services:

_____

_____

_____

e. I plan to obtain work after high school in one of the following jobs:

_____

_____

_____

Signature _____ (Date) _____ (Date) _____ (Date)

Student   Parent   Counselor

A-33

APPENDIX C

CAREER COUNSELING COMPETENCIES OF THE NATIONAL CAREER DEVELOPMENT ASSOCIATION (NCDA)

INTRODUCTION TO CAREER COUNSELING COMPETENCY STATEMENTS

These competency statements are for those professionals interested and trained in the field of career counseling. For the purpose of these statements, career counseling is defined as the process of assisting individuals in the development of a life career with focus on the definition of the worker role and how that role interacts with other life roles.

NCDA's Career Counseling Competencies are intended to represent minimum competencies for those professionals at or above the master's degree level of education. These competencies are reviewed on an ongoing basis by the NCDA Professional Standards Committee, the NCDA Board, and other relevant associations. Professional competency statements provide guidance for the minimum competencies necessary to perform effectively a particular occupation or job within a particular field. Professional career counselors (master's degree or higher) or persons in career development positions must demonstrate the knowledge and skills for a specialty in career counseling that the generalist counselor might not possess. Skills and knowledge are represented by designated competency areas, which have been developed by professional career counselors and counselor educators. The Career Counseling Competency Statements can serve as a guide for career counseling training programs or as a checklist for persons wanting to acquire or to enhance their skills in career counseling.

CAREER DEVELOPMENT THEORY

(Chapters 2 and 3)
Theory base and knowledge considered essential for professionals engaging in career counseling and development. Demonstration of knowledge of:

1. Counseling theories and associated techniques.
2. Theories and models of career development.
3. Individual differences related to gender, sexual orientation, race, ethnicity, and physical and mental capacities.
4. Theoretical models for career development and associated counseling and information-delivery techniques and resources.
5. Human growth and development throughout the life span.
6. Role relationships which facilitate life-work planning.
7. Information, techniques, and models related to career planning and placement.

INDIVIDUAL AND GROUP COUNSELING SKILLS

(Chapters 1, 8)
Individual and group counseling competencies considered essential to effective career counseling. Demonstration of ability to:

1. Establish and maintain productive personal relationships with individuals.
2. Establish and maintain a productive group climate.
3. Collaborate with clients in identifying personal goals.
4. Identify and select techniques appropriate to client or group goals and client needs, psychological states, and developmental tasks.
5. Identify and understand clients' personal characteristics related to career.
6. Identify and understand social contextual conditions affecting clients' careers.
7. Identify and understand familial, sub-cultural, and cultural structures and functions as they are related to clients' careers.
8. Identify and understand clients' career decision-making processes.

Source: National Career Development Association, (2009). Career Counseling Competencies. Broken Arrow, OK: Author.

9. Identify and understand clients' attitudes toward work and workers.
10. Identify and understand clients' biases toward work and workers based on gender, race, and cultural stereotypes.
11. Challenge and encourage clients to take action to prepare for and initiate role transitions by: locating sources of relevant information and experience, obtaining and interpreting information and experiences, and acquiring skills needed to make role transitions.
12. Assist the client to acquire a set of employability and job search skills.
13. Support and challenge clients to examine life-work roles, including the balance of work, leisure, family, and community in their careers.

INDIVIDUAL/GROUP ASSESSMENT

(Chapters 1, 5, 6, 7 and 8)
Individual/group assessment skills considered essential for professionals engaging in career counseling. Demonstration of ability to:

1. Assess personal characteristics such as aptitude, achievement, interests, values, and personality traits.
2. Assess leisure interests, learning style, life roles, self-concept, career maturity, vocational identity, career indecision, work environment preference (e.g., work satisfaction), and other related life style/development issues.
3. Assess conditions of the work environment (such as tasks, expectations, norms, and qualities of the physical and social settings).
4. Evaluate and select valid and reliable instruments appropriate to the client's gender, sexual orientation, race, ethnicity, and physical and mental capacities.
5. Use computer-delivered assessment measures effectively and appropriately.
6. Select assessment techniques appropriate for group administration and those appropriate for individual administration.
7. Administer, score, and report findings from career assessment instruments appropriately.
8. Interpret data from assessment instruments and present the results to clients and to others.
9. Assist the client and others designated by the client to interpret data from assessment instruments.
10. Write an accurate report of assessment results.

INFORMATION/RESOURCES

(Chapters 6 and 7)
Information/resource base and knowledge essential for professionals engaging in career counseling. Demonstration of knowledge of:

1. Education, training, and employment trends; labor market information and resources that provide information about job tasks, functions, salaries, requirements, and future outlooks related to broad occupational fields and individual occupations.
2. Resources and skills that clients utilize in life-work planning and management.
3. Community/professional resources available to assist clients in career planning, including job search.
4. Changing roles of women and men and the implications that this has for education, family, and leisure.
5. Methods of good use of computer-based career information delivery systems (CIDS) and computer-assisted career guidance systems (CACGS) to assist with career planning.

PROGRAM PROMOTION, MANAGEMENT, AND IMPLEMENTATION

(Chapters 10, 11, 12, 13, and 14)
Knowledge and skills necessary to develop, plan, implement, and manage comprehensive career development programs in a variety of settings. Demonstration of knowledge of:

1. Designs that can be used in the organization of career development programs.
2. Needs assessment and evaluation techniques and practices.
3. Organizational theories, including diagnosis, behavior, planning, organizational communication, and management useful in implementing and administering career development programs.
4. Methods of forecasting, budgeting, planning, costing, policy analysis, resource allocation, and quality control.
5. Leadership theories and approaches for evaluation and feedback, organizational change, decision-making, and conflict resolution.
6. Professional standards and criteria for career development programs.
7. Societal trends and state and federal legislation that influence the development and implementation of career development programs.

Demonstration of ability to:

8. Implement individual and group programs in career development for specified populations.
9. Train others about the appropriate use of computer-based systems for career information and planning.
10. Plan, organize, and manage a comprehensive career resource center.
11. Implement career development programs in collaboration with others.
12. Identify and evaluate staff competencies.
13. Mount a marketing and public relations campaign in behalf of career development activities and services.

COACHING, CONSULTATION, AND PERFORMANCE IMPROVEMENT

(Chapters 8, 9, 10, 11, 12, 13, and 14)
Knowledge and skills considered essential in relating to individuals and organizations that impact the career counseling and development process. Demonstration of ability to:

1. Use consultation theories, strategies, and models.
2. Establish and maintain a productive consultative relationship with people who can influence a client's career.
3. Help the general public and legislators to understand the importance of career counseling, career development, and life-work planning.
4. Impact public policy as it relates to career development and workforce planning.
5. Analyze future organizational needs and current level of employee skills and develop performance improvement training.
6. Mentor and coach employees.

DIVERSE POPULATIONS

(Chapter 4)
Knowledge and skills considered essential in relating to diverse populations that impact career counseling and development processes. Demonstration of ability to:

1. Identify development models and multicultural counseling competencies.
2. Identify developmental needs unique to various diverse populations, including those of different gender, sexual orientation, ethnic group, race, and physical or mental capacity.

3. Define career development programs to accommodate needs unique to various diverse populations.
4. Find appropriate methods or resources to communicate with limited-English-proficient individuals.
5. Identify alternative approaches to meet career planning needs for individuals of various diverse populations.
6. Identify community resources and establish linkages to assist clients with specific needs.
7. Assist other staff members, professionals, and community members in understanding the unique needs/characteristics of diverse populations with regard to career exploration, employment expectations, and economic/social issues.
8. Advocate for the career development and employment of diverse populations.
9. Design and deliver career development programs and materials to hard-to-reach populations.

SUPERVISION

(Chapter 8)
Knowledge and skills considered essential in critically evaluating counselor or career development facilitator performance, maintaining and improving professional skills. Demonstration of:

1. Ability to recognize own limitations as a career counselor and to seek supervision or refer clients when appropriate.
2. Ability to utilize supervision on a regular basis to maintain and improve counselor skills.
3. Ability to consult with supervisors and colleagues regarding client and counseling issues and related to one's own professional development as a career counselor.
4. Knowledge of supervision models and theories.
5. Ability to provide effective supervision to career counselors and career development facilitators at different levels of experience.
6. Ability to provide effective supervision to career development facilitators at different levels of experience by: knowledge of their roles, competencies, and ethical standards; determining their competence in each of the areas included in their certification; further training them in competencies, including interpretation of assessment instruments; monitoring and mentoring their activities in support of the professional career counselor; and scheduling regular consultations for the purpose of reviewing their activities.

ETHICAL/LEGAL ISSUES

(Chapter 15)

Information base and knowledge essential for the ethical and legal practice of career counseling. Demonstration of knowledge of:

1. Adherence to ethical codes and standards relevant to the profession of career counseling (e.g. NBCC, NCDA, APA, and ACA).
2. Current ethical and legal issues which affect the practice of career counseling with all populations.
3. Current ethical/legal issues with regard to the use of computer-assisted career guidance systems.
4. Ethical standards relating to consultation issues.
5. State and federal statutes relating to client confidentiality.

RESEARCH/EVALUATION

(Chapters 1, 2, 3, 10, 11, 12, 13, and 14)

Knowledge and skills considered essential in understanding and conducting research and evaluation in career counseling and development. Demonstration of ability to:

1. Write a research proposal.
2. Use types of research and research designs appropriate to career counseling and development research.
3. Convey research findings related to the effectiveness of career counseling programs.

4. Design, conduct, and use the results of evaluation programs.
5. Design evaluation programs which take into account the need of various diverse populations, including persons of both genders, differing sexual orientations, different ethnic and racial backgrounds, and differing physical and mental capacities.
6. Apply appropriate statistical procedures to career development research.

TECHNOLOGY

(Chapters 6 and 7)

Knowledge and skills considered essential in using technology to assist individuals with career planning. Demonstration of knowledge of:

1. Various computer-based guidance and information systems as well as services available on the Internet.
2. Standards by which such systems and services are evaluated (e.g., NCDA and ACSCI).
3. Ways in which to use computer-based systems and Internet services to assist individuals with career planning that are consistent with ethical standards.
4. Characteristics of clients which make them profit more or less from use of technology-driven systems.
5. Methods to evaluate and select a system to meet local needs.

REFERENCE

National Career Development Association (2009). *Career Counseling Competencies.* Broken Arrow, OK: Author.

2016 CACREP Standards Related to Career Development

Career Development—studies that provide an understanding of career development and related life factors, including all of the following:

Book Chapter	CACREP Standard
2, 3	a. theories and models of career development, counseling, and decision making;
1, 2, 3, 8	b. approaches for conceptualizing the interrelationships among and between work, mental well-being, relationships, and other life roles and factors;
6, 7	c. processes for identifying and using career, avocational, educational, occupational and labor market information resources, technology, and information systems;
1, 2, 3, 4	d. approaches for assessing the conditions of the work environment on clients' life experiences;
1, 2, 3, 5, 7, 8, 9	e. strategies for assessing abilities, interests, values, personality, and other factors that contribute to career development;
10, 11, 12, 13, 14	f. strategies for career development program planning, organization, implementation, administration, and evaluation;
1, 4	g. strategies for advocating for diverse clients' career and educational development and employment opportunities in a global economy;
8, 9, 10, 11, 12, 13, 14	h. strategies for facilitating client skill development for career, educational, and life-work planning and management;
1, 8	i. methods of identifying and using assessment tools and techniques relevant to career planning and decision making;
4, 15	j. ethical and culturally relevant strategies for addressing career development.

Source: Council for the Accreditation of Counseling and Related Educational Programs. (2015). 2016 CACREP Standards. Alexandria, VA: Author.

NATIONAL CAREER DEVELOPMENT GUIDELINES (NCDG) FRAMEWORK

UNDERSTANDING THE NCDG FRAMEWORK

Domains and Goals

Domains, goals, and indicators organize the NCDG framework. The **three domains** Personal Social Development (PS), Educational Achievement and Lifelong Learning (ED), and Career Management (CM) describe content. Under each domain are **goals** (eleven in total). The goals define broad areas of career development competency.

Personal Social Development Domain

- GOAL PS1: Develop understanding of self to build and maintain a positive self-concept.
- GOAL PS2: Develop positive interpersonal skills including respect for diversity.
- GOAL PS3: Integrate growth and change into your career development.
- GOAL PS4: Balance personal, leisure, community, learner, family, and work roles.

Educational Achievement and Lifelong Learning Domain

- GOAL ED1: Attain educational achievement and performance levels needed to reach your personal and career goals.
- GOAL ED2: Participate in ongoing, lifelong learning experiences to enhance your ability to function effectively in a diverse and changing economy.

Career Management Domain

- GOAL CM1: Create and manage a career plan that meets your career goals.
- GOAL CM2: Use a process of decision making as one component of career development.
- GOAL CM3: Use accurate, current, and unbiased career information during career planning and management.
- GOAL CM4: Master academic, occupational, and general employability skills in order to obtain, create, maintain, and/or advance your employment.

- GOAL CM5: Integrate changing employment trends, societal needs, and economic conditions into your career plans.

Indicators and Learning Stages

Under each goal in the framework are indicators of mastery that highlight the knowledge and skills needed to achieve that goal. Each indicator is presented in **three learning stages** derived from *Bloom's Taxonomy*: knowledge acquisition, application, and reflection. The stages describe learning competency. They are not tied to an individual's age or level of education.

Knowledge Acquisition (K). Youth and adults at the knowledge acquisition stage expand knowledge awareness and build comprehension. They can recall, recognize, describe, identify, clarify, discuss, explain, summarize, query, investigate, and compile new information about the knowledge.

Application (A). Youth and adults at the application stage apply acquired knowledge to situations and to self. They seek out ways to use the knowledge. For example, they can demonstrate, employ, perform, illustrate, and solve problems related to the knowledge.

Reflection (R). Youth and adults at the reflection stage analyze, synthesize, judge, assess, and evaluate knowledge in accord with their own goals, values, and beliefs. They decide whether or not to integrate the acquired knowledge into their ongoing response to situations and adjust their behavior accordingly.

Coding System

The NCDG framework has a simple **coding system** to identify domains, goals, indicators, and learning stages. The coding system makes it easy for you to use the NCDG for program development and to track activities by goal, learning stage, and indicator. However, you do **not** need to know or include the codes to use the NCDG framework.

Domains

- PS—Personal Social Development
- ED—Educational Achievement and Lifelong Learning
- CM—Career Management

Goals

(Coded by domain and then numerically.)

For example, under the Personal Social Development domain:

- Goal PS1: Develop understanding of yourself to build and maintain a positive self-concept.
- Goal PS2: Develop positive interpersonal skills including respect for diversity.

Indicators and Learning Stages

(Coded by domain, goal, learning stage, and then numerically.)

Learning Stages:

- K—Knowledge Acquisition
- A—Application
- R—Reflection

For example, the second indicator under the first goal of the Personal Social Development domain:

- PS1.K2: Identify your abilities, strengths, skills, and talents.
- PS1.A2: Demonstrate use of your abilities, strengths, skills, and talents.
- PS1.R2: Assess the impact of your abilities, strengths, skills, and talents on your career development.

  If you have questions about the NCDG framework, in general, or its technical development, please contact the National Training Support Center (703-416-1840).

THE FRAMEWORK

National Career Development Guidelines Revision 09/30/04

PERSONAL SOCIAL DEVELOPMENT DOMAIN

Goal PS1	Develop understanding of yourself to build and maintain a positive self-concept.
PS1.K1	Identify your interests, likes, and dislikes.
PS1.A1	Demonstrate behavior and decisions that reflect your interests, likes, and dislikes.
PS1.R1	Assess how your interests and preferences are reflected in your career goals.
PS1.K2	Identify your abilities, strengths, skills, and talents.
PS1.A2	Demonstrate use of your abilities, strengths, skills, and talents.
PS1.R2	Assess the impact of your abilities, strengths, skills, and talents on your career development.
PS1.K3	Identify your positive personal characteristics (e.g., honesty, dependability, responsibility, integrity, and loyalty).
PS1.A3	Give examples of when you demonstrated positive personal characteristics (e.g., honesty, dependability, responsibility, integrity, and loyalty).
PS1.R3	Assess the impact of your positive personal characteristics (e.g., honesty, dependability, responsibility, integrity, and loyalty) on your career development.
PS1.K4	Identify your work values/needs.
PS1.A4	Demonstrate behavior and decisions that reflect your work values/needs.
PS1.R4	Assess how your work values/needs are reflected in your career goals.
PS1.K5	Describe aspects of your self-concept.
PS1.A5	Demonstrate a positive self-concept through your behaviors and attitudes.
PS1.R5	Analyze the positive and negative aspects of your self-concept.
PS1.K6	Identify behaviors and experiences that help to build and maintain a positive self-concept.

Goal PS1	Develop understanding of yourself to build and maintain a positive self-concept.
PS1.A6	Show how you have adopted behaviors and sought experiences that build and maintain a positive self-concept.
PS1.R6	Evaluate the effect of your behaviors and experiences on building and maintaining a positive self-concept.
PS1.K7	Recognize that situations, attitudes, and the behaviors of others affect your self-concept.
PS1.A7	Give personal examples of specific situations, attitudes, and behaviors of others that affected your self-concept.
PS1.R7	Evaluate the effect of situations, attitudes, and the behaviors of others on your self-concept.
PS1.K8	Recognize that your behaviors and attitudes affect the self-concept of others.
PS1.A8	Show how you have adopted behaviors and attitudes to positively affect the self-concept of others.
PS1.R8	Analyze how your behaviors and attitudes might affect the self-concept of others.
PS1.K9	Recognize that your self-concept can affect educational achievement (i.e., performance) and/or success at work.
PS1.A9	Show how aspects of your self-concept could positively or negatively affect educational achievement (i.e., performance) and/or success at work.
PS1.R9	Assess how your self-concept affects your educational achievement (performance) and/or success at work.
PS1.K10	Recognize that educational achievement (performance) and/or success at work can affect your self-concept.
PS1.A10	Give personal examples of how educational achievement (performance) and/or success at work affected your self-concept.
PS1.R10	Assess how your educational achievement (performance) and/or success at work affect your self-concept.
Goal PS2	**Develop positive interpersonal skills including respect for diversity.**
PS2.K1	Identify effective communication skills.
PS2.A1	Demonstrate effective communication skills.
PS2.R1	Evaluate your use of effective communication skills.
PS2.K2	Recognize the benefits of interacting with others in a way that is honest, fair, helpful, and respectful.
PS2.A2	Demonstrate that you interact with others in a way that is honest, fair, helpful, and respectful.
PS2.R2	Assess the degree to which you interact with others in a way that is honest, fair, helpful, and respectful.
PS2.K3	Identify positive social skills (e.g., good manners and showing gratitude).
PS2.A3	Demonstrate the ability to use positive social skills (e.g., good manners and showing gratitude).
PS2.R3	Evaluate how your positive social skills (e.g., good manners and showing gratitude) contribute to effective interactions with others.
PS2.K4	Identify ways to get along well with others and work effectively with them in groups.
PS2.A4	Demonstrate the ability to get along well with others and work effectively with them in groups.
PS2.R4	Evaluate your ability to work effectively with others in groups.
PS2.K5	Describe conflict resolution skills.
PS2.A5	Demonstrate the ability to resolve conflicts and to negotiate acceptable solutions.
PS2.R5	Analyze the success of your conflict resolution skills.
PS2.K6	Recognize the difference between appropriate and inappropriate behavior in specific school, social, and work situations.

(Continued)

Goal PS2	Develop positive interpersonal skills including respect for diversity.
PS2.A6	Give examples of times when your behavior was appropriate and times when your behavior was inappropriate in specific school, social, and work situations.
PS2.R6	Assess the consequences of appropriate or inappropriate behavior in specific school, social, and work situations.
PS2.K7	Identify sources of outside pressure that affect you.
PS2.A7	Demonstrate the ability to handle outside pressure on you.
PS2.R7	Analyze the impact of outside pressure on your behavior.
PS2.K8	Recognize that you should accept responsibility for your behavior.
PS2.A8	Demonstrate that you accept responsibility for your behavior.
PS2.R8	Assess the degree to which you accept personal responsibility for your behavior.
PS2.K9	Recognize that you should have knowledge about, respect for, be open to, and appreciate all kinds of human diversity.
PS2.A9	Demonstrate knowledge about, respect for, openness to, and appreciation for all kinds of human diversity.
PS2.R9	Assess how you show respect for all kinds of human diversity.
PS2.K10	Recognize that the ability to interact positively with diverse groups of people may contribute to learning and academic achievement.
PS2.A10	Show how the ability to interact positively with diverse groups of people may contribute to learning and academic achievement.
PS2.R10	Analyze the impact of your ability to interact positively with diverse groups of people on your learning and academic achievement.
PS2.K11	Recognize that the ability to interact positively with diverse groups of people is often essential to maintain employment.
PS2.A11	Explain how the ability to interact positively with diverse groups of people is often essential to maintain employment.
PS2.R11	Analyze the impact of your ability to interact positively with diverse groups of people on your employment.
Goal PS3	**Integrate personal growth and change into your career development.**
PS3.K1	Recognize that you will experience growth and changes in mind and body throughout life that will impact on your career development.
PS3.A1	Give examples of how you have grown and changed (e.g., physically, emotionally, socially, and intellectually).
PS3.R1	Analyze the results of your growth and changes throughout life to determine areas of growth for the future.
PS3.K2	Identify good health habits (e.g., good nutrition and constructive ways to manage stress).
PS3.A2	Demonstrate how you have adopted good health habits.
PS3.R2	Assess the impact of your health habits on your career development.
PS3.K3	Recognize that your motivations and aspirations are likely to change with time and circumstances.
PS3.A3	Give examples of how your personal motivations and aspirations have changed with time and circumstances.
PS3.R3	Assess how changes in your motivations and aspirations over time have affected your career development.
PS3.K4	Recognize that external events often cause life changes.
PS3.A4	Give examples of external events that have caused life changes for you.
PS3.R4	Assess your strategies for managing life changes caused by external events.

Goal PS3	**Integrate personal growth and change into your career development.**
PS3.K5	Identify situations (e.g., problems at school or work) in which you might need assistance from people or other resources.
PS3.A5	Demonstrate the ability to seek assistance (e.g., with problems at school or work) from appropriate resources including other people.
PS3.R5	Assess the effectiveness of your strategies for getting assistance (e.g., with problems at school or work) from appropriate resources including other people.
PS3.K6	Recognize the importance of adaptability and flexibility when initiating or responding to change.
PS3.A6	Demonstrate adaptability and flexibility when initiating or responding to change.
PS3.R6	Analyze how effectively you respond to change and/or initiate change.

Goal PS4	**Balance personal, leisure, community, learner, family, and work roles.**
PS4.K1	Recognize that you have many life roles (e.g., personal, leisure, community, learner, family, and work roles).
PS4.A1	Give examples that demonstrate your life roles including personal, leisure, community, learner, family, and work roles.
PS4.R1	Assess the impact of your life roles on career goals.
PS4.K2	Recognize that you must balance life roles and that there are many ways to do it.
PS4.A2	Show how you are balancing your life roles.
PS4.R2	Analyze how specific life role changes would affect the attainment of your career goals.
PS4.K3	Describe the concept of lifestyle.
PS4.A3	Give examples of decisions, factors, and circumstances that affect your current lifestyle.
PS4.R3	Analyze how specific lifestyle changes would affect the attainment of your career goals.
PS4.K4	Recognize that your life roles and your lifestyle are connected.
PS4.A4	Show how your life roles and your lifestyle are connected.
PS4.R4	Assess how changes in your life roles would affect your lifestyle.

EDUCATIONAL ACHIEVEMENT AND LIFELONG LEARNING DOMAIN

Goal ED1	**Attain educational achievement and performance levels needed to reach your personal and career goals.**
ED1.K1	Recognize the importance of educational achievement and performance to the attainment of personal and career goals.
ED1.A1	Demonstrate educational achievement and performance levels needed to attain your personal and career goals.
ED1.R1	Evaluate how well you have attained educational achievement and performance levels needed to reach your personal and career goals.
ED1.K2	Identify strategies for improving educational achievement and performance.
ED1.A2	Demonstrate strategies you are using to improve educational achievement and performance.
ED1.R2	Analyze your educational achievement and performance strategies to create a plan for growth and improvement.
ED1.K3	Describe study skills and learning habits that promote educational achievement and performance.
ED1.A3	Demonstrate acquisition of study skills and learning habits that promote educational achievement and performance.
ED1.R3	Evaluate your study skills and learning habits to develop a plan for improving them.
ED1.K4	Identify your learning style.

(Continued)

Goal ED1	Attain educational achievement and performance levels needed to reach your personal and career goals.
ED1.A4	Show how you are using learning-style information to improve educational achievement and performance.
ED1.R4	Analyze your learning style to develop behaviors to maximize educational achievement and performance.
ED1.K5	Describe the importance of having a plan to improve educational achievement and performance.
ED1.A5	Show that you have a plan to improve educational achievement and performance.
ED1.R5	Evaluate the results of your plan for improving educational achievement and performance.
ED1.K6	Describe how personal attitudes and behaviors can impact educational achievement and performance.
ED1.A6	Exhibit attitudes and behaviors that support educational achievement and performance.
ED1.R6	Assess how well your attitudes and behaviors promote educational achievement and performance.
ED1.K7	Recognize that your educational achievement and performance can lead to many workplace options.
ED1.A7	Show how your educational achievement and performance can expand your workplace options.
ED1.R7	Assess how well your educational achievement and performance will transfer to the workplace.
ED1.K8	Recognize that the ability to acquire and use information contributes to educational achievement and performance.
ED1.A8	Show how the ability to acquire and use information has affected your educational achievement and performance.
ED1.R8	Assess your ability to acquire and use information in order to improve educational achievement and performance.
Goal ED2	**Participate in ongoing, lifelong learning experiences to enhance your ability to function effectively in a diverse and changing economy.**
ED2.K1	Recognize that changes in the economy require you to acquire and update knowledge and skills throughout life.
ED2.A1	Show how lifelong learning is helping you function effectively in a diverse and changing economy.
ED2.R1	Judge whether or not you have the knowledge and skills necessary to function effectively in a diverse and changing economy.
ED2.K2	Recognize that viewing yourself as a learner affects your identity.
ED2.A2	Show how being a learner affects your identity.
ED2.R2	Analyze how specific learning experiences have affected your identity.
ED2.K3	Recognize the importance of being an independent learner and taking responsibility for your learning.
ED2.A3	Demonstrate that you are an independent learner.
ED2.R3	Assess how well you function as an independent learner.
ED2.K4	Describe the requirements for transition from one learning level to the next (e.g., middle school to high school, high school to postsecondary).
ED2.A4	Demonstrate the knowledge and skills necessary for transition from one learning level to the next (e.g., middle to high school, high school to postsecondary).
ED2.R4	Analyze how your knowledge and skills affect your transition from one learning level to the next (e.g., middle school to high school, high school to postsecondary).
ED2.K5	Identify types of ongoing learning experiences available to you (e.g., two- and four-year colleges, technical schools, apprenticeships, the military, online courses, and on-the-job training).
ED2.A5	Show how you are preparing to participate in ongoing learning experiences (e.g., two- and four-year colleges, technical schools, apprenticeships, the military, online courses, and on-the-job training).

Goal ED2	**Participate in ongoing, lifelong learning experiences to enhance your ability to function effectively in a diverse and changing economy.**
ED2.R5	Assess how participation in ongoing learning experiences (e.g., two- and four-year colleges, technical schools, apprenticeships, the military, online courses, and on-the-job training) affects your personal and career goals.
ED2.K6	Identify specific education/training programs (e.g., high school career paths and courses, college majors, and apprenticeship programs).
ED2.A6	Demonstrate participation in specific education/training programs (e.g., high school career paths and courses, college majors, and apprenticeship programs) that help you function effectively in a diverse and changing economy.
ED2.R6	Evaluate how participation in specific education/training programs (e.g., high school career paths and courses, college majors, and apprenticeship programs) affects your ability to function effectively in a diverse and changing economy.
ED2.K7	Describe informal learning experiences that contribute to lifelong learning.
ED2.A7	Demonstrate participation in informal learning experiences.
ED2.R7	Assess, throughout your life, how well you integrate both formal and informal learning experiences.

CAREER MANAGEMENT DOMAIN

Goal CM1	**Create and manage a career plan that meets your career goals.**
CM1.K1	Recognize that career planning to attain your career goals is a lifelong process.
CM1.A1	Give examples of how you use career planning strategies to attain your career goals.
CM1.R1	Assess how well your career planning strategies facilitate reaching your career goals.
CM1.K2	Describe how to develop a career plan (e.g., steps and content).
CM1.A2	Develop a career plan to meet your career goals.
CM1.R2	Analyze your career plan and make adjustments to reflect ongoing career management needs.
CM1.K3	Identify your short-term and long-term career goals (e.g., education, employment, and lifestyle goals).
CM1.A3	Demonstrate actions taken to attain your short-term and long-term career goals (e.g., education, employment, and lifestyle goals).
CM1.R3	Reexamine your career goals and adjust as needed.
CM1.K4	Identify skills and personal traits needed to manage your career (e.g., resiliency, self-efficacy, ability to identify trends and changes, and flexibility).
CM1.A4	Demonstrate career management skills and personal traits (e.g., resiliency, self-efficacy, ability to identify trends and changes, and flexibility).
CM1.R4	Evaluate your career management skills and personal traits (e.g., resiliency, self-efficacy, ability to identify trends and changes, and flexibility).
CM1.K5	Recognize that changes in you and the world-of-work can affect your career plans.
CM1.A5	Give examples of how changes in you and the world-of-work have caused you to adjust your career plans.
CM1.R5	Evaluate how well you integrate changes in you and the world-of-work into your career plans.
Goal CM2	**Use a process of decision making as one component of career development.**
CM2.K1	Describe your decision-making style (e.g., risk taker, cautious).
CM2.A1	Give examples of past decisions that demonstrate your decision-making style.
CM2.R1	Evaluate the effectiveness of your decision-making style.
CM2.K2	Identify the steps in one model of decision making.

(Continued)

Goal CM2	Use a process of decision making as one component of career development.
CM2.A2	Demonstrate the use of a decision-making model.
CM2.R2	Assess what decision-making model(s) work best for you.
CM2.K3	Describe how information (e.g., about you, the economy, and education programs) can improve your decision making.
CM2.A3	Demonstrate use of information (e.g., about you, the economy, and education programs) in making decisions.
CM2.R3	Assess how well you use information (e.g., about you, the economy, and education programs) to make decisions.
CM2.K4	Identify alternative options and potential consequences for a specific decision.
CM2.A4	Show how exploring options affected a decision you made.
CM2.R4	Assess how well you explore options when making decisions.
CM2.K5	Recognize that your personal priorities, culture, beliefs, and work values can affect your decision making.
CM2.A5	Show how personal priorities, culture, beliefs, and work values are reflected in your decisions.
CM2.R5	Evaluate the effect of personal priorities, culture, beliefs, and work values in your decision making.
CM2.K6	Describe how education, work, and family experiences might impact your decisions.
CM2.A6	Give specific examples of how your education, work, and family experiences have influenced your decisions.
CM2.R6	Assess the impact of your education, work, and family experiences on decisions.
CM2.K7	Describe how biases and stereotypes can limit decisions.
CM2.A7	Give specific examples of how biases and stereotypes affected your decisions.
CM2.R7	Analyze the ways you could manage biases and stereotypes when making decisions.
CM2.K8	Recognize that chance can play a role in decision making.
CM2.A8	Give examples of times when chance played a role in your decision making.
CM2.R8	Evaluate the impact of chance on past decisions.
CM2.K9	Recognize that decision making often involves compromise.
CM2.A9	Give examples of compromises you might have to make in career decision making.
CM2.R9	Analyze the effectiveness of your approach to making compromises.
Goal CM3	Use accurate, current, and unbiased career information during career planning and management.
CM3.K1	Describe the importance of career information to your career planning.
CM3.A1	Show how career information has been important in your plans and how it can be used in future plans.
CM3.R1	Assess the impact of career information on your plans and refine plans so that they reflect accurate, current, and unbiased career information.
CM3.K2	Recognize that career information includes occupational, education and training, employment, and economic information and that there is a range of career information resources available.
CM3.A2	Demonstrate the ability to use different types of career information resources (i.e., occupational, educational, economic, and employment) to support career planning.
CM3.R2	Evaluate how well you integrate occupational, educational, economic, and employment information into the management of your career.
CM3.K3	Recognize that the quality of career information resource content varies (e.g., accuracy, bias, and how up-to-date and complete it is).
CM3.A3	Show how selected examples of career information are biased, out-of-date, incomplete, or inaccurate.

Goal CM3	Use accurate, current, and unbiased career information during career planning and management.
CM3.R3	Judge the quality of the career information resources you plan to use in terms of accuracy, bias, and how up-to-date and complete it is.
CM3.K4	Identify several ways to classify occupations.
CM3.A4	Give examples of how occupational classification systems can be used in career planning.
CM3.R4	Assess which occupational classification system is most helpful to your career planning.
CM3.K5	Identify occupations that you might consider without regard to your gender, race, culture, or ability.
CM3.A5	Demonstrate openness to considering occupations that you might view as nontraditional (i.e., relative to your gender, race, culture, or ability).
CM3.R5	Assess your openness to considering nontraditional occupations in your career management.
CM3.K6	Identify the advantages and disadvantages of being employed in a nontraditional occupation.
CM3.A6	Make decisions for yourself about being employed in a nontraditional occupation.
CM3.R6	Assess the impact of your decisions about being employed in a nontraditional occupation.
Goal CM4	Master academic, occupational, and general employability skills in order to obtain, create, maintain, and/or advance your employment.
CM4.K1	Describe academic, occupational, and general employability skills.
CM4.A1	Demonstrate the ability to use your academic, occupational, and general employability skills to obtain or create, maintain, and advance your employment.
CM4.R1	Assess your academic, occupational, and general employability skills and enhance them as needed for your employment.
CM4.K2	Identify job-seeking skills such as the ability to: write a resume and cover letter, complete a job application, interview for a job, and find and pursue employment leads.
CM4.A2	Demonstrate the following job-seeking skills: the ability to write a resume and cover letter, complete a job application, interview for a job, and find and pursue employment leads.
CM4.R2	Evaluate your ability to: write a resume and cover letter, complete a job application, interview for a job, and find and pursue employment leads.
CM4.K3	Recognize that a variety of general employability skills and personal qualities (e.g., critical thinking, problem solving, resource, information, and technology management, interpersonal skills, honesty, and dependability) are important to success in school and employment.
CM4.A3	Demonstrate attainment of general employability skills and personal qualities needed to be successful in school and employment (e.g., critical thinking, problem solving, resource, information, and technology management, interpersonal skills, honesty, and dependability).
CM4.R3	Evaluate your general employability skills and personal qualities (e.g., critical thinking, problem solving, resource, information, and technology management, interpersonal skills, honesty, and dependability).
CM4.K4	Recognize that many skills are transferable from one occupation to another.
CM4.A4	Show how your skills are transferable from one occupation to another.
CM4.R4	Analyze the impact of your transferable skills on your career options.
CM4.K5	Recognize that your geographic mobility impacts on your employability.
CM4.A5	Make decisions for yourself regarding geographic mobility.
CM4.R5	Analyze the impact of your decisions about geographic mobility on your career goals.
CM4.K6	Identify the advantages and challenges of self-employment.
CM4.A6	Make decisions for yourself about self-employment.

(Continued)

Goal CM4	Master academic, occupational, and general employability skills in order to obtain, create, maintain, and/or advance your employment.
CM4.R6	Assess the impact of your decision regarding self-employment on your career goals.
CM4.K7	Identify ways to be proactive in marketing yourself for a job.
CM4.A7	Demonstrate skills that show how you can market yourself in the workplace.
CM4.R7	Evaluate how well you have marketed yourself in the workplace.
Goal CM5	Integrate changing employment trends, societal needs, and economic conditions into your career plans.
CM5.K1	Identify societal needs that affect your career plans.
CM5.A1	Show how you are prepared to respond to changing societal needs in your career management.
CM5.R1	Evaluate the results of your career management relative to changing societal needs.
CM5.K2	Identify economic conditions that affect your career plans.
CM5.A2	Show how you are prepared to respond to changing economic conditions in your career management.
CM5.R2	Evaluate the results of your career management relative to changing economic conditions.
CM5.K3	Identify employment trends that affect your career plans.
CM5.A3	Show how you are prepared to respond to changing employment trends in your career management.
CM5.R3	Evaluate the results of your career management relative to changes in employment trends.

REFERENCE

Bloom, B. S., Engelhart, M. D., Furst, E. J., Hill, W. H., & Krathwohl, D. R. (Eds.). (1956). *Taxonomy of educational objectives: Handbook I: Cognitive domain.* New York: David McKay.

References

Chapter 1

American School Counselor Association (ASCA). (2003). *The ASCA National Model: A framework for school counseling programs.* Alexandria, VA: American School Counselor Association.

Amundson, N. E. (2009). *Active engagement: Enhancing the career counseling process* (3rd ed.). Vancouver, Canada: Ergon Press.

Anderson, W. P., & Niles, S. G. (1995). Career and personal concerns expressed by career counseling clients. *The Career Development Quarterly, 43,* 240–245.

Anderson, W. P., Jr., & Niles, S. G. (2000). Important events in career counseling: Client and counselor descriptions. *The Career Development Quarterly, 48,* 251–263.

Ardichvili, A., & Kuchinke, K. (2009). International perspectives on the meanings of work and working: Current research and theory. *Advances in Development Human Resources, 11,* 155–167.

Bingham, R. P., & Ward, C. M. (1994). Career counseling with ethnic minority women. In W. B. Walsh & S. H. Osipow (Eds.), *Career counseling for women* (pp. 165–196). Hillsdale, NJ: Erlbaum.

Bingham, W. V. (1937). *Aptitudes and aptitude testing.* New York, NY: Harper & Brothers.

Blustein, D. L. (1994). "Who am I?" The question of self and identity in career development. In M. L. Savickas & R. W. Lent (Eds.), *Convergence in career development theories: Implications for science and practice* (pp. 139–154). Palo Alto, CA: Consulting Psychologists Press.

Blustein, D. L. (2006). *The psychology of working: A new perspective for career development, counseling, and public policy.* New York, NY: Routledge.

Blustein, D. (2013). *The Oxford handbook of the psychology of working.* New York, NY: Oxford University Press.

Blustein, D. L., & Spengler, P. M. (1995). Personal adjustment: Career counseling and psychotherapy. In W. B. Walsh & S. H. Osipow (Eds.), *Handbook of vocational psychology: Theory, research, and practice* (2nd ed., pp. 295–330). Mahwah, NJ: Lawrence Erlbaum Associates.

Borchert, M., & Landherr, G. (2009). The changing meanings of work in Germany. *Advances in Developing Human Resources, 11,* 204–217.

Borow, H. (Ed.). (1964). *Man in a world at work.* Boston, MA: Houghton Mifflin.

Bowlsbey, J. H., Dikel, M. R., & Sampson, J. P. (2002). *The Internet: A tool for career planning* (2nd ed.). Tulsa, OK: National Career Development Association.

Brewer, J. M. (1942). *History of vocational guidance.* New York, NY: Harper.

Bridges, W. (1994). *Jobshift: How to prosper in a workplace without jobs.* Reading, MA: Addison-Wesley.

Brief, A., & Nord, W. (1990). Work and meaning: Definitions and interpretations. In A. Brief & W. Nord (Eds.), *The meaning of occupational work* (pp. 21–45). Lexington, MA: Lexington.

Bureau of Labor Statistics. (2004, August 25). *Number of jobs held, labor market activity, and earnings among younger baby boomers: Recent results from a longitudinal study.* Washington, DC: United States Department of Labor.

Bureau of Labor Statistics. (2011). Retrieved from bls.gov.

Bureau of Labor Statistics. (2015). The employment situation–February 2015. Washington, DC: Bureau of Labor Statistics. Retrieved from bls.gov/news.release/pdf/empsit.pdf.

Byars-Winston, A., & Fouad, N. (2006). Metacognition and multicultural competence: Expanding the culturally appropriate career counseling model. *The Career Development Quarterly, 54,* 187–201.

Cahill, M., & Martland, S. (1996). Community career counseling for rural transition. *Canadian Journal of Counseling, 30,* 155–164.

Chope, R. C. (2006). *Family matters: The influence of the family in career decision making.* Austin, TX: Pro-Ed.

Chung, Y. B. (2001). Work discrimination and coping strategies: Conceptual frameworks for counseling lesbian, gay, and bisexual clients. *The Career Development Quarterly, 50,* 33–44.

Cochran, L. (1997). *Career counseling: A narrative approach.* Thousand Oaks, CA: Sage.

Dawis, R. (2002). Person-environment correspondence theory. In D. Brown & Associates (Eds.), *Career choice and development* (4th ed., pp. 427–464). San Francisco, CA: Jossey-Bass.

Dawis, R. V. (1996). The theory of work adjustment and person-environment correspondence counseling. In D. Brown, L. Brooks, & Associates (Eds.), *Career choice and development* (3rd ed., pp. 75–120). San Francisco, CA: Jossey-Bass.

Dawis, R. V. (2005). The Minnesota theory of work adjustment in career development and counseling. In S. D. Brown & R. W. Lent (Eds.), *Career development and counseling: Putting theory and research to work* (pp. 3–23). Hoboken, NJ: Wiley.

Dawis, R. V., England, G. W., & Lofquist, L. H. (1964). A theory of work adjustment. *Minnesota Studies in Vocational Rehabilitation, XV,* 1–27.

Doherty, M. (2009). When the working day is through: The end of work as identity? *Work, Employment, & Society, 23,* 84–101.

Enright, M., Conyers, L., & Szymanski, E. M. (1996). Career and career-related educational concerns of college students with disabilities. *Journal of Counseling & Development, 74,* 103–114.

Ferrar, L., Nota, L., Soresi, S., Blustein, D., Murphy, K., & Kenna, A. (2009). Construction of work among adolescents in transition. *Journal of Career Assessment, 17,* 99–115.

Fouad, N. A., & Byars-Winston, A. M. (2005). Cultural context of career choice: Meta-analysis of race/ethnicity differences. *The Career Development Quarterly, 53,* 223–233.

Friedman, T. H. (2005). *The world is flat: A brief history of the 21st century.* New York, NY: Farrar, Straus, and Giroux.

Fritzche, B. A., & Parrish, T. J. (2005). Theory and research on job satisfaction. In S. D. Brown & R. W. Lent (Eds.), *Career development and counseling: Putting theory and research to work* (pp. 180–202). Hoboken, NJ: Wiley.

Gomez, M. J., Fassinger, R. E., Prosser, J., Cooke, K., Mejia, B., & Luna, J. (2001). *Voces abriendo caminos* (Voices forging paths): A qualitative study of the career development of notable Latinas. *Journal of Counseling Psychology, 48,* 286–300.

Gysbers, N. C., Heppner, M. J., & Johnston, J. A. (2009). *Career counseling: Process, issues, and techniques* (3rd ed.). Boston: Allyn & Bacon.

Hall, D. T., & Associates. (1996). *The career is dead—long live the career: A relational approach to careers.* San Francisco, CA: Jossey-Bass.

Harpaz, I. (1999). The transformation of work values. *Israel Monthly Review, 122,* 46–50.

Hartung, P. J. (2002). Development through work and play. *Journal of Vocational Behavior, 61,* 424–438.

Hartung, P. J., Speight, J. D., & Lewis, D. M. (1996). Individualism-collectivism and the vocational behavior of majority culture college students. *The Career Development Quarterly, 45,* 87–96.

Heppner, M. J., O'Brien, K. M., Hinkelman, J. M., & Flores, L. Y. (1996). Training counseling psychologists in career development: Are we our own worst enemies? *The Counseling Psychologist, 24,* 105–125.

Herr, E. L. (1989). Career development and mental health. *Journal of Career Development, 16,* 5–18.

Herr, E. L. (1997). Super's life-span, life-space approach and its outlook for refinement. *The Career Development Quarterly, 45,* 238–246.

Herr, E. L. (2001). Career development and its practice: A historical perspective. *The Career Development Quarterly, 49,* 196–211.

Herr, E. L. (2003). The future of career counseling as an instrument of public policy. *The Career Development Quarterly, 52,* 8–17.

Herr, E. L., & Cramer, S. H. (1996). *Career guidance and counseling through the lifespan: Systemic approaches* (5th ed.). New York, NY: HarperCollins.

Herr, E. L., Cramer, S. H., & Niles, S. G. (2004). *Career guidance and counseling through the lifespan: Systemic approaches* (6th ed.). Boston, MA: Allyn & Bacon.

Herr, E. L., & Niles, S. G. (1998). Career: Social action in behalf of purpose, productivity, and hope. In C. Lee & G. R. Walz (Eds.), *Social action: A mandate for counselors* (pp. 117–156). Alexandria, VA: American Counseling Association.

Hershenson, D. B. (2005). INCOME: A culturally inclusive and disability-sensitive framework for organizing career development concepts and interventions. *The Career Development Quarterly, 54,* 11–23.

Hoyt, K. B., Evans, R., Mackin, E., & Magnum, G. L. (1972). *Career education: What is it and how to do it?* Salt Lake City, UT: Olympus Publishing Company.

Hull, C. L. (1928). *Aptitude testing.* Yonkers, NY: World Book Company.

Isaacson, L. (1985). *Basics of career counseling.* Boston, MA: Allyn & Bacon.

Isaacson, L. E., & Brown, D. (2000). *Career information, career counseling, and career development.* Boston, MA: Allyn & Bacon.

Kalton, C. A. (2001). Client psychological distress: An important factor in career counseling. *The Career Development Quarterly, 49,* 324–335.

Kapes, J. T., & Whitfield, E. A. (2002). *A counselor's guide to career assessment instruments* (4th ed.). Alexandria, VA: National Career Development Association.

Kim, B. S. K., Li, L. C., & Liang, C. T. H. (2002). Effects of Asian American client adherence to Asian cultural values, session goal, and counselor emphasis of client expression on career counseling process. *Journal of Counseling Psychology, 49,* 3–13.

Kitson, H. D. (1925). *The psychology of vocational adjustment.* Philadelphia, PA: Lippincott.

Krumboltz, J. D. (1993). Integrating career and personal counseling. *The Career Development Quarterly, 42,* 143–148.

Lee, C. C. (1989). Needed: A career development advocate. *The Career Development Quarterly, 37,* 218–220.

Lee, C. C. (2012). A conceptual framework for culturally competent career counseling practice. *Career Planning and Adult Development Journal, 28,* 7.

Lee, C. C., & Richardson, B. L. (Eds.). (1991). *Multicultural issues in counseling: New approaches to diversity.* Alexandria, VA: American Counseling Association.

Lent, R. W., Brown, S. D., & Hackett, G. (2002). Social cognitive career theory. In D. Brown & Associates (Eds.), *Career choice and development* (4th ed., pp. 255–311). San Francisco, CA: Jossey-Bass.

Lent, R. W., & Worthington, R. L. (1999). Applying career development theories to the school-to-work transition process. *The Career Development Quarterly, 47,* 291–296.

Leong, F. T. L. (1995). *Career development and vocational behavior of racial and ethnic minorities.* Mahwah, NJ: Erlbaum.

Leong, F. T. L. (2002). Challenges for career counseling in Asia: Variations in cultural accommodation. *The Career Development Quarterly, 50,* 277–284.

Leong, F. T. L., & Hartung, P. J. (2000). Adapting to the changing multicultural context of career. In A. Collin & R. A. Young (Eds.), *The future of career* (pp. 212–227). Cambridge, England: Cambridge University Press.

Leong, S. A. (1995). Career development and counseling: A multicultural perspective. In J. G. Ponterotto, J. M. Casas, L. A. Suzuki, & C. M. Alexander (Eds.), *Handbook of multicultural counseling* (pp. 549–566). Thousand Oaks, CA: Sage.

Liem, R., & Rayman, P. (1982). Health and social costs of unemployment. *American Psychologist, 37,* 1116–1123.

Ludwikowski, W., Vogel, D., & Armstrong, P. (2009). Attitudes toward career counseling: The role of public and self-stigma. *Journal of Counseling Psychology, 56,* 408–416.

Luzzo, D. A. (2000). *Career counseling of college students: An empirical guide to strategies that work.* Washington, DC: American Psychological Association.

Lyons, H. Z., Mehta, M., Velez, B. L., & Neill, N. (2014). Tests of the theory of work adjustment with economically distressed African Americans. *Journal of Counseling Psychology, 61,* 473–483. DOI: 10.1037/cou0000017.

Maccoby, M., & Terzi, K. (1981). What happened to the work ethic? In J. O'Toole, J. L. Scheiber, & L. C. Wood (Eds.), *Working, changes, and choices* (pp. 162–171). New York, NY: Human Sciences Press.

Madonna, M. G., Miville, M. L., Warren, M. K., Gainor, K. A., & Lewis-Coles, M. E. L. (2006). Religion, spirituality, and career development in African American college students: A qualitative inquiry. *The Career Development Quarterly, 54,* 227–241.

Mannheim, B. (1993). Gender and the effects of demographics status and work values on work centrality. *Work and Occupations, 20,* 3–22.

McCortney, A. L., & Engels, D. W. (2003). Revisiting the work ethic in America. *The Career Development Quarterly, 52,* 132–140.

Moore, H. (2013, February 1). The unemployment crisis that lies behind the US monthly jobs report. *The Guardian.* Retrieved from theguardian.com/commentisfree/2013/feb/01/unemployment-crisis-us-monthly-jobs-report

Mortimer, J. T., Zimmer-Gembeck, T., Holmes, M., & Shanahan, M. J. (2002). The process of occupational decision making: Patterns during the transition to adulthood. *Journal of Vocational Behavior, 61,* 439–465.

Multon, K. D., Heppner, M. J., Gysbers, N. C., Zook, C., & Ellis-Kalton, C. A. (2001). Client psychological distress: An important factor in career counseling. *The Career Development Quarterly, 49,* 324–335.

National Career Development Association. (1999). *Career connecting in a changing context: A summary of key findings of the 1999 national survey of working America.* Tulsa, OK: Author.

National Career Development Association. (2003a). *The professional practice of career counseling and consultation: A resource document.* Tulsa, OK: Author.

National Career Development Association. (2003b). *Career counseling competencies.* Tulsa, OK: Author.

National Career Development Association. (2009). *Career counseling competencies.* Tulsa, OK: Author.

National Career Development Association. (2011). *National survey on working America.* Broken Arrow, OK, Author.

Niles, S. G. (2003). Career counselors confront critical crossroads: A vision of the future. *The Career Development Quarterly, 52,* 70–77.

Niles, S. G., Amundson, N. E., & Neault, R. A. (2011). *Career flow: A hope-centered approach to career development.* Columbus, OH: Merrill Prentice Hall.

Niles, S. G., & Anderson, W. P. (1993). Career development and adjustment: The relation between concerns and stress. *Journal of Employment Counseling, 30,* 79–87.

Niles, S. G., & Anderson, W. P. (1995). A content analysis of career and personal concerns expressed by career counseling clients. *Educational and Vocational Guidance Bulletin, 57,* 59–62.

Niles, S. G., & Pate, P. H., Jr. (1989). Competency and training issues related to the integration of career counseling and mental health counseling. *Journal of Career Development, 16,* 63–71.

O'Brien, K. M. (2001). The legacy of Parsons: Career counselors and vocational psychologists as agents of social change. *The Career Development Quarterly, 50,* 66–76.

O'Toole, J. (1981). Work in America. In J. O'Toole, J. L. Schiber, & L. C. Wood (Eds.), *Working: Changes and choices* (pp. 12–17). New York, NY: Human Sciences Press.

Parmer, T., & Rush, L. C. (2003). The next decade in career counseling: Cocoon maintenance or metamorphosis? *The Career Development Quarterly, 52,* 26–34.

Parsons, F. (1909). *Choosing a vocation.* Boston, MA: Houghton Mifflin.

Paul, P. (2008). Applying a constructive-developmental approach to issues of sexual orientation and religion in career counseling. *The Career Development Quarterly, 56,* 344–352.

Pepper, S., & Lorah, P. (2008). Career issues and workplace considerations for the transsexual community: Bridging a gap of knowledge for career counselors and mental health care providers. *The Career Development Quarterly, 56,* 330–343.

Perrone, K. M. (2005). Work-family interface for same-sex dual-earner couples: Implications for counselors. *The Career Development Quarterly, 53,* 317–325.

Perrone, K. M., Webb, L. K., Blalock, R. H. (2005). The effects of role congruence and role conflict on work, marital and life satisfaction. *Journal of Career Development, 31,* 225–238.

Pew Research Center. (2014). *Millennials in adulthood: detached from institutions, networked with friends.* Washington, DC: Author.

Pope, M. (2000). A brief history of career counseling in the United States. *The Career Development Quarterly, 48,* 194–211.

Pope, M. (2012). Embracing and harnessing diversity in the US workforce: What have we learned? *International Journal for Educational and Vocational Guidance, 12,* 17–30.

Pope-Davis, D. B., & Dings, J. G. (1995). The assessment of multicultural counseling competencies. In J. G. Ponterotto & J. M. Casas (Eds.), *Handbook of multicultural counseling* (pp. 287–311). Thousand Oaks, CA: Sage.

Powell, G., & Greenhaus, J. (2012). When family considerations influence work decisions: Decision-making process. *Journal of Vocational Behavior, 81,* 322–329.

Richardson, M. S. (1993). Work in people's lives: A new location for counseling psychology. *Journal of Counseling Psychology, 40,* 425–433.

Riegle, D. W., Jr. (1982). Psychological and social effects of unemployment. *American Psychologist, 21,* 113–115.

Rifkin, J. (1995). *The end of work.* New York, NY: Putnam.

Rogers, C. R. (1942). *Counseling and psychotherapy: Newer concepts in practice.* Boston, MA: Houghton Mifflin.

Savickas, M. L. (1993). Predictive validity criteria for career development measures. *Journal of Career Assessment, 1,* 93–104.

Savickas, M. L. (2009). Career studies as self-making and life designing. *Career Research & Development, 24,* 15–17.

Savickas, M. L. (2010). Vocational counseling. In I. B. Weiner & W. E. Craighead (Eds.), *Corsini's encyclopedia of psychology* (4th ed., pp. 1841–1844). Hoboken, NJ: Wiley.

Sears, S. (1982). A definition of career guidance terms. A National Vocational Guidance Association perspective. *Vocational Guidance Quarterly, 31,* 137–143.

Shanahan, M. J., & Porfeli, E. (2002). Integrating the life course and life-span: Formulating research questions with dual points of entry. *Journal of Vocational Behavior, 61,* 398–406.

Spokane, A. R. (1991). *Career interventions.* Upper Saddle River, NJ: Prentice Hall.

Strong, E. K., Jr. (1943). *Vocational interests of men and women.* Stanford, CA: Stanford University Press.

Subich, L. M. (1993). How personal is career counseling? *The Career Development Quarterly, 42,* 129–131.

Subich, L. M. (2001). Introduction: Special section on contextual factors in career services delivery. *The Career Development Quarterly, 50,* 20.

Sue, D. W., Bernier, Y., Durran, A., Feinberg, L., Pedersen, P., Smith, E. J., & Nuttall, E. V. (1982). Position paper: Cross-cultural counseling competencies. *The Counseling Psychologist, 10*(2), 45–52.

Super, D. E. (1951). Vocational adjustment: Implementing a self-concept. *Occupations, 51,* 88–92.

Super, D. E. (1976). *Career education and the meaning of work.* Washington, DC: Office of Education.

Super, D. E. (1980). A life-span, life-space approach to career development. *Journal of Vocational Behavior, 16,* 282–298.

Super, D. E., Savickas, M. L., and Super, C. M. (1996). The life-span, life-space approach to careers. In D. Brown, L. Brooks, & Associates (Eds.), *Career choice development: Applying contemporary theories to practice* (3d ed., pp. 121–178). San Francisco, CA: Jossey–Bass.

Swanson, J. L., & Gore, P. A., Jr. (2000). Advances in vocational psychology theory and research. In S. D. Brown & R. W. Lent (Eds.), *Handbook of counseling psychology* (3rd ed., pp. 233–269). New York, NY: Wiley.

Tabuchi, H., & Barbaro, M. (2015, April 1). Walmart emerges as unlikely social force. *New York Times,* p. B1.

Toporek, R. L. (2006). An integrative approach for competence: Career counseling, social justice advocacy and the multicultural counseling competencies. *Career Planning and Adult Development Journal, 4,* 34–50.

Toporek, R. L., & Liu, W. M. (2001). Advocacy in counseling: Addressing race, class, and gender oppression. In D. B. Pope-Davis & H. L. K. Coleman (Eds.), *The intersection of race, class, and gender in multicultural counseling* (pp. 285–413). Thousand Oaks, CA: Sage.

United Nations. (2000). *The global compact.* New York, NY: Author.

Viteles, M. S. (1932). *Industrial psychology.* New York, NY: Norton.

Vondracek, F. W., Lerner, R. M., & Schulenberg, J. E. (1986). *Career development: A life-span developmental approach.* Hillsdale, NJ: Erlbaum.

Watkins, C. E., Jr., & Savickas, M. L. (1990). Psychodynamic career counseling. In W. B. Walsh & S. H. Osipow (Eds.), *Career counseling: Contemporary topics in vocational psychology* (pp. 79–116). Hillsdale, NJ: Erlbaum.

Williams, J. C., & Boushey, H. (2010). *The three faces of work-family conflict: The poor, the professionals and the missing middle.* Washington, DC: The Center for American Progress.

Williamson, E. G. (1939). *How to counsel students.* New York, NY: McGraw-Hill.

Wrenn, C. G. (1962). The culturally encapsulated counselor. *Harvard Educational Review, 32,* 444–449.

Zytowski, D. G. (2001). Frank Parsons and the progressive movement. *The Career Development Quarterly, 50,* 57–65.

Chapter 2

Anderson, W. P., & Niles, S. G. (1995). Career and personal concerns expressed by career counseling clients. *The Career Development Quarterly, 43,* 240–245.

Bandura, A. (1977). *Social learning theory.* Englewood Cliffs, NJ: Prentice Hall.

Bandura, A. (1986). *Social foundations of thought and action: A social-cognitive theory.* Upper Saddle River, NJ: Prentice Hall.

Behrens, E. L., & Nauta, M. M. (2014). The Self-Directed Search as a stand-alone intervention with college students. *The Career Development Quarterly, 62,* 224–238.

Betz, N. E., & Corning, A. F. (1993). The inseparability of "career" and "personal" counseling. *The Career Development Quarterly, 42,* 137–148.

Blanchard, C. A., & Lichtenberg, J. W. (2003). Compromise in career decision making: A test of Gottfredson's theory. *Journal of Vocational Behavior, 62,* 250–271.

Blustein, D. L. (1994). "Who am I?" The question of self and identity in career development. In M. L. Savickas & R. W. Lent (Eds.), *Convergence in career development theories: Implications for science and practice* (pp. 139–154). Palo Alto, CA: Consulting Psychologists Press.

Borgen, F. H. (1991). Megatrends and milestones in vocational behavior: A 20-year counseling psychology perspective. *Journal of Vocational Behavior, 39,* 263–290.

Borodovsky, L., & Ponterotto, J. (1994). A family-based approach to multicultural career development. In P. Pedersen & J. Carey (Eds.), *Multicultural counseling in schools* (pp. 195–206). Boston, MA: Allyn & Bacon.

Brown, D. (1996). Brown's values-based, holistic model of career and life-role choices and satisfaction. In D. Brown, L. Brooks, & Associates (Eds.), *Career choice and development* (3rd ed., pp. 337–372). San Francisco, CA: Jossey-Bass.

Brown, M. T., Lum, J. L., & Voyle, K. (1997). Roe revisited: A call for the reappraisal of the theory of personality development and career choice. *Journal of Vocational Behavior, 51,* 283–294.

Buehler, C. (1933). *Der menschliche lebenslauf als psychologisches problem.* Leipzig, Germany: Hirzel.

Cairo, P. C., Kritis, K. J., & Myers, R. M. (1996). Career assessment and the Adult Career Concerns Inventory. *Journal of Career Assessment, 4,* 189–204.

Cochran, D. B., Wang, E. W., Stevenson, S. J., Johnson, L. E., & Crews, C. (2011). Adolescent occupational aspirations: Test of Gottfredson's Theory of Circumscription and Compromise. *The Career Development Quarterly, 59,* 412–427.

Coltrane, S., & Adams, M. (1997). Work-family imagery and gender stereotypes: Television and the reproduction of difference. *Journal of Vocational Behavior, 50,* 323–347.

Donahue, R. (2006). Person-environment congruence in relation to career change and career persistence. *Journal of Vocational Behavior, 68,* 504–515.

Downes, M., & Kroeck, K. G. (1996). Discrepancies between existing jobs and individual interests: An empirical investigation of Holland's model. *Journal of Vocational Behavior, 48,* 107–117.

Eagle, B. W., Miles, E. W., & Icenogle, M. L. (1997). Interrole conflicts and the permeability of work and family domains: Are there gender differences? *Journal of Vocational Behavior, 50,* 168–184.

Ginzberg, E., Ginsburg, S. W., Axelrad, S., & Herma, J. (1951). *Occupational choice: An approach to a general theory.* New York, NY: Columbia University Press.

Gottfredson, L. S. (1981). Circumscription and compromise: A developmental theory of occupational aspirations. *Journal of Counseling Psychology, 28,* 545–579.

Gottfredson, L. S. (1996). A theory of circumscription and compromise. In D. Brown, L. Brooks, & Associates (Eds.), *Career choice and development* (3rd ed., pp. 179–281). San Francisco, CA: Jossey-Bass.

Gottfredson, L. S. (2002). Gottfredson's theory of circumscription, compromise, and self-creation. In D. Brown & Associates (Eds.), *Career choice and development* (4th ed., pp. 85–148). San Francisco, CA: Jossey-Bass.

Gottfredson, L. S. (2003). The challenge and promise of cognitive career assessment. *Journal of Career Assessment, 11,* 115–135.

Gottfredson, L. S. (2005). Applying Gottfredson's theory of circumscription and compromise in career guidance and counseling. In S. D. Brown & R. W. Lent (Eds.), *Career development and counseling: Putting theory and research to work* (pp. 71–100). Hoboken, NJ: Wiley.

Gottfredson, L. S., & Holland, J. L. (1996). *Position classification inventory.* Odessa, FL: Psychological Assessment Resources.

Gottfredson, L. S., & Richards, J. M. (1999). The meaning and measurement of environments in Holland's theory. *Journal of Vocational Behavior, 42,* 200–211.

Hackett, G., Lent, R., & Greenhaus, J. (1991). Advances in vocational theory and research: A 20-year retrospective. *Journal of Vocational Behavior, 38,* 3–38.

Hannah, J., & Kahn, S. (1989). The relationship of socioeconomic status and gender to the occupational choices of grade 12 students. *Journal of Vocational Behavior, 34,* 161–178.

Harmon, L. W., Hansen, J. C., Borgen, F. H., & Hammer, A. L. (1994). *Strong Interest Inventory applications and technical guide.* Stanford, CA: Stanford University Press.

Hartung, P. J. (2013). The life-span, life-space theory of careers. In S. Brown & R. Lent (Eds.), *Career development and counseling* (pp. 83–114). Hoboken, NJ: Wiley.

Hartung, P. J., Vandiver, B. J., Leong, F. T. L., Pope, M., Niles, S. G., & Farrow, B. (1998). Appraising cultural identity in career development assessment and counseling. *The Career Development Quarterly, 46,* 276–293.

Havighurst, R. J. (1951). Validity of the Chicago Attitude Inventory as a measure of personal adjustment in old age. *Journal of Abnormal and Social Psychology, 46,* 24–29.

Havighurst, R. J. (1953). *Human development and education.* New York, NY: Longmans Green.

Helwig, A. A. (2001). A test of Gottfredson's theory using a ten-year longitudinal study. *Journal of Career Development, 28,* 77–95.

Henderson, S., Hesketh, B., & Tuffin, A. (1988). A test of Gottfredson's theory of circumscription. *Journal of Vocational Behavior, 32,* 37–48.

Herr, E. L., Cramer, S. H., & Niles, S. G. (2004). *Career guidance and counseling through the lifespan: Systematic approaches* (6th ed.). Boston, MA: Allyn & Bacon.

Hesketh, B., Elmslie, S., & Kaldor, W. (1990). Career compromise: An alternative account to Gottfredson's theory. *Journal of Counseling Psychology, 37,* 49–56.

Holland, J. L. (1959). A theory of vocational choice. *Journal of Counseling Psychology, 6,* 35–45.

Holland, J. L. (1966). *The psychology of vocational choice.* Waltham, MA: Blaisdell.

Holland, J. L. (1973). *Making vocational choices: A theory of careers.* Upper Saddle River, NJ: Prentice Hall.

Holland, J. L. (1985a). *Making vocational choices: A theory of vocational personalities and work environments* (2nd ed.). Upper Saddle River, NJ: Prentice Hall.

Holland, J. L. (1985b). *Vocational Preference Inventory.* Odessa, FL: Psychological Assessment Resources.

Holland, J. L. (1992). *Making vocational choices* (2nd ed.). Odessa, FL: Psychological Assessment Resources.

Holland, J. L. (1994). Separate but unequal is better. In M. L. Savickas & R. W. Lent (Eds.), *Convergence in career development theories: Implications for science and practice* (pp. 45–51). Palo Alto, CA: CPP Books.

Holland, J. L. (1996). Integrating career theory and practice: The current situation and some potential remedies. In M. L. Savickas & W. B. Walsh (Eds.), *Handbook of career counseling theory and practice* (pp. 1–12). Palo Alto, CA: Davies-Black.

Holland, J. L. (1997). Current status of Holland's theory of careers: Another perspective. *The Career Development Quarterly, 36,* 31–44.

Holland, J. L., Gottfredson, G., & Power, P. (1980). Some diagnostic scales for research in decision-making and personality: Identity, information, and barriers. *Journal of Personality and Social Psychology, 39,* 1191–1200.

Holmberg, K., Rosen, D., & Holland, J. L. (1990). *Leisure activities finder.* Odessa, FL: Psychological Assessment Resources.

Jepsen, D. A. (1994). The thematic-extrapolation method: Incorporating career patterns into career counseling. *The Career Development Quarterly, 43,* 43–53.

Johannson, C. B. (1986). *The Career Assessment Inventory.* Minneapolis, MN: NCS Assessments.

Kelly, G. A. (1955). *The psychology of personal constructs.* New York, NY: Norton.

Kim, B., Jung, S. H., Jang, S. H., Lee, B., Rhee, E., Cho, S. H, & Lee, S. M. (2014). Construction and initial validation of the Planned Happenstance Career Inventory. *The Career Development Quarterly, 62,* 239–253.

Krumboltz, J. D. (1976). A social learning theory of career choice. *Counseling Psychologist, 6,* 71–80.

Krumboltz, J. D. (1988). *Career Beliefs Inventory.* Palo Alto, CA: Consulting Psychologists Press.

Krumboltz, J. D. (1993). Integrating career and personal counseling. *The Career Development Quarterly, 42,* 143–148.

Krumboltz, J. D. (1994). The Career Beliefs Inventory. *Journal of Counseling and Development, 72,* 9–31.

Krumboltz, J. D. (1996). A learning theory of career counseling. In M. Savickas & B. Walsh (Eds.), *Integrating career theory and practice* (pp. 233–280). Palo Alto, CA: CPP Books.

Krumboltz, J. D., & Henderson, S. J. (2002). A learning theory for career counselors. In S. Niles (Ed.), *Adult career development: Concepts, issues, and practices* (pp. 39–56). Tulsa, OK: National Career Development Association.

Krumboltz, J. D., Mitchell, A., & Gelatt, H. G. (1976). Applications of social learning theory of career selection. *Focus on Guidance, 8,* 71–81.

Krumboltz, J. D., & Thoresen, C. E. (1969). *Behavioral counseling: Cases and techniques.* New York, NY: Holt, Rinehart and Winston.

Lent, E. B., & Lopez, F. G. (1996). Congruence from many angles: Relations of multiple congruence indices to job satisfaction among adult workers. *Journal of Vocational Behavior, 49,* 24–37.

Lent, R. W., Brown, S. D., Nota, L., & Soresi, S. (2003). Testing social cognitive interest and choice hypotheses across Holland types in Italian high school students. *Journal of Vocational Behavior, 62,* 101–118.

Leong, S. A., & Plake, T. S. (1990). A choice dilemma approach for examining the relative importance of sex type and prestige preferences in the process of career choice compromise. *Journal of Counseling Psychology, 37,* 399–406.

Lewis, D. M., Savickas, M. L., & Jones, B. J. (1996). Career development predicts medical school success. *Journal of Vocational Behavior, 49,* 86–98.

Loscocco, K. A. (1997). Reactions to blue-collar work: A comparison of men and women. *Work and Occupations, 17,* 152–177.

Lucas, M. S. (1993). A validation of types of career indecision at a counseling center. *Journal of Counseling Psychology, 40,* 440–446.

Maslow, A. H. (1954). *Motivation and personality.* New York, NY: Harper & Row.

McLennan, N. A., & Arthur, N. (1999). Applying the cognitive information processing approach to career problem solving and decision making to women's career development. *Journal of Employment Counseling, 36,* 82–96.

Mihalik, J. R. (1996). Client vocational interests as predictors of client reactions to counselor intentions. *Journal of Counseling and Development, 74,* 416–421.

Miller, D. C., & Form, W. H. (1951). *Industrial sociology.* New York, NY: Harper & Row.

Miller, M. J. (1997). Error rates on two forms on the Self-Directed Search and satisfaction with results. *Journal of Employment Counseling, 34,* 98–103.

Miller, M. J. (2002). A longitudinal examination of a three-letter Holland code. *Journal of Employment Counseling, 39,* 43–48.

Miller, M. J., & Bass, C. (2003). Application of Holland's theory to a nonprofessional occupation. *Journal of Employment Counseling, 40,* 17–23.

Mitchell, L. K., & Krumboltz, J. D. (1984). Social learning approach to career decision making: Krumboltz's theory. In D. Brown, L. Brooks, & Associates (Eds.), *Career choice and development: Applying contemporary theories to practice* (2nd ed., pp. 235–280). San Francisco, CA: Jossey-Bass.

Mitchell, L. K., & Krumboltz, J. D. (1996). Krumboltz's theory of career choice and counseling. In D. Brown, L. Brooks, & Associates (Eds.), *Career choice development* (3rd ed., pp. 233–280). San Francisco, CA: Jossey-Bass.

Mitchell, A., Levin, A., & Krumboltz, J. D. (1999). Planned happenstance: Constructing unexpected career opportunities. *Journal of Counseling and Development, 77,* 115–124.

Murray, H. (1938). *Explorations in personality.* New York, NY: Oxford University Press.

Nevill, D. D., & Calvert, P. D. (1996). Career assessment and the Salience Inventory. *Journal of Career Assessment, 4,* 399–412.

Nevill, D. D., & Kruse, S. J. (1996). Career assessment and the Values Scale. *Journal of Career Assessment, 4,* 383–397.

Nevill, D. D., & Super, D. E. (1986). *The Values Scale: Theory, application, and research manual* (research ed.). Palo Alto, CA: Consulting Psychologists Press.

Niles, S. G., & Anderson, W. P. (1993). Career development and adjustment: The relation between concerns and stress. *Journal of Employment Counseling, 30,* 79–87.

Niles, S. G., Anderson, W. P., & Goodnough, G. (1998). Exploration to foster career development. *The Career Development Quarterly, 46,* 262–275.

Niles, S. G., & Goodnough, G. E. (1996). Life-role salience and values: A review of recent research. *The Career Development Quarterly, 45,* 65–86.

Oleski, D., & Subich, L. M. (1996). Congruence and career change in employed adults. *Journal of Vocational Behavior, 49,* 221–229.

Oliver, K. E., & Waehler, C. A. (2005). Investigating the validity of Holland's (1959, 1997) RIASEC typology among Native Hawaiians. *Journal of Counseling Psychology, 52,* 448–452.

Osipow, S. H., & Fitzgerald, L. F. (1996). *Theories of career development* (4th ed.). Needham, MA: Allyn & Bacon.

Parasuraman, S., Purhoit, Y. S., Godshalk, V. M., & Beutell, N. J. (1996). Work and family variables, entrepreneurial career success, and psychological well-being. *Journal of Vocational Behavior, 48,* 275–300.

Perdue, S., Reardon, R., & Peterson, G. (2007). Person-environment congruence, self-efficacy, and environmental identity in relation to job satisfaction: A career decision theory perspective. *Journal of Employment Counseling, 44,* 29–39.

Perrone, K. M. (2005). Work-family interface for same sex, dual-earner couples: Implications for counselors. *The Career Development Quarterly, 53,* 317–324.

Phillips, S. D. (1982). Career exploration in adulthood. *Journal of Vocational Behavior, 20,* 129–140.

Richardson, M. S. (1993). Work in people's lives: A location for counseling psychologists. *Journal of Counseling Psychology, 40,* 425–433.

Roe, A. (1956). *The psychology of occupations.* New York, NY: Wiley.

Roe, A. (1957). Early determinants of vocational choice. *Journal of Counseling Psychology, 4,* 212–217.

Rogers, C. R. (1951). *Client-centered therapy, its current practice, implications, and theory.* Boston, MA: Houghton Mifflin.

Rounds, J., & Tracey, T. J. G. (1996). Cross-cultural structural equivalence of RIASEC models and measures. *Journal of Counseling Psychology, 43,* 310–329.

Ryan, J. M., Tracey, T. J. G., & Rounds, J. (1996). Generalizability of Holland's structure of vocational behavior interest across ethnicity, gender, and socioeconomic status. *Journal of Counseling Psychology, 43,* 330–337.

Salomone, P. R. (1996). Tracing Super's theory of vocational development: A 40-year retrospective. *Journal of Career Development, 22,* 167–184.

Savickas, M. L. (1993). Predictive validity criteria for career development measures. *Journal of Career Assessment, 1,* 93–104.

Savickas, M. L. (1997). Career adaptability: An integrative concept for life-span, life-space theory. *The Career Development Quarterly, 45,* 247–259.

Savickas, M. L. (2002). Career construction: A developmental theory of vocational behavior. In D. Brown & Associates (Eds.), *Career choice and development* (4th ed., pp. 149–205). San Francisco, CA: Jossey-Bass.

Savickas, M. L. (2005). The theory and practice of career construction. In S. D. Brown & R. W. Lent (Eds.), *Career development and counseling: Putting theory and research to work* (pp. 42–70). Hoboken, NJ: Wiley.

Savickas, M. L., & Hartung, P. J. (1996). The Career Development Inventory in review: Psychometric and research findings. *Journal of Career Assessment, 4,* 171–188.

Savickas, M. L., & Porfeli, E. J. (2011). Revision of the Career Maturity Inventory: The adaptability form. *Journal of Career Assessment, 19,* 355–374.

Spokane, A. (1985). A review of research on person-environment congruence in Holland's theory of careers. *Journal of Vocational Behavior, 26,* 306–343.

Spokane, A. (1996). Holland's theory. In D. Brown, L. Brook, & Associates (Eds.), *Career choice and development* (3rd ed., pp. 33–74). San Francisco, CA: Jossey-Bass.

Spokane, A. R., & Cruza-Guet, M. C. (2005). Holland's theory of vocational personalities in work environments. In S. D. Brown & R. W. Lent (Eds.), *Career development and counseling: Putting theory and research to work* (pp. 24–41). Hoboken, NJ: Wiley.

Spokane, A. R., Fouad, N., & Swanson, J. (2001). *Culture-centered career intervention. Paper presented at a symposium on career intervention.* (S. Whiston, Chair). San Francisco, CA: American Psychological Association.

Spokane, A., Luchetta, E., & Richwine, M. (2002). Holland's theory of personalities. In D. Brown & Associates (Eds.), *Career choice and development* (4th ed., pp. 373–426). San Francisco, CA: Jossey-Bass.

Spranger, E. (1928). *Types of men: The psychology and ethics of personality* (Paul J. W. Pigors, Trans.). Halle, Germany: Max Niemeyer Verlag.

Subich, L. M. (1993). How personal is career counseling? *The Career Development Quarterly, 42,* 129–131.

Super, D. E. (1953). A theory of vocational development. *American Psychologist, 8,* 185–190.

Super, D. E. (1954). Career patterns as a basis for vocational counseling. *Journal of Counseling Psychology, 1,* 12–20.

Super, D. E. (1957). *The psychology of careers.* New York, NY: Harper & Row.

Super, D. E. (1961). The self concept in vocational development. *Journal of Vocational and Educational Guidance, 8,* 13–29.

Super, D. E. (1963). Toward making self-concept theory operational. In D. E. Super, R. Starishevsky, N. Matlin, & J. P. Jordaan (Eds.), *Career development self-concept theory* (pp. 17–32). New York, NY: College Entrance Examination Board.

Super, D. E. (1969). Vocational development theory: Persons, positions, processes. *The Counseling Psychologist, 1,* 2–9.

Super, D. E. (1980). A life-span, life-space approach to career development. *Journal of Vocational Behavior, 16,* 282–298.

Super, D. E. (1981). Approaches to occupational choice and career development. In A. G. Watts, D. E. Super, & J. M. Kidd (Eds.), *Career development in Britain* (pp. 28–42). Cambridge, England: Hobsons Press.

Super, D. E. (1983). Assessment in career guidance: Toward truly developmental counseling. *Personnel and Guidance Journal, 61,* 555–562.

Super, D. E. (1984). Leisure: What it is and might be. *Journal of Career Development, 11,* 71–80.

Super, D. E. (1990). A life-span, life-space approach to career development. In D. Brown, L. Brook, & Associates (Eds.), *Career choice and development: Applying contemporary theories to practice* (2nd ed., pp. 197–261). San Francisco, CA: Jossey-Bass.

Super, D. E. (1992). Toward a comprehensive theory of career development. In D. Montross & C. Shinkman (Eds.), *Career development: Theory and practice* (pp. 35–64). Springfield, IL: Charles C Thomas.

Super, D. E. (1993). The two faces of counseling: Or is it three? *The Career Development Quarterly, 42,* 132–136.

Super, D. E., & Bachrach, P. (1957). *Scientific careers and vocational development theory.* New York, NY: Teachers College Press.

Super, D. E., & Knasel, E. G. (1981). Career development in adulthood: Some theoretical problems and a possible solution. *British Journal of Guidance and Counselling, 9,* 194–201.

Super, D. E., & Nevill, D. D. (1986). *The Salience Inventory.* Palo Alto, CA: Consulting Psychologists Press.

Super, D. E., Osborne, W. L., Walsh, D. J., Brown, S. D., & Niles, S. G. (1992). Developmental assessment and counseling: The C-DAC model. *Journal of Counseling and Development, 71,* 74–80.

Super, D. E., Savickas, M. L., & Super, C. (1996). A life-span, life-space approach to career development. In D. Brown, L. Brook, & Associates (Eds.), *Career choice and development* (3rd ed., pp. 121–178). San Francisco, CA: Jossey-Bass.

Super, D. E., Thompson, A. S., & Lindeman, R. H. (1988). *Adult Career Concerns Inventory: Manual for research and exploratory usage in counseling.* Palo Alto, CA: Consulting Psychologists Press.

Super, D. E., Thompson, A. S., Lindeman, R. H., Jordaan, J. P., & Myers, R. A. (1981). *Career Development Inventory.* Palo Alto, CA: Consulting Psychologists Press.

Sverko, I., Babarovic, T., & Medugorac, V. (2014). Pictorial assessment of interests: Development and evaluation of pictorial and descriptive interest inventory. *Journal of Vocational Behavior, 84,* 356–366.

Thompson, A. S., Lindeman, R. H., Super, D. E., Jordaan, J. P., & Myers, R. A. (1984). *Career Development Inventory: Technical manual.* Palo Alto, CA: Consulting Psychologists Press.

Tinsley, H. E. A. (1994). Construct your reality and show us its benefits: Comment on Richardson. *Journal of Counseling Psychology, 40,* 108–111.

Tracey, T. (2008). Adherence to RIASEC structure as a key career decision construct. *Journal of Counseling Psychology, 55,* 146–157.

Tracey, T. J. B., Wille, B., Durr, M. R., & Fruyt, F. (2014). An enhanced examination of Holland's consistency and differentiation hypotheses. *Journal of Vocational Behavior, 84,* 237–247.

U.S. Department of Defense. (1993). *Technical supplement to the counselor's manual for the Armed Services Vocational Aptitude Battery.* North Chicago, IL: U.S. Military Entrance Processing Command.

Vondracek, F. W., Lerner, R. M., & Schulenberg, J. E. (1986). *Career development: A life-span developmental approach.* Hillsdale, NJ: Erlbaum.

Weinrach, G. (1984). Determinants of vocational choice: Holland's theory. In D. Brown, L. Brooks, & Associates (Eds.), *Career choice and development: Applying contemporary theories to practice* (3rd ed., pp. 61–93). San Francisco, CA: Jossey-Bass.

Weinrach, S. G. (1996). The psychological and vocational interest patterns of Donald Super and John Holland. *Journal of Counseling and Development, 75,* 5–16.

Chapter 3

Ali, S. R., & Menke, K. A. (2014). Rural Latino youth career development: An application of social cognitive career theory. *The Career Development Quarterly, 62*(2), 175–186.

Bandura, A. (1986). *Social foundations of thought and action: A social cognitive theory.* Upper Saddle River, NJ: Prentice Hall.

Bloch, D. P., & Richmond, L. J. (1998). *Soul work: Finding the work you love, loving the work you have.* Palo Alto, CA: Davies-Black.

Bolles, R. N. (1998). *What color is your parachute?* Berkeley, CA: Ten Speed Press.

Bright, J. E. H., Pryor, R. G. L., Wilkenfield, S., & Earl, J. (2005). The role of social context and serendipitous events in career decision making. *International Journal for Educational and Vocational Guidance, 5,* 19–36.

Brown, S. D., & Lent, R. W. (1996). A social cognitive framework for career choice counseling. *The Career Development Quarterly, 44,* 354–366.

Cardoso, P., Silva, J. R., Gonçalves, M. M., & Duarte, M. E. (2014). Innovative moments and change in Career Construction Counseling. *Journal of Vocational Behavior, 84,* 11–20.

Carlsen, M. B. (1988). *Making meaning: Therapeutic processes in adult development.* New York, NY: W. W. Norton.

Choi, B., Park, H., Yang, E., Lee, S., Lee, Y., & Lee, Y. (2012). Understanding career decision self-efficacy: A meta-analytic approach. *Journal of Career Development, 39,* 443–460.

Clemens, E., & Milsom, A. (2008). Enlisted service members' transition into the civilian world of work: A cognitive information processing approach. *The Career Development Quarterly, 56,* 246–256.

Cochran, L. (1985). *Position and nature of personhood.* Westport, CT: Greenwood.

Cochran, L. (1994). What is a career problem? *The Career Development Quarterly, 42,* 204–215.

Cochran, L. (1997). *Career counseling: A narrative approach.* Thousand Oaks, CA: Sage.

Cochran, L. R. (1990). Narrative as a paradigm for career research. In K. A. Young & W. E. Borgen (Eds.), *Methodological approaches to the study of careers* (pp. 71–86). New York, NY: Praeger.

Di Fabio, A., & Maree, J. G. (2012). Group-based life design counseling in an Italian context. *Journal of Vocational Behavior, 80,* 100–107.

Diegelman, N. M., & Subich, L. M. (2001). Academic and vocational interests as a function of outcome expectancies in social cognitive career theory. *Journal of Vocational Behavior, 59,* 394–405.

Ecke, Y. (2007). Attachment style and dysfunctional career thoughts: How attachment style can affect the career counseling process. *The Career Development Quarterly, 55,* 339–350.

Flores, L. Y., & O'Brien, K. M. (2002). The career development of Mexican American adolescent women: A test of social cognitive career theory. *Journal of Counseling Psychology, 49,* 14–27.

Gainor, K. A. & Lent, R. W. (1998). Social cognitive expectations and racial identity attitudes in predicting the math choice of Black college students. *Journal of Counseling Psychology, 45,* 403–413.

Gelatt, H. B. (1989). Positive uncertainty: A new decision-making framework for counseling. *Journal of Counseling Psychology, 36,* 252–256.

Gibbons, M. M., & Borders, L. D. (2010). Prospective first-generation college students: A social-cognitive perspective. *The Career Development Quarterly, 56,* 194–208.

Goldman, L. (1992). Qualitative assessment: An approach for counselors. *Journal of Counseling and Development, 70,* 616–621.

Hackett, G., & Betz, N. (1981). A self-efficacy approach to the career development of women. *Journal of Vocational Behavior, 18,* 326–329.

Hackett, G., & Byars, A. (1996). Social cognitive theory and the career development of African American women. *The Career Development Quarterly, 44,* 322–340.

Hansen, L. S. (1997). *Integrative life planning: Critical tasks for career development and changing life patterns.* San Francisco, CA: Jossey-Bass.

Hansen, L. S. (2002). *Integrative life planning: A holistic theory for career counseling with adults.* In S. G. Niles (Ed.), *Adult career development: Concepts, issues, and practices* (3rd ed., pp. 59–76). Tulsa, OK: National Career Development Association.

Hansen, L. S., Hage, S., & Kachgal, M. (1999). *Integrative life planning inventory.* University of Minnesota, MN: Integrative Life Planning, Counseling and Student Personnel Psychology.

Helwig, A. A. (1992). Book review of career development and services. *Journal of Employment Counseling, 29,* 77–78.

Herr, E. L., & Cramer, S. H. (1996). *Career guidance and counseling through the lifespan* (5th ed.). New York, NY: HarperCollins.

Hinkle, D. (1965). *The change of personal constructs from the viewpoint of a theory of implications.* Unpublished doctoral dissertation, Ohio State University, Columbus, Ohio.

Hirshi, A., & Lage, D. (2008). Increasing the career choice readiness of young adolescents: An evaluation study. *International Journal for Educational and Vocational Guidance, 8,* 95–110.

Holland, J. L. (1985). *Making vocational choices: A theory of vocational personalities and work environments* (2nd ed.). Upper Saddle River, NJ: Prentice Hall.

Howard, G. S. (1989). *A tale of two stories: Excursions into a narrative approach to psychology.* Notre Dame, IN: Academic.

Hsieh, H. H., & Huang, J. T. (2014). The effects of socioeconomic status and proactive personality on career decision self-efficacy. *The Career Development Quarterly, 62* 29–43.

Janis, I. L., & Mann, L. (1977). *Decision-making: A psychological analysis of conflict, choice, and commitment.* New York, NY: Free Press.

Kelly, G. A. (1955). *A theory of personality: The psychology of personal constructs.* New York, NY: Norton.

Ledwith, K. E. (2014). Academic advising and career services: A collaborative approach. *New Directions for Student Services, 2014,* 49–63.

Lent, R. W. (2005). A social cognitive view of career development and counseling. In S. D. Brown & R. W. Lent (Eds.), *Career development and counseling: Putting theory and research to work* (pp. 101–127). New York, NY: Wiley.

Lent, R. W. (2013). Career-life preparedness: Revisiting career planning and adjustment in the new workplace. *The Career Development Quarterly, 61,* 2–14.

Lent, R. W., & Brown, S. D. (1996). Social cognitive approach to career development: An overview. *The Career Development Quarterly, 44,* 310–321.

Lent, R. W., & Brown, S. D. (2002). Social cognitive career theory and adult career development. In S. Niles (Ed.), *Adult career development: Concepts, models, and practices* (3rd ed., pp. 77–98). Tulsa, OK: National Career Development Association.

Lent, R. W., & Brown, S. D. (2006). On conceptualizing and assessing social cognitive constructs in career research: A measurement guide. *Journal of Career Assessment, 14,* 12–35.

Lent, R. W., Brown, S. D., Brenner, B., Chopra, S. B., Davis, T., Talleyrand, R., & Suthakaran, V. (2001). The role of contextual supports and barriers in the choice of math/science educational options: A test of social cognitive hypotheses. *Journal of Counseling Psychology, 48,* 474–483.

Lent, R. W., Brown, S. D., & Hackett, G. (1994). Toward a unifying social cognitive theory of career and academic interests, choice, and performance. *Journal of Vocational Behavior, 45,* 79–122.

Lent, R. W., Brown, S. D., & Hackett, G. (1996). Career development from a social cognitive perspective. In D. Brown, L. Brooks, & Associates (Eds.), *Career choice and development* (3rd ed., pp. 373–416). San Francisco, CA: Jossey-Bass.

Lent, R. W., Brown, S. D., & Hackett, G. (2002). Social cognitive career theory. In D. Brown & Associates (Eds.), *Career choice and development* (4th ed., pp. 255–311). San Francisco, CA: Jossey-Bass.

Lent, R. W., & Hackett, G. (1987). Career self-efficacy: Empirical status and future directions. *Journal of Vocational Behavior, 30,* 347–382.

Lewis, R. A., & Gilhousen, M. R. (1981). Myths of career development: A cognitive approach to vocational counseling. *The Personnel and Guidance Journal, 5,* 296–299.

Lindley, L. D. (2005). Perceived barriers to career development in the context of social cognitive career theory. *Journal of Career Assessment, 13,* 271–287.

McLennan, N. A., & Arthur, N. (1999). Applying the cognitive information processing approach to career problem solving and decision making to women's career development. *Journal of Employment Counseling, 36,* 82–96.

Meichenbaum, D. (1977). *Cognitive behavior modification.* New York, NY: Plenum.

Miller-Tiedeman, A. L. (1997). The Lifecareer Process Theory: A healthier choice. In D. P. Bloch & L. J. Richmond (Eds.), *Connection between spirit and work in career development* (pp. 87–114). Palo Alto, CA: Davies-Black.

Mitchell, L. K., & Krumboltz, J. D. (1996). Krumboltz's learning theory of career choice counseling. In D. Brown, L. Brooks, & Associates (Eds.), *Career choice and development* (3rd ed., pp. 233–276). San Francisco, CA: Jossey-Bass.

Mitchell, L. K., Levin, A. S., & Krumboltz, J. D. (1999). Planned happenstance: Constructing unexpected career opportunities. *Journal of Counseling & Development, 77,* 115–124.

Morrison, R. F. (1994). Biodata applications in career development research and practice. In G. S. Stokes, M. D. Mumford, & W. A. Owens (Eds.), *Biodata handbook: Theory, research and use of biographical information in selection and performance prediction* (pp. 451–484). Palo Alto, CA: Consulting Psychologists Press.

Nauta, M. M., Kahn, J. H., Angell, J. W., & Cantarelli, E. A. (2002). Identifying the antecedent in the relation between career interests and self-efficacy: Is it one, the other, or both? *Journal of Counseling Psychology, 49,* 290–301.

Neimeyer, G. J. (1989). Personal constructs systems in vocational development and information processing. *Journal of Career Development, 16,* 83–96.

Neimeyer, G. J. (1992). Personal construct and vocational structure: A critique of poor status. In R. A. Neimeyer & G. J. Neimeyer (Eds.), *Advances in personal construct psychology* (pp. 91–120). Greenwich, CT: JAI Press.

Niles, S. G., & Pate, R. H. (1989). Competency and training issues related to the integration of career counseling and mental health counseling. *Journal of Career Development, 16,* 63–71.

Ochs, L. A., & Roessler, R. T. (2004). Predictors of career exploration and intentions: A social cognitive career theory perspective. *Rehabilitation Counseling Bulletin, 47,* 224–233.

Osborn, D. S., Howard, D. K., & Leierer, S. J. (2007). The effect of a career development course on the dysfunctional career thoughts of racially and ethnically diverse college freshmen. *The Career Development Quarterly, 55,* 365–377.

Osborn, D. S., Peterson, G. W., Sampson, J. P., Jr., & Reardon, R. C. (2003). Client anticipations about computer-assisted career guidance system outcomes. *The Career Development Quarterly, 51,* 356–367.

Patton, W., & McIlveen, P. (2009). Practice and research in career counseling and development—2008. *The Career Development Quarterly, 58,* 118–161.

Patton, W., & McMahon, M. (1999). *Career development and systems theory: A new relationship.* Pacific Grove, CA: Brooks/Cole.

Peavy, R. V. (1992). A constructivist model of training for career counselors. *Journal of Career Development, 18,* 215–228.

Peterson, G. W., Sampson, J. P., Jr., Lenz, J. G., & Reardon, R. C. (2002). A cognitive information processing approach to career problem solving and decision making. In D. Brown & Associates (Eds.), *Career choice and development* (4th ed., pp. 312–372). San Francisco, CA: Jossey-Bass.

Peterson, G. W., Sampson, J. P., Jr., & Reardon, R. C. (1991). *Career development and services: A cognitive approach.* Pacific Grove, CA: Brooks/Cole.

Peterson, G. W., Sampson, J. P., Jr., Reardon, R. C., & Lenz, J. G. (1996). A cognitive information processing approach. In D. Brown, L. Brooks, & Associates (Eds.), *Career choice and development* (3rd ed., pp. 423–476). San Francisco, CA: Jossey-Bass.

Polkinghorne, D. E. (1988). *Narrative knowing and the human sciences.* Albany, NY: State University of New York Press.

Pryor, R., & Bright, J. (2011). *The chaos theory of careers: A new perspective on working in the twenty-first century.* New York, NY: Routledge.

Raque-Bogdan, T. L., Klingaman, E. A., Martin, H. M., & Lucas, M. S. (2013). Career-related parent support and career barriers: An investigation of contextual variables. *The Career Development Quarterly, 61,* 339–353.

Reardon, R. C., & Wright, L. K. (1999). The case of Mandy: Applying Holland's theory and cognitive informational processing theory. *The Career Development Quarterly, 47,* 195–203.

Reed, C. A., Reardon, R. C., Lenz, J. G., & Leierer, S. J. (2001). A cognitive career course: From theory to practice. *The Career Development Quarterly, 50,* 158–167.

Rehfuss, M. C., Cosio, S., & Del Corso, J. (2011). Counselors' perspectives on using the career style interview with clients. *The Career Development Quarterly, 59,* 208–218.

Rogers, M. E., Creed, P. A., & Glendon, A. I. (2008). The role of personality in adolescent career planning and exploration: A social cognitive perspective. *Journal of Vocational Behavior, 73,* 132–142.

Rokeach, M. (1973). *The nature of human values.* New York, NY: Free Press.

Sampson, J. P., Jr., Peterson, G. W., Lenz, J. G., & Reardon, R. C. (1992). A cognitive approach to career services: Translating concepts into practice. *The Career Development Quarterly, 41,* 67–74.

Sampson, J. P., Peterson, G. W., Lenz, J. G., Reardon, R. C., & Saunders, D. E. (1996). *The Career Thoughts Inventory (CTI).* Odessa, FL: Psychological Assessment Resources.

Sampson, J. P., Jr., Reardon, R. C., Peterson, G. W., & Lenz, J. G. (2004). *Career counseling and services: A cognitive information processing approach.* Pacific Grove, CA: Brooks/Cole.

Saunders, D. E., Peterson, G. W., Sampson, J. P., Jr., & Reardon, R. C. (2000). Relation of depression and dysfunctional career thinking to career indecision. *Journal of Vocational Behavior, 56,* 288–298.

Savickas, M. L. (1995). Constructivist counseling for career indecision. *The Career Development Quarterly, 43,* 363–373.

Savickas, M. L. (1997). The spirit in career counseling: Fostering self-completion through work. In D. P. Bloch & L. J. Richmond (Eds.), *Connections between spirit and work in career development* (pp. 3–25). Palo Alto, CA: Davies-Black.

Savickas, M. L. (1998). Career style assessment and counseling. In T. Sweeney (Ed.), *Adlerian counseling: A practitioner's approach* (4th ed., pp. 329–359). Philadelphia, PA: Accelerated Development.

Savickas, M. L. (2005). The theory and practice of career construction. In S. D. Brown & R. W. Lent (Eds.), *Career development and counseling* (pp. 42–70). Hoboken, NJ: Wiley.

Savickas, M. L. (2009). Career-style counseling. In T. J. Sweeney (Ed.), *Adlerian counseling and psychotherapy: A practitioners' approach* (5th ed., pp. 183–207). New York, NY: Routledge.

Savickas, M. L. (2013). Career construction theory and practice. In S. D. Brown & R. W. Lent (Eds.), *Career development and counseling* (2nd ed., pp. 147–186). Hoboken, NJ: Wiley.

Shen, F. C., Liao, K. Y. H., Abraham, W. T., & Weng, C. Y. (2014). Parental pressure and support toward Asian Americans' self-efficacy, outcome expectations, and interests in stereotypical occupations: Living up to parental expectations and internalized stereotyping as mediators. *Journal of Counseling Psychology, 61,* 241.

Stein-McCormick, C., Osborn, D. S., Hayden, S. C. W., & Van Hoose, D. (2013). *Career development for transitioning veterans.* Broken Arrow, OK: National Career Development Association.

Strauser, D. R. (2013). *Career development, employment, and disability in rehabilitation: From theory to practice.* New York, NY: Springer Publishing Company

Strauser, D. R., Lustig, D. C., Cogdal, P. A., & Uruk, A. C. (2006). Trauma symptoms: Relationship with career thoughts, vocational identity, and developmental work personality. *The Career Development Quarterly, 54,* 346–360.

Strauser, D. R., Lustig, D. C., & Uruk, A. C. (2004). Differences in career thoughts between individuals with and without disability: Do they really exist? *Journal of Applied Rehabilitation Counseling, 35,* 25–31.

Sverko, I., Babarovic, T., & Medugorac, V. (2014). Pictorial assessment of interests: Development and evaluation of pictorial and descriptive interest inventory. *Journal of Vocational Behavior, 84*(3). DOI:10.1016/j.jvb.2014.02.008

Taber, B. J., Hartung, P. J., Briddick, H., Briddick, W. C., & Rehfuss, M. C. (2011). Career style interview: A contextualized approach to career counseling. *The Career Development Quarterly, 59,* 274–287.

Tang, M., Pan, W., & Newmeyer, M. D. (2008). Factors influencing high school students' career aspirations. *Professional School Counseling, 11,* 285–295.

Thrift, E., & Amundson, N. (2005). Hermeneutic-narrative approach to career counseling: An alternative to postmodernism. *Perspectives in Education, 23,* 9–21.

Watkins, C. E., Jr., & Savickas, M. L. (1990). Psychodynamic career counseling. In W. B. Walsh & S. H. Osipow (Eds.), *Career counseling: Contemporary topics in vocational psychology* (pp. 79–116). Hillsdale, NJ: Erlbaum.

Watson, J., Lenz, J., & Melvin, B. (2013). Response to Raven: The case of the righteous paralegal. In S. G. Niles, J. Goodman, & M. Pope (Eds.). *The career counseling casebook* (2nd ed., pp. 315–324). Broken Arrow, OK: NCDA.

Yanckak, K. V., Lease, S. H., & Strauser, D. R. (2005). Relation of disability type and career thoughts to vocational identity. *Rehabilitation Counseling Bulletin, 48,* 130–138.

Chapter 4

Arons, J. (2008). *Lifetime losses: The career wage gap.* Washington, DC: Center for American Progress.

Arthur, N., & Collins, S. (2011). Infusing culture in career counseling. *Journal of Employment Counseling, 48,* 147–149.

Atkinson, D. R., Morten, G., & Sue, D. W. (1989). A minority identity development model. In D. R. Atkinson, G. Morten, & D. W. Sue (Eds.), *Counseling American minorities* (pp. 35–52). Dubuque, IA: William C. Brown.

Atkinson, D. R., Morten, G., & Sue, D. W. (Eds.). (1993). *Counseling American minorities* (4th ed.). Madison, WI: Brown & Benchmark.

Atkinson, D. R., Morten, G., & Sue, D. W. (Eds.) (1998). *Counseling American minorities: A cross cultural perspective* (5th ed.). New York, NY: McGraw Hill.

Axelson, J. A. (1985). *Counseling and development in a multicultural society.* Pacific Grove, CA: Brooks/Cole.

Bandura, A. (1986). *Social foundations of thought and action: A social cognitive theory.* Englewood Cliffs, NJ: Prentice Hall.

Berg-Cross, L., & Zoppetti, L. (1991). Person-in-Culture Interview: Understanding culturally different students. *Journal of College Student Psychotherapy, 5,* 5–21.

Bimrose, J., Watson, M., McMahon, M., Haasler, S., Tomassini, M., & Suzanne, P. A. (2014). The problem with women? Challenges posed by gender for career guidance practice. *International Journal for Educational and Vocational Guidance, 14,* 77–88.

Blustein, D. (2013). *The Oxford handbook of the psychology of working.* New York, NY: Oxford University Press.

Bohart, A. C. (2002). Focusing on the positive, focusing on the negative: Implications for psychotherapy. *Journal of Clinical Psychology, 58,* 1–7.

Bureau of Labor Statistics. (2010). Employment status of the civilian population by sex, age, and disability status. Retrieved from http://www.bls.gov/news.release/empsit.t06.htm.

Bureau of Labor Statistics. (2015). The employment situation–February 2015. Washington, DC: Bureau of Labor Statistics. Retrieved from www.bls.gov/news.release/pdf/empsit.pdf.

Casella, C. (2002). Using Super's theory in career counseling with lesbian clients. *The Career Development Quarterly, 50,* 306–310.

Cashwell, C. S., & Young, J. S. (Eds.). (2005). *Integrating spirituality and religion into counseling: A guide to competent practice.* Alexandria, VA: American Counseling Association.

Cass, V. C. (1979). Homosexual identity formation: A theoretical model. *Journal of Homosexuality, 7,* 219–235.

Center for American Progress. (2014, October). *The facts on immigration today.* Washington, DC: Author.

Chan, C. (1992). Cultural considerations in counseling Asian American lesbians and gay men. In S. Dworkin & F. Gutierrez (Eds.), *Counseling gay men and lesbians* (pp. 115–124). Alexandria, VA: American Association for Counseling and Development.

Chapman, B. E., & Brannock, J. C. (1987). Proposed model of lesbian identity development: An empirical examination. *Journal of Homosexuality, 14,* 69–80.

Chung, Y. B. (2001). Work discrimination and coping strategies: Conceptual frameworks for counseling lesbian, gay, and bisexual clients. *The Career Development Quarterly, 50,* 33–44.

Chung, Y. B. (2003). Career counseling with lesbian, gay, bisexual, and transgender persons: The next decade. *The Career Development Quarterly, 52,* 78–86.

Chung, Y. B., Williams, B., & Dispenza, F. (2009). Validating work discrimination and coping strategy models for sexual minorities. *The Career Development Quarterly, 58,* 162–170.

Colby, S. L., & Ortman, J. M. (2015). *Predictions of the size and composition of the U.S. population: 2014 to 2060.* Washington, DC: U.S. Census Bureau.

Constantine, M. G. (1997). Facilitating multicultural competency in counseling supervision: Operationalizing a practical framework. In D. B. Pope-Davis & H. L. K. Coleman (Eds.), *Multicultural counseling competencies: Assessment, education and training, and supervision* (pp. 310–324). Thousand Oaks, CA: Sage.

Cook, D. W. (1981). Impact of disability on the individual. In R. M. Parker & C. E. Hansen (Eds.),

Rehabilitation counseling (pp. 169–197). Boston, MA: Allyn & Bacon.

Cook, E. (1994). Role salience and multiple roles: A gender perspective. *The Career Development Quarterly, 43,* 85–95.

Cook, E., Heppner, M. J., & O'Brien, K. M. (2002). Feminism and women's career development: An ecological perspective. In S. Niles (Ed.), *Adult career development: Concepts, models, and practices* (3rd ed., pp. 169–190). Tulsa, OK: National Career Development Association.

Cross, W. E. (1971). The Negro-to-Black conversion experience: Toward a psychology of Black liberation. *Black World, 20,* 13–27.

Cross, W. E. (1995). The psychology of Nigrescence: Revising the Cross model. In J. G. Ponterotto, J. M. Casas, L. A. Suzuki, & C. M. Alexander (Eds.), *Handbook of multicultural counseling* (pp. 93–122). Thousand Oaks, CA: Sage.

Cross, W., & Strauss, L. (1998). The everyday functions of African American identity. In J. Swim & C. Stangor (Eds.), *Prejudice: The target's perspective* (pp. 267–279). San Diego, CA: Academic Press.

Cummings, R., Maddux, C. D., & Casey, J. (2000). Individualized transition planning for students with learning disabilities. *The Career Development Quarterly, 49,* 60–72.

Daire, A. P., LaMothe, S., & Fuller, D. P. (2007). Differences between Black/African American and White college students regarding influences on high school completion, college attendance, and career choice. *The Career Development Quarterly, 55,* 275–279.

Datti, P. (2009). Applying the social learning theory of career decision making to gay, lesbian, bisexual, transgender, and questioning young adults. *The Career Development Quarterly, 58,* 54–64.

Degges-White, S., & Shoffner, M. (2002). Career counseling with lesbian clients: Using the theory of work adjustment as a framework. *The Career Development Quarterly, 51,* 87–96.

Dipeolu, A., Sniatecki, J. L., Storlie, C. A., & Hargrave, S. (2013). Dysfunctional career thoughts and attitudes as predictors of vocational identity among young adults with attention deficit hyperactivity disorder. *Journal of Vocational Behavior, 82,* 79–84.

Dispenza, F., Watson, L. B., Chung, Y. B., & Brack, G. (2012). Experience of career-related discrimination for female-to-male transgender persons: A qualitative study. *The Career Development Quarterly, 60,* 65–81.

Downing, N. E., & Roush, K. L. (1985). From passive acceptance to active commitment: A model of feminist identity development for women. *The Counseling Psychologist, 13,* 195–209.

Eggerth, D. E., DeLaney, S. C., Flynn, M. A., & Jacobson, C. J. (2012). Work experiences of Latina immigrants: A qualitative study. *Journal of Career Development, 39,* 13–30.

Eggerth, D. E., & Flynn, M. A. (2012). Applying the theory of work adjustment to Latino immigrant workers: An exploratory study. *Journal of Career Development, 39,* 76–98.

Ettinger, J. (1996). Meeting the career development needs of individuals with disabilities. In R. Feller & G. Walz (Eds.), *Career transitions in turbulent times: Exploring work, learning and careers* (pp. 239–244). Greensboro, NC: Educational Resources Information Center, Counseling and Student Services Clearinghouse.

Fassinger, R. E. (1995). From invisibility to integration: Lesbian identity in the workplace. *The Career Development Quarterly, 44,* 148–167.

Fischer, A. R., Jome, L. M., & Atkinson, D. R. (1998). Reconceptualizing multicultural counseling: Universal healing conditions in a culturally specific context. *Counseling Psychologist, 26,* 525–588.

Fiske, S. T. (1998). Stereotyping, prejudice, and discrimination. In D. T. Gilbert, S. T. Fiske, & G. Lindzey (Eds.), *Handbook of social psychology* (4th ed., Vol. 2, pp. 357–411). New York, NY: McGraw-Hill.

Flores, L. Y., Spanierman, L. B., & Obasi, E. M. (2003). Professional and ethical issues in career assessment with diverse racial and ethnic groups. *Journal of Career Assessment, 11,* 76–95.

Fouad, N. A. (1993). Cross-cultural vocational assessment. *The Career Development Quarterly, 42,* 4–13.

Frome, P. M., Alfeld, C. J., Eccles, J. S., & Barber, B. L. (2006). Young women who changed their occupational aspirations. *Educational Research and Evaluation, 12,* 359–372.

Gati, I., & Perez, M. (2014). Gender differences in career preferences from 1990 to 2010: Gaps reduced but not eliminated. *Journal of Counseling Psychology, 61,* 63.

Gilligan, C. (1982). *In a different voice.* Cambridge, MA: Harvard University Press.

Goleman, D. (1990, July 10). Homophobia: Scientists find clues to its roots. *New York Times,* pp. C1, C11.

Gottfredson, L. S. (1981). Circumscription and compromise: A developmental theory of occupational aspirations. *Journal of Counseling Psychology, 28,* 545–579.

Gottfredson, L. S. (2002). Gottfredson's theory of circumscription, compromise, and self-creation. In D. Brown & Associates (Eds.), *Career choice and development* (4th ed., pp. 85–148). San Francisco, CA: Jossey-Bass.

Grieger, I., & Ponterotto, J. G. (1995). A framework for assessment in multicultural counseling. In J. G. Ponterotto, J. M. Casas, L. A. Suzuki, & C. M. Alexander (Eds.), *Handbook of multicultural counseling* (pp. 357–374). Thousand Oaks, CA: Sage.

Gysbers, N. C., Heppner, M. J., & Johnston, J. A. (2003). *Career counseling: Process, issues, and techniques* (2nd ed.). Boston, MA: Allyn & Bacon.

Gysbers, N. C., Heppner, M. J., & Johnston, J. A. (2014). *Career counseling: Holism, diversity, and strengths.* Alexandria, VA: American Counseling Association.

Hageman, M. B., & Gladding, S. T. (1983). The art of career exploration: Occupational sex-role stereotyping among elementary school children. *Elementary School Guidance and Counseling, 17,* 280–287.

Hartung, P. J., Speight, J. D., & Lewis, D. M. (1996). Individualism-collectivism and the vocational behavior of majority culture college students. *The Career Development Quarterly, 45,* 87–96.

Hayes, J. A. (2002). Playing with fire: Countertransference and clinical epistemology. *Journal of Contemporary Psychotherapy, 32,* 93–100.

Hernandez, T. J., & Morales, N. E. (1999). Career, culture, and compromise: Career development experiences of Latinas working in higher education. *The Career Development Quarterly, 48,* 45–58.

Herr, E. L., Cramer, S. H., & Niles, S. G. (2004). *Career guidance and counseling through the lifespan: Systemic approaches* (6th ed.). Boston, MA: Allyn & Bacon.

Herring, R. D. (2002). Multicultural counseling for career development. In J. Trusty, E. J. Looby, & D. S. Sandhu (Eds.), *Multicultural counseling: Context, theory and practice, and competence* (pp. 219–246). Huntington, NY: Nova Science.

Hussar, W. J., & Bailey, T. M. (2014). *Projections of education statistics to 2022.* Washington, DC: National Center for Education Statistics.

Innovative Placements. (2010). *The facts about employing people with disabilities.* Retrieved from http://innovativeplacementswny.com/facts.

Ivey, A. E., D'Andrea, M., Ivey, M. B., & Simek-Morgan, L. (2009). *Theories of counseling and psychotherapy: A multicultural perspective* (7th ed.). Pacific Grove, CA: Brooks/Cole.

Kluckhohn, C., & Murray, H. A. (1950). Personality formation: The determinants. In C. Kluckhohn & H. A. Murray (Eds.), *Personality in nature, society, and culture* (pp. 35–48). New York, NY: Knopf.

Lease, S. H. (2003). Testing a model of men's nontraditional occupational choices. *The Career Development Quarterly, 51,* 244–258.

Lee, C. C. (2012). A conceptual framework for culturally competent career counseling practice. *Career Planning and Adult Development Journal, 28,* 7.

Lee, C. C., & Richardson, B. L. (Eds.). (1991). *Multicultural issues in counseling: New approaches to diversity.* Alexandria, VA: American Association for Counseling and Development.

Lee, D. L., & Ahn, S. (2012). Discrimination against Latina/os: A meta-analysis of individual-level resources and outcomes. *The Counseling Psychologist, 40,* 28–65.

Lent, R. W., Brown, S. D., & Hackett, G. (2002). Social cognitive career theory. In D. Brown & Associates (Eds.), *Career choice and development* (4th ed., pp. 255–311). San Francisco, CA: Jossey-Bass.

Leong, F. T. L. (1993). The career counseling process with racial-ethnic minorities: The case of Asian Americans. *The Career Development Quarterly, 42,* 26–40.

Leong, F. T. L. (2010). A Cultural Formulation Approach to career assessment and career counseling: Guest editor's introduction. *Journal of Career Development, 37,* 375–390.

Leong, F. T. L., & Brown, M. T. (1995). Theoretical issues in cross-cultural career development: Cultural validity and cultural specificity. In W. B. Walsh & S. H. Osipow (Eds.), *Handbook of vocational psychology: Theory, research, and practice* (2nd ed., pp. 143–180). Mahwah, NJ: Erlbaum.

Leong, F. T. L., Hardin, E., & Gupta, A. (2007). Culture and self in vocational psychology: A cultural formulations approach to career assessment and career counseling. An invited paper presented at the Society for Vocational Psychology Biennial Conference, University of Akron, May 29–June 1.

Leong, F. T., & Pearce, M. (2014). Indigenous models of career development and vocational psychology. In G. Arumani, G. Bakshi, A. J. Leong, and F. T. L. Watts (Eds.), *Handbook of career development: International perspectives* (pp. 67–79). New York, NY: Springer.

Levinson, E. M. (1998). *Transition: Facilitating the post-school adjustment of students with disabilities.* Boulder, CO: Westview Press.

Levinson, H. (1994). Why the behemoths fell: Psychological roots of corporate failure. *American Psychologist, 49,* 428–436.

Lewin, T. (2010). Once a leader, U.S. lags in college degrees. *New York Times.* Retrieved from http://www.nytimes.com/2010/07/23/education/23college.html.

Lindstrom, L., Doren, B., Post, C., & Lombardi, A. (2013). Building career PATHS (Postschool Achievement Through Higher Skills) for young women with disabilities. *The Career Development Quarterly, 61,* 330–338.

Louis, L. (2006). Life as a mother-scientist. *The Chronicle of Higher Education, 53,* C1.

Luzzo, D. A., Hitchings, W. E., Retish, P., & Shoemaker, A. (1999). Evaluating differences in college students' career decision making on the basis of disability status. *The Career Development Quarterly, 46,* 142–156.

McMahon. B. T., Roessler, R., Rumrill, P. D., Hurley, J. E., West, S. L., Chan, F., & Carlson, L. (2008). Hiring discrimination against people with disabilities under the ADA: Characteristics of charging parties. *Journal of Occupational Rehabilitation, 18,* 111–132.

Morgan, K. S., & Brown, L. S. (1991). Lesbian career development, work behavior, and vocational counseling. *Counseling Psychologist, 19,* 273– 291.

Nassar-McMillan, S., & Zagzebski-Tovar, L. (2012). Career counseling with Americans of Arab descent. *Career Planning and Adult Development Journal, 28,* 72.

National Council on Disability. (2000). *Transition and post-school outcomes for youth with disabilities: Closing the gaps to post-secondary education and employment.* Washington, DC: National Council on Disability, Social Security Administration.

Niles, S. G., & Goodnough, G. (1996). Life-role salience and values: A review of recent research. *The Career Development Quarterly, 45,* 65–86.

Nguyen, A. M., & Benet-Martínez, V. (2013). Biculturalism and adjustment: A meta-analysis. *Journal of Cross-Cultural Psychology, 44,* 122–159.

O'Neil, W. M. (1982). Gender role conflict and strain in men's lives: Implications for psychiatrists, psychologists, and other human-service providers. In K. Solomon & N. B. Levy (Eds.), *Men in transition* (pp. 5–44). New York, NY: Plenum.

Organization for Economic Co-operation and Development. (2010). Babies and bosses: Key outcomes of the United States compared to OECD average. Retrieved from http://www.oecd.org/els/family/babiesandbosses-keyoutcomesofunitedstatescomparedtooecdaverage.htm.

Orzek, A. M. (1992). Career counseling for the gay and lesbian community. In S. H. Dworkin & F. J. Guitierrez (Eds.), *Counseling gay men and lesbians: Journey to the end of the rainbow* (pp. 23–24). Alexandria, VA: American Association for Counseling and Development.

Park, R. E. (1928). Human migration and the marginal man. *American Journal of Sociology, 33,* 881–893.

Park, R. E., & Burgess, E. W. (1921). *Introduction to the science of sociology.* Chicago, IL: University of Chicago Press.

Paul, P. (2008). Applying a constructivist-developmental approach to issues of sexual orientation and religion in career counseling. *The Career Development Quarterly, 56,* 344–352.

Pepper, S., & Lorah, P. (2008). Career issues and workplace considerations for the transsexual community: Bridging a gap of knowledge for career counselors and mental health care providers. *The Career Development Quarterly, 56,* 330–343.

Pew Research Center. (2014). *Millennials in adulthood: Detached from institutions, networked with friends.* Washington, DC: Author.

Piña-Watson, B., Jimenez, N., & Ojeda, L. (2014). Self-construal, career decision self-efficacy, and perceived barriers predict Mexican American women's life satisfaction. *The Career Development Quarterly, 62,* 210–223.

Ponterotto, J. G., Rivera, L., & Sueyoshi, L. A. (2000). The career-in-culture interview: A semi-structured protocol for the cross-cultural intake interview. *The Career Development Quarterly, 49,* 85–95.

Pope, M. (1995). Gay and lesbian career development: Introduction to the special section. *The Career Development Quarterly, 44,* 146–147.

Pope, M. (2012). Embracing and harnessing diversity in the US workforce: What have we learned? *International Journal for Educational and Vocational Guidance, 12,* 17–30.

Pope, M., & Barret, B. (2002). Providing career counseling to gay and lesbian clients. In S. G. Niles (Ed.), *Adult career development* (3rd ed., pp. 215–232). Tulsa, OK: National Career Development Association.

Pope-Davis, D. B., Toporek, R. L., Ligiero, D., Ortega, L., Bashshur, M. L., Brittan Powell, ... & Liang, C. (2002). A qualitative study of clients' perspectives of multicultural counseling competence. *The Counseling Psychologist, 30,* 355–393.

Powell, G. N., & Butterfield, D. A. (2015). The preference to work for a man or a woman: A matter of sex and gender? *Journal of Vocational Behavior, 86,* 28–37.

Prati, G., & Pietrantoni, L. (2014). Coming out and job satisfaction: A moderated mediation model. *The Career Development Quarterly, 62,* 358–371.

Prince, J. P. (1995). Career assessment with lesbian, gay, and bisexual individuals. *Journal of Career Assessment, 5,* 168–177.

Richards, P. S., & Bergin, A. E. (1997). *A spiritual strategy for counseling and psychotherapy.* Washington, DC: American Psychological Association.

Rogers, C. R. (1957). The necessary and sufficient conditions of therapeutic personality change. *Journal of Consulting Psychology, 21,* 95–103.

Sage, G. P. (1991). Counseling American Indian adults. In C. C. Lee & B. L. Richardson (Eds.), *Multicultural issues in counseling: Approaches to diversity* (pp. 23–36). Alexandria, VA: American Association for Counseling and Development.

Sangganjanavanich, V. F., & Headley, J. A. (2013). Facilitating career development concerns of gender transitioning individuals: Professional standards and competencies. *The Career Development Quarterly, 61,* 354–366.

Scheuermann, T. S., Tokar, D. M., & Hall, R. J. (2014). An investigation of African-American women's prestige domain interests and choice goals using Social Cognitive Career Theory. *Journal of Vocational Behavior, 84,* 273–282.

Scholl, M. B. (1999). The career path tournament: Developing awareness of sociological barriers to career advancement. *The Career Development Quarterly, 47,* 230–242.

Siperstein, G. N., Parker, R. C., & Drascher, M. (2013). National snapshot of adults with intellectual disabilities in the labor force. *Journal of Vocational Rehabilitation, 39,* 157–165.

Skovholt, T. M. (1990). Career themes in counseling and psychotherapy with men. In D. Moore & F. Leafgren (Eds.), *Problem solving strategies and interventions for men in conflict* (pp. 39–53). Alexandria, VA: American Association for Counseling and Development.

Sophie, J. (1986). A critical examination of stage theories of lesbian identity development. *Journal of Homosexuality, 12,* 39–51.

Stead, G. B. (2004). Culture and career psychology: A social constructionist perspective. *Journal of Vocational Behavior, 64,* 389–406.

Stein, J. (1975). *The Random House college dictionary* (rev. ed.). New York, NY: Random House.

Sue, D. W., & Sue, D. (1990). *Counseling the culturally different: Theory and practice* (2nd ed.). New York, NY: Wiley.

Sun, K. (1995). The definition of race. *American Psychologist, 50,* 43–44.

Torrey, E. F. (1986). *Witchdoctors and psychiatrists: The common root of psychotherapy and its future.* New York, NY: Harper and Row.

U.S. Census Bureau. (2010). *Demographic profiles.* Retrieved from census.gov/2010census/news/press-kits/demographic-profiles.html.

U.S. Census Bureau. (2015). *About Hispanic origin.* Retrieved from www.census.gov/topics/population/hispanic-origin/about.html.

U.S. Department of Justice. (1991). *Americans with disabilities handbook.* Washington, DC: U.S. Government Printing Office.

U.S. Department of Labor. (2010). *Occupational outlook handbook.* Washington, DC: Author.

Velez, B. L., & Moradi, B. (2012). Workplace support, discrimination, and person–organization fit: Tests of the theory of work adjustment with LGB individuals. *Journal of Counseling Psychology, 59,* 399.

Walsh, W. B., & Betz, N. E. (1990). *Tests and assessment* (3rd ed.). Englewood Cliffs, NJ: Prentice Hall.

Wohl, J. (1995). Traditional individual psychotherapy and ethnic minorities. In J. F. Aponte, R. Y. Rivers, & R. Young (Eds.), *Psychological interventions and cultural diversity* (pp. 74–91). Boston, MA: Allyn & Bacon.

Worthington, R. L., Flores, L. Y., & Navarro, R. L. (2005). Career development in context: Research with people of color. In S. D. Brown & R. W. Lent (Eds.), *Career development and counseling: Putting theory and research to work* (pp. 225–252). Hoboken, NJ: Wiley.

Wrenn, C. G. (1962). The culturally encapsulated counselor. *Harvard Educational Review, 32,* 444–449.

Young, R. A., Marshall, S. K., & Valach, L. (2007). Making career theories more culturally sensitive: Implications for counseling. *The Career Development Quarterly, 56,* 4–18.

Zunker, V. G. (2006). *Using assessment results in career counseling* (7th ed.). Monterey, CA: Brooks/Cole.

Chapter 5

ACT, Inc. (2007). *EXPLORE.* Iowa City, IA: Author.

ACT, Inc. (2011). *PLAN.* Iowa City, IA: Author.

ACT, Inc. (2015a). *ACT Assessment Program.* Iowa City, IA: Author.

ACT, Inc. (2015b). *WorkKeys.* Iowa City, IA: Author.

Campbell, D. (2000). *Campbell Intand Skill Survey.* Bloomington, MN: Pearson.

Carlson, J. F., Geisinger, K. F., & Jonson, J. L. (Eds.). (2014). *The nineteenth mental measurements yearbook*. Lincoln, NE: Buros Institute.

Chartrand, J. M., Robbins, S. B., & Morrill, W. H. (1997). *The Career Factors Inventory*. Mountain View, CA: Consulting Psychologists Press.

College Entrance Examination Board. (2015). *Scholastic Aptitude Test (SAT)*. New York, NY: Author.

Crites, J., & Savickas, M. (1995). *Career Maturity Inventory*. Boulder, CO: Crites Career Consultants.

Flores, L. Y., Spanierman, L. B., Armstrong, P. I., & Velez, A. D. (2006). Validity of the Strong Interest Inventory and Skills Confidence Inventory with Mexican American high school students. *Journal of Career Assessment, 14,* 183–202. Retrieved from http://onlinesagepub.com.

Golden, J. (2004). *The Golden Personality Type Profiler.* San Antonio, TX: Pearson.

Harris-Bowlsbey, J., Dikel, M. R., & Sampson, J. P., Jr. (2002) *The Internet: A tool for career planning,* 2nd ed. Broken Arrow, OK: National Career Development Association.

Holland, J. L. (1996). *Self-Directed Search, Form E.* Odessa, FL: Psychological Assessment Resources.

Holland, J. L. (1997). *Making vocational choices: A theory of vocational personalities and work environments* (3rd ed.). Odessa, FL: Psychological Assessment Resources.

Holland, J. L., Daiger, D. C., & Power, P. G. (1980). *My vocational situation*. Retrieved from saens.hi.is.

Holland, J. L., & Gottfredson, G. D. (1991). *Position Classification Inventory.* Odessa, FL: Psychological Assessment Resources.

Holland, J. L., & Gottfredson, G. D. (1994). *Career Attitudes and Strategies Inventory.* Lutz, FL: Psychological Assessment Resources.

Holland, J. L., & Messer, M. A. (2015). *Self-Directed Search,* 5th ed. Odessa, FL: Psychological Assessment Resources.

Jackson, D. N. (1999). *Jackson Vocational Interest Survey.* Port Huron, MI: Sigma Assessment Systems.

Johansson, C. B. (1986). *Career Assessment Inventory.* Bloomington, MN: Pearson.

Johansson, C. B. (1993). *Interest Determination, Exploration, and Assessment System (IDEAS).* Bloomington, MN: Pearson.

Joint Committee on Testing Practices. (2004). *Code of fair testing practices.* Washington, DC: Author.

Jones, L. K. (1986). *Career Decision Profile.* Raleigh, NC: CareerKey, Inc.

Jung, C. G. (1959). The archetypes and the collective unconscious. In C. G. Jung, *Collected works* (vol. 9, part I). Princeton, NJ: Princeton University Press.

Kapes, J. T., & Whitfield, E. A. (2002). *Counselor's guide to career assessment instruments.* Broken Arrow, OK: National Career Development Association.

Knapp, R. R., & Knapp, L. (1995). *Career Occupational Preference Survey.* San Diego, CA: EdITs.

Krumboltz, J. D. (1991). *The Career Beliefs Inventory.* Menlo Park, CA: Mind Garden, Inc.

Kuder, Inc. (1998). *Iowa Career Learning Assessment.* Adel, IA: Author.

Kuder, Inc. (2013a). *Kuder Career Interests Assessment.* Adel, IA: Author.

Kuder, Inc. (2013b). *Kuder Skills Confidence Assessment.* Adel, IA: Author.

Miller, C. H. (1961). *Foundations of guidance.* New York, NY: Harper & Row.

Miller, M. J. (2007). Examining the degree of congruency between a traditional career instrument and an online self-assessment exercise. *Journal of Employment Counseling, 44,* 11–16. Retrieved from http://proquest.libguides.com/ABI.

Myers, I., & Briggs, K. (2012). *The Myers-Briggs Type Indicator.* Palo Alto, CA: Consulting Psychologists Press.

National Council on Measurement in Education. (1995). *The code of professional responsibilities in educational measurement.* Washington, DC: Author.

O'Shea, A., & Feller, R. (2000). *Career Decision Making System – Revised (CDM-R).* Bloomington, MN: Pearson.

Osipow, S. H., Carney, C. G., Winer, J., Yanico, B., & Kosshier, M. (1997). *Career Decision Scale.* Odessa, FL: Psychological Assessment Resources.

Parsons, F. (1909). *Choosing a vocation.* Boston, MA: Houghton Mifflin.

Psychological Assessment Resources. (2015). *Educational opportunities finder.* Odessa, FL: Author.

Real Game. (2015). *The real game series.* Toronto, Canada: Career Cruising.

Riverside Publishing. (1998). *Interest Explorer.* Rolling Meadows, IL: Author.

Sampson, J. P., Peterson, G. W., Lenz, J. G., Reardon, R. C., & Saunders, D. E. (1996). *Career Thoughts Inventory.* Odessa, FL: Psychological Assessment Resources.

SkillScan. (1987). *SkillScan Professional Pack.* Martinez, CA: Author.

SkillScan. (2009). *Career Driver Online.* Martinez, CA: Author.

SkillScan. (2014). *SkillScan Express*. Martinez, CA: Author.

Strong, E. K. (2004). *The Strong Interest Inventory*. Palo Alto, CA: Consulting Psychologists Press.

Super, D. E. (1957). *The psychology of careers*. New York, NY: Harper.

Super, D. E., Starishevsky, R., Matlin, N., & Jordaan, J. P. (1963). *Career development: Self-concept theory* (Research Monograph No. 4). New York, NY: College Entrance Examination Board.

Super, D. E., Thompson, A. S., Lindeman, R. H., Jordaan, J. P., & Myers, R. A. (1984). *Career Development Inventory*. Palo Alto, CA: Consulting Psychologists Press.

Super, D. E., & Zytowski, D. G. (2006). *Super's Work Values Inventory, Revised*. Adel, IA: Kuder, Inc.

Swaney, K. B. (1995). *Technical manual: Revised unisex edition of the ACT Interest Inventory (UNIACT)*. Iowa City, IA: ACT, Inc.

U.S. Census Bureau. (2014). *2014 National Population Projections*. Washington, DC: Author.

U.S. Department of Defense. (2005). *Armed Services Vocational Aptitude Battery*. Monterey, CA: Author.

U.S. Department of Labor, Employment and Training Administration. (2001a). *O*Net Interest Profiler*. Washington, DC: Author.

U.S. Department of Labor, Employment and Training Administration. (2001b). *O*Net Ability Profiler*. Washington, DC: Author.

U.S. Department of Labor, Employment and Training Administration. (2001c). *O*Net Work Importance Profiler*. Washington, DC: Author.

Wood, C., & Hays, D. G. (2013). *A counselor's guide to career assessment instruments*. Broken Arrow, OK: National Career Development Association.

Chapter 6

ACT, Inc. (1989a). *Inventory of Work-Relevant Abilities*. Iowa City, IA: Author.

ACT, Inc. (1989b). *UNIACT Interest Inventory*. Iowa City, IA: Author.

ACT, Inc. (2015). *ACT profile* [Computer software]. Iowa City, IA: Author.

Association of American Medical Colleges. (2014). *The official guide to medical school admissions 2014: How to prepare for and apply to medical school*. Washington, DC: Author.

Barron's Educational Publications. (2015). *Profiles of American colleges 2015*. Hauppauge, NY: Author.

Campbell, D. (2000). *Campbell Interest and Skill Survey*. Minneapolis, MN: NCS Assessments.

Career Cruising. (2015). *Career cruising*. Toronto, Canada: Author.

Carnevale, A. P., Smith, N., & Strohl, J. (2013). *Recovery: Job growth and education requirements through 2020*. Washington, DC: Georgetown Public Policy Institute.

College Board. (2015a). *College board scholarship handbook*. New York, NY: Author.

College Board. (2015b). *The book of majors*. New York, NY: Author.

Dinklage, L. B. (1968). *Decision strategies of adolescents*. Unpublished doctoral dissertation, Harvard University, Cambridge, MA.

Fedorko, J., & Allott, D. (2006). *The internship files: How to get, keep, and make the most of your internship*. New York, NY: Simon & Schuster.

Fiske, E. (2015). *Fiske guide to colleges 2015*. Naperville, IL: Sourcebooks, Inc.

Gottfredson, G. D., & Holland, J. L. (1996). *The dictionary of Holland occupational codes*. Odessa, FL: Psychological Assessment Resources.

Holland, J. L. (1997). *Making vocational choices: A theory of vocational personalities and work environments* (3rd ed.). Odessa, FL: Psychological Assessment Resources.

Holland, J. L., & Messer, M. A. (2015). *The Self-Directed Search* (5th ed.). Odessa, FL: Psychological Assessment Resources.

J. G. Ferguson Publishing. (2014). *Encyclopedia of careers and vocational guidance*. Chicago, IL: Author.

Johansson, C. B. (1984). *Career Assessment Inventory*. Minneapolis, MN: NCS Assessments.

Krumboltz, J. D. (1991). *The Career Beliefs Inventory*. Palo Alto, CA: Consulting Psychologists Press.

Kuder, Inc. (2013a). *Kuder Career Interests Assessment*. Adel, IA: Author.

Kuder, Inc. (2013b). *Kuder Skills Confidence Assessment*. Adel, IA: Author.

Kuder, Inc. (2013c). *Galaxy* [Computer software]. Adel, IA: Author.

Kuder, Inc. (2015a). *Journey* [Computer software]. Adel, IA: Author.

Kuder, Inc. (2015b). *Navigator* [Computer software]. Adel, IA: Author.

Kuder, Inc. (2015c). *Kuder Career Planning System*. Adel, IA: Author.

Landes, M. (2004). *The back door guide to short-term job adventures: Internships, extraordinary experiences, seasonal jobs, volunteering, work abroad*. Berkeley, CA: Ten Speed Press.

Margolis, W. (Ed.). (2013). *ABA-LSAC official guide to ABA-approved law schools: 2013 Edition*. Lawrenceville, NJ: Arco.

Mayne, T. J., Norcross, J. G., & Sayette, M. A. (2014). *Insider's guide to graduate programs in clinical and counseling psychology 2014–15*. New York, NY: Guilford Press.

National Career Development Association. (1991). *Guidelines for the preparation and evaluation of career and occupational information literature*. Broken Arrow, OK: Author.

O'Shea, A. J., & Feller, R. (2000). *Career Decision-Making System*. Circle Pines, MN: American Guidance Service.

Peterson's Publishing. (2015a). *Graduate programs in engineering and applied science*. Lawrenceville, NJ: Author.

Peterson's Publishing. (2015b). *Peterson's four-year colleges 2015*. Lawrenceville, NJ: Author.

Peterson's Publishing. (2015c). *Peterson's two-year colleges 2015*. Lawrenceville, NJ: Author.

Pope, L., & Oswald, H. M. (2012). *Colleges that change lives: 40 colleges that will change the way you think about colleges*. New York, NY: Penguin.

Prediger, D. P. (1981). Aid for mapping occupations and interests: A graphic for vocational guidance and research. *Vocational Guidance Quarterly, 30,* 21–36.

Princeton Review. (2005). *The internship bible* (10th ed.). New York, NY: Author.

Princeton Review. (2013). *The best 168 medical schools*. New York, NY: Author.

Princeton Review. (2015a). *Paying for college without going broke*. New York, NY: Author.

Princeton Review. (2015b). *The complete guide to colleges 2015*. New York, NY: Author.

Psychological Assessment Resources. (2015a). *The occupations finder*. Odessa, FL: Author.

Psychological Assessment Resources. (2015b). *The educational opportunities finder*. Odessa, FL: Author.

Psychological Assessment Resources. (2015c). *The leisure activities finder*. Odessa, FL: Author.

Sampson, J. P., Reardon, R., Lenz, J., & Peterson G. (2003). *Career counseling and services: A cognitive information processing approach*. Florence, KY: Brooks/Cole.

Tanabe, G., & Tanabe, K. (2015). *The ultimate scholarship book 2015: Billions of dollars in scholarships, grants, and prizes*. Belmont, CA: SuperCollege.

Tiedeman, D., & O'Hara, R. (1963). *Career development: Choice and adjustment*. New York, NY: College Entrance Examination Board.

U.S. Department of Education. (2010). *Classification of instructional programs*. Washington, DC: Author.

U.S. Department of Labor. (1991). *The dictionary of occupational titles*. Washington, DC: U.S. Government Printing Office.

U.S. Department of Labor. (1992). *What work requires of schools. SCANS Report*. Washington, DC: U.S. Government Printing Office.

U.S. Department of Labor. (2014). *The occupational outlook handbook 2014–15*. Washington, DC: U.S. Government Printing Office.

U.S. Department of Labor. (2015). *O*NET occupational database*. Washington, DC: Author.

U.S. News and World Report. (2015). *Best graduate schools 2015*. Washington, DC: Author.

Wischnitzer, S., & Wischnitzer, E. (2012). *Barron's guide to medical and dental schools*. Hauppauge, NY: Barron's Educational Publishers.

Xap Corporation. (2015a). *CHOICES Explorer*. [Computer software]. Culver City, CA: Author.

Xap Corporation. (2015b). *CHOICES Planner*. [Computer software]. Culver City, CA: Author.

Chapter 7

Betz, N., & Borgen, F. (2010). The CAPA integrative online system for college major exploration. *Journal of Career Assessment, 18,* 317–327.

Bobek, B. L., Robbins, S. B., Gore, P. A., Harris-Bowlsbey, J., Lapan, R. T., Dahir, C. A., & Jepsen, D. A. (2005). Training counselors to use computer-assisted career guidance systems more effectively: A model curriculum. *The Career Development Quarterly, 53,* 363-371.

D'Achiardi-Ressler, C. (2008). *The impact of using the Kuder Career Planning System: School performance, career decision making, and educational transitions*. Adel, IA: Kuder, Inc.

Fowkes, K. M., & McWhirter, E. H. (2007). Evaluation of computer-assisted career guidance in middle and secondary education settings: Status, obstacles, and suggestions. *Journal of Career Assessment, 15,* 388–400.

Gati, I. G., Reuma, D., & Shemesh, N. (2006). The predictive validity of a computer-assisted career decision-making system: A six-year follow-up. *Journal of Vocational Behavior, 68*(2), 205–219.

Gore, P. A., Jr., Bobek, B. L., Robbins, S. B., & Shayne, L. (2006). Computer-based career exploration: Usage patterns and a typology of users. *Journal of Career Assessment, 14,* 421–436.

Gore, P. A., Jr., & Leuwerke, W. C. (2008). Computer-assisted career counseling. In F. T. L. Leong (Ed.),

Encyclopedia of counseling (pp. 1510–1514). Thousand Oaks, CA: Sage.

Harris-Bowlsbey, J. (2009). *Take hold of your future*. Adel, IA: Kuder, Inc.

Herman, S. (2010). Career HOPES: An Internet-delivered career development intervention. *Computers in Human Behavior, 26,* 339–344.

Holland, J. L., & Messer, M. A. (2015). *The Self-Directed Search* (5th ed.). Odessa, FL: Psychological Assessment Resources.

Hooley, T. (2012). How the Internet changed career: Framing the relationship between career development and online technologies. *Career Research & Development, 29,* 3–12.

Kettunena, J., Vuorinena, R., & Sampson, J. P., Jr. (2014). Career practitioners' conceptions of social media in career services. *British Journal of Guidance & Counselling, 41,* 302–317.

Kolek, E. A., & Saunders, D. (2008). Online disclosure: An empirical examination of undergraduate Facebook profiles. *NASPA Journal, 45,* 2–35.

Kuder, Inc. (2015). *Journey*. [Computer software] Adel, IA: Author.

Maples, M. R., & Luzzo, D. A. (2005). Evaluating DISCOVER's effectiveness in enhancing college students' social cognitive career development. *The Career Development Quarterly, 53,* 274–285.

Osborn, D. S., Kronholz, J. F., Finklea, T. & Cantonis, A. M. (2014). Technology-savvy career counselling. *Canadian Psychology, 55,* 258–265.

Parsons, F. (1909). *Choosing a vocation*. Boston, MA: Houghton-Mifflin.

Pyle, K. R. (2001). Career counseling in an information age. *The Career Planning and Adult Development Journal, 16*. San Jose, CA: Career Research and Testing.

Sampson, J. P., Jr., & Makala, J. P. (2014). Ethical issues associated with information and communication technology in counseling and guidance. *International Journal of Educational and Vocational Guidance, 14*. Dordrecht, The Netherlands: Springer.

Savickas, M. L. (2005). The theory and practice of career construction. In S. D. Brown and R. W. Lent (Eds.), *Career development and counseling: Putting theory and research to work* (pp. 42–70). Hoboken, NJ: Wiley.

Spivack, N. (2007). *Web 3.0: The third generation Web is coming*. Minden, NV: Lifeboat Foundation. Retrieved from lifeboat.com/ex/web.3.0.

Taber, B. J., & Luzzo, D. A. (1999). *ACT Research Report 99–3: A comprehensive review of research evaluating the effectiveness of DISCOVER in promoting career development*. Iowa City, IA: ACT, Inc.

Trusty, J. (2014). *Study of outcomes associated with use of the Kuder Career Search with Person Match at a public research university in Greater Miami, Florida*. Adel, IA: Kuder, Inc.

U.S. Department of Labor. (2014). *The occupational outlook handbook 2014–15*. Washington, DC: U.S. Government Printing Office. Retrieved from bls.gov/ooh.

Whiston, S. C., Brecheisen, B. K., & Stephens, J. (2003). Does treatment modality affect career counseling effectiveness? *Journal of Vocational Behavior, 62,* 390–410.

Chapter 8

Amundson, N. E. (1995). An interactive model of career decision making. *Journal of Employment Counseling, 32,* 11–21.

Amundson, N. E. (2009). *Active engagement: The being and doing of career counseling*. Richmond, BC: Ergon Communications.

Amundson, N. E., Harris-Bowlsbey, J., & Niles, S. G. (2013). *Essential elements of career counseling* (3rd ed.). Upper Saddle River, NJ: Merrill/Prentice Hall.

Anderson, W. P., & Niles, S. G. (1995). Career and personal concerns expressed by career counseling clients. *The Career Development Quarterly, 43,* 240–245.

Anderson, W. P., & Niles, S. G. (2000). Important events in career counseling: Client and counselor descriptions. *The Career Development Quarterly, 48,* 251–263.

Blustein, D. L., & Spengler, P. M. (1995). Personal adjustment: Career counseling and psychotherapy. In W. B. Walsh & S. H. Osipow (Eds.), *Handbook of vocational psychology* (2nd ed., pp. 295–329). Hillsdale, NJ: Erlbaum.

Brammer, L. M. (1993). *The helping relationship: Process and skills* (5th ed.). Boston, MA: Allyn & Bacon.

Brehm, S. S. (1987). Social support and clinical practice. In J. Maddux, C. Stoltenberg, & R. Rosenwein (Eds.), *Social processes in clinical and counseling psychology* (pp. 26–38). New York, NY: Springer-Verlag.

Brown, D., & Brooks, L. (1985). Career counseling as a mental health intervention. *Professional Psychology: Research and Practice, 16,* 860–867.

Brown, D., & Brooks, L. (1991). *Career counseling techniques*. Needham Heights, MA: Allyn & Bacon.

Brown, S. D., Ryan, J. M., & Krane, N. E. (2000). Four (or five) sessions and a cloud of dust: Old assumptions and new observations about career counseling. In S. D. Brown & R. W. Lent (Eds.), *Handbook of counseling psychology* (3rd. ed., pp. 740–766). New York, NY: Wiley.

Carlsen, M. B. (1988). *Making meaning: Therapeutic processes in adult development.* New York, NY: W. W. Norton.

Carson, K. D., Carson, P. P., Phillips, J. S., & Roe, C. W. (1996). A career retrenchment model: Theoretical development and empirical outcomes. *Journal of Career Development, 22,* 273–286.

Chung, Y. B., & Gfroerer, M. C. A. (2003). Career coaching: Practice, training, professional, and ethical issues. *The Career Development Quarterly, 52,* 141–152.

Council for Accreditation of Counseling and Related Educational Programs (CACREP). (2015). *2016 CACREP Standards.* Alexandria, VA: Author.

Crites, J. O. (1976). A comprehensive model of career development in early adulthood. *Journal of Vocational Behavior, 9,* 105–118.

Crites, J. O. (1981). *Career counseling: Models, methods, and materials.* New York, NY: McGraw-Hill.

Dorn, F. J. (1992). Occupational wellness: The integration of career identity and personal identity. *Journal of Counseling & Development, 71,* 176–178.

Fouad, N. A. (1993). Cross-cultural vocational assessment. *The Career Development Quarterly, 42,* 4–13.

Fouad, N. A., Chen, Y. L., Guillen, A., Henry, C., Kantamneni, N., Novakovic ... Terry. (2007). Role induction in career counseling. *The Career Development Quarterly, 56,* 19–33.

Galassi, J. P., Crace, R. K., Martin, G. A., James, R. M., & Wallace, R. L. (1992). Client preferences and anticipations in career counseling: A preliminary investigation. *Journal of Counseling Psychology, 39,* 46–55.

Gati, I., Krausz, M., & Osipow, S. H. (1996). A taxonomy of difficulties in career decision making. *Journal of Counseling Psychology, 43,* 510–526.

Gysbers, N. C., Heppner, M. J., & Johnston, J. A. (2003). *Career counseling: Process, issues, and techniques.* Boston, MA: Allyn & Bacon.

Gysbers, N. C., Heppner, M. J., & Johnston, J. A. (2014). *Career counseling: Holism, diversity, and strengths* (4th ed.). Alexandria, VA: American Counseling Association.

Hansen, J. C., & Cramer, S. H. (Eds.). (1971). *Group guidance and counseling in the schools.* New York, NY: Appleton-Century-Crofts.

Heppner, M. J., & Hendricks, F. (1995). A process and outcome study examining career indecision and indecisiveness. *Journal of Counseling & Development, 73,* 426–437.

Heppner, M. J., Multon, K. D., Gysbers, N. C., Ellis, C. A., & Zook, C. E. (1998). The relationship of trainee self-efficacy to the process and outcome of career counseling. *Journal of Counseling Psychology, 45,* 393–402.

Heppner, M. J., O'Brien, K. M., Hinkelman, J. M., & Flores, L. Y. (1996). Training counseling psychologists in career development: Are we our own worst enemies? *The Counseling Psychologist, 24,* 105–125.

Herr, E. L., Cramer, S. H., & Niles, S. G. (2004). *Career guidance and counseling through the lifespan: Systemic approaches* (6th ed.). Boston, MA: Allyn & Bacon.

Herr, E. L., & Niles, S. G. (1998). Career: Social action in behalf of purpose, productivity, and hope. In C. Lee & G. Walz (Eds.), *Social action: A mandate for counselors* (pp. 117–136). Alexandria, VA: American Counseling Association.

Hershenson, D. B. (1996). Work adjustment: A neglected area in career counseling. *Journal of Counseling & Development, 74,* 442–446.

Highlen, P. S., & Hill, C. E. (1984). Factors affecting client change in individual counseling: Current status and theoretical speculations. In S. Brown & R. Lent (Eds.), *Handbook of counseling psychology* (pp. 334–396). New York, NY: Wiley.

Holland, J. L., Magoon, T. M., & Spokane, A. R. (1981). Counseling psychology: Career interventions, research, and theory. *Annual Review of Psychology, 32,* 279–300.

House, J. S. (1981). *Work stress and social support.* Reading, MA: Addison-Wesley.

Ibrahim, F. A., Ohnishi, H., & Wilson, R. P. (1994). Career assessment in a culturally diverse society. *Journal of Career Assessment, 2,* 276–288.

Kahn, R. L., & Antonucci, T. (1980). Convoys over the life course: Attachment, roles, and social support. In P. B. Baltes & O. Brim (Eds.), *Life-span development and behavior* (vol. 3). Boston, MA: Lexington Press.

Kalton, C. A. (2001). Client psychological distress: An important factor in career counseling. *The Career Development Quarterly, 49,* 324–335.

Kirschner, T. (1988). *Process and outcome of career counseling.* Unpublished doctoral dissertation, University of Maryland, College Park.

Kirschner, T., Hoffman, M. A., & Hill, C. E. (1994). Case study of the process and outcome of career counseling. *Journal of Counseling Psychology, 35,* 216–226.

Kivlighan, D. M. (1990). Career group therapy. *The Counseling Psychologist, 18,* 64–80.

Krumboltz, J. D. (1988). *Career Beliefs Inventory.* Palo Alto, CA: Consulting Psychologists Press.

Krumboltz, J. D. (1996). *A social learning theory of career counseling.* Stanford, CA: Stanford University.

Leong, F. T. L. (1993). The career counseling process with racial-ethnic minorities: The case of Asian Americans. *The Career Development Quarterly, 42,* 26–40.

Leong, F. T. L., & Chervinko, S. (1996). Construct validity of career indecision: Negative personality traits as predictors of career indecision. *Journal of Career Assessment, 4,* 315–329.

Luzzo, D. A. (1996). Exploring the relationship between the perception of occupational barriers and career development. *Journal of Career Development, 22,* 239–248.

Mawson, D. L., & Kahn, S. E. (1993). Group process in a women's career intervention. *The Career Development Quarterly, 41,* 238–245.

Meichenbaum, D., & Turk, D. C. (1987). *Facilitating treatment adherence: A practitioner's guidebook.* New York, NY: Plenum Press.

Multon, K. D., Heppner, M. J., Gysbers, N. C., Zook, C., & Ellis-Kalton, C. A. (2001). Client psychological distress: An important factor in career counseling. *The Career Development Quarterly, 49,* 324–325.

National Career Development Association. (2009). *Career counseling competencies.* Broken Arrow, OK: Author.

Neimeyer, G. J. (1992). Personal constructs in career counseling and development. *Journal of Career Development, 18,* 163–174.

Niles, S. G., & Anderson, W. P. (1995). A content analysis of career and personal concerns expressed by career counseling clients. *Educational and Vocational Guidance Bulletin, 57,* 59–62.

Niles, S. G., Anderson, W. P., Jr., & Cover, S. (2000). Comparing intake concerns and goals with career counseling concerns. *The Career Development Quarterly, 49,* 135–145.

Niles, S. G., & Pate, R. H. (1989). Competency and training issues related to the integration of career counseling and mental health counseling. *Journal of Career Development, 16,* 63–71.

Oliver, L. W., & Spokane, A. R. (1988). Career-intervention outcome: What contributes to client gain? *Journal of Counseling Psychology, 35,* 447–462.

Otani, A. (1989). Client resistance in counseling: Its theoretical rationale and taxonomic classification. *Journal of Counseling and Development, 67,* 458–461.

Peavy, R. V. (1994). A constructivist perspective for counseling. *Educational and Vocational Guidance Bulletin, 55,* 31.

Pope-Davis, D. B., & Dings, J. G. (1995). The assessment of multicultural counseling competencies. In J. G. Ponterotto, J. M. Casas, L. A. Suzuki, & C. M. Alexander (Eds.), *Handbook of multicultural counseling* (pp. 287–311). Thousand Oaks, CA: Sage.

Pyle, K. R. (2000). A group approach to career decision-making. In N. Peterson & R. C. Gonzalez (Eds.), *Career counseling models for diverse populations: Hands-on applications for practitioners* (pp. 121–136). Belmont, CA: Wadsworth/Thompson Learning.

Pyle, K. R. (2007). *Group career counseling: practices and principles.* Broken Arrow, OK: National Career Development Association.

Riordan, R. J., & Kahnweiler, W. (1996). Job support groups: Three configurations. *Journal of Counseling & Development, 74,* 517–520.

Rounds, J. B., & Tinsley, H. E. A. (1984). Diagnosis and treatment of vocational problems. In S. Brown & R. Lent (Eds.), *Handbook of counseling psychology* (pp. 137–177). New York, NY: Wiley.

Salomone, P. R. (1982). Difficult cases in career counseling: II. The indecisive client. *The Personnel and Guidance Journal, 60,* 496–500.

Sampson, J. P., Vacc, N. A., & Loesch, L. C. (1998). The practice of career counseling by specialists and counselors in general practice. *The Career Development Quarterly, 46,* 404–415.

Savickas, M. L. (1993). Career counseling in the postmodern era. *Journal of Cognitive Psychotherapy: An International Quarterly, 7,* 205–215.

Savickas, M. L. (2012). Life design: A paradigm for career intervention in the 21st century. *Journal of Counseling & Development, 90,* 13–19.

Savickas, M. L. (2013). Career construction theory and practice. In S. D. Brown & R. W. Lent (Eds.), *Career development and counseling* (2nd ed., pp. 147–186). Hoboken, NJ: Wiley & Sons.

Schlossberg, N. K., Lynch, A. Q., & Chickering, A. W. (1989). *Improving higher education environments for adults.* San Francisco, CA: Jossey-Bass.

Spokane, A. R. (1991). *Evaluating career interventions.* Upper Saddle River, NJ: Prentice Hall.

Subich, L. M. (1993). How personal is career counseling? *The Career Development Quarterly, 42,* 129–131.

Sue, D. W., Bernier, J. E., Durran, A., Feinberg, L., Peterson, P., Smith, E. J., & Vasquez-Nutall, E. (1982). Position paper: Cross-cultural counseling competencies. *The Counseling Psychologist, 10,* 45–52.

Sullivan, K. R., & Mahalik, J. R. (2000). Increasing career self-efficacy for women: Evaluating a group intervention. *Journal of Counseling & Development, 78,* 54–62.

Super, D. E. (1957). *The psychology of careers.* New York, NY: Harper & Row.

Super, D. E. (1980). A life-span, life-space approach to career development. *Journal of Vocational Behavior, 16,* 282–298.

Super, D. E. (1990). A life-span, life-space approach to career development. In D. Brown, L. Brooks, & Associates (Eds.), *Career choice and development: Applying contemporary theories to practice* (2nd ed., pp. 197–261). San Francisco, CA: Jossey-Bass.

Super, D. E., Savickas, M. L., & Super, C. (1996). A life-span, life-space approach to career development. In D. Brown, L. Brooks, & Associates (Eds.), *Career choice and development* (3rd ed.). San Francisco, CA: Jossey-Bass.

Swanson, J. L. (1995). The process and outcome of career counseling. In W. B. Walsh & S. H. Osipow (Eds.), *Handbook of vocational psychology: Theory, research, and practice* (pp. 217–259). Hillsdale, NJ: Erlbaum.

Ward, C. M., & Bingham, R. P. (1993). Career assessment of ethnic minority women. *Journal of Career Assessment, 1,* 246–257.

Watkins, C. E., Jr., & Savickas, M. L. (1990). Psychodynamic career counseling. In W. B. Walsh & S. H. Osipow (Eds.), *Career counseling: Contemporary topics in vocational psychology* (pp. 79–116). Hillsdale, NJ: Erlbaum.

Whiston, S. C. (2002). Applications of the principles: Career counseling and interventions. *The Counseling Psychologist, 30,* 218–237.

Whiston, S. C. (2003). Career counseling: 90 years old yet still healthy and vital. *The Career Development Quarterly, 52,* 35–42.

Whiston, S. C., & Blustein, D. L. (2013). *The impact of career interventions: Preparing our citizens for the 21st century jobs.* (Research Report). Broken Arrow, OK: National Career Development Association and the Society for Vocational Psychology.

Chapter 9

ACT, Inc. (2000). *World-of-work map, 2000 revision.* Iowa City, IA: Author.

American School Counselor Associations. (2004). *ASCA national standards for students.* Alexandria, VA: Author. Retrieved from http://static.pdesas.org/content/documents/ASCA_National_Standards_for_Students.pdf.

Harris-Bowlsbey, J. (2010a). *Take hold of your future.* Adel, IA: Kuder, Inc.

Harris-Bowlsbey, J. (2010b). *Direct your future.* Adel, IA: Kuder, Inc.

Holland, J. L. (1997). *Making vocational choices: A theory of vocational personalities and work environments* (3rd ed.). Odessa, FL: Psychological Assessment Resources.

Joint Committee on Standards for Educational Evaluation. (2011). *The program evaluation* (3rd ed.). Thousand Oaks, CA: Sage.

Patrick, J., & Niles, S. G. (1988). Establishing accountability and evaluation procedures in student affairs offices. *NASPA Journal, 25,* 291–296.

Super, D. E. (1957). *The psychology of careers.* New York, NY: Harper.

Super, D. E. (1980). A life-span, life-space approach to career development. *Journal of Vocational Behavior, 16,* 282–298.

U.S. Department of Education, Office of Vocational and Adult Education, in collaboration with several professional organizations. (2003). *The national career development guidelines.* Washington, DC: Author. Retrieved from http://acrn.ovae.org/ncdg/ncdg_what.htm.

Wood, C., & Hays, D. G. (2013). *A counselor's guide to career assessment instruments.* Broken Arrow, OK: National Career Development Association.

Chapter 10

American School Counselor Association. (2003). *The ASCA National Model: A framework for school counseling programs.* Alexandria, VA: Author.

American School Counselor Association. (2012). *ASCA National Model: A framework for school counseling.* Alexandria, VA: Author.

American School Counselor Association. (2014). *Mindsets and behaviors for student success: K-12 college- and career-readiness standards for every student.* Alexandria, VA: Author.

Beale, A. V. (2000). Elementary school career awareness: A visit to a hospital. *Journal of Career Development, 26,* 65–72.

Beale, A. V., & Williams, C. J. (2000). The anatomy of an elementary school career day. *Journal of Career Development, 26,* 205–213.

Bloom, B. S., Engelhart, M. D., Furst, E. J., Hill, W. H., & Krathwohl, D. R. (Eds.). (1956). *Taxonomy of educational objectives – The classification of educational goals – Handbook 1: Cognitive domain.* London, WI: Longmans, Green & Co. Ltd.

Campbell, C. A., & Dahir, C. A. (1997). *The national standards for school counseling programs.* Alexandria, VA: American School Counselor Association.

Dimmitt, C., & Carey, J. (2007). Using the ASCA National Model to facilitate school transitions. *Professional School Counseling, 10,* 227–232.

Erikson, E. H. (1963). *Childhood and society.* New York, NY: W. W. Norton.

Gottfredson, L. S. (2002). Gottfredson's theory of circumscription, compromise, and self-creation. In D. Brown & Associates (Eds.), *Career choice and development* (4th ed., pp. 85–148). San Francisco, CA: Jossey-Bass.

Gysbers, N. C., & Henderson, P. (1998). *Developing and managing your school guidance program.* Alexandria, VA: American Counseling Association.

Gysbers, N. C., & Henderson, P. (2001). Comprehensive guidance and counseling programs: A rich history and a bright future. *Professional School Counseling, 4,* 246–256.

Havighurst, R. J. (1972). *Developmental tasks and education* (3rd ed.). New York, NY: D. McKay.

Herr, E. L., Cramer, S. H., & Niles, S. G. (2004). *Career guidance and counseling through the lifespan: Systematic approaches* (6th ed.). Boston, MA: Allyn & Bacon.

Holcomb-McCoy, C. (2007). Transitioning to high school: Issues and challenges for African American students. *Professional School Counseling, 10,* 253–260.

Howard, K., & Walsh, M. E. (2010). Conceptions of career choice and attainment: Developmental levels in how children think about careers. *Journal of Vocational Behavior, 76,* 143–152.

Howard, K., & Walsh, M. E. (2011). Children's conceptions of career choice and attainment: Model development. *Journal of Career Development, 38,* 256–271.

Jackson, M., & Grant, D. (2004). Fostering positive career development in children and adolescents. In R. Perusse & G. Goodnough (Eds.), *Leadership, advocacy, and direct service strategies for professional school counselors* (pp. 125–154). Belmont, CA: Brooks/Cole.

Lapan, R. T. (2004). *Career development across the K–16 years.* Alexandria, VA: American Counseling Association.

Lee, C. C. (1984). Predicting the career choice attitudes of rural Black, White, and Native American high school students. *Vocational Guidance Quarterly, 32,* 177–184.

Magnuson, C. S., & Starr, M. F. (2000). How early is too early to begin life career planning? The importance of the elementary school years. *Journal of Career Development, 27,* 89–101.

Marcia, J. E. (1966). Development and validation of ego-identity status. *Journal of Personality and Social Psychology, 3,* 551–558.

Miller, J. (1977). *Career development needs of nine-year-olds: How to improve career development programs.* Washington, DC: National Advisory Council for Career Education.

Myrick, R. (1993). *Developmental guidance and counseling: A practical approach* (2nd ed.). Minneapolis, MN: Educational Media.

National Occupational Information Coordinating Committee (NOICC). (1992). *The National Career Development Guidelines Project.* Washington, DC: U.S. Government Printing Office.

Niles, S. G., Trusty, J., & Mitchell, N. (2004). Fostering positive career development in children and adolescents. In R. Perusse & G. Goodnough (Eds.), *Leadership, advocacy, and direct service strategies for professional school counselors* (pp. 102–124). Belmont, CA: Brooks/Cole.

No Child Left Behind. Pub. L. 107-110, 115 Stat. 1425 (2001).

Perkins, G. W. (2012). *School counselors' and teachers' perceptions of elementary school counselor roles related to person/social, academic, and career counseling.* Retrieved from www.counseling.org/resources/library/VISTAS/vistas12/2012_Vol_1_45-66/Article_53.pdf.

Perusse, R., & Goodnough, G. (2004). *Leadership, advocacy, and direct service strategies for professional school counselors.* Belmont, CA: Brooks/Cole.

Porfeli, E. J., Hartung, P. J., & Vondracek, F. W. (2008). Children's vocational development: A research rationale. *The Career Development Quarterly, 57,* 25–37.

Schmidt, J. J. (2003). *Counseling in schools: Essential services and comprehensive programs* (4th ed.). Boston, MA: Allyn & Bacon.

Super, D. E. (1957). *A psychology of careers.* New York, NY: Harper & Row.

Super, D. E. (1990). Career and life development. In D. Brown & L. Brooks (Eds.), *Career choice and development: Applying contemporary theories to practice* (2nd ed., pp. 197–261). San Francisco, CA: Jossey-Bass.

Super, D. E. (1994). A life-span, life-space perspective on convergence. In M. L. Savickas & R. W. Lent (Eds.), *Convergence in career development theories: Implications for science and practice* (pp. 63–74). Palo Alto, CA: CPP Books.

Super, D. E., Savickas, M. L., & Super, C. M. (1996). The life-span, life-space approach to careers. In D. Brown & L. Brooks (Eds.), *Career choice and development: Applying contemporary theories to practice* (3rd ed., pp. 121–178). San Francisco, CA: Jossey-Bass.

Tracey, T. J. G., & Caulum, D. (2015). Minimizing gender differences in children's interest assessment: Development of the Inventory of Children's Activities-3 (ICA-3). *Journal of Vocational Behavior, 87,* 154–160.

U.S. Department of Education, Office of Career, Technical, and Adult Education. (2007). *America's Career Resource Network: Career development resources and training.* Retrieved from www2.ed.gov/about/offices/list/ovae/pi/cte/acrnres.html.

Walz, G. R., & Benjamin, L. (1984). A systems approach to career guidance. *Vocational Guidance Quarterly, 33,* 26–34.

Watts, A. G., Super, D. E., & Kidd, J. M. (1981). *Career development in Britain.* Cambridge, UK: Hobsons Press.

Young, R. A. (1994). Helping adolescents with career development: The active role of parents. *The Career Development Quarterly, 42,* 195–203.

Chapter 11

Akos, P. (2004). Transition programming for school counselors. In B. Erford (Ed.), *Professional school counseling: A handbook of theories, programs, and practices* (pp. 881–888). Austin, TX: CAPS Press, an imprint of PRO-ED.

Akos, P., Konold, T., & Niles, S. G. (2004). A career readiness typology and typal membership in middle school. *The Career Development Quarterly, 53,* 53–66.

American School Counselor Association. (2003). *The ASCA National Model: A framework for school counseling programs.* Alexandria, VA: Author.

American School Counselor Association. (2004). The role of the school counselor in career guidance: Expectations and responsibilities. *The School Counselor, 29,* 164–168.

American School Counselor Association. (2012). *ASCA National Model: A framework for school counseling.* Alexandria, VA: Author.

Berardi-Demo, L. (2012). Seventh graders' perceptions of college and career ready supports in two urban charter middle schools. Doctoral dissertation, University of Pittsburgh, Pittsburgh, PA.

Bireley, M., & Genshaft, J. (1991). Adolescence and giftedness: A look at the issues. In M. Bireley & J. Genshaft (Eds.), *Understanding the gifted adolescent: Educational, developmental, and multicultural issues.*

Education and psychology of the gifted series (pp. 1–17). New York, NY: Teachers College Press.

Blustein, D. (1994). "Who am I?" The question of self and identity in career development. In M. L. Savickas & R. W. Lent (Eds.), *Convergence in career development theories* (pp. 139–154). Palo Alto, CA: Consulting Psychologists Press.

Campbell, C. A., & Dahir, C. A. (1997). *The national standards for school counseling programs.* Alexandria, VA: American School Counselor Association.

Conley, D. T. (2012). *The complexity of college and career readiness.* Presentation delivered at The Role of Technical Assistance in Actualizing College and Career Readiness, Arlington, VA.

Council of Chief State School Officers. (2014). *Opportunities and options: Making career preparation work for students.* Washington, DC: Author.

Erikson, E. H. (1963). *Childhood and society.* New York, NY: W. W. Norton.

Havighurst, R. J. (1972). *Developmental tasks and education* (3rd ed.). New York, NY: D. McKay.

Herr, E. L., Cramer, S. H., & Niles, S. G. (2004). *Career guidance and counseling through the lifespan* (6th ed.). Boston, MA: Allyn & Bacon.

Hutchinson, A. (2013). Expanding your horizons: An engaging opportunity for middle and high school girls in STEM career exploration. *Career Convergence.* Retrieved from ncda.org/aws/NCDA/pt/sp/career_convergence_features.

Kuder, Inc. (2015). *Navigator* [Computer software]. Adel, IA: Author.

National Association of State Directors of Career Technical Education Consortium. (2015). *Career clusters.* Retrieved from www.careertech.org/career-clusters.

Stott, K. A., & Jackson, A. P. (2005). Using service learning to achieve middle school comprehensive guidance program goals. *Professional School Counseling, 9,* 156–159.

Super, D. E. (1981). Approaches to occupational choice and career development. In A. G. Watts, D. E. Super, & J. M. Kidd (Eds.), *Career development in Britain.* Cambridge, UK: Hobsons Press.

Super, D. E. (1984). Leisure: What it is and might be. *Journal of Career Development, 11,* 71–80.

Super, D. E. (1990). Career and life development. In D. Brown & L. Brooks (Eds.), *Career choice and development: Applying contemporary theories to practice* (2nd ed., pp. 197–261). San Francisco, CA: Jossey-Bass.

Super, D. E., Savickas, M. L., & Super, C. M. (1996). The life-span, life-space approach to careers. In D. Brown

& L. Brooks (Eds.), *Career choice and development: Applying contemporary theories to practice* (3rd ed., pp. 121–178). San Francisco, CA: Jossey-Bass.

Vernon, A. (1993). *Developmental assessment and intervention with children and adolescents.* Alexandria, VA: American Counseling Association.

Chapter 12

Akos, P. (2004). Transition programming for school counselors. In B. Erford (Ed.), *Professional school counseling: A handbook of theories, programs, and practices* (pp. 881–888). Austin, TX: CAPS Press–PRO-ED.

Alliance for Excellent Education. (2006). *Paying double: Inadequate high schools and community college remediation.* Washington, DC: Author. Retrieved from all4ed.org/reports-factsheets/paying-double-inadequate-high-schools-and-community-college-remediation.

American School Counselor Association. (2003). *The ASCA National Model: A framework for school counseling programs.* Alexandria, VA: Author.

American School Counselor Association. (2012). *ASCA National Model: A framework for school counseling.* Alexandria, VA: Author.

Amundson, N. E., & Penner, K. (1998). Parent involved career exploration. *The Career Development Quarterly, 47,* 135–144.

Anctil, T. M., Smith, C. K., Schenck, P., & Dahir, C. (2012). Professional school counselors' career development practices and continuing education needs. *The Career Development Quarterly, 60,* 109–121.

Baker, S. (2000). *School counseling for the 21st century* (3rd ed.). Upper Saddle River, NJ: Merrill/Prentice Hall.

Baker, S. B., & Gerler, E. R. (2008). *School counseling for the twenty-first century* (5th ed.). Upper Saddle River, NJ: Merrill/Prentice Hall.

Barton, P. (2003). *Parsing the achievement gap: Baselines for tracking progress.* Princeton, NJ: Educational Testing Service.

Bennett, G. K., Seashore, H. G., & Wesman, A. G. (1992). *Technical manual: Differential Aptitude Tests* (5th ed.). San Antonio, TX: The Psychological Corporation.

Casselman, B. (2014). More high school grads decide college isn't worth it. *FiveThirtyEightEconomics.* Retrieved from fivethirtyeight.com/features/more-high-school-grads-decide-college-isnt-worth-it.

Crites, J. O. (1978). *Theory and research handbook for the Career Maturity Inventory.* Monterey, CA: CTB, McGraw-Hill.

Erford, B. T. (2003). *Transforming the school counseling profession.* Upper Saddle River, NJ: Merrill/Prentice Hall.

Feller, R. W. (2003). Aligning school counseling, the changing workplace, and career development assumptions. *Professional School Counseling, 6,* 262–271.

Froeschle, J. G. (2009). Using career counseling to influence minority dropout rates. In G. R. Walz, J. C. Bleuer, & R. K. Yep (Eds.), *Compelling counseling interventions: VISTAS* (pp. 11–20). Alexandria, VA: American Counseling Association.

Gibbons, M. M., Borders, L. D., Wiles, M. E., Stephan, J. B., & Davis P. E. (2006). Career and college planning: Needs of ninth graders—as reported by ninth graders. *Professional School Counseling, 10,* 168–178.

Greene, J. P., & Winters, M. A. (2005). *Public high school graduation and college readiness rates: 1991–2002* (Working Paper No. 8). New York, NY: Manhattan Institute for Policy Research [Online]. Retrieved from manhattan-institute.org/html/ewp_08.htm.

Hansen, L. S. (1999). Beyond school-to-work: Continuing contributions of theory and practice to career development of youth. *The Career Development Quarterly, 47,* 353–358.

Harrington, T. (1996). *Ability Explorer.* Itasca, IL: Riverside Publishing.

Haycock, K. (2004, May 10). Testimony of Kati Haycock [president of the Education Trust], before the National Commission on Accountability in Higher Education. Retrieved from edtrust.org/press_release/testimony-of-kati-haycock-before-the-national-commission-on-accountability-in-higher-education.

Herr, E. L., Cramer, S. H., & Niles, S. G. (2004). *Career guidance and counseling through the lifespan* (6th ed.). Boston, MA: Allyn & Bacon.

Holland, J. L. (1985). *Making vocational choices: A theory of vocational personalities and work environments* (2nd ed.). Upper Saddle River, NJ: Prentice Hall.

Jerald, C. D. (2006). *Measured progress: A report on the high school reform movement* (Educator Sector Reports). Washington, DC: Educator Sector.

Johansson, C. B. (1986). *Career Assessment Inventory.* Minneapolis, MN: NCS Assessments.

Keller, B. K., & Whiston, S. C. (2008). The role of parental influences on young adolescents' career development. *Journal of Career Development, 16,* 198–217.

Kolodinsky, P., Schroder, V., Montopoli, G., McLean, S., Managan, P. A., & Pedersen, W. (2006). The career fair as a vehicle for enhancing occupational self-efficacy. *Professional School Counseling, 10,* 161–167.

Krumboltz, J. D., & Worthington, R. (1999). The school-to-work transition from a learning theory perspective. *The Career Development Quarterly, 47,* 312–325.

Lapan, R. T., Whitcomb, S. A., & Aleman, N. M. (2012). Connecticut professional school counselors: College and career counseling services and smaller ratios benefit students. *Professional School Counseling, 16,* 117–124.

Marcia, J. E. (1966). Development and validation of ego-identity status. *Journal of Personality and Social Psychology, 3,* 551–558.

Marcia, J. E. (1980). Identity in adolescence. In J. Adelson (Ed.), *Handbook of adolescent psychology* (pp. 159–187). New York, NY: Wiley.

McLaughlin, J., Sum, A., & Fogg, N. (with Khatiwada, I., & Palma, S.). (2006, April). *The summer teen job market in 2005 and the predicted outlook for 2006: Implications of summer employment for Jobs for America's Graduates' programs* (prepared for Jobs for America's Graduates, Alexandria, VA). Boston, MA: Center for Labor Market Studies, Northeastern University.

Muuss, R. L. (1998). Marcia's expansion of Erikson's theory of identity formation. In R. Muuss, H. Porton, & Associates (Eds.), *Adolescent behavior and society: A book of readings* (5th ed., pp. 260–270). New York, NY: McGraw-Hill.

National High School Center. (2008). *Linking research and resources for better high schools.* Retrieved from betterhighschools.org.

Niles, S. G., & Goodnough, G. E. (1996). Life-role salience and values: A review of recent research. *The Career Development Quarterly, 45,* 65–86.

Pathways to College Network. (2004). *A shared agenda: A leadership challenge to improve college access and success.* Boston, MA: Author.

Perusse, R., & Goodnough, G. (2004). *Leadership, advocacy, and direct service strategies for professional school counselors.* Belmont, CA: Brooks/Cole.

Rosenbaum, J. E. (2001). *Beyond college for all.* New York, NY: Russell Sage.

Rosenbaum, J. E., & Person, A. E. (2003). Beyond college for all: Policies and practices to improve transitions into college and jobs. *Professional School Counseling, 6,* 252–261.

Savickas, M. L. (1990). The career decision-making course: Description and field test. *The Career Development Quarterly, 38,* 275–284.

Savickas, M. L. (1993). Predictive validity criteria for career development measures. *Journal of Career Assessment, 1,* 93–104.

Savickas, M. L. (1999). The transition from school to work: A developmental perspective. *The Career Development Quarterly, 47,* 326–336.

Savickas, M. L., Stilling, S. M., & Schwartz, S. (1984). Time perspective in vocational maturity and career decision making. *Journal of Vocational Behavior, 25,* 258–269.

Sum, A., McLaughlin, J., & Khatiwada, I. (2006, September). *The 2006 summer job market for the nation's teens: Who got the jobs and who didn't and why we should care* (prepared for Jobs for America's Graduates, Alexandria, VA). Boston, MA: Center for Labor Market Studies, Northeastern University.

Super, D. E. (1955). Transition: From vocational guidance to counseling psychology. *Journal of Counseling Psychology, 2,* 3–9.

Super, D. E. (1957). *A psychology of careers.* New York, NY: Harper & Row.

Super, D. E. (1970). *The Work Values Inventory.* Boston, MA: Houghton Mifflin.

Super, D. E. (1980). A life-span, life-space approach to career development. *Journal of Vocational Behavior, 16,* 282–298.

Super, D. E. (1983). Assessment in career guidance: Toward truly developmental counseling. *Personnel and Guidance Journal, 61,* 555–562.

Super, D. E. (1990). Career and life development. In D. Brown & L. Brooks (Eds.), *Career choice and development: Applying contemporary theories to practice* (2nd ed., pp. 197–261). San Francisco, CA: Jossey-Bass.

Super, D. E., Osborne, W. L., Walsh, D. J., Brown, S. D., & Niles, S. G. (1992). Developmental assessment and counseling: The C-DAC model. *Journal of Counseling and Development, 71,* 74–80.

Super, D. E., Savickas, M. L., & Super, C. M. (1996). The life-span, life-space approach to careers. In D. Brown & L. Brooks (Eds.), *Career choice and development: Applying contemporary theories to practice* (3rd ed., pp. 121–178). San Francisco, CA: Jossey-Bass.

Super, D. E., Thompson, A. S., Lindeman, R. H., Jordaan, J. P., & Myers, R. M. (1988). *Adult Career Concerns Inventory: Manual for research and exploratory use in counseling.* Palo Alto, CA: Consulting Psychologists Press.

Turner, S., & Lapan, R. T. (2002). Career self-efficacy and perceptions of parent support in career development. *The Career Development Quarterly, 51,* 44–55.

Wagner, M., Newman, L., Cameto, R., Garza, N., & Levine, P. (2005, April). Postsecondary education: Participation of youth with disabilities. In *After high school:*

A first look at the postschool experiences of youth with disabilities. A report from the National Longitudinal Transition Study-2 (NLTS2) (Chap. 4). Menlo Park, CA: SRI International. Retrieved from nlts2.org/reports/2005_04/nlts2_report_2005_04_complete.pdf.

Wise, R. (2007, June). Systems of support for high school improvement. Presented at the National High School Center Summer Institute, June 11–13, 2007, Washington, DC. Retrieved from betterhighschools.org/summerinst/SI2007SystemsofSupport.asp.

Chapter 13

American College Health Association. (2012). *American College Health Association national college health assessment.* Washington, DC: Author. Retrieved from www.acha-ncha.org/docs/ACHA-NCHA-II_ReferenceGroup_DataReport_Spring2012.pdf.

American Council on Education. (1999). *The American freshman national norms for fall 1998.* Washington, DC: Author.

Americans with Disabilities Act of 1990, Pub. L. No. 101-336, 104 Stat. 328 (1990).

Americans with Disabilities Amendments Act (ADAAA), Pub. L. No. 110-325, § 2(b)(1), 122 Stat. 3553 (2008).

Association for Career and Technical Education. (2011). *CTE information.* Washington, DC: Author. Retrieved from acteonline.org/cte_info.aspx.

Bureau of Labor Statistics. (2014). *College enrollment and work activity of 2013 high school graduates.* Washington, DC: U.S. Department of Labor. Retrieved from bls.gov/news.release/archives/hsgec_04222014.pdf.

Chan, A., & Derry, T. (2013). *Rethinking success: From the liberal arts to careers in the 21st century.* Retrieved from rethinkingsuccess.wfu.edu/files/2013/05/A-Roadmap-for-Transforming-The-College-to-Career-Experience.pdf.

College Placement Council. (1991, July). *Career Planning and Placement Survey. Special report. Spotlight.* Bethlehem, PA: Author.

Collins, M. (1998). Snapshot of the profession. *Journal of Career Planning and Employment, 41,* 51–55.

Colozzi, E. A. (2000). Toward the development of systemic career guidance. In D. A. Luzzo (Ed.), *Career counseling of college students* (pp. 285–310). Washington, DC: American Psychological Association.

Complete College America. (2014). *Four-year myth: Make college more affordable.* Washington, DC: Author.

Conyers, L. M., & Szymanski, E. M. (1998). The effectiveness of an integrated career intervention for college students with and without disabilities. *Journal of Postsecondary Education and Disability, 13,* 23–34.

Council for the Advancement of Standards in Higher Education. (2010). *Career services: CAS standards and guidelines.* Washington, DC: Author.

Davidson, M. M. (2001). The computerization of career services: Critical issues to consider. *Journal of Career Development, 27,* 217–228.

Fassinger, R. E., & O'Brien, K. M. (2000). Career counseling with college women: A scientist-practitioner-advocate model of intervention. In D. A. Luzzo (Ed.), *Career counseling of college students* (pp. 253–265). Washington, DC: American Psychological Association.

Friehe, M., Aune, B., & Leuenberger, J. (1996). Career service needs of college students with disabilities. *The Career Development Quarterly, 44,* 289–300.

Halasz, T., & Kempton, C. B. (2000). Career planning workshops and courses. In D. A. Luzzo (Ed.), *Career counseling of college students* (pp. 157–169). Washington, DC: American Psychological Association.

Hardesty, P. H. (1991). Undergraduate career courses for credit: A review and meta-analysis. *Journal of College Student Development, 32,* 184–185.

Healy, C. C., & Reilly, K. C. (1989). Career needs of community college students: Implications for services and theory. *Journal of College Student Personnel, 30,* 541–545.

Herr, E. L. (1989). Career development and mental health. *Journal of Career Development, 16,* 5–18.

Herr, E. L., Cramer, S. H., & Niles, S. G. (2004). *Career guidance and counseling through the lifespan: Systematic approaches* (6th ed.). Boston, MA: Allyn & Bacon.

Herr, E. L., Rayman, J., & Garis, J. W. (1993). *Handbook for the college and university career center.* Westport, CT: Greenwood Press.

Hess, F. (2011). Old school: College's most important trend is the rise of the adult student. *The Atlantic.* Retrieved from theatlantic.com/business/archive/2011/09/old-school-colleges-most-important-trend-is-the-rise-of-the-adult-student/245823.

Higher Education Research Institute. (2012). *More freshmen than ever say they go to college to get better jobs and make more money.* Los Angeles, CA: Author. Retrieved from heri.ucla.edu/pr-display.php?prQry=111.

Hitchings, W. E., & Retish, P. (2000). The career development needs of students with learning disabilities. In D. A. Luzzo (Ed.), *Career counseling of college students* (pp. 253–265). Washington, DC: American Psychological Association.

Institute of International Education. (2014). *Open door report on international educational exchange.* Washington, DC: Author. Retrieved from iie.org/Who-We-Are/News-and-Events/Press-Center/Press-Releases/2014/2014-11-17-Open-Doors-Data.

Johnson, R. H. (1978). Individual styles of decision-making: A theoretical model for counseling. *Personnel and Guidance Journal, 56,* 531–536.

Kingkade, T. (2014). *Only 1 state's college students graduate with less than $20,000 of debt, report finds.* Retrieved from www.huffingtonpost.com/2014/11/13/college-student-debt-states_n_6146242.html.

Kuder, Inc. (2015). *Journey* [Computer software]. Adel, IA: Author.

Luzzo, D. A. (2000). Career development of returning-adult and graduate students. In D. A. Luzzo (Ed.), *Career counseling of college students* (pp. 191–200). Washington, DC: American Psychological Association.

Marklein, M. (2009). *4-year colleges graduate 53 percent of students in 6 years.* Retrieved from usatoday30.usatoday.com/news/education/2009-06-03-diploma-graduation-rate_N.htm.

Marron, D., & Rayman, J. R. (2002). Addressing the career development needs of adult students in research university settings. In S. Niles (Ed.), *Adult career development: Concepts, models, and practices* (3rd ed., pp. 319–334). Tulsa: OK: National Career Development Association.

Miller, K. L., & McDaniels, R. M. (2001). Cyberspace, the new frontier. *Journal of Career Development, 27,* 199–206.

National Association of Colleges and Employers. (2010). *Professional standards for college and university career services–2009.* Bethlehem, PA: Author.

National Center for Education Statistics. (2014a). *Fast facts: Enrollment.* Washington, DC: U.S. Department of Education. Retrieved from nces.ed.gov/fastfacts/display.asp?id=98.

National Center for Education Statistics. (2014b). *Fast facts: Graduation rates.* Washington, DC: U.S. Department of Education. Retrieved from nces.ed.gov/fastfacts/display.asp?id=40.

National Occupational Information Coordinating Committee (NOICC), U.S. Department of Labor. (1992). *The National Career Development Guidelines Project.* Washington, DC: U.S. Department of Labor.

Niles, S. G., Erford, B. T., Hunt, B., & Watts, R. H. (1997). Decision-making styles and career development of college students. *Journal of College Student Development, 38,* 479–488.

Noel-Levitz. (2013). *2014 National freshman attitudes report: Exploring college readiness among college freshmen.* Coralville, IA: Author. Retrieved from www.noellevitz.com/documents/shared/Papers_and_Research/2013/2013_National_Freshman_Attitudes.pdf.

Normyle, M. (2014). *Nine ways to provide the career planning assistance that incoming college freshmen want: Part one.* Coralville, IA: Ruffalo Noel Levitz. Retrieved from blog.noellevitz.com/2014/04/09/nine-ways-provide-career-planning-assistance-incoming-college-freshmen-want-part-one.

Ohler, D. L., Levinson, E. M., & Barker, W. F. (1996). Career maturity in college students with learning disabilities. *The Career Development Quarterly, 44,* 278–288.

Pew Research Center. (2009, October). *College enrollment hits all-time high, fueled by community college surge.* Washington, DC: Author. Retrieved from www.pewsocialtrends.org/2009/10/29/college-enrollment-hits-all-time-high-fueled-by-community-college-surge.

Pope, M. S., Prince, J. P., & Mitchell, K. (2000). Responsible career counseling with lesbian and gay students. In D. A. Luzzo (Ed.), *Career counseling of college students* (pp. 267–281). Washington, DC: American Psychological Association.

Powell, R., & Kirts, D. K. (1980). *Career services today: A dynamic college profession.* Bethlehem, PA: The College Placement Council.

Rayman, J. R. (1996). Apples and oranges in the career center: Reaction to R. Reardon. *Journal of Counseling and Development, 74,* 286–287.

Rayman, J. R. (1999). Career services imperative for the next millennium. *The Career Development Quarterly, 48,* 175–184.

Reardon, R. C. (1996). A program and cost analysis of a self-directed career decision-making program in a university career center. *Journal of Counseling and Development, 74,* 280–285.

Reardon, R. C., Lenz, J. G., Sampson, J. P., Jr., & Peterson, G. W. (2000). *Career development and planning: A comprehensive approach.* Pacific Grove, CA: Brooks/Cole.

Reardon, R. C., Zunker, V., & Dyal, M. A. (1979). The status of career planning programs and career centers in colleges and universities. *Vocational Guidance Quarterly, 28,* 154–159.

Reed, C. A., Reardon, R. C., Lenz, J. G., & Leirer, S. J. (2001). A cognitive career course: From theory to practice. *The Career Development Quarterly, 50,* 158–167.

Rehabilitation Act of 1973, Section 504, 34 C.F.R. Part 104. Retrieved from www2.ed.gov/policy/rights/reg/ocr/34cfr104.pdf.

Sampson, J. P., Jr. (2008). *Designing and implementing career programs: A handbook for effective practice.* Broken Arrow, OK: National Career Development Association.

Super, D. E. (1984). Leisure: What it is and might be. *Journal of Career Development, 11,* 71–80.

U.S. Department of Education, National Center for Education Statistics. (2009). *Students with disabilities at postsecondary education institutions.* Washington, DC: Author. Retrieved from nces.ed.gov/pubs2011/2011018.pdf.

Vickers, M. Z. (2010). *Accommodating college students with learning disabilities: ADD, ADHD, and dyslexia.* Raleigh, NC: The John William Pope Center for Higher Education Policy.

Washington University. (n.d.). *About the Career Center.* St. Louis, MO: Author. Retrieved from careercenter.wustl.edu/about/Pages/Mission.aspx.

Weissberg, M., Berenstein, M., Cote, A., Cravey, B., & Heath, K. (1982). An assessment of the personal, career, and academic needs of undergraduate students. *Journal of College Student Personnel, 23,* 415–422.

Whiston, S. C., Sexton, T. L., & Lasoff, D. L. (1998). Career-intervention outcome: A replication and extension of Oliver and Spokane. *Journal of Counseling Psychology, 45,* 150–165.

Whiteley, S. M., Mahaffey, P. J., & Geer, C. A. (1987). The campus counseling center: A profile of staffing patterns and services. *Journal of College Student Personnel, 28,* 71–81.

Chapter 14

AllAboutKids.com. (n.d.) *Parents corner: Glossary.* Retrieved from allaboutkidsny.com/glossary.html.

AllPsychologyCareers. (n.d.). *Community counselor.* Retrieved from allpsychologycareers.com/career/community-counselor.html.

The Career Development Quarterly. (2004). Special Issue: Career Counseling in the Next Decade. *The Career Development Quarterly, 52*(1), 89. Retrieved May 11, 2004, from bartlyeby.com/59/10/churchill.win.html.

Churchill, W. (1940, August). *The Few.* Downers Grove, IL: The Churchill Centre. Retrieved from winstonchurchill.org/resources/speeches/1940-the-finest-hour/the-few.

Dougherty, A. M. (1990). *Consultation: Practice and perspectives.* Pacific Grove, CA: Brooks/Cole.

Goodman, P. S. (2010, February 20). Despite signs of recovery, chronic joblessness rises. *New York Times,* p. A1.

Goodwill. (2015). *About us.* Retrieved from http://www.goodwill.org/about-us.

Hershenson, D. B., Power, P. W., & Waldo, M. (1996). *Community counseling: Contemporary theory and practice.* Boston, MA: Allyn & Bacon.

Kuder, Inc. (2015). *Journey* [Computer software]. Adel, IA: Author.

National Occupational Information Coordinating Committee. (1989). *National career development guidelines.* Retrieved from acrn.ovae.org/ncdg/ncdg_what.htm.

Philanthropedia. (2010). *Ranked nonprofits: National workforce development 2010.* Retrieved from myphilanthropedia.org/top-nonprofits/national/workforce-development/2010#non-profits.

Schlossberg, N. K. (1989). *Overwhelmed: Coping with life's ups and downs.* Lexington, KY: Lexington Press.

Chapter 15

American Counseling Association (ACA). (2014). *Code of Ethics.* Alexandria, VA: Author. Retrieved from www.counseling.org/resources/aca-code-of-ethics.pdf.

American Psychological Association (APA). (2010). *Ethical principles of psychologists and code of conduct.* Washington, DC: Author. Retrieved from www.apa.org/ethics/code/index.aspx.

American School Counselor Association. (2010). *ASCA code of ethics.* Alexandria, VA: Author.

Anderson, W. P., Jr., & Niles, S. G. (1995). Career and personal concerns expressed by career counseling clients. *The Career Development Quarterly, 43,* 240–245.

Beauchamp, T. L., & Childress, J. F. (2001). *Principles of biomedical ethics* (5th ed.). New York, NY: Oxford University Press.

Bergin, A. E. (1985). Proposed values for guiding and evaluating counseling and psychotherapy. *Counseling and Values, 29,* 99–115.

Commonwealth of Virginia Board of Counseling. (2007). *Regulations Governing the Practice of Professional Counseling.* (18 VAC 115-20-10 et seg.)

Family Educational Rights and Privacy Act of 1974, 20 U. S. C. § 1232g; 34 CFR Part 99. Retrieved from www2.ed.gov/policy/gen/guid/fpco/ferpa/index.html.

Forester-Miller, H. & Davis, T. (1996). *A practitioner's guide to ethical decision making.* Alexandria, VA: American Counseling Association.

Glosoff, H. L., & Freeman, L. T. (2007). Report of the ACA Ethics Committee: 2005–2006. *Journal of Counseling and Development, 85,* 251–254.

Herlihy, B., & Corey, G. (2006). *ACA Ethical Standards Casebook* (6th ed.). Alexandria, VA: American Counseling Association.

Herlihy, B., & Remley, T. P. (1995). Unified ethical standards: A challenge for professionalism. *Journal of Counseling & Development, 74,* 130–133.

Herlihy, B. R., & Watson, Z. E. (2006). Gender issues in career counseling. In D. Capuzzi & M. D. Stauffer (Eds.), *Career counseling: Foundations, perspectives, and applications* (pp. 363–385). Boston, MA: Pearson Education.

Herr, E. L., & Niles, S. G. (1988). The values of counseling: Three domains. *Counseling and Values, 33,* 4–17.

International Association for Educational and Vocational Guidance. (1995). *IAEVG Ethical Standards.* Berlin, Germany: Author. Retrieved from iaevg.net/iaevg.org/IAEVG/nave1ba.html?lang=2&menu=1&submenu=2.

Kidder, R. M. (1995). *How good people make tough choices: Resolving the dilemmas of ethical living.* New York, NY: Fireside.

Lee, G. (1994). *Honor and duty.* New York, NY: Knopf.

London, P. (1964). *The modes and morals of psychotherapy.* New York, NY: Holt, Rinehart, and Winston.

National Association for College Admission Counseling. (2007). *Statement of principles of good practice.* Alexandria, VA: Author.

National Association of Social Workers. (2010). *Code of Ethics of the National Association of Social Workers.* Washington, DC: Author.

National Career Development Association. (1997). *NCDA guidelines for the use of the Internet for provision of career information and planning services.* Columbus, OH: Author.

National Career Development Association. (2015). *Code of ethics.* Broken Arrow, OK: Author. Retrieved from www.ncda.org/aws/NCDA/asset_manager/get_file/3395.

Niles, S. G., & Pate, R. H. (1989). Competency and training issues related to the integration of career counseling and mental health counseling. *Journal of Career Development, 16,* 63–71.

Sampson, J. P., Dikel, M. R., & Osborn, D. S. (2012). *The Internet: A tool for career planning* (3rd ed.). Broken Arrow, OK: National Career Development Association.

Subich, L. M. (1993). How personal is career counseling? *The Career Development Quarterly, 42,* 129–131.

Super, D. E. (1983). Assessment in career guidance: Toward truly developmental counseling. *Personnel and Guidance Journal, 61,* 555–562.

Tjeltveit, A. C. (1986). The ethics of value conversion in psychotherapy: Appropriate and inappropriate therapist influence on client values. *Clinical Psychology Review, 6,* 515–537.

VanHoose, W. H. (1986). Ethical principles in counseling. *Journal of Counseling and Development, 65,* 168–169.

Index